Handbook
of Evangelical
Theologians

Baker Reference Library

Handbook
of Evangelical
Theologians

Edited by

Walter A. Elwell

Baker Books

A Division of Baker Book House Co.
Grand Rapids, Michigan 49516

Published by Baker Books
a division of Baker Book House Company
P.O. Box 6287, Grand Rapids, Michigan 49516-6287

Printed in the United States of America

Library of Congress Cataloging-in-Publication Data

Handbook of Evangelical theologians / edited by Walter A. Elwell.
     p.   cm.
    Includes bibliographical references.
    ISBN 0-8010-3212-1
    1. Evangelicalism—History—20th century. 2. Theology, Doctrinal—History—20th century. 3. Theologians. I. Elwell, Walter A.
    BR1640.H363   1993
    230'046—dc20   93-5606

Scripture quotations are taken from the King James Version (KJV), the New American Standard Bible (NASB), the New International Version (NIV), the New King James Version (NKJV), and the Revised Standard Version (RSV).

Sketches by Jack Brouwer

Contents

Preface

The last thirty years have seen a recrudescence of evangelicalism in America. Accordingly, there has been increased interest in what evangelicalism actually is, what its roots are, who was influential in its earlier days, where it is going, and myriad similar topics. Fortunately, on most of these subjects competent individuals are expending a good bit of energy, and many of the gaps are being filled in.[1] Yet it remains difficult, if not impossible, to find some of the basic information regarding the theologians who have played a role in informing and sustaining evangelicalism in the twentieth century, especially the earlier part. We have in view here biographical facts, theological development and stance, major writings, and evaluation of where a particular theologian might fit into the overall scheme of things. It was to provide this information that the *Handbook of Evangelical Theologians* has been put together.

Two major questions presented themselves at the outset—What is evangelicalism anyway? and What criteria should be used to determine who among the many possibilities should be included in this volume? Neither one of these questions was particularly easy to handle. It turned out that no single, simple answer could be given to the first question. Everyone seems to know, in some intuitive kind of way, what evangelicalism means; but when it comes to writing that meaning down on paper, no two definitions turn out exactly alike. They run the spectrum from the very broad understanding of evangelicalism as synonymous with Protestantism to some very specific formulations that entail acceptance of a lengthy list of precise theological statements; various middle positions define evangelicalism as commitment to the tenets of historical orthodoxy. David Bebbington, in a very fine volume entitled *Evangelicalism in Modern Britain*, speaks of the "enormous variation in Evangelicalism

1. See, for example, Bernard Ramm, *The Evangelical Heritage: A Study in Historical Theology* (Waco: Word, 1973); Donald G. Bloesch, *The Evangelical Renaissance* (Grand Rapids: Eerdmans, 1973); *The Gospel in America: Themes in the Story of America's Evangelicals*, ed. John D. Woodbridge, Mark A. Noll, and Nathan O. Hatch (Grand Rapids: Zondervan, 1979); *Evangelicalism and Modern America*, ed. George M. Marsden (Grand Rapids: Eerdmans, 1984); Mark A. Noll, *Between Faith and Criticism: Evangelicals, Scholarship, and the Bible in America* (San Francisco: Harper and Row, 1986; 2d ed., Grand Rapids: Baker, 1991); George M. Marsden, *Reforming Fundamentalism: Fuller Seminary and the New Evangelicalism* (Grand Rapids: Eerdmans, 1987); James Davison Hunter, *Evangelicalism: The Coming Generation* (Chicago: University of Chicago Press, 1987); Donald W. Dayton, *Discovering an Evangelical Heritage* (Peabody, Mass.: Hendrickson, 1988); George M. Marsden, *Understanding Fundamentalism and Evangelicalism* (Grand Rapids: Eerdmans, 1990). For a comprehensive survey of materials relating to evangelicalism, see *Twentieth-Century Evangelicalism: A Guide to the Sources*, ed. Edith L. Blumhofer and Joel A. Carpenter (New York: Garland, 1990); *Researching Modern Evangelicalism: A Guide to the Holdings of the Billy Graham Center, with Information on Other Collections*, comp. Robert D. Shuster et al. (Westport, Conn.: Greenwood, 1990).

over time" in his country.[2] The same holds true for America as well.[3] For along the way considerations in the areas of sociology, economics, philosophy, and even the matter of personal style have made a single comprehensive definition of evangelicalism even more elusive.

For all of the complicating factors, however, there remained a feeling that evangelicalism could still be roughly defined and understood. The uncertainties obviously did not stop books from being written on the subject! Having to make a decision, we opted for a middle-of-the-road definition.[4] Too broad a definition would have meant that almost anyone could be included: Karl Barth, after all, produced a volume entitled *Evangelical Theology: An Introduction.* Too narrow a definition would have meant that B. B. Warfield and perhaps even Gordon H. Clark (if Cornelius Van Til had his way) would have been left out. So rather than enter into a complex and, for our purposes, unnecessary discussion as to the exact nature of evangelicalism, we opted for a definition somewhat more on the broad rather than on the narrow side. That we have included theologians who by some definitions are not solidly evangelical goes without saying, but our purpose has been to allow for the inclusion of theologians who have had a marked influence on the evangelical movement and considered themselves evangelical, even if not everyone agreed. In the end, the reader will have to decide.

2. David Bebbington, *Evangelicalism in Modern Britain: A History from the 1730s to the 1980s* (Grand Rapids: Baker, 1992), 276.
3. Timothy Smith uses the terms *mosaic* and *kaleidoscope* (see *Evangelicalism and Modern America,* ed. Marsden, viii). Robert Webber has found fourteen varieties (*Common Roots: A Call to Evangelical Maturity* [Grand Rapids: Zondervan, 1978], 32).
4. For a good discussion see *Evangelicalism and Modern America,* ed. Marsden, vii–xix; and Kenneth S. Kantzer, "Unity and Diversity in Evangelical Faith," in *The Evangelicals: What They Believe, Who They Are, Where They Are Changing,* ed. David F. Wells and John D. Woodbridge, rev. ed. (Grand Rapids: Baker, 1977), 58–87.

Once the first question was for all practical purposes settled, we established some criteria for deciding which theologians to include in our list:

1. Twentieth-century figures (i.e., for a theologian to be included, at least part of his career must have taken place in the present century)
2. Representatives from both halves of the century (i.e., pre- and post-1950)
3. Identification with the evangelical movement
4. Significant influence on or in the evangelical movement
5. Representatives of various denominational points of view; these include (a) Arminian/Wesleyan, (b) Calvinist/Reformed, (c) charismatic, (d) dispensationalist, (e) Lutheran, (f) Baptist, and (g) Anglican (of course, some of these categories may overlap)
6. Major interest in theology rather than biblical studies

By using these criteria we were able to come up with a fairly good cross section of evangelicalism in the twentieth century. We knew at the outset that not everyone could be included and that some biblical scholars would eminently qualify. But our criteria were set, and the choices made. There might be legitimate discussion about some theologians who have not been included in this volume, but we doubt that many would exclude those who have been.

The next task was to choose writers for the various articles. It would have made excellent sense to have some of our subjects write on the earlier theologians. But that seemed too ingrown an idea. So we decided not to have anyone who was being written about write on someone else. That settled, where it was possible we chose people who were in one way or another close to the theologian being written about. For example, Glen Scorgie had written a biography of James Orr, and the general editor's position at Wheaton College made Henry C.

Thiessen's literary output readily accessible. We hoped that this would provide a sense of freshness and immediacy to the essays.

Let me end on a brief personal note. Going over the material contained in this volume produced in me an interesting mixture of feelings, some positive, some negative, some rather indefinable. The books of so many of these men played such a significant role in my own theological development that at times it is hard to know where their thoughts end and my own begin. James Orr's *Christian View of God and the World*, B. B. Warfield's *Inspiration and Authority of the Bible*, Augustus H. Strong's *Systematic Theology*, J. Gresham Machen's *Christianity and Liberalism*, Henry C. Thiessen's *Lectures in Systematic Theology* are still on my shelf, marked up from college days. Sometimes it was the man himself that was influential. The commanding presence of Cornelius Van Til, Gordon H. Clark, John Murray, and Edward John Carnell, to mention only a few, was something not soon forgotten. And yet time does have a way of blurring the edges, so the memory needs something to jog it, and the biographical vignettes in this volume did just that, bringing the past back to life again.

It is a sad fact that our theologians are probably little more than names to members of the younger generation. This volume can introduce them to venerable thinkers now gone, but also to those of our generation, who are shaping the thought of today, such as Carl F. H. Henry, J. I. Packer, and John Walvoord. Such is our aim, at any rate. This volume is offered in the sincere hope that the evangelical theologians will be understood better, and that evangelicalism will be strengthened as a result.

Contributors

Bauman, Michael. Ph.D., Fordham University. Associate Professor of Theology and Culture, Hillsdale College, Hillsdale, Michigan; Lecturer and Tutor in Renaissance Literature and Theology, Centre for Medieval and Renaissance Studies, Oxford, England.

Blaising, Craig A. Th.D., Dallas Theological Seminary; Ph.D., University of Aberdeen. Professor of Systematic Theology, Dallas Theological Seminary, Dallas, Texas.

Burgess, Stanley M. Ph.D., University of Missouri–Columbia. Professor of Religious Studies, Southwest Missouri State University, Springfield, Missouri.

Clendenin, Daniel B. Ph.D., Drew University. Visiting Professor of Christian Studies, Moscow State University, Moscow, Russia.

Cragoe, Thomas H. Th.D., Dallas Theological Seminary. Pastor, Believer's Bible Church, Lufkin, Texas.

Duriez, Colin. B.A. (Honours), University of Ulster–Coleraine. General Books Editor, InterVarsity Press, Leicester, England.

Elwell, Walter A. Ph.D., University of Edinburgh. Professor of Biblical and Theological Studies, Wheaton College Graduate School, Wheaton, Illinois.

Enns, Paul P. Th.D., Dallas Theological Seminary. Provost and Dean, Tampa Bay Theological Seminary, Tampa, Florida.

Ferguson, Sinclair B. Ph.D., University of Aberdeen. Professor of Systematic Theology, Westminster Theological Seminary, Philadelphia, Pennsylvania.

Frame, John M. M.Phil., Yale University. Professor of Apologetics and Systematic Theology, Westminster Theological Seminary in California, Escondido, California.

Fry, C. George. Ph.D., Ohio State University. Teaching Theologian, Lutheran College of Health Professions, Fort Wayne, Indiana.

Hannah, John D. Th.D., Dallas Theological Seminary; Ph.D., University of Texas–Dallas. Department Chairman and Professor of Historical Theology, Dallas Theological Seminary, Dallas, Texas.

Hart, D. G. Ph.D., Johns Hopkins University. Director, Institute for the Study of American Evangelicals, Wheaton College, Wheaton, Illinois.

Hustad, L. Arnold. Ph.D., New York University. Professor of Theology and Philosophy, Crown College, St. Bonifacius, Minnesota.

Johnston, Robert K. Ph.D., Duke University. Provost, Fuller Theological Seminary, Pasadena, California.

Klooster, Fred H. Th.D., Free University, Amsterdam. Professor of Systematic Theology, Emeritus, Calvin Theological Seminary, Grand Rapids, Michigan.

Lewis, Gordon R. Ph.D., Syracuse University. Professor of Theology and Philosophy, Denver Seminary, Denver, Colorado.

McKim, Donald K. Ph.D., University of Pittsburgh. Academic Dean and Professor of Theology, Memphis Theological Seminary, Memphis, Tennessee.

Marquart, Kurt E. M.A., University of Western Ontario. Associate Professor of Systematic Theology, Concordia Theological Seminary, Fort Wayne, Indiana.

Nash, Ronald H. Ph.D., Syracuse University. Professor of Philosophy and Theology, Reformed Theological Seminary, Orlando, Florida.

Nettles, Thomas J. Ph.D., Southwestern Baptist Theological Seminary. Professor of Church History, Trinity Evangelical Divinity School, Deerfield, Illinois.

Nicole, Roger. Th.D., Gordon Divinity School; Ph.D., Harvard University. Visiting Professor of Theology, Reformed Theological Seminary, Orlando, Florida.

Noll, Mark A. Ph.D., Vanderbilt University. McManis Professor of Christian Thought, Wheaton College, Wheaton, Illinois.

Pointer, Steven R. Ph.D., Duke University. Associate Academic Dean and Associate Professor of History, Trinity College, Deerfield, Illinois.

Purdy, Richard A. Ph.D., New York University. Vice President of Operations, The J. R. Reeves Company, Cheshire, Connecticut.

Scaer, David P. Th.D., Concordia Theological Seminary–St. Louis. Professor of Systematic Theology and New Testament, Concordia Theological Seminary, Fort Wayne, Indiana.

Scorgie, Glen G. Ph.D., University of St. Andrews. Academic Dean, North American Baptist College, Edmonton, Alberta, Canada.

Tyson, John R. Ph.D., Drew University. Professor of Theology, Houghton College, Houghton, New York.

Vanhoozer, Kevin J. Ph.D., Cambridge University. Lecturer in Theology, New College, University of Edinburgh, Scotland.

Venema, Cornelis P. Ph.D., Princeton Theological Seminary. Associate Professor of Doctrinal Studies, Mid-America Reformed Seminary, Orange City, Iowa.

Watts, Gary L. Ph.D., Fuller Theological Seminary. Associate Professor of Religion and Philosophy, Jamestown College, Jamestown, North Dakota.

Williams, Peter. Ph.D., University of London. Vicar, Ecclesall Parish Church, Sheffield, England.

Wilson, Charles R. Ph.D., Vanderbilt University. Professor Emeritus, Taylor University, Upland, Indiana.

Augustus H. Strong

Steven R. Pointer

Baptist theologian and longtime seminary president Augustus Hopkins Strong was one of the most influential conservative Protestant thinkers in the United States in the late nineteenth and early twentieth centuries. Born on August 3, 1836, in Rochester, New York, Strong would spend the lion's share of his lengthy life identified with that city. His parents, Alvah Strong and Catherine Hopkins, were early pioneers of Rochester. As proprietor of the *Rochester Democrat*, the local newspaper, Alvah Strong achieved a measure of social prominence. Converted at a Charles Finney revival service in 1830, Alvah Strong blazed the spiritual trail for his son, who, while home in Rochester on spring break from college in April 1856, also succumbed to Finney's "new measures." In his autobiography, begun on his sixtieth birthday, Strong would later refer to his coming to faith as "a purely New School conversion," that is to say, heavy emphasis was placed on the human decision.[1]

Earning his undergraduate degree at Yale in 1857, Strong cited the positive personal influence upon him by the likes of Theodore Woolsey, James Hadley, Noah Porter, and George Park Fisher. However, he lamented the fact that college instruction at that time discouraged discussion and cultivated only "a narrow accuracy" in a curriculum still dominated by the classical languages.[2] Happily, that deficiency was rectified for him in his studies at Rochester Theological Seminary and in a fifteen-month excursion to Europe and the Middle East. Together, those experiences allowed Strong to find his tongue and cultivate a love for both theology and travel.

Though he followed his profession of faith with baptism and membership at the First Baptist Church of Rochester and then attended a Baptist seminary, Strong was

1. Augustus H. Strong, *Autobiography of Augustus Hopkins Strong*, ed. Crerar Douglas (Valley Forge, Pa.: Judson, 1981), 86.

2. Ibid., 63–68.

1

not yet convinced as to his ultimate denominational affiliation. In fact, he later confessed that had he heeded "worldly ambition and personal preference," he would have become a Congregationalist or Presbyterian, but instead "conscience and Scripture compelled me to be a Baptist."[3] Resolving for himself that immersion is the proper form of baptism—"What other form could set forth the merging of the believer into Christ and the believer's participation in the death and resurrection of his Lord?"[4]—and that baptism was the New Testament prerequisite to participation in the Lord's Supper, Strong overcame the last hurdle and became a convinced Baptist.

After brief service as pulpit supply to North Baptist Church in Chicago, Strong accepted a call to pastor the First Baptist Church in Haverhill, Massachusetts, where he was ordained in August 1861. Thus Haverhill, a small shoemaking town of about ten thousand in northeastern Massachusetts, was the place where Strong spent the years of the Civil War. An enthusiastic supporter of the Union cause, nonetheless, when drafted, Strong secured a replacement (a typical practice at that time) with the help of his congregation, who raised $350 to keep their young preacher. During his four-year pastorate in Haverhill, Strong showed himself to be innovative in his leadership, encouraging women to speak and pray in the church. But on the whole he found change difficult to implement at Haverhill, and so he accepted a call to the First Baptist Church of Cleveland in August 1865.

Cleveland in 1865 was a bustling city of sixty thousand, and First Baptist was a church of six hundred, making it "one of the largest, wealthiest, and most prestigious in the denomination."[5] In his seven-year tenure there, Strong gained renown as a preacher of "meaty, meticulously prepared sermons on the great themes of Christian faith."[6] Enlarging his study beyond the Bible, Strong read avidly in science, history, and philosophy with the intention of being, in his own words, "a proper interpreter of the Bible."[7] He systematically preached doctrinal sermons on the second Sunday of each month, but wisely pitched them at a teenager's level of comprehension, and always offered numerous captivating illustrations and practical applications.

Strong's growing reputation earned him his first honorary degree: the D.D. from Brown University in 1870. Subsequently, he would also receive a D.D. from Yale (1890) and Princeton (1896), an LL.D. from Bucknell (1891) and Alfred (1894), and a Litt.D. from the University of Rochester (1912).[8] He also gained new career opportunities as several offers in academia were received and declined. In 1872, however, he accepted the offer of his alma mater, Rochester Theological Seminary, to return home at age thirty-six as both president and professor of systematic theology.

For the next forty years Strong adroitly handled both positions. By 1897 Strong had presided over impressive growth at the seminary: 250 percent in enrolment (up to 148 students), over 400 percent in property value, and almost 600 percent in the school's endowment. Clearly, Strong was not bashful when it came to fundraising. On the contrary, he moved comfortably and forcefully among the well-to-do and secured many benefactors for Rochester Theological Seminary. Undoubtedly the most significant was Strong's close friend John D. Rockefeller. In fact, one of Rockefeller's daughters married Strong's elder son, Charles. Yet Rockefeller was to hand Strong one of the greatest disappointments of his life by choosing to fund the University of Chicago

3. Ibid., 150.
4. Ibid., 143.
5. Grant Wacker, *Augustus H. Strong and the Dilemma of Historical Consciousness* (Macon, Ga.: Mercer University Press, 1985), 45.

6. Ibid.
7. Strong, *Autobiography*, 180.
8. Wacker, *Strong*, xi.

instead of a major Baptist university in New York City, for which Strong had lobbied long and aggressively.[9]

Strong's family life during these years was also both a blessing and a burden to him. Rebounding from a broken engagement with Julia Finney (daughter of Charles), he met Harriet Louise Savage (1839–1914) in Rochester in the summer of 1861; and, as he later put it, "I came, I saw, and I was conquered."[10] Three months later they were married; their union produced six children—Charles, Mary, John Henry, Cora, Kate, and Laura. Unhappily, Harriet contracted cerebral meningitis in the 1880s, leaving her virtually an invalid and recluse for the rest of her life. Following her death, Strong married Marguerite Jones, a widow also of Rochester. His sons distinguished themselves: John Henry delighted his father by joining him as a professor at the seminary; Charles became a success in academia, though he crushed his father by renouncing the Christian faith.[11]

During his Rochester reign, Strong also served as president of the American Baptist Foreign Mission Society (1892–95), the General Convention of Baptists of North America (1905–10), and the Rochester Historical Society (1890), and as chairman of the board of trustees of Vassar College (1906–11), thus eliciting the judgment that "at the turn of the century he was one of the most visible churchmen in the United States."[12] Witty, affable, urbane, and gracious, Strong made many trips to Europe. On those occasions he dispensed with his teetotaling practice, quipping, "I once told Theodore Bacon that I had to draw the line

somewhere, and I drew mine in the middle of the Atlantic Ocean."[13]

Despite the affability, one did not have to look hard to see "that there was considerable flint in Strong's personality."[14] A tireless worker, some of his contemporaries found him to be autocratic, dogmatic, and domineering. The complexities in Strong's character also extended to his theology. Was he essentially a conservative or a liberal in his theological orientation? We must now attend to the task of sorting out the somewhat ambiguous evidence.

Systematic Theology

The dominant influence at Rochester Theological Seminary when Strong was a student there was Ezekiel Robinson. As a preacher and theologian, Robinson made a great impression on Strong, shaping his theology into a Calvinist mold and his philosophy into a reflection of Sir William Hamilton's synthesis of Scottish and Kantian epistemology. In so doing Robinson formed Strong's thinking in a way that was difficult for him to shake. Yet Strong intuitively realized that he must make his own way through theological thickets; and so, when he succeeded Robinson in 1872 at the seminary, he resolved not to use Robinson's notes in teaching theology to the seminarians, but to create his own.

Those lecture notes, showing Strong's careful reading of orthodox German Lutherans such as Isaak Dorner, Gottfried Thomasius, and Friedrich Philippi, were printed in 1876 as Lectures on Theology for his students at the seminary.[15] With another decade of study and teaching, those notes were enlarged and became the basis for the first edition of Strong's Systematic Theology, published in 1886. Over the next quarter century that work would be reissued in seven more editions, finally ex-

9. For Strong's side of the story, see Strong, *Autobiography*, 247–51, 308–9.

10. Ibid., 157.

11. On Strong's anguish over Charles's renouncing the faith, see Wacker, *Strong*, 102. Charles studied philosophy under Josiah Royce and William James at Harvard, did graduate work in Europe, and went on to teach psychology and philosophy at Chicago, Cornell, and Columbia.

12. Wacker, *Strong*, 5.

13. Strong, *Autobiography*, 207.

14. Wacker, *Strong*, 3.

15. Augustus H. Strong, *Lectures on Theology* (Rochester: E. R. Andrews, 1876).

panding to become a three-volume work with a thousand pages of text, bristling with erudite encounters with biblical material and major thinkers.[16] That work became a widely used textbook in theological seminaries.

With his definition of theology on page 1 as "the science of God and of all the relations between God and the universe," Strong positioned himself in the venerable camp of Protestant orthodox rationalism. Not unaware of the challenge Immanuel Kant had posed for modern theology by his assertion that humans can know only phenomena and not noumena, Strong was confident that Hamilton and Hermann Lotze had healed that epistemological rift, making it possible for him to affirm that the human mind has the capacity to know God, that God has revealed himself, and that faith is the highest kind of knowing. Therefore, theological knowledge is not meaningless; to the contrary, "a scientific theology is possible" and even "a rational necessity," since all human beings have organizing, reflective minds. So then, every individual has a personal theology; unfortunately, however, many of those theologies are "meager and blundering."[17]

Against the Enlightenment contention that human reason is the ultimate authority in assessing truth, even religious truth, Strong presumed that the foundation for systematic theology is a God who has taken the initiative in revelatory self-disclosure. Thus, against the nineteenth-century liberal Protestant tradition that had arisen out of that Enlightenment contention, Strong affirmed the primacy of doctrine as over against either religious feeling (with Friedrich Schleiermacher) or morality (with Albrecht Ritschl).[18]

Ethical Monism

Equally compelling for Strong was the intellectual revolution in historical consciousness washing over Western culture in the late nineteenth century. The sense that life and all knowledge are dynamic and developing, not static, and as such are vitally linked to consciousness and perspective, which, in turn, are strongly conditioned by cultural context, had a revolutionary impact on Christian doctrine. Grant Wacker has presented Augustus Strong as a conservative thinker allured by this modernist impulse and thus "torn between the ahistorical world of orthodox rationalism and the historically informed world of Protestant liberalism."[19]

By his own admission Strong did experience a significant intellectual shift, probably in the early 1890s. Though more philosophical than theological, the change in point of view did have implications for all the old doctrines. As he put it, "I seem to myself to have reached a fundamental truth which throws new light upon them all."[20] This new outlook was publicly disclosed in a series of articles published in 1894–95[21] and then reissued in book form in 1899 as *Christ in Creation and Ethical Monism*. It represented a shift from dualism to a form of philosophical monism as Strong now saw all of reality as one and the divine as immanent within human history and nature: "That Christ is the one and only Revealer of God in nature as well as in Scripture is in my judgement the key to theology. This view implies a monistic and idealistic conception of the world, together with an evolutionary idea of its origin and progress."[22]

Perhaps Strong adopted this new outlook as quickly and decisively as he did to

16. Augustus H. Strong, *Systematic Theology*, 8th ed., rev. and enlarged, 3 vols. (Philadelphia: Griffith and Rowland, 1907–09); 3 vols. in 1 (Philadelphia: Judson, 1960).

17. Ibid., 1, 5, 11, 16.

18. Ibid., 20–21.

19. Wacker, *Strong*, 12.

20. Strong, *Autobiography*, 338.

21. Augustus H. Strong, "Christ in Creation," *Examiner*, 6 October 1894; idem, "Ethical Monism Once More," *Examiner*, 17 October, 24 October, and 3 November 1895.

22. Strong, *Autobiography*, 339.

ease the tension between his modernist impulse and traditional orthodoxy. Clearly, it allowed Strong to appropriate a historical consciousness and gave him an openness to modernity without jettisoning the classical standards of Christian orthodoxy. Thus he could state that "theology is a progressive science, not because the truth itself changes, but because human apprehension and statement of the truth improve from age to age."[23]

Strong created the term "ethical monism" to differentiate his view from the personalistic idealism of Borden Parker Bowne at Boston University and Hermann Lotze in Germany.[24] In like manner, his definition of ethical monism was intended to contrast his system with materialism, materialistic idealism, and idealistic pantheism:

> *Ethical Monism:* Universe = Finite, partial, graded manifestation of the divine Life; Matter being God's self-limitation under the law of necessity, Humanity being God's self-limitation under the law of freedom, Incarnation and Atonement being God's self-limitations under the law of grace. Metaphysical Monism, or the doctrine of one Substance, Principle, or Ground of Being, is consistent with Psychological Dualism, or the doctrine that the soul is personally distinct from matter on the one hand and from God on the other.[25]

That is to say, all reality is one substance, God. Christ, the eternal Word of God, is the only complete and perfect expression of God. The universe is Christ's finite manifestation of God in time. The universe is not itself God, only a partial disclosure of God's wisdom and power, adapted for human comprehension and displaying the inherent limitations that an infinite, eternal Word must endure under the restrictions of time and space.[26]

Although critics warily sniffed the heresy of pantheism lurking under this guise of monism, Strong repeatedly denied the accusation. Pantheism, he countered, always denies the personality and the transcendence of God; his monistic version affirmed both. When pressed, Strong admitted that his ethical monism was really a "dualistic monism." That is, he had no desire to deny "the dualism of matter and mind" or "the dualism of man and God." But these truths, which Strong called "psychological dualism," were deemed to be consistent with metaphysical monism in view of the complementary greater truth that "matter and mind, man and God, have underground connections and a common life, because all things, humanity included, live, move, and have their being in God."[27] Pantheism rightly stresses the truth of divine immanence, but limits God by imprisoning him in the universe. On the contrary, Strong's monism acknowledges God's transcendence by affirming that the universe does not exhaust God: "The universe is a manifestation of God, but it is not God . . . [for] all things . . . are only the partial, temporal, graded, finite unfoldings of a Being infinitely greater than they."[28]

Strong's monism was also *ethical*—it safeguarded the moral character of both God and humanity. By retaining the concepts of freedom, responsibility, sin, and guilt, it retained the concepts of moral action and accountability. Thus Strong contended not for a deterministic monism, but for one that acknowledged free will and distinctive personality for both God and humanity. As he put it, ethical monism admits that "sin and righteousness, God and the world, remain—two in one and one in two—with their antagonisms as well as their ideal unity."[29]

23. Augustus H. Strong, *Christ in Creation and Ethical Monism* (Philadelphia: Roger Williams, 1899), 1.

24. Wacker, *Strong*, 62.

25. Strong, *Systematic Theology*, 90.

26. Strong, *Christ in Creation*, 45.

27. Ibid., 53–54.

28. Ibid., 63–64.

29. Ibid., 27.

Strong's new worldview of ethical monism was radically and thoroughly christocentric as well. In the economy of the Triune God it is the Second Person, the Word, who expresses, manifests, and reveals God. Accordingly, "we may say that God never thought, said, or did anything except through Christ" (the Word of God in both time and eternity).[30] While orthodoxy has long recognized the redemptive work of Christ, the biblical testimony to his work in creation has been underplayed. Strong pointed to passages such as Colossians 1:16–17 ("For by him all things were created: things in heaven and on earth, visible and invisible, whether thrones or powers or rulers or authorities; all things were created by him and for him. He is before all things, and in him all things hold together," NIV) and John 1:3 ("Through him all things were made; without him nothing was made that has been made," NIV). Strong regarded such texts as foundational for redressing an evangelical theology overly skewed in a soteriological direction.

Just as faithful Christians affirm that salvation lies in the incarnate Christ, who made atonement for sin by his death on the cross, so also, urged Strong, must we recognize "the universe as created, upheld, and governed by the same Being."[31] In so doing we will see Christ as supplying the very coherence of our universe, physically, morally, and intellectually, "for in him we live and move and have our being" (Acts 17:28 NIV). And thus, just "as the attraction of gravitation and the principle of evolution are only other names for Christ, so he is the basis of inductive reasoning and the ground of moral unity in the creation."[32] Though we are isolated spiritually through sin, there is in creation a natural bond uniting all humanity and Christ. Through this bond, which cannot be severed, "all men are naturally one with Christ by physical birth, before they become morally one with him by spiritual birth."[33]

Strong was convinced, then, that there was a happy convergence between his new philosophy of ethical monism and what Scripture says about Christ's work in creation. There was another major impetus towards this new outlook, namely, the spirit of the age: "The tendency of modern thought in all its departments, whether physics, literature, theology, or philosophy, is to monism."[34] From the writings of Robert Browning to the geological hypotheses of Thomas Chamberlin at the newly established University of Chicago, Strong saw philosophical monism sweeping through the Western world. In a telling passage, he offered this candid challenge:

> It is of great importance, both to the preacher and to the Christian, to hold the right attitude toward the ruling idea of our time. This universal tendency toward monism, is it a wave of unbelief set agoing by an evil intelligence in order to overwhelm and swamp the religion of Christ? Or is it a mighty movement of the Spirit of God, giving . . . a deeper understanding of truth. . . ? I confess that I have come to believe the latter alternative.[35]

If indeed monism was to be the philosophy of the future, the only issue for Strong was whether it would be "an ethical and Christian, or a non-ethical and anti-Christian monism."[36] The challenge of capturing monism for Christ, lest any materialistic or pantheistic alternatives prevail, exhilarated Strong: "Let us see in this forward march of thought a sign that Christ and his kingdom are conquering and to conquer."[37]

Such triumphalist bravado has sounded foreign to the ears of most twentieth-century American evangelicals, whose eschatological and cultural orientations dif-

---

30. Ibid., 2.
31. Strong, *Systematic Theology*, 109.
32. Ibid.

33. Ibid., 110.
34. Strong, *Christ in Creation*, 16.
35. Ibid., 22.
36. Ibid.
37. Ibid.

fer from Strong's. A staunch postmillennialist to the end of his life, he assumed and expected a continuing Christian hegemony over American culture.[38] Along with many of his contemporaries he was "swept up in a powerful longing to hear the rhythms of the divine in the cadence of modern life."[39]

Even in his own time, Strong's attempted reconciliation of philosophical monism with evangelical doctrine was not persuasive to many critics. Emerging conservative and liberal Protestant positions—magnified and polarized dramatically by the modernist-fundamentalist controversies of the 1920s—were readily apparent in the 1890s; and representatives from both sides assailed him for perceived inadequacies. From the conservative side, critics such as the Baptist Alvah Hovey, the Methodist A. J. F. Behrends, and the Presbyterian Caspar Wistar Hodge, complained that Christian faith and philosophical monism were not as harmonious as Strong imagined. Unconvinced that he had successfully skirted the dangers of pantheism, they feared that his reformulation of some doctrines compromised biblical fidelity more than he realized.[40] Yet the liberal critic William Adams Brown had the opposite lament: monism's emphasis on divine immanence necessitated a complete overhaul of traditional doctrine, a task left undone by Strong. Thus, on the whole, Strong's views "won only a partial acceptance" and "were received with equal caution by conservative and liberal alike."[41]

Caution has continued to characterize twentieth-century evangelical responses to Strong. Carl Henry charges that ethical monism led Strong to subscribe "to a new theory of religious knowledge" that "weakened the objective authority of Scripture."[42] Wacker has also focused on Strong's "shifting epistemic assumptions," but suggests that his developing historical consciousness had a greater impact.[43] Wacker notes as well that Strong is now largely ignored by both liberals and conservatives.[44]

Though Strong's ethical monism failed to win a fervent following among his contemporaries and has languished in relative obscurity since then, he himself was undaunted in singing its virtues. He was sure that monism, far from denying or threatening any cherished articles of faith, profoundly enriched the old doctrines. Furthermore, he expected that perennial theological thorns (e.g., the difficulty of reconciling divine sovereignty and human freedom) would be, if not completely resolved, at least made less thorny from a monistic perspective. In addition, theological truths that were formerly obscured would emerge. For example, the profound truth of human solidarity would help keep theology from being, as it had been in the past, merely individualistic.[45]

Strong's adoption of a form of philosophical monism seems to have allowed him to make peace with, if not wholly capitulate to, historicism and its epistemological ramifications. Wacker has cataloged some of the characteristics of Strong's theology after his adoption of monism: (1) an inclination to blur the distinction between special and general revelation; (2) a greater stress on the developmental nature of the matrix in which revelation was given; (3) an affirmation of spiritual progress in modern culture as the work of Christ; and (4) an

38. For Strong's millennial views see *Systematic Theology*, 1003–14; for a more popular, succinct statement see his *What Shall I Believe?* (New York and Chicago: Revell, 1922), 104–8.

39. Wacker, *Strong*, 134.

40. For the most complete analysis of Strong's views and an assessment of his critics, see Carl F. H. Henry, *Personal Idealism and Strong's Theology* (Wheaton, Ill.: Van Kampen, 1951).

41. Ibid., 196. Wacker concurs: "[Between 1886 and 1907] the review literature did become increasingly perceptive about, and astringent toward, Strong's work." To be fair, however, Wacker notes that the publication of *Christ in Creation* in 1899 was hardly noticed (*Strong*, 88, 94).

42. Henry, *Personal Idealism*, 228, 205.

43. Wacker, *Strong*, 9, 46–54.

44. Ibid., 5–6.

45. Strong, *Christ in Creation*, 41–44; idem, *Systematic Theology*, 106.

abiding conviction that the truth of Christianity, nonetheless, does not change.[46] The last point, it would seem, was most crucial in Strong's retaining his evangelical credentials, for it both limited and colored the preceding three.

View of Biblical Inspiration and Authority

More visible than the epistemological shifts in the shadowy, subterranean world of Strong's consciousness were the accommodations made in his theological superstructure. Here Strong's views on biblical inspiration and authority were primary. From his *Lectures on Theology* (1876) through the sixth edition of his *Systematic Theology* (1899) Strong defined inspiration as "that special divine influence upon the minds of the Scripture writers in virtue of which their productions, apart from errors of transcription, and when rightly interpreted, together constitute an infallible and sufficient rule of faith and practice."[47] To that definition was added the following statement in the seventh edition of *Systematic Theology* (1902): "Inspiration is that influence of the Spirit of God upon the minds of the Scripture writers which made their writings the record of a progressive divine revelation, sufficient . . . to lead every honest inquirer to Christ and salvation."[48] Whether Strong intended this addition as a new definition is ambiguous, but the differences are clear: the Bible is referred to not as God's revelation, but as merely a record of God's revelation; and the term "progressive" is added while "infallible" is dropped. The eighth and final edition of Strong's *Systematic Theology* included only the latter statement about inspiration; the original definition was dropped.

Strong still affirmed his belief that inspiration had secured "a trustworthy trans-

mission by the sacred writers of the truth they were commissioned to deliver"; he did not think that inspiration was verbal, however, and he was uncertain as to the method.[49] He also denied that Christianity stands or falls with the doctrine of inspiration or with some particular theory thereof. He professed to be content "to let science and criticism tell us what inspiration is." After all, "the supremacy of Christ, and not any theory of inspiration," was the foundation of his faith.[50] But if one had to opt for a specific theory, Strong favored regarding inspiration as "neither natural, partial, nor mechanical, but supernatural, plenary, and dynamical."[51]

Strong's ideas about biblical inspiration were, of course, intimately linked with his views about the Bible's authority and purpose. He believed that Scripture has divine authority; but like that of the church, the human conscience, and civil rulers, its authority is "delegated [by] and subordinate" to the ultimate source of authority, Christ himself. Specifically, biblical authority is "limited to the sphere in which it was meant to move and to the purposes for which it was designed."[52] Those purposes, Strong maintained, are redemptive, and not historical or scientific. The Bible "was not meant to teach us mathematics, but it was meant to teach us of Christ. It was not meant to teach us how the heavens go, but to teach us how to go to heaven."[53]

Scripture, then, was intended to answer only two fundamental questions: "What has God done to save me? and what must I do to be saved?"[54] Apart from that soteriological thrust, biblical inspiration "did not guarantee inerrancy."[55] Not that Strong admitted that Scripture contains proved er-

46. Wacker, *Strong*, 75–81.
47. Quoted in Wacker, *Strong*, 67.
48. Ibid.

49. Strong, *Systematic Theology*, 215–18.
50. On this issue see Strong's essay "The Authority of Scripture," in *Christ in Creation*, 113–36 (the quotations are from p. 126).
51. Strong, *Systematic Theology*, 211.
52. Strong, *Christ in Creation*, 123.
53. Ibid.
54. Strong, *Systematic Theology*, 218.
55. Ibid., 215.

rors in other matters. To the contrary, he declared that "what is charged as such is simply truth presented in popular and impressive forms."[56] Nevertheless, he was conceptually comfortable with the possibility of error: "The propositions of Euclid are not invalidated by the fact that he believed the earth to be flat. The ethics of Plato would not be disproved by his mistakes with regard to the solar system. So religious authority is independent of merely secular knowledge."[57]

Such an outlook made Strong utterly sanguine about accepting the results of higher criticism. He reasoned that if inductive scholarly study of Scripture should necessitate reversing long-held traditions about authorship, date of composition, and historical exactness, then so be it. For the Bible, with its self-authenticating character, would still offer overwhelming proof of its divine (as well as human) origin and therefore warrant acceptance by Christians as their "sufficient rule of faith and practice."[58]

View of Creation

Flexibility (or laxity, depending on one's judgment!) in interpreting the biblical record also gave Strong a mediating view on the issue of creation. Rejecting allegorical and mythical renderings of Genesis 1–2 as well as a variety of literalist positions that sought precise correspondence between science and the biblical text, Strong favored what he called a "pictorial-summary interpretation." By this he meant that he regarded the opening chapters of Genesis as a rough sketch of the history of creation, "true in all its essential features, but presented in a graphic form suited to the common mind and to earlier as well as to later ages." Revelation was given in

"pregnant language" so that it could accord with scientific understanding at all times.[59]

Though Strong was certain that humanity was the result of the creative work of God, and not the "mere product of unreasoning natural forces,"[60] he was, nevertheless, quite open to the possibility of evolutionary means for the creation of the human race. Genesis, he believed, was not explicit as to whether or not the human body was derived by natural descent from lower animals: "The forming of man 'of the dust of the ground' (Gen. 2:7) does not in itself determine whether the creation of man's body was mediate or immediate."[61]

Strong conceded a partial truth to Darwin's theory of natural selection—homologous structures and similarity in embryonic development apparently link humanity to the animal world. Nonetheless, he disputed the notion that evolution makes the Creator superfluous. On the contrary, "evolution is only the method of God."[62] Moreover, the overwhelming differences between humanity and other life forms evidence divine intervention; thus, human creation was both mediated and immediate. In a favorite phrase Strong exclaimed that "man came not *from* the brute, but *through* the brute."[63]

Strong's theistic evolutionism was reinforced by his conversion to philosophical monism. The foundational reality of the oneness of creation pulsating in the divine Christ meant that the naturalistic, atheistic, nonteleological implications of Darwin's evolutionary theory could be exchanged for a Christianized version. Strong could also readily embrace the traducianist position on the origin of the human soul and the Augustinian position on the imputation of Adam's sin to his posterity through his natural headship. Indeed, Strong considered these

56. Ibid., 223.
57. Ibid., 218.
58. See Strong, *Autobiography*, 346, and *Systematic Theology*, 145–46, 171–72, 214, 223, 238–41.

59. Strong, *Systematic Theology*, 393–94.
60. Ibid., 465.
61. Ibid.
62. Ibid., 466.
63. Ibid., 467.

positions to be enriched by an evolutionary monistic perspective.[64]

Final Years and Theological Legacy

Clearly, Strong was not a typical American conservative Protestant at the turn of the century. His views reveal both his willingness to rethink and revise inherited orthodoxy and his indebtedness to the Zeitgeist. Indeed, Grant Wacker has suggested that by 1900 Strong "was more worried about the pretentiousness of rationalistic orthodoxy" than the doctrinal errors of liberalism.[65] He was responsible for the addition of a number of liberal Protestants to the faculty at Rochester, including Conrad Moehlman, Walter Betteridge, Joseph W. A. Stewart, Cornelius Woelfkin, and most famous of all, Walter Rauschenbusch.[66] Though all turned out to be more liberal than Strong, he did not restrict their teaching and writing.

For most of his career Strong shunned involvement in theological controversy. His own views attempted to mediate the growing rift between evangelical orthodoxy and Protestant liberalism; and, ecclesiastically, he balanced denominational loyalty with a spirit of catholicity. Yet events following his resignation in 1912 after forty years as both president and professor at Rochester Theological Seminary soon dictated a new outlook for him. Rapid theological change at the school ensued as Clarence Barbour, a man Strong believed to be adversely influenced by the Chicago School of Theology, was selected as the new president. Even worse was the appointment of George Cross as professor of systematic theology,

which Strong pronounced to be "the greatest calamity that has come to the seminary since its foundation." Because Cross viewed the Bible as "only the record of man's gropings after God," Strong regarded him as an agnostic and skeptic for whom systematic theology, at least in the traditional sense, was impossible.[67] Strong regretted that he had not lobbied intensively for his son John Henry, a professor at the seminary, to succeed him as president.

A worldwide tour of Baptist missions in 1916 also added to Strong's alarm about the pernicious effects of liberalism. His book *A Tour of the Missions*, based on his observations, raised the concern that evangelistic outreach was being replaced on the mission field by social services. Missionaries no longer had a gospel to preach, claimed Strong, and the fault lay with modernistic liberalism. This extreme version of liberalism, gaining force since 1900, had a "perverted historical method" at its foundation. That is, the modernist teacher not only used critical methods in interpreting Scripture, something Strong had accepted for years, but joined such methods with utterly naturalistic and historicist presuppositions, and thus became a "blind leader of the blind." Ask such a teacher, averred Strong, "if he believes in the preexistence, deity, virgin birth, miracles, atoning death, physical resurrection, omnipresence, and omnipotence of Christ, and he denies your right to require of him any statement of his own beliefs. He does not conceive it to be his duty to furnish his students with any fixed conclusions as to doctrine but only to aid them in coming to conclusions for themselves."[68]

Not surprisingly, then, as his own Northern Baptist Convention became embroiled in open conflict between fundamentalists and modernists, Strong cast his lot with the

64. Ibid., 488–97, 619–37.
65. Wacker, *Strong*, 85.
66. For the fullest discussion see LeRoy Moore, Jr., "The Rise of American Religious Liberalism at the Rochester Theological Seminary, 1872–1928," Ph.D. diss., Claremont Graduate School, 1966; see also D. Dennis Hesselgrave, "The Relationship between A. H. Strong and Walter Rauschenbusch at Colgate-Rochester Divinity School," M.A. thesis, Trinity Evangelical Divinity School, 1970.

67. Strong, *Autobiography*, 357.
68. Augustus H. Strong, *A Tour of the Missions: Observations and Conclusions* (Philadelphia: Griffith and Rowland, 1918), 187–90.

former in the summer of 1921.[69] To be sure, the fit was not entirely comfortable, but "Strong had every reason to believe that he could champion their cause without compromising his intellectual integrity."[70] His final word was a rebuke of both sides. "So-called fundamentalists [were] not fundamental enough," failing to appreciate the historical dimensions of the incarnation. Liberals, armed with their trusty telescopes, could "see a fly on a barn door a half mile off, but they cannot see the door." The two sides, then, were "sincere but imperfectly informed parties."[71] Little wonder that Strong often caught flak from each camp: "The conservatives at Waco and Princeton think me too radical, and the radicals of Union and of Chicago think me too conservative."[72] Yet the other side of the coin was that both camps "had ample reason to believe that in his heart of hearts, he was one of them."[73]

The threat of modernism was one of Strong's two great concerns in the last years of his life. The other, reinforced by the events of World War I, was the ongoing conviction "that Christ is the immanent energizing force in history."[74] Since his death on November 29, 1921, Strong's legacy has been rather enigmatic. His adoption of ethical monism, ready acceptance of theistic evolution and biblical criticism, and attraction to the modernist view of historical consciousness clearly distanced him from many of his conservative contemporaries. Yet his faithful championing of orthodox doctrine and his persistent confession of

the Bible as divine revelation positioned him on the evangelical side of the divide. The suggestion that Strong played a mediatorial role in the United States similar to that of Peter Taylor Forsyth in Great Britain is probably the best assessment.[75] No other American evangelical theologian of his generation, with the exception of Princeton's B. B. Warfield, could match Strong's erudition or his vision of the dimensions of Christian faith. A man who devoured literature, who traveled constantly, "and who could not bear to be anywhere except in the driver's seat of every organization he joined,"[76] Strong had a great passion for theology and learning that is worthy of scrutiny by his spiritual descendants.

Primary Sources

Strong, Augustus H. *Christ in Creation and Ethical Monism.* Philadelphia: Roger Williams, 1899.

_____. *Systematic Theology.* 8th ed., revised and enlarged. 3 vols. Philadelphia: Griffith and Rowland, 1907–09. Reprint (3 vols. in 1). Philadelphia: Judson, 1960.

Secondary Sources

Henry, Carl F. H. *Personal Idealism and Strong's Theology.* Wheaton, Ill.: Van Kampen, 1951.

Strong, Augustus H. *Autobiography of Augustus Hopkins Strong.* Edited by Crerar Douglas. Valley Forge, Pa.: Judson, 1981.

Wacker, Grant. *Augustus H. Strong and the Dilemma of Historical Consciousness.* Macon, Ga.: Mercer University Press, 1985.

69. For his public announcement see Augustus H. Strong, "Confessions of Our Faith," *Watchman-Examiner,* 21 July 1921, p. 910.

70. Wacker, *Strong,* 120.

71. Strong, *What Shall I Believe?* 62–63. These ten essays, written by Strong in the fall of 1921 on the main themes of Christian faith, were first published jointly in the conservative *Watchman-Examiner* and the liberal *Baptist* in the winter of 1921–22.

72. Quoted in Wacker, *Strong,* 97.

73. Wacker, *Strong,* 129.

74. Ibid., 121.

75. For other ways to categorize Strong, see Wacker, *Strong,* 7–9; for the similarities between Strong and Forsyth, see pp. 164–66.

76. Wacker, *Strong,* 131. For Strong's theological interaction with literature, see his *Great Poets and Their Theology* (Philadelphia: American Baptist Publication Society, 1897) and *American Poets and Their Theology* (Philadelphia: Griffith and Rowland, 1916). For a collection of his addresses, sermons, and essays, see his *Miscellanies,* 2 vols. (Philadelphia: Griffith and Rowland, 1912); see also *One Hundred Chapel-Talks to Theological Students* (Philadelphia: Griffith and Rowland, 1913).

James Orr

Glen G. Scorgie

James Orr (not to be confused with J. Edwin Orr, a more recent chronicler of revivals) was born in Glasgow on April 11, 1844. He was orphaned at an early age; subsequent apprenticeship (of economic necessity) to a bookbinder and the postponement of his university entrance until age twenty-one give some suggestion of a Spartan adolescence. As a young man he came in touch with the United Presbyterians and identified with their egalitarian tradition. In 1865 he enrolled as an arts student at the University of Glasgow with a view to the Christian ministry, and in 1868 he began to attend summer sessions at the United Presbyterian Divinity Hall in Edinburgh. He took a string of prizes at Glasgow and graduated in 1870 with first-class honors as a master of arts in mental philosophy. His crowning achievement as an undergraduate was winning a prestigious Ferguson Scholarship for his work in philosophy. Most Ferguson scholars elected to attend Oxford or Cambridge, but Orr used his funding to remain at the University of Glasgow and study divinity there from 1870 to 1872.

Scottish philosophy was in transition when Orr began his university studies, and the University of Glasgow was the eye of the storm, for it employed both John Veitch, one of the last of Scotland's commonsense philosophers, and Edward Caird, who was soon to establish himself as a champion of Hegelian idealism. Orr went against the general student trend by attaching himself more to Veitch than to Caird, and his philosophical viewpoint was shaped by commonsense assumptions, not least of which was the tenet that every person (hence, *common* sense) has the potential to judge what is true. Still, Orr's position was sufficiently mediating that Caird felt able to commend publicly an essay by Orr on David Hume—an essay that earned a share of the university's Lord Rector's Prize in 1872 and that became the basis for Orr's book entitled *David Hume and His Influence on Philosophy and Theology* (1903). Significantly, he emerged from his philosophical studies with an affirmative and confident perspective on metaphysics and epistemology, a perspective that allowed reason a healthy role in the realm of theology.

Orr received a bachelor of divinity degree from Glasgow in 1872, and completed his final session at the United Presbyterian Divinity Hall shortly thereafter. Towards the end of 1873 he accepted a call from the East Bank United Presbyterian Church in the Borders town of Hawick, and for the next seventeen years performed ministerial duties there. He took an active role in community affairs yet managed to devote a substantial portion of his time to theological study. At some point he learned German, and in 1885 earned the doctor of divinity degree from Glasgow.

In Scotland, theological reappraisal prompted by the refining fires of the nineteenth century eventually focused on the Westminster Confession and the scholastic brand of Calvinism contained therein. During the 1870s Orr was among those who campaigned for modified subscription to the confession. He helped draft the United Presbyterian Declaratory Statement of 1879, which qualified and effectively relaxed the extent to which a minister was obliged to affirm the content of the church's subordinate standards. The United Presbyterian approach was accorded the flattery of being imitated by the other main wings of Scottish Presbyterianism, and served to undermine the rule of Calvinism in Scotland.

While Orr believed that John Calvin's disposition "tended to severity" and that Calvinism (and especially the Westminster Confession) reflected more the holiness than the love of God, he denied that Calvinism was "that monstrosity of cold-blooded logic, destroying freedom, and consigning myriads, without fault of their own, by biased decree of reprobation, to the pit, which some have imagined."[1] His qualified appreciation for Calvinism was to a large extent a

consequence of the distinction he drew between the component evangelical doctrines of Calvinism and the means by which they were organized. Observing that these components were far older than Calvin's organization of them, Orr insisted that they had special value and were destined to endure.[2]

The Christian View of God and the World

A turning point in Orr's career came when he was invited to deliver in 1891 the initial series of Kerr Lectures at the United Presbyterian Theological College (formerly Divinity Hall). Three years in preparation, these lectures revealed Orr's remarkable grasp of contemporary philosophical and theological literature. They were published two years later as *The Christian View of God and the World, as Centring in the Incarnation.* This work, which proved to be his magnum opus, was widely acclaimed and launched him on a prolific academic career. In the remaining two decades of his life, Orr wrote sixteen books, contributed hundreds of articles and reviews to religious and secular periodicals, edited a denominational magazine and a major reference work, and frequently lectured abroad. The cumulative effect was that his voice seemed omnipresent in his day.

The central thesis of Orr's *Christian View*, a thesis that later directly influenced Carl F. H. Henry among others, is that there is inherent in the Christian faith a uniquely adequate and coherent interpretation of existence. Though Christianity is a religion and not a philosophy, it does offer among its benefits a supremely satisfying worldview. Humanity's irrepressible need for a worldview makes urgent the church's task of proclaiming its own. The Christian

1. James Orr, "Calvinism and Protestantism," *Missionary Record of the United Free Church* 9 (1909): 197–98.

2. James Orr, "Calvinism," in *Encyclopaedia of Religion and Ethics,* ed. James Hastings, 13 vols. (New York: Scribner, 1924–27), 3:148; see also James Orr, "Calvin," in *The Reformers,* ed. James Brown (Glasgow: Maclehose, 1885), 241–95; and idem, *The Progress of Dogma* (London: Hodder and Stoughton, 1901), 292–94.

worldview has to be presented with force and appeal, or people will look elsewhere for intellectual satisfaction.

It is the coherency of the Christian worldview, its harmony with reason and moral experience, that makes it compelling. To use a word that Orr favored, the Christian worldview has verisimilitude. Thus the systematic presentation of evangelical doctrine (which is nothing other than the setting forth of this worldview) is in fact the most comprehensive apologetic for the Christian faith. Accordingly, *The Christian View* does not begin with an apology for Scripture and then proceed to confident deduction therefrom. To the contrary, Scripture is not treated at all. The Christian system of belief is commended on the basis of its own intrinsic merits and the correspondence assumed to exist between its claims and humanity's capacity to recognize truth intuitively and rationally. In this sense, then, the Christian faith is self-authenticating.

Having retreated from a strict adherence to confessional Calvinism, Orr gave notice in *The Christian View* of what he considered the substance of the Christian faith. The subtitle of the work, *As Centring in the Incarnation*, points to Orr's selection of the incarnation as the unifying principle of his system. This departure from the traditional focus on the atonement reflected a popular tendency in late-nineteenth-century British theological scholarship. Orr ventured to suggest that the incarnation was more than a mere declaration of God's purpose to save the world. "It is itself a certain stage in that reconciliation, and the point of departure for every other. In the Incarnation, God and man are already in a sense one."[3] He also stressed the high view of humanity implied by the incarnation. Among other things the incarnation showed that there is "a natural kinship between the human spirit and the Divine" and that "the bond between God and man is inner and essential." A capacity for the divine is inherent in humanity: "If there were not already a God-related element in the human spirit, no subsequent act of grace could confer on man this spiritual dignity."[4]

Such suggestive (one might say provocative) remarks are rare in *The Christian View*. In both its structure and content, the work basically followed traditional lines. Christianity, Orr insisted, is more than a source of ethical instruction, social-reform principles, and philanthropic impulse. It is "a great Divine economy for the recovery of men from guilt and the power of sin—from a state of estrangement and hostility to God—to a state of holiness and blessedness in the favour of God, and of fitness for the attainment of their true destination."[5] This conception of Christianity as a religion of personal redemption, Orr believed, found its essential undergirding in the central tenets of evangelical orthodoxy. Everything hung upon the doctrines, first of all, of God as personal, ethical, and self-revealing; then, of humanity as created in his image yet horribly defiled by an inherited moral evil; of incarnation and redemption; of forgiveness, regeneration, and immortality. Exactly these doctrines, and not the minutiae of some historic creed, had to be vigorously defended. With respect to the atonement, for example, Orr considered it sufficient, given the hostile theological climate, simply to insist that Christ's death had sacrificial and expiatory value. As for the various interpretative theories of the atonement (including that of John McLeod Campbell, who startled and stimulated Scottish theology by depicting Christ's death as an act of vicarious repentance), Orr was content to explore them all with a view to synthesizing, with Hegelian-style magnanimity, their profoundest insights.

The Christian View anticipates some significant features of Orr's subsequent theological mind-set. In the first place, it con-

---

3. James Orr, *The Christian View of God and the World, As Centring in the Incarnation* (Edinburgh: A. Elliot, 1893), 296.

4. Ibid., 119–21.

5. Ibid., 287.

tains a clear statement of Orr's conviction that Christianity is undeniably and irreducibly supernatural. By this Orr meant that Christianity assumes the existence of two distinct realms, the natural and the supernatural, which periodically and miraculously intersect in the interests of religion. This assumption of the supernatural (which Rudolf Bultmann later rejected as unscientific biblical cosmology) is woven inextricably into the very fabric of the Christian religion and cannot be excised without dealing a mortal blow to the religion itself. Orr made it plain that for him this point was absolutely nonnegotiable.[6]

In the second place, Orr gravitated toward dichotomous conflict as his basic paradigm for understanding his times. Christianity with its supernaturalistic assumption was in cosmic struggle with naturalism. No eclecticism was possible. Quoting Franz Delitzsch's *Deep Gulf between the Old and Modern Theology* (1890), Orr held that "the answer can only be yes or no. The deep gulf remains. It will remain to the end of time."[7] Given the centrality of the supernatural to Orr's conception and defense of the Christian faith, we should note how he tried to prove its plausibility. Basically he stressed the reasonableness of the idea that a personal, loving God would take nature-suspending initiatives to communicate with, and maintain fellowship with, his creatures. According to Orr, then, theism makes supernatural activity plausible.[8]

With Orr's confidence in the self-authenticating character of the Christian faith, he might have lapsed quite easily into an insular fideism were it not for a third noteworthy conviction, namely, the rational unity of all truth. James Denney, Orr's colleague and close friend, noted that "nothing marks

[Orr's] whole work as a teacher of theology more strongly than his sense of the unity of knowledge."[9] He held that everything within the scope of human experience has the potential either to confirm or to undermine the claims of evangelical orthodoxy. The range of possible challenges to orthodoxy is, according to this view, very extensive indeed. To his credit, Orr responded with an equally broad apologetic agenda. And no less remarkable than the sheer scope of his work was his degree of competence in all these endeavors. He was a rare polymath.

Though in principle Orr was prepared to be dislodged from his position if the facts warranted, he remained confident. "I do not believe," he said, "that in order to preserve [the Christian view] one single truth we have been accustomed to see shining in that constellation will require to be withdrawn."[10] This comment set the tone for Orr's subsequent theological contribution, which may best be described as a call for continued adherence to the central tenets of evangelical orthodoxy. In the course of his career, he urged such continued adherence in the face of challenges from Ritschlianism, Old Testament criticism, evolutionary theory, and the quest of the historical Jesus.

Responses to Challenges to Evangelical Orthodoxy

Ritschlianism

Shortly after the completion of Orr's lecture series, the chair of church history at the United Presbyterian Theological College fell vacant, and on the strength of his recent success the post was offered to him. When Orr accepted the chair, a Scotswoman noted that the "big and burly" professor coming up from the Borders was not the kind to be intimidated physically nor, she suggested shrewdly, was it likely that

6. Ibid., 10.
7. Ibid., 372.
8. Ibid., 51, 76; see also James Orr, *David Hume and His Influence on Philosophy and Theology* (Edinburgh: T. and T. Clark, 1903), 192–216; idem, *Revelation and Inspiration* (New York: Scribner, 1910), 109–30; and idem, *The Faith of a Modern Christian* (London: Hodder and Stoughton, 1910), 61–78.

9. James Denney, "The Late Professor Orr," *British Weekly*, 11 September 1913, p. 576.
10. Orr, *Christian View*, 347.

one of his temper would be pushed around theologically either.[11]

This image of theological sturdiness was immediately put to a great test as Scottish religious thought began to feel the impact of Albrecht Ritschl, the dominant figure in German theology in the latter part of the nineteenth century. His reconstruction of Christian theology stressed the historical revelation of God in Jesus Christ and took the shape of an ellipse with twin foci: the religious experience of justification and the practical mandate of the kingdom of God. Ritschl emphasized Christ's role as the supreme revealer of God's fatherly love and shifted the balance of concern from theoretical to ethical matters. At the same time Ritschl sought to fortify religious confidence against any possible assaults from historical criticism or scientific advance.

It was not long before Orr focused his considerable energies upon an analysis of Ritschlianism, and in 1897 he published *The Ritschlian Theology and the Evangelical Faith*, the first book-length assessment of Ritschlian theology by a British writer. Thereafter he commented from time to time on developments within the Ritschlian school.[12] His assessment was profoundly negative, and in 1901 a Ritschlian enthusiast lamented that "Professor Orr . . . has done more than any other critic to discredit Ritschl in the estimation of the English public."[13]

Focusing on Ritschl's philosophical premises, Orr sought to trace their effects on Ritschl's theology as a whole. Orr believed

that Ritschl's theology without metaphysics amounted to a Kantian phenomenalism that limited the exercise of reason to empirical data. Despite this limitation of reason Ritschl felt that religious knowledge could be obtained through what he termed "value judgments." The red-flag issue for Orr was the Ritschlian claim that religious and theoretical knowledge operate in mutually exclusive spheres and consequently cannot contradict one another. In this regard, Orr considered Wilhelm Herrmann to be representative of the Ritschlians.

Herrmann claimed that the certitude of faith springs from an immediate impression of Christ upon the soul. This faith is itself the guarantee that attacks upon the truth of Christianity (in its general character, though not necessarily in its details) will prove false. Orr agreed with Herrmann on the immediate certitude of faith, which Orr equated with the old doctrine of "the self-evidencing character of the Gospel revelation."[14] Where Herrmann and the other Ritschlians went wrong, Orr averred, was in pushing faith's independence of critical results too far. "Instead of using their principle of faith as a check against the inroads of destructive criticism—as, if it has any worth, they ought to do—they make concessions to opponents which practically mean the cutting away of the bough they themselves are sitting on."[15]

The comment is significant, for it shows just how close to, and yet how far from, the Ritschlian position Orr stood. On the one hand, for Orr no less than for the Ritschlians, faith was a means of knowing. He readily acknowledged that "reason is not the only power in my being," and that the roots of his faith were nourished by "many other elements besides the intellectual." In a statement reflective of the commonsense epistemology he had learned from Veitch, Orr explained: "It is when a word, message, revelation, comes to us which accords with these laws of the spiri-

---

11. Deas Cromarty [Elizabeth S. Watson], *Scottish Ministerial Miniatures* (London: Hodder and Stoughton, 1892), 50–53.

12. See, e.g., James Orr, *Ritschlianism: Expository and Critical Essays* (London: Hodder and Stoughton, 1903). In *The Progress of Dogma* Orr tried to counter Ritschlian Adolf von Harnack's negative assessment of the history of dogma by arguing that it has unfolded according to a recognizable inner logic. By regarding this logical development as a manifestation of God's hand in history, Orr sought to vindicate the orthodox doctrines that it produced.

13. Albert T. Swing, *The Theology of Albrecht Ritschl* (New York: Longmans, Green, 1901), 4.

14. Orr, *Ritschlianism*, 14.

15. Ibid., 16.

tual being—which strikes and awakens the verifying chord within—that faith is generated."[16] On the other hand, Orr, unlike the Ritschlians, held that the confidence granted to faith cannot be sustained if it is subsequently contradicted by other faculties of the intuitive soul. Thus Orr considered it myopic to ignore the points of contact between faith and reason. The two can be distinguished, but in the end they have to harmonize. In short, Orr believed that the Ritschlian theology demanded a violation of rationality itself.

Having laid this groundwork, Orr proceeded to expose the deleterious effects of Ritschl's philosophical assumptions on the fabric of his theological system. Those assumptions had led to "an imperfect and mutilated, and in many ways wholly inadmissible version of Christianity."[17] With respect to the incarnation, for example, Orr asserted that Ritschl's agnostic stand regarding the metaphysical doctrine of the person of Christ was a departure from apostolic belief. It was incorrect, he argued, to say that apostolic Christianity had to do only with Christ's historical manifestation. The immediate impression of Christ's person and work upon the first disciples had grown in a natural and legitimate way into their conviction of his ontological divinity. The later Athanasian confession that Christ is of the same substance as God the Father was not an unfortunate and speculative accretion to the faith, but a legitimate formulation necessary to preserve the apostolic conviction. Orr dismissed as "no real Deity at all" the Godhead of religious value that Ritschl ascribed to Christ. Ritschl, he added, "asks us to value as God one who is not God in fact. . . . Value-predicates in this case are but stilts to raise a little higher one who is after all but Man."[18]

There was one Ritschlian emphasis that Orr seemed to applaud. He claimed to welcome Ritschl's stress on the kingdom of God as a needed corrective to previous Protestant neglect; he agreed that the church should reject any otherworldly outlook and demonstrate the power it possessed to transform society. Nevertheless, it was clear that Orr's primary concern within any new theological climate stressing the kingdom was to preserve the soteriological emphasis of traditional evangelical theology. He stressed personal regeneration as a precondition to, and mystical communion with Christ as an ongoing requirement of, fulfilling the social agenda of the kingdom. The kingdom is not only patterned on Christ's teaching, but obtains its vital impulse from his resurrected life.[19]

Old Testament Criticism

Orr, as the United Presbyterians' leading theologian after 1892, played a key role in their merger with the Free Church of Scotland to form the United Free Church (1900). With that merger the United Presbyterian Theological College became redundant, and Orr was transferred to his native city, where he teamed up with George Adam Smith, T. M. Lindsay, and James Denney to form what became an internationally renowned faculty at the Glasgow United Free Church College. There, from his new chair of systematic theology and apologetics, Orr turned to the task of articulating and defending an evangelical doctrine of Scripture in the face of the challenge of biblical criticism. Orr expressed his doctrine of Scripture most fully in his *Revelation and Inspiration* (1910). In a significant departure from the customary pattern, Orr drew a clear distinction between revelation and its record—between divine disclosures in history and the accounts thereof

---

16. Ibid., 256, 260, 249.
17. James Orr, *The Ritschlian Theology and the Evangelical Faith* (London: Hodder and Stoughton, 1897), 234.
18. Ibid., 262–65; see also 131.

19. Ibid., 258; see also James Orr, "The Coming of the Kingdom in the Church," *United Presbyterian Magazine* 12 (1895): 485–86; and idem, "Kingdom of God, of Heaven," in *Dictionary of the Bible,* ed. James Hastings, 5 vols. (New York: Scribner, 1906), 2:856.

preserved in Scripture. Reflecting the historical consciousness that accompanied higher criticism, Orr stressed the distinct and historical character of revelation. Orr's main concerns were to defend, first, the actuality of what he called supernatural historical revelation and, second, the concept of Scripture as a trustworthy record of such revelation.

Ever since his public face-off with Hegelian Otto Pfleiderer in 1894, when Pfleiderer came to give the Gifford Lectures in Edinburgh, Orr had insisted that the only sure grounds for Christian conviction was authoritative supernatural revelation. He sharply distinguished supernatural from all forms of natural revelation. Against believing critics like his own colleague George Adam Smith, Orr quite pointedly refused to label as supernatural any instance of revelation that worked itself out through natural processes. For Orr, genuine supernatural revelation was something altogether different; it was unabashedly miraculous. It was God himself taking personal revelatory initiative that cut through and suspended the operations of natural law. This, Orr maintained, was the only concept of revelation that adequately represented the direct divine communication and the other sorts of encounters that the various authors of Scripture alleged had occurred.

It was also necessary to demonstrate that the Bible is a trustworthy record of such revelations. If the revelation really was from God and for human benefit, Orr argued, then it seems reasonable to assume some divine superintendence to ensure that the record is sufficiently accurate to accomplish its purposes. The existing Scriptures, he urged, are the objective fulfilment of just such an assumption. The proofs of Scripture's genuineness lie, externally, in its enlightening and transforming effects and, internally, in a number of qualities among which teleology (an unwavering sense of direction and design) stands foremost.

But then comes a very sensitive issue. What degree of accuracy is implied by the

Bible's claim to be inspired? Orr maintained that the Scriptures, specifically the classic *theopneustos* ("God-breathed") text of 2 Timothy 3:16, claim functional effectiveness, but do not explicitly claim inerrancy in any precise scientific sense. Nonetheless, Scripture is free from any defects that might interfere with or nullify its utility for its specified ends. Back in 1894 Orr had already written, "A hard-and-fast inerrancy in minute matters of historical, geographical, chronological and scientific detail—for the most part indifferent to the substance of the revelation—it seems to me to be a mistake to bind up with the essence of the doctrine of inspiration."[20] Sixteen more years of biblical study did nothing to alter his conviction. In *Revelation and Inspiration* he urged that it would be suicidal to rest the case for scriptural authority on a supposed inerrancy of the biblical record in its minutest details: "One may plead, indeed, for 'a supernatural providential guidance' which has for its aim to exclude all, even the least error or discrepancy in statement, even such as may inhere in the sources from which the information is obtained, or may arise from corruption from anterior documents. But this is a violent assumption which there is nothing in the Bible really to support. It is perilous, therefore, to seek to pin down faith to it as a matter of vital moment."[21]

Yet the extent of Orr's concession could easily be overestimated. His disavowal of inerrancy was more tactical than substantive. He did not wish to be trapped in an awkward corner, but, on the other hand, he was really unwilling to concede very much at all. He held that the assurance of Scripture's profitability in 2 Timothy 3:16 implies a very high degree of historical and factual accuracy. He held, in fact, that the degree of accuracy is so high as to be itself an argument for the supernatural origin of Scripture. Moreover, he sympathized with

20. James Orr, "Revelation and Inspiration," *Thinker* 6 (1894): 43.

21. Orr, *Revelation and Inspiration*, 197–98, 213–14.

the general direction of the inerrantists' regard for Scripture, believing that it was in line with apostolic conviction and historic Christianity.[22] Orr had taken a difficult intermediate position. On the one side he failed to please the inerrantists, and on the other he frustrated those who had dispensed with the concept of a direct propositional revelation in favor of a subjective apprehension of God's voice mediated through the recorded religious experiences of others. Ultimately, Orr insisted on retaining the unpopular concepts of supernatural revelation and its accurate recording in Scripture because he believed any departure from them would prove extremely damaging to the life and future of the church.

These were the convictions which shaped Orr's *Problem of the Old Testament* (1906), with which he burst into print with all the delicacy of an exploding volcano. It was a startling, ringing rejection of the Graf-Wellhausen hypothesis and indeed of any theory that postulated a synthesis of documents to account for the Pentateuch. For his work Orr was awarded the lucrative Bross Prize by an American foundation, and became recognized thereafter as the most formidable champion of the anti-Wellhausen forces. Israel's religion, he held, was categorically distinct from and superior to all other religions by reason of its unique origins in supernatural and authoritative revelation. Orr charged that German criticism was rationalistic and consequently approached the Old Testament with a naturalistic bias. It adhered to a nonsupernatural model of the development of religions and then forced the data of the Old Testament to fit that model, at the cost of great injustice to those data. Orr was particularly severe with the believing critics—those who basically accepted the Graf-Wellhausen scheme, but ascribed the highest insights of Israel's religion to supernatural revelation. He charged them with fundamental inconsistency for endorsing a reconstruction of Old Testament history that was dependent for its very existence on naturalistic presuppositions that they did not share.

Orr perceived in the Graf-Wellhausen hypothesis not only opposition to the concept of supernatural revelation, but also hostility to a high view of its written record. The critics' reconstruction of Old Testament history was so distant from the apparent intentions of the biblical writers that to accept the reconstruction was to damage the writers' credibility almost beyond repair. To preserve the trustworthiness and authority of Scripture, countered Orr, we are compelled to hold to its historical "structure."[23]

Evolutionary Theory

The quintessential thinker of the nineteenth century was not Ritschl, not Graf nor Wellhausen, but Charles Darwin. Perhaps it is not too much to describe Darwin as the catalyst for a paradigm shift in the understanding of reality. After *Origin of Species* (1859), only a theologian akin to the fabled ostrich could ignore Darwinism and its implications for the faith, and Orr had already proven that he did not belong to that species. His instinctive suspicion of the notion that there are mutually exclusive types of truth, a suspicion now further sensitized by his encounter with Ritschlianism, made it unthinkable for him to evade the Darwinian challenge through recourse to the idea that religious truth claims are completely independent of science and thus

---

22. Ibid., 216–17. The affinities between Orr and B. B. Warfield are explored in Robert J. Hoefel, "The Doctrine of Inspiration in the Writings of James Orr and B. B. Warfield: A Study in Contrasting Approaches to Scripture," Ph.D. diss., Fuller Theological Seminary, 1983.

23. James Orr, *The Problem of the Old Testament* (New York: Scribner, 1906), 4–20; see also Orr, *Revelation and Inspiration*, ix; idem, "Need and Basis of a Doctrine of Holy Scripture," *Review and Expositor* 6 (1909): 379–93; and idem, "Holy Scripture and Modern Negations," in *The Fundamentals*, ed. Reuben A. Torrey et al., 4 vols. (Grand Rapids: Baker, 1970), 1:94–110.

invulnerable to scientific refutation. As it turned out, Orr came to the conclusion that evolutionary theory, or more precisely Darwin's theory of origins, did challenge certain doctrines, in particular, creation, humanity, and sin.

The foundation of Orr's response to Darwinian theory was his allowance that organic evolution of some kind or other is quite likely. In *The Christian View* he wrote, "On the general hypothesis of evolution, as applied to the organic world, I have nothing to say, except that, within certain limits, it seems to me extremely probable, and supported by a large body of evidence." Later in the same work he declared that "we need not reject the hypothesis of evolution within the limits in which science has really rendered it probable." It is noteworthy that he never backed away from this position, even in his later contributions to *The Fundamentals.*[24]

With respect to the doctrine of creation, first of all, Orr was not concerned to exonerate a literal interpretation of the biblical account and in fact expressed some reservations about such a line of interpretation. He urged his right-wing opponents to quit "carping and pettifogging" about the details of the account and to agree with him that "the main point is the absolute derivation of all things from God, and on this truth the Scripture as a whole gives no uncertain sound."[25] For Orr, the doctrine of creation was a necessary presupposition of the elemental religious belief that all things depend upon and are controlled by God. This notion of dependence upon God was being threatened by the Darwinian denial of any need for or evidence of a creative cause. Belief in a Creator and creation needed to be buttressed by a recognition of the manifestly teleological character of nature. Orr allowed that the operations of natural selection are real enough, but insisted that

Darwin had overrated their significance. Trying to redress this imbalance, Orr highlighted the teleology of organic life by stressing the determinants of change that are internal to organisms.

Orr's second, and indeed greater, concern was to defend the biblical doctrine of humanity, and he did so in both *The Christian View* and his 1903 Stone Lectures at Princeton Seminary, later published as *God's Image in Man* (1905). Once again Orr was not concerned to defend a literal interpretation of the Genesis account. His broader concern was to confirm the view that humans are creatures categorically distinct from animals and immortal. He was convinced that any theory of gradual evolution from animal forms is fatal to the assumption that humanity possesses a spiritual nature and immortality. A series of insensible gradations simply allows no opportunity for the introduction of these categorically new qualities. A decisive "leap" (an abrupt and definite advance prompted by forces immanent in the evolutionary process itself) must have occurred. An interesting shift in Orr's thought by the time of his Stone Lectures was his tendency to speak of such a leap as an opportunity for a supernatural initiative or cause to come into play. He actually went as far as to speak of "the production of something perfectly new by the direct act of God."[26] This was plainly the language of direct intervention and breaks in the natural scheme of things, yet Orr continued to imply that such a creative event could occur through the operation of immanent teleological forces. B. B. Warfield, detecting Orr's apparent ambivalence on this point, argued that supernaturalism should be understood in more explicitly interventionist terms.[27] Orr replied that ultimately it did not matter. For

---

24. Orr, *Christian View*, 99, 182–83; James Orr, "Science and Christian Faith," in *Fundamentals*, 1:345.

25. Orr, *Christian View*, 122; see also 402–21.

26. James Orr, *God's Image in Man and Its Defacement in the Light of Modern Denials* (London: Hodder and Stoughton, 1905), ch. 3 and p. 123.

27. B. B. Warfield, review of *God's Image in Man*, by James Orr, *Princeton Theological Review* 4 (Oct. 1906): 557.

him, the only real issue was whether human beings had come into possession of unique and transcendental qualities. If we had, Orr was sure that we had acquired these qualities, and through them our identity as humans, instantly.

Orr's third, and greatest, concern was to defend the evangelical doctrine of sin. He was adamant that evolution never could serve, as Darwin in *The Descent of Man* (1871) had attempted to make it serve, as an explanation of humanity's moral history. Evolutionary ascent is the absolute inversion of descent. The two are irreconcilable. Orr was convinced that only inadequate concepts of sin and guilt could follow from the evolutionists' inversion of human moral history. Theories of moral evolution make sin a natural necessity, not a fault for which humanity is entirely and personally responsible. Conscience, he said, can never be reconciled to the evolutionary rationalization of guilt. Along these lines Orr interpreted the biblical account of the fall very cautiously. Probably it reflects an "old tradition clothed in oriental allegorical dress," he said. The abiding truth of the account is that humanity fell from an original state of purity. Though inferior to modern persons in some respects, Adam had "high and noble faculties, a pure and harmonious nature, rectitude of will, capability of understanding his creator's instructions, and power to obey them."[28]

In the first few years of the twentieth century, Frederick Tennant of Cambridge University launched, on moral evolutionary premises, a devastating attack on the doctrine of original sin. In his *Origin and Propagation of Sin* (1902) and *Sources of the Doctrines of the Fall and Original Sin* (1903), Tennant defined sin as failure in terms of what evolving moral consciousness has come to regard as right and not, as in traditional doctrine, as failure in terms of a fixed and absolute standard.

Both Orr's *God's Image in Man* and his subsequent *Sin as a Problem of Today*

(1910) were direct responses to Tennant's work. Orr had at least three basic criticisms. First, he argued that on the assumption of moral evolution sin becomes inevitable, and ultimate responsibility for it therefore falls upon the Creator. But then sin would be the result not of humanity's free volition, but of our God-given constitution, and our liability to punishment would be unreasonable. Second, Orr complained that the theories of moral evolution implied that humans are not absolutely helpless and hopeless. Given sufficient time, our condition will right itself. If that were possible, Orr asked, "How should a redeemer be necessary . . . to secure for [man] a gain which evolutionary processes infallibly secure for him without supernatural help?"[29] Third, Orr was concerned that the seriousness of sin would be diminished by indexing it to the relative standards of the evolutionary process rather than to a fixed norm. And so in *Sin as a Problem of Today* he defined sin in relation to three standards: absolute moral law, divine holiness, and the teleological end of the kingdom of God. The last of these was an obvious genuflection in the direction of Ritschl. Orr's stress was clearly upon the first two criteria: absolute moral law and divine holiness. Sin is a violation of an absolute standard and an affront to the living God. One can almost hear Orr shouting his conception of sin: that which absolutely ought not to be.[30] But his shout was like the voice of one crying in the wilderness. Not many other voices joined in chorus with Orr's on that more innocent side of the Great World War.

The Quest of the Historical Jesus

Orr responded to the challenges to evangelical orthodoxy that were posed not only by Ritschlianism, Old Testament criticism, and evolutionary theory, but also by the rigorous investigation that came to be known as the quest of the historical Jesus. Particu-

---

28. Orr, *Christian View*, 185–86.

29. Orr, *God's Image in Man*, 204ff., quotation 20.
30. James Orr, *Sin as a Problem of Today* (London: Hodder and Stoughton, 1910), 1.

larly prominent in Germany, this line of investigation often led to conclusions that called for revisions in the traditional view of Christ, and especially of his supernatural attributes and divine nature. Orr realized that there was a tremendous amount at stake here. While endorsing the growing recognition of Jesus' humanity and human development, he was convinced that the most important truth about Jesus to maintain in the current milieu was his full divinity. And Orr was unwilling to accept just any definition of divinity; only the bold, ontological Christology of Chalcedon was adequate. Any retreat from the credal formulations, he warned, would bring disaster. He claimed that the logic of history operates in its own inexorable fashion to eliminate intermediate Christologies. Inevitably the options are reduced to two: a truly divine Christ or simply a human one.

Orr put forward a number of arguments designed to underscore the importance of retaining belief in Christ's divinity. First, theism finds its logical fulfilment and vindication in the incarnation. If the historic incarnation is denied, we must either doubt the existence of the personal, loving God of Christianity or look beyond Jesus for a superior revelation of such a God. Second, only a divine Christ was adequate to provide the salvation humans need (here Orr is following Anselm and Calvin). And third, the viability of Christianity hinges on continued belief in Christ's divinity. Historically, Orr argued, a merely human Christ could not have inspired congregational activity, aggressive evangelism, and sacrificial philanthropy on such a scale, nor served so effectually as a source of personal consolation and strength. It is vain, therefore, to hope that a Christ of such reduced proportions can perform such essential functions in the present age. Orr's populist sympathies surfaced in his remark that orthodox Christology is an expression of the church's "instinct for what is, and is not, vital to Christian faith," while Christologies that see Jesus as merely human are the work of "closet-recluses" who are more at home in critical studies than in experiential religion and the practical work of the church.[31]

It is one thing to insist that the divinity of Christ is necessary for the survival of Christianity, and quite another to hold that there are firm grounds for maintaining such a doctrine. The challenge Orr faced as an apologist for orthodox Christology was to demonstrate that the Jesus of history was indeed divine. The task had vast dimensions, so Orr chose to concentrate his energies on two particular events in the life of Jesus: the virginal conception and the resurrection. In *The Virgin Birth of Christ* (1907) and *The Resurrection of Jesus* (1908), companion volumes of similar outline and purpose, Orr defended his position that the doctrine of Christ's divinity has indeed been verified by history.

Orr believed that the virgin birth is an essential doctrine; it can be relegated to the periphery only if faith does not clearly recognize its own presuppositions. He suggested that there is some truth to the time-honored opinion that the virgin birth was the necessary means by which the incarnate Christ evaded the taint of original sin, but he declined to press this line of argument. Instead, he stressed that the divine Christ's entrance into history necessarily demanded "a supernatural act in the production of Christ's bodily nature." He drew this conclusion on the basis of the psychosomatic unity of each human being and Christ's spiritual discontinuity with the rest of humanity. The incarnation, Orr reasoned, had to entail a moral and spiritual miracle ensuring that there would be "a suitable humanity on the physical side to match the perfection of the spirit." Though this remark has a docetic ring, Orr believed that a physical body suitable to the unique spiritual creation could be obtained only through a complementary supernatural act of physical creation. This line of reasoning obviously does not specify the precise form

31. James Orr, "Christ in the Thought of Today," *Baptist Review and Expositor* 1 (1904): 294–300.

the miracle had to take. Orr countered that only history could disclose the particular manner in which the necessary miracle actually occurred. As it turned out, the Gospel accounts of the virgin birth provided a trustworthy description of the manner in which the requirement of a supernatural physical creation found its historical fulfilment.[32]

To all of this Orr added a tactical consideration. He had been much impressed by A. B. Bruce's remark that "with belief in the Virgin Birth is apt to go belief in the Virgin Life." He too saw the virgin birth as a Maginot Line for evangelical orthodoxy in its war with rationalism. To abandon the doctrine of the virgin birth would be to give way to a thoroughgoing conquest of the doctrine of the divine Christ.[33]

Similarly, Orr's main reason for expending effort on *The Resurrection of Jesus* was to strengthen the grounds for belief in the transcendent nature of Jesus Christ. To be sure, he was motivated in part by the conviction that the resurrection is a constitutive part of the gospel and the necessary culmination of Christ's redemptive work.[34] But he was equally concerned about a truth to which he believed the event pointed. "The Resurrection," he said, "is a retrospective attestation that Jesus was indeed the exalted and divinely-sent Person he claimed to be."[35] It was historical evidence that Jesus had transcended death, the ultimate limit and sine qua non of postlapsarian humanity.

Orr's strategy of marshaling evidence and arguments in support of the New Testament's supernatural portrait of Christ was not without its serious limitations. At best Orr's books weakened criticisms and eliminated certain problems, but by them-

selves did not hold back the sea. What quality or quantity of human testimony could ever be sufficient to outweigh experience-based bias against the probability of a miracle? What Orr needed was a means of turning the tide, of positively commending the supernatural and putting skepticism on the defensive.

This is precisely what Orr set out to do in an extensive encyclopedia article on Jesus Christ. He accepted the Gospel narratives fairly much at face value and attempted a moderate harmonization of their contents. None of the supernatural incidents described was suppressed; everything was allowed to stand as recorded in the most reliable manuscripts. Orr commented that this "treatment of the subject is guided by the conviction that, while critical discussion cannot be ignored, a simple and straightforward presentation of the narrative of this transcendent life, in its proper historical and chronological setting, is itself the best antidote to the vagaries of much current speculation."[36] Orr's strategy was based on the assumption that there is a self-authenticating quality to the New Testament portrait of Christ that guarantees eventual confirmation of its historicity.

Writings for the General Christian Reader

Orr's deep-seated populist instincts and commonsense convictions produced in him a strong sense of responsibility for the religious welfare of the general Christian public. He scorned the label "ivory-tower theologian" and anyone he considered deserving of that appellation. In addition, he maintained a high regard for the Christian public's competence to judge in crucial matters of religious concern. James Denney remarked that "the traditional Scottish ideal of an intelligent Christian public, be-

32. Orr, *Ritschlianism*, 221–38.
33. James Orr, *The Virgin Birth of Christ* (New York: Scribner, 1907), 192; idem, "The Virgin Birth of Christ," in *Fundamentals*, 2:248.
34. James Orr, *The Resurrection of Jesus* (London: Hodder and Stoughton, 1908), 274–88.
35. Ibid., 270–71.
36. James Orr, Introduction to *International Standard Bible Encyclopedia*, ed. James Orr, 5 vols. (Chicago: Howard-Severance, 1915), 1:x. The article itself is "Jesus Christ," 3:1624–68.

fore which all Christian causes must be argued out, was deeply rooted in [Orr's] mind."[37] To state the matter another way, Orr did not believe that issues of great significance to the faith could safely be left to scholarly specialists. The fairly widespread academic resistance to Orr's views only intensified his resolve in this direction.

The Bible under Trial (1907) and *The Faith of a Modern Christian* (1910) were especially prepared for "the general Christian reader." From Winnipeg, where Orr's public lectures were attended by lawyers and doctors, and with unflagging zeal by numbers of "intellectual ladies" (so the *Manitoba Morning Free Press* reported), to G. Campbell Morgan's Mundesley Bible Conference in England, where another publication judged that "he did much to strengthen faith," Orr labored tirelessly. He mounted open-air platforms as willingly as he lectured at prestigious seminaries, and wrote for city newspapers as readily as for scholarly journals. Over the years he crisscrossed North America to speak at Bible institutes and summer conferences. He contributed four essays to *The Fundamentals* (1910–15) and assumed the duties of general editor for the *International Standard Bible Encyclopedia*. He explained, in words that reveal the man, that he believed there was room for a reference work "adapted more directly to the needs of the average pastor and Bible student." First published in five volumes in 1915, the encyclopedia has enjoyed steady sales to the present day and has been one of the more important means of extending evangelical orthodoxy's line of defense in twentieth-century America. Orr died on September 6, 1913, with the encyclopedia essentially finished. Close friends suspected that his dogged determination to complete it had hastened his death.

Legacy

Many of Orr's works, as a result of their preoccupation with literature and opinions of transitory interest, eventually became dated and have been largely forgotten. However, there are some significant exceptions. *The Christian View*, which went through ten editions in Orr's lifetime, was reprinted in 1948, in 1954, and again in 1989. In the foreword to the most recent edition, Vernon Grounds, president emeritus of Denver Seminary, testifies that Orr's work intellectually grounded his own fledgling faith as a seminarian in the late 1930s, and that since that time he has taken Orr as a model for his own theological career. Likewise, Carl Henry was greatly impressed in his student days at Wheaton College by Orr's concept of an evangelical worldview. Henry has edited a series of monographs, Studies in a Christian World View, that seeks to spell out the multidisciplinary implications of such a worldview. In the first volume of that series, *Contours of a World View* (1983), Arthur Holmes quotes Orr at the outset.

In addition, Orr's *Revelation and Inspiration* has been held on both sides of the Atlantic to offer the most articulate conservative alternative to the inerrantist doctrine of Scripture championed by the Princeton giant B. B. Warfield.[38] It has not been overlooked in the recent American evangelical debate over the nature and implications of inspiration.[39] Unfortunately, Orr's book has not been reprinted since 1969, though a significant chapter-length excerpt may be found in *The Living God* (1973), volume 1 of the Readings in Christian Theology series edited by Millard Erickson. Moreover, there are a number of references to *Revelation and Inspiration*, and other of Orr's writings, in Erickson's influential *Christian Theology* (1986).

37. Denney, "Late Professor Orr," 576.

38. I. Howard Marshall, *Biblical Inspiration* (Grand Rapids: Eerdmans, 1983), 40; Edward John Carnell, *The Case for Orthodox Theology* (Philadelphia: Westminster, 1959), 99ff.

39. Jack B. Rogers and Donald K. McKim, *The Authority and Interpretation of the Bible: An Historical Approach* (San Francisco: Harper and Row, 1979), 385–88.

The Problem of the Old Testament continued to be reprinted through the turbulent 1920s, reaching a sixth and final edition in 1931. *The Progress of Dogma* was last printed in 1952. Presently just three of Orr's books are in print. In addition to *The Christian View*, which we have already noted, Orr's *Virgin Birth of Christ* has been combined with a study on the same subject by H. P. Liddon and retitled *The Birth of Christ* (1980). In a similar fashion, Orr's *Resurrection of Jesus* has been joined with a cognate work by H. C. G. Moule in a single volume bearing the title *The Resurrection of Christ* (1980). More than any other, however, Orr's last great work, the *International Standard Bible Encyclopedia,* has pressed the stamp of his influence on several generations of conservative Protestant pastors and leaders in North America. A recent major revision (1979–88) under the general editorship of Geoffrey Bromiley ensures the continuation of this influence.

But Orr's legacy to contemporary evangelicals consists of more than the arguments and perspectives with which he defended and commended orthodox belief. It consists also of his example of responsibility to and respect for the general Christian public—the *laos* of God. To the evangelical theologians of today Orr would undoubtedly commend the opinion of his great liberal foe Adolf von Harnack: "The theologians of every country only half discharge their duties if they think it enough to treat of the Gospel in the recondite language of learning and bury it in scholarly folios."[40]

Secondary Sources

Scorgie, Glen G. *A Call for Continuity: The Theological Contribution of James Orr.* Macon, Ga.: Mercer University Press, 1988.

Sell, Alan P. F. *Defending and Declaring the Faith: Some Scottish Examples, 1860–1920,* ch. 7. Colorado Springs: Helmers and Howard, 1987.

Toon, Peter. *The Development of Doctrine in the Church,* 53–73. Grand Rapids: Eerdmans, 1979.

40. Adolf von Harnack, Preface to *What Is Christianity?* trans. Thomas B. Saunders (Philadelphia: Fortress, 1986), vi.

B. B. Warfield

Mark A. Noll

At the end of the nineteenth and the beginning of the twentieth centuries, Benjamin Breckinridge Warfield was the most widely known American advocate of confessional Calvinism. Today, Warfield continues to exert an influence mostly through his defense of biblical inerrancy, although his convictions about the role of reason in apologetics also stimulate discussion and debate. Three-quarters of a century after his death, many of his works remain in print, and his opinions continue to count, not only among conservative Presbyterians and modern advocates of inerrancy, where such attention could be expected, but also with Southern Baptists, Wesleyans, some neo-orthodox theologians, and others whose interest in Warfield's views might be regarded as a surprise.[1]

Warfield was born on November 5, 1851, at Grasmere, his family's estate in the vicinity of Lexington, Kentucky.[2] Warfield's lin-

1. As examples of the former, see D. Clair Davis, "Inerrancy and Westminster Calvinism," and Moisés Silva, "Old Princeton, Westminster, and Inerrancy," in *Inerrancy and Hermeneutic*, ed. Harvie M. Conn (Grand Rapids: Baker, 1988), 37–39, 67–80; and John H. Gerstner, "Warfield's Case for Biblical Inerrancy," in *God's Inerrant Word*, ed. John Warwick Montgomery (Minneapolis: Bethany, 1974), 115–42. As examples of the latter, see L. Russ Bush (for Southern Baptists), "The Roots of Conservative Perspectives on Inerrancy (Warfield)," in *Proceedings of the Conference on Biblical Inerrancy, 1987* (Nashville: Broadman, 1987), 273–88; *A Contemporary Wesleyan Theology:*

Biblical, Systematic, and Practical, ed. Charles W. Carter, 2 vols. (Grand Rapids: Francis Asbury [Zondervan], 1983), 1:289, 296, 301–2; T. F. Torrance, review of *Inspiration and Authority of the Bible*, by B. B. Warfield, *Scottish Journal of Theology* 7 (March 1954): 104–8; and David H. Kelsey, *The Uses of Scripture in Recent Theology* (Philadelphia: Fortress, 1975), 17–24.

2. On Warfield's life see Ethelbert D. Warfield, "Biographical Sketch," in *Works of Benjamin B. Warfield*, 10 vols. (New York: Oxford University Press, 1927–32; Grand Rapids: Baker, 1981), 1:v–ix; Francis L. Patton, "Benjamin Breckinridge Warfield—A Memorial Address," *Princeton Theological Review* 19 (July 1921): 369–91; and James C. Klotter, *The Breckinridges of Kentucky, 1760–1981* (Lexington: University Press of Kentucky, 1986). Especially helpful for this essay was Hugh T. Kerr, "Warfield: The Person behind the Theology" (Lecture presented at Princeton Theological Seminary, Spring 1982).

eage was distinguished. On the side of his mother, Mary Cabell Breckinridge, Warfield's great-grandfather was John Breckinridge, one of Thomas Jefferson's attorneys general; and a first cousin once removed was John C. Breckinridge, vice president of the United States under James Buchanan. His father, William Warfield, who was a prosperous gentleman farmer, served as a Union officer in the Civil War. It may not be unrelated to B. B. Warfield's later ability to reconcile his conservative Calvinist faith with a modified form of Darwinian evolution that William Warfield bred cattle and horses scientifically and authored a study entitled *The Theory and Practice of Cattle Breeding* (1888). Wallis Warfield Simpson, for whom Edward VIII gave up the British throne in 1936, was a distant relation. Warfield's works were edited by his brother Ethelbert Dudley (1861–1936), who was a lawyer and then president of Lafayette College.

Warfield was privately schooled by two young college graduates, Lewis Barbour and James Kennedy Patterson, both of whom later became successful college teachers and administrators. Their instruction in mathematics and science made a particularly strong impression on the young Warfield. For most of his late adolescence, the family took it for granted that he would pursue a scientific field. Warfield's entrance into the sophomore class at the College of New Jersey (later Princeton University) in 1868 coincided with the arrival of President James McCosh, who had been called to Princeton from his post as professor of moral philosophy at Queen's University, Belfast. McCosh was the last great American exponent of the Scottish philosophy of common sense. He was also an early promoter of the idea that traditional Christian faith and nonnaturalistic forms of evolution are compatible. In both his philosophy and his desire to maintain harmony between science and faith, McCosh set out a path that Warfield would follow.

After graduating from college in 1871, Warfield traveled in Europe for a year and then surprised his family by announcing his intention to prepare for the ministry. Before entering Princeton Theological Seminary in 1873, he pursued the family's interest in livestock breeding by serving briefly as an editor with Lexington's *Farmer's Home Journal*. At Princeton Seminary, Warfield was particularly influenced by Charles Hodge, who, though well into his seventies, was still the theological mainstay of the institution. Warfield later memorialized Hodge as a great teacher of Scripture who nevertheless lacked technical expertise as an exegete.[3] After graduating from the seminary in 1876, Warfield married Annie Pearce Kinkead, a descendant of the early American explorer George Rogers Clark. Warfield then returned to Europe with his bride for study at Leipzig.

During their European stay tragedy struck when the young couple was caught in a violent thunderstorm. Warfield's wife was severely traumatized; for the rest of her life she was a semi-invalid. In order to remain near her, and perhaps also in keeping with a reflective, even reclusive temperament, Warfield did not mix in society or pursue involvement in Presbyterian affairs as his predecessors at Princeton had done. Rarely was he absent from home for more than two hours during the third of a century he taught at Princeton.

When Warfield returned to the United States, he served briefly as a supply minister in Baltimore. In 1878 he accepted a call to teach New Testament at Western Theological Seminary near Pittsburgh. In 1887, upon the death of Archibald Alexander Hodge, the son of Charles, Warfield returned to Princeton Seminary as professor of didactic and polemic theology. During thirty-four years in that position, he taught more than twenty-seven hundred students. As a teacher, he was exacting but also fair. Warfield died at Princeton late in the evening of

3. "Dr. Charles Hodge as a Teacher of Exegesis," in *Selected Shorter Writings of Benjamin B. Warfield*, ed. John E. Meeter, 2 vols. (Nutley, N.J.: Presbyterian and Reformed, 1970, 1973), 1:437–40.

February 16, 1921, after teaching his classes earlier that day.

Warfield's incredibly prolific output of books, learned essays, and reviews (which were frequently accomplished monographs in their own right) was a product of his devotion to the confessional standards of Presbyterianism and, behind those standards, to his conception of classic Christian faith. Indefatigable efforts as editor for a series of Presbyterian journals (1889, *Presbyterian Review;* 1890–1903, *Presbyterian and Reformed Review;* 1903–21, *Princeton Theological Review*) were directed to the same ends. Almost all of Warfield's most penetrating work—on Scripture as well as on the theology of Augustine and John Calvin, on the continuing importance of the Westminster Confession, on the threats (as he perceived them) of rationalism, perfectionism, Pentecostalism, mysticism, the Higher Life movement, and naturalistic science—arose in response to issues either taken up formally by the Presbyterian churches or seeming in his eye to affect their course and direction.

Even in the long line of outstanding conservative, Old School theologians that stretched from Archibald Alexander (who in 1812 became the first professor at Princeton Seminary) to J. Gresham Machen (who left the seminary in 1929), Warfield stood out. In that distinguished company, he was the most widely read, had the greatest skill in European languages, displayed the most patience in unpacking arguments, and wrote clearly on the widest range of subjects. Some of Warfield's convictions—especially his conception of the inerrancy of Scripture in its original autographs—have generated a great quantity of polemical attack and defense. But despite helpful work by John Meeter, Roger Nicole, and a few other industrious scholars, there exists no comprehensive account of Warfield's theology.[4]

And there is nothing close to an adequate biography.

One reason for the absence of such work may be directly related to Warfield's conception of his task. He was, in the strictest sense of the terms, a polemical and a conserving theologian. Despite comprehensive learning, he never attempted a full theological statement, primarily because he found Charles Hodge's *Systematic Theology* satisfactory for himself and his students. Because he was entirely content with the positions of the Westminster Confession and Catechisms, he was also satisfied throughout his long career to explicate their meaning, fend off misreadings, and defend their content against the modernizing, subjective, and naturalistic tendencies of his day.

Warfield was also content with what had been handed down to him by his Princeton predecessors on questions concerning the larger framework of thought. He did not delight in speculation (and so would mildly criticize Jonathan Edwards for his "individualisms," while praising Edwards for being "a convinced defender of Calvinism").[5] Rather, he gave himself wholeheartedly to Princeton's deeply ingrained commitment to theology as a scientific task (with "science" defined in the conventional positivistic terms of the Enlightenment). He shared just as fully Princeton's equally longstanding confidence in a philosophy of commonsense realism. That philosophy owed something to its formal statement by the cautious savants of the Scottish Enlightenment like Thomas Reid and Dugald Stewart. But it owed even more to a concrete, antispeculative turn of mind that the Old School theologians liked to think of as a simple Anglo-Saxon inheritance. From the perspective of the late twentieth century, the attitude lying behind this philosophy of common sense looks mostly like a gentlemanly, Victorian, and dignified Presbyterian adaptation of the practical bent so

---

4. See especially John E. Meeter and Roger R. Nicole, *A Bibliography of Benjamin Breckinridge Warfield, 1851–1921* (Nutley, N.J.: Presbyterian and Reformed, 1974).

5. B. B. Warfield, "Edwards and the New England Theology," in *Works,* 9:530–31.

common at all levels in nineteenth-century American culture.

Warfield seems to have thought that his most significant work was his ardent defense of the theology of Calvin and the Westminster divines. Later attention, however, has focused more on his exposition of individual issues that engaged Presbyterians around the turn of the century, for example, the inerrancy of Scripture and the place of apologetics. The result has been that, although several of Warfield's positions continue to exert considerable influence, the defense of Calvinism that loomed large in his own estimation receives far less attention today. Despite the varying degrees of interest, however, it is Warfield's positions on Scripture, on apologetics, and on Calvinism that constitute his most important legacies.

Defender of Biblical Inerrancy

Princeton Seminary, with its traditional conservatism as well as its steady interest in European theological debate, responded quite early (by American standards) to the higher criticism of Scripture. In 1857, Charles Hodge took the occasion of the publication of a book on the Bible by William Lee of Trinity College, Dublin, to reaffirm his belief that the authors of Scripture, though their writings were not mechanically dictated to them, yet communicated truth infallibly. They were preserved from error in what they wrote.[6] Hodge repeated these opinions in his *Systematic Theology*, but without a full consideration of the latest opinions from Europe.[7] On Scripture, as on many other subjects, Warfield picked up where Charles Hodge left off.

By the early 1880s, American Presbyterians were being drawn more directly into the European debates over the Bible. Presbyterian leaders realized that the new criti-

cal proposals touched the heart of their faith as it had developed in Britain and America. They knew as well that the controversies raging in Scotland over modern criticism, especially concerning the work of William Robertson Smith of the Free Church, would soon arrive in America. Smith's acceptance of Old Testament higher criticism was especially significant for Princeton Seminary because it had been an American champion of the Free Church since its founding in 1843. So it came about that Archibald Alexander Hodge of Princeton and Charles Briggs of Union Theological Seminary in New York agreed that the journal they jointly edited, the *Presbyterian Review*, should consider these matters. Briggs, who was predisposed toward the newer opinions, enlisted several colleagues to write in favor of adjusting the traditional views. Hodge too sought assistance in supporting his opposing conviction that the new views were a threat to the church. His first recruit was B. B. Warfield, then still a young New Testament professor at Western Theological Seminary.

The essay, entitled simply "Inspiration," that Hodge and Warfield published in the April 1881 issue of the *Presbyterian Review* both recapitulated many of the themes that had been prominent in previous Princeton writing and anticipated most of the points that Warfield would make over the next forty years in a wealth of publications. What was new in this essay was its precision in stating the doctrine of Scripture and its detailed response to modern views. The essay's burden was to show that proper scholarship on Scripture and its background supported, rather than undercut, a high view of verbal inspiration. The doctrine this essay defended was the belief in "God's continued work of superintendence, by which, his providential, gracious and supernatural contributions having been presupposed, he presided over the sacred writers in their entire work of writing, with the design and effect of rendering that writing an errorless record of the matters he de-

6. Charles Hodge, "Inspiration," *Biblical Repertory and Princeton Review* 29 (Oct. 1857): 660–87.
7. Charles Hodge, *Systematic Theology*, 3 vols. (New York: Scribner, 1872–73), 1:151–90.

signed them to communicate, and hence constituting the entire volume in all its parts the word of God to us."[8]

Throughout the essay, as indeed throughout Warfield's entire career, great care was taken to qualify the doctrine of verbal inspiration. Hodge and Warfield stated almost at the outset that the doctrine of plenary verbal inspiration is not "a principle fundamental to the truth of the Christian religion" as such, nor is it the case "that the truth of Christianity depends upon any doctrine of inspiration whatever."[9] They also maintained at length that the verbal inspiration of Scripture did not rule out a full, active participation of the human authors in its production. In fact, the biblical authors "were in large measure dependent for their knowledge upon sources and methods in themselves fallible, and . . . their personal knowledge and judgments were in many matters hesitating and defective, or even wrong."[10] Hodge and Warfield further insisted that the key to interpreting the Bible is to discover the intent of its authors, a pursuit that might require discriminating study. They held that for an accusation that there are errors in Scripture to hold any weight, it must have reference to "some part of the original autograph" rather than to some phrasing drawn from what might be a corrupted transmission of the text.[11] And they acknowledged that the doctrine of verbal inspiration, which they held to be the plain teaching of many scriptural passages, needed to be confirmed by paying full attention and responding to all possible objections arising from the study of the Bible itself (e.g., questions of mistaken history or geography, inaccurate quotations from the Old Testament in the New, internal lack of harmony, and the like). Yet once they made these qualifications, Hodge and Warfield insisted that the Bible is fully inspired. Absolutely without error, it is to be regarded not just as a bearer of the Word of God, but as that Word itself.

In Warfield's day and since, there have been countless objections to the doctrine of biblical inspiration. Warfield's most concentrated writing on the subject came in the five-year period from 1889 to 1894, when the Presbyterian church was both considering a revision of the Westminster Confession and deciding what to do about Charles Briggs, who had continued in the attempt to adapt the hereditary evangelical faith to moderate critical conclusions about Scripture. But works from Warfield both before and after this period, for example, the essays on "Inspiration" and "Revelation" that he wrote at the request of James Orr for the *International Standard Bible Encyclopedia* (1915), maintained consistently the position he had outlined in 1881.

Warfield himself responded at length to many of the objections that have been raised against his view of inspiration. Among the charges are: (1) it cannot be found in Scripture; (2) it is an innovation in the history of the church; (3) it amounts to mechanical dictation; (4) it explains away difficulties by referring to the inerrancy of the "original autographs," which, conveniently, are no longer extant; (5) it does not take full account of the phenomena of Scripture; and (6) it is a rationalistic view that fails to provide adequate scope for the indwelling work of the Holy Spirit.[12]

---

8. Archibald A. Hodge and Benjamin B. Warfield, *Inspiration,* ed. Roger R. Nicole (Grand Rapids: Baker, 1979), 17–18.

9. Ibid., 8.

10. Ibid., 28.

11. Ibid., 36.

12. Examples of these arguments can be found in James D. G. Dunn, "The Authority of Scripture according to Scripture," *Churchman* 96 (1982): 104–22, 201–25; Ernest R. Sandeen, *The Roots of Fundamentalism: British and American Millenarianism, 1800–1930* (Chicago: University of Chicago Press, 1970); William J. Abraham, *The Divine Inspiration of Holy Scripture* (New York: Oxford University Press, 1981); Jack B. Rogers and Donald K. McKim, *The Authority and Interpretation of the Bible: An Historical Approach* (San Francisco: Harper and Row, 1979), 323–51; James Barr, *Beyond Fundamentalism* (Philadelphia: Westminster, 1984), 141; and John C. Vander Stelt, *Philosophy and Scripture: A Study in Old Princeton and Westminster Theology* (Marlton, N.J.: Mack, 1978), 166–84.

Each of these contentions is worthy of full consideration. We must both look closely at what Warfield actually wrote and evaluate how his view comports with a proper understanding of the Bible's character and purpose. In doing so, it is important for us to realize that Warfield himself was aware of these issues and sought to address them.

1. In some of his strongest exegetical work, Warfield painstakingly examined the meaning of biblical words and phrases like "Scripture," "it says," "Scripture says," and "God says."[13] Warfield's conclusion after studying such terms exhaustively was that the biblical writers themselves equated the words of Scripture with the words of God and meant them to be read with all of the respect due to God himself.

2. Warfield expended his greatest historical energy in arguing that his view of inspiration was simply a modern restatement of the Westminster divines' belief in the "verbal inspiration and the inerrancy of Scripture."[14] Already in the 1881 essay itself, Warfield accumulated references to show that many of his theological predecessors "have so handled the divine Word"—Clement of Rome, Tertullian, Clement of Alexandria, Origen, the Council of Trent, the Second Helvetic Confession, and "all the great world-moving men, as Luther, Calvin, Knox, Wesley, Whitefield and Chalmers."[15]

3. Repeatedly Warfield tried to show that his view entailed *concursus*, as he phrased it in 1894, rather than mechanical dictation. This meant that "the Scriptures are the joint product of divine and human activities, both of which penetrate them at every point, working harmoniously together to the production of a writing which is not

divine here and human there, but at once divine and human in every part, every word and every particular."[16]

4. After objection arose to the argument that only the texts that came directly from the hands of the biblical authors were, in a strict sense, inerrant, Warfield conceded that "the phrase 'the inerrancy of the original autographs' is not an altogether happy one to express the doctrine of the Scriptures as given by God." Yet he went on to ridicule the objection that, since we do not have any of the original autographs, we do not possess an inerrant Scripture. Warfield responded that while the "codex" of Scripture (i.e., the physical parchment upon which the words were originally written) is indeed lost, the "autographic text" is to be found in "practically the whole" scope of the best critical editions of Scripture.[17]

5. To the charge that his view was deductive and so rode roughshod over actual discrepancies, inconsistencies, and disharmonies discovered by empirical study, Warfield insisted time and again, and buttressed his insistence with arsenals of learned exegesis, that the number of truly difficult passages is very small indeed. Even the most doubtful passages are far short of showing conclusively any contradiction between the intention of the biblical author and an empirically verified fact.[18]

6. In responding to the question of whether one becomes convinced of the verbal inerrancy of Scripture through rational argument or through the testimony of the Holy Spirit, Warfield discussed Calvin's memorable treatment of this subject *(Institutes* 1.7.4–5), which emphasizes that the witness of the Spirit is stronger than all proof. Warfield conceded that Calvin speaks of the ineffectiveness of the *indicia* (demonstrations of the Bible's divine char-

13. B. B. Warfield, "'Scripture,' 'The Scriptures,' in the New Testament," "'It Says:' 'Scripture Says:' 'God Says,'" and "The Oracles of God," in *Works*, 1:115–65, 283–332, 335–91.

14. B. B. Warfield, "The Doctrine of Inspiration of the Westminster Divines," in *Works*, 6:333; see also "The Westminster Doctrine of Holy Scripture," in *Works*, 6:155–257.

15. Hodge and Warfield, *Inspiration*, 32–33.

16. B. B. Warfield, "The Divine and Human in the Bible," in *Selected Shorter Writings*, 2:547.

17. B. B. Warfield, "The Inerrancy of the Original Autographs," in *Selected Shorter Writings*, 2:582, 584.

18. For examples see Hodge and Warfield, *Inspiration*, 45–71.

acter) in producing strong faith in the unbeliever: "He sometimes even appears to speak of them rather as if they lay side by side with the testimony of the Spirit than acted [as Warfield taught] along with it as co-factors" to convince people of the truth of the Bible.[19] Yet after an involved argument Warfield concluded that Calvin meant to say, as Warfield himself did, that the Holy Spirit always exercises his convicting power through the *indicia*.

Of these rejoinders to the objections to his view of inspiration, Warfield's response is least satisfactory for the last issue. Andrew Hoffecker, one of the best students of the subject, concludes simply, "The passages [Warfield] cites from Calvin on the relationship between the Spirit's testimony and the *indicia* do not support his position."[20] On the other issues, Warfield's reasoning has not received unanimous support, but has sharpened understanding of the view of biblical inerrancy to which he devoted such great energy.

Nonfundamentalist

The rise of fundamentalism placed Warfield and other confessional conservatives in an ambiguous situation. While they applauded the fundamentalists' adherence to biblical infallibility and their defense of a supernatural faith, they found fundamentalism theologically eccentric and methodologically suspect. Many later fundamentalists would employ Warfield's formulation of biblical inerrancy as a definition of their own beliefs about Scripture, but Warfield himself maintained several views that set him apart from fundamentalism.

In the first instance, Warfield held that fundamentalist proof-texting represented a retrograde step in studying the Bible. He questioned, for example, the method which Reuben A. Torrey of the Moody Bible Institute used in *What the Bible Teaches* (1898). The problem was that Torrey's method embodied "a tendency . . . to formulate doctrine on the basis of a general impression derived from a cursory survey of the Scriptural material or on the basis of the specific study of a few outstanding texts isolated from their contexts, and then to seek support for it in more or less detached passages." Far different and far better, in Warfield's view, was "the thorough understanding" to be found in the truly "inductive" exegesis of recent decades.[21] While commending Torrey for his understanding of the need for God's grace, Warfield had doubts about his ability to interpret the Scriptures as a whole.

Warfield, in addition, was thoroughly unimpressed by the dispensationalism that became so important in American fundamentalism. To Warfield, the confessions of the Reformation Era provided the best guides to the coherence of Christian truth. By contrast, he saw in the modern theologies associated with John Nelson Darby, C. I. Scofield, and the other promoters of dispensationalism faulty exegesis, questionable theological construction, and errors on the work of the Holy Spirit. Either an amillennialist or postmillennialist himself, Warfield felt that the reference to the thousand-year reign of Christ in Revelation 20 was obviously a symbol for the peace enjoyed by saints who have died in the Lord.[22]

Finally, Warfield, like his college teacher McCosh and his predecessor Archibald Hodge, found little difficulty in aligning his sturdy confessional Calvinism with a nonnaturalistic view of evolution. To be sure, Warfield's opposition to naturalistic forms of evolution never wavered. On several occasions he wrote on Darwin and, in so do-

19. B. B. Warfield, "Calvin's Doctrine of the Knowledge of God," in *Works*, 5:88.

20. W. Andrew Hoffecker, *Piety and the Princeton Theologians* (Phillipsburg, N.J.: Presbyterian and Reformed, 1981), 107.

21. B. B. Warfield, review of *What the Bible Teaches*, by Reuben A. Torrey, *Presbyterian and Reformed Review* 39 (July 1899): 562–64.

22. B. B. Warfield, "The Millennium and the Apocalypse," in *Works*, 2:643–64.

ing, took pains to show that if Darwinism meant random, purposeless change, then it must be opposed by every Christian. On the other hand, Warfield moved throughout his career to ever stronger assertions about the compatibility between scriptural truth and forms of evolution that do not entail random ateleology. Drawing on the exegesis of Genesis by William Henry Green, his Old Testament colleague at Princeton, Warfield wrote in 1911 that "the question of the antiquity of man has of itself no theological significance."[23] And expounding in 1915 on Calvin's view of creation, Warfield argued that Calvin's doctrine of providence allowed for "not only evolutionism but pure evolutionism."[24] Warfield may or may not have understood Calvin correctly, but he was certainly making an important personal statement of his own. As Warfield saw it, God at a point in time had supernaturally created all of the potential for subsequent development, and at a later point in time had supernaturally created the human soul. Warfield was content to think that everything else in nature, including the human body, could have developed through forces ordained by God in creation and sustained by him in providence. So convinced was Warfield of the compatibility between biblical inerrancy and evolution that he once chided James Orr for unnecessarily worrying about accepting "a purely evolutionary theory" of natural development. In making this point, Warfield called on his family's expertise in cattle raising to note that "nothing is commoner in the experience of breeding" than the origination of new variations through gradual change.[25]

The idea of *concursus* that Warfield had used in talking about Scripture was helpful also in thinking about God's relationship to the physical world. Just as the authors of

Scripture exercised their individual humanity in writing the Bible, even while they enjoyed the full inspiration of the Holy Spirit, so too could all forms of life have developed fully (with the exception of the original creation and the human soul) through natural means. The key for Warfield was a doctrine of providence that saw God working in and with, instead of completely apart from, the processes of nature. Late in his career, this stance also grounded Warfield's opposition to faith healing. In his eyes, physical healing through medicine and the agency of physicians was as much God's action (though through secondary means) as were the cures claimed to be the direct result of divine intervention.[26]

In his views on Bible study, dispensationalism, and evolution, therefore, Warfield was far from a fundamentalist. To note these differences is not a judgment on where Warfield or the fundamentalists were right or wrong (independent study of the various issues would be required for such conclusions). Rather, it is a recognition that Warfield's carefully qualified view of biblical inerrancy, far from necessarily entailing the particulars of fundamentalist theology, could in fact lead to specific judgments on nature, the character of biblical theology, and the approach to biblical scholarship that were almost diametrically opposed to what was found among fundamentalists.

Apologist

When Warfield was called to Princeton Seminary in 1887, he chose to speak at his inaugural on "The Idea of Systematic Theology Considered as a Science." It was fitting that Warfield chose such a topic, since it set out clearly his conception of theology and pointed directly to the high value he placed on apologetics. Warfield viewed theology as a straightforward science. God is the object of this science, and

23. B. B. Warfield, "On the Antiquity and the Unity of the Human Race," in *Works*, 9:235.

24. B. B. Warfield, "Calvin's Doctrine of the Creation," in *Works*, 5:305.

25. B. B. Warfield, review of *God's Image in Man*, by James Orr, in *Works*, 10:140–41.

26. See B. B. Warfield, *Counterfeit Miracles* (New York: Scribner, 1918).

Scripture provides the most important evidence for valid conclusions about him. Useful as other forms of divine revelation might be (whether conscience, nature, or religious experience), the fulness of God's revelation in the Bible "all but supersedes their necessity," as Warfield put it in 1896.[27] Scriptural revelation, moreover, conveys facts which the various subdivisions of theology (exegesis, biblical theology, historical theology) develop for the use of the systematician. Systematic theology makes progress just as natural science makes progress, incrementally, with each generation building on the foundation of the one before. With this conception of theology, Warfield was continuing a viewpoint that had become a hallmark of the Princeton Theology.

But Warfield's understanding of theology also marked several new tendencies at Princeton. For one, Warfield placed less emphasis on the role of religious experience than had his predecessors Archibald Alexander and Charles Hodge. To be sure, Warfield did believe that theology has its proper end in the stirring of heart, will, and emotion. In 1911, for example, he could say that "in every moment of faith . . . from the lowest to the highest, there is an intellectual, an emotional, and a voluntary element."[28] Yet, in the end, he remained much more rational than voluntarist or affectional in conceiving the essence of Christianity. The kind of statement that Charles Hodge could make as a young theologian— "opinions on moral and religious subjects depend mainly on the state of the moral and religious feelings"[29]—was for Warfield beyond the pale.

With such a view of theology, Warfield naturally placed a very heavy emphasis on

the apologetic foundations of the faith. He was convinced, as he put it in 1896, that "philosophical apologetics is . . . presupposed in and underlies the structure of scientific theology. . . . Apologetical Theology prepares the way for all theology by establishing its necessary presuppositions without which no theology is possible—the existence and essential nature of God, the religious nature of man which enables him to receive a revelation from God, the possibility of a revelation and its actual realization in the Scriptures."[30] That is, a theologian must use reason to establish the foundations from which the specific claims of Christianity arise. In a 1908 essay on "Apologetics," Warfield made this idea explicit: "Though faith be a moral act and the gift of God, it is yet formally conviction passing into confidence; and . . . all forms of conviction must rest on evidence as their ground, and it is not faith but reason which investigates the nature and validity of this ground. . . . We believe in Christ because it is rational to believe in Him." Warfield went on to acknowledge that "of course mere reasoning cannot make a Christian." Nonetheless, the Holy Spirit never works "apart from evidence, but along with evidence."[31]

These convictions lay behind one of Warfield's most quoted conclusions about the power of reason. In the introduction to an apologetical textbook by Francis R. Beattie, Warfield makes clear that while he is "not absurdly arguing that Apologetics has in itself the power to make a man a Christian," nonetheless, apologetics is still absolutely vital, since faith, "in all its exercises," is "a form of conviction, and is, therefore, necessarily grounded in evidence." Because of this relationship between faith and evidence, apologetics plays "a primary part, . . . a conquering part," in spreading the Christian faith. Warfield concludes, "It is the distinction of Christianity that it has come into

27. B. B. Warfield, "The Idea of Systematic Theology," in *Works*, 9:61.

28. B. B. Warfield, "On Faith in Its Psychological Aspects," in *Works*, 9:341.

29. Charles Hodge, "Lecture, Addressed to the Students of the Theological Seminary," *Biblical Repertory and Princeton Review* 1 (Jan. 1829): 90.

30. Warfield, "Idea of Systematic Theology," 55, 64.

31. B. B. Warfield, "Apologetics," in *Works*, 9:15.

the world clothed with the mission to *reason* its way to its dominion. Other religions may appeal to the sword, or seek some other way to propagate themselves. Christianity makes its appeal to right reason, and stands out among all religions, therefore, as distinctively 'the Apologetic religion.' It is solely by reasoning that it has come thus far on its way to its kingship."[32]

Warfield's view of the character of theology set him in opposition to what the Princeton tradition had long called rationalists, that is, modern thinkers who used reason to argue against historic Christianity. It also made him an opponent of evangelical "enthusiasm," which Warfield consistently espied in movements like Higher Life and Victorious Living. Perhaps most intriguingly, it also set him against contemporary Reformed theologians in the Netherlands with whom he otherwise had much in common.

Warfield studied the works of the Dutch Calvinists, especially Abraham Kuyper (1837–1920) and Herman Bavinck (1854–1921), with a mixture of delight and exasperation. When he provided an introduction for the English translation of Kuyper's *Encyclopedia of Sacred Theology* in 1898, he praised the work highly for both its substance and its form. And Warfield often expressed similar appreciation for the work of Bavinck and other theologians in Kuyper's orbit. But when it came to Dutch apologetics, it was another story. Historian George Marsden does not exaggerate when he concludes that Warfield was "utterly mystified by this approach."[33]

In particular, Warfield could not fathom why the Dutch theologians gave apologetics so little authority. Nor could he understand their insistence that all argumentation, even about the most basic epistemological matters, is at root religious and therefore slanted by the stance of the one making the argument. So when Kuyper stated in his *Encyclopedia* that facts of religious experience like regeneration and an implicit belief in God's ability to perform miracles inform theological thought at even the most preliminary level, Warfield begged to differ. As he put it in his introduction to Beattie's study, "It is easy, of course, to say that a Christian man must take his standpoint not *above* the Scriptures, but *in* the Scriptures. He very certainly must. But surely he must first *have* Scriptures, authenticated to him as such, before he can take his standpoint in them."[34]

Warfield consistently held that the world of facts is open to all people, and that all can be convinced of God's existence and the truth of Scripture by the proper reasoning of a redeemed thinker. This opinion, which had been a standard (though never unopposed) theme in Western Christendom, was particularly strong in the nineteenth century, when confidence in the power of scientific reasoning rose to its greatest height. In the twentieth century, by contrast, a different situation has prevailed. It has become very common (though not without opposition) to say that knowledge is always situated within the experience of the knower. Given this modern situation, it is not surprising that a major divide now exists, just as it did during the Dutch-American theological debates in which Warfield took part, between evangelical theologians on the proper form and place of apologetics. It is a testimony to the power of Warfield's work that modern discussions continue to feature it as an outstanding example of the evidentialist approach. In general, scholars whose work is influenced by Kuyper or Kuyper's successors find Warfield excessively rationalistic and unconvincing.[35] Those, on the other hand, who

32. B. B. Warfield, Introduction to *Apologetics*, by Francis R. Beattie, in *Selected Shorter Writings*, 2:99–100.

33. George M. Marsden, *Fundamentalism and American Culture* (New York: Oxford University Press, 1980), 115.

34. Warfield, Introduction to *Apologetics*, 2:98.

35. E.g., Rogers and McKim, *Authority and Interpretation;* Vander Stelt, *Philosophy and Scripture;* and Cornelius Van Til, *The Defense of the Faith* (Philadelphia: Presbyterian and Reformed, 1955), 262–65.

defend the older Scottish and American apologetics find in Warfield a convincing guide for how apologetics should be done.[36]

When Warfield spoke of theology as a science, he was speaking out of his own experience as a theologian of painstaking diligence and a lay scientist of wide and careful reading. In the late twentieth century, the temptation is almost overwhelming to submit Warfield's ardent defense of scientific theology, along with the evidentialist apologetics that was part of his view, to psychological analysis. Did Warfield argue so forcefully for the reasonableness of Christianity out of a need to convince himself? The question is perhaps worth pondering, but only after a full investigation of Warfield's extensive corpus. Such perusal of his work will demonstrate—even to those who side with Kuyper—how exhaustively thorough and unremittingly plausible were the arguments Warfield marshaled both for the truth of classic Christianity and for the power of reason.

Calvinist

Important as Warfield felt it was to contend for the reasonableness of orthodoxy, he exerted even more energy throughout his long career expounding that orthodoxy itself. In other words, while he was very much concerned to establish the Bible as the ground of theology and reason as a prime theological tool, he was (at least usually) even more interested in the theology he felt the Bible teaches and reason supports.

Warfield was not in the least embarrassed to say what that theology was and where he felt it had been best represented in the history of the church. Time and again throughout his historical, exegetical, and polemical works (it is not easy to disengage these categories from each other), Warfield

defined true Christianity as the pure religion of the Reformation or, in a phrase that to him meant the same thing, as the Augustinian grasp of human sin and divine grace as that understanding was recovered by Luther and especially Calvin or, even more fully, as the Pauline summation of the biblical gospel passed on especially to Augustine and then renewed by the magisterial Reformers. "Calvinism," he wrote in 1904, "is just religion in its purity. We have only, therefore, to conceive of religion in its purity, and that is Calvinism."[37]

Four years later Warfield spelled out explicitly what he meant by Calvinism—"a profound apprehension of God in His majesty, with the inevitably accompanying poignant realization of the exact nature of the relation sustained to Him by the creature as such, and particularly by the sinful creature." In the same essay Warfield suggested that he was not using "Calvinism" as a label for a narrow theological position, but that he regarded Calvinism as a way of life before God which over the course of history had been most satisfactorily described by those Protestant Reformers who had recovered an Augustinian understanding of the biblical message. If Warfield's claims for Calvinism were arrogant, his conception of it was broadly catholic:

> He who believes in God without reserve, and is determined that God shall be God to him in all his thinking, feeling, willing—in the entire compass of his life-activities, intellectual, moral, spiritual, throughout all his individual, social, religious relations—is, by the force of that strictest of all logic which presides over the outworking of principles into thought and life, by the very necessity of the case, a Calvinist. . . . Whoever believes in God; whoever recognizes in the recesses of his soul his utter dependence on God; whoever in all his thought of salvation hears in his heart of hearts the echo of the *soli Deo gloria* of the evangelical profession—by whatever name he may call

36. E.g., R. C. Sproul, John H. Gerstner, and Arthur Lindsley, *Classical Apologetics* (Grand Rapids: Zondervan, 1984), 38, 209, 256, 327.

37. B. B. Warfield, "What Is Calvinism?" in *Selected Shorter Writings*, 1:389.

himself, or by whatever intellectual puzzles his logical understanding may be confused—Calvinism recognizes as implicitly a Calvinist.[38]

Although Warfield is today better known for his views on the Bible, a solid case can be constructed that his commitment to classic Protestantism was deeper and more comprehensive than even his commitment to inerrancy. By "classic Protestantism" Warfield meant theological commitment to an Augustinian view of God, of the sinful human condition, and of salvation in Christ, but also a broadly open acceptance of the world as the arena of God's creative activity. For Warfield, the heart of both theology and active religion was the glory of the God who rescues sinful humans from self-imposed destruction and who enables them to share the work of his kingdom in every sphere of life.

Much of Warfield's most creative historical theology went into the exposition of these convictions. For example, major monographs on Augustine's response to Pelagius, the theology of the Reformers, the theology of the Reformation's confessional statements, and the debate that went into the Westminster Confession's chapter on the divine decree were devoted to promoting what Warfield called "the Augustinianism of grace."[39] While some of these essays had other purposes (e.g., to discourage efforts to revise the Westminster Confession), the theological engine that drove Warfield's polemical activity was very frequently the doctrines of sin and grace as they were expounded by the classical Reformation.

Toward the end of his life Warfield devoted immense effort to refuting a species of theological error that he called "perfectionism." The perfectionists Warfield attacked were an oddly assorted lot—German modernists like Albrecht Ritschl, pietists like Theodor Jellinghaus, Holiness teachers like Robert Pearsall Smith and William Boardman, Asa Mahan and Charles Finney of Oberlin College, the communitarian John Humphrey Noyes, and various promoters of Victorious Living like Charles Trumbull of the *Sunday School Times*. Warfield justified lumping them together because of what he considered their common tendency to exalt human capability and so diminish both reliance upon God and God's glory.

Perfectionism of whatever kind—whether the pretensions to exalted knowledge by academics or the assumption of perfected hearts among evangelical enthusiasts—was rendered, in Warfield's words, "impossible in the presence of a deep sense or a profound conception of sin." Warfield also held that perfectionists inevitably tended to trivialize the person and work of God. "The practical effect of the teaching" that people could gain a "second blessing," achieve a "victorious life," or attain "sinless perfection" was, as Warfield saw it, "to encourage men to look upon [God] as a force existing for them and wholly at their command. . . . [Perfectionism] tends to looking upon Him as the instrument which we use to secure our ends, and that is a magical rather than a religious attitude. In the end it inhibits religion which includes in its essence a sense of complete dependence on God."[40] The problem of perfectionism, which Warfield saw in so many deviant movements, was at root a turning away from the biblical teaching, championed by both Augustine and the Reformers, concerning the constant need of all people, even the redeemed, for the grace of God. The modern movements, in sum, hastened to forget that, as Augustine, Luther, and Calvin had stressed, "we must always be ac-

---

38. B. B. Warfield, "Calvinism," in *Works*, 5:354–56.

39. B. B. Warfield, "Augustine and the Pelagian Controversy," in *Works*, 4:289–412; "The Theology of the Reformation," in *Works*, 9:461–79; "Predestination in the Reformed Confessions," in *Works*, 9:117–231; and "The Making of the Westminster Confession, and Especially of Its Chapter on the Decree of God," in *Works*, 6:75–151.

40. B. B. Warfield, "The 'Higher Life' Movement," in *Works*, 8:554–55.

cepted for Christ's sake, or we cannot ever be accepted at all."[41]

Given this conception of what true religion involves, Warfield's positive theology, which sometimes did verge on abstraction when he was defending the rationality of true religion, became warm, lively, and even passionate. In a lengthy essay on predestination, for example, the peroration is not a neat academic summary, but a burning cry: "The hope of the world, the hope of the Church, and the hope of the individual alike, is cast solely on the mercy of a freely electing God, in whose hands are all things, and not least the care of the advance of His saving grace in the world."[42] Similarly vivid language can be found in an address delivered at Princeton's opening convocation in 1911. Warfield urged the students to combine hard study and fervent prayer. The point in striving to grow both as Christian thinkers and as Christian pietists was not merely to gain new insight into biblical teaching; it was also to be able, like the angels, "to sound the trumpets." Warfield urged the students to so prepare themselves day and night that "when you come to sound the trumpet the note will be pure and clear and strong, and perchance may pierce even to the grave and wake the dead."[43]

Finally, we should note that even Warfield's defense of inerrancy, which often seems to have been undertaken in behalf of a bare notion of biblical veracity, was probably a product of his overarching Calvinism. In Warfield's view, what was at stake in defending traditional views of the Bible was not so much the Bible itself as what the Bible taught. Consider, for example, Warfield's review of the autobiography of William Newton Clarke, a Northern Baptist whose definition of the Bible gradually changed from an inerrant revelation from God to a refined record of religious encounter with God. Warfield rehearsed the arguments he had made many times before concerning Jesus' own testimony to the infallibility of Scripture. But in the end the critical matter was not just Scripture: "He who no longer holds to the Bible of Jesus—the word of which cannot be broken—will be found on examination no longer to hold to the Jesus of the Bible," the Jesus who communicates forgiveness to needy sinners.[44]

L. Russ Bush has made the important observation that Warfield's understanding of the Bible follows his general view of theology.[45] The same Calvinistic conception of sovereignty that governs Warfield's soteriology—God is the initiator and enabler of human repentance and faith—governs his view of Scripture. Closely related to the *concursus* of salvation—God acting in and with humanity—is a *concursus* that yields an infallible Bible, as well as a *concursus* linking nature and providence.

It is sometimes difficult to see the ties between Warfield's defense of biblical inerrancy and the theocentric concerns of his Calvinist theology. It is even more difficult to say how his high view of evidentialist apologetics fit into a Calvinism that, as he described it, undermined all human self-congratulation. For could not the same Augustinian theology that he employed in criticizing perfectionists for their excessive confidence in the moral capacities of redeemed human nature be used to criticize his own confidence in its reasoning capacities?

No modern evangelical has defended biblical inerrancy better than has Warfield. Nor has anyone more securely tied inerrancy to classical Protestant orthodoxy on the one hand, and to a full deployment of modern science on the other. One of the

---

41. B. B. Warfield, "'Miserable-Sinner Christianity' in the Hands of the Rationalists," in *Works*, 7:113.

42. B. B. Warfield, "Predestination," in *Works*, 2:66.

43. B. B. Warfield, "The Religious Life of Theological Students," in *Selected Shorter Writings*, 1:425.

44. B. B. Warfield, review of *Sixty Years with the Bible*, by William Newton Clarke, *Princeton Theological Review* 8 (Jan. 1910): 167.

45. Bush, "Roots of Conservative Perspectives," 280–81.

reasons that those who have adopted Warfield's view of inerrancy have by and large not shared his Calvinism or his enjoyment of modern science may be that the rationalistic principles of his theological method undermine the bonds that, in his greatest contribution to modern evangelical theology, he saw between scriptural inerrancy and both the Augustinian religion and appreciation of natural knowledge wherever it is found.

Primary Sources

B. B. Warfield. *Counterfeit Miracles.* New York: Scribner, 1918.

_____. *Faith and Life: "Conferences" in the Oratory of Princeton Seminary.* New York: Longmans, Green, 1916.

_____. *An Introduction to the Textual Criticism of the New Testament.* London: Hodder and Stoughton, 1886.

_____. *Selected Shorter Writings of Benjamin B. Warfield.* Edited by John E. Meeter. 2 vols. Nutley, N.J.: Presbyterian and Reformed, 1970, 1973.

_____. *Works of Benjamin B. Warfield.* 10 vols. New York: Oxford University Press, 1927–32. Reprint. Grand Rapids: Baker, 1981. Vol. 1, *Revelation and Inspiration,* 1927; vol. 2, *Biblical Doctrines,* 1929; vol. 3, *Christology and Criticism,* 1929; vol. 4, *Studies in Tertullian and Augustine,* 1930; vol. 5, *Calvin and Cal-vinism,* 1931; vol. 6, *The Westminster Assembly and Its Work,* 1931; vols. 7–8, *Perfectionism,* 1931–32; vol. 9, *Studies in Theology,* 1932; vol. 10, *Critical Reviews,* 1932.

Secondary Sources

Fuller, Daniel P. "Benjamin B. Warfield's View of Faith and History." *Bulletin of the Evangelical Theological Society* 11 (Spring 1968): 75–83.

Hoffecker, W. Andrew. "Benjamin B. Warfield." In *The Princeton Theology: Reformed Theology in America,* edited by David F. Wells, 65–91. Grand Rapids: Baker, 1989.

Noll, Mark A., ed. *The Princeton Defense of Plenary Verbal Inspiration.* New York: Garland, 1988.

_____. *The Princeton Theology 1812–1921: Scripture, Science, and Theological Method from Archibald Alexander to Benjamin Warfield.* Grand Rapids: Baker, 1983.

Rogers, Jack B. *Scripture in the Westminster Confession.* Grand Rapids: Eerdmans, 1967.

Spencer, Stephen R. "A Comparison and Evaluation of the Old Princeton and Amsterdam Apologetics." Th.M. thesis, Grand Rapids Baptist Seminary, n.d.

Woodbridge, John D., and Randall H. Balmer. "The Princetonians and Biblical Authority: An Assessment of the Ernest Sandeen Proposal." In *Scripture and Truth,* edited by D. A. Carson and John D. Woodbridge, 251–79. Grand Rapids: Zondervan, 1983.

Francis Pieper

David P. Scaer

Francis (Franz) August Otto Pieper was born on June 27, 1852, in Pomerania, a Prussian province on the Baltic Sea.[1] A son of the mayor of Carwitz, Pieper would become the most influential confessional Lutheran theologian in twentieth-century America. The English translation of his *Christliche Dogmatik* still sets the tone in large part for the theology of the Lutheran Church–Missouri Synod, which he served as president from 1899 to 1911.[2] When he joined the faculty of Concordia Seminary (St. Louis) in 1878, the Missouri Synod numbered an estimated 150,000 members. By the time of his death in 1931, the synod had added a million members and had become completely acclimated to America.

Influences on Pieper and His Impact on the Missouri Synod

In accordance with nineteenth-century German academic tradition, Pieper received an education in the classical languages. He attended first the gymnasium (a junior-college-level institution) in Köslin, then completed his degree at Kolberg in

1. In the year of Pieper's death appeared what amounted to an official biography—Theodore Graebner, *Dr. Francis Pieper: A Biographical Sketch* (St. Louis: Concordia, 1931). This work was intended more as a tribute than a critical analysis. (To date no critical analysis of his theology has been published.) Many personal details are set forth in glowing terms. Throughout the book Pieper is referred to as "the Doctor," an appropriate title for the man who is still revered as the Missouri Synod's most significant theologian.

2. Pieper's abiding influence over the Missouri Synod is the subject of a series of three articles by Richard E. Koenig—"Church and Tradition in Collision," *Lutheran Forum* 6 (Nov. 1972): 17–20; "Missouri Turns Moderate: 1938–1965," *Lutheran Forum* 7 (Feb. 1973): 19–20, 29; and "Conservative Reaction: 1965–1969," *Lutheran Forum* 7 (March 1973): 18–21. Labeling the theology of the Missouri Synod "the Pieper tradition" and "the Pieper legacy," the articles criticize it for rendering the synod incapable of fellowship outside of its own heritage. At the time of writing, Koenig was a clergyman in the Missouri Synod and editor of the *Lutheran Forum,* but he later left for the Evangelical Lutheran Church in America.

1870. In the year of his graduation, he along with his widowed mother and three younger brothers emigrated from Prussia to join two older brothers already living in Wisconsin. His older brother Reinhold would become a professor of homiletics and then president of Concordia Theological Seminary in Springfield, Illinois. Younger brother August became a professor at the seminary of the Wisconsin Evangelical Lutheran Synod, a church body that was a member of the Evangelical Lutheran Synodical Conference, an association of conservative Lutheran bodies that also included the Missouri Synod. Francis took an additional two years of college education at the Wisconsin Synod's Northwestern College in Watertown. At his graduation at the age of twenty he delivered an oration in Latin on the theme "Which Characteristics of the German People Should Be Retained in This Country and Which Should Be Discarded?" This title reflects the desire of the recent German immigrants to integrate into the life of their adopted country without giving up certain fundamentals, including commitment to the Lutheran faith for which their forefathers had contended since the Reformation.

Memories of weathering three centuries in the inhospitable political climate that reflected the Reformed bias of Prussia's ruling family helped shape the conservative confessional Lutheran theology of Francis Pieper and of the Missouri Synod, as it continues to be influenced by him. Philip of Hesse had attempted to merge the Lutheran and Reformed traditions by bringing Martin Luther and Ulrich Zwingli together at the Marburg Colloquy in 1529. Luther's opposition to a religious accommodation for the sake of political alliance was reinforced by the Lutherans in the Formula of Concord (1577), which rejected John Calvin's view on the Lord's Supper and on the person of Christ. Though Marburg failed to provide a national Protestant religion for the German states, this was achieved in Prussia in 1817 during the commemoration of the three hundredth anniversary of the Reformation. Friedrich Wilhelm III forced an administrative union of the Lutheran and Reformed churches—the Evangelical (Protestant) Church, which was known as the Union. A liturgical union followed in 1830 to mark the three hundredth anniversary of the Augsburg Confession. Included under these measures was Pomerania, Pieper's home province. At peril was the characteristic Lutheran teaching that the elements of the Lord's Supper are actually Christ's body and blood, a doctrine repudiated by the Reformed. Lutheran pastors were permitted to occupy their pulpits, but liturgies compromising the Lutheran understanding of the Lord's Supper were distributed by the king. Failure to utilize them could result in fines, loss of property, and imprisonment. Some of the Lutherans chose migration to Australia and America, and took with them an aversion to the Reformed faith.[3] Pieper's Christology and doctrine of the Lord's Supper, which are the most fully developed sections in his *Christian Dogmatics,* are marked by a strongly anti-Reformed bias that reflects this Lutheran struggle for survival in Prussia. In 1861 the Lutheran minority within the Union received some relief from Wilhelm I. They were allowed Luther's Small Catechism with its classical Lutheran positions on Christ's person and work, the Lord's Supper, and justification, themes that later proved important in Pieper's theology.

Various eighteenth- and nineteenth-century religious and philosophical movements were among the other factors shaping Pieper's thought. Though Pietism was short-lived as an intellectual movement in Germany, it made intense inroads among the people. Its emphasis on sanctification began to erode the differences between Lutheran and Reformed teachings, and pre-

3. For a recent critical appraisal see David Schuber, "Should We Be Here? A New Look at Why the First Lutherans Came to Australia," *Lutheran Theological Journal* 25 (Dec. 1991): 147–56.

pared the way for Frederick the Great's introduction of the Enlightenment into Prussia in the mid-1700s. Rationalism not only made light of denominational differences, but questioned the uniqueness of Christianity. Religion came to be viewed as having less to do with the supernatural and more with morality. Though Christianity may have been superior, it was no longer thought to be the exclusive religious expression. The Lutheran struggles over the exclusivity of Christianity surface throughout Pieper's three-volume *Christian Dogmatics*. In fact, a section entitled "Christianity the Absolute Religion" is part of the prolegomena.[4] He addressed the same topic in more detail in his 1926 essay "The Christian Religion in Its Relation to All Other Religions."[5]

Pieper's theology is also a reaction to Friedrich Schleiermacher, who, combining Pietism and the rationalist disregard for the supernatural, viewed the collective consciousness of the Christian community as the basis for religious truth. Pieper considered Schleiermacher a pantheist who had replaced the Scriptures as the source of religious truth with experience.[6] Pieper also gave a great deal of attention in his *Christian Dogmatics* to the Erlangen School, a group of Lutheran theologians who had been heavily influenced by Schleiermacher.

In the theological spectrum of his time, Pieper's restatement of Lutheranism as derived from sixteenth- and seventeenth-century sources occupied a position on the right. He quoted extensively from, for example, Luther, the Lutheran confessions, Martin Chemnitz, Johann Gerhard, and J. A. Quenstedt. To Pieper's left was the Erlangen School, which attempted reformulating confessional Lutheran theology to fit Schleiermacher's emphasis on collective Christian consciousness. Among them were

Franz von Frank, Ludwig Ihmels, Johann Hoefling, Christoph Luthardt, and Gottfried Thomasius. As part of the nineteenth-century revival of the Reformation and post-Reformation Lutheranism, they played a large role in making sources from those periods available. At the same time they attempted to make what Pieper regarded as an accommodation with the new thought of rationalism and of Schleiermacher. Rationalism had opened the world of biblical criticism, which they were unwilling to surrender. While the Bible remained a source of theology, verbal inspiration was deemed impossible. Like Schleiermacher the Erlangen School appealed to collective Christian consciousness as the basic source of religious truth.[7] Later Paul Tillich would call attention to the philosophical impossibility of the Erlangen attempt to derive a Lutheran theology from Christian consciousness. Like Tillich, Emil Brunner and Karl Barth, the neo-orthodox theologians, show no acquaintance with Pieper in their criticisms of nineteenth-century liberal theology and the subjectivism introduced by Schleiermacher. For Pieper's critique of the Erlangen School was based on his understanding that the Bible is the Word of God; the neo-orthodox theologians, on the other hand, saw the Word of God as the source of theology, but defined it as an encounter.

Also having significant impact on Pieper was repristination theology, the early-nineteenth-century revival of confessional Lutheranism. Ironically, the events sounding the death knell for Lutheranism as the official religion in Prussia encouraged its reawakening as a confessional movement. The three-hundredth anniversaries of the Reformation and the Augsburg Confession alerted Lutherans to the old Reformation sources which had fallen into disuse because of the ascendancy of rationalism. Similarly, Schleiermacher's examination of Christian consciousness as the source of religious truth, though rejected later by Lu-

---

4. Francis Pieper, *Christian Dogmatics*, 3 vols. (St. Louis: Concordia, 1950–53), 1:34–40.

5. Francis Pieper, "Die christliche Religion in ihrem Verhältnis zu allen andern Religionen," *Lehre und Wehre* 72.9 (Sept. 1926): 257–68.

6. Pieper, *Christian Dogmatics*, 2:6, 367.

7. Ibid., 1:30.

therans, proved a stimulus for the reevaluation of Reformation sources. Luther, the Lutheran confessions, and the sixteenth- and seventeenth-century Lutheran theologians were part of the culture which informed the collective Christian consciousness in the religious life of Germany. By the time Pieper did his work in the last quarter of the nineteenth century, confessional Lutheranism had already taken shape as an independently viable theology. His accomplishment was to preserve this revived confessional Lutheran theology and reformulate it for the Lutheran situation in America.

Among the repristination theologians who reintroduced Reformation sources into the theological task was Carl F. W. Walther, under whom Pieper studied at Concordia Seminary (St. Louis) and whom he succeeded as professor of theology and eventually as president. Walther had direct influence on Pieper's theological development. Pieper was dependent on Walther for his views on various crucial issues for the Missouri Synod—the ministry, the church, and predestination.[8] The Baier-Walther *Compendium*, a seventeenth-century Lutheran dogmatics updated and edited by Walther, was often cited by Pieper and frequently provided his ancient sources.[9] Unlike Walther, Pieper had no direct experience with the theology of the German universities. He was dependent, instead, on his wide reading, as evidenced by his encyclopedic citations. It would be difficult to identify any American Lutheran, even today, so thoroughly immersed in both the Anglo-Saxon and German theological scenes of his era. It is no wonder that he succeeded Walther as the chief theologian of the Missouri Synod. Certain of its characteristic views, for example, on divine election and verbal inspiration, were formulated by Pieper. His influence outside of this circle, however, has been limited.

The chief reason for Pieper's lack of influence outside the Missouri Synod is the language factor. He was a German-speaking theologian not only in an English-speaking country, but in a church body which had adopted the language of its new homeland. He was accomplished in English, but preferred German. Before he died, the Missouri Synod's first theological journal, *Lehre und Wehre*, which he served as editor, was absorbed into the *Concordia Theological Monthly*.[10] His *Christliche Dogmatik* appeared in its complete form in 1924; but World War I had, of course, made it impossible for the synod to use German. Only in 1950 did his magnum opus appear in English translation.

As Pieper was a bridge between the German and English worlds of the Missouri Synod, he also spanned different theological worlds. On one side he dealt with the rationalism of late-eighteenth-century Germany and on the other with the Calvinism and Arminianism of twentieth-century American Protestantism. He knew about Adolf von Harnack and Albert Schweitzer, but he was clearly a nineteenth-century theologian with an American audience.[11] He knew the German theologians better than they knew him, the one exception being Friedrich Adolph Philippi of the Univer-

---

8. Koenig, "Church and Tradition," 19, claims that Pieper moved away from Walther's emphasis on justification to "a preoccupation with the doctrine of the Holy Scripture." But one can reasonably argue that Pieper was more obsessed with the doctrine of justification than Walther was.

9. Johann Wilhelm Baier, *Compendium theologiae positivae*, ed. Carl F. W. Walther (St. Louis: Concordia, 1879).

10. For a bibliography of Pieper's last articles to appear in *Lehre und Wehre* and its successor, the *Concordia Theological Monthly*, see P. E. Kretzmann, "Prof. Franz August Otto Pieper, D.theol.," *Concordia Theological Monthly* 2.8 (Aug. 1931): 563–65. All of these articles are in German.

11. An invaluable tool in studying Pieper's *Christian Dogmatics* is the index prepared by Walter W. F. Albrecht, which was eventually added as a fourth volume to the set (St. Louis: Concordia, 1957). From the exhaustive list of Pieper's references to theologians it is evident that he was not at home in the twentieth-century theological world.

sity of Rostock, with whom Pieper entered into dialogue on the topic of verbal inspiration.[12]

Though largely unknown elsewhere, Pieper's impact on the Missouri Synod has been, as we have already suggested, immense. At the age of twenty-six, three years after graduation, he began his fifty-three-year teaching career at Concordia Seminary. At the time of his death, the graduating classes numbered near two hundred. In addition, his *Christian Dogmatics* continues to be used in the seminaries of the Missouri Synod. His influence both directly on his students and through his dogmatics cannot be overestimated.

An abridged English-language version of the *Christliche Dogmatik* was prepared by John Theodore Mueller, Pieper's successor as professor of theology at Concordia Seminary, and published in 1934. Entitled *Christian Dogmatics: A Handbook of Doctrinal Theology for Pastors, Teachers, and Laymen*, the abridgment has been translated into Spanish, Swedish, French, Finnish, and, ironically, German, the language of the original dogmatics. Omitting some of Pieper's more complex refutations of nineteenth-century theologians, Mueller's version has assisted students for whom the theological arguments in the three-volume *Christian Dogmatics* are too detailed. Mueller's abridgment is really Pieper's work, though Pieper is not mentioned on the title page (there is a reference to him in the preface). Students from other denominations are likely to use the abridgment to determine the classical Lutheran position.

Basic Approach to Theology

Essential to understanding Pieper's method is recognition that he designed his theology to serve nineteenth-century confessional Lutheranism in the Missouri Synod. Even today he is frequently cited to settle theological disputes in that church body. Especially significant in this connec-

tion is the "Brief Statement of the Doctrinal Position of the Missouri Synod," of which Pieper was the principal author.[13] First circulated in 1931 and accepted as the official position of the synod in 1932, one year after Pieper's death, the "Brief Statement" remains the hallmark for conservative Lutheran theology in America. Though Walther's edition of the Baier *Compendium* had alerted the synod's first theological students to the older Lutheran treasures from the Reformation and post-Reformation eras, it was not an original dogmatics. Consequently, Pieper's dogmatics became and remains the standard theology for the Missouri Synod.

As his dogmatics was constructed almost directly from his classroom lectures and convention speeches, which frequently took the form of reactions to various nineteenth-century theologians, Pieper's discussion more often than not is polemical, as he himself admitted.[14] Thus his dogmatics is as much biographical theology as it is systematics. The dogmatic works of Adolf Hoenecke, the theologian of the Wisconsin Synod, and Friedrich Adolph Philippi, who shared Pieper's concern for confessional Lutheranism and whose works he recommended, more closely followed a predeter-

---

12. Pieper, *Christian Dogmatics*, 1:224.

13. The official form of the "Brief Statement" was written in German and entitled "Thesen zur kurzen Darlegung der Lehrstellung der Missourisynod," *Concordia Theological Monthly* 2.5 (May 1931): 321–36. The English translation appeared in the next issue (pp. 400–416). From 1959 to 1962 the "Brief Statement" was given virtual confessional status in the Missouri Synod and is still an honored document today. Its forty-eight numbered paragraphs cover the following topics: the Holy Scriptures, God, creation, man and sin, redemption, faith in Christ, conversion, justification, good works, the means of grace, the church, public ministry, church and state, the election of grace, Sunday, the millennium, the Antichrist, open questions, and the symbols of the Lutheran church.

14. "We Missourians, so-called, are well aware that we are opposed in principle to the aim of modern theology. Nor is the fact hidden from us that we are *persona ingrata* with the greater part of the ecclesiastical public"—quoted in W. H. T. Dau, "Dr. Francis Pieper the Churchman," *Concordia Theological Monthly* 2.10 (Oct. 1931): 734.

mined order.[15] Exegetical, historical, and contemporary questions were handled separately. Pieper, by contrast, merges these categories into a general discussion. In an almost Luther-like manner he will interrupt the orderly flow of his exposition to engage current theologians. He quotes them at length and then with biblical and confessional references refutes them in order to validate his own position. The length of a section betrays his interests. Pieper makes no attempt to be evenhanded in allotting space to the various loci. Whereas only two pages are devoted to infant baptism, more than one hundred pages are devoted to the means of grace.[16] The means of grace was a prominent issue between Lutherans and Reformed; infant baptism was not. Seeing grace as the fundamental Christian doctrine, he was extremely disturbed by the Reformed denial of what Lutherans considered to be some of the means through which grace comes to the Christian. It is arguable that if the Missouri Synod had been surrounded by a Baptist majority, there would have been a lengthier treatment of infant baptism.

Theology for Pieper is a totality: a tear at a corner can rip the entire garment. For this reason biblical inerrancy and infallibility are essential.[17] Accordingly, while he allows less than one page for the theology of creation, he spends thirteen pages defending the six-day creation. And because of the

Reformed threat, Pieper centers his Christology on a discussion of the communication of attributes, with considerably less attention to the events in the life of Christ.[18] Fittingly the concluding section on the person of Christ is entitled "Summary Critique of Reformed Christology."[19] Later on he identifies the pope as the Antichrist on the grounds of the Roman Catholic denial of justification by grace. This leads Pieper to reintroduce the chief elements of the doctrine of justification.[20] Thus his theology takes shape as confrontation with error.

Pieper's presentation of individual topics often begins not with his own view, but with a summary and repudiation of his adversaries' positions. There is no doubt where Pieper stands, but sometimes the arguments for his own position must be sifted from his polemics. While he on occasion cites his opponents' opinions in support of his own arguments, he does not always analyze the method that was used to determine their conclusions. For example, he cites the rationalist Karl August von Hase to demonstrate that the congregation is the source of all church authority; in doing so he ignores the fact that Hase was arguing against the divine institution of the office of the ministry, a concept which Pieper upheld against the rationalists.[21]

That theology was the preserve of the congregations was reinforced by the custom of seminary professors serving as pastors of local parishes. During his tenure as seminary professor, Pieper was assistant pastor of Immanuel Lutheran Church in St. Louis, where he lies buried. So in a very real sense his theology developed in a close relationship to the people. Half of the delegates to the church conventions for which his essays were prepared were laymen. He firmly believed that theology is not scholarship for its own sake, but for the church's.

---

15. Adolf Hoenecke, *Kirchliche Dogmatik* (Milwaukee: Northwestern, 1909); Friedrich Adolph Philippi, *Kirchliche Glaubenslehre*, 7 vols. (Gütersloh: Bertelsmann, 1854–82).

16. Pieper, *Christian Dogmatics*, 3:277–78; 3:104–219.

17. At the time of Pieper's death, his colleague Ludwig Fürbringer made the following assessment: "Without any hesitation or doubt he committed himself to the highest principle of theology, that the Holy Scriptures are the Word of God, infallible and without error in matters of doctrine and life, and in the so-called side issues of historical, archaeological, geographical, astronomical, and similar details. The Scriptures are the absolute and only source and norm of all doctrine" ("Dr. F. Pieper als Theolog," *Concordia Theological Monthly* 2:10 [Oct. 1931]: 724).

18. Pieper, *Christian Dogmatics*, 2:129–271; 2:305–30.

19. Ibid., 2:271–79.

20. Ibid., 2:555–57.

21. Ibid., 3:458–59; 3:443–49.

This does not mean that theology is not an academic discipline,[22] but that its basic purpose is to serve the people. Hence it is a practical discipline. It may involve the theologian to the point of actual suffering. Pieper summarized this concept with the Latin phrase *Oratio, meditatio, tentatio faciunt theologicum* ("Prayer, contemplation on the Scriptures, and tribulations make the theologian").[23] To sum up: Pieper viewed theology as the task of the militant church confronting false doctrine. Practical theology is the final goal and crown of all theology, since everything in theology is for the people's benefit.

Fundamental Themes

Election—Universal Grace and Salvation by Grace Alone

In addition to his duties as professor of theology (1878–1931) and seminary president (1887–1931), Pieper served for thirteen years as president of the Missouri Synod (1899–1911)—a physically taxing combination. During that period he was heavily involved in maintaining the confessional integrity of the Evangelical Lutheran Synodical Conference. After his tenure as synod president, he witnessed the weakening of the synodical conference with the withdrawal of the Norwegian Synod over the matter of predestination, an issue over which the Ohio Synod had left during Walther's time. Pieper, like Walther before him, had to defend himself against the charge of Calvinism for his position on election. Ironically, opposition to Calvin's doctrines on the person of Christ and the Lord's Supper had been among the primary reasons for the founding of the Missouri Synod. Pieper's doctrine of election resembles the Reformed position in that salvation depends not on the believer, but totally on God. Unlike the Reformed, however, Pieper does not base election in divine sovereignty or providence, but in the cross as a neces-

sary concomitant of the doctrine of grace. Accordingly, he places election at the conclusion of his dogmatics and not at the beginning.[24] The topic does not belong to human speculations about God, but relates to God's comforting of the sinner.[25] There is no suggestion of a predestination to damnation.[26] Pieper's interest in the doctrine of election was evident already in 1885, when he took up its implication for the Christian life in the essay "The Certainty of Our Salvation Viewed in Its Importance for Spiritual Life." Near the end of his life he took up the subject again in his 1928 essay "How May a Christian Become Certain of His Eternal Election?"[27] To Pieper, election or predestination was a facet of salvation by grace alone, and not a separate doctrine.

Though Pieper, like Walther, was dependent on the seventeenth-century Lutheran theologians, he was not uncritical in his use of them. For instance, they were sometimes interpreted as teaching that faith is a cause of salvation.[28] Pieper's arguments against regarding faith as a cause of salvation depended on Article 11 of the Formula of Concord. Quoting the confessions gave him an advantage over his Lutheran opponents. The problem of divine election was an American one, but it had its roots in the assertion of the seventeenth-century Lutheran theologians that God has elected believers *intuitu fide* ("in view of faith"). Originally this may have meant simply that faith was somehow entailed in God's electing of the believer. Regardless of the original intent, *intuitu fide* was interpreted first by the Ohio Synod and then by a group within the Norwegian Synod as a declaration that faith is a cause of election, which means that humans contribute to their conversion. This was a denial of the Reforma-

---

22. Ibid., 1:106–10.
23. Ibid., 1:186–90.

24. Ibid., 3:473–503.
25. Ibid., 3:490–94.
26. Ibid., 3:494–501.
27. Francis Pieper, "Wie wird ein Christ seiner ewigen Erwählung gewiß?" *Lehre und Wehre* 74.4 (April 1928): 97–110; 74.5 (May 1928): 129–42.
28. Pieper, *Christian Dogmatics*, 3:501–3.

tion principle of salvation by grace alone and accordingly labeled as Arminianism. As far as Pieper was concerned, the theological argument could begin with either conversion by grace alone or election—each doctrine complemented and required the other. By placing election near the end of his final volume, Pieper completed his theological circle, which began in the prolegomena with the introduction of the doctrine of grace as the standard of theology. No other issue absorbed Pieper as much as did divine election, for he had to face the political consequences of the denial of this doctrine in the dissolution of the synodical conference. Surfacing in the introduction of his *Christian Dogmatics,*[29] it is arguable that the controversy over election is the reason he made divine grace the basis of his theological program.

Pieper rejected all notions of human cooperation as synergistic. He let stand the apparent contradiction between universal grace (*gratia universalis*) and salvation by grace alone (*sola gratia*), rather than allow any suggestion that salvation depends to some extent on the human believer. The grace by which salvation is seriously offered to all, Christ's atonement being unlimited in scope, is the same grace that underlies the salvation of those who are ultimately saved. The impossibility of resolving universal grace and salvation by grace alone is the *crux theologorum* ("the cross or burden of theologians"). To favor one over the other distorts Christianity. At stake for Pieper was not only the characteristic Lutheran doctrine of justification, but Christ's incarnation and atonement.

Given Pieper's insistence on the divine inspiration of the Bible, he expectedly musters the necessary biblical evidences in support of his positions: *Quod non est biblicum, non est theologicum* ("What is not biblical is not theological").[30] The biblical data are reinforced with confessional references. Still Pieper's theological method is more complex than mere citation of the Bible and the Lutheran confessions. At the base of his theology is a carefully worked out Christology which challenges both Calvinism and Arminianism. The Reformed doctrine of the incarnation is not only inadequate, but an actual denial of the fact. The *extra Calvinisticum*, the Reformed argument that in the incarnation the Second Person of the Trinity was not totally contained in the human nature of Jesus, allows only a limited atonement. The Arminians, on the other hand, are right about universal grace, but by viewing salvation as partially dependent on the human believer, nullify salvation by grace alone and the atonement.

Not only is Pieper's Christology crucial here, but as the basis of his doctrine of justification, it serves as the basis of all his doctrine.[31] The importance of Christology for Pieper is further seen in that the second volume of *Christian Dogmatics*, which contains his Christology, was published first and provides the assumptions for the first and third volumes. Without reading the prefaces to these volumes, one would not be immediately aware of the primacy of Christology in Pieper's theology. But even his markedly polemical approach in stating his opponents' position first is for the sake of defending his Christology. Moreover, determination to keep his Christology intact accounts for his refusal to resolve the dilemma of *cur alii, alii non* ("why some are saved and others are not"). Better that theologians leave the problem unresolved than to provide an answer requiring a false Christology and denial of grace.

It is apparent from the foregoing that Pieper was not a twentieth-century theologian, though more than half of his career was spent in this period. Neo-orthodoxy,

---

29. Ibid., 1:9–34.
30. Ibid., 1:52.

31. Koenig, "Church and Tradition," 17–20, faults Pieper for devoting two hundred pages to the doctrine of Holy Scripture and only about sixty to justification. This fails to consider that Pieper regarded justification as a subsidiary article of Christology, to which he devoted over three hundred pages, and that the discussion of election is really about justification.

which discredited Schleiermacher and the optimism of the nineteenth-century theologians for their subjectivism, had obviated much of Pieper's polemic before *Christian Dogmatics* was published. The complete set appeared in 1924, when he was seventy-two years old and his theological work done. In the preface he notes his appreciation of the works of Ernst Sartorius, who in the 1820s found a basis for religion outside of reason and the Christian consciousness.[32] This was not an issue in the twentieth century, at least not in this form. During Pieper's lifetime the older world had passed away. In his last ten years he was absorbed with reconstructing a confessional alliance with the American Lutheran Church, which included the Ohio Synod, a former partner in the Evangelical Lutheran Synodical Conference. In his late seventies he was working on the "Brief Statement." Virtually oblivious to twentieth-century neo-orthodoxy, Pieper worked on and lived his theology within the tension of his own dialectical understanding of grace as universal (*gratia universalis*) and as the only cause of salvation (*sola gratia*). Luther's dialectic involved the tension of reconciling the gracious God who appeared in Christ and doubts of his own salvation. Pieper's dialectic was the problem of why some are saved and others are not. Luther agonized over his own damnation. For Pieper it was the damnation of others. Universal grace seemed to contradict the damnation of any one. Caught between universal grace and grace alone, he refused to accept one and reject the other. The issue surfaces in the prolegomena of his *Christian Dogmatics* and remains central throughout.[33]

The True Church, Visible (Lutheran) and Invisible—Correct Understanding of All Doctrine and Correct Understanding of Grace

Though Pieper concentrated on the doctrines of Christ and grace, he required be-

lief in all doctrines. For lack of agreement on any doctrine disrupts church unity. In "The Unity of Faith" he claimed that those who do not accept the doctrines which Lutherans recognize are knowingly rejecting clear biblical truth.[34] Here he assumes the clarity of the Scriptures, with some sections having a translucence which others do not.[35] The clearer sections, called *sedes doctrinae* ("proof passages"), form an operative canon for interpreting the less clear sections and for doing theology.[36] Though the Missouri Synod does not require agreement on exegetical questions, in practice it follows Pieper in requiring agreement on the *sedes doctrinae*, placing the highest value on them in the doing of theology.[37] In his 1889 article "The Difference between Orthodox and Unorthodox Churches" Pieper charges Christians to avoid those churches which do not teach the truth and to join those which do. Receiving communion and serving as baptismal sponsors at the former are disallowed.

Pieper's doctrine of the church and church fellowship is connected with his understanding of Scripture and grace. For outward or visible church unity Pieper requires agreement on all the articles of Scripture. At the same time he recognizes those who have an understanding of divine grace as belonging to the *una sancta eccle-*

32. Pieper, *Christian Dogmatics*, 1:x.
33. Ibid., 1:28–34.

34. Francis Pieper, "Von der Einigkeit im Glauben," *Lehre und Wehre* 34.10 (Oct. 1888): 289–95.
35. Koenig, "Church and Tradition," 20, observes, "From Pieper's writings it is obvious that he assumed the Missouri Synod were in possession of the truth in all its purity and were passing it on for the benefit of future generations."
36. Pieper, *Christian Dogmatics*, 1:362. Koenig, "Church and Tradition," 20, may have slightly overstated the case that Pieper considered the Bible free from "all ambiguity or uncertainty." For Pieper's emphasis on the *sedes doctrinae* presupposes that while some passages are easy to interpret, others present difficulties.
37. According to the "Brief Statement" (p. 416), "the (confessional) obligation does not extend to historical statements, 'purely exegetical questions,' and other matters not belonging to the doctrinal content of the symbols. All *doctrines* of the symbols are based on clear statements of Scripture."

sia, the true church. This point is elaborated in his 1919 essay, "The Ecumenical Character of the Lutheran Church in Doctrine and Practice." Fundamental here is a dual understanding of the true church: (1) the visible church—those who hold to the clearly revealed teachings of Scripture; and (2) the invisible church—those who by grace believe in Christ. This dualism prevents Pieper from a sectarianism that allows only Lutherans to claim salvation and from a doctrinal relativism that would view Lutheran teaching as only one of several expressions of Christian truth. For his definition of the invisible church he begins with faith; for his definition of the visible church he begins with a correct understanding of the Bible's teachings.

In a similar vein, Philipp Melanchthon in the Augsburg Confession (1530) and its Apology (1531) provided historical evidence to show Roman Catholics that the Lutherans and their teachings stood in continuity with the ancient church. Similar evidence was presented in the Catalog of Testimonies that was appended to the Book of Concord (1580). Pieper reverses the argument. It is not that Lutherans are true Catholics, but that true Christians in other churches are, by their adherence to grace, really Lutherans. The Lutheran church with its understanding of grace is the true visible church, but Lutherans can be found in other churches as well, for all those who believe that they are saved by grace, even if they do not articulate this doctrine correctly, are Lutheran. Pieper's position here is consistent with his argument that grace is the basis of Christianity. (Whether he was always consistent with his principles is another question. In the "Brief Statement," for example, he asserted that the doctrines of the church and ministry are clearly defined.[38] But he did not let differences on these issues disrupt fellowship with the Wisconsin Synod, whose

leading theologian was his brother August.)[39]

A chief evidence of grace is the substitutionary atonement, a theme that is introduced in the prolegomena of *Christian Dogmatics.* The reader soon becomes acquainted with the phrase *satisfactio vicaria.* Indeed, a denial of any doctrine is logically connected with rejection of the atonement, for this doctrine provides all the others with their content. While Pieper holds to what is called the Latin or Anselmic theory of the atonement (i.e., vicarious satisfaction), he avoids a detailed discussion. He does, however, in confrontation with the ethic-oriented Christianity of rationalism, Schleiermacher, and Albrecht Ritschl, specifically reject the moral theory of the atonement.[40] In contrast to rationalism and Schleiermacher, Pieper asserts that reason has a place in theology as a servant (*usus rationis ministerialis*) but not as a source (*usus rationis magisterialis*).[41] Zwingli in his debate with Luther had let reason rule his theology, as all Reformed theologians do.[42] Schleiermacher, who is said to have adopted the methods of Calvin and Zwingli, and the Erlangen theologians made the individual the source of their theologies, as is clear from their emphasis on "Christian consciousness," "experience," and "pious self-consciousness."[43] Pieper's code words for subjectivism are the Latin

38. "Brief Statement," 415.

39. For a discussion of the differences between the two brothers, see Erling Teigen, "The Universal Priesthood in the Lutheran Confessions," *Confessional Lutheran Research Newsletter* 25 (Advent 1991). Whereas Francis held that the ministry is a divine institution, August saw it as an unnecessary human deduction from the universal priesthood of all believers. Teigen contends that Francis Pieper's refutation of Johann Hoefling's position on this matter (*Christian Dogmatics,* 3:443–49) was really a refutation of his brother's. Though Francis Pieper held that a doctrinal issue was at stake here, the Missouri Synod never broke fellowship with the Wisconsin Synod.

40. Pieper, *Christian Dogmatics,* 2:342; 1:67; 2:18.

41. Ibid., 1:197–99.

42. Ibid., 1:25.

43. Ibid., 1:185, 226–27.

Ego and the German *Ichtheologie*.[44] He includes under subjective theology the pope, who makes his heart the source of Christian truth. All error in all non-Lutheran churches originates in human experience and not in the Holy Scriptures.

Pieper is particularly troubled by "Reformed" theology, which can have two meanings. In his discussion on grace it is synonymous with Calvinism as opposed to Arminianism;[45] this is the more commonly recognized meaning among non-Lutherans. In his discussion of the Lord's Supper it refers to all Protestants who reject the Lutheran doctrine of Christ's real presence in the sacrament. While he takes exception to the Roman doctrine of transubstantiation,[46] Pieper's real opponent is the Reformed principle that finite nature is incapable of the infinite (*finitum non capax infiniti*), a frequent phrase in his dogmatics. This Reformed principle strikes at the heart of Christianity by denying Christ's physical presence with the sacramental elements and limiting the incarnation. Going back to Zwingli, the sacramental denial is symptomatic of a deeper christological problem.[47]

On what, one might ask, did Pieper base his strong views? The phrase *Scriptura sacra locuta, res decisa est* ("the Holy Scriptures have spoken, the matter is decided") is axiomatic to his theology.[48] At the start of his dogmatics Pieper without argumentation lays down the doctrines of Christ and the Scriptures as the poles around which theology revolves.[49] Together the Scriptures and Christology are the principles for doing theology. Theology comes from the

Scriptures and finds its conclusion in Christ. Denial of one suggests denial of the other. The gospel, that is, the proclamation of Christ's atonement, is thus the touchstone of all theology.[50] All other doctrines are either antecedent or consequent to Christology and have meaning only in relation to it.[51]

Critics have charged that under Pieper faith in Christ has been replaced as the touchstone of theology by trust in the authority of the Bible.[52] It is true that Pieper made an uncompromising defense of biblical inspiration and inerrancy. It should be borne in mind, however, that this doctrine serves Christology and the doctrine of justification. *Christian Dogmatics* begins not with an abstract discussion of God, nor of the Bible as the source of theology, but with Christianity as the religion of grace. For Pieper, then, the doctrine of grace derived from Christology is the standard in judging the truth claims first of non-Christian religions and then of other Christian denominations.[53] Error not only contradicts clear biblical passages (*sedes doctrinae*), but denies sound Christology. Using the doctrine of grace as the standard, Pieper concludes that Lutheranism is the only true religion. All others are false.

Pieper's argument begins with the observation that all religions fall into two basic categories—grace (gospel) and works (law).

44. Ibid., 1:6–7.
45. Ibid., 1:29.
46. Ibid., 3:301–2.
47. Ibid., 3:323.
48. Ibid., 1:4.
49. Ibid., 1:6. Koenig's critical analysis ("Church and Tradition") seems to be completely unaware that this is Pieper's position. Pieper does not flesh out his arguments for the authority of Scripture and Christology until the sections devoted to those doctrines (*Christian Dogmatics*, 1:193–367; 2:55–394).

50. Pieper, *Christian Dogmatics*, 1:xi.
51. Ibid., 2:v.
52. Koenig, "Church and Tradition," 19.
53. Koenig, "Missouri Turns Moderate," 20, approves of Martin Scharlemann's introduction of the christological principle into the Missouri Synod: "'By insisting on a Christological principle of interpretation,' [Scharlemann] wrote, 'we can . . . distinguish between [those] facts [of Holy Scripture] that matter and those that do not.'" Compare this with Walther's statement, "If anyone would not rightly know and believe this doctrine [i.e., justification], it would not do him any good if he knew correctly all other doctrines, as, for instance, those of the Holy Trinity, of the person of Christ, and the like"—cited in Francis Pieper, "Dr. C. F. W. Walther as Theologian," trans. John Theodore Mueller, *Concordia Theological Monthly* 26.12 (Dec. 1955): 915.

Non-Christian religions teach salvation by works and thus are false.[54] Their idolatry plays no major part in Pieper's argument. Roman Catholicism's condemnation of the Reformation principle of salvation by grace without works marks it as false. Non-Lutheran Protestantism is more problematical for Pieper, because its denominations claim as their own the Reformation theme of salvation by grace through faith without works. But Pieper sees the Reformed separation of the Holy Spirit from the means of grace as an implicit denial of grace, which is confirmed by their disavowal of universal grace.[55] They are forced to find certainty of their salvation and election in works.[56] Arminianism in making human will or free choice a factor in conversion denies salva-

tion by grace alone and is thereby marked as a false religion.[57] It is clear, then, that, contrary to the critics' charge that Pieper bases his theology on an abstract principle of biblical authority, he has in fact made the basic premise of Luther's Reformation, salvation by grace alone, his operating theological principle.

At first glance it may appear that Pieper has isolated the doctrine of justification by grace, since he calls it the doctrine by which the church stands and falls.[58] This is a false reading of Pieper, however, for it is clear that in his view Christology is at the heart of justification and all of theology. Justification by grace is a necessary conclusion of Pieper's Christology and is not simply a forensic decision of divine sovereignty.

Rudolf Bultmann also made justification the touchstone for theology. Thus his position superficially resembles Pieper's. But Bultmann provided an existential definition for justification: becoming aware of one's situation. The history of Jesus was incidental to Bultmann's Christology and definition of the gospel. For Pieper, on the other hand, justification, God's declaring the sinner righteous for Christ's sake, is a necessary conclusion of his Christology, which involves a historic incarnation, resurrection, and a real atonement at the center. Justification by grace "is directly based on the doctrine of Christ, on the doctrine of Christ's theanthropic Person and theanthropic work."[59]

Inasmuch as Christology is the premise for justification, a fault in the understanding of justification may be symptomatic of a deeper error in Christology. On the other hand, the value and truth of Christology are not necessarily compromised by a faulty view of justification. Non-Lutheran churches do not always carry false doctrines of justification to their logical conclusions; thus they can still proclaim Christ and salvation in spite of an inherent contra-

54. Pieper, *Christian Dogmatics*, 1:9–21. To prove his claims that all religions can be neatly divided into the categories of works and grace, and that only Christianity fits the latter category, Pieper depends on conclusions drawn from the discipline of comparative religions (pp. 15–16). There are several problems here. First, by depending on the discipline of comparative religions he may have contradicted his own principle that theology be taken only from the Scriptures. There is also the bothersome issue of whether the division of religions into law and grace is a scientific finding or simply the imposition of a Christian theologoumenon on the study of religions. Finally, it has been pointed out that salvation by grace is not unknown in Hinduism. For a fascinating article on Pieper's claims see William J. Danker, "Who Wrote the Pivotal Quotation in Francis Pieper's *Christian Dogmatics?*" *Currents in Theology and Mission* 4 (Aug. 1970): 235–39.

55. In his 1890 essay on Walther, Pieper had already taken the position that a denial of what Lutherans regard as the means of grace is a denial of grace; see Francis Pieper, "Dr. C. F. W. Walther as Theologian," trans. John Theodore Mueller, *Concordia Theological Monthly* 27.1 (Jan. 1956): 29. Though Pieper recognized that Reformed theologians like Charles Hodge defended the doctrine of biblical inspiration (*Christian Dogmatics*, 1:25), he challenged them for ascribing regeneration to the Spirit but not to Scripture as well (3:120, 129). According to Pieper, the Holy Spirit, having given the Scripture, continues to work not merely outside or alongside, but in and through it to bring sinners to faith in Christ. Biblical authority rests, then, on both inspiration and the divine efficacy of Scripture as a means of grace to salvation (1:315–17).

56. Pieper, *Christian Dogmatics*, 1:26.

57. Ibid., 1:29.
58. Ibid., 2:55.
59. Ibid.

diction in their theologies. Roman Catholicism for the most part has an acceptable Christology, but a false doctrine of justification. Calvinists have an inadequate Christology: the *extra Calvinisticum*, the belief that not all of the Son of God became incarnate, entails a limited atonement. Arminians are like Roman Catholics in seeing humans as contributing to their own salvation; there is, then, a cause of salvation outside of Christ.

Since justification by grace is brought about by the proclamation of the gospel, the distinction between law and gospel is vital. Only the gospel, the preaching of the atonement, and not the law, creates and preserves the *una sancta ecclesia*. Confusing gospel with law makes faith impossible.[60] False religions and errant denominations are recognized not by their faulty interpretations of the Bible, but by their stress on law rather than on the gospel of grace.[61]

The tension between the *una sancta ecclesia*, which believes the gospel, and the true visible church, which believes all scriptural truth, gives Pieper a framework for classifying Christian doctrine. From the standpoint of the Scriptures, all doctrines are necessary; but from the standpoint of the salvation of the individual, some doctrines are less significant than others.[62] This distinction leads Pieper to divide all doctrines into fundamental and nonfundamental. Fundamental doctrines are further divided into primary and secondary. The most fundamental is the gospel, the proclamation of the forgiveness of sins. While insistent on requiring belief in all doctrines for outward church unity, Pieper approaches a bare doctrinal minimum in defining the *una sancta ecclesia*. Since proclamation of the gospel is always for the sake of Christ, Pieper expands his primary fundamental doctrines to include sin, the divinity and humanity of Christ (the Trinity is

included here), his mediatorial work, the necessity of faith in the Word, resurrection and eternal life.[63] Without belief in the fundamental doctrine of justification by grace through faith, a correct understanding of all other doctrines is without value.[64] Pieper is here reflecting the vision of the Augsburg Confession, which makes justification and Christology the content of the other articles. The Smalkald Articles also make Christology the foundation on which all other doctrine rests (2.1.1–5). In the category of secondary fundamental doctrines are issues dividing traditional Christianity, for instance, baptism and the Lord's Supper. The only doctrines listed as nonfundamental are the Antichrist and angels.

Pieper provides another category: open questions and theological problems. These issues are unresolvable on earth and hence should be avoided.[65] He places the origin of the soul among the open questions, but later argues forcefully for traducianism.[66] His doctrine of original sin hardly allows the creationist view of the origin of the soul.

Pieper was hardly the first to rank doctrines, but he did so with a view to their necessity for salvation and not, like the rationalists, on the basis of the relative strength of their claims to truth. Schleiermacher ranked doctrines according to their contribution to corporate Christian consciousness. Pieper, like the rationalists and Schleiermacher, placed belief in angels on the periphery. But Pieper made this judgment not because there is a relative lack of evidence, but because belief in angels is not necessary for salvation by faith. Similarly, while affirming the divine institution of baptism and the ministry, he denies that they are necessary to salvation.[67] They seem to belong to the secondary fundamental doctrines.

60. Ibid., 3:222–52, esp. 243–47.
61. Ibid., 1:19–21.
62. Ibid., 1:80–93.
63. Ibid., 1:82–85.
64. Pieper, "Walther," *Concordia Theological Monthly* 26.12 (Dec. 1955): 915.
65. Pieper, *Christian Dogmatics*, 1:93–96.
66. Ibid., 1:119, 488–89.
67. Ibid., 3:280–81, 449–50.

Pieper's classification of doctrines is related to his definition of the church. The invisible church is defined by its belief in the primary fundamental doctrines, which are necessary for salvation. But fellowship with other Christians is limited to those who hold to both the fundamental and nonfundamental doctrines. The distinction between the church invisible and the church visible allows Pieper to recognize non-Lutheran denominations as Christian but refuse them fellowship. In addition, by defining the term *church* in two ways he can say of a particular group that it is both a true church and a false church.

At this point it will be instructive to compare Pieper's approach with Schleiermacher's. Each begins with what he considers to be the church's position. Schleiermacher begins with what he views as the common faith of the various Reformation churches, Pieper with the faith of the church of the Lutheran confessions. Schleiermacher blends the contradictions into a totality that can support a union of churches. For Pieper, the contradictions are evidence of false doctrine and reason for continued division. Moreover, different definitions of faith lead to different perspectives on the church. Schleiermacher sees faith in the common piety and conduct of the Christian community. The church, then, is in essence a sociological reality. In Pieper's theology, faith is known only to God, and thus the invisible church is beyond human ken. The true visible church is recognized by profession of true doctrine. Finally, Schleiermacher views Scripture as the work of the community of the earliest believers; it reveals what they thought to be true. Pieper sees Scripture as a direct work of the Holy Spirit revealing what God wants us to believe. The writers are the secretaries and pens of the Holy Spirit. Viewing Scripture as the product of the community allows Schleiermacher to accept biblical criticism. Pieper's understanding leads to the doctrines of inspiration and inerrancy.

The Missouri Synod's insistence on biblical inspiration and inerrancy can be traced to Pieper. Thus the synod's successful defense of this doctrine in the 1970s brought him a recognition long denied. Those who left the synod, on the other hand, held him responsible for its uncompromising position on inspiration and inerrancy and for its intransigent denial of fellowship to other Christians. Today, phrases from Pieper's *Christian Dogmatics* are still in common use in the synod's theology. In particular, his doctrine of grace (*sola gratia*), which entails a complete incarnation of God in Christ and a universal atonement (*gratia universalis*), helps keep the Missouri Synod true to its Lutheran heritage. Clearly, Pieper is still an extraordinarily influential theologian in America sixty years after his death.

Edgar Young Mullins

Thomas J. Nettles

Edgar Young Mullins served as president of Southern Baptist Theological Seminary in Louisville, Kentucky, from 1899 till his death in 1928. A native of Franklin County, Mississippi, he was born on January 5, 1860, the fourth of eleven children. His father, Seth Granberry Mullins, was "of New England stock and traced his lineage back to the Pilgrim Fathers."[1] A graduate of Mississippi College, the elder Mullins was a preacher, teacher, and farmer. In 1863 the family moved to Copiah County to escape the menacing presence of Union troops, who had become much more plentiful around Franklin County since the Confederacy lost the battle of Vicksburg. When Edgar was eight, the family moved to Corsicana, Texas, where his father organized and became pastor of the First Baptist Church. While working as a telegraph operator and dispatcher for the Associated Press, Edgar entered Texas A&M, where he finished his course of study in 1879.

Mullins admired the legal profession and was preparing to enter it himself. In the fall of 1880 he heard that a former lawyer, Major William Evander Penn, was holding a series of evangelistic services at First Baptist Church, Dallas. The first full-time Southern Baptist evangelist, Penn has been described as using "reason and persuasion without denunciation."[2] Converted in one of Penn's services, Mullins was shortly thereafter baptized by his father in Corsicana.

Feeling called to Christian ministry, Mullins entered Southern Baptist Theolog-

---

1. A. T. Robertson, "A Sketch of the Life of President Mullins," *Review and Expositor* 22.1 (Jan. 1925): 7. More detailed biographical information can be found in Isla May Mullins, *Edgar Young Mullins: An Intimate Biography* (Nashville: Sunday School Board of the Southern Baptist Convention, 1929); see also William E. Ellis, *A "Man of Books and a Man of the People"* (Macon, Ga.: Mercer University Press, 1985).

2. *Encyclopedia of Southern Baptists*, ed. Norman W. Cox (Nashville: Broadman, 1958), s.v. "Penn, William Evander."

ical Seminary in 1881. The seminary had just experienced difficult years financially and theologically. In the fall of 1877 it had moved from Greenville, South Carolina, to Louisville in an attempt to avert closing. A new major effort to build up the endowment eventually proved successful.

Theologically, the seminary was firmly committed to the plenary inspiration of Scripture. The school's confession comprised "a complete exhibition of the fundamental doctrines of grace." Its ecclesiology was Baptist, but flexible on details. William Williams, a member of the original faculty, had come under attack from several churches in various parts of the South over an ecclesiological detail. James Petrigru Boyce, founder of the seminary and chairman of its faculty, protected and encouraged Williams. This controversy ended only with the death of Williams in February 1877.

Another controversy involved Old Testament professor C. H. Toy's views of the doctrine of inspiration. As a result of his higher-critical studies, Toy spoke of inaccuracies, discrepancies, and errors in the Bible in scientific, geographic, historical, and political areas. The trustees did not share Toy's position and, to his surprise, accepted his resignation in 1879.

The Williams controversy concerned a matter that the seminary decided to leave to the individual conscience. The Toy controversy, by contrast, centered on a theological issue about which there was clear confessional assertion and, in Boyce's assessment, no room for disagreement.[3] Mullins in his own time would contemplate the relationship between individual conscience and standard confessional statements and seek a balance in the tension between them.

Boyce taught Mullins systematic theology. One contemporary remarked, "Though the young men were generally rank Arminians when they came to the Seminary, few went through this course under [Boyce] without being converted to his strong Calvinistic views."[4] At the same time, New Testament professor John A. Broadus was reaching the full flower of his powers as teacher, scholar, and preacher. Replacing Toy as professor of Old Testament interpretation was Basil Manly, Jr. A member of the original faculty, Manly had authored the "Abstract of Principles," the school's confessional basis. And in 1888 Manly published *The Bible Doctrine of Inspiration*, a clear and comprehensive investigation of an issue he had studied for twenty-five years. With the Toy controversy so fresh, this subject doubtless received special attention during the years Mullins was on campus.

Mullins graduated in 1885, having concentrated on theology and philosophy. On the strong advice of a doctor, he surrendered plans to go to the mission field and accepted a call to pastor Harrodsburg Baptist Church in Harrodsburg, Kentucky. In 1886 he married Isla May Hawley, who described him as "a slender, graceful figure of six feet, two inches, very erect. [He had] an abundant shock of very dark hair [and] a beard of soft fineness which was then attractive and added much to his look of maturity."[5] From Kentucky the Mullinses moved to Maryland, where Edgar became pastor of Lee Street Baptist Church in Baltimore. After serving for seven years, Mullins spent a brief period of time with the Southern Baptist Foreign Mission Board as an associate secretary and then became pastor of the Baptist Church of Newton

3. In his inaugural address as a teacher of theology at Furman University, Boyce had asserted that a theological seminary must be governed by a confession of faith: "No difference, however slight, no peculiar sentiment, however speculative, is here allowable. [The professor's] agreement with the standard should be *exact*" (James Petigru Boyce, *Three Changes in Theological Institutions* [Greenville, S.C.: C. J. Elford's Book and Job Press, 1856], 35).

4. John A. Broadus, *Memoir of James Petigru Boyce* (New York: A. C. Armstrong and Son, 1893), 265. Broadus is quoting E. E. Folk, editor of the *Baptist Reflector* of Chattanooga.

5. Mullins, *Edgar Young Mullins*, 15.

Center, Massachusetts. While there he developed contacts with the educational centers at Newton Theological Seminary, Harvard, Wellesley, and Brown.

Another controversy at Southern Seminary culminated with the resignation of William H. Whitsitt from the presidency in 1899. Without his knowledge or consent, the trustees elected Mullins as president. Puzzled as to why a Louisville paper, the *Baptist Argus*, requested a picture of him, Mullins went to the Newton Center telegraph office to send off an inquiry about the request. While he was there, a message came asking him to become president of the seminary. The former telegrapher received permission to send his own response and immediately wired his acceptance of the position.

On the Relationship between Religion and Science

Into the stream of Southern Protestant orthodoxy came Edgar Young Mullins fresh from the cerebrally stimulating air of New England. There he had learned to co-exist with modern thinkers. He commended, as far as he could, their discoveries and accomplishments, and, when necessary, fenced with them, using their methods. Against the backdrop of the rise of modern scientific scholarship, he contended that the "need is great for a restatement of the grounds of our Christian belief."[6] Without discarding traditional theology and apologetics the task was to "establish the Christian position by means of the principles of investigation employed by the opposition, so far as those principles are valid."[7] He maintained this stance throughout his ministry.

In 1925, three years before Mullins's death, Thornton Whaling, professor of theology and apologetics at the Presbyte-

rian Theological Seminary in Louisville, described Mullins in dithyrambic terms. As a competent scholar, wrote Whaling, Mullins is well acquainted with the historic attacks on the Christian faith and is equally a master of the historic answers. But as a "modern scholar up to date in every particular," he also knows the nature of the modern mind and the extraordinary progress of recent thought. He is well aware that "some opponents of the Christian religion make use of these marvelous recent achievements" as an occasion for an attack on the faith. The apologete cannot use old weapons for new wars, but must meet on their own ground these opponents who "are perplexing the minds even of thoughtful, earnest and scholarly" Christians. Eschewing the "anachronism which builds on the base of nineteenth century scholarship," Mullins comes to the ground of twentieth-century science, psychology, criticism, and philosophy. There he demonstrates that the recent achievements "in no sense demolish but really confirm the Christian faith."[8]

This movement away from the nineteenth century inserted real ambivalence into Mullins's status as a genuine theological hero in his own denomination. His grasp of modernity and his ability to interpret it endeared him to thousands who felt that "whether we like it or not we are sailing out on other seas than our fathers sailed and are driven about by other winds."[9] There was a growing feeling among others, however, that Mullins had left more of nineteenth-century Baptist life behind than was warranted. Some truths are timeless and cannot be considered "anachronisms." Among the charges leveled against Mullins were: (1) his tentative attitude toward creeds limited their usefulness; (2) his axiomatic emphasis on human freedom led to

6. Edgar Young Mullins, *Why Is Christianity True?* (Philadelphia: American Baptist Publication Society, 1905), vii.

7. Ibid., 4.

8. Thornton Whaling, review of *Christianity at the Cross Roads*, by Edgar Young Mullins, *Review and Expositor* 22.1 (Jan. 1925): 108–13.

9. Henry Alfred Porter, "An Interpreter, One among a Thousand," *Review and Expositor* 22.1 (Jan. 1925): 15.

changes in soteriology; and (3) his position on revelation and inspiration created the possibility of fissure in the Southern Baptist approach to inerrancy (for Mullins's specific views in these areas, see pp. 62–65).

The conflict over evolution will serve to illustrate Mullins's theological stance. This debate brought into clear view issues he considered paramount as well as the position of those who resisted any semblance of friendship toward the modern spirit. In 1923 Mullins was scheduled to give the presidential address at the yearly meeting of the Southern Baptist Convention. According to George W. Truett, "the whole land was nervous with the wide-spread agitation concerning the relation of science and religion." Mullins's statement on "Science and Religion" at this meeting proved to be the "crucial word, the interpretative word, the certain word, the word that settled things, just at the right time":[10]

> We recognize the greatness and value of the service which modern science is rendering to the cause of truth in uncovering the facts of the natural world. We believe that loyalty to fact is a common ground of genuine science and the Christian religion. We have no interest or desire in covering up any fact in any realm of research. But we do protest against certain unwarranted procedures on the part of some so-called scientists; first, in making discoveries or alleged discoveries in physical nature a convenient weapon of attack upon the facts of religion; second, using the particular sciences, such as psychology, biology, geology and various others as if they necessarily contained knowledge pertaining to the realm of the Christian religion, setting aside the supernatural; third, teaching as facts what are merely hypotheses. The evolution doctrine has long been a

working hypothesis of science, and will probably continue to be because of its apparent simplicity in explaining the universe. But its best exponents freely admit that the causes of the origin of species have not been traced. Nor has any proof been forthcoming that man is not the direct creation of God as recorded in Genesis. We protest against the imposition of this theory upon the minds of our children in denominational or public schools as if it were a definite and established truth of science. We insist that this and all other theories be dealt with in a truly scientific way, that is, in conformity to established facts.

> We record again our unwavering adherence to the supernatural elements in the Christian religion. The Bible is God's revelation of Himself through man moved by the Holy Spirit, and is our sufficient, certain and authoritative guide in religion. Jesus Christ was born of the Virgin Mary through the power of the Holy Spirit. He was the divine and eternal Son of God. He died as the vicarious atoning Saviour of the world and was buried. He arose again from the dead. The tomb was empty of its contents. In His risen body He appeared many times to His disciples. He ascended to the right hand of the Father. He will come again in person, the same Jesus who ascended from the Mount of Olives.

> We believe that adherence to the above truths and facts is a necessary condition of service for teachers in our Baptist schools. These facts of Christianity in no way conflict with any fact in science. We do not sit in judgment upon the scientific views of teachers of science. We grant them the same freedom of research in their realm that we claim for ourselves in the religious realm. But we do insist upon a positive content of faith in accordance with the preceding statements as a qualification for acceptable service in Baptist schools. The supreme issue today is between naturalism and super-naturalism. We stand unalterably for the supernatural in Christianity. Teachers in our schools should be careful to free themselves from any suspicion of disloyalty on this point. In the present period of agitation and unrest they are obligated to make their positions clear.

---

10. George W. Truett, "A Quarter of a Century of World History," *Review and Expositor* 22.1 (Jan. 1925): 62. Truett's exalted estimate is from a speech delivered at a celebration of Mullins's twenty-fifth year as president of Southern Seminary (Sept. 24, 1924). Porter's judgments (n. 9) were delivered on the same occasion.

We pledge our support to all schools and teachers who are thus loyal to the facts of Christianity as revealed in the Scripture.[11]

Though some were dissatisfied that Mullins had not made a specific disavowal of evolutionary theory, the Southern Baptists adopted his statement as an official appendage to their 1925 Confession of Faith. The statement reflects several of his characteristic emphases. First is his determination to preserve religion as a separate sphere of reality, not unrelated to all other spheres, but certainly not defined in their terms nor reduced to their categories. His position here is in perfect agreement with what he had written ten years earlier: "We must then recognize the independence of religion, its autonomy, so to speak, in its relations with other forms of human activity."[12] Second is his emphasis on facts and acceptance of the scientific method. He resisted any position that pictured science as based on fact and religion as based on "mere beliefs or fancies or forms of unreality." He relentlessly insisted that religion is "empirical in that it starts from actually given data of experience."[13] The most often overlooked or misinterpreted fact of existence is religious experience. Mullins sought to give this fact a place of prominence in his system. Third is his affirmation of the reality of the supernatural elements in the Christian religion. Fourth is his unyielding commitment to a central core of teachings that he considered clearly demonstrated facts and inviolable for Christian faith.

Mullins's emphasis on religion as constituting a sovereign, inviolable sphere was fundamental to his thought. His concern was to protect religion as a genuine reality, an irreducible fact, in the life of the human race. Occupying a sphere of truth all its own, it cannot be collapsed into any other reality. Like the scientist, however, Mullins believed in the final unity of all truth. "Somewhere," Mullins assumed, "is to be found a force or principle or bond which unites all things." This belief is essential to thought and is "a first principle of all modern research."[14] But on the other hand Mullins firmly rejected those attempts to understand all truth that utilize only one method of arriving at knowledge or reduce all reality to one factor. Some opt for pure materialism, others for idealism; but it is philosophy, not science, that drives them to such a conclusion. Mullins resisted the "monistic passion to exalt some one factor of being to the supreme place, to cancel half of the world in order to save the other half." All reductionists, even the scientist who seeks to explain everything on the principle of continuity, must submit to the fact that "reality has more than one dimension."[15]

The clearest example of reductionism is naturalism. Naturalism (or any other system that tends to see all of reality in terms of one basic factor) will starve itself to death. It will be swept away by the ongoing tide of life itself. It "is an outrage against human nature, . . . a million miles away from the great struggling heart of the world."[16] The organ of humankind's religious nature has a wide keyboard running "into the heights of the intellectual, and down to the depths of the emotional yearnings of the soul." Any theory, scientific or religious, which tries to "evoke the music by cutting out all the octaves but one will soon be compelled to yield its place to a better player."[17]

The view of reality as multidimensional was essential to Mullins's approach to theology, apologetics, polemics, and evangelism. On this point Mullins had great appreciation for William James. Although re-

11. Edgar Young Mullins, "Science and Religion," *Review and Expositor* 22.1 (Jan. 1925): 64.

12. Edgar Young Mullins, *Freedom and Authority in Religion* (Philadelphia: Griffith and Rowland, 1913), 212.

13. Ibid., 213.

14. Mullins, *Why Is Christianity True?* 6–7.

15. Mullins, *Freedom and Authority*, 246–47.

16. Edgar Young Mullins, *Christianity at the Cross Roads* (New York: George H. Doran, 1924), 148.

17. Ibid., 144.

jecting James's pluralism and his view of God as a "finite struggler,"[18] Mullins regarded James as "one of the most discerning of modern thinkers" and rarely equaled in "judicial breadth of view and fairmindedness."[19] James was no "sectarian scientist" nor a devotee of "scientific absolutism." To his credit, James's research on religious experience was inductively scientific and reached the conclusion that "there is a divine and genuinely miraculous power which regenerates men."[20]

Mullins felt that the fact of religious experience could no longer be seriously disputed. Friedrich Schleiermacher's definition of religion as the sense of absolute dependence is axiomatic. But while supplying a much-needed emphasis on the inescapable fact of religious consciousness, such a definition is too indistinct. Schleiermacher himself could not escape pantheism.[21]

A similar shortcoming plagues F. S. Hoffman's twofold definition of religion: our recognition that a power other than ourselves pervades the universe, and our endeavor to put ourselves in harmonious relations with this power. According to Mullins, this definition does not distinguish religion from a herd of buffalo running from a prairie fire. Mullins would add four points: (1) the object of religion is personal; (2) an adjustment is made in personal terms and on the basis of personal relationship; (3) religion includes cognitive and voluntaristic elements in addition to the emotional; and (4) the aim of religion is redemption. Mullins defends each of these points as essential and, once understood, as axiomatic in religion. Definitions omitting one of these points make religion something indistinct and attempt to take refuge in a "citadel which the scientific man cannot successfully assail." The pity is that in constructing such a citadel, religion is lost.[22]

The value of religion lies in its distinctiveness. Though it does not contradict any other sphere of reality, we are on a false trail when we strive to make religion conform to science or philosophy. The Christian religion is autonomous and free; it has its own tests and criteria of truth, and must be judged by its own standards. Redefining it in terms of science, philosophy, historical criticism, or comparative religion in order to defend it or deny it leaves out the vital and essential factors of religion itself. "Converting religion into something which may be defended from a non-religious standpoint [empties] religion of all that makes it valuable and desirable."[23]

Scientific absolutism, to use James's phrase, had trampled the rights of other disciplines under its feet. Ruthless in its radicalism and unlawful in its intellectual processes and methods, it branded Christianity a chief offender because of its powerful influence and claim to supernatural origin. In opposing Christianity, however, scientific absolutism had to run roughshod over a mountain of stubborn facts. An impartial investigation of those facts and comparison with the various philosophies would demonstrate that only Christianity can absorb all the facts of the natural world, human personality, and history. Christianity is the only view of reality that can give them meaning and coherence: "We maintain that the only adequate hypothesis to account for a vast mass of facts is the Christian hypothesis, and that verification in all its legitimate forms in the personal and moral realm may be applied to the hypothesis successfully."[24]

The conscientious quest for facts the Christian holds in common with the scientist. Mullins was committed to true science and the scientific method, that is, inductive reasoning. He had little use for *a priori* as-

18. Ibid., 161–62, 168.
19. Mullins, *Freedom and Authority*, 149.
20. Mullins, *Cross Roads*, 269.
21. Mullins, *Freedom and Authority*, 198.
22. Ibid., 195–207.
23. Mullins, *Cross Roads*, 233.
24. Mullins, *Why Is Christianity True?* 6.

sumptions and deductive reasoning built on them. He also argued that pure syllogistic logic, while valid, cannot produce those facts of "living vital experience" which are "incalculably richer and fuller than those few phases of it which we reduce to rational and logical form."[25] But he opposed neither syllogisms nor deductive reasoning that followed from an inductive process.

Mullins maintained that every theory must be open to modification when new facts come to light. Accordingly, he was very cautious not to make too many affirmations at the points where natural science and religion were beginning to merge. He was quite protective of the central facts of the Christian faith, but did not want to intrude on the scientific process by excluding *a priori* the possibility of some type of evolutionary development. Nor did he want to give any quarter to science to intrude in the sphere where only religion is competent. In fact, religion challenges the arrogance of those scientists who try to construct a religion out of the narrow limits of one scientific hypothesis. "Religious experience knows more than biological science has discovered"; any system that "flattens out the personality of God and man to [the] biological level is contrary to the best attested items of our spiritual experience."[26]

The Facts of Christianity

In his emphasis on facts, Mullins focuses on the two great facts of Christianity, Christian experience and Christ. Not only are large sections of several monographs given over to the topic of Christian experience,

but also the first 136 pages of his systematic theology, *The Christian Religion in Its Doctrinal Expression,* discuss various of its aspects. Mullins notes that the authority for doctrinal development consists of four elements: (1) the facts of the historical Jesus; (2) the Scriptures, especially the New Testament; (3) the work of the Holy Spirit; and (4) Christian experience. Accordingly, he includes discussions of the impact of experience on the formulation and understanding of each major doctrine. Five advantages accrue to the inclusion of experience as an explicit element in the development of doctrine: (1) it enables us to avoid a false intellectualism in theology; (2) it provides the necessary factual basis for a scientific presentation of the truths of Christian theology; (3) it offers the best apologetic foundation; (4) it demonstrates the reality, autonomy, and freedom of the Christian religion; and (5) it helps define the nature of the authority of the Bible.[27]

In winnowing out the essential elements of Christian experience, Mullins recorded the testimonies of various individuals, including well-known figures of church history and contemporary Christians. He observed that conversion, which involves the moral, emotional, volitional, and intellectual aspects of experience, becomes an ineradicable fact of consciousness, a subjective certainty of the objective reality of Christ. Current psychology cannot reduce it to a mere impact of the subconscious, because it is undeniably a *new* thing, a *new* direction, the awareness of a personal dimension completely consonant with the claims of Christ in the New Testament. Mullins subjected Christian experience to current criteria of verification and found it powerfully and cumulatively confirmed. Further examination found the New Testament Christ the only sufficient explanation for the cumulative witness of the totality of Christian experience. At one point Mullins

25. Mullins, *Freedom and Authority*, 160.

26. Mullins, *Cross Roads*, 65–67, 97. Writing near the time of the *Scopes* trial, Mullins said, "Nothing could be more ill-advised than for Americans to attempt to employ legislative coercion in the realm of scientific opinion." The Christian thinker "is perfectly willing to admit that God made the world gradually through long eras of time" and also "refuses to dogmatize in the scientific realm." On the other hand, Mullins insisted as well that "science should practice the same modesty that it enjoins upon others."

27. Edgar Young Mullins, *The Christian Religion in Its Doctrinal Expression* (Philadelphia: Judson, 1917; 1974 reprint), 4–12.

used his own life to illustrate his contention that "the experience of Christians does not render theology less biblical, or less systematic, or less historical":[28]

> If, therefore, in the exercise of repentance and faith a face answers my face, a heart responds to my heart, and I am acted on from without in personal ways, I have, for me at least, irrefutable evidence of the objective existence of the Person so moving me. When to this personal experience I add that of tens of thousands of living Christians, and an unbroken line of them back to Christ, and when I find in the New Testament a manifold record of like experiences, together with a clear account of the origin and cause of them all, my certainty becomes absolute. One of the most urgent of all duties resting upon modern Christians is to assert with clearness and vigor the certainties of Christian experience.[29]

Mullins's separation of the facts of the historical Jesus from the New Testament as sources of Christian doctrine may seem an attempt to delicately untie the Gordian knot. His intent, however, was to take advantage of the latest conclusions of New Testament criticism. He distilled his facts from the Synoptic Gospels and four Pauline Epistles. The portrait of Christ that emerges is fully supernatural: virgin-born and sinless, he accomplished all the facts of the kerygma, dying a substitutionary, sacrificial, propitiatory death. Mullins concluded, "Scientific exegesis yields the doctrine of the deity of Christ, and his atoning death and resurrection from the dead. There is no longer any serious controversy on the interpretation of these passages."[30] The ascertaining of such facts, including Jesus' promise of the work of the Spirit within the apostles (John 14:26), leads naturally to an affirmation of the rest of the New Testament, though such an affirma-

tion is not necessary to establish the irreducible facts concerning Christ. Mullins explains that in omitting the other New Testament books he was "not rejecting them, nor evading any issues about them. [He was] simply seeking the ultimate bases for the historical facts of our religion. . . . Modern scientific criticism holds that [the books on which he concentrated] are our oldest documents."[31]

Mullins is very disapproving of those critics who dismiss the radical elements of the Synoptic Gospels and the four Pauline Epistles through philosophical *a priori*. James Martineau, Adolf von Harnack, and Albert Schweitzer err, not in too closely applying the historical-critical tools, but in abandoning them for mere speculative theory. To begin by assuming the impossibility of a supernatural event annuls the evidence before it is brought forward.[32]

On the other hand, Mullins appreciated James Moffatt's contribution to historical study. Moffatt "set forth no doctrinal system" and "bowed to no dogmatic authority." Apparently he believed the universe is fireproof, for he did not hesitate "to drop burning matches around anywhere and everywhere." He was willing to see anything which can be burned go up in flames. Though cautious about other aspects of Moffatt's thinking, Mullins valued his pointing to the harmony, magnetism, and credibility of the New Testament witness to Jesus.[33]

No amount of genuine historical criticism, observed Mullins, can remove the resurrection from the New Testament records. The supernatural elements rejected by the critics "are so inwrought and interwoven with the entire New Testament that they cannot be taken out without leaving the entire fabric in shreds and tatters."[34] If the Jesus of evangelical faith does not exist, there is no Jesus. And not only is there no

28. Ibid., 3.
29. Mullins, *Why Is Christianity True?* 284.
30. Mullins, *Cross Roads*, 197.

31. Ibid., 195–96.
32. Ibid., 189–209.
33. Ibid., 184–88, 225–29.
34. Ibid., 202.

Jesus, there can be no religious experience! Those who reject the miraculous in order to protect experience misperceive the nature of religion. They fail to realize that what is essential to the miracles in Scripture—the "coming of a force from without"—is essential everywhere in redemption. The supernatural cannot be reduced to only the immanence of God, nor the miraculous defined merely in terms of the continuous outflow of divinity on the natural order. Leave the matter there, and depraved natures, moral despair, and evil will still dominate. Reducing the New Testament miracles to the plane of the purely natural will produce a similar and unacceptable result in the area of Christian experience. Extraneous power offending in one order would offend in another. So as reasonable as reducing the miraculous to the immanence of God might seem, it is unacceptable.[35]

Furthermore, it should be noted that the miraculous in Scripture is virtually always restorative or redemptive. It is not a violation of natural order, but a superior intelligence's use of it to promote the ends of a higher order. Miracles are means of mercy, judgment, and revelation; and, instead of disturbing the order of the world, they unify it. Dualism is not the final truth. To the mind seeking final truth the biblical miracles bring rest "by suggesting the bond which secures a moral, theological, and philosophical unity" in the world. The cosmos is not bound together by physical force but by personality—purposive, intelligent, just, and compassionate.[36]

Shifts toward Moderatism

Mullins considered theology the "systematic and scientific explanation" of the facts of religion. Thus the title of his systematic theology, *The Christian Religion in Its Doctrinal Expression*. His doctrinal positions were consonant for the most part with Baptist theology of the Augustinian strain.

He considered the central core of doctrines to include the virgin birth, the deity and humanity of Christ, the vicarious propitiatory atonement, the necessity of regeneration, justification by imputed righteousness, the certainty and progressive nature of sanctification, the historical reality of Christ's physical return, and the bodily resurrection of believers.

Yet Mullins also introduced some shifts in Baptist doctrine. His chosen approach made him more anthropocentric than theocentric and purposefully hesitant to engage in inferential theology. His dislike for the *a priori* method virtually precluded any construction of unassailable dogma in the form of creed or theory of inspiration. Whereas, prior to Mullins, Baptists in the South had been strongly confessional at the associational and institutional level, Mullins encouraged a tentative and mediating approach toward confessions. He still maintained that creeds "help rather than hinder," especially as tools to educate us "to unity of faith and practice." In addition, he believed it proper for a group united by confession to "judge when an individual or group within the larger body has departed from the common view sufficiently to warrant separation."[37] Nonetheless, his emphasis on the superiority of experience to creed, his clear warnings about the dangers of creeds, and the vivid images he evoked in speaking of their oppressive use tended to neutralize their employment as instruments of education, definition, and discipline. He spoke of creeds as becoming "stereotyped and formal" and used as "death masks for defunct religion" or "lashes to chastise others." A creed without life "becomes a chain to bind, not wings on which the soul may fly." Nothing is more distasteful than a barren intellectualism, void of life, where creeds may become "whips to coerce men into uniformity of belief by carnally-minded champions of the faith."[38]

35. Mullins, *Why Is Christianity True?* 170–78.
36. Ibid., 179–87.

37. Edgar Young Mullins, *Baptist Beliefs* (Valley Forge, Pa.: Judson, 1962), 8.
38. Ibid., 9–10.

In a fashion similar to his tentativeness toward creeds, Mullins hesitated to identify himself with either Calvinism or Arminianism as a system, preferring to "adhere more closely than either to the Scriptures, while retaining the truth in both systems."[39] He dismisses the issue of the extent of the atonement in paragraphs totaling less than one page, affirming a universal atonement.[40] He does not discuss bondage of the will, but does say that "without God's prevenient grace the will inevitably chooses evil."[41] But even more forcefully he insists that neither prevenient nor regenerating grace acts upon the will by way of compulsion, "but always in accordance with its freedom."[42] For Mullins, human freedom was a fact of consciousness. In order to protect that freedom, God reduces "his own action to the minimum lest he compel the will."[43] "God will not do violence to the will of man."[44] Election is true, but it is not based on God's mere pleasure, or partiality, or arbitrariness. God saves all that he possibly can, given the factors of human sin and freedom and the necessity of accomplishing salvation within the normal flow of history, God's purposes being incorporated by slow degrees into human character and human society. Not surprisingly, the clear and precise commitment of Southern Baptists to Calvinism diminished rapidly after the time of Mullins.

Mullins showed this same spirit of moderatism in his discussion of revelation and inspiration. The positions arising from agnosticism, pantheism, and naturalism were so clearly wrong and so thoroughly antagonistic to historic Christianity that Mullins rejected them outright. More dangerous because more subtle were the subjectivist views of thinkers in the tradition of Schleiermacher. They sought to salvage Christianity by rendering it completely subjective, denying not only any external cause for its origin, but also any external authority for its definition. Any external objective authority was, in their view, barely distinguishable from Roman Catholic repressiveness. Mullins outlines their chief emphases:

> Over against Roman Catholic authority and in sharpest antithesis to it is the modern principle of freedom. The advocates of this principle in Germany and France, in England and America, are far too numerous to mention. They are idealists of the most pronounced type in their view of freedom in the religious sphere. They emphasize the likeness rather than the unlikeness of man to God; the immanence rather than the transcendence of God; man's unaided and native capacity rather than his incapacity in religion; the pedagogic rather than the redemptive aspects of salvation; and the Christian consciousness rather than the Bible or the church as the ultimate seat of authority in religion.[45]

Mullins saw this as a recrudescence of the spirit of Clement of Alexandria, restored by Schleiermacher, and modified by Albrecht Ritschl. While Mullins also objected to the kind of external authority wielded by the Roman Catholic hierarchy, he did not view external authority as inconsistent with true religion.

Mullins sketched two conservative views of authority, the traditional and the inductive. The traditional was characteristic of scholastic Protestantism. Mullins infelicitously chose to describe this view in its most extreme and caricatured form. According to Mullins, it begins with an abstract principle not derived from Scripture: "the biblical writers [were] mere unintelligent instruments or pens used by the Holy Spirit to dictate the truths of revelation." His own view, that is, the inductive view, on the other hand, "refuses to adopt any abstract or *a priori* starting point, but rather

39. Mullins, *Christian Religion*, vii.

40. Ibid., 336, 340.

41. Edgar Young Mullins, *The Axioms of Religion* (Philadelphia: American Baptist Publication Society, 1908), 84.

42. Ibid.

43. Mullins, *Christian Religion*, 349.

44. Mullins, *Axioms*, 90.

45. Mullins, *Freedom and Authority*, 16.

goes directly to the Bible itself for the evidence of its own inspiration."[46] Among others who took this approach he listed James Orr, Marcus Dods, and William Sanday. The inductive approach focuses on God at work in history as well as in the biblical literature; recognizes a gradually developing clarity in the unfolding revelation, which culminated only in the person of Jesus Christ; takes into account the language and culture of the individual writers; distinguishes the various literary forms and realizes that they call for different principles of interpretation; and sees the Bible as essentially a religious book, and thus refrains from looking for "premature revelations of science through prophets and apostles."[47]

Mullins believed that both in revelation and in the ministry of Christ there was a certain accommodation to human ignorance and theological immaturity. On this issue Mullins used very careful wording. For example, he spoke of "the pedagogic adaptation of the method and means of revelation to the state of mind and degree of religious maturity of hearer and reader."[48] This "gradual and progressive" aspect of revelation sheds light on three perplexing biblical phenomena: the appearance of arbitrariness and vindictiveness on the part of God, low standards of morality, and overly severe punitive measures in the life of Israel. These can be understood "if we think of the Bible as the record of God's self-disclosure to a people incapable of more rapid development."[49] Mullins does not say if he considers these puzzling phenomena to be errors or just the first parts of larger truths.

Recognizing the progressive nature of revelation helps one comprehend the ripening of God's purposes until the fulness of time and the coming of Christ. Christ came "as soon as the incarnation could be effective for the end in view."[50] Progression in revelation also explains the appearance of development and growth in theological maturity. Epochal events such as the exodus and the incarnation-crucifixion-resurrection are not, then, anomalous. Instead, they are logical culminations from one era to another and are most clearly understood as extensions of everything that preceded them.

In harmony with this principle, Mullins saw Christ as adopting "the language of his contemporaries in order to instruct or refute them on the basis of their own assumptions." In doing this, Christ was "free from all error in his revelation to men of the mind and will of God."[51] Mullins never discussed, however, whether prophet, apostle, or Christ may actually have employed error, something indeed false, to teach spiritual truth.

Even though Mullins stopped short of affirming the doctrine of inerrancy, it is extremely doubtful that he would have set himself against it. He did not deny inerrancy; he simply felt that the argument, which he viewed as an *a priori* approach, was not to the point of the contemporary issue. It presents Scripture as an ideological intrusion somewhat alien to the heartbeat of human life. Mullins preferred to see the literature of Scripture as arising out of genuine discoveries from religious experience, that is, the Christian life. The life produced the literature; in turn, the literature gives life. The Bible has withstood the withering blast of criticism because it arose in life and creates life. "Authoritative revelations of truth," preached Mullins, "are designed to become human discoveries of truth."[52] Indeed, in ministering to his disciples, Christ "desired that his revelation might become their discovery."[53]

We must note here that Mullins strongly rejected the idea that religious truth arises strictly from immanent processes. Without

46. Ibid., 379.
47. Ibid., 380.
48. Ibid., 381.
49. Mullins, *Christian Religion*, 146.
50. Ibid., 147.

51. Mullins, *Freedom and Authority*, 381.
52. Edgar Young Mullins, *The Life in Christ* (New York: Revell, 1917), 16.
53. Mullins, *Christian Religion*, 156.

transcendent revelation, we would not have Christian truth. Neither can Christian experience sit in judgment on Scripture so as to reject any of its teaching. Though it has arisen from the fabric of Christian life, the true understanding of inspiration and revelation "leaves an authoritative Scripture which Christian experience does not and cannot transcend."[54]

Mullins emphasized the apartness and the interdependence of the biblical literature and life. At other times he spoke of faith and history as dependent on, but independent of each other. That confusing language was designed to seal the point that faith is dependent on the reality of history and has as one of its constituent elements a positive belief in historical facts, but goes far beyond mental assent to those facts.

In keeping with that tension, Mullins often speaks of a view of Scripture which, left by itself, imparts no life. He describes a skeptic who is "unconvinced by arguments for an infallible or inerrant Bible" and, being unconvinced, accuses those who believe of "bibliolatry."[55] Such a person has missed the crucial fact that the Bible points beyond itself to him who is life. By contrast, Mullins, keenly aware of the interdependence of the Bible and life in Christ, has come to the view of plenary inspiration, which rendered the writers capable of declaring "truth unmixed with error."[56] And so, when he speaks about the "needless confusion of science and religion," he adds the disclaimer that this "must not be taken to justify the sweeping assertions as to error and discrepancy so often made about the Scripture."[57] At this point he approves James Orr's affirmation that the Bible, "impartially interpreted and judged, is free from demonstrable error in its statements, and harmonious in its teachings."[58]

In summing up his own inductive view as contrasted with the traditional view, Mullins notes that there is no difference as to the "reality of the supernatural revelation," its sufficiency for our "religious needs," and the "finality and authoritativeness of the Bible."[59] The difference between the two, which accounts for the passion that informed Mullins's view of Scripture and indeed all of his writings, is that the inductive approach sees the Bible as the natural outflow of genuine religious life, that is, Christian life—Christ's encounter with sinful humans corporately and individually.

Though in comparison with most other theologians Mullins was conservative and a self-professed evangelical, he desired, for most of his theological career, to be seen as a man of openness, understanding, and moderation. His mediating position is clear in this midcareer (1908) description of the theological spectrum:

> On one side is the ultra-conservative, the man of the hammer and anvil method, who relies chiefly upon denunciation of opponents, and who cannot tolerate discussion on a fraternal basis; on the other is the ultra-progressive whose lofty contempt of the "traditionalist" shuts him out from the ranks of sane scholarship and wise leadership. The really safe leaders of thought, however, are between these extremes. They are men who have sympathy on the one hand with those who are perplexed by the difficulties to faith occasioned by modern science and philosophy, and on the other are resolved to be loyal to Christ and his gospel.[60]

This spirit of moderation should not be mistaken for lack of conviction in theology. It appears that Mullins considered unbelieving philosophers and scientists capable of being wooed to faith if they were treated delicately and not too soon excluded through dogmatism. That his confi-

54. Mullins, *Freedom and Authority*, 382.
55. Ibid., 352.
56. Mullins, *Christian Religion*, 144.
57. Mullins, *Freedom and Authority*, 380.
58. Ibid., 381, quoting James Orr, *Revelation and Inspiration* (New York: Scribner, 1910), 215–16.

59. Ibid., 382.
60. Mullins, *Axioms*, 14.

dence in their pliability diminished by the end of his life is evident in the spirit of aggressive confrontation that characterizes his *Christianity at the Cross Roads* (1924).

The tone of *Christianity at the Cross Roads* is one of gentlemanly indignation. Christians are not dreamers, Mullins asserts, but "the dreamers and visionaries are those who are blind to so palpable a fact as Christianity and who imagine they can overthrow it by imposing fabrics of speculative thought."[61] And he is similarly out of patience when he notes "with what vehemence the modern scientist can preach modesty to his theological opponent" and at the same time "practice dogmatism and arrogance in the realm of theological opinion."[62] His confrontation with liberalism exhibits something of the spirit of J. Gresham Machen, for he represents it as virtually something other than Christianity.[63] Modern liberalism, he observes, disagrees with the evangelical experience on such crucial issues as the reality of sin, atonement, grace, supernatural regeneration, Christian holiness, and the person of Christ. The formula of modernism will not work. Liberalism deludes itself. Thinking its opponent is a backward, crass, literalistic reactionary, it fails to realize that it is actually attacking the very foundations of religious life. Liberalism's assault is in fact aimed back through the Christian centuries at the most central and vital truths of the New Testament.[64]

Perhaps a growing dissatisfaction with Mullins's theological methodology in combination with the necessity of raising money for building projects at Southern Seminary pushed Mullins toward the traditionalist onslaught against modern thought. More likely, however, it was Mullins's own growing conviction. After all, he changed nothing in his theology or even in his methodology, but merely threw down the gauntlet of confrontation. "There is little likelihood," he declared, "that evangelical Christianity will yield to the moderns who have laid so extensive a plan for its overthrow."[65] He had himself reached the Cross Roads.

Primary Sources

Mullins, Edgar Young. *The Axioms of Religion.* Philadelphia: American Baptist Publication Society, 1908.

_____. *Christianity at the Cross Roads.* New York: George H. Doran, 1924.

_____. *The Christian Religion in Its Doctrinal Expression.* Valley Forge, Pa.: Judson, 1974.

_____. *Freedom and Authority in Religion.* Philadelphia: Griffith and Rowland, 1913.

_____. *Why Is Christianity True?* Philadelphia: American Baptist Publication Society, 1905.

Secondary Sources

Ellis, William E. *A "Man of Books and a Man of the People."* Macon, Ga.: Mercer University Press, 1985.

Mullins, Isla May. *Edgar Young Mullins: An Intimate Biography.* Nashville: Sunday School Board of the Southern Baptist Convention, 1929.

Thomas, Bill Clark. "Edgar Young Mullins: A Baptist Exponent of Theological Restatement." Ph.D. diss., Southern Baptist Theological Seminary, 1963.

---

61. Mullins, *Cross Roads,* 174.
62. Ibid., 58.
63. Ibid., 238–43.
64. Ibid., 243.

65. Ibid.

W. H. Griffith Thomas

Thomas H. Cragoe

William Henry Griffith Thomas was a scholar of great distinction, a theologian of international reputation, and one of the leaders of the evangelical wing of the Church of England in England, Canada, and the United States.[1] Both the man himself and his ministry were characterized first and foremost by a reliance upon Scripture. Indeed, his commitment to the Bible as the authoritative Word of God so distinguished his ministry that a memorial tribute observed, "One cannot think of Dr. Thomas apart from the Bible. He was essentially a teacher of the Word of God, and it was upon this work he brought his learning and his powers chiefly to bear."[2]

Another key mark of the man and his ministry was scholarship. Possessing a thorough knowledge of the Scripture in the original languages, Griffith Thomas became renowned as a biblical scholar and for a grasp of the truth that was both comprehensive and balanced.[3] His scholarship was "thorough and accurate, and his interpretations beyond question reliable. But with this accurate and thorough scholarship there was coupled a remarkable clearness of spiritual vision, a clearness of spiritual perception that is rarely coupled with thorough scholarship."[4]

Griffith Thomas's ministry was also characterized by simplicity. He possessed a remarkable ability to express profound biblical and theological truths simply, clearly, and attractively.[5] In so doing, Griffith Thomas was not an original thinker, but contented himself with crystalizing and

1. While W. H. Griffith Thomas's surname was simply Thomas, he preferred to be called Griffith Thomas.

2. John McNicol, "What Dr. Griffith Thomas Meant to Us," *Sunday School Times*, 19 July 1924, p. 437.

3. W. Graham Scroggie, "Dr. Griffith Thomas—Scholar, Teacher, Friend," *Sunday School Times*, 21 June 1924, p. 383.

4. Reuben A. Torrey, "What Dr. Griffith Thomas Meant to Us," *Sunday School Times*, 5 July 1924, p. 412.

5. Arno C. Gaebelein, "One of God's Noblemen, Dr. Griffith Thomas," *Sunday School Times*, 26 July 1924, p. 450.

communicating the deep truths of Christianity. With his remarkable powers of analysis and synthesis, he consistently succeeded in clarifying the truth in a manner which indelibly impressed his audiences.[6]

Griffith Thomas was also a man of genuine spirituality. He has been described, for example, as "a good man and full of the Holy Spirit and of faith,"[7] a man of God who "always and everywhere . . . lived the life he professed."[8] His ministry was so distinguished by service that a contemporary described him as "the most selfless man I have ever known."[9] Such were the basic qualities for which he is remembered.

Early Life

W. H. Griffith Thomas was born in Oswestry, Shropshire, England on January 2, 1861. His mother had been widowed before he was born, and so he spent the early years of his life in the care of his grandfather. After the death of his grandfather, protracted litigation over the estate, and the remarriage of his mother, the family's financial circumstances forced Griffith Thomas to leave school at the age of fourteen. Later recognized as a brilliant educator and scholar, he had obtained his education only with great difficulty and sacrifice.

At the age of sixteen, Griffith Thomas was asked to teach a Sunday-school class at Holy Trinity Church, Castle Fields, Oswestry. For four months he did his best, but during that time he became increasingly aware that he was trying to teach what he had never experienced in his own life.[10]

The next year two evangelical Christians were used of the Lord to bring him to salvation. Griffith Thomas wrote concerning his experience of March 23, 1878, "My soul was simply overflowing with joy, and since then I have never doubted that it was on that Saturday night I was born again, converted to God."[11] He was confirmed in May of that same year.

At the age of eighteen, Griffith Thomas moved to London to work for his stepfather's brother, William Charles. During the three years he labored in his stepuncle's office, he obtained a good knowledge of Greek through disciplined study (often from 10:30 P.M. to 2:30 A.M.).[12] Then the vicar of the church which he attended, B. Oswald Sharp, offered him a lay curacy which enabled him to devote greater time to study. As a curate, Griffith Thomas assisted the vicar in the discharge of his parish duties. Each morning Griffith Thomas attended lectures at King's College, London, and then spent his afternoons and evenings in parish work.[13] After three years of course work he received an associate's degree with distinction.

One of the most formative influences on Griffith Thomas's life occurred at King's College. Henry Wace, who had been appointed principal (i.e., president) of the college in 1883, became a lifelong friend. Indeed, Griffith Thomas acknowledged his debt to Wace in the preface of his *Principles of Theology*.

Pastoral Ministry and Teaching in England

Griffith Thomas was ordained to the order of deacon within the Anglican church in 1885. At the service of ordination the bishop of London, Frederick Temple, charged Griffith Thomas to read from his Greek New Testament daily. He kept that

6. J. I. Packer, Preface to *Principles of Theology*, by W. H. Griffith Thomas (Grand Rapids: Baker, 1979), iii.

7. Scroggie, "Dr. Griffith Thomas," 383.

8. James M. Gray, "What Dr. Griffith Thomas Meant to Us," *Sunday School Times*, 28 June 1924, p. 395.

9. J. Harvey Borton, "What Dr. Griffith Thomas Meant to Us," *Sunday School Times*, 19 July 1924, p. 437.

10. Warren W. Wiersbe, *Listening to the Giants: A Guide to Good Reading and Great Preaching* (Grand Rapids: Baker, 1980), 140.

11. M. Guthrie Clark, *William Henry Griffith Thomas* (London: Church Book Room, 1949), 5.

12. Ibid., 6.

13. Ibid.

promise for the rest of his life by faithfully reading a chapter every day.[14] In addition he annually re-signed a statement he drew up in 1888: "On this the Third anniversary of my Ordination, I desire to renew my vows to God and reconsecrate myself to His service. May He fill me entirely with His Spirit. May I be holy in character, and earnest in work. May He continually keep me, 'All for Jesus,' W. H. G. Thomas."[15]

Griffith Thomas served as an Anglican clergyman out of firm conviction and loyal devotion. He resolutely held to evangelical Anglicanism as "that which is the most Scriptural, most historical, most useful form of Church government and life."[16] Indeed, it was the central place of Scripture within the Church of England that made him a firmly committed churchman:

There is no Church in Christendom which uses so much of Scripture or gives it so prominent a place in its services.

1. In the Articles it is the supreme standard of doctrine and the final court of appeal.

2. In the Lessons, Epistles, and Gospels it is used daily and weekly for instruction.

3. In the Psalms it is employed for worship daily through the month.

4. In the Prayers, the substance of the petitions is often verbally identical with, or evidently based on, Holy Scripture.

5. In the Ordination Services special prominence is given to the Bible by the presentation of a Testament to the Deacon and a Bible to the Priest. . . . Our Ordinal . . . lays the chief emphasis on our work as Ministers of the Word.[17]

Of course, along with his devotion to the Church of England, Griffith Thomas demonstrated firm loyalty and adherence to both the Book of Common Prayer and the Thirty-nine Articles as well.

As an ordained deacon, Griffith Thomas served as a curate under Sharp for another three-and-a-half years. The work of a deacon included a number of ministerial responsibilities: "The Deacon is to assist in Divine Service, to help at Holy Communion, to read the Holy Scriptures and Homilies in Church, to instruct the youth in the Catechism, to baptize, and to preach. His paramount duties are therefore spiritual, and this element must ever predominate."[18]

In February of 1889, Griffith Thomas was appointed senior curate on the staff at St. Aldate's Church, Oxford.[19] This began an association with Oxford which lasted for over twenty years. The seven years spent at the church were of great importance in his life and ministry. It was during this period that he pursued his education at Oxford. In 1894 he was awarded the Hall-Houghton Junior Septuagint Prize and subsequently won second prize in the Ellerton Theological Essay competition.[20] He wrote on the Synoptic Problem with special reference to the Gospel of Mark. He earned his B.D. from Christ Church, Oxford, in 1895, and an M.A. in 1898.

While at Oxford, Griffith Thomas was invited by the vicar of Islington to read a paper at the Islington Clerical Conference on January 14, 1896. It has been said that this is the only time that a curate was ever honored in this way.[21] He spoke on the subject of the doctrine of the church, and "received the cordial recognition and praise of the entire Meeting."[22] As a result, he began to be noticed within the broader fellowship of the Anglican church, and in 1896 he accepted a call to the distinguished congrega-

14. Wiersbe, *Listening to the Giants*, 140.

15. Clark, *Griffith Thomas*, 7.

16. W. H. Griffith Thomas, *The Work of the Ministry* (London: Hodder and Stoughton, 1911), 119. This volume was later abridged by his widow, Alice Griffith Thomas, and retitled *Ministerial Life and Work* (Chicago: Bible Institute Colportage Association, 1927; Grand Rapids: Baker, 1974).

17. Ibid., 126–27.

18. Ibid., 135.

19. Clark, *Griffith Thomas*, 8.

20. Ibid., 9.

21. Ibid., 10.

22. *Record*, 17 January 1896, cited by Wiersbe, *Listening to the Giants*, 141.

tion of St. Paul's, Portman Square, London. There he experienced nine years of fruitful ministry.

At the age of thirty-seven, Griffith Thomas married Alice Monk. Their only child, Winifred, was born in 1902. Griffith Thomas's devotion as husband and father was testified to in a posthumous tribute:

> While I have often heard Dr. Thomas speak, and have, as often, admired his scholarship, his Scripturalness and his spirituality, . . . I do not think of him as in the pulpit or on the platform, but rather as within the confine of his home. . . . There he was what he was, altogether natural, and there it was that he was most to be esteemed. For it was at such a time and within such a setting that the Doctor revealed himself at his best. . . . According to my mind, if a man stands the test of his home relaxation, he may be reckoned as pure gold; and it is my conviction that Dr. Thomas did stand this test.[23]

Griffith Thomas's ministry at St. Paul's, Portman Square, was fueled by prayer. No fewer than six prayer meetings were held each week. There was also a weekly afternoon Bible study for which Griffith Thomas prepared "a printed syllabus outlining the course . . . and then weekly notes for study. Much ground was covered in this way, and the author's books on Peter's life and letters, the Epistle to the Romans, and the book of Genesis were first given in the form of these weekly lectures."[24] Indeed, his literary output increased considerably during his nine years of ministry in London. *Methods of Bible Study* was issued originally in 1902, and *The Catholic Faith*, the substance of which was taught to his confirmation classes, was first published in 1904.

Griffith Thomas's ministry at St. Paul's (1896–1905) proved to be one of the most joyful experiences of his life. In his farewell letter to the congregation he wrote:

> These nine years of happy ministry have left a deep mark on my heart and life, and I lay down my work here with keenest regret, even though I am fully convinced that I have taken the right step in so doing. I can understand now from personal experience what I have long known from the testimony of others that "Portman Chapel is one of the dearest spots on earth." It will be specially dear to me as the place of my first incumbency, as the place of my first home, and as the place where we have had our first experiences of home joys and sorrows.[25]

In October 1905, Griffith Thomas accepted the position of principal of Wycliffe Hall, Oxford, a training center for evangelical Anglicans. During his five years of ministry there, he trained more than eighty students. Apparently he bore the brunt of the lecturing, instructing his students in the Pentateuch, the historical books of the Old Testament, doctrine, the Gospels, apologetics, and pastoral theology.[26] The lectures on Christian doctrine constitute the substance of his posthumous *Principles of Theology* (1930). The addresses on the pastoral ministry appear in his *Work of the Ministry* (1911).

Griffith Thomas's literary work also included contributing a column to the *Record*. In this column, which was entitled "In Conference," he answered questions that subscribers to the journal had asked on biblical, spiritual, and theological matters. He planned a series of Anglican handbooks, to which he contributed *Christianity Is Christ* (1909). He also served as the editor of the quarterly periodical *The Churchman*. The dissertation that he submitted to Christ Church, Oxford, for his D.D. (1906) was published in the same year as *A Sacrament of Our Redemption*.

---

23. Henry W. Frost, "Dr. Griffith Thomas' Home Life," *Sunday School Times*, 30 August 1924, p. 516.
24. Clark, *Griffith Thomas*, 13.
25. Cited by Clark, *Griffith Thomas*, 14.
26. Clark, *Griffith Thomas*, 16.

The Work of the Ministry

In 1903 Griffith Thomas traveled across the Atlantic for the first time to address the annual Northfield Conference, which had been associated with Dwight L. Moody during his later years. Griffith Thomas also began to minister at the British Keswick Convention in 1906. In 1910 he was approached about assuming a professorship at Wycliffe College in Toronto. By this time in his life, his philosophy of pastoral ministry was well established. He outlined its principles in *The Work of the Ministry*. The substance of this volume was, as we have seen, first delivered in his lectures at Wycliffe Hall, Oxford, but the experience on which it was based was largely gained from St. Paul's, Portman Square.

In all Christian work and ministry, says Griffith Thomas, there are three absolutely indispensable elements, "the Spirit of God as the power, the Word of God as the message, and the man of God as the instrument."[27] These three vital ingredients—the Spirit, the Scriptures, and the servant—are interconnected, for the Holy Spirit uses the message (the Scripture) as proclaimed by the man (his servant).

The presence of the Spirit is the secret of all spiritual power in the life of the minister. The Holy Spirit "makes the Truth real to the soul, and keeps it vital in life and service."[28] His indwelling presence "will enlighten the judgment, control the feelings, direct the will, and possess and energize every faculty. The natural temperament will be glorified, the natural wisdom illuminated, and the natural determination set on fire."[29] Thus the power of true ministry comes from God alone, a power which is always imparted through the Holy Spirit.[30] In fact, ministerial duty is not measured by the ability of the minister. Rather, it is measured by the ability of the Lord and his indwelling Spirit, and ministerial responsibility is really *"our* response to *His* ability."[31]

> Christ does not give *inherent* ability to any worker. He does not expect grace to be used apart from Himself and then to be replenished when exhausted. Grace is nothing so material as this. Grace is relationship, and its power depends on the maintenance of that relationship by a constant attitude of faith and obedience. . . . By prayer we speak to God; by the Bible God speaks to us, and when these two are made real by the Spirit Who is "the Spirit of grace and supplication," we find the contact maintained, and the life kept, blessed, energized, used to the glory of God.[32]

The second indispensable element in ministry is the Scripture. It must be prominent in every sphere of ministerial work.[33] For while "the Word without the Spirit is dry and useless; the Spirit without the Word has no message."[34] Accordingly, the deepest need of the minister is for "solitary and prayerful study of the Word of God."[35] Indeed, "no ministry can ever be of service to men which does not start here, in the definite, conscious, blessed possession of the Word of God."[36]

To possess the Word of God, the minister must engage in constant, thorough, firsthand study of the Scripture in the original languages. The goal of such study is to master the contents of the Bible, assimilate its truth into one's own life, and use it in the work of the ministry.[37] As the perfect and constant standard of truth,[38] the Word of God must be both the substance of ministry and the standard of the life of the minister.[39] Reliance on Scripture will guard the

27. Griffith Thomas, *Work of the Ministry*, 86.
28. Ibid., 77.
29. Ibid., 103.
30. Ibid., 170.
31. Ibid., 38.
32. Ibid., 40.
33. Ibid., 127.
34. Ibid., 406.
35. Ibid., 94.
36. Ibid., 15.
37. Ibid., 128–29.
38. Ibid., 152.
39. Ibid., 20.

minister from error; we know this to be true because "every error comes in some way or other from a neglect of God's Word, and every safeguard against error comes from the closest adherence thereto."[40] In truth, the Word of God is the secret of ministerial power in Christian service,[41] because it is "the greatest power in the universe."[42]

The reason for steadfast adherence to the Scripture is its nature, for in it the Lord has "handed over to us His glorious Gospel, His Divine message, and we are the trustees of so weighty a charge."[43] Being divinely inspired ("God-breathed"),[44] the Scriptures are the supreme authority in all matters of faith and practice.[45] Belief in the truth revealed in Scripture means that we will agree as well with the fundamentals of the faith. "The doctrines of God, of Christ, of the Holy Spirit, and the various aspects of the Divine Redemptive Person and Work of our Lord, as taught by the Church, will be accepted because they 'may be proved by most certain warrants of Holy Scripture.'"[46] Because of our conviction concerning the Bible we will view the Christian message as having its source in God himself.

The final essential ingredient of the ministry is the servant, the man of God. The minister is first and foremost, and at all times, a man of God, a servant of God to God's people. He is an ambassador on behalf of Christ,[47] a "Messenger of Redemption."[48] As such, he possesses an assured conviction concerning the message which he delivers. This message is certain—definite, positive, and unchanging.[49] In fact, "herein lies the supreme secret of Christian ministry: a man who knows God, who

knows God's truth, who knows by experience what Christianity is, and who intends at all costs to tell what he knows and give what he has received. The man who is in doubt can never be a messenger of the Lord of Hosts."[50]

Use of the Bible is essential to the minister, for it gives his preaching the authority of a divine message.[51] Preaching is, after all, "God's Word to man through man, and the motto of every preacher should be, 'I have a message from God to thee.'"[52] The task of preaching, then, is to so elucidate the text of Scripture as to communicate its true meaning; and the message will be "a portion of Divine truth, selected, prepared, and delivered under the guidance and in the power of the Holy Spirit, and adapted to present needs."[53]

Also essential to the servant of God is a godly character in harmony with the message. Indeed, the chief requirement of the minister is character,[54] for "there is no greater danger, no more serious peril, than that of a gulf between word and deed, between message and character, between preaching and practice."[55] To be a man of character, the servant of God must be filled with the Spirit of love, truth, and wisdom—love which is guided by the truth, truth which is inspired by love, and a resulting spiritual wisdom which comes from on high.[56] Doing God's work in his way, the minister "will be 'wise' in his efforts to instruct and feed. He will be 'faithful' in the discharge of his duties. And he will be 'good' both inwardly and outwardly . . . in that attractiveness which ministers and wins for Christ."[57]

Godly character is based upon and springs out of a vital communion with God. This fellowship "comes in a simple way . . .

40. Ibid., 154.
41. Ibid., 93.
42. Ibid., 11.
43. Ibid., 77.
44. Ibid., 87.
45. Ibid., 122.
46. Ibid., 117.
47. Ibid., 67.
48. Ibid., 7.
49. Ibid., 55.

50. Ibid., 165.
51. Ibid., 220–21.
52. Ibid., 205.
53. Ibid., 235.
54. Ibid., 69.
55. Ibid., 70.
56. Ibid., 160.
57. Ibid., 164.

in the twofold method of prayer and meditation. In prayer we speak to God; in the Bible God speaks to us. And prayer is the response of the soul to the Bible as the Word of God."[58] Communion with God through both prayer and the Bible, and obedience to him by responding to his will, are the guarantees of a perpetual fellowship with the Lord which is the heart of the Christian ministry.[59] As a servant of God and a man of character, the minister will lead a consistent, exemplary life, walking "ever in the light of Holy Scripture."[60]

Griffith Thomas sees the goal of the ministry as fourfold: "to witness to Christ; to win men for Him; to set them at work for Him; and to keep watch for their souls as those who belong to Him."[61] The first two goals relate to the biblical task of evangelizing through the gospel, which is the main work of the church.[62] In sharing the gospel, the minister's aim is that individuals come to trust in God's revelation and experience genuine, personal contact of the soul with Christ as Savior and Master.[63] The second two goals relate to the biblical task of edification—the building up of believers in the faith. The minister uses the Scriptures to guide and equip believers.[64] This ministry of the Word establishes within the local assembly an agreement in faith and knowledge, maturity in Christian experience, and Christ-like character and conduct.[65]

Professorship in Canada

It was in the autumn of 1910 that Griffith Thomas joined the staff of Wycliffe College, Toronto, a school devoted to the training of evangelical Anglicans. Initially invited to be a professor of systematic theology, he found upon arrival in Toronto that this

chair had been given to a Wycliffe graduate. So he was asked to teach Old Testament literature and exegesis, a task which he faithfully performed for the nine years he was in Toronto. Toward the end of this period he was asked to teach systematic theology as well. While the change in position from principal of Wycliffe Hall to the subordinate role of professor at the school in Toronto was no doubt very difficult (especially when coupled with the change in teaching responsibilities), Griffith Thomas submitted to the change "with Christian grace, and never lost sight of the validity of his call to Canada."[66] Indeed, it was during the years in Toronto that he became known to the Christian public throughout the American continent.

As a professor Griffith Thomas was very popular with his students. This popularity can be traced to two features of his teaching style—his conviction concerning the Scriptures and his concern for his students. No matter what subject he taught, the lectures he delivered had the ring of biblical authority and definite conviction. A colleague later recalled that "the students who listened to his lectures in . . . Wyclif [sic] College, Toronto, heard the words of a man whose voice never quivered with an accent of doubt. No words of distrust or disbelief were ever evoked by his teachings. No student ever went away from his classes with a sickening sense of sinking faith with regard to the inspiration of the Scriptures, the authority of the Word, the Deity of Christ."[67] Griffith Thomas's conviction was not born out of ignorance, but rather out of a profound and well-versed understanding of contemporary and modernist thought. "All the latest material was incorporated into his work and carefully examined but there was never any uncertainty as to where he stood in his loyalty to Holy Scripture."[68] It

58. Ibid., 142.
59. Ibid., 402.
60. Ibid., 141.
61. Ibid., 352.
62. Ibid., 347.
63. Ibid., 302, 316.
64. Ibid., 89–91.
65. Ibid., 168–69.

66. Clark, *Griffith Thomas*, 22.
67. Dyson Hague, "What Dr. Griffith Thomas Meant to Us," *Sunday School Times*, 28 June 1924, p. 395.
68. Clark, *Griffith Thomas*, 23.

was this blend of informed scholarship with evangelical conviction that cast Griffith Thomas into an increasingly prominent role as a strong witness for the truth,[69] one who stood in "outspoken opposition to those who have drifted from the creedal standards of the evangelical churches."[70] Yet he did so in a way which consistently reflected "the method and spirit of the Master."[71]

The second endearing quality of Griffith Thomas's teaching style was his concern for his students. He "was ever a believer in the 'personal touch,' and subsequent letters from all over the world show that this side of his work was appreciated as much as any other. These contacts were maintained afterwards and men in their parishes and the Mission field used to write to their old Professor for counsel and guidance."[72] Bound up with his rich scholarship, then, there was a love which rendered him accessible. He was "so simple and approachable that the most sensitive or retiring student might call upon him at his rooms at any time and receive a genial welcome, a patient hearing, and the help he asked."[73]

In addition to his duties as a professor at Wycliffe College, Griffith Thomas engaged in various other ministries. He was a regular lecturer at the Toronto Bible College, where he taught the Book of Genesis, the Book of Romans, Old Testament interpretation, and biblical theology. Twice during this period he returned to England to minister. He was the featured speaker at the Westminster Bible Conference, Mundesley, in 1912; and he spoke at the Keswick Convention in 1914. He also became an increasingly familiar figure at American Bible conferences.

The Last Years

Toward the end of his nine years in Toronto, opportunities for wider ministry increasingly presented themselves to Griffith Thomas. As a result, he left Wycliffe College in 1919 and moved to Philadelphia to engage in what he referred to as a "continent-wide ministry."[74] During this final stage in his life he participated in many conferences and wrote extensively.

Griffith Thomas had long been sought after as a guest lecturer and conference speaker. As has been noted, he was involved in the Keswick Convention in England, speaking there in 1906, 1907, 1908, and 1914. When the Victorious Life movement (a chain of local "Keswicks") was established in America, Griffith Thomas was a featured speaker at its first conference (1913).[75] From that date on, if he was in the country, he always led the Bible Hour at the major conference in July.[76] He was a speaker at the Montrose Bible Conference every year.[77] He was invited to lecture at the Moody Bible Institute, the Bible Institute of Los Angeles, the National Bible Institute of New York, and the Bible Institute of Pennsylvania.[78] Griffith Thomas was also invited by B. B. Warfield to visit Princeton Theological Seminary and to deliver the Stone Lectures for 1913. He lectured six times on the Holy Spirit—twice on the biblical revelation of the doctrine, once on its historical development, twice on theological considerations, and once on the spiritual application. These lectures formed the substance of his book *The Holy Spirit of God*.

69. William L. Pettingill, "What Dr. Griffith Thomas Meant to Us," *Sunday School Times*, 5 July 1924, p. 412.

70. *Toronto Globe*, "What Dr. Griffith Thomas Meant to Us," *Sunday School Times*, 5 July 1924, p. 412.

71. Scroggie, "Dr. Griffith Thomas," 383.

72. Clark, *Griffith Thomas*, 22–23.

73. Gray, "What Dr. Griffith Thomas Meant to Us," 395.

74. Clark, *Griffith Thomas*, 23.

75. Borton, "What Dr. Griffith Thomas Meant to Us," 437.

76. Ibid.

77. Torrey, "What Dr. Griffith Thomas Meant to Us," 412.

78. Clark, *Griffith Thomas*, 24.

Griffith Thomas traveled to China and Japan in the summer of 1920 to strengthen the missionaries by means of Bible teaching. While there, he saw many undeniable evidences of modernism among the missionaries, which he disclosed upon his return. He traveled to England for the last time in 1922.

Together with Lewis Sperry Chafer and A. B. Winchester, Griffith Thomas was a co-founder of Evangelical Theological College, which later became Dallas Theological Seminary. He was to serve as a visiting professor of Bible until he could move to Dallas, when he would become a professor of theology. However, he died in Philadelphia on June 2, 1924, before this new field of ministry could be realized. Through the benevolence of William Nairn of Dundee, Scotland, the library of Griffith Thomas, some forty-five hundred books and fifteen hundred pamphlets, was purchased for the seminary.

Griffith Thomas's literary contribution during his years in Canada and the United States was considerable. He wrote devotional commentaries on Romans (1911), Colossians (1923), and Hebrews (1923). Other devotional works include *The Prayers of St. Paul* (1914) and *Grace and Power* (1916), a series of addresses on the spiritual life. He also wrote a biographical work on the apostle John (1923). The major theological work written during this period was *The Principles of Theology*. In all, he published twenty-six booklets and twenty-four larger works, many of which are still in print.[79]

In addition, Griffith Thomas made regular contributions to numerous periodicals, including the *Sunday School Times*, the *Evangelical Christian*, *Bibliotheca Sacra*, and the *Toronto Globe*. He was also the editor of the *Canadian Churchman* (1910–13), an associate editor of *Bibliotheca Sacra* (1911–24), and a contributing editor of the *Bible Champion* (1923). He authored the ar-

ticles on "Adam in the New Testament," "Ascension," and "Resurrection of Jesus Christ" in the *International Standard Bible Encyclopedia*. What is truly remarkable about the literary contributions of Griffith Thomas is that not only are they soundly scriptural and scholarly, as well as simple and clear, but they also consistently create in the reader "a deeper love of and desire for God as revealed in His word."[80]

The Principles of Theology

The theological contribution of Griffith Thomas is best seen in his major treatise, *The Principles of Theology*. The manuscript of this work was complete when he died in 1924, and was published in both London and New York in 1930. The work is cast into the form of a study of each of the Thirty-nine Articles of the Church of England. The purpose was both to distinguish the established theology of the Church of England from the opinions of various individual Anglicans, and to demonstrate where the Church of England actually stood on doctrinal truth.

The work itself is not original or speculative. Rather, it collects, crystalizes, and communicates the thoughts of other Anglican scholars on the Articles. Griffith Thomas's clearly defined task was "magisterially and definitively to spell out, on the basis of others' minute researches and debates, what the Articles actually affirm, both in principle and in detail; what biblical warrant there is for making such affirmations; and what their implications are in relation to various forms of Catholic tradition and (less fully) of shallow rationalism."[81] He acknowledged a special debt to the lectures on the Articles by Henry Wace, his principal at King's College, London. He also acknowledged his indebtedness to E. A. Litton's *Introduction to Dogmatic Theology* and T. P. Boultbee's *Commentary on the Thirty-nine Articles Forming an Introduc-*

79. Wiersbe, *Listening to the Giants*, 143.

80. Scroggie, "Dr. Griffith Thomas," 383.
81. Packer, Preface to *Principles of Theology*, x.

tion to the Theology of the Church of England.

As an exposition of the Thirty-nine Articles, *The Principles of Theology* methodically relates Scripture, reason, and church history (both past and present). Because of its basic approach the work partakes of some of the weaknesses of the Articles themselves. In fact, Griffith Thomas acknowledges that "the Articles do not present a complete system of doctrine because they were largely due to the historical circumstances which called them forth."[82] The areas of anthropology (the doctrine of man), pneumatology (the doctrine of the Holy Spirit), and eschatology (the doctrine of future things) are not fully developed. Furthermore, the work specifically addresses concerns that were relevant in the early twentieth century (e.g., Anglo-Catholic claims concerning the ministry, the priesthood, the sacraments, and salvation). And of course it fails to address concerns that arose later in the twentieth century with the works of Karl Barth, Rudolf Bultmann, and others. Yet in *The Principles of Theology* one finds a clear, orderly, and nontechnical presentation of the Christian faith. It is evangelical by conviction and Anglican by creed, because Griffith Thomas believed that "by historical and theological right real Anglicanism is evangelicalism in a pure form."[83] Despite its minor shortcomings his analysis of the basics of Christian theology is an enduring contribution to the church, since the fundamentals of the faith are unchanging.

The Principles of Theology begins with a discussion of several introductory matters, the first of which is revelation. The possibility of revelation is established on two grounds—the nature of God as a supreme personal being, which necessarily involves the power of self-revelation; and the nature of man, which involves a capacity for communion with a higher being.[84] The method of revelation is

> first and foremost one of *Life;* that is, it is a revelation of a Person to persons. Christianity is primarily a religion of facts with doctrines arising out of the facts. All through the historic period of God's manifestation, from patriarchal times to the period of Christ and His Apostles, Revelation was given to life and manifested through personality. But the Divine life has been expressed in *Word,* first oral and then written. Both in the Old Testament and in the New Testament we see first what God was and did to men, and afterwards what He said. So that while we distinguish between the Revelation and the Record, the former being necessarily prior to the latter, yet the Revelation needed the Record for accuracy, and also for accessibility to subsequent ages.[85]

Being mediated through history, revelation is also of necessity progressive. "In Jesus Christ the self-disclosure of God reached its climax, and the New Testament is the permanent, written embodiment of the uniqueness of Christianity in the world."[86]

Faith is the human response to this divine revelation, the attitude of the soul to Christ as the manifestation of God. Griffith Thomas makes it clear that

> trust is the only adequate answer to God's Revelation. . . . Trust is thus the correlative of truth. Faith in man answers to grace in God. As such, it affects the whole of man's nature. It commences with the conviction of the mind based on adequate evidence; it continues in the confidence of the heart or emotions based on the above conviction, and it is crowned in the consent of the will, by means of which the conviction and confidence are expressed in conduct.[87]

---

82. Griffith Thomas, *Principles of Theology,* lix.
83. Packer, Preface to *Principles of Theology,* xi.
84. Griffith Thomas, *Principles of Theology,* xviii.
85. Ibid., xviii–xix.
86. Ibid., xix.
87. Ibid., xx.

Note that faith begins as a cognitive assent to propositional truth:

> In all true faith, therefore, there will of necessity be the three elements of knowledge, assent, and confidence, and anything short of these will never give the full Christian trust. . . . [Holy Scripture] is the guide and standard of our faith, and the supreme authority as to what we are to believe. . . . God has given His people a written Revelation of Himself, and this tells us clearly all that it is necessary for us to know about God.[88]

This cognitive response to propositional truth eventually involves the entire person: "While the intellect is not to be neglected, faith is very much more than knowledge. It is not mere belief in a thought, or conception, or idea. It is the expression of the whole nature of man in response to God's approach in Christ. As such, it involves personal committal and confidence."[89] The revelation of Christ, then, is met by a response of the whole individual—intellect, emotion, and will.

The discussion then moves from faith to doctrine, which is simply defined as "the fundamental truths of revelation arranged in systematic form."[90] "Theology" denotes the technical expression of the revelation of God. It is the task of theology "to examine all the spiritual facts of revelation, to estimate their value, and to arrange them into a body of teaching."[91] The result is a "systematised statement of truth deduced from the Bible, the intellectual expression in technical language of what is contained in the Word of God."[92]

With regard to the systematizing of theological truth, Griffith Thomas showed a decided preference for a credal approach:

88. Ibid., xxii.
89. Ibid., xxi.
90. Ibid., xxiii.
91. Ibid.
92. Ibid.

> There is obvious danger in every attempt at systematising Christian truth, as we may see from the great works of men like Aquinas and Calvin. The human mind is unable to find a place for every single Christian doctrine, and it is far better to be content with "Articles," or "points," with gaps unfilled, because it is impossible for thought to be covered by them. General lines of Christian truth are far safer and also truer to the growth of thought and experience through the ages. This method prevents teaching becoming hardened into a cast-iron system which cannot expand. It is the virtue of the Church of England Articles that they take this line and do not commit Churchmen to an absolute, rigid system of doctrine from which there is no relief and of which there is no modification.[93]

Though he adhered strictly to the fundamentals of the Christian faith, Griffith Thomas treasured the room for refinement and mental enterprise which the Articles afforded the theologian.

Griffith Thomas concludes his introductory remarks with a discussion of the place of creeds, confessions, and the Thirty-nine Articles of the Church of England. The Articles are of particular value for the church and the theologian. As part of the Reformation, they have historical value, representing the position of the Church of England especially in relation to Roman Catholicism. They have doctrinal value in that they serve as the standard of belief of the Church of England. Expressed with exactness, balance, and fulness, they provide a test of orthodoxy,[94] and yet are subject to Scripture as the ultimate authority.[95] In addition, Griffith Thomas observes that they have practical value:

> The Articles express the intellectual position involved in being a believer, the explicit, intellectual sign of what is spiritually implicit from the first moment of faith

93. Ibid., xxiv.
94. Ibid., xxx, liv, lvi.
95. Ibid., lviii.

in Christ. When He is accepted as Saviour, Lord, and God, everything else is involved and possessed in germ. We commence by *faith* and go on to *knowledge*. It is inevitable that we should think out our position. St. Peter tells us to be ready to give a reason for the hope that is in us (1 Pet. 3:15), and we see the natural order of experience followed by expression. (1) Hope possessed; (2) having a reason for our hope; (3) giving a reason. The intellectual grasp of Christianity is essential for a strong Christian life, for giving balance and force to experience, for protection against error, for equipment for service.[96]

This practical and experiential dimension brings in personal, emotional, and ethical elements that are an absolute necessity in theology:

> It is, of course, essential to remember that theology is not merely a matter of intellect, but also of experience. Theology is concerned with spiritual realities, and must include personal experience as well as ideas. . . . The feeling equally with the reason must share in the consideration of theology, because theology is of the heart, and the deepest truths are inextricably bound up with personal needs and experiences.[97]

This experiential dimension is closely tied to the person and work of Jesus Christ:

> The sole and sufficient guarantee of Christian doctrine being at once intellectual and experimental is its constant and close association with the Person of Jesus Christ. In order to avoid anything dry and lifeless we must relate every truth to the living Person of Him Who declared, "I am the Way, the Truth, and the Life." When it is realised that "Christianity is Christ," that Christ Himself is the substance, source, and spring of all doctrine, our theology will be truly Christian.[98]

With this conviction Griffith Thomas begins a point-by-point examination of the Articles—historically, doctrinally, and practically.

The first five Articles are grouped under the general heading "The Substance of Faith." This section includes a detailed consideration of the Trinity, the person and work of Christ, and the Holy Spirit. The chapter on Article I provides a thorough discussion of theology proper, including proofs from both natural and special revelation for the existence of God, the nature and attributes of God, and the Trinity.

In treating Article II, Griffith Thomas discusses the person and work of Christ in terminology that is in keeping with the formula of Chalcedon. Jesus Christ is essential deity and perfect humanity united in one person. This uniqueness of his person is essential for his work, for salvation is possible only by divine grace, and grace can come to us only through a Savior who is both divine and human.

With regard to the work of Christ, Griffith Thomas focuses upon the substitutionary atonement. In harmony with the formula of Chalcedon and the teaching of the New Testament, he declares that the heart of the Christian faith is Jesus Christ's dying in the place of sinners and paying the price of their sins: "The Atonement means that God in the Person of His Eternal Son took upon Himself in vicarious death the sin of the whole world. The offer of mercy is made to everyone, since there is no sinner for whom Christ did not die, and every sin, past, present, and future, is regarded as laid on and borne by Him."[99] The death of Christ accomplished "(*a*) the removal of sin by expiation; (*b*) the removal of enmity by means of the moral and spiritual dynamic of the indwelling Christ; (*c*) the provision and guarantee of fellowship with Christ by means of our oneness with Him."[100] This understanding of the atonement both meets the demand for peace with God and

---

96. Ibid., xxvi.
97. Ibid., xxvii.
98. Ibid., xxviii.

99. Ibid., 58–59.
100. Ibid., 59.

assures the conscience burdened with sin and guilt.

Article IV affirms the bodily resurrection of Christ, his ascension, and his return in judgment. In discussing the return of Christ, Griffith Thomas espouses premillennialism[101] and intimates a belief in pretribulationism.[102] In his exposition of the doctrine of the Holy Spirit (Article V), he affirms the personality and deity of the Holy Spirit, as well as the vital and essential place which the Spirit occupies in the Christian system of belief.

The next three Articles are grouped under the heading "The Rule of Faith." They deal respectively with the Scriptures (Article VI), the Old Testament (Article VII), and the three creeds (Article VIII).

In the chapter on Article VI, Griffith Thomas discusses the canon, character, sufficiency, and supremacy of the Scriptures. Divine inspiration is the key to the character of the Bible. It *is the Word of God in the sense that it conveys to us an accurate record of everything God intended man to know and learn in connection with His will.*[103] The divine element was paramount in the process of inspiration—it was "not the Divine *and* the human, but the Divine *through* the human."[104] The result of inspiration is that the Holy Scriptures preserve for us God's revelation in its purest accessible form.[105] This written revelation is certain, permanent, and universally available.[106] It is also inerrant, in that "the widest learning and the acutest ingenuity of scepticism have never pointed to one complete and demonstrable error of fact or doctrine in the Old or New Testament."[107] Moreover, the Scriptures

are sufficient in that they contain everything that is necessary for salvation. Indeed, the Bible is a book of and for redemption.[108] The Scriptures are, then, "the supreme and final authority in all matters of faith and practice."[109] They are supreme over reason, over the church, and over church tradition.[110] Whatever doctrine, creed, or practice is received and accepted by the church must be proved by the "most certain warrants of Holy Scripture," or at least found to be in harmony with its teaching.[111]

In his discussion of the Old Testament (Article VII), Griffith Thomas shows himself to be a dispensationalist in his approach to interpreting Scripture.[112]

Article VIII affirms belief in the Apostles' Creed, the Nicene Creed, and the Athanasian Creed. Their thorough reception by the church is based upon their agreement with Scripture.[113] Creeds are valuable in that they amplify Scripture.[114] They state explicitly what is implicit in Scripture, and thereby are useful as conditions of fellowship and tests of orthodoxy.[115] As intellectual statements of the truth, they are designed to guide the believer to a more perfect trust in the Lord.

The next major division of the Articles is entitled "The Life of Faith." In this section Griffith Thomas discusses those doctrines connected with both justification (Articles IX–XIV) and sanctification (Articles XV–XVIII).

Article IX deals with original sin or "inborn sinfulness," which is that "principle of evil which has infected human nature by reason of the original connection of the race with Adam."[116] There are two effects

101. Ibid., 87.
102. Ibid., 88, 256. Like the pretribulationists Griffith Thomas makes the distinction between Christ's coming for his people and coming with his people.
103. Ibid., 119.
104. Ibid., 118.
105. Ibid., 117.
106. Ibid.
107. Frederic W. Farrar, "Inspiration," in *Cassell's Biblical Educator*, 1:207, cited by Griffith Thomas, *Principles of Theology*, 501.

108. Griffith Thomas, *Principles of Theology*, 120.
109. Ibid., 132.
110. Ibid., 124–32.
111. Ibid., 123.
112. Ibid., 140–41; see also W. H. Griffith Thomas, *The Holy Spirit of God* (London: Longmans, Green, 1913), 46–49, 70.
113. Griffith Thomas, *Principles of Theology*, 147.
114. Ibid., 150.
115. Ibid., 151.
116. Ibid., 159.

of original sin upon the individual. The first is deprivation of moral ability; that is, "man has been so thoroughly deprived of moral and spiritual power that he is incapable of doing the will of God."[117] The second is the actual existence of an evil principle within man.[118] As a result, evil has touched every part of man's nature.

With regard to the condemnation that falls on all humans Griffith Thomas writes, "While everyone is born into this world with the evil principle within derived and inherited, it is only as the individual asserts himself and does what is wrong that he is personally subject to the Divine condemnation."[119] The guilt associated with original sin is covered by the atonement of Christ, so that original sin, considered in and by itself, does not carry with it the penalty of eternal condemnation.[120] What does bring condemnation, on the other hand, are the actual sins that are committed because of the evil principle within and that have not been forgiven. This evil principle remains even in the regenerate to the end of this life.[121]

Article X observes that fallen man has the faculty of will, the ability to determine the course of his action and to select what he desires.[122] Yet "behind the will is the nature, and as is the nature so is the will. Moral inability is thus due to the corruption of nature."[123] Given the ability to choose, man is accountable; but sin is inevitable because his reason and will have been corrupted. The divine response to this human weakness and inability is the provision of grace.

Justification denotes the restoration of a true relationship with God (Article XI). "It includes (a) the removal of condemnation by the gift of forgiveness; (b) the removal of

guilt by the reckoning (or imputation) of righteousness; (c) the removal of separation by the restoration to fellowship."[124] The basis of justification is the atoning work of Christ, and it is received only by faith in him.[125]

Of particular interest in Griffith Thomas's discussion of the doctrine of sanctification is his advocacy of the Keswick teaching that the Christian's tendency to sin is not eradicated, but rather is counteracted by victorious living in the Spirit. Griffith Thomas writes:

> While Scripture teaches something that is very near eradication, in order that we may not be satisfied with anything less than the highest type of Christian living, on the other hand, it as clearly teaches that the evil principle has not been removed. . . . On the one hand we must insist that even in the regenerate the evil principle remains and will remain to the end of this life; on the other hand, we must be clear that this evil principle need not and ought not to produce evil results in practice, since the grace of God has been provided to overcome it.[126]

Sanctification, then, is best described as counteraction—"the presence and power of evil within are counteracted by the presence and greater power of the Holy Spirit. So that evil though mighty is subjugated by the mightier force of the Spirit of God."[127] And spirituality, accordingly, is the life of Christ that the power of the Holy Spirit reproduces in the believer through the Word of God and prayer.

The final major division of *The Principles of Theology* is designated "The Household of Faith" (Articles XIX–XXXIX). In this section Griffith Thomas discusses the church —its nature, purpose, characteristics, and authority. He then examines the work of the pastoral ministry and in so doing espe-

117. Ibid., 164.
118. Ibid., 165.
119. Ibid., 166.
120. Ibid., 167.
121. Ibid., 171, 174–75.
122. Ibid., 180.
123. Ibid., 181.

124. Ibid., 185–86.
125. Ibid., 191–92.
126. Ibid., 174–75.
127. Ibid., 233.

cially refutes the Roman Catholic concept of the priesthood. Additional topics include church discipline, the role of tradition, the use of homilies, and the consecration of bishops and ministers.

In dealing at length with the sacraments of the church Griffith Thomas contrasts the Anglican and Roman Catholic views. He rejects five of the seven Roman Catholic sacraments (confirmation, penance, orders, matrimony, and extreme unction).[128] He also refutes the *ex opere operato* view, that is, the idea that if no barriers are present, the sacraments invariably convey grace.[129] He rejects as well the Roman Catholic doctrines of baptismal regeneration, transubstantiation, and the mass.[130] Only water baptism and the Lord's Supper are to be understood as sacraments in that they are divinely appointed means through which God's presence and blessing are received in faith.[131] They are visible expressions of membership in the community of those who are professed followers of Christ; at the same time they are divine assurances and pledges of the fulfilment of the promises proclaimed in the Word.[132]

Finally, there is a discussion of the relationship between the church and state. Elements distinctive of Anglicanism abound as the relationship between the church and the king of England is defined and defended. The Articles establish the right of believers to possess private property and take oaths in court. The state possesses the right to exercise capital punishment and to conscript its citizens into military service.

The value of *The Principles of Theology*, as of all the literary contributions of W. H. Griffith Thomas, lies in its analysis of Scripture and the basics of the Christian faith. In that the essentials do not change, his works represent a lasting contribution to the church. He is masterful in his ability

to interpret Scripture, and in his ability to relate Scripture, reason, and church history (both past and present). His powers of analysis, synthesis, and clarification impress the mind. Yet his writings also consistently create in the reader a deeper love for the Lord as revealed in his Word. One may well concur with the assessment of William Pettingill: "I found in him a wonderful blending of strength and gentleness, wisdom and teachableness, profundity and simplicity, firmness and tenderness; and in all this he resembled his Master and Lord, of Whom it is written that He was 'full of truth and grace.'"[133]

Primary Sources

Griffith Thomas, W. H. *The Apostle John: His Life and Writings.* Grand Rapids: Kregel, 1984.

_____. *The Apostle Peter: His Life and Writings.* Grand Rapids: Kregel, 1984.

_____. *The Catholic Faith: A Manual of Instruction for Members of the Church of England.* New York: Longmans, Green, 1920.

_____. *Christianity Is Christ.* Grand Rapids: Kregel, n.d.

_____. *Genesis: A Devotional Commentary.* Grand Rapids: Kregel, n.d.

_____. *Grace and Power.* New York: Revell, 1916.

_____. *Hebrews: A Devotional Commentary.* Grand Rapids: Eerdmans, 1962.

_____. *The Holy Spirit of God.* London: Longmans, Green, 1913. Reprint. Grand Rapids: Kregel, 1986.

_____. *Ministerial Life and Work.* Abridged by Alice Griffith Thomas from *The Work of the Ministry.* Chicago: Bible Institute Colportage Association, 1927. Reprint. Grand Rapids: Baker, 1974.

_____. *Outline Studies in Luke.* Edited by Winifred G. T. Gillespie. Grand Rapids: Kregel, 1984.

_____. *Outline Studies in Matthew.* Edited by Winifred G. T. Gillespie. Grand Rapids: Kregel, 1985.

128. Ibid., 351–57, 362.
129. Ibid., 357–64.
130. Ibid., 381, 393–400, 415–26.
131. Ibid., 357, 362.
132. Ibid., 343, 357.

133. Pettingill, "What Dr. Griffith Thomas Meant to Us," 412.

_____. *Outline Studies in the Acts of the Apostles.* Edited by Winifred G. T. Gillespie. Grand Rapids: Eerdmans, 1956.

_____. *The Prayers of St. Paul.* New York: Scribner, 1914.

_____. *The Principles of Theology: An Introduction to the Thirty-nine Articles.* New York: Longmans, Green, 1930. Reprint. Grand Rapids: Baker, 1979.

_____. *St. Paul's Epistle to the Romans.* Grand Rapids: Eerdmans, 1946.

_____. *Sermon Outlines on Christian Living.* Grand Rapids: Kregel, 1988.

_____. *Studies in Colossians and Philemon.* Edited by Winifred G. T. Gillespie. Grand Rapids: Kregel, 1986.

_____. *Through the Pentateuch Chapter by Chapter.* Grand Rapids: Kregel, 1985.

_____. *The Work of the Ministry.* New York: Hodder and Stoughton, n.d.

Secondary Source

Clark, M. Guthrie. *William Henry Griffith Thomas (1861–1924): Minister, Scholar, Teacher.* London: Church Book Room, 1949.

Lewis Sperry Chafer

Craig A. Blaising

From a background of ministry in turn-of-the-century revivalism and teaching at Bible conferences, Lewis Sperry Chafer (1871–1952) founded Dallas Theological Seminary and served as its first president and principal theologian. An author of several books on evangelism, prophecy, and the Christian life, Chafer is best known for his eight-volume *Systematic Theology*, which was the first dispensational, premillennial systematic theology. Although many works have helped spread the influence of dispensationalism, the institutional and theological efforts of Lewis Sperry Chafer have been foremost in establishing it as a viable feature of twentieth-century evangelical thought and ministry.

Life

Lewis Chafer was born in Rock Creek, Ohio, where his father later became the Congregational minister.[1] Following up on

an early interest in music, Lewis studied at Oberlin College and Conservatory. In 1889 he joined the evangelistic team of A. T.

1. For Chafer's life and ministry see Charles F. Lincoln, "Lewis Sperry Chafer," *Bibliotheca Sacra* 109 (Oct.–Dec. 1952): 332–37; idem, "Biographical Sketch of the Author," in Lewis Sperry Chafer, *Systematic Theology*, 8 vols. (Dallas: Dallas Seminary Press, 1947–48), 8:3–6; John F. Walvoord, "Lewis Sperry Chafer," *Sunday School Times*, 11 October 1952, pp. 855, 868–70; John D. Hannah, "The Early Years of Lewis Sperry Chafer," *Bibliotheca Sacra* 144 (Jan.–March 1987): 3–23; idem, "Chafer, Lewis Sperry (1871–1952)," in *Dictionary of Christianity in America*, ed. Daniel G. Reid et al. (Downers Grove, Ill.: Inter-Varsity, 1990), 237–38; and Jeffrey J. Richards, *The Promise of Dawn: The Eschatology of Lewis Sperry Chafer* (Lanham, Md.: University Press of America, 1991). For histories of Dallas Theological Seminary see Lewis Sperry Chafer, "Twenty Years of Experience," *Dallas Theological Seminary Bulletin* 19 (July–Sept. 1943): 3–4; Rudolf A. Renfer, "A History of Dallas Theological Seminary," Ph.D. diss., University of Texas, 1959; and John D. Hannah, "The Social and Intellectual History of the Origins of the Evangelical Theological College," Ph.D. diss., University of Texas at Dallas, 1988. The work by Hannah offers the most extensive analysis of archival material and corrects other histories on important points. The biographical summary given here is indebted primarily to Hannah's work.

Reed. Because his activities had increased, Chafer withdrew from Oberlin in 1891. For five years he ministered with Reed (and occasionally other evangelists) as a revivalist singer and choir director.

In 1896 Lewis married Ella Loraine Case, whom he had met during student days at Oberlin. Together they formed their own evangelistic team with Lewis preaching and singing and Ella accompanying at the piano. For the next ten years they held revival meetings throughout Ohio, Pennsylvania, New York, and New Jersey. Eventually these meetings extended to the southeastern states as well.

Soon after they formed their own ministry team, the Chafers became acquainted with key figures in the music ministry of Dwight L. Moody's evangelistic empire, notably Ira Sankey and George Stebbins. After a two-year position as assistant pastor of the First Congregational Church in Buffalo (where Lewis was ordained), the Chafers moved in 1901 to East Northfield, Massachusetts, the site of the Moody summer conference. In addition to his ongoing revivalism, Lewis became more and more a part of the Moody ministry, directing singing at the Northfield Conference and then helping to establish (in 1904) and eventually presiding over (in 1909) the Southfield Conference in Crescent City, Florida.

The Northfield Conference was a primary forum for the Victorious Life movement and for expositions of the Bible in the style of the popular Niagara Bible Conferences. Some of the well-known speakers at that time included F. B. Meyer, G. Campbell Morgan, W. H. Griffith Thomas, Reuben Torrey, and George F. Pentecost. Through various conferences over the years, Chafer also came into contact with James Orr, James M. Gray, A. C. Gaebelein, Harry A. Ironside, A. T. Pierson, and Charles Trumbull.[2] But by far the one person who had the most profound impact upon Chafer was C. I. Scofield.

At the time that Chafer moved to Northfield, Scofield not only was a speaker at the summer conference, but lived in the community, presiding over the Northfield Bible Training School and pastoring the Trinitarian Congregational Church. Before coming to Northfield in 1895, Scofield had already established himself both in Congregationalist circles (as a pastor and superintendent of home missions in Dallas) and in interdenominational ministry (as founder of the Central American Mission, director of a Bible correspondence course, and featured speaker at various Bible and prophecy conferences). But in 1901 Scofield, with the encouragement of colleagues like Gaebelein, committed himself to a new undertaking, the preparation of a reference Bible with notes presenting expositional and doctrinal themes which he had taught and shared with others at the Bible conferences.

Soon after Chafer arrived in Northfield, he attended the Bible training school. That year, 1901, brought few revival meetings, so Chafer devoted much of his time to study under Scofield's tutelage. Scofield's impact can be seen in Chafer's own testimony: "Until that time, I had never heard a real Bible teacher. . . . My first hearing of Dr. Scofield was at a morning Bible class at the Bible School. He was teaching the sixth chapter of Romans. I am free to confess that it seemed to me at the close that I had seen more vital truth in God's Word in that one hour than I had seen in all my life before. It was a crisis for me. I was captured for life."[3]

The two men developed a teacher-disciple relationship that grew over the years despite Scofield's frequent relocations for the purpose of working on his reference Bible. When Scofield challenged him to redirect his ministry from evangelism to Bible teaching, Chafer became increasingly active as a teacher at Bible conferences. In 1909 the Scofield Reference Bible was published, and Chafer also published his first theological book, *Satan,*

---

2. Hannah, "Social and Intellectual History," 114–17; Chafer, "Twenty Years of Experience," 3.

3. Lewis Sperry Chafer, "What I Learned from Dr. Scofield," *Sunday School Times,* 4 March 1922, p. 120.

which had been composed with Scofield's assistance.[4] Two years later, Scofield established the Scofield School of the Bible in New York City. Chafer was appointed director of the Department of Oral Extension. In this capacity he traveled widely, teaching at conferences and holding seminars called "Bible Institutes." In 1914 Chafer helped Scofield found a second school, the Philadelphia School of the Bible. Chafer served on the faculty and developed the curriculum. To serve the two schools, in Philadelphia and New York, as well as continue his conference teaching, Lewis and Ella moved in 1915 from Northfield to East Orange, New Jersey.

Chafer continued in his capacity as a teacher of Bible and theology until Scofield's death in 1921. Most of Chafer's theological views were shaped and finalized in those years, and it was during this time that he published most of his books. *True Evangelism*, published in 1911 but written in 1901, was a critique of the methods and practices of many revivalists.[5] *The Kingdom in History and Prophecy* (1915) offered a systematic presentation of Scofieldian eschatology.[6] *Salvation* (1917), while claiming to be an evangelistic rather than a theological work, nevertheless presented doctrinal features which were later taken up in Chafer's *Systematic Theology*.[7] *He That Is Spiritual* (1918) presented Chafer's version of the Victorious Life movement.[8] Finally, *Grace* (1922), published the year after Scofield's death and dedicated to him, comprehensively distinguished between law and grace.[9]

In 1922, Chafer moved to Dallas, where he assumed Scofield's former pastorate at the First Congregational Church, which at Chafer's suggestion was renamed the Scofield Memorial Church. He was also appointed general secretary of the Central American Mission, a ministry which Scofield had founded. However, Chafer's real interest remained in theological education.

From his days at Northfield on through his work with Scofield, Chafer had nurtured the vision of a theological seminary which would train ministers as Bible teachers matching the skills of those who expounded so effectively at Bible conferences. Conversations with many pastors about their seminary training and informal discussions with students during a lecture tour of some colleges and seminaries in 1912 led him to believe that the typical seminary curriculum failed to impart both a knowledge of the spiritual content of the Bible and skill in teaching and applying it.[10] Consequently, he determined to establish a school which would redress that omission in the regular course of seminary studies. Reflecting the Bible conference movement, the school would not affiliate with any denomination. This would allow it the widest possible sphere of ministry in American evangelicalism. As for his own affiliation, Chafer maintained his ordination in the Presbyterian church (having in 1906 transferred his credentials from the Congregational church to the Presbyterian Church in the U.S.A., and then in 1912 to the Presbyterian Church in the United States). As a re-

4. Lewis Sperry Chafer, *Satan: His Motive and Methods* (New York: Gospel, 1909).

5. Lewis Sperry Chafer, *True Evangelism* (New York: Gospel, 1911; Philadelphia: Sunday School Times, 1919).

6. Lewis Sperry Chafer, *The Kingdom in History and Prophecy* (New York: Revell, 1915).

7. Lewis Sperry Chafer, *Salvation* (New York: C. C. Cook, 1917).

8. Lewis Sperry Chafer, *He That Is Spiritual* (New York: Our Hope, 1918).

9. Lewis Sperry Chafer, *Grace* (Philadelphia: Sunday School Times, 1922).

10. Chafer apparently saw impartation of this knowledge and skill as a corrective to the critical study of the Bible that was being done in many schools. The issue was not simply modernism, but their focus on philological and exegetical matters apart from a devotional use of the text. Chafer felt that the teaching at the Bible conferences was well received by the churches precisely because it was devotional and applicable. As he saw it, the need of his day was for a seminary that would combine philological and devotional study of the Bible. See Chafer, "Twenty Years of Experience," 3–4; Hannah, "Social and Intellectual History," 164–93.

sult, a majority of the first students in his new seminary would be Presbyterian.

After considering several possible locations for the new seminary, Dallas was chosen. Backing came principally from the Scofield Memorial Church, which Chafer pastored, and the First Presbyterian Church, pastored by William M. Anderson, Jr. The school began in 1924 as the Evangelical Theological College, a name suggested by W. H. Griffith Thomas to reflect the British model of theological colleges. In 1936 the name was changed to Dallas Theological Seminary.

From 1924 to 1952 Chafer served as president and professor of systematic theology at the school he had founded. In order to devote full attention to the school, he resigned from the Central American Mission in 1925 and from his pastorate in 1926. But he continued to travel widely, teaching and preaching in churches and at Bible conferences. He wrote in various periodicals including the *Sunday School Times* and *Our Hope*. In 1926 a collection of Chafer's theological articles in the *Sunday School Times* was published as *Major Bible Themes*.[11] In 1933 the seminary acquired ownership of *Bibliotheca Sacra*. Rollin T. Chafer (Lewis's brother) served as editor. After Rollin's death in 1940, Lewis took over as sole editor. He used the journal to publish installments of his final and most noteworthy writing, the *Systematic Theology*. When this work was fully published in 1948, it covered eight volumes, incorporating a fair amount of material from his earlier books.

The financial and administrative burden of carrying a school without denominational support through the depression years took its toll. Rising controversy about Scofieldian dispensationalism added to Chafer's concerns. In June 1935 he suffered a heart attack while participating in a conference on the West Coast and was out of the classroom for most of 1935–36. Ella Chafer died in 1944 after a four-year illness. Hav-

ing experienced recurring health problems in 1945 and 1948, Lewis Chafer died while ministering in Seattle in August 1952.

Systematic Theology

Systematic Theology is clearly Chafer's magnum opus.[12] The product of years of study under Scofield and as professor of systematic theology at Dallas, it represents the culmination of Chafer's dream of bringing the teaching found in the Bible conferences into formal theological instruction. The work is basically Reformed in its theological orientation.[13] There are many discussions which follow the scholastic pattern of nineteenth-century systematic theologies. Chafer's moderate Calvinism is seen in his discussion of the decrees of God, predestination, and the atonement.[14] His position on the inspiration and authority of Scripture is identical to that of the Old Princeton theology of Charles Hodge and B. B. Warfield, the Bible conferences, and the fundamentalist movement in general. The uniqueness of Chafer's *Systematic Theology* is found in what he called its unabridged scope, which refers to its inclusion of material popularized in the Bible conferences and the Scofield Reference Bible. It claimed to be the first premillennial systematic theology; and by virtue of its inclusion of various emphases of the Scofield Reference Bible, Chafer's work was also

11. Lewis Sperry Chafer, *Major Bible Themes* (Philadelphia: Sunday School Times, 1926).

12. A recent abridgment of this work appeared as Lewis Sperry Chafer, *Systematic Theology*, ed. John F. Walvoord, Donald K. Campbell, and Roy B. Zuck, 2 vols. (Wheaton, Ill.: Victor, 1988). While following Chafer's outline, this work is a thorough revision which alters some of his unique theological views.

13. John F. Walvoord, "A Review of Lewis Sperry Chafer's 'SYSTEMATIC THEOLOGY,'" *Bibliotheca Sacra* 105 (Jan.–March 1948): 120–23. Walvoord also hailed it as the first systemization of modern fundamentalism (p. 127). In a review of Henry Meeter's *Calvinism*, Chafer himself noted, "It may be assumed that Bible expositors almost without exception are Calvinists" (*Bibliotheca Sacra* 96 [Oct.–Dec. 1939]: 491).

14. Chafer's "moderate Calvinism" is self-defined as an infralapsarian view of the divine decrees to which he has added the position of unlimited atonement (Chafer, *Systematic Theology*, 3:179–88).

seen as the first dispensational systematic theology ("dispensational" is here a reference to the views expressed in Scofield's notes).

The preface of *Systematic Theology* reprints the substance of "Evils of an Abridged Systematic Theology," an article published by Chafer in 1934. Here Chafer outlines seven areas (he was fond of the number seven) which in his estimation were either lacking or received inadequate treatment in other systematic theologies:

1. *The divine program of the ages.* Chafer gives an account of the dispensations and ages included in the scope of divine revelation. His concern is not only their order, but also their different purposes.
2. *The church, the body of Christ.* For various reasons, several nineteenth-century Reformed systematic theologies produced in the United States paid no attention to ecclesiology.[15] But Chafer's *Systematic Theology* not only included traditional ecclesiological issues, but carefully elaborated the themes of the universal church and what he called the church's unique rule of life vis-à-vis other dispensations. The volume on ecclesiology summarizes Chafer's earlier work in the area of dispensationalism.
3. *Human conduct and the spiritual life.* Repeating the themes of *He That Is Spiritual,* Chafer extends some dispensational distinctions to his discussion of the Christian life (found in the volumes on ecclesiology and pneumatology). Here he also distinguishes between the rule of life and Christian conduct. In this dispensation the rule of life concerns spirituality—living by the Spirit. Christian conduct is the result of following this rule of life—one adjusts one's behavior in accordance with the energizing power of the Holy Spirit.

4. *Angelology.* Chafer organizes in a somewhat scholastic fashion the biblical data on angels. He includes a study of Satan which incorporates much of his first publication. A special section covers the relationship between Satan and sin. This material supports Chafer's dispensational view of grace as distinguished from moralism and modernism.
5. *Typology.* While Chafer does not devote any specific division of his systematic theology to the subject of typology, he frequently draws upon it to support his theological studies, especially in Christology. The study of types was popular in the Bible conferences and a major feature in the notes of the Scofield Reference Bible.
6. *Prophecy and premillennial eschatology.* Chafer's lists and classifications of various prophecies are unique among the standard theologies.
7. *Christ's present session in heaven.* In a section bridging his Christology and ecclesiology, Chafer analyzes various biblical images of Christ's relation to the church and his threefold priestly ministry as Giver of gifts, Intercessor, and Advocate.

Chafer's *Systematic Theology* is a synthesis of a traditional scholastic study of theology with the outlines and topical classification schemes made popular in the Bible conferences. The result is a unique treatment of many themes. It is no wonder that *Systematic Theology* became in its day the definitive statement of dispensational theology.

Key Theological Ideas

Grace

The key to Chafer's theology is his doctrine of grace, which supports a highly spiritual, mystical view of Christianity.[16] As Chafer sees it, true Christianity is the in-

---

15. This omission is also noted by Louis Berkhof, *Systematic Theology,* rev. ed. (Grand Rapids: Eerdmans, 1941), 553–54.

16. The extent to which this doctrine pervades all of Chafer's writings is especially evident in *Grace.*

dwelling of God in human beings: God, by the Holy Spirit, first regenerates us and then directly enacts works of service through us. This divine action is completely free—God is not obligated to do it. Yet this action can and will take place whenever a sinner believes or a believer yields to the Holy Spirit. At such times the manifestation of divine power is full and complete. On the other hand, God's action in and through us can be fully hindered by failure on our part to believe or yield. Except for this simple response of believing or yielding (which Chafer calls a "right adjustment of the heart"), the Christian life is in no way dependent on us. It is, rather, God's directly acting in us. It is heaven's living a heavenly mode of life in us.

Chafer acknowledges that this idea of Christianity is imperfectly realized by Christians now; it will, however, be fully realized in heaven. Part of the problem, as Chafer sees it, is confusion caused by the ethical teachings of postmillennialism, liberalism, moralism, some varieties of revivalism, and the works-righteousness inculcated by Roman Catholicism, Arminianism, and various cults.[17] All of these lead in one way or another to self-directed activities which, while they envision ideals that are good and moral in themselves, fall short of the Christian standards taught in the New Testament. Worse still, these self-directed activities miss, hinder, and even oppose the only effectual power of Christian living! God cannot and will not live in someone who is trying to merit divine approval or to carry out the divine commands by human will. In true Christianity, one can be made righteous only by God and in the way that he requires.

Another reason why Christianity is imperfectly realized today is the forces which support and affirm the self-directed, merit-seeking form of living. These forces include the devil, the world system, and our "flesh."

By "flesh" Chafer means not only "the sin nature," depravity, our disposition to sin, but the human self—its self-directed planning and volition.[18]

Dispensations

In teaching that Christianity is a religion of pure grace, Chafer faced the difficulty that the Bible can be and sometimes is used to support a religion in which divine favor is merited and righteousness is understood as human accomplishments of divine commands. As Chafer saw it, the problem here is that the Scripture actually presents more than one religion, more than one rule of life. In interpreting the Scripture, we must be careful to discern the rule of life which is applicable to Christians today and to distinguish it from rules of life which characterized other dispensations.[19]

Chafer held to Scofield's division of seven dispensations. He defended Scofield's definition of a dispensation—"a period of time during which man is tested in respect of obedience to some *specific* revelation of the will of God."[20] And he accepted Scofield's idea that the seven dispensations are united in the purpose of revealing human sin.[21] Most of Chafer's writings on dispensations, however, are concerned with distinguishing the present dispensation of grace from the past dispensation of law and the future dispensation of

---

17. Chafer, *Grace*, xii–xiv; idem, *He That Is Spiritual*, 8–9; idem, *Satan*, 46, 66, 104–11; idem, *Systematic Theology*, 4:168.

18. Chafer takes the Pauline term *flesh* to refer to humanity as such. The struggle in the Christian life, then, is not simply between the Spirit and human depravity, but between the Spirit and humanity, between Spirit-initiated activity and human-directed activity. See Chafer, *Grace*, 49–50, 55, 339–40; idem, *He That Is Spiritual*, 48 (cf. 46), 140–42; idem, *Satan*, 26, 47, 92–95.

19. Chafer noted that while these different rules of life are to some extent mixed in Scripture, they should not be confused in the mind of the interpreter (*Grace*, 124, 128–29, 232, 245).

20. Lewis Sperry Chafer, *Dispensationalism* (Dallas: Dallas Theological Seminary, 1936), 9. He later defined a dispensation as "a period [of time] which is identified by its relation to some particular purpose of God—a purpose to be accomplished within that period" (*Systematic Theology*, 1:40).

21. Chafer, *Grace*, 135.

the kingdom. A distinct rule of life governs each of these three dispensations. But in actual fact Chafer concentrated on the even more fundamental twofold division between law and grace. For although the kingdom carries features not found in the Old Testament—the Messiah rules on earth in fulfilment of Old Testament prophecies and a new covenant is enacted—nevertheless, both the old dispensation under the Mosaic law and the dispensation of the kingdom are "pure law."[22] Chafer characterizes both as Judaism in contrast to Christianity, the religion and rule of life of the present dispensation.[23]

Unfortunately, at this point many have misunderstood Chafer, and he himself seems to have had difficulty in clearing up the misunderstanding.[24] These two fundamentally different rules of life, these two religions, and these three distinct dispensations do not really have the same concern. They are not different ways of achieving the same type of salvation. (Nor, on the other hand, are two different ways of salvation possible in the same dispensation.)[25] Rather, these two religions presented in Scripture entail *completely different kinds of salvation!* Judaism, as Chafer presents it, is an earthly religion. It concerns prosperity, peace, and security on the earth for a particular race and nation of people. When

Chafer says that in the past these blessings were merited by works, he is not talking about salvation as understood in the present dispensation, but about the theocratic blessings of Israel (found, e.g., in Deut. 28). There was, however, unmerited grace even in that dispensation, for the Jews were born into their covenant standing (quite apart from their own personal efforts) and were, like Abraham, justified by faith.[26] With this foundation, God gave them a legal rule of life which marked a dispensational change: at Sinai they voluntarily relinquished the rule of grace.[27]

It is important to understand that the Bible presents two peoples of God related to him by two different religions. The Jews are an earthly people with earthly promises about an earthly inheritance.[28] In the past dispensation they had (and in the future dispensation they will have) a rule of life which was (will be) pure law, a rule that actually appealed to the flesh and consequently is designated earthly. When Chafer spoke of the eternal salvation of Israel, he distinguished between national salvation, that is, the eternal endurance of the nation, and personal salvation, which is eternal life in the earthly kingdom. While this personal salvation is secured by observing the law as a rule of life, it should be kept in mind that the law itself is a system which includes God's gracious acceptance of the Jews through their sacrifices, which is in turn based on the unconditional covenants into which the descendants of Abraham are born.[29] (It is curious that throughout these discussions Chafer is silent about Gentiles in the past and future dispensations.)

22. Ibid., 124. In order to distinguish these two dispensations, Chafer teaches that the legal requirements are more severe in the kingdom than under the law (p. 125; see also Chafer, *Systematic Theology,* 4:167, 169–70).

23. Chafer, *Kingdom in History and Prophecy,* 64; idem, *Dispensationalism,* 41; idem, *Systematic Theology,* 4:14–15. Various of Chafer's editorials also make this distinction between Christianity and Judaism: "Theology," *Bibliotheca Sacra* 104 (Jan.–March 1947): 1–2; "Judaism," *Bibliotheca Sacra* 104 (April–June 1947): 129–30; "Dispensationalism," *Bibliotheca Sacra* 106 (Jan.–March 1949): 2; "Judaism," *Bibliotheca Sacra* 106 (Oct.–Dec. 1949): 385–86.

24. Lewis Sperry Chafer, "Inventing Heretics through Misunderstanding," *Bibliotheca Sacra* 102 (Jan.–March 1945): 1–2.

25. Lewis Sperry Chafer, "Are There Two Ways to Be Saved?" *Bibliotheca Sacra* 105 (Jan.–March 1948): 1–2.

26. Ibid., 1; Chafer, *Systematic Theology,* 4:15; idem, "Inventing Heretics through Misunderstanding," 2; Lewis Sperry Chafer, "Justification," *Bibliotheca Sacra* 103 (April–June 1946): 129–34.

27. Chafer, *Grace,* 114–16.

28. On the two distinct religions see n. 23; on the complete contrast between the heavenly and earthly nature of these religions, see Chafer, *Systematic Theology,* 4:47–53.

29. Chafer, *Systematic Theology,* 4:24–25.

The present dispensation concerns not an earthly people, but a heavenly people—the church—made up of believing Jews and Gentiles without earthly (racial, political) distinctions. These people do not have an earthly inheritance, but a heavenly home. When raised from the dead or transformed at the rapture, they will enter into heaven, their eternal abode. Their salvation is heavenly; it is a manifestation of divine life and power not only in justification by grace through faith, but also in regeneration, indwelling by the Holy Spirit, and adoption as children of the household of God. As their salvation differs from that of the earthly people of the dispensation of law, so does their rule of life. It is not a rule of works or merit, which is fleshly, earthly, but a heavenly rule, an energizing by divine power. The principles (to distinguish them from the rule of merit, Chafer avoids the word *commands*) of this heavenly rule presume the values of the old law, but are higher, more heavenly, and in fact impossible from an earthly, fleshly perspective.[30] Divine empowerment, which is not merited in any way but "released" through a "right adjustment of the heart," is the only means for accomplishing those heavenly principles.

In the present dispensation, the rule is blessing followed by "beseechings" (rather than "commands"). In the past and future dispensations, the order is commandment followed by blessing.[31] The rules of life are different, their relations to works are different, and the blessings are different.

Chafer's distinction between law and grace has sometimes been accused of antinomianism. But the accusation is usually the result of a misunderstanding. Chafer certainly did not advocate lawlessness;

quite the contrary, he believed that the moral values of law are upheld in grace. And though the rule of law—the meriting of divine favor—is absent in grace, there are divine imperatives for Christians in this dispensation.[32] Sometimes Chafer referred to them as the law of Christ, but mostly as divine beseechings, to emphasize that blessing precedes law in this dispensation. These beseechings, divine imperatives, define Christian conduct, which is distinguishable (but not separate) from the rule of grace. The responsibility of the believer in the rule of grace is confession of sin and a right adjustment of the heart. When this responsibility is carried out, divine power will accomplish the beseechings (which include many imperatives from the law of the earlier dispensation), and Christian conduct will be manifest. While condemning lawlessness, understood as sin or approval of sin, Chafer, in contrast to legalism, emphasizes a radical faith-mysticism as the key to fulfilling the righteous requirements of the law, which are found in the divine beseechings given to Christians in this dispensation. Chafer's key concern might be summed up as a Pauline revision of James's maxim: apart from faith, works are dead!

Chafer taught that Christians are required to conduct themselves as citizens of heaven. The key here is yieldedness to the Spirit (right adjustment of the heart). When we yield to him, God works through us. We are conscious of exercising our faculties in carrying out the divine beseechings and thus experience victory in the Christian life.[33]

Premillennialism

A primary focus of the premillennialism which Chafer inherited from Scofield and late-nineteenth-century conferences on the Bible and prophecy was an opposition to postmillennialism. Chafer interpreted postmillennialism as another form of legalism,

---

30. Chafer, *Grace*, 199. Unfortunately, Chafer's attempt to relate the teachings of law and grace is obscured by contradictory terminology. For example, he says that the teachings of grace contain the principles of the law but not its precepts (pp. 90, 104), but later on he says that they restate the precepts of the law (p. 153).

31. Ibid., 182–85.

32. Ibid., 344; Chafer, *Systematic Theology*, 4:184.

33. Chafer, *Grace*, 338–39; idem, *He That Is Spiritual*, 49, 59, 122, 171–72, 185.

another attempt to reform human beings and society apart from the specific means that God has purposed. By contrast the premillennial view relegates the biblical predictions of an eschatological kingdom to the future, making it clear that a reformation of society based on human self-effort is not God's plan for the present, although it does fit the divine plan for history after the return of Christ. In the meantime, we should attend to the biblical teachings on grace in order to understand present Christian existence.[34]

After the return of Christ, Israel's legal relationship with God will be reestablished; and their social, political, and earthly blessings will be restored. Consequently, all legal teachings connected with predictions about the kingdom should be relegated to that future period. On this basis Chafer, following Scofield, deferred to the future dispensation the primary application of the ethic of Jesus in the Gospels, including, for example, the Sermon on the Mount.[35] Only its basic values and principles find application today.

The present dispensation was to Chafer an intercalation in the divine plan for Israel; it is wholly unrelated to that plan, having instead its own divinely ordained purpose.[36] To emphasize the distinctiveness of the present dispensation, he stressed pretribulationism. Pretribulationism maintains the hope for the imminent return of Christ, a doctrine that clearly distinguishes premillennialism from postmillennialism.[37] Pretribulationists keep their hopes fixed on heaven, as is proper for a heavenly people. They do not fix their expectations on developments on earth.

The pretribulational hope ought to prevent premillennialists from identifying present events of history as part of the tribulation, as fulfilments of the visions of Daniel, Ezekiel, and Revelation. However, the controversy with postmillennialism, the conviction that the present was an evil age in decline toward the apocalypse, and the events of the early twentieth century led some pretribulationists to speculate about the relationship of present events to the tribulation events which would follow the rapture of the church. In 1919 Chafer published a pamphlet entitled *Seven Major Biblical Signs of the Times*.[38] Most of the signs he mentions are general. Nevertheless, the pamphlet demonstrates Chafer's willingness to utilize social and political developments of the early twentieth century as a basis for speculating about the proximity of the Lord's coming.[39] He declines, however, to speculate about the date of the Lord's return. For Chafer the rapture is ever an imminent event.[40]

During the 1940s Chafer avoided identifying events of World War II with prophecy, preferring instead to issue warnings to political powers about policies that *could* lead to divine judgment, and comforting believers that such trials are bound to happen and will in fact characterize the period before the Lord's return to rule.[41] Other editorial writers also warned against falsely identifying present events as fulfilments of prophecy.[42]

Chafer's view of the kingdom was essentially the same as Scofield's. He distinguished between the kingdom of heaven and the kingdom of God, identifying the former as the divine government on the

34. Chafer, *Satan*, 29, 40, 42–43, 66–68, 73, 93–95; idem, *Kingdom in History and Prophecy*, 148–50.

35. Chafer, *Systematic Theology*, 5:99; idem, *Grace*, 161–81.

36. Chafer, *Systematic Theology*, 4:41 (cf. 34); 5:321.

37. Chafer, *Kingdom in History and Prophecy*, 103, 125.

38. Lewis Sperry Chafer, *Seven Major Biblical Signs of the Times* (Philadelphia: Sunday School Times, 1919).

39. See also Chafer, *Satan*, 102–3.

40. "It is 'timeless, signless, and unrelated,' excepting to that which is to follow" (Chafer, *Seven Major Biblical Signs*, 10).

41. See the editorials in *Bibliotheca Sacra* 97 (1940): 257–60, 388–89; 98 (1941): 129–31, 257–60; 99 (1942): 1–2.

42. E.g., Miner B. Stearns, "Is It the End?" *Bibliotheca Sacra* 99 (July–Sept. 1942): 259–61.

earth. It is manifest in three stages: (1) the kingdom as offered by Christ; (2) its present mystery form; and (3) its millennial form.[43] The key to understanding the kingdom of heaven is the millennial form, that is, the dispensation of the kingdom—the time in which the political promises to national Israel will be fulfilled under the rule of Jesus Christ. This will be a dispensation of pure law. Conditions will be much improved for earthly people during this period of Christ's reign on the earth (the church will be in heaven during this time). Jesus offered this kingdom to the Jews in his precross ministry. (That is why, according to Chafer, one must tie Jesus' ethic in the Gospels to the future kingdom as a legal ethic of works-righteousness.) Jesus was rejected, however, and a mystery form of the kingdom ensued and is now manifest. This form of the kingdom is Christendom, the current governmental state of the world.[44] Although present in this form of the kingdom, the church is not the kingdom. Its ethic is separate, its rule of life is different. It is one of the mysteries present in this second stage of the kingdom.

Chafer's view of the rule of grace along with his distinction of the church from the kingdom led him to criticize various efforts toward social reform. In his mind social reform was a wrongheaded goal of postmillennialism and modernism, and he did not hesitate to denounce it as misguided, even deluded by Satan.[45] His view of Christianity was conditioned by a strong individualism; political and social concern were wholly a matter for the future kingdom.[46]

In *Systematic Theology*, Chafer's ultimate work, amillennialism receives more criti-

cism than does postmillennialism, reflecting not only the decline of the latter during the two world wars, but also the increasing popularity of the former in Reformed circles and the rising debate between premillennialism and amillennialism during that same period. Chafer also connected amillennialism with the increased criticism of dispensationalism, criticism in which he was often the target.[47]

A Theology of Evangelism

Chafer's view of grace and its dispensational uniqueness had an important effect on his view of the message and practice of evangelism. The message of the gospel is simply the need to believe in Jesus Christ for salvation. It is not an appeal for any self-directed reformation of character, but for complete reliance upon God for regeneration. Accordingly, the evangelist is to avoid manipulation and high-pressure methods. Rather, the evangelist is to follow the rule of grace—confession of sin and complete reliance upon the Holy Spirit. The Spirit will then work through the evangelist to present the call directly to the heart of the hearer.[48]

Controversy

Chafer's attempt to systematize the theology of Scofield and of the Bible conference movement was not without opposition. For three decades, battles erupted in print regarding the purity and loyalty of Chafer's Reformed theology. It was natural

---

43. Chafer, *Kingdom in History and Prophecy*, 52–55.

44. Ibid., 95–117.

45. Chafer, *Satan*, 40, 66–68, 93.

46. Chafer saw a clear dichotomy between individual regeneration and social improvement of earthly conditions (*Satan*, 46). See also Michael D. Williams, "Where's the Church? The Church as the Unfinished Business of Dispensational Theology," *Grace Theological Journal* 10 (1989): 175–81.

47. Chafer, *Systematic Theology*, 5:255–63, 279–84.

48. These themes are developed in Chafer, *True Evangelism*; see also Lewis Sperry Chafer, "An Attack upon a Book," *Bibliotheca Sacra* 104 (April–June 1947): 130–34. Chafer felt that his theology of evangelism was consistent with the development of radio preaching and the methods of parachurch organizations such as Inter-Varsity Christian Fellowship, Young Life, and Child Evangelism Fellowship. See Lewis Sperry Chafer, "Salient Facts regarding Evangelism," *Bibliotheca Sacra* 101 (Oct.–Dec. 1944): 385–88; idem, "Modern Evangelism," *Bibliotheca Sacra* 103 (Oct.–Dec. 1946): 385–86; and idem, "Public Evangelism," *Bibliotheca Sacra* 105 (Oct.–Dec. 1948): 386.

that controversy should flare up in these circles since Chafer maintained his ordination in the Presbyterian church. To the end of his life he remained a member in good standing with his presbytery. But the controversies which ignited over his theological views led many other dispensationalists to depart from Presbyterianism.

In a 1919 review of Chafer's *He That Is Spiritual,* B. B. Warfield claimed that Chafer was in the "very uncomfortable condition of having two inconsistent systems of religion struggling together in his mind."[49] One was Reformed theology and the other was a Wesleyan Arminianism which pervaded the Higher Life movement and, according to Warfield, was promulgated by many of the Bible teachers and evangelists of the day. Warfield was at that time engaged in a critique of the Victorious Life movement.[50] He objected to Chafer's distinction between carnal and spiritual Christians, but even more to his teaching that the reception of divine power for sanctification depends on the believer's yielding, the right adjustment of one's heart. To Warfield, this seemed to say that while God makes sanctification possible, a human act makes it actual.

Warfield's criticism was not entirely just. Chafer repeatedly denied that the rule of grace has anything to do with merit—the blessings of God's grace in sanctification are not acquired or earned by human effort. And on this basis Chafer frequently criticized Arminianism. However, Chafer did not seem to be aware of the psychological effort which Victorious Life teaching entailed and which seemed to reside in his own notion that if we rightly adjust our heart, sanctification is total and complete, but if we do not, victory eludes us.

However, more fundamental was the conflict between what has since been called created and uncreated grace. Chafer took the view of uncreated grace: spirituality is actually the indwelling of God in the soul. Warfield, in his criticism of Chafer, took the view that grace is the creation of new character, new habits in a human being.

Controversy flared up again in 1936 with the appearance of several articles accusing dispensationalism, as taught by Scofield and Chafer, of denying the unity of the covenant of grace as expressed in the Westminster Confession.[51] The specific issue of dispute was the central motif in Chafer's (and Scofield's) theology: the existence of two different religions in the Bible. Chafer held that there are two peoples of God, one earthly and the other heavenly. They are governed by two different rules of life, law and grace; they experience two different kinds of blessing and have different eternal destinies, earthly for the one group and heavenly for the other.

The belief that the covenant of grace unifies the Scripture entailed the belief that the divine purpose expressed in the past dispensation was not substantially different from God's purpose in the present dispensation. Since this unity in the divine purpose was understood in Reformed circles as one way of salvation, Chafer's idea of two different divine purposes in the Bible was interpreted as two ways of salvation. It did not matter to his detractors that he viewed the death of Christ as equally foundational for both systems, law and grace, a fact which he himself believed exonerated him from the charge. That he saw in the Bible two substantially different religions (Christianity and Judaism) which entailed differ-

49. B. B. Warfield, review of *He That Is Spiritual,* by Lewis Sperry Chafer, *Princeton Theological Review* 17 (April 1919): 322.

50. B. B. Warfield, "The Victorious Life," *Princeton Theological Review* 16 (July 1918): 321–73.

51. Oswald T. Allis, "Modern Dispensationalism and the Doctrine of the Unity of Scripture," *Evangelical Quarterly* 8 (1936): 22–35. Several critical articles appeared in the 1936–37 issues of the *Presbyterian Guardian.* A review of the controversy is provided in the editorial "A Clarification of Some Issues," *Presbyterian Guardian,* 13 March 1937, pp. 217–20. Also note James E. Bear, "Dispensationalism and the Covenant of Grace," *Union Seminary Review* 49 (1938): 285–307. Bear offered an insightful and penetrating criticism that defined the issue for the investigative committee appointed five years later by the General Assembly of the Presbyterian Church in the United States. (Bear served on that committee.)

ent and opposed rules of life and different eternal destinies (heavenly vs. earthly) was sufficient in the minds of many to make stand the charge that he believed in two different kinds of salvation and thus two ways of salvation.

Objection was also raised to the way Chafer (and the Scofield Reference Bible) treated the Sermon on the Mount as pure law, distinguished between the kingdom of heaven and the kingdom of God in the Scripture,[52] and excluded the Lord's Prayer from use in the present dispensation. It was pointed out, for example, that the Westminster Shorter Catechism has an extended discussion of the meaning of the Lord's Prayer for Christians in this dispensation.

In 1936 Chafer responded with a lengthy article in *Bibliotheca Sacra* entitled "Dispensationalism," which Dallas Theological Seminary also published as a separate booklet by the same name. In it he reasserted his basic proposals and argued that, while covenant theology is relatively recent, theologians throughout the history of the church have recognized dispensations. He also argued that dispensationalism cannot be properly evaluated by reference to the Westminster Confession but only by reference to the Scripture.

Chafer acknowledged that he worked from premises different from those of the covenant theologians. He did not deny the charge that he rejected the concept of a unifying covenant of grace (although he would later teach it in his *Systematic Theology*). Furthermore, under his editorship *Bibliotheca Sacra* published an article both criticizing that belief and labeling covenantal theology a recent innovation.[53]

In 1943 the Presbyterian Church in the United States appointed an ad interim committee to study the matter of whether dis-

pensationalism was in accord with the Westminster Confession. Ernest Thompson summarizes the result: "This committee, composed of representatives from the theological seminaries, to whom a couple of old-fashioned premillenarians were later added, brought in a lengthy and carefully worded report, adopted practically without debate, which ended with the unanimous judgment of the committee that dispensationalism was 'out of accord with the system of the doctrine set forth in the Confession of Faith, not primarily or simply in the field of eschatology, but because it attacks the very heart of the theology of our church.'"[54] The General Assembly took no official action on the report. Nevertheless, it circulated widely and was seen by many Presbyterians as a sufficient basis for excluding dispensationalists from ministerial positions in their churches.[55]

When his loyalty to the Westminster Confession was attacked, Chafer repeatedly appealed to Scripture, which all acknowledged to be foundational to that creed. His opponents steadfastly refused to engage the issue on this level, defining their purpose strictly as a matter of adherence to the confession. In two lengthy editorials in *Bibliotheca Sacra*—the first during the deliberations of the ad interim committee and the second immediately after the presentation of its conclusions—Chafer challenged the General Assembly to revise the confession to include the teaching of dispensationalism.[56] He appealed to the authority of

52. John Murray, "The 'Kingdom of Heaven' and the 'Kingdom of God,'" *Presbyterian Guardian*, 9 January 1937, pp. 139–41.

53. Charles F. Lincoln, "The Development of the Covenant Theory," *Bibliotheca Sacra* 100 (Jan.–March 1943): 134–63.

54. Ernest Trice Thompson, *Presbyterians in the South*, 3 vols. (Richmond: John Knox, 1963–73), 3:488.

55. *Dispensationalism and the Confession of Faith. Report of the Ad Interim Committee on Changes in the Confession of Faith and Catechisms on the Question as to Whether the Type of Bible Interpretation Known as Dispensationalism Is in Harmony with the Confession of Faith* (Richmond: Board of Christian Education, Presbyterian Church in the United States, 1944).

56. Lewis Sperry Chafer, "Dispensational Distinctions Challenged," *Bibliotheca Sacra* 100 (July–Sept. 1943): 337–45; idem, "Dispensational Distinctions Denounced," *Bibliotheca Sacra* 101 (July–Sept. 1944): 257–60.

Scripture over the confession and presented dispensational teachings as newly discovered doctrinal truths. Pointing out that the confession acknowledged its dependence on the Bible, Chafer called for an evaluation of dispensationalism on biblical grounds to determine whether the creed should be revised.

When Chafer published his *Systematic Theology* in 1947–48, he included several harsh comments reflecting the controversies of the preceding years. Critical comments were made about the covenant of grace, although in the first volume he affirmed a traditional three-covenant structure.[57] Moreover, in editorials in *Bibliotheca Sacra* up to the time of his death, Chafer defended the notion of two religions in the Bible. Even though he denounced the charge that he believed in two ways of salvation (which offended him more than did the charge that he denied the unity of the covenant of grace), he continued to insist that the requirements for and benefits of salvation are distinct in Judaism and Christianity.[58]

Legacy

Lewis Chafer served a movement which had already become a major feature in American evangelicalism, but his theological and institutional efforts provided a framework not only to maintain but also to broaden its influence. Many of those who founded dispensationalist colleges and seminaries, who served as faculty in those institutions, and who wrote dispensational

theologies in the next generation were trained by him. The controversies in which he became embroiled led to a decline of dispensational influence in Presbyterian circles. They also produced a sharpness and divisiveness that troubled both fundamentalists and the newly forming evangelical coalitions. Yet Chafer himself encouraged evangelical cooperation. He hailed the formation of the National Association of Evangelicals and applauded the work of such organizations as Young Life, Youth for Christ, and Inter-Varsity Christian Fellowship.[59] Many graduates of his seminary served in these organizations as well as in churches, schools, and missions around the world. Thus, in spite of tensions and controversies, Chafer maintained an evangelical ecumenical vision which carried over from the days of the great Bible conferences.

By systematizing the theology of Scofield and the Bible conference movement, Chafer helped maintain the continuing influence of the dispensational tradition. In his own way he passed on to a later generation those features which continue to characterize that tradition: a commitment to the authority of Scripture, emphasis on the theological relevance of biblical prophecy and apocalyptic, futurist premillennialism, the expectation of a national future for Israel in the plan of God, and an encouragement of evangelical cooperative ministries which is based on the reality of the universal body of Christ. Few of Chafer's successors, however, have followed him in drawing his particular distinction between Christianity and Judaism. Although they speak of a distinction between Israel and the church in biblical theology, they nevertheless see a unified salvation and even abandon Chafer's notion of dual spheres of eternal life—heaven and

57. Chafer, *Systematic Theology*, 1:42; 4:156. In his book *Grace*, Chafer uses the terms "covenant of works" and "covenant of grace" to refer to the two rules of life, law and grace, which are distinguished by dispensation. This, of course, is not the way the terms were ordinarily used by Reformed theologians. Chafer also uses the phrase "covenant of faith" as a synonym for covenant of grace (*Grace*, 102, 106, 121, 157, 164–65, 187, 193). The incorporation of this material in volume 4 of the *Systematic Theology* leads to conflicting statements about the covenant of grace (cf. 4:156 with 4:229).

58. See n. 23.

59. Lewis Sperry Chafer, "United Action of Evangelicals," *Bibliotheca Sacra* 99 (Oct.–Dec. 1942): 385–86; idem, "Salient Facts regarding Evangelism," *Bibliotheca Sacra* 101 (Oct.–Dec. 1944): 385.

earth.[60] Many speak of a unified participation in the biblical covenants, regard all aspects of Jesus' teaching in the Gospels as relevant to the church, and even believe that the covenant of grace unifies Scripture.[61] Nevertheless, Chafer's emphasis on the distinctiveness of the forms of religion in biblical revelation has won widespread appreciation for the dispensationalist interpretation of the Old Testament. And his views have helped pave the way, especially in dispensational circles, for the acceptance of a biblical theology which sees development and progress in the history of revelation.

60. *Dispensationalism, Israel and the Church: The Search for Definition*, ed. Craig A. Blaising and Darrell L. Bock (Grand Rapids: Zondervan, 1992), 25. Today, in contrast to Chafer, progressive dispensationalism has completely abandoned the notion of two peoples of God and sees a single divine purpose in which all the dispensations interrelate as progressive stages focusing on the eschatological kingdom of God (pp. 380–84).

61. John F. Walvoord, *Major Bible Prophecies* (Grand Rapids: Zondervan, 1991), 188–90.

Primary Sources

Chafer, Lewis Sperry. *Dispensationalism*. Dallas: Dallas Theological Seminary, 1936.

_____. *The Ephesian Letter*. New York: Loizeaux, 1935.

_____. *Grace*. Philadelphia: Sunday School Times, 1922.

_____. *He That Is Spiritual*. New York: Our Hope, 1918.

_____. *The Kingdom in History and Prophecy*. New York: Revell, 1915.

_____. *Major Bible Themes*. Philadelphia: Sunday School Times, 1926.

_____. *Must We Dismiss the Millennium?* Crescent City, Fla.: Florida Testimony Association, 1921.

_____. *Salvation*. New York: C. C. Cook, 1917.

_____. *Satan: His Motive and Methods*. New York: Gospel, 1909.

_____. *Seven Major Biblical Signs of the Times*. Philadelphia: Sunday School Times, 1919.

_____. *Systematic Theology*. 8 vols. Dallas: Dallas Seminary Press, 1947–48.

_____. *True Evangelism*. New York: Gospel, 1911; Philadelphia: Sunday School Times, 1919.

Louis Berkhof

Fred H. Klooster

Louis Berkhof was born on October 13, 1873, in Emmen, the province of Drenthe, the Netherlands.[1] He was eight years old when the family immigrated to the United States and settled in Grand Rapids, Michigan, where his father continued his trade as a baker. Coming from the Christelijke Gereformeerde Kerk in the Netherlands, which originated in the 1834 secession from the Nederlandse Hervormde Kerk, the family joined the Christian Reformed Church, the denomination to which Louis would devote his life.

As a teenager Louis Berkhof was the secretary of the first Reformed young men's society organized in Grand Rapids. Gaining a knowledge of Reformed doctrine and Calvinistic principles for all areas of life made a profound impact on him. In the process he learned to study and express himself and gradually came to feel called to the ministry of the gospel. In later life he acknowledged that he owed more to the young men's society than he would ever be able to repay.[2] In

1893, at the age of nineteen, he made public profession of his Christian faith and enrolled in the Theological School of the Christian Reformed Church, which was later called Calvin Theological Seminary and from which Calvin College eventually emerged. He received his college diploma in 1897 and his seminary diploma in 1900.

In 1898 Abraham Kuyper, the leader of a dynamic revival of Calvinism in the Netherlands, came to the United States to deliver the Stone Lectures at Princeton Theological Seminary. Then he made a triumphal tour of Dutch-American communities, including the Grand Rapids seminary campus, where Berkhof must have seen and heard him. Kuyper had already gained fame as the founder of the Free University of Amsterdam (1880) and the leader of a secession from the national church (1886). In 1892

---

1. Louis Berkhof is not to be confused with Hendrikus Berkhof (1914–), professor emeritus of systematic theology at the University of Leiden, the Netherlands.

2. Editorial, *Young Calvinist* 38.7 (July 1957): 4.

the secession movements of 1834 and 1886 were brought together to form the Gereformeerde Kerken in Nederland. The Dutch immigrants in the Christian Reformed Church, Berkhof one of them, followed these developments with great interest.

After graduation from the seminary Berkhof married Reka Dijkuis and on September 16, 1900, he was ordained as the pastor of the Christian Reformed Church in Allendale, Michigan. After two years he requested leave to pursue further study at Princeton Theological Seminary, where he received the B.D. degree in 1904. Among his teachers at Princeton were the well-known B. B. Warfield and Geerhardus Vos, whom the Christian Reformed Church always considered her son. Vos came from the Netherlands in 1881 at the age of nineteen. He graduated from the theological school in 1883, pursued further study at Princeton and Berlin, and earned a Ph.D. at the University of Strasbourg. Declining an invitation from Kuyper to teach at the Free University of Amsterdam, he returned to Grand Rapids, where he taught dogmatics for five years. In 1893 he left for Princeton Theological Seminary, where he pioneered in the development of biblical theology from a Reformed perspective. Berkhof studied Vos's syllabi on dogmatics before going to Princeton. Vos's *Teaching of Jesus concerning the Kingdom of God and the Church* must have been of special interest to him.[3] In later years Berkhof claimed that his insight into Reformed theology was more indebted to Vos than to anyone else.

In 1904 Berkhof returned to Grand Rapids to become the pastor of the Oakdale Park Christian Reformed Church. He gained a reputation for his biblically insightful, well-prepared, and effectively delivered sermons.[4] During his two-year pastorate he took correspondence courses, mainly in philosophy, from the University of Chicago. Berkhof never had the opportunity to pursue resident graduate studies or to earn a doctorate in theology. His vital interest in education was evident, however, in "Christian Education and Our Church's Future," a lecture that was published in Dutch in 1905.[5] In fact, his life's work as the chief theological educator of the Christian Reformed Church was soon to begin. And by means of his series of textbooks on systematic theology his influence would eventually be felt in conservative circles throughout the world.

As early as 1902 Berkhof was being considered for appointment to the theological school. That year his name was included in the list of nominees for a new chair in exegetical theology. Ralph Janssen with a Ph.D. from the University of Halle in Germany received the appointment. But the board of trustees did not recommend his reappointment in 1906. The Christian Reformed synod that year, of which Berkhof was the vice-president, again included Berkhof's name in the list of nominees. This time he was elected by a large majority, thus beginning a thirty-eight-year career as a theology professor at his alma mater. At his installation on September 5, 1906, Berkhof delivered his inaugural address (in Dutch) on "The Interpretation of Holy Scripture."[6] He emphasized the importance of hermeneutics for ministers and insisted that proper interpretation requires acknowledgment of the uniqueness of Scripture as the authoritative Word of God. He also pointed out that the Reformed perspectives were being threatened by higher criticism, liberalism, and some other trends in theology.

3. Geerhardus Vos, *The Teaching of Jesus concerning the Kingdom of God and the Church* (New York: American Tract Society, 1903).

4. H. Henry Meeter, "Professor Louis Berkhof—1873–1957," *De Wachter* 90 (June 11, 1957): 5.

5. Louis Berkhof, *Het christelijk onderwijs en onze kerkelijke toekomst* (Holland, Mich.: H. Holkeboer, 1905).

6. Louis Berkhof, "De verklaring der Heilige Schrift," *De Wachter* 39 (Sept. 19, 1906): 1–2.

Early Teaching Career (1906–14)

The first twenty years (1906–26) of Berkhof's long teaching career were devoted to the biblical departments, and the final eighteen years (1926–44) to the department of systematic theology. During those four decades the globe was embroiled in two world wars. Liberalism and the social gospel dominated the theological scene before the First World War. In the United States, fundamentalism was the major conservative reaction to those trends. In Europe the neo-orthodoxy of Karl Barth and Emil Brunner developed out of the ashes of war, but it did not have much influence in the United States until the 1940s. Berkhof and Calvin Seminary vigorously maintained the heritage of Reformed theology, especially as it was developed in the Netherlands by Kuyper and Herman Bavinck.

The Dutch language was still dominant in preaching and teaching during the first decades of the 1900s. Berkhof's predecessor in dogmatic theology, F. M. Ten Hoor, lectured in the Dutch language throughout his tenure from 1900 to 1924. Berkhof himself was bilingual and was able to write and speak equally well in either language. After its fragile beginnings as a denomination in 1857, the Christian Reformed Church had remained small and paid little attention to its American environment. But during the 1880s immigrants from the Netherlands, the Berkhofs among them, swelled the size of the church so that by 1900 the denomination had increased by almost 500 percent in the number of its families, individual members, and ministers. The size of its congregations, largely rural, grew significantly, and the total number of congregations increased from 39 to 144. Yet almost a third of those congregations were without a regular minister in 1900. One of the tasks of Berkhof and his colleagues was to confront the demands of Americanization while they instructed their students in the precious Reformed heritage, which they were convinced was relevant to all areas of life in America as well as in the Netherlands.

That was the historical and cultural context in which Berkhof began his teaching career. From 1906 to 1914 he was responsible for all the courses in the biblical area, both Old and New Testament. He taught Old and New Testament introduction, exegesis, and history as well as the biblical languages. Of course, the student body was small, and so were his classes. Consequently, Berkhof had various other denominational responsibilities. As a gifted speaker, Berkhof was in great demand. He was a regular contributor to the denominational weekly periodicals, the *Banner* and *De Wachter*, as well as to a number of other periodicals read widely in Christian Reformed circles. The number of such contributions as well as the range of subjects is amazing. In addition to a variety of theological subjects and reviews of theological publications, Berkhof wrote on social issues, Christian education, evangelism, missions, and many practical problems faced by the churches. Only the most significant of his writings can be referred to in this essay.

During the first period of his teaching career, when he was responsible for all the Old and New Testament courses, Berkhof published three pamphlets and a book on hermeneutics. The hermeneutical issues raised in his 1906 inaugural address were developed in his lectures. They led to the book *Beknopte bijbelsche hermeneutiek* (*Concise Biblical Hermeneutics*), which was published in 1911 by the Dutch firm of J. H. Kok. Hermeneutics was not as complex a subject then as it has become recently, but a book on this subject by a Reformed theologian was itself significant. An English edition, *Principles of Biblical Interpretation*, appeared in 1950.[7] After historical chapters on hermeneutical principles among the

7. Louis Berkhof, *Principles of Biblical Interpretation* (Grand Rapids: Baker, 1950). A complete bibliography of Berkhof's writings, including articles and addresses, is found in *Bibliography of the Writings of the Professors of Calvin Theological Seminary,* ed. Peter DeKlerk (Grand Rapids: Calvin Theological Seminary, 1980), 2.1–52.

Jews and in the Christian church, Berkhof has a key chapter on "The Proper Conception of the Bible, the Object of Hermeneutica Sacra." This is followed by a hundred pages describing in three chapters the grammatical-historical-theological method of biblical exegesis.

One of Berkhof's three pamphlets published during this period dealt with the Book of Judges. It appeared in 1914 and was entitled *Life under the Law in a Pure Theocracy*. The other two published pamphlets discussed sociocultural issues. In *Christendom en leven* (*Christianity and Life*) Berkhof addressed some of the complexities of Americanization faced by Dutch-American people of Reformed persuasion. The Dutch denominational paper, *De Wachter*, described the pamphlet as drawing clear lines, setting forth basic issues, and providing valuable counsel and advice.[8] The third pamphlet, which was published in 1913, was his first to appear originally in English. Its twenty-three pages contain the text of an address Berkhof presented to the full student body. Entitled *The Church and Social Problems*, it merits extensive attention.[9]

In the year before the First World War, liberalism was still widespread, the social gospel was at its peak, and fundamentalism had not yet discovered its "uneasy conscience."[10] A vigorous debate was going on in the Christian Reformed Church. The convergence of Kuyper's influence and the awakened social conscience in the United States and Canada led to three conflicting positions. One group reflected the spirit of the 1834 secession and lacked a kingdom vision; the other two groups embraced the Reformed vision of the kingdom, but differed as to how it should be promoted in North America. Following in Kuyper's di-

rection, Berkhof expressed the hope that his message would "promote the proper activity of the church along social lines" and "lead to an ever increasing establishment of God's rule in every sphere of life."

"The greatest liberating force in the world is the gospel of Jesus Christ." Those opening words from Berkhof's 1913 address sound like a voice from the 1960s. "No other single agency can be pointed out that wrought such momentous changes," he added. That was clear during the Apostolic Age and during the great emancipatory age of the Reformation. And now the church of 1913 was facing massive social problems that called for similar change. Berkhof pointed to four major revolutions that had forced the issue of social reform. First, the French Revolution at the end of the eighteenth century broke radically with the past, placed primary emphasis on individual rights, accentuated class distinction, and led to industrial war. It was, in Thomas Carlyle's words, "truth clad in hell-fire." Then the Industrial Revolution brought in machines to replace human workers and completely changed the conditions of the working class. Industry became centralized in the cities, agricultural machines drove thousands more into the city, magnifying its great social problems. The Socialist Revolution then reacted against the rank individualism of the age; this sociopolitical movement attempted a radical reorganization of society as the panacea for all social evils and promoted a new morality for the working class. Finally, the Educational Revolution made education available to all and thus heightened general awareness of the widespread social injustice inherent in the capitalistic system.

Berkhof disapproved of socialism, but generally applauded attempts to correct present social evils by less radical means such as the labor movement and trade unions, settlement houses and recreation centers, the Anti-Saloon League, and similar efforts to promote social justice. The church, in contrast, had no effect on the

8. *De Wachter* 46 (Dec. 10, 1913): 5.

9. Louis Berkhof, *The Church and Social Problems* (Grand Rapids: Eerdmans-Sevensma, 1913).

10. See Carl F. H. Henry, *The Uneasy Conscience of Modern Fundamentalism* (Grand Rapids: Eerdmans, 1947).

rich, did not reach the poor, but influenced only the comfortable middle class, especially its women. In the words of Henry Carter, an English writer, "The church is confronted by a paradox. Within her borders, loss; beyond her borders, gain for the Kingdom of God."[11]

Berkhof went on to mention seven causes of the church's insensitivity and indifference to the socioeconomic injustices of the day. This list also sounds like something from the 1960s: (1) The church sanctioned the existing social order by favoring the rich and helping capitalism to subjugate the working class. (2) While the laboring world cried out for justice, the church preached a gospel of contentment. (3) Remaining aloof from the suffering masses, the church brought them neither hope nor comfort. (4) The church had abandoned the inner city and fled to the suburbs. (5) The church discouraged reform movements and criticized those who did the work she neglected. (6) Focusing exclusively on the salvation of the individual, the church showed little concern for the social renewal that ought to follow. (7) The church preached an otherworldly gospel which did not touch the realities of everyday life. In a word, "to the hungry she preaches that the righteous shall live by faith; to the homeless that God is the eternal dwelling-place for all his people. It seems like mockery."[12]

Whether one regards the church as guilty of such charges depends on one's conception of the church. Berkhof summarized the Anabaptist, Roman Catholic, and social-gospel conceptions and their responses to the question whether the church has a duty in the area of social reform. He declared that the spiritual sons of Calvin cannot be satisfied with any of them. Calvinists recognize that the church has a social responsibility and that there is no dualism between nature and grace, natural and supernatural, body and soul. Whether one

views the church as a social organism or as an institution, the office of deacon is itself clear proof that the church has a social responsibility. The goal of the church's social activity is the furtherance of the kingdom of God. There are both a present and a future, an "already" as well as a "not yet," to God's kingdom. Christians must look and work for the manifestation of God's kingdom on this earth. That is implied in praying, "Your will be done on earth as it is in heaven." Calvin, John Knox, and Kuyper, whatever their faults, were on the right track!

Berkhof then proposed a far-reaching program by which the institutional church can promote the kingdom of God through social action: (1) Since society cannot be renewed without individual renewal, the church must promote a healthy spiritual life for all her members. (2) The pulpit must proclaim the social message of Scripture and seek the realization of the kingdom of God on earth, thus avoiding both the danger of exclusive otherworldliness and the danger of simply becoming a platform for sociology. The cross and kingdom are not alternatives, for the kingdom is to be founded on the cross. (3) There is no place for social injustice, social sin, or social misery within the church itself; the church must exemplify the gospel in her deeds, since actions speak louder than words. (4) The church may not neglect the inner city or ghetto; missionaries have pointed out that many American cities are worse than cities in pagan lands. (5) The church must carefully study the issues and take an informed stand on social reform. To that end every denomination should have a standing committee of experts to study current social problems and propose biblical solutions; and theological seminaries should have a required course in social ethics so that future ministers may be alert to their kingdom responsibilities. (6) The church should encourage its members to promote independent Christian organizations that advance the kingdom of God in the various areas of life—social, economic, political. In

---

11. Quoted in Berkhof, *Church and Social Problems*, 10.
12. Ibid., 12.

such ways, Berkhof suggested, Christians will become "the leaven permeating the lump, God's spiritual force for the regeneration of the world, his chosen agents to influence every sphere of life, to bring science and art, commerce and industry in subjection to God."[13]

Berkhof emphasized that enactment of his six proposals would make the Christian Reformed Church more Calvinistic, not less so. In this way the momentous significance of Calvinism in the past could be recaptured, for Calvinism "contains the principles and forces that make for industrial democracy, for the establishment of God's rule in every sphere of life, for the introduction of a better social day, and for an ever increasing fulfillment of the church's constant prayer" that God's will be done on earth as in heaven.[14]

Berkhof's essay on *The Church and Social Problems* has been described as "the most significant work to appear in the [Christian Reformed Church] on the task of the church in society."[15] This pamphlet "better than any other single source illustrates the breadth of Berkhof's interests and sympathies, his knowledge of contemporary American theological literature, his capacity for balanced judgment, and his ability to engage discursively and critically in theological issues and problems."[16] Students who know Berkhof only from his books on systematic theology are usually surprised to discover that he also wrote this striking piece on social responsibility. It is unfortunate that Berkhof did not bring these insights and convictions into his later systematic works. The world was on the brink of the First World War when he presented this address. That war shattered

the hopes of liberalism and the social gospel. It is a disappointing fact that kingdom interest and practice also waned in the Christian Reformed Church during the following decades.

A Decade of Controversies (1914–26)

The Christian Reformed Synod of 1914 decided to reduce Berkhof's work load and divide the Old and New Testament courses between two professors. Ralph Janssen, who had not been reappointed in 1906, was now appointed to the Old Testament chair, and Berkhof continued with the New Testament courses. The following year he published a textbook on *New Testament Introduction* and another on *Biblical Archaeology* in which he showed how the history and culture of the ancient Near East aid in understanding the Bible.[17] A booklet on *Paul the Missionary* was also published in 1915.

In 1916 Berkhof again turned his attention to a critical social issue. In his 1913 publication on *The Church and Social Problems* he had noted that labor unions had made some positive contributions to social justice. But in a new publication on *The Christian Laborer in the Industrial Struggle* he argued that it was not legitimate for members of the Christian Reformed Church to join religiously neutral labor unions. He favored the establishment of separate Christian organizations. The Christian Reformed Synod of 1916 had this issue on its agenda, but it did not adopt Berkhof's point of view. The synod advised Christian workers that if their jobs compelled them to join neutral unions, they should witness powerfully "by word and deed within the unions to the fact that they belonged to Christ and sought his honor."[18] This was perhaps the only in-

13. Ibid., 20.

14. Ibid.

15. Henry Zwaanstra, *Reformed Thought and Experience in a New World: A Study of the Christian Reformed Church and Its American Environment, 1890–1918* (Kampen: J. H. Kok, 1973), 196.

16. Henry Zwaanstra, "Louis Berkhof," in *Reformed Theology in America: A History of Its Modern Development,* ed. David F. Wells (Grand Rapids: Eerdmans, 1985), 158.

17. Louis Berkhof, *New Testament Introduction* (Grand Rapids: Eerdmans-Sevensma, 1915); idem, *Biblical Archaeology* (Grand Rapids: Eerdmans-Sevensma, 1915).

18. *Acta der Synode van de Christelijke Gereformeerde Kerk 1916,* Grand Rapids, 21–30 June 1916, pp. 38–39.

stance in which the synod ever differed with Berkhof on a major issue.

During the next decade the Christian Reformed Church was rocked by three very serious doctrinal controversies, and Berkhof was the churchman most often called on for advice. The first conflict concerned the premillennial views of Harry Bultema, a Christian Reformed minister in Muskegon, Michigan. In 1917 Bultema published *Maranatha: A Study on Unfulfilled Prophecy*.[19] Berkhof was invited to present a public lecture on "Premillennialism: Its Scriptural Basis and Some of Its Practical Consequences." He expressed appreciation for the premillennialists' high view of and devotion to Scripture, a striking contrast, he added, to the "icebergs of higher criticism." But he also pointed to four major objections to premillennialism. His most basic objection was to the strictly literal interpretation of prophecy. That meant neglect of the principle that difficult passages are best interpreted by comparison with other Scripture texts (the analogy of Scripture). The strict literalism also involved a hermeneutic different from that of the historic Christian church. Berkhof expressed his support for the amillennial interpretation of Revelation 20:4–6 endorsed by Kuyper, Bavinck, Seakle Greydanus, and Hendrik Hoekstra in the Netherlands and by Warfield, Vos, Ezra Milligan, and George Eckman in the United States. He questioned the scriptural basis of the premillennial view of a thousand-year kingdom of Christ, a second resurrection, the absolute separation of Israel and the church, and the distinction between the kingdom and the church in the New Testament. Berkhof was requested to publish his address in the Dutch language to make it available to a wider audience. So an expanded Dutch edition appeared in April

1918.[20] In June the synod judged Bultema's *Maranatha* to be in conflict with Scripture and the Reformed confessions on the issue of Israel and the church as well as on the issue of the church and the kingdom. The synod ruled that his views denied the spiritual unity between Israel and the church as well as the present kingship of Christ. Eventually deposed, Bultema went on to found the Berean Church in Muskegon.

The second controversy was initiated by Berkhof and three of his seminary colleagues. In a letter to the board of trustees they suggested that Janssen, their Old Testament colleague, held higher-critical views of Scripture. Later the four professors— Berkhof, William Heyns, F. M. Ten Hoor, and Samuel Volbeda—provided "further light on the Janssen case" in a pamphlet published in the Dutch language.[21] On the basis of notes that students had taken at his lectures the four professors charged that Janssen denied the Mosaic authorship of the Pentateuch, the historicity of biblical miracles, and the messianic significance of certain Old Testament passages. Hence they questioned Janssen's views on the authority, infallibility, and trustworthiness of Scripture. The bitter controversy continued through 1922 when Janssen was deposed. A few ministers left the denomination as a result, but no major schism followed synod's action.

The Christian Reformed Church became embroiled in yet another theological conflict in 1924, this one dealing with a denial of common grace. Two ministers, Herman Hoeksema and Henry Danhof, rejected the doctrine of common grace. In the Netherlands, Kuyper had championed the doctrine and published a three-volume work on the subject. The 1924 synod adopted the following three points as flowing from

---

19. Harry Bultema, *Maranatha: Eene studie over de onvervulde profetie* (Grand Rapids: Eerdmans-Sevensma, 1917; Eng. trans., Grand Rapids: Kregel, 1985).

20. Louis Berkhof, *Premillennialisme: Zijn schriftuurlijke basis en enkele van zijn practische gevolgtrekkingen* (Grand Rapids: Eerdmans-Sevensma, 1918).

21. Louis Berkhof et al., *Nadere toelichting omtrent de zaak Janssen* (Holland, Mich.: Holland Printing, 1921).

Scripture and the Reformed confessions: the existence of a general or common grace of God that is shown to all, a restraint of sin by the general work of the Holy Spirit, and the ability of unregenerate persons to perform civic good though they are unable to perform any saving good. Berkhof was not directly involved in the dispute before synod's action, but when protests and appeals were submitted to the next synod, Berkhof published a pamphlet (in Dutch) in which he maintained that the three points were in every respect Reformed.[22] The protests and appeals were not sustained, and synod's disciplinary measures against the two ministers led to their resignation from the Christian Reformed Church and the formation of the Protestant Reformed Church.

When Berkhof retired twenty years later, his longtime colleague, Clarence Bouma, commented on Berkhof's role in controversy: "The Christian Reformed Church has gone through doctrinal controversies coupled with ecclesiastical upheavals, and in every case the quiet, steady hand and mind of Louis Berkhof was in the background." But, Bouma added, Berkhof "was no 'fighter.' He disliked controversy. He was no organizer of a group to fight a battle. But his pervasive influence and his careful, balanced, sober thinking on all issues was sure to be found controlling many a situation. His church respected and still respects him."[23]

During those critical, controversial years, Louis Berkhof's reputation as a Reformed churchman and theologian rose significantly, both within the Christian Reformed Church and without. In 1919 he was invited to become the president of Calvin College, and in 1921 to become the editor of De Wachter. Berkhof declined both invitations. But he did accept an invitation to deliver the prestigious Stone Lectures at Princeton in 1920–21. Earlier in that series

Kuyper had lectured on *Calvinism* (1898) and Bavinck on *The Philosophy of Revelation* (1908). Berkhof's Stone Lectures were on *The Kingdom of God*. Although during the years 1919–20 he had published in *De Wachter* a long series of articles on the kingdom, his Stone Lectures were not published until 1951, seven years after he had retired.[24]

Systematic Theology

Berkhof had been teaching biblical subjects for twenty years when synod appointed him to the chair of dogmatic theology in 1926. Synod had considered shifting him to that department in 1924, when Ten Hoor retired, but appointed Clarence Bouma to the dogmatics chair, which then included ethics and apologetics. Two years later synod decided to divide the department into two branches; Bouma was assigned to ethics and apologetics, and Berkhof became professor of dogmatics. Bouma wrote in 1944 that "this was an ideal to which [Berkhof] had aspired for some years. The field of dogmatics had the love of his heart."[25] For the next eighteen years, until his retirement in 1944, Berkhof's field of teaching, research, and writing was dogmatics or systematic theology. This is the field in which he was to make his name and for which he is chiefly remembered today.

Teaching biblical subjects, both Old and New Testament, was excellent preparation for teaching Reformed systematic theology. B. B. Warfield began his teaching career in the New Testament field. J. Gresham Machen, the eminent New Testament scholar from Princeton and Westminster seminaries, stated that he always regarded the study of the New Testament as "ancillary" to that of systematic theology: "New Testament study has its own methods, indeed;

22. Louis Berkhof, *De drie punten in alle deelen gereformeerd* (Grand Rapids: Eerdmans, 1925).

23. Clarence Bouma, "Professor Berkhof Retires," *Calvin Forum* 10.3 (Oct. 1944): 35.

24. Louis Berkhof, *The Kingdom of God: The Development of the Idea of the Kingdom, Especially since the Eighteenth Century* (Grand Rapids: Eerdmans, 1951).

25. Bouma, "Professor Berkhof Retires," 35.

but ultimately its aim should be to aid in the establishment of that system of doctrine that the Scriptures contain."[26] Berkhof shared that perspective. Dogmatic or systematic theology is the capstone of the entire theological enterprise where all the fruits of the other disciplines, especially the biblical, are brought together into a systematic whole that reflects all the riches of Scripture and the Christian faith.[27]

The years Berkhof taught systematic theology, 1926–44, were relatively free from doctrinal controversy within the Christian Reformed Church. That was quite a contrast to the preceding decade. Now there was "an amazing theological consensus, basically conservative and deeply rooted in traditional Reformed confessional orthodoxy."[28] Berkhof contributed much to that situation, and he would do much more for its continuation. In that peaceful context he concentrated on teaching and research in his new, cherished field, the first fruit of which was a small doctrinal study on *The Assurance of Faith* (1928).[29]

In 1931 Berkhof became the first president of Calvin Theological Seminary. Since its founding in 1876, the school had followed the European style of a rotating rectorate. Berkhof was both the last rector and the first president. On September 9, 1931, he was installed as president and honored on the same occasion for his twenty-five years as a professor. His inaugural address on "Our Seminary and the Modern Spirit" expressed both the seminary's goals and the direction of his own thought. He traced the "modern spirit" to the rise of the scientific method, the development of liberalism since Friedrich Schleiermacher, and the appearance of the social gospel of Walter Rauschenbusch. Adopting those modern trends, many seminaries had raised the banner of academic freedom, broken away from church control, and denied the final authority of Scripture. In such seminaries the curriculum showed a shift away from dogmatics to practical theology and from church-centered to social concerns. Calvin Seminary, however, would continue its unique role: "We accept the Reformed system of truth which was handed down to us by previous generations, attempt to exhibit it in all its comprehensiveness and in all its beauty and logical consistency, seek to defend it against all opposing systems, and endeavor to carry it forward to still greater perfection in harmony with the structural lines that were clearly indicated in its past development."[30] The four principles thus enunciated, especially the first three, were ably upheld in the following years by Berkhof himself as president and professor of systematic theology.

The added responsibility of the presidency of a relatively small seminary did not curtail Berkhof's research, teaching, and publication. In fact, the final thirteen years of his seminary career proved to be the most productive. He prepared for publication the lecture materials he had compiled for the classroom. The time was opportune for their use in conservative schools throughout the world. What became his magnum opus, his *Systematic Theology*, began as mimeographed syllabi (1927), was published in two volumes as *Reformed Dogmatics* (1932), and then was revised and enlarged in a comprehensive but compact single volume of 784 pages (1941). In the fifty years since then, *Systematic Theology* has gone through more than twenty printings and sold over one hundred thousand copies. By means of this work Berkhof has been able to promote Reformed theology throughout the world.

26. J. Gresham Machen, "Christianity in Conflict," in *Contemporary American Theology*, ed. Vergilius Ferm, 2 vols. (New York: Round Table, 1932–33), 1:253.

27. See Fred H. Klooster, *The Adjective in "Systematic Theology"* (Grand Rapids: Calvin Theological Seminary, 1963).

28. Zwaanstra, "Louis Berkhof," 163.

29. Louis Berkhof, *The Assurance of Faith* (Grand Rapids: Smitter, 1928).

30. Louis Berkhof, "Our Seminary and the Modern Spirit," *Banner* 67 (Sept. 11, 1931): 806.

Berkhof also prepared companion volumes to *Systematic Theology*, which, like the major work, were first published under the title *Reformed Dogmatics*. A prolegomenon was published in 1932 with the title *Reformed Dogmatics: Introductory Volume;* a revised edition carries the title *Introduction to Systematic Theology*. To augment this series of seminary-level textbooks, *Reformed Dogmatics: Historical Volume* appeared in 1937 and was reissued in 1949 as *The History of Christian Doctrines*. To further assist students in their study, a *Textual Aid to Systematic Theology* was added in 1942. It contained the main source texts, the proof texts, for each section of *Systematic Theology*, where Berkhof had generally cited biblical passages only by chapter and verse. As a twenty-year teacher of biblical subjects, he was able to quote many passages from memory with relevant exegetical comments when he used his own textbook in the classroom. The aim of the *Textual Aid* was to make sure the students had ready access to the relevant biblical passages.

The need for doctrinal textbooks on other academic levels led Berkhof to comply with requests to condense his *Reformed Dogmatics*. In 1933 his *Manual of Reformed Doctrine* was published to meet the needs of college courses and adult-education classes. When this volume was reprinted in 1939, the title was changed to *Manual of Christian Doctrine*. An even more extensive condensation of *Reformed Dogmatics* led to the publication in 1938 of the *Summary of Christian Doctrine for Senior Classes*, which was intended for high schools (later editions dropped the reference to "senior classes" in the title). These condensed systematic-theology textbooks have also experienced extraordinary acceptance. The *Manual* has sold more than fifty-five thousand copies, and the *Summary* more than eighty thousand. The *Summary* has also appeared in Spanish and Portuguese translations, while the *Manual* has been published in Japanese, Chinese, Spanish, and Portuguese. What more could a systematic theologian hope for? A representative of the publisher reports that a contract was signed in 1990 for a Russian translation of the *Manual!*

Within the Christian Reformed Church and its network of parent-controlled Christian schools, it was not uncommon, at least up to the 1960s, to find seminary students who had already studied Berkhof's *Summary* in a Christian high school and his *Manual* in college. That was probably too much of a good thing, "overkill" some might say, and led to negative attitudes toward the massive *Systematic Theology*. Yet when more-recent publications were substituted at Calvin Seminary, it was not uncommon to hear some students plead for a return to the orderly, compact work of the renowned Berkhof. Given their background in the *Summary* and the *Manual*, they were well prepared to tackle the *Systematic Theology*.

In the wake of liberal theology and early fundamentalism, doctrinal studies were not popular and works on systematic theology rare. Neo-orthodox publications were hardly textbooks. In that context Berkhof's works met a growing need. During almost four decades of teaching, Berkhof had a total of only some three hundred students at Calvin Seminary. By contrast, during five decades of teaching at Princeton, Charles Hodge taught more than three thousand students. But after Berkhof's death in 1957, he continued to be influential; his books were purchased in surprising numbers. By 1991 the combined sales of his *Systematic Theology, Manual,* and *Summary* totaled approximately a quarter million. While he rests from his labors, Berkhof's deeds certainly follow him (Rev. 14:13). Indeed, like Abel, "he still speaks, even though he is dead" (Heb. 11:4 NIV). Through Berkhof's publications Calvin Theological Seminary has undoubtedly made one of its most significant contributions to the cause of Christ and his kingdom throughout the world.

Goals

Though Louis Berkhof produced a very influential series of textbooks in systematic theology, he did not create a Berkhofian theology, nor did he introduce distinctly Berkhofian doctrines. He had no such desires nor ambitions; he made no such claims. His goals were essentially the four principles enunciated in his 1931 presidential inaugural address. He certainly spoke for himself as a systematic theologian when he said, "We accept the Reformed system of truth which was handed down to us by previous generations." For Berkhof that was a personal confession as well as a goal. He accepted the Reformed system because he was convinced that it was in basic accord with Scripture, which he wholeheartedly accepted as the authoritative Word of God, inspired and infallible, normative for theology and all of life. In his day that conviction led some to label him, as they did Machen and others, a fundamentalist. Berkhof recognized fundamentalists as fellow believers, but he was a Calvinist, a Reformed theologian rather than a fundamentalist. Though Berkhof and other Reformed theologians had much in common with the fundamentalists, his 1913 address on *The Church and Social Problems* revealed basic differences. His recognition of the role of hermeneutics also served to distinguish him from the fundamentalists. While always opposing higher criticism, he was opposed to literalism as well. Indeed, he had emphasized the need for biblical hermeneutics as early as his inaugural address of 1906, a point he elaborated in his book on the *Principles of Biblical Interpretation* (1911).

Berkhof's many years of teaching biblical subjects were an asset to him as professor of systematic theology. Limitations of space, however, prevented him from incorporating into his *Systematic Theology* and textbooks as much exegetical material as one might expect. Even his professed indebtedness to Geerhardus Vos is scarcely evident in his publications. This is one of the disadvantages of a systematic style, which, like the advantages, become clear on even superficial analysis.

Berkhof's textbooks draw on the biblical sources largely as they had been treated in the Reformed system handed down by previous generations. For Berkhof that meant the Reformed confessions first of all— especially the Belgic Confession, the Heidelberg Catechism, and the Canons of Dort. He did not often quote those confessions directly, but they formed the background and context of his theology. He accepted the classic doctrines and dogmas of the historic Christian church as they had been developed in the ecumenical councils of the Patristic Age and further elaborated in the Reformation Era. Rejecting Adolf von Harnack's view that Christian dogma had been so molded by Greek thought that the essence of Jesus' teachings was lost, Berkhof embraced the dogmas of the church as crucial to Reformed theology. That was undoubtedly the reason for his personal preference for the title *Reformed Dogmatics* even though he consented to the more popular designation of *Systematic Theology*. While the titles of his textbooks changed, the contents remained basically unaltered.

The Reformed system had been handed down to Berkhof by several theologians with whom he was in basic agreement. John Calvin was on the top of that list. Among American theologians, Charles Hodge and B. B. Warfield were quite high on the list. But, after Calvin, Berkhof favored Vos, and especially Kuyper and Bavinck from the Netherlands. Ethnic reasons played a role, perhaps, but Berkhof's preference was due primarily to the revival and development of Reformed theology in the Netherlands in its direct confrontation with liberalism. He valued the repristination of Reformed theology that occurred there, and he shared the main lines of Kuyper's kingdom vision. But Berkhof was most dependent on the Reformed system as it was handed down by Bavinck's four-volume *Gereformeerde Dogmatiek*.[31] In fact, the preface to Berkhof's *Reformed Dogmatics: Introductory Volume* (1932) states that "the general plan of the work is based on that of the first volume of Dr. Bavinck's *Gereformeerde Dogmatiek*. In a few of the chapters," Berkhof adds, "I have followed his line of argumentation as well, but in the greater part of the work I have followed a somewhat independent course."[32] Though this acknowledgment was dropped from later printings, the indebtedness to Bavinck remained. It was undoubtedly far greater than the preface in the first printing indicates.[33]

Berkhof's dependence on Reformed theologians from the past led Brevard Childs to characterize *Systematic Theology* as a "repristination of seventeenth-century dogmatics."[34] He would likely say the same of Bavinck's dogmatics. Millard Erickson has pointed out the "erroneous conception" that underlies this characterization—Childs fails to take into account that "the orthodox form of theology is not the theology of any one particular period, not even a fairly recent one." Accordingly, "a theology should not be assessed as being nothing but a ver-

sion of an earlier theology simply because it happens to agree with the theology of an earlier time." Erickson notes that this is true of any theology that makes "the elements found within the Bible normative for its basic structure" and thus recognizes "the timeless essence of the doctrines."[35]

Berkhof's second goal, as stated in the 1931 address, was to "attempt to exhibit [Reformed theology] in all its comprehensiveness and in all its beauty and logical consistency." That goal is reflected in his personal love for the field of dogmatics and the energy he expended in bringing his lecture materials into print. He never dreamed that his textbooks would have such a market, even fifty years after publication. One of the reasons for their success is that they clearly interrelate the various doctrines and exhibit the wholeness of the Reformed system. Was he successful in also displaying its beauty? Textbooks rarely endear themselves to students required to master their contents. Indeed, beauty is in the eyes of the beholder. Berkhof, like many other Reformed theologians, saw something beautiful and majestic in the way in which Reformed theology reflects the wonderful message of Scripture. Unfortunately, those who have the privilege of growing up with such a treasure are often the least likely to recognize its beauty. Excitement about a volume such as *Systematic Theology* is more likely to be experienced by evangelicals who have had little previous acquaintance with a system of doctrine that beautifully integrates the various facets of the Christian faith. That beauty Berkhof exhibits in various textbooks, though not every reader may sense it.

Berkhof's third goal was "to defend [Reformed theology] against all opposing systems." He effectively carried out that goal. His general approach in lectures, ad-

31. Herman Bavinck, *Gereformeerde Dogmatiek*, 4th ed., 4 vols. (Kampen: J. H. Kok, 1928–30).

32. Louis Berkhof, *Reformed Dogmatics: Introductory Volume* (Grand Rapids: Eerdmans, 1932), 5.

33. Zwaanstra, "Louis Berkhof," 162–68.

34. Brevard S. Childs, *Biblical Theology in Crisis* (Philadelphia: Westminster, 1970), 20. David W. Soper, *Major Voices in American Theology*, 2 vols. (Philadelphia: Westminster, 1953, 1955), 2:152–67, characterizes Berkhof's position as "A Theology of Biblical Literalism": "Louis Berkhof specifically states that he believes in God only because an infallible Bible tells him that God exists. To believe in the Bible first and God second—is not this idolatry?" (p. 152). In spite of several appreciative comments, Soper has so obvious a dislike of Reformed theology that his evaluation is filled with caricature. W. E. Garrison, review of *Major Voices in American Theology*, vol. 1, by David W. Soper, *Christian Century* 70 (Dec. 30, 1953): 1529, observes that "we need a word or phrase to denote the kind of theology which is conservatively evangelical and supernaturalistic but which does not have the specific characteristics that 'Fundamentalist' implies." He suggests the term "classical Protestantism."

35. Millard J. Erickson, *Christian Theology* (Grand Rapids: Baker, 1986), 64–65. On the recent explosion of works in systematic theology see Gabriel Fackre, "Reorientation and Retrieval in Systematic Theology," *Christian Century* 108 (June 26–July 3, 1991): 653–55.

dresses, essays, and especially his textbooks, was to begin with a historical review. For example, with his unusual gift for efficient and accurate condensation he introduced every section of the *Systematic Theology* with a brief, comprehensive, and accurate historical survey. This survey included the major contributors to a doctrine, its variations, its main opponents, and alternative views. He set forth the Reformed position and then defended it against, for example, Roman Catholic, Lutheran, and liberal perspectives. He was less successful in dealing with the emerging neo-orthodoxy of his own time. That theology was still developing, its complexities did not lend themselves to easy condensation, and its rejection of liberalism together with its claims to be a return to classic Reformed theology made it appealing. Berkhof attempted to understand neo-orthodoxy and in the expanded 1941 edition of *Systematic Theology* made a noble effort to identify its serious deficiencies in the light of the history of authentic Reformed thought. But *Systematic Theology* does not really take students reliably and competently beyond the liberalism of Friedrich Schleiermacher and Albrecht Ritschl. In dealing with theological systems through nineteenth-century liberalism, however, and even with some contemporaries, Berkhof did achieve his third goal. The reader is not left in doubt as to the superiority of the Reformed system, even though the major opposing systems are treated with fairness and appreciation for certain features.

The fourth goal Berkhof mentioned in his presidential inaugural of 1931 was to carry the Reformed system "forward to still greater perfection in harmony with the structural lines that were clearly indicated in its past development." Here his appreciation of the contemporary theology of Kuyper and Bavinck came into play. Berkhof recognized that they had contributed to a resurgence and development of Reformed theology by overcoming many of the errors and weaknesses of seventeenth-century Protestant scholasticism. He regretted that Kuyper's and Bavinck's works were not available in English; hence he paraphrased much of their thought in English. Beyond that it is difficult to point to specific contributions Berkhof made toward his fourth goal. He may have considered his series of textbooks as contributing toward that goal, and they may well have had that effect. We should mention here, however, a few possibilities for development that Berkhof might have pursued.

In the area of prolegomena Berkhof made only brief reference to the radical differences between Warfield and Kuyper concerning the place and role of apologetics. He made no contribution to that challenging field where battles are still raging in the evangelical world today.

Another area where Berkhof chose not to enter the fray is the doctrine of predestination. Prior to the First World War the advocates of infralapsarianism and supralapsarianism had engaged in frequent verbal battles within the Christian Reformed Church. Berkhof's *Systematic Theology* carefully sets up the arguments for and against each position and emphasizes the lack of convincing evidence one way or the other. He favored the infralapsarian position but did not rise above the dispute to ask whether the whole issue of the logical order of God's decree(s) might actually be an illegitimate question.

On the subject of the covenant(s), Berkhof painstakingly reviewed many of the positions within Reformed theology. Yet he made no contribution to clarifying and further developing the issues along biblical lines. Identifying covenant membership with election, he neglected the historical dimensions of God's covenantal dealings. The questions concerning the interrelations of covenant, church, and kingdom did not challenge Berkhof to make personal contributions on the subject. His colleague in practical theology, Samuel Volbeda, made some very creative suggestions on this subject, but Berkhof gives no evidence of similar efforts.[36] Especially disappointing and somewhat baffling is the fact, mentioned earlier, that the kingdom vision reflected in *The Church and Social Problems* finds no echo in his *Systematic Theology*. What a difference the overall impact of that work might have had, especially in the 1960s, if the author had developed the social-economic-political implications of the biblical doctrine of the kingdom of God.

This analysis is not meant to detract from the significant contributions Berkhof made. It does indicate, however, that his stated goals, especially the fourth, were not fully achieved. There is still work to be done! Berkhof's *Introduction to Systematic Theology* continues to remind readers that systematic theology, in addition to its constructive and defensive tasks, has a critical task to perform.

The Years of Retirement

Berkhof retired at the age of seventy in 1944. He was scheduled to deliver the commencement address at the combined graduation ceremonies of the college and seminary. But June 6, 1944, was D Day when the Allied forces landed in France in the deadly campaign to liberate Europe. The commencement program was changed to fit that somber occasion. His scheduled address on "The Value of a Calvinistic Training in a Disillusioned World" was not delivered, but presented later in the *Calvin Forum*. The editor referred to it as "an appropriate academic swan song from his virile mind and facile pen."[37]

In his retirement year Berkhof was a member of a committee that presented to the Christian Reformed synod a trailblazing report on ecumenicity.[38] Recognizing that there is no scriptural warrant for the large number of separate denominations, the report emphasized that the Christian Reformed Church has an ecumenical responsibility to all churches in the world—Eastern Orthodox, Roman Catholic, non-Reformed Protestant, and other Reformed-Presbyterian churches. The type of responsibility and action to be taken depends on the nature of each church's confession and the degree of its faithfulness to that confession and to Scripture. The report recommended that the Christian Reformed Church begin by consulting with other Reformed churches and then move out in ever-widening circles. Some kind of Reformed ecumenical synod had been contemplated for years but was delayed by the war. Finally, as a result of the impetus of the 1944 report, the first such synod was convened in Grand Rapids in 1946. Berkhof preached a sermon on Ephesians 4:12–15 and was elected president.[39] That organization, now called the Reformed Ecumenical Council, continues to function today, and the 1944 report continues to guide the Christian Reformed Church's ecumenical activity as well.

Still physically and mentally vigorous when he retired, Berkhof enjoyed another thirteen years of good health. He read the current theological literature, wrote scores of reviews, and provided the denominational publications with articles on a wide variety of subjects. Eighteen of the fifty-two pages in the bibliography of his writings cover his retirement years.[40] A lecture on "Recent Trends in Theology," first presented at Moody Bible Institute and highly praised by Wilbur M. Smith, was published in 1944.[41] Ten expository sermons ap-

---

36. On Volbeda, Vos, and Berkhof, see Fred H. Klooster, "The Kingdom of God in the History of the Christian Reformed Church," in *Perspectives on the Christian Reformed Church*, ed. Peter DeKlerk and Richard R. DeRidder (Grand Rapids: Baker, 1983), 203–24.

37. Bouma, "Professor Berkhof Retires," 35–36.

38. *Acts of Synod 1944 of the Christian Reformed Church*, Grand Rapids, 14–23 June 1944, pp. 330–67.

39. *Acts of the First Reformed Ecumenical Synod, 1946*, Grand Rapids, 14–30 August 1946, pp. 75–83.

40. *Bibliography*, ed. DeKlerk, 2.35–52.

41. Louis Berkhof, *Recent Trends in Theology* (Grand Rapids: Eerdmans, 1944).

peared in 1948 under the title *Riches of Divine Grace.*[42] And in 1951 a collection of his lectures on *Aspects of Liberalism* was issued. One of those lectures, "The Missing Chain in Liberal Theology," focuses on certain legal or judicial facets of Scripture which "constitute a logically progressive chain or series" anchored in God's justice.[43] (In an earlier treatise, *Vicarious Atonement through Christ,* Berkhof had held forth on the neglected and frequently rejected doctrine that Christ's substitutionary atonement satisfies God's justice.)[44] *Aspects of Liberalism* is significant as well for revealing Berkhof's growing disillusionment with Karl Barth, Emil Brunner, Reinhold Niebuhr, and other contemporaries who had also reacted to liberalism. Increasingly Berkhof came to share Cornelius Van Til's view that the neo-orthodox theologians reflected a modified modernism.[45]

Retirement provided the opportunity for a long-neglected responsibility, the publication of the Stone Lectures delivered at Princeton three decades earlier. In 1951 *The Kingdom of God* came from the press with "the original material . . . left intact" except for chapter divisions and an added chapter.[46] After introductory chapters on the New Testament and the Reformation, Berkhof deals with Albrecht Ritschl, the social gospel, Johannes Weiss and Albert Schweitzer, Barth and Brunner, and premillennial views. Covering a wide range of writers, Berkhof is mainly critical of the positions he reviews. Unfortunately, the book lacks the fire of *The Church and Social Problems* and fails to set forth constructively the kingdom vision that Berkhof had expressed on earlier occasions.

During the last years of his life Berkhof turned repeatedly to eschatological subjects. *The Second Coming of Christ* appeared in 1953.[47] Opposing the dispensational view, he stressed the "already" as well as the "not yet" of Christ's return. He also discussed the manner, purpose, glory, and comfort of the second coming. During the last year of his life Berkhof wrote articles on the influence Christians should exert in cultural life, on the preacher's training and task, on rejoicing in God's grace, and a series on "The Biblical Conception of Hope."[48]

The reflections of his colleague Clarence Bouma provide a fitting summary of the life and work of Louis Berkhof. In Berkhof there was "a fusion of simple piety, a high theology, and unswerving devotion to the Reformed faith." When the spiritual heritage which he had received had been "enriched and deepened in the alembic of his capacious mind by way of pulpit and professor's desk," he passed it on to "the minds and hearts of the rising generation and the coming ministry of the church." Bouma's characterization seems even more fitting almost five decades later. There was in Louis Berkhof, he continued,

a remarkable combination of whole-souled loyalty and devotion to the Reformed Faith with a breadth of outlook and sympathy coupled with fairness of judgment also in dealing with opponents' views that is refreshing. He had no sympathy with the extremism of certain recent Reformed writers who, though boasting of their superior soundness, in reality narrowed the great classic tradition of the Reformed Faith as represented in the writings of Bavinck and Kuyper, of Warfield and Vos. His *Systematic Theology* is the

42. Louis Berkhof, *Riches of Divine Grace* (Grand Rapids: Eerdmans, 1948).

43. Louis Berkhof, *Aspects of Liberalism* (Grand Rapids: Eerdmans, 1951), 115.

44. Louis Berkhof, *Vicarious Atonement through Christ* (Grand Rapids: Eerdmans, 1936).

45. Berkhof, *Aspects of Liberalism,* 138–63; see also Louis Berkhof, review of *The New Modernism,* by Cornelius Van Til, *Banner* 82 (Nov. 14, 1947): 1264; and idem, "Is Neo-Orthodoxy Tainted by Liberalism?" *Banner* 85 (Nov. 3, 1950): 1353.

46. Berkhof, *Kingdom of God,* 4.

47. Louis Berkhof, *The Second Coming of Christ* (Grand Rapids: Eerdmans, 1953).

48. See "Bibliography," ed. DeKlerk, 2.51–52. The last article in the series, "The New Jerusalem," appeared on the day of his death.

crystallization, condensation and reproduction in his own original way of the best he had imbibed from such master minds in Reformed Theology as these. The vagaries of Premillennialism had no fascination for him. Thoroughly committed to the particularism of the Reformed Faith, he had a no less deep appreciation of the significance of God's common grace. He has been a lifelong champion of the cause of Christian education, primary, secondary, and higher. He has raised his voice to plead for Christian social action in the industrial sphere. In standpoint, outlook, and vision he is a true spiritual son of John Calvin.[49]

49. Bouma, "Professor Berkhof Retires," 35.

Secondary Sources

Bratt, James D. *Dutch Calvinism in Modern America: A History of a Conservative Subculture.* Grand Rapids: Eerdmans, 1984.

DeKlerk, Peter, ed. *Bibliography of the Writings of the Professors of Calvin Theological Seminary,* 2.1–52. Grand Rapids: Calvin Theological Seminary, 1980.

DeKlerk, Peter, and Richard R. DeRidder, eds. *Perspectives on the Christian Reformed Church: Studies in Its History, Theology, and Ecumenicity.* Grand Rapids: Baker, 1983.

Wells, David F., ed. *Reformed Theology in America: A History of Its Modern Development.* Grand Rapids: Eerdmans, 1985.

H. Orton Wiley

John R. Tyson

Henry Orton Wiley (1877–1961) was born in a sod house near Marquette, Nebraska. His life soon shifted farther west as he attended Oregon State Normal School in Ashland, graduating in 1898. While in school, Wiley worked in a drug store and subsequently became a registered pharmacist. He also served as a minister in the United Brethren Church for a short time prior to enrolling in the University of California. Wiley then united with the Church of the Nazarene in Berkeley, serving as its pastor from 1905 to 1909. During that period he received an A.B. from the University of California, as well as a B.D. from the Pacific School of Religion, and was ordained to the ministry of the Church of the Nazarene. From the pastorate at Berkeley he was called to service at Pasadena College.[1]

Pasadena College was founded in 1910 by Phineas Bresee, patriarch of the Church of the Nazarene, with the vision of its becoming a Nazarene university, "a center of holy fire." Wiley served first as dean and then as president during his stay at the college from 1910 to 1916. He simultaneously continued his own education, working toward an S.T.M. from the Pacific School of Religion. As dean, Wiley established the curriculum for the degree program of the college of liberal arts. During its infancy, Pasadena College was chronically short of funds and qualified instructors. In the academic year 1911–12, for example, President Edgar P. Ellyson was responsible for classroom instruction in three fields, theology, astronomy, and geology, while Dean Wiley taught in two areas, philosophy and education.[2] Ellyson resigned after only two years

1. For a useful examination of the emergence of the Church of the Nazarene and Wiley's significant role in the formative years of that church and her educational institutions, see Timothy L. Smith, *Called unto Holiness; The Story of the Nazarenes: The Formative Years* (Kansas City, Mo.: Nazarene, 1962).

2. Ibid., 261.

of service, and Wiley was elected to replace him in 1912.

Wiley's tenure as president of Pasadena College proved to be tumultuous. Controversy and schism soon compounded the continuing financial and curricular challenges faced by the fledgling institution. The University Church, which was associated with the college, was placed in the hands of Seth C. Rees, a powerful revivalist, as Wiley came to the presidency. In 1913 Wiley brought A. J. Ramsay, a former Baptist minister and a graduate of Union Theological Seminary in Richmond, to join the faculty as professor of Bible. Though the labors of these men led to dynamic revivals, their strong views and strong personalities produced tensions that threatened to divide the community. In the aftermath of a great revival in the spring of 1915, the small campus divided into camps of conflicting loyalties. Professor Ramsay and A. O. Hendricks—who was simultaneously a student at Pasadena, pastor of the downtown Nazarene church, and a member of the college's board of trustees—reacted unfavorably to the "freedom of the Spirit" which Rees and Wiley viewed as being necessary to worship in the Nazarene tradition. Charges and countercharges flew back and forth. Rees charged Ramsay with harboring Calvinist doctrine, and because of his Congregationalist tendencies Rees was in turn charged with attempting to take the University Church out of the denomination. The board of trustees mounted investigations to assess the theological propriety of Ramsay and other faculty members. The fatherly counsel of Phineas Bresee papered over the dispute, but his death in October of 1915 signaled a renewal of hostilities. As he lay on his deathbed, Bresee begged Wiley to "stay by the college." But after the founder's death and the renewal of Rees's attacks upon Ramsay, Wiley resolved to resign if he could not rid himself and the school of the ongoing interventions by the college's board of trustees and other outside influ-

ences. Because his stipulations were not met, he resigned his post in March of 1916.[3]

Wiley intended to return to the Nazarene congregation at Berkeley and to complete his master's degree at Pacific School of Religion. He was, however, soon elected to the presidency of Northwest Nazarene College in Nampa, Idaho, a position he held until 1926. The trustees of Northwest were so anxious to have Wiley come to the school that they deferred his appointment till May of 1917, so that he could finish his S.T.M. The controversy at Pasadena also colored Wiley's first two years at Northwest Nazarene College, but he eventually engineered a reconciliation between the principal figures of both parties. The role of reconciler is sometimes without honor, and Wiley operated under a cloud of suspicion for several years. His friends among the more independent Nazarenes, including Seth Rees, saw Wiley as turning away from the rights of the local congregation, while the leadership of the denomination were somewhat dubious regarding his loyalty to the Church of the Nazarene. Gradually, through a vigorous campaign of speaking engagements and letter writing, the breach was healed and the cloud of suspicion dissipated. The centerpiece of Wiley's campaign was his urging revisions to correct organizational problems that arose from weaknesses in the Nazarene *Manual of Discipline.* Seeking to maintain the traditional Nazarene balance between congregational and hierarchical polity, Wiley urged changes in the *Manual* which would make it impossible for a functioning church to disorganize and leave the denomination; on the other side of the issue, he also urged that the general superintendents of the Church of the Nazarene function not like independent bishops, but like a board in conversation with the church. "I can see no reason," Wiley said, "why the people who prefer a distinctively Holiness Church should be compelled to submit to an autocratic government."[4]

3. Ibid., 275–77.
4. Ibid., 284–85.

Although his ten-year presidency did not solve the financial problems which plagued the early years of Northwest Nazarene College, Wiley's educational vision, fervent piety, and denominational loyalty left an indelible mark upon the school. At the very beginning of his tenure, Wiley had declared his resolve to make Northwest a missionary school. His resolve bore fruit, and by 1922 there were on campus six vital student organizations focused on missions, and thirteen Northwest alumni had become missionaries in foreign lands. Former students like Fairy Chism, who served as a Nazarene missionary to Africa, remembered Wiley's dictum, "The symbol of Christianity is neither a cross, nor a crown, but a towel," an allusion to Christ's servantlike washing of the disciples' feet. The curriculum which Wiley shaped sent forth Christian scholar-servants who had received rudimentary medical training in addition to the more typical religious preparation.[5]

Timothy Smith's assessment of Wiley's work at Northwest Nazarene College is worth quoting: "The measure of Dr. Wiley's achievement in this his second major assignment from the church seems large indeed. He kept his own heart strong and loving under severe pressure and inspired a band of devoted young preachers and prospective missionaries to stay by the denomination. He led the way in reforms aimed at maintaining within the communion the spirituality which Rees believed could exist only outside. The institution at Nampa became during his administration the strongest Nazarene college."[6] As a result of his efforts, Wiley was selected in 1928 by the General Conference of the Church of the Nazarene to serve on the commission appointed to revise the *Manual*.[7]

Having been awarded a D.D. from Pasadena College in 1925, Wiley returned to the presidency of that institution in 1926. Its financial struggles continued unabated. Af-

ter two years in that position, he left again to undertake the editorship of the denominational journal, the *Herald of Holiness*. In 1929 he received an S.T.D. from the Pacific School of Religion, and in 1933 he returned to the presidency of Pasadena again, where he was immediately met by an institutional debt of over $135,000.[8] Through the ensuing efforts of Wiley and James B. Chapman, who served as officers with the General Department of Education of the Church of the Nazarene, the marriage between the denominational colleges and the church was stabilized, and gradually the colleges' financial hurdles were overcome through sacrificial giving and denominational support. Orton Wiley served as president of Pasadena College until his retirement in 1949, when he was named president emeritus.

In sum, we might say that while Wiley's ministry embraced the pastorate, it focused on the educational institutions of his church. He was substantially involved in the leadership of the Church of the Nazarene, serving as the secretary of the General Department of Education from its organization in 1917 onwards. One of his first acts as secretary was to begin a series of department-authorized communications which gradually enabled the Nazarene colleges to work in closer cooperation with the aims of the department and the church. In concert with Chapman, who was chairman of the department, and others of like mind, Wiley worked tirelessly in behalf of Christian liberal-arts colleges affiliated with the Church of the Nazarene. In an address delivered in 1920, Chapman urged that only an educated ministry could conserve and spread the Wesleyan message. However important Holiness seminaries and Bible schools were to the mission of the church, the Nazarenes had to concentrate their efforts on building first-rate liberal-arts colleges, and had to be willing to spend money for gymnasiums, laboratories, and the like, even though some pious people deemed such items un-

5. Ibid., 285–88.
6. Ibid., 288.
7. Ibid., 295.

8. Ibid., 328.

necessary for the training of ministers and missionaries. Through his formative and forward-looking work with the General Department of Education, Wiley along with several others set the Church of the Nazarene on the educational path it has followed ever since.[9]

Christian Theology

Its Purpose and Sources

Wiley's magnum opus was his three-volume *Christian Theology* (1941). The fruit of "nearly twenty years of constant study and teaching," it took shape at Chapman's request for a work on systematic theology which could be used in the training of ministers.[10] The work was subsequently abridged by Paul T. Culbertson and released in 1946 as a one-volume edition with the title *Introduction to Christian Theology*.[11] Both the original and the abridged versions have become mainstays of evangelical Wesleyan Arminianism.

Wiley's commitment to the Christian church and her ministry is voiced in the dedication of his *Christian Theology*: "To the young men and young women who, feeling the call of God to the work of the ministry, desire to 'take heed to the doctrine' that they may be able to direct others in the way that leads to God and life eternal, this work is affectionately dedicated." The preface signals similar concerns, indicating that the book is "offered with a prayer that it may find at least some small place in the preparation of young men and women who look forward to the work of the ministry. . . . My purpose and aim has been to review the field of theology in as simple a manner as possible for the use of those who, entering the ministry, desire to be informed concerning the great doctrines of the

church."[12] The author's prayer was certainly answered; as late as 1984, a survey of evangelical Wesleyan theologians identified Wiley's *Christian Theology* as the greatest influence upon their own scholarly development.[13]

Wiley's self-conscious commitment to doing theology in and for the church significantly determined the resources from which his doctrine was derived. He followed the Wesleyan practice of focusing concretely upon Scripture and the Christian tradition; each theological doctrine is examined in the light of both its biblical bases (there is substantial exegetical study of the Old and New Testaments) and the historical foundations of the Christian church. Striving for a systematic theology that embraces the Bible and the church catholic, Wiley cites Augustine, the ancient church councils and creeds, Cyprian, Gregory Nazianzen, Irenaeus, Origen, Tertullian, and Thomas Aquinas more frequently than James Arminius.[14] Wiley's Wesleyan-Arminian posture emerges in his exposition of specific theological doctrines, but he utilizes resources and addresses a readership that go beyond the bounds of his own denomination and tradition. Thus the works of John Wesley (though not those of Charles Wesley) are cited with predictable frequency, and with an emphasis that suggests that they are at the core of the author's own theological tradition. But evangelical theologians of other traditions—A. A. and Charles Hodge (Reformed) and Augustus H. Strong (Baptist), for example—are also cited with approval. Equally telling, however, is the absence of any reference to the work of Karl Barth or Emil Brunner, who

9. Ibid., 324–25.

10. H. Orton Wiley, *Christian Theology*, 3 vols. (Kansas City, Mo.: Beacon Hill, 1941), 1:3.

11. H. Orton Wiley and Paul T. Culbertson, *Introduction to Christian Theology* (Kansas City, Mo.: Beacon Hill, 1946).

12. Wiley, *Christian Theology*, 1:3.

13. Mark A. Noll, *Between Faith and Criticism: Evangelicals, Scholarship, and the Bible in America* (San Francisco: Harper and Row, 1986), 209, 213. Twenty-five of ninety-five respondents identified Wiley as the theologian who had most influenced them. Twenty-one named *Christian Theology* as the most influential work.

14. Augustine, for example, is cited forty-six times, as compared to only ten citations of Arminius.

were well into their productive years when Wiley's *Christian Theology* was written. Wiley's chief partners in dialogue were theologians of the nineteenth century, writers of the old evangelicalism, and generally (though not exclusively) those who stood within the Wesleyan tradition.

Wiley's Wesleyan resources were of two varieties. The one group, including Richard Watson, John Miley, and William Burt Pope, constituted what was best in mainstream, classical Methodist theology (both in England and in the United States); the other group, including Phineas Bresee, Edgar P. Ellyson, and A. M. Hills, represented the distinctive contributions of the American Holiness tradition.[15] Wiley's *Christian Theology* built a bridge between these two types of Wesleyan theology without losing the distinctives of the Holiness tradition, and without degenerating into the extreme anti-Calvinist, anti-Catholic rhetoric that had characterized earlier Holiness theologies.[16] He sought to draw sectarian Wesleyan theology into dialogue with the parent tradition, to the mutual benefit of both. It is also clear that Wiley was primarily interested in the classical expressions of the Wesleyan tradition, for while he cited Wesley along with Watson, Miley, and Pope with great frequency, he showed little interest in more modern—and more liberal—Methodist figures like Borden Parker Bowne and Edgar S. Brightman.[17]

The structure of Wiley's *Christian Theology* follows the same basic pattern that had been laid down for Protestant theologians by John Calvin's *Institutes of the Christian Religion* (1559). It moves from prolegomena through the doctrines of God and humanity to Christology, soteriology, the church, and finally eschatology. Wiley's most immediate precursor seems to be the three-volume *Compendium of Christian Theology* of William Burt Pope (1875–76).[18] Pope was tutor of theology at Didsbury College, Manchester, England. His *Compendium* was very popular among Methodists in Britain and the United States, and remained as one of the classical expressions of Wesleyan theology long after it disappeared from required-reading lists. That the basic structure of Wiley's *Christian Theology* follows Pope's *Compendium* throughout is not especially surprising since Pope's work, while representing mainstream Methodist theology, stood remarkably close to Wiley's views. Both works, for example, included a substantial section on entire sanctification and Christian perfection at a time when Methodist theologians had begun to eschew these distinctive doctrines of their tradition.[19]

The Definition and Sources of Theology

Wiley begins with various concerns preliminary to doing theology in the evangelical Wesleyan mode. After considering the definitions for "theology" offered by the leading lights of classical Christianity, Wiley characteristically opts for one that he believes to be the most synthetic and most succinct: "Christian Theology is the systematic presentation of the doctrines of the Christian Faith."[20] His own approach

---

15. For a discussion of the theological background of Wiley's work, see Thomas A. Langford, *Practical Divinity: Theology in the Wesleyan Tradition* (Nashville: Abingdon, 1983), 137–40.

16. A. M. Hills, *Fundamental Christian Theology*, 2 vols. (Pasadena: Kinne, 1931), represents the older, sectarian Nazarene theology, which was stridently anti-Calvinist at points.

17. For an examination of the theological trends and shifts within American Methodism, see Langford, *Practical Divinity*, and Robert E. Chiles, *Theological Transition in American Methodism, 1790–1935* (Nashville: Abingdon, 1965).

18. William Burt Pope, *A Compendium of Christian Theology*, 3 vols., 2d ed. (New York: Phillips and Hunt, 1880–81).

19. Pope, *Compendium*, 3:27–100; Wiley, *Christian Theology*, 2:440–517. It is clear, from the sheer amount of coverage, that entire sanctification, which receives direct exposition in seventeen pages of the *Compendium*, is an area in which Wiley's treatment goes well beyond that of Pope.

20. Wiley, *Christian Theology*, 1:16.

closely follows the synthetic method which he observed in Strong, Pope, Miley, Hills, and others. This method has been described "as one which 'starts from the highest principle, God, and proceeds to man, Christ, redemption, and finally to the end of all things.' The basic principle of organization is its logical order of cause and effect."[21]

Another of Wiley's preliminary concerns is the fundamental relationships that theology has with religion, revelation, and the church.[22] His aim here is to demonstrate that "every branch of this science is sacred. It is a temple which is filled with the presence of God. . . . Therefore all fit students are worshipers as well as students."[23] In Wiley's view, Christian theology as a didactic or positive science is best categorized under the traditional fourfold classification: (1) biblical (or exegetical), (2) historical, (3) systematic, and (4) practical.[24] In this approach Wiley followed the precedent of Philip Schaff, Strong, Miley, and Pope.[25]

As Wiley turns to survey "The Sources of Theology" (ch. 2), his posture as an evangelical Wesleyan theologian begins to emerge more distinctively. Under the subhead "Authoritative Sources" he asserts that "Christian Theology as the science of the one true and perfect religion is based upon the documentary records of God's revelation of Himself in Jesus Christ. The Bible, therefore, is the Divine Rule of faith and practice, and the only authoritative source of theology."[26] Yet "this statement needs ex-plication if not qualification," for "in a stricter and deeper sense, Jesus Christ himself as the Personal and Eternal Word is the only true and adequate revelation of the Father." The revelatory interconnection of Christ and Scripture is supported by an examination of biblical passages; Wiley concludes that "the Oracle and the oracles are one."[27]

Wiley embraces the dynamic theory of inspiration, which "maintains that there was an 'elevation' on the part of the sacred writers which prepared their minds and hearts for the reception of the message, but insists that . . . there must be in addition a divine communication of truth."[28] He uses the term "plenary inspiration" to describe his understanding "that the whole and every part [of Scripture] is divinely inspired."[29] So saying, Wiley clearly aligns himself with evangelicals like B. B. Warfield, J. Gresham Machen, and Pope, but in a way that is characteristic of the Wesleyan preference for using biblical words to describe biblical doctrines. (Ironically, the only reference to "infallibility" that is listed in the index of the massive *Christian Theology* directs the reader to a discussion of papal infallibility.) Wiley's extensive investigation of the doctrine of Scripture leads him to conclude with the ancient church that the Bible is the Christian's only rule of faith and practice. For proof of the Bible's authority, Wiley looks to the inner witness of the Holy Spirit as well as various historical evidences.[30]

Among Wiley's secondary or subsidiary sources for doing theology are four elements: (1) "experience, which is commonly known as the vital source of theology in that it conditions a right apprehension of its truths"; (2) confessions or articles of faith, which are "generally termed the traditional source"; (3) philosophy, "which is the formal or shaping source of theology"; and

---

21. Ibid., 1:58.
22. Ibid., 1:16–20.
23. Ibid., 1:17, following Pope, *Compendium*, 1:4–5.
24. Wiley, *Christian Theology*, 1:20–32.
25. Ibid., 1:21.
26. Ibid., 1:33. Wiley and Culbertson, *Introduction*, 26–27, offers a similar succinct statement: "Christian theology as the science of the one true and perfect religion is based upon the documentary records of God's revelation of Himself in Jesus Christ. Thus the Bible is the divine rule of faith and practice, and the only authoritative and primary source of Christian theology. The Holy Scriptures constitute the quarry out of which are mined the glorious truths utilized in constructing the edifice of Christian doctrine."

27. Wiley, *Christian Theology*, 1:33.
28. Ibid., 1:177.
29. Ibid., 1:184.
30. Ibid., 1:205–14.

(4) nature, "a fundamental and conditioning source."[31] His emphasis upon experience as a theological source is characteristically Wesleyan, reaching back to John Wesley's insistence that true religion and vital piety go hand in hand.[32] Yet Wiley is not interested in human experience per se, nor in emotionalism, but in "Christian experience, in the sense of an impartation of spiritual life through the truth as vitalized by the Holy Spirit."[33] Wiley returns to his doctrine of Holy Scripture to observe that theological truth and Christian experience become intertwined through the action of Word and Spirit upon the human heart. Having reaffirmed the written Word's interconnection with and subordination to the personal Word (Jesus Christ), Wiley suggests "that the formal principle of the Word may through the Personal Word, so coincide with the material principle of faith as to become the *engrafted word* which is able to save the soul. Truth in its ultimate nature is personal."[34] To emphasize the personal quality of Christian truth, Wiley points out that Jesus "knocks at the door of men's hearts—not as a proposition to be apprehended, but as a Person to be received and loved."[35] Moreover, "granting that all personal knowledge must have its root in ethical sympathy, or a likeness in character between the knower and the known, then the knowledge of God involves a filial relationship between the Incarnate Son and the souls of men, a relationship begotten and nourished by the Holy Spirit. This filial relationship is spiritual knowledge."[36]

After an extensive examination of the Apostles', Nicene, and Athanasian creeds, which constitute Wiley's second subsidiary source of theology, he affirms the value of philosophy as a device for "systematizing and rationalizing truth, so that it may be presented to the mind in proper form for assimilation."[37] Recognizing the conflict between theology and philosophy, Wiley traces it briefly through Christian history. He concludes that the truth about the relationship between theology and philosophy lies somewhere between Tertullian's characterization of all philosophy as fiction ("What has Athens to do with Jerusalem?") and the Alexandrian school's affirmation that Christianity is the truest philosophy.[38]

Wiley's recognition of nature as a source for theological reflection seems particularly pertinent in the current ecological crisis; his rationale for so doing lay in a robust affirmation of general revelation.[39] While he did not explicitly discuss the plausibility of natural theology, a topic which had been the focus of much controversy between his contemporaries Karl Barth and Emil Brunner,[40] Wiley did not leave much room for it. Consider, for example, his observation that "the language of nature falls upon darkened intellects and dulled sensibilities and must be read in the dim light of a vitiated spiritual nature."[41]

The Doctrine of the Father

The second main section of *Christian Theology* is devoted to "The Doctrine of the Father." The reader is shepherded through

31. Ibid., 1:37.
32. See John Wesley, "Letter to Mr. C——," in *The Works of John Wesley*, 14 vols. (Kansas City, Mo.: Beacon Hill, 1979), 13:132, where Wesley writes: "'What then is religion?' It is happiness in God, or in the knowledge and love of God. It is 'faith working by love;' producing 'righteousness, and peace, and joy in the Holy Ghost.' In other words, it is a heart and life devoted to God; or, communion with God the Father and the Son; or, the mind which was in Christ Jesus, enabling us to walk as He walked." See also John Wesley, "A Letter to the Reverend Dr. Conyers Middleton," in *Works*, 10:67–77, where Wesley describes the interconnection between Christian doctrine and Christian experience.
33. Wiley, *Christian Theology*, 1:38.
34. Ibid.
35. Ibid.
36. Ibid.
37. Ibid., 1:49.
38. Ibid., 1:50.
39. Ibid., 1:125–34.
40. See *Natural Theology*, trans. Peter Fraenkel (London: Geoffrey Bles, 1946); this work comprises Brunner's "Nature and Grace" and Barth's spirited "No!"
41. Wiley, *Christian Theology*, 1:127–28.

thorough discussions of "The Existence and Nature of God" (ch. 9), "The Divine Names and Predicates" (ch. 10), and the traditional conceptions of "God as Absolute Reality" (ch. 11) and "God as Infinite Efficiency" (ch. 12). Wiley's most distinctive contribution in this section may be his meditation upon "God as Perfect Personality" (ch. 13). Here the personalist tradition, which had strongly influenced Methodism, merges with the traditional conceptions to create a synthesis that points to their inner coherence.[42] As Wiley explains, "the Christian conception of God must therefore include the idea of Absolute Reality as the ground of existence, His Infinite Efficiency as its cause, and His Perfect Personality as the reason or end of all things."[43] After examining the perfections of the divine personality, Wiley points to the correlation that exists between divine and human personalities and the potential of renewal through a saving relationship with God: "God as Perfect Personality is the only worthy object of human choice, and love to God the fulfilling of the law. With perfect love to God and man, the soul must forever unfold in the light of this Supreme Good, and at every stage of its progress will embrace enlarged conceptions of the true, and the right, the perfect and the good."[44] Contemplation of the perfections of the divine personality foreshadows the wholeness that can come to the saved and sanctified human soul.

Wiley's treatment of "The Attributes of God" (ch. 14) classifies them in three distinct categories: (1) the absolute attributes, "those qualities which belong to God apart from His creative work"; (2) the relative attributes, "those arising out of the relation existing between the Creator and the created"; and (3) the moral attributes, "those which belong to the relation between God and the moral beings under His government, more especially as they concern mankind."[45] Wiley's discussion of divine omniscience includes the common ground as well as the differences between Calvinistic and Arminian conceptions of that attribute: "Both the Arminian and Calvinistic theologians hold to . . . the knowledge that God has of Himself, and . . . the free knowledge that God has of persons and things outside of Himself. However, they differ as to the ground of this foreknowledge, the Arminians generally maintaining that God has a knowledge of pure contingency, while the Calvinistic theologians connect it with the decrees which God has purposed in Himself."[46]

In a similar fashion Wiley delineates three classical positions taken with respect to the relationship of divine foreknowledge and predestination: (1) "The Arminian position holds that the power of contrary choice is a constituent element of human freedom, and that foreknowledge must refer to free acts and therefore to pure contingency." Rejecting the medieval scholastics' approach which located divine foreknowledge in the eternal now, Wiley follows Pope in viewing predestination as having a sequential connection to human actions. At the same time, Wiley also refuses, along with Pope, to identify divine foreknowledge with predestination: "Predestination must have its rights; all that God wills to do is foredetermined. But what human freedom accomplishes, God can only foreknow; otherwise freedom is no longer freedom."[47] (2) "The Calvinist position identifies foreknowledge and foreordination, maintaining that the divine decrees are the ground for the occurrence of all events, including

---

42. John Miley, *Systematic Theology*, 2 vols. (New York: Hunt and Eaton, 1892, 1894), 1:177–80, uses personality as the organizing principle for presenting the divine attributes.

43. Wiley, *Christian Theology*, 1:290.

44. Ibid., 1:312.

45. Ibid., 1:329. This is essentially the pattern laid down by Pope, who delineated the divine attributes under three heads: (1) attributes of absolute essence; (2) attributes related to the creation; and (3) attributes related to moral government. For a discussion of this method of classifying the divine attributes, see Pope, *Compendium*, 1:289–91.

46. Wiley, *Christian Theology*, 1:356.

47. Ibid., 1:357, citing Pope, *Compendium*, 1:318ff.

the voluntary actions of men. On this theory, foreknowledge depends upon the certainty of the decrees, and is not strictly a knowledge of contingent events."[48] Calvin, Francis Turretin, and Charles Hodge are cited as examples of the Calvinist position. (3) "The Socinian position denies that God has any foreknowledge of contingent events."[49] Predictably, Wiley concludes that the Arminian view forms a more coherent whole with the nature of God and the doctrines of salvation: "The Arminian position . . . is in reality the Catholic view of the Church, and is the only one which can be consistently maintained in harmony with the great doctrines of salvation."[50] Though Wiley wrote at a time when the lines separating the three traditional positions were being blurred through reformulation of the doctrine, his preference for classical theological sources precluded any conversation with emergent modern alternatives. His attention was focused upon the three traditional approaches to the question at hand.

Wiley's treatment of "Cosmology" (ch. 16) concludes the first volume of his trilogy. He affirms creation out of nothing, though recognizing that it is not demanded on purely linguistic grounds.[51] In the face of mounting scientific theories to the contrary, he maintains that creation occurred by divine fiat. His treatment of the six days of creation seeks to merge elements of both an instantaneous and a gradual creation into a coherent whole that is not at variance with the best scientific evidence: "In the sense of origination, creation is instantaneous; but as formation it is gradual and cumulative. There is a progressive revelation in an ascending scale of creative acts. . . . The study of the Genesis account reveals certain facts which take on added significance with each new scientific discovery."[52] Furthermore, when surveying the various approaches to the doctrine of providence, classical and scientific, Wiley seems to lean towards a view that emphasizes concurrence, "that activity of God which concurs in second causes, and co-operates with living creatures."[53] He accepts, however, Pope's criticism that this view gives too much weight to the actions of the second causes, implying that the first and second causes contribute equally to the resultant action. Also given some favorable attention is the notion of continuous creation, which was pioneered by Augustine; it is deemed preferable to a determinist model based on the belief that everything depends directly upon God without any intervening second causes.

Wiley's anthropology is presented under the heading "The Doctrine of God the Father," because the creation of humanity in the *imago Dei* ("image of God") is the foundation of his understanding of human nature and destiny.[54] Emphasis on creation in God's image and thus on the primitive holiness of humanity's original nature later provides a useful counterpoint to Wiley's robust doctrine of human depravity, as well as lays the foundation for his Wesleyan-Holiness exposition of Christian perfection as the restoration of humanity's created nature. Other aspects of Wiley's anthropology seem less useful, such as his rather extensive treatment of the classical theories on the origin of the human soul, a subject he discusses without any recourse to psychological theory.[55]

In his treatment of the fall of humanity, Wiley follows Pope in bemoaning the myopic approach of some of the more orthodox theologians of the nineteenth century who, "in their efforts to defend the historical character of the Mosaic account, failed to

48. Wiley, *Christian Theology*, 1:357–58.
49. Ibid., 1:358.
50. Ibid., 1:359. Wiley cites Richard Watson, *Theological Institutes*, 2 vols. (New York: Lane and Scott, 1851), 1:365ff., as the best-known apologetic for the Arminian conception of divine foreknowledge and predestination.
51. Wiley, *Christian Theology*, 1:458. Here Wiley cites Miley, *Systematic Theology*, 1:283.
52. Wiley, *Christian Theology*, 1:462–63.
53. Ibid., 1:480.
54. Ibid., 2:29–50.
55. Ibid., 2:23–29.

do justice to its rich symbolism."[56] Wiley would prefer to follow the pattern of Paul, whose hermeneutic allowed him to see the ancient figures historically and allegorically without placing those two approaches in opposition (see Gal. 4:24). This, in Wiley's estimate, was also the approach of "the earlier Arminian and Wesleyan theologians[, who] were not under the necessity of combating destructive criticism, and hence took a truer and more scriptural position."[57] Wiley's exegesis of the Genesis account allows that "Adam's will was holy, and therefore created with a tendency in the right direction, but not indefectibly so; that is, it had the power of reversing its course and moving in the opposite direction, and this solely through its own self-determination."[58] Resorting to classical theological categories, Wiley describes this as the *posse non peccare* view (Adam was "able not to sin"), which he identifies as being "generally accepted as the orthodox position."[59] Distinguishing between the "natural" image of God which humanity still bears today and the "moral" image allows Wiley to sharply contrast the depth of human depravity with the history of our higher nature and the hope of our higher destiny: "If now we examine the fall in its external relations, we shall find that man no longer bears the glory of his moral likeness to God. The natural image in the sense of his personality he retained, but the glory was gone. From his high destination in communion with God, he fell into the depths of deprivation and sin. Having lost the Holy Spirit, he began a life of external discord and internal misery."[60]

Utilizing a word-study approach the author proceeds to examine "The Nature and Penalty of Sin." Wiley explores various biblical terms (*hamartia, parabasis, parapiptein, adikia, anomia,* and *asebeia*) and clas-

sical definitions to show the nuances of the term *sin* as well as the unanimity among orthodox theologians in emphasizing that sin is both act and state or condition.[61]

Though unwilling to distinguish between the Reformed and Wesleyan views of the nature of sin, Wiley does distinguish between the Reformed, Arminian, and Wesleyan conceptions of original sin or inherited depravity. In an extensive section on the development of the doctrine of original sin, Wiley characterizes Calvin and the Reformed churches as making "no distinction between imputed guilt and inherited depravity. Original sin include[s] both elements—guilt and corruption."[62] Wiley subsequently points out that this approach gives Reformed theologians a more negative understanding of total depravity than is prevalent among Wesleyan theologians, who view original sin primarily in terms of corruption.[63]

Wiley also distinguishes between Wesleyan (Pope preferred the term *Methodist*) theologians and the Arminians. Here he approvingly cites a summation by the Reformed theologian Charles Hodge: "Wesleyanism (1) admits entire moral depravity; (2) denies that any men in this state have any power to co-operate with the grace of God; (3) asserts that the guilt of all through Adam was removed by justification of all through Christ; and (4) ability to co-operate is of the Holy Spirit, through the universal influence of the redemption of Christ."[64] Pope made the same point, in a more characteristically Methodist fashion, by dwelling upon the Wesleyan doctrine of prevenient or preventing grace, which goes before and enables human cooperation with the Holy Spirit. Wiley's willingness to cite Hodge instead of Pope reveals his

56. Ibid., 2:54.
57. Ibid.
58. Ibid., 2:59.
59. Ibid.
60. Ibid., 2:65.

61. Ibid., 2:86.
62. Ibid., 2:100–137; here Wiley is largely dependent on Pope, *Compendium,* 2:72–86. The quote is from *Christian Theology,* 2:106.
63. Wiley, *Christian Theology,* 2:128–30.
64. Ibid., 2:108; Charles Hodge, *Systematic Theology,* 3 vols. (New York: Scribner, 1872–73), 2:329–30.

irenic spirit. He sacrificed a bit of theological precision in an effort to bridge the rancorous separation between earlier evangelicals. The nineteenth-century debates and acrimony between Reformed and Wesleyan evangelicals made no sense in the context of the twentieth-century struggle with liberalism. Yet Wiley would not have his own position misunderstood. For classical Wesleyan theology comes, as John Wesley himself said, "within a hair's breadth" and "to the very edge of Calvinism . . . (1) In ascribing all good to the free grace of God. (2) In denying all natural free-will, and all power antecedent to grace. And, (3) In excluding all merit from man; even for what he has or does by the grace of God."[65] In contradistinction to Wesleyan theology, some of the Remonstrant theologians who followed Arminius, having a less severe view of human depravity, saw a measure of human ability in the process of salvation. This view (perhaps justifiably) has been styled semi-Pelagian, which is very much like saying semiheretical.[66]

Christology

The Trinity is the principle around which Wiley organized his *Christian Theology.* Accordingly, he turns next to "The Doctrine of the Son." Wiley's Christology follows classical patterns in treating first the person (ch. 21) and then the work ("The Estates and Offices of Christ," ch. 22). He affirms the biblical teachings, examines the historical debates, and embraces orthodox interpretations. For example, he follows classical Protestant theology in identifying redemption through sacrifice as the chief aim of Christ's incarnation.[67] The traditional threefold offices of Christ— Prophet, Priest, and King—receive surprisingly sparse attention, while the doctrine of

the atonement is the focus of two separate chapters and nearly one hundred pages.[68] The reason for this emphasis is that in Wiley's day adherence to the orthodox doctrine of the atonement seemed to be eroding.

Wiley's emphasis upon the atoning work of Christ would later receive extended treatment in his commentary on *The Epistle to the Hebrews.*[69] The central section of the commentary, as is indeed the case with the epistle itself, deals with the priestly intercession of Jesus Christ. This work complements Wiley's earlier interest in the atonement of Christ and its purifying effects in the Christian's life. Wiley's exposition of Hebrews 6:4–12 follows Bresee in identifying "Christian Perfection as the normal standard of spiritual experience, but also the high level of living which should characterize holy men and women."[70]

The last chapter of Wiley's Christology in *Christian Theology* treats the nature and extent of the atonement in a predictably evangelical and Wesleyan fashion. First, over against liberalism he emphasizes "that the idea of propitiation is the dominant note in the Wesleyan type of Arminian theology."[71] Second, over against Calvinism he points out that "Arminianism with its emphasis upon moral freedom and prevenient grace, has always held to the universality of the atonement; that is, as a provision for the salvation of all men, conditioned upon faith. Calvinism on the other hand . . . has always been under the necessity of accepting the idea of a limited atonement."[72]

The Doctrine of the Holy Spirit

Ironically, Wiley's soteriology begins—as Calvin's did before him—with a detailed

---

65. John Wesley, "Minutes of Some Late Conversations between the Rev. Mr. Wesley and Others," in *Works,* 8:284–85.
66. Wiley, *Christian Theology,* 2:102–4, 108–9; Pope, *Compendium,* 2:79–86.
67. Wiley, *Christian Theology,* 2:185.

68. Ibid., 2:213–15, 217–300.
69. H. Orton Wiley, *The Epistle to the Hebrews* (Kansas City, Mo.: Beacon Hill, 1959); see especially ch. 6.
70. Ibid., 210.
71. Wiley, *Christian Theology,* 2:284.
72. Ibid., 2:296.

treatment of the doctrine of the Holy Spirit.[73] His examination of biblical terms describing the soteriological function of the Spirit (birth, baptism, anointing, and sealing) is an interesting synthesis of Wesleyan and Holiness theology.[74] Without embracing distinctively Pentecostal conceptions, Wiley's approach gives ample evidence of the heritage shared by Wesleyan and Pentecostal evangelicals.[75] (1) "The birth of the Spirit" is defined as "the impartation of divine life to the soul. It is not merely a reconstruction or working over of the old life; it is the impartation to the soul, or the implantation within the soul, of the new life of the Spirit."[76] (2) "Baptism with the Spirit" is "the induction of newborn individuals into the full privileges of the New Covenant."[77] This Spirit baptism is treated without reference to the sacrament of baptism, and is thought of as being subsequent to and consequent upon Christian initiation. Being subsequent to justification, it is described as a second work of grace. Further, it "must be considered under a twofold aspect; *first*, as a death to the carnal [fallen] nature; and *second*, as the fullness of life in the Spirit. Since entire sanctification is effected by the baptism with the Spirit, it likewise has a twofold aspect—the

cleansing from sin and full devotion to God."[78] (3) The "anointing with the Spirit" Wiley describes as "a further aspect of this second work of grace—that which regards it as a conferring of authority and power. It refers, therefore, not to the negative aspect of cleansing [from sin], but to the positive phase of the indwelling Spirit as 'empowering the believers for life and service.'"[79] (4) The "sealing with the Spirit" is the sign of "God's ownership and approval" of the believer; "this approval is not only a claim upon the service of the sanctified as involved in ownership, but the seal of approval upon that service as rendered through the Holy Spirit. The seal is also the guaranty of full redemption in the future."[80] Thus the distinctiveness of Wiley's Wesleyan-Holiness soteriology can be encapsulated under the rubric of the work of the Holy Spirit in the life of the believer: "The pentecostal gift of the Holy Spirit, which under one aspect is the baptism which purifies the heart; and under another, the anointing which empowers for life and service, is under still another aspect, the seal of God's ownership and approval."[81]

Wiley turns next to the various facets of salvation. John Wesley's emphasis upon sanctification or holiness of heart and life is well known. When describing "The Principles of a Methodist," for example, Wesley wrote: "Our main doctrines, which include all the rest, are three—that of repentance, of faith, and of holiness. The first of these we account, as it were, the porch of religion; the next, the door; the third, religion itself."[82] Wiley follows Wesley's subsumption of most of his soteriology within the doctrine of sanctification. Thus he characterizes vocation (the gospel call), prevenient grace, repentance, saving faith, and

73. The third book of Calvin's *Institutes of the Christian Religion,* which explains "The Way in Which We Receive the Grace of Christ," begins with a chapter entitled "The Things Spoken concerning Christ Profit Us by the Secret Working of the Holy Spirit. . . ."
74. Wiley, *Christian Theology,* 2:321–26.
75. See Donald W. Dayton, *Theological Roots of Pentecostalism* (Grand Rapids: Zondervan, 1987), 35–115.
76. Wiley, *Christian Theology,* 2:322.
77. Ibid., 2:323. It is often suggested that the identification of entire sanctification with "baptism with the Spirit" is more a product of the American Holiness tradition than a perspective derived directly from Wesley and the earliest Methodist preachers. See Langford, *Practical Divinity,* 140–43; Donald W. Dayton, "The Doctrine of the Baptism of the Holy Spirit," *Wesleyan Theological Journal* 13 (Spring 1978): 114–26. The Pentecostal imagery was present in the work of John Fletcher, but was most fully developed by Charles Finney, Asa Mahan, and other American revivalists.

78. Wiley, *Christian Theology,* 2:323–24.
79. Ibid., 2:324.
80. Ibid., 2:325.
81. Ibid.
82. John Wesley, "The Principles of a Methodist Farther Explained," in *Works,* 8:472.

conversion as "The Preliminary States of Grace" (ch. 26), since they precede and prepare the way for Christian righteousness and sanctification.[83] Justification, regeneration, adoption, the witness of the Spirit, and entire sanctification are described as the "conditional benefits of the atonement."[84] Justification, regeneration, adoption, and the witness of the Spirit are given due attention, but Wiley's most characteristic emphasis is upon the sanctifying role of the Holy Spirit in the life of the Christian.

At the beginning of his discussion of the preliminary states of grace, Wiley presents a summary of the Calvinist view of election and predestination. Predictably, he prefers to think of election and predestination in general (as opposed to particular) and conditional terms. Thus he writes: "Arminianism holds that predestination is the gracious purpose of God to save mankind from utter ruin. It is not an arbitrary, indiscriminate act of God intended to secure the salvation of so many and no more. It includes provisionally, all men in its scope, and is conditioned solely on faith in Jesus Christ."[85]

There follows an extensive discussion on prevenient grace, which is one of the most useful portions of volume 2 of *Christian Theology*. After a historical survey of comparative soteriologies—including Augustinian, Pelagian, and Arminian—Wiley appropriately locates Wesleyan-Arminian theology between soteriological determinism and a Pelagian position that speaks of salvation by the agency of a free human will. Now both great wings of evangelical Protestantism share a belief that fallen people cannot choose God: "The true Arminian as fully as the Calvinist, admits the depravity of human nature, and thereby magnifies the grace of God in salvation."[86] Arminianism, however, holds to the doctrine of prevenient grace. Prevenient grace, which

Wiley (quoting Wesley) describes as "all the drawings of the Father; the desires after God, which if we yield to them, increase more and more; . . . all the convictions which His Spirit, from time to time, works in every child of man; although it is true the generality of men stifle them as soon as possible," enables fallen people to turn toward God, but does not compel them to do so.[87] Thus synergism, or the cooperation of divine grace and the human will, is a basic truth of the Arminian system.[88] This synergism maintains both the seriousness of human sin and the human moral responsibility to act: "Arminianism holds that salvation is all of grace, in that every movement of the soul toward God is initiated by divine grace; but it recognizes also in a true sense, the co-operation of the human will, because in the last stage, it remains with the free agent, as to whether the grace thus proffered is accepted or rejected."[89]

As we hinted earlier, one of the most distinctive aspects of Wiley's *Christian Theology* is his extensive treatment of "Christian Perfection or Entire Sanctification" (ch. 29).[90] Christian perfection and entire sanctification, as the author notes, "are terms used to express the fullness of salvation from sin, or the completeness of the Christian life."[91] After examining "The Scriptural Basis for the Doctrine" and "The Historical Approach to the Subject," Wiley considers "The Meaning and Scope of Sanctification." Here he notes that the primary biblical term in this connection is "holiness," and that while its "primary meaning is a setting apart, or a separation, this in the New Testament takes on the deeper significance of a cleansing from all sin."[92]

"Entire sanctification" is defined in terms characteristic of the Wesleyan-Holiness tradition: "that act of God, subsequent to regeneration, by which believers are made

---

83. Wiley, *Christian Theology*, 2:334–79.
84. Ibid., 2:299.
85. Ibid., 2:337.
86. Ibid., 2:354.

87. Ibid., 2:355.
88. Ibid.
89. Ibid., 2:356.
90. Ibid., 2:440–517.
91. Ibid., 2:440.
92. Ibid., 2:466.

free from original sin, or depravity, and brought into a state of entire devotement to God, and the holy obedience of love made perfect."[93] Or more succinctly, "entire sanctification is a term applied to the fullness of redemption, or the cleansing of the heart from all sin."[94] Understood as being wrought both "by the baptism with the Holy Spirit" and "instantaneously by faith," it "comprehends in one experience the cleansing of the heart from sin and the abiding, indwelling presence of the Holy Spirit."[95] Following Wesley, Wiley affirms that there is a sense in which sanctification is gradual and progressive; but Wiley argues that there is also a single, discernible moment in which entire sanctification takes place: "While there is a gradual approach to sanctification, and a gradual growth in grace following it, the sanctifying act by which we are made holy, must of necessity be instantaneous."[96] To support the latter view, Wiley is able to cite one of the earliest theologians of Methodism, Adam Clarke, but not John Wesley himself; subsequent refinements of the doctrine are illustrated from Bresee's sermons and other documents representative of the American Holiness tradition.

Whereas "entire sanctification" applies more to the cleansing from sin, "Christian perfection" describes "the cluster and maturity of graces which compose the Christian character in the Church militant."[97] Following Wesley's famous treatise, Wiley emphasizes that Christian perfection is not (1) absolute perfection (this belongs to God alone), (2) the sort of perfection as inheres in angelic or unfallen beings, (3) the perfection that Adam and Eve enjoyed, (4) perfection in knowledge, or (5) immunity from temptation.[98] To state constructively precisely what Christian perfection is, Wiley turns to the concept of perfect love (1 John 4:17–18). The human heart is filled and purified by an infusion of divine love: "This is the full life of love, made perfect in the heart by the agency of the Holy Spirit. Pure love reigns supreme without the antagonisms of sin. Love is the spring of every activity."[99]

Wiley is careful to make several important "distinctions" (one might say "qualifications") in connection with the doctrine of Christian perfection, most notably a recognition that "infirmities must be distinguished from sins. Sin in the sense used here is a voluntary transgression of a known law. Infirmities on the other hand, are involuntary transgressions of the divine law, known or unknown, which are consequent on the ignorance and weakness of fallen men."[100] Since Christian perfection is a matter of the heart (motives and attitudes) rather than of knowledge, willful sin is inconsistent with Christian perfection, but infirmities (i.e., involuntary transgressions) are not.

In the final volume of his trilogy, Wiley draws a close correlation between Holiness soteriology and the life of the Christian. A pivotal discussion emerges in a section entitled "The Law of Love," where the Christian perfection that is realizable through an infusion of divine love is seen as entailing the ability to live a life that corresponds to the revealed will of God.[101] A shortcoming in Wiley's exposition of Christian ethics is that the virtues and duties enjoined are primarily of a personal or individualistic nature; matters of social reform or social holiness, which had been a formative part of Wesley's message, receive rather meager treatment.[102] The right to private property is singled out for particular attention, but little is said about other human rights such

93. Ibid., 2:466–67.
94. Ibid., 2:487.
95. Ibid., 2:467.
96. Ibid., 2:483.
97. Ibid., 2:496.
98. Ibid., 2:497–98; John Wesley, "A Plain Account of Christian Perfection," in Works, 11:441–43.

99. Wiley, Christian Theology, 2:502.
100. Ibid., 2:507.
101. Ibid., 3:29–35.
102. Ibid., 3:68–79, chiefly as an exposition of the Ten Commandments.

as social equality, economic opportunity, and freedom from exploitation.

The Doctrines of the Church and Last Things

Wiley's exposition of the church gives ample attention to the biblical and historical resources for examining its nature and function. After surveying the three major types of church organization—episcopal, congregational, and presbyterian—he allows for a combination of the best elements of each approach. In this way the spiritual function of the church can determine the shape of its polity.[103] Although Wiley affirms the role of women as prophets and deacons in the apostolic church, he stops short of applying these examples as models for ordaining women to the ministry of modern congregations.[104]

Turning to the sacraments, Wiley affirms the suitability of various modes of baptism and argues strongly against the necessity of immersion. In reference to the proper subjects of Christian baptism, he notes that "in addition to adult believers the church has always held that the children of believers are, likewise, the proper subjects of baptism; nor does it deny baptism to the children of unbelievers."[105] And after surveying the classical views of the presence of Christ in the Lord's Supper, Wiley correctly aligns Wesleyanism with Calvin's conception of spiritual presence: "Christ is spiritually present, so that [the communicants] may truly and emphatically be said to be partakers of His body and blood."[106] Stressing that the Lord's Supper is to be offered to all the people of God, Wiley repeats with approval the words of eucharistic invitation: "Let all those who have with true repentance forsaken their sins, and have believed in Christ unto salvation, draw near and take these emblems, and, by faith, partake of the life of Jesus Christ."[107]

Wiley's treatment of "The Doctrine of Last Things" runs to almost two hundred pages, which seems to be out of proportion with classical Protestantism's interest in eschatology. The extended discussion is, perhaps, more reflective of the milieu of American evangelicalism than of classical Wesleyanism or Continental Protestantism. In the face of modern skepticism the author argues for the immortality of the human soul and the resurrection of the dead. He gives a lengthy, but somewhat disinterested account of the intermediate state,[108] placing most of his constructive emphasis upon the return of Christ or "The Second Advent" (ch. 34).[109] His treatment of "The Final Consummation" (ch. 36) attacks certain "Heretical Theories concerning the Final State of the Wicked" (e.g., destructionism, universalism, annihilationism) on the way to an affirmation of a belief in the eternal punishment of the wicked and eternal blessedness of the saints. Both heaven and hell are thought of as states of being as well as places.[110] A succinct historical survey leads to the conclusion that premillennialist eschatology has always been the dominant view of classical Christianity and Protestantism.[111] There follows a review of "Modern Types of Millennial Theory," which considers various approaches but gives no attention to the dispensationalist eschatology popularized by the Scofield Reference Bible.[112]

H. Orton Wiley's *Christian Theology* remains one of the clearest and most comprehensive systematic theologies that are both distinctively evangelical in posture and distinctively Wesleyan in construction of doctrine. Drawing readily upon the Bible and classical Christian tradition, Wiley fuses Wesleyan and evangelical concerns into an indissoluble whole. His academic work also

---

103. Ibid., 3:120–21.
104. Ibid., 3:131–34.
105. Ibid., 3:183.
106. Ibid., 3:205.
107. Ibid., 3:207.

108. Ibid., 3:224–42.
109. Ibid., 3:243–319.
110. Ibid., 3:365–86.
111. Ibid., 3:264–79.
112. Ibid., 3:280–97.

evidences the irenic spirit that characterized his ministry as a pastor and educator. His mediation between mainstream Methodist theology and the Holiness movement mirrors his personal efforts as a reconciler of divergent parties within his own tradition. Thus Thomas Langford's assessment of *Christian Theology* is apt: "Both Wiley's relationship to received Methodist theology and the special emphases derived from his Holiness tradition are evident. His constructive statement is the most complete systematic theology the Holiness movement has produced, and it is an important marker of that movement's theological expression."[113] It might also be said that Wiley's preference for evangelical resources linked his *Christian Theology* to works as well as to issues of the late nineteenth century, and that his work is—to some degree—dated by that association. But his lack of interaction with other contemporary theologians is more than offset by his

invaluable development of foundational Christian doctrines from an evangelical, Wesleyan-Arminian perspective.

Primary Sources

Wiley, H. Orton. *Christian Theology*. 3 vols. Kansas City, Mo.: Beacon Hill, 1941.

_____. *The Epistle to the Hebrews*. Kansas City, Mo.: Beacon Hill, 1959. 2d ed. Kansas City, Mo.: Beacon Hill, 1985.

_____, and Paul T. Culbertson. *Introduction to Christian Theology*. Kansas City, Mo.: Beacon Hill, 1946.

Secondary Sources

Langford, Thomas. *Practical Divinity: Theology in the Wesleyan Tradition*, 131–47. Nashville: Abingdon, 1983.

Smith, Timothy L. *Called unto Holiness; The Story of the Nazarenes: The Formative Years*. Kansas City, Mo.: Nazarene, 1962.

Tyson, John R. "H. Orton Wiley." In *Dictionary of Christianity in America*, edited by Daniel G. Reid et al., 1256. Downers Grove, Ill.: Inter-Varsity, 1990.

---

113. Langford, *Practical Divinity*, 140.

J. Gresham Machen

D. G. Hart

In his day, J. Gresham Machen was widely regarded in the United States as one of conservative Protestantism's most intelligent and zealous defenders. A professor of New Testament at Princeton Theological Seminary for most of his career, Machen was among the few major conservative voices in the academic world, publishing works on the apostle Paul and the virgin birth that merited serious attention from secular and Christian scholars alike. Yet his complex scholarship was not the sole reason for his prominence. In 1923, Machen wrote *Christianity and Liberalism,* a popular statement of Protestant orthodoxy and polemic against liberalism.

The significance of *Christianity and Liberalism,* which is still in print, did not lie in its author nor its clear presentation of Christian doctrine. Rather, with its straightforward case that liberal Protestantism was not just a departure from orthodoxy but an entirely different religion, the book put Machen at the center of the modernist-fundamentalist controversy. Leading fundamentalists immediately recognized Machen as an ally, and his correspondence swelled with invitations to speak at rallies, Bible conferences, and church conventions. *Christianity and Liberalism* also attracted the attention of secular intellectuals. Journalists Walter Lippmann and H. L. Mencken both acknowledged the forcefulness and cogency of Machen's arguments, and editors of newspapers and magazines, as well as members of academe, regularly sought Machen to speak on behalf of fundamentalism. The only constituency that failed to appreciate Machen's stand was his own communion, the Northern Presbyterians (the Presbyterian Church in the U.S.A.). They understandably perceived fundamentalism as a threat to the church's harmony and unity. As a result, Machen's call for the removal of liberals from the denomination met with resistance.

Eventually, Machen's opposition to religious modernism led him to found Westminster Theological Seminary in 1929 and the Presbyterian Church of America (later re-

129

named the Orthodox Presbyterian Church) in 1936, two institutions that increased Machen's reputation and nurtured a young generation of leaders who contributed mightily to the post–World War II resurgence of American evangelicalism. Indeed, when he suddenly died of pneumonia on January 1, 1937, Princeton Seminary's Caspar Wistar Hodge declared that evangelical Christianity had "lost its greatest leader," while the religion editor for the *Boston Evening Transcript* wrote that Machen was "as learned and valiant" a theologian as "the Protestant church has produced in modern times."[1]

Early Academic Career

Born on July 28, 1881, Machen grew up the son of a prominent Baltimore lawyer, Arthur W. Machen. From his father Machen inherited a keen logical mind and a deep interest in classical literature. The legal background would later become especially evident during his battles in the Presbyterian church, where he devoted considerable time to constitutional and procedural questions. Through the influence of his mother, Mary Gresham, Machen acquired a thorough knowledge of the Bible and the Westminster Catechism. Machen's father, who hailed from Virginia, had been reared an Episcopalian. But his mother, a devout Old School Presbyterian from Georgia, insisted upon membership in Baltimore's Franklin Street Presbyterian Church. The Presbyterianism in which Machen grew up was not, however, the Old School tradition that had expelled the New School Presbyterians in 1837.[2] The preaching of Harris E. Kirk, Machen's minister, repeated far more the sentimental plati-

tudes of Victorian Protestantism than it did the Calvinistic and denominational concerns of the Old School tradition.

Machen chose to pursue his undergraduate degree at Johns Hopkins University, an institution just a few blocks from his parents' home. Majoring in classics deepened his interest in ancient literature. Machen graduated in 1901 first in his class and stayed on for a year of graduate work with one of the leading classicists in America, Basil L. Gildersleeve, who was also an elder in Machen's church. While enhancing Machen's language skills, the university ethos also stimulated his academic interests. Johns Hopkins was the first university in the United States dedicated to graduate study and specialized research in all areas of the curriculum. Founded without ecclesiastical ties, it is generally cited as an example of the secularization of American higher education. Still, Machen had nothing but good to say about his experience there and became a strong advocate of the scientific ideals of modern learning.

Nevertheless, during the summer of 1902 Machen considered a career in banking and international law before enrolling with reluctance at Princeton Theological Seminary. He immediately disliked his seminary courses and complained that the routine was too restrictive compared with the open atmosphere at Johns Hopkins. In fact, he regularly cut classes to attend Princeton football games, go ice skating on the Delaware Canal, or play tennis. Of far more interest academically were the classes across the street at Princeton University, where he simultaneously earned an M.A. in philosophy.

Machen's ambivalence about his theological training stemmed from his doubts about a career in the ministry. No family precedent existed for him to pursue an ecclesiastical career. Machen's grandfathers had been successful in law and politics respectively (his maternal grandfather a judge and his paternal grandfather a secretary for the United States Senate), and his

---

1. Caspar Wistar Hodge, quoted in "Recent Tributes to Dr. Machen," *Presbyterian Guardian* 3 (Feb. 13, 1937): 189; and Albert C. Dieffenbach, "The Passing of a Great Fundamentalist," *Boston Evening Transcript*, 9 January 1937.

2. George M. Marsden, *The Evangelical Mind and the New School Presbyterian Experience* (New Haven: Yale University Press, 1970), 59–87.

brothers gave the ministry little consideration. His older brother, Arthur, Jr., followed their father into law; and his younger brother, Thomas, became an architect. In addition, the culture in which Machen grew up did not make the ministry attractive to one with his academic instincts.

Victorian culture made sharp distinctions between the intellect and the emotions, between materialism and idealism, and between science and faith.[3] Because of its eternal, moral, and spiritual concerns, Christianity was considered part of the ideal realm. Religion had little to do with science, not because science was irreligious, but because scientists studied the material world, while ministers and theologians were concerned with the world of the spirit. Romantic and evangelical influences furthered the divorce between religion and the world of science by placing a premium on experience and heartfelt faith. Although the Victorians valued rationality and order in the workplace, they also loved preachers who could move their souls. Henry Ward Beecher and Phillips Brooks, two of the most popular American preachers, relied upon poetic images and figurative language to convey religious truth. At the same time the revivalist Dwight L. Moody used sentimental stories to win souls and further his crusade against urban vice. In such preaching was a highly optimistic message that assured the middle class that changes and uncertainty in the spheres of science, politics, and business would be ultimately resolved through faith in God and adherence to a strict moral code. Because religion appeared to be cut off from the scientific pursuits of the university, Machen was reluctant to go into the ministry. From his perspective, American Protestantism was inherently anti-intellectual and sentimental.

Still, Machen persevered at Princeton Seminary, and in 1905 completed his

course of study there. When he graduated, he was convinced that becoming ordained was out of the question. He thought the only way he could combine his academic interests and faith was through advanced study of the New Testament.

Thanks to a fellowship from Princeton Seminary and the encouragement of William Park Armstrong, professor of New Testament and Machen's mentor while a student there, he left to study in Germany for the academic year 1905–06. At Marburg the main attraction was Adolf Jülicher, well known for his *Introduction to the New Testament* and *Parables of Jesus.* But the teacher who captivated Machen was Wilhelm Herrmann, professor of theology and a disciple of Albrecht Ritschl.[4] Like Protestant preachers in America who viewed Christianity in idealistic terms, Herrmann made a sharp distinction between the competing methods of science and religion. Reflecting Ritschl's disdain for metaphysics, he held that Christianity is primarily moral and active. In contrast to philosophy, which is concerned with the world of science, religion is concerned with the highest good and the way in which it might be achieved. At Göttingen Machen studied with the New Testament scholars Wilhelm Bousset and Wilhelm Heitmüller. Rather than having his faith shaken, Machen saw that religious scholarship held a prominent place in German intellectual life. Unlike America, where the best-known figures were popular preachers who were marginal to the university, Germany's church leaders were also important members of academe. To be sure, Machen recognized that the views of his German professors were incompatible with traditional Protestant beliefs. But the fact that religion was not isolated from the world of learning gave him some hope for a career in the ministry.

While a student in Germany Machen also began to view his education at Prince-

3. See Paul A. Carter, *The Spiritual Crisis of the Gilded Age* (DeKalb, Ill.: Northern Illinois University Press, 1971).

4. See Wilhelm Herrmann, *The Communion of the Christian with God,* ed. Robert T. Voelkel (Philadelphia: Fortress, 1971), xxii–xlii.

ton Seminary in a different light. He looked back upon his studies especially with Armstrong as genuine university work. In one letter to his family, Machen praised Princeton for not hiding from "the real state of affairs in Biblical study." For Machen, this attitude distinguished Princeton from those evangelical institutions that stuck with conservative scholarship just because it was safe. With his estimation of Princeton rising, Machen accepted an offer to become an instructor there beginning in the fall of 1906. His initial duties included teaching elementary Greek, exegesis, and an introductory course on the New Testament. Teaching elementary Greek prepared him well to compose his *New Testament Greek for Beginners,* a grammar originally published in 1923 and still used widely at seminaries and divinity schools.

Nevertheless, Machen's doubts about the ministry continued. In fact, he accepted the position at Princeton on the condition that he would not have to be licensed, ordained, or even placed under the jurisdiction of a presbytery. His tenure at Princeton did, however, begin to acclimate him to the seminary's theological convictions. Indeed, Princeton's historic defense of the intellectual and objective nature of Christianity provided him with the necessary environment to work out his doubts.

Signs of Machen's intellectual and spiritual resolve came in an address he gave at Princeton in the fall of 1912 at the opening of the academic year. Entitled "Christianity and Culture," the talk was intended to be a defense of the aims of theological education, but it was also his confession of faith.[5] As Machen saw it, the problem facing the church was to define the relation between knowledge and piety. Tension was evident in the growing rift between evangelists and theologians, but also between theology and other areas of learning. At seminary these

antagonisms were particularly striking. The Bible was no longer studied solely for the purpose of moral and spiritual improvement; it was also studied for the sake of knowledge. Three approaches could be taken. The liberal Protestant option was to subordinate the gospel to science and eliminate the supernatural. The second solution prevailed in the emerging fundamentalist movement. It preserved the supernatural element of the gospel by rejecting scientific pursuit. Though Machen preferred this solution over that of liberal Protestantism, he thought it inadequate because it denied the intellectual gifts that God has given to humankind. Thus the only legitimate approach was to consecrate the pursuit of knowledge to the religious endeavor. Instead of rejecting or being indifferent to the arts and sciences, Machen thought Christians should cultivate them with all the enthusiasm of the "veriest humanist," while at the same time consecrating them to the service of God. This vision of the Christian scholar was the calling to which Machen would dedicate himself as a seminary professor. And with his intellectual doubts resolved, he was ordained in 1914 and promoted to assistant professor.

Pauline Scholarship

A crucial factor in Machen's intellectual maturation was his scholarship on the apostle Paul, which he first presented in 1920 as the Sprunt Lectures at Union Theological Seminary in Richmond. These lectures were published the next year under the title *The Origin of Paul's Religion.*[6] Ironically, most of Machen's early research, both as a seminarian and then as a professor, had concerned Christ's virgin birth. This subject, in fact, was to be the topic for his second scholarly work, *The Virgin Birth of Christ* (1930), a book he would refer to as his magnum opus. But it was his study of Paul that was pivotal for

5. J. Gresham Machen, "Christianity and Culture," in J. Gresham Machen, *What Is Christianity?* ed. Ned B. Stonehouse (Grand Rapids: Eerdmans, 1951), 156–69.

6. J. Gresham Machen, *The Origin of Paul's Religion* (New York: Macmillan, 1921).

his critique of liberal Protestantism and his eventual involvement in the fundamentalist controversy, laying the foundation for his *Christianity and Liberalism*, which has been called the "chief theological ornament of American fundamentalism."[7]

Within the history of New Testament scholarship the early dates of the Pauline corpus had proved immensely difficult for liberal Protestants, who wanted to retain the teachings of Jesus, but had little sympathy for the particulars of Paul's theology. Many critics argued that Paul was the second founder of Christianity and had, in a certain sense, perverted Christ's teachings. Machen countered, however, that recent scholarship on the Epistles made such an argument dubious. If Paul deviated from Christ, for example, why do his Epistles make up such a large part of the New Testament? Machen also drew upon the recent conclusion of more-radical biblical scholars that it is impossible to separate the ethical teachings of Jesus from the supernaturalism of the New Testament. This led Machen to argue that Pauline theology with its supernaturalistic emphasis does not deviate from Jesus' teaching, but reflects the faith and creed of the apostles and the early church. Liberal Protestants unwilling to own up to the theology of original Christianity should, Machen implied, think about calling themselves by a different name.

The character of early Christian doctrine is, according to Machen, remarkably plain and accords well with the beliefs of conservative Protestants. Paul taught that Jesus Christ is a heavenly being who came to earth, died on the cross for the sins of believers, rose from the dead, and is present with the Christian church through the Holy Spirit. Machen noted the apostle's stress upon the historical nature of the gospel. By contrast, liberal biblical criticism maintained that Christ's significance

resides in the realm of ideals. According to this view, Jesus' ethical teachings are eternally and absolutely true, while his miracles, death, and resurrection are creative symbols by which the apostles and early church sought to show his superiority. In Machen's reading of Paul, however, the works of Christ, especially his death and resurrection, are not merely the product of the early church's nostalgia for their deceased leader. Rather, Christ's work on the cross and his resurrection from the dead are fundamental to the gospel. Without Christ's atonement for sin, Machen argued, the whole Christian conception of salvation and redemption falls to the ground. In sum, what Paul taught, according to Machen, is that without Christ's vicarious sacrifice the Christian gospel becomes a totally different religion.[8]

Another important feature of Machen's first book that would influence his arguments during the fundamentalist controversy was his selective appropriation of recent German scholarship. During the early twentieth century many German scholars, some of whom Machen had studied with, began to apply the methods of comparative religion to the New Testament. The advocates of this approach became known as the history-of-religions school. In Pauline studies scholars were prompted to explain the apostle's teachings as the product of either his Jewish religious upbringing or his education in the Hellenistic world. The danger here, of course, was that Christianity might be stripped of its unique and absolute character. Indeed, some American scholars, primarily at the University of Chicago, began to stress that Christianity is an amalgam of other religions.[9] Such historians of early Christianity as Shirley

8. Machen, *Origin*, 314–17.
9. See Archibald M. Hunter, *Interpreting the New Testament, 1900–1950* (Philadelphia: Westminster, 1951), 68–76; Robert W. Funk, "The Watershed of American Biblical Tradition: The Chicago School, First Phase, 1892–1920," *Journal of Biblical Literature* 95 (1976): 4–22.

7. Sydney E. Ahlstrom, *A Religious History of the American People* (New Haven: Yale University Press, 1972), 912.

Jackson Case and Shailer Mathews argued that the genius of the early church was its ability to incorporate the ideals and practices of other faiths. This view of Christianity was also congenial to liberal Protestants who hoped that denominations would give up their distinctive doctrines in order to work together in ecumenical projects that would extend the church's impact upon the culture.

Machen drew on some of the insights of the history-of-religions school to explore the human and cultural factors in the development of Christianity. For instance, he argued that Paul's Hellenistic background made him the perfect instrument for preaching the gospel among Greeks and Gentiles, and helps to explain how Christianity, initially a Jewish sect, came to such prominence in a society dominated by Greek and Roman culture. He also maintained that, "to almost as great an extent as any great historical movement can be ascribed to one man," the establishment of Christianity as a world religion was the work of Paul. Jesus' teaching, Machen explained, was not sufficient for the spread of Christianity. In making this assertion, Machen did not intend to diminish the traditional Protestant beliefs about the centrality of Christ's work and ministry. But he did want to underscore the apostle's historical importance. Jesus had only implied, but not made explicit, the universal mission of the church; he had not clarified how Gentiles were to be admitted into the church. These limitations made necessary "the epoch-making work of Paul," who understood the death of Christ "in its full historical and logical relations" and established the principles of the Christian movement. Rather than viewing the spread of the church as simply an act of God and nothing more, Machen followed those Princeton theologians before him who had recognized that the human component, not just divine initiative, is crucial

to understanding Scripture and the history of redemption.[10]

Yet Machen opposed all efforts to classify Christianity as just one among the many religions that sought to win the ancient world by incorporating the beliefs of other faiths. In fact, what struck Machen about Paul's teaching was how exclusive and intolerant it was of other faiths. Not only did Paul's preaching differ significantly from other religions, but the apostle demanded exclusive devotion from converts to Christianity. This interpretation of Paul undoubtedly followed from Machen's concerns as an apologist to defend the uniqueness and normative status of the Christian gospel. But it also reflected his training as a classicist. Classicists and philologists are more inclined than are scholars of comparative religion to focus on ideas and to notice the differences between the various religions and philosophies.[11] They tend to approach ancient writings from the perspective of the history of ideas. The discipline of comparative religion, in contrast, is influenced by developments in the social sciences and tends to view the biblical writings as the outgrowth of political, economic, and social realities. In distinguishing Paul's thought from other religions in the ancient world, Machen was defending the uniqueness of Christianity and also putting into practice what he had learned at Johns Hopkins and Princeton,

10. Machen, *Origin*, 8, 16–17, 19. For Princeton's exploration of inerrancy and the human aspects of revelation, see B. B. Warfield, "The Divine and Human in the Bible," in *Selected Shorter Writings of Benjamin B. Warfield*, ed. John E. Meeter, 2 vols. (Nutley, N.J.: Presbyterian and Reformed, 1970, 1973), 2:542–48; and Moisés Silva, "Old Princeton, Westminster, and Inerrancy," in *Inerrancy and Hermeneutic*, ed. Harvie M. Conn (Grand Rapids: Baker, 1988), 67–80.

11. Laurence Veysey, "The Pluralized Worlds of the Humanities," in *The Organization of Knowledge in Modern America*, ed. Alexandra Oleson and John Voss (Baltimore: Johns Hopkins University Press, 1979), 51–106.

namely, to regard human thought as independent of social and political conditions.

Machen and Fundamentalism

The Origin of Paul's Religion anticipated most of the arguments Machen would use during the fundamentalist controversy. It strongly affirmed the exclusiveness of Christianity, the centrality of Christ's death and resurrection, and the truthfulness of the Bible; it also admonished liberals for reducing Christianity to humanitarianism and for minimizing the importance of traditional theology. These were positions that Machen popularized in *Christianity and Liberalism,* a book written at the height of the fundamentalist controversy. Yet Machen was not a likely fundamentalist. Indeed, his views on a number of significant issues were at odds with the aims and methods of fundamentalism. To be sure, the term *fundamentalist* has become increasingly pejorative throughout the twentieth century. But even by the standards of the 1920s Machen always looked somewhat out of step in the ranks of the fundamentalists. He himself did not like the term because it sounded like "some strange new sect."[12]

One obvious point of dissimilarity concerned Machen's cultural and educational background. Fundamentalism was by no means as socially backward and anti-intellectual as its detractors claimed. But it was a movement that was isolated from the cultural establishment, and in many respects it was a religious expression of popular resentment against the social elite. Fundamentalists put a premium on doctrine and intellectual assent in their understanding of the Christian faith, and they established schools, usually Bible institutes and colleges, to perpetuate their views. Yet for all of their concern for theology and education, fundamentalists were a world removed from academic life in American colleges and universities.[13] Machen, by contrast, not only grew up in polite society and attended a prominent American university, but maintained close ties to influential circles in American culture throughout his life.

Machen differed from the fundamentalists on theological matters as well, two of which were dispensational premillennialism and evolution. Most fundamentalists were committed to a dispensationalist understanding of history and Christ's second coming. Dividing the history of salvation into different epochs of human faithlessness followed by divine judgment, this perspective taught that the present age, the age of the church, would witness another round of apostasy and punishment leading up to the Lord's return. Dispensationalist pessimism about the future of American churches and society contrasted sharply with liberal Protestant optimism that God's presence ensured the progress of human civilization. Machen was by no means enamored of liberal estimates about the advance of society. But he was also quite critical of dispensationalism and refused to join any fundamentalist organization whose statement of faith included it. Machen maintained that dispensationalism displayed a faulty method of interpreting the Bible and a poor understanding of the pervasive effects of the fall upon all of humanity throughout all periods of history.[14]

Fundamentalism was also defined by its opposition to evolution.[15] Indeed, the most

---

12. J. Gresham Machen, "What Fundamentalism Stands for Now," in *What Is Christianity?* 253.

13. On fundamentalism's declining cultural prestige see George M. Marsden, *Fundamentalism and American Culture* (New York: Oxford University Press, 1980); and on fundamentalist education see Virginia Lieson Brereton, *Training God's Army* (Bloomington: Indiana University Press, 1990).

14. J. Gresham Machen, *Christianity and Liberalism* (New York: Macmillan, 1923), 49. On dispensationalism see Timothy P. Weber, *Living in the Shadow of the Second Coming* (New York: Oxford University Press, 1979). For Machen's views see D. G. Hart, "'Doctor Fundamentalis': An Intellectual Biography of J. Gresham Machen, 1881–1937," Ph.D. diss., Johns Hopkins University, 1988, pp. 130–34, 356–58.

15. Marsden, *Fundamentalism,* ch. 16.

widely publicized event of the fundamentalist controversy was the showdown between Clarence Darrow and William Jennings Bryan during the *Scopes* trial (1925). Fundamentalists believed that evolutionary theory and the scientific establishment that had nurtured it were responsible for German barbarism during World War I and for the decline of Christian civilization in the United States. Opposition to teaching evolution in public schools followed logically from this perspective. Fundamentalists did not want schools to undermine the faith and morals of their children. In contrast, Machen believed that evolution was a conceivable way for God to have created the earth. Questioning whether the human species could have evolved from lower animals, he insisted that God must have intervened in the process of natural development to create the human soul. Yet by acknowledging that the divine image in humans is a spiritual, not a physical, characteristic, Machen left unresolved the issue of whether the human form actually evolved from lower forms of life.[16]

The one doctrine upon which Machen and fundamentalists agreed was biblical inerrancy. This doctrine was, according to many, the link between the learned theology of Princeton Seminary and the revivalistic preaching of popular fundamentalism. Indeed, many fundamentalists adopted a definition of biblical authority and infallibility that mirrored that of B. B. Warfield, the Princeton theologian who was the principal advocate of the doctrine of inerrancy.[17] Moreover, the doctrine of inerrancy was on every fundamentalist list of necessary and essential doctrines. This affirmation of the truthfulness of the Bible, many presume, drove Machen to align himself with a movement that otherwise gave him pause.

Writings against Liberalism

Affirming the doctrine of inerrancy, Machen never wavered in his defense of the full integrity and reliability of the Bible. Yet in *Christianity and Liberalism*, the book in which he most pointedly argues that modernist theology is an entirely different religion from historic Christianity, Machen barely mentions inerrancy. He discusses the doctrine on only three pages, a paltry sum compared to Warfield's extended explanations; in fact, the chapter on the Bible is the shortest one in the book.[18] If Machen's opposition to liberalism was rooted in his understanding of the authority and infallibility of the Bible, his most popular book gives little indication.

Instead of serving as a defense of Princeton's doctrine of inerrancy, *Christianity and Liberalism* reads more like a primer in the rudiments of Reformed theology. Machen devotes separate chapters to the doctrines of God, man, Christ, the Bible, salvation, and the church. The most enormous differences between liberalism and historic Christianity are found on the issue of salvation. Indeed, the chapter on this subject is the longest and contains the heart of Machen's objection to liberalism. To put it in simple terms: Christianity and liberalism have entirely different views of salvation. Christians have traditionally held, according to Machen, that Jesus provided salvation, not by inspiring emulation of the life he led, but by bearing the guilt of human sin upon the cross. Machen thus launches his thirty-five-page defense of the doctrine of vicarious atonement. The very term *gospel*, Machen asserts, implies this conception of Christ's death. "Gospel," he explains,

16. J. Gresham Machen, *The Christian View of Man* (London: Banner of Truth Trust, 1965), 114–20, 145.

17. See Ernest R. Sandeen, *The Roots of Fundamentalism: British and American Millenarianism, 1800–1930* (Chicago: University of Chicago Press, 1970), 126–27.

18. Machen, *Christianity and Liberalism*, ch. 4; cf. B. B. Warfield's elaborate rendering, "The Real Problem of Inspiration," in *The Inspiration and Authority of the Bible*, ed. Samuel G. Craig (Philadelphia: Presbyterian and Reformed, 1948), 169–226.

means "'good news,' tidings, information about something that has happened." Christianity, he argues, "must be abandoned altogether unless at a definite point in history Jesus died as a propitiation for the sins of men." With their divergent attitudes toward the death of Christ, Christianity and liberalism are clearly two different religions. For liberals Christ's death is a symbol of self-sacrifice and a model for the Christian life, but for conservatives it is the only remedy for human sinfulness.[19]

Christianity and Liberalism thus was a popular expression of a major theme of Machen's work on Paul. His aim in *The Origin of Paul's Religion* had been to show the centrality of Christ's death and resurrection to the faith and theology of the first Christians. Now in *Christianity and Liberalism* Machen was making a similar point about modern Christianity. The message of the New Testament is that Jesus was no mere prophet, no mere inspired teacher of righteousness, but rather a supernatural person, a heavenly Redeemer come to earth for the salvation of sinners. Machen regarded this message as the great current of the church's life, flowing down from the apostles through Augustine, Martin Luther, and John Calvin, and in America finding expression in Charles Hodge and B. B. Warfield. This theological tradition was what motivated Machen to side with the fundamentalists.[20]

Though his critique of liberalism was primarily theological and though he avoided the public controversy over evolution, Machen did not avoid the subject of science. He was deeply concerned about the widespread notion that conservative Protestants were hostile to science and therefore anti-intellectual. So Machen added to his theological critique the somewhat surprising argument that liberal Protestantism was unscientific and anti-intellectual.

The unscientific character of liberalism, according to Machen, was particularly evident in biblical studies. The proper way of studying Scripture, Machen held, was to discover the author's intention by situating the text in its historical setting. Conservatives made the best biblical scholars because they were not troubled by the Bible's supernaturalism. They did not feel compelled to explain away miracles. Liberals, in contrast, foisted their own religious views onto the text. They often interpreted the supernatural component of Scripture as the cultural husk in which the kernel of Christ's ethical teachings resided. Thus, rather than following their investigations wherever they might lead, liberals let their presuppositions get in the way of good scholarship.[21]

This argument is implicit in Machen's scholarly monograph *The Virgin Birth of Christ* (1930), a compilation of his Thomas Smyth Lectures at Columbia (S.C.) Theological Seminary. Through intricate literary and historical analysis, he makes the relatively simple argument that a well-formulated belief in the virgin birth was not a late addition to Christianity, but can be traced to the early second century. Such evidence suggests that the best historical explanation for the belief is that the virgin birth actually occurred.[22]

Machen also used the occasion to attack the liberal habit of trying to separate Christianity's ethical instruction from its historical realities. Many liberals, in order to accommodate modern science, had separated religion and science into two spheres. Religious truths, they said, transcend scientific investigation. Using this logic, liberals hoped to retain basic Christian ideals while getting rid of those biblical accounts that are rooted in a prescientific concept of nature. In Machen's view this approach was a

19. Machen, *Christianity and Liberalism*, 117, 124, 128, 132.

20. J. Gresham Machen, "Dr. Machen Declines the Presidency of Bryan University," *Moody Monthly* 28 (Sept. 1927): 16.

21. J. Gresham Machen, "The Modern Use of the Bible," in *What Is Christianity?* 185–200.

22. J. Gresham Machen, *The Virgin Birth of Christ* (New York: Harper, 1930), 320–23, 379.

colossal mistake. The Bible is not merely a book of inspiration, but also a book of history. "There can scarcely be a greater error," he wrote, than to regard religious truth "as in some way distinct" from scientific truth. The virgin birth cannot be true in the realm of religion and false in the realm of science. By treating the Bible as a book of inspiration rather than as a book of "external history," liberals had embraced a halfway position that was "utterly inconsistent and absurd." While the popular exponents of liberalism went "cheerfully on asserting that the authority of the Bible lies altogether in the sphere of ideals," that is, in the superiority of Jesus' teaching, they failed to recognize that even this assertion depended on the external historical facts that Jesus really lived in first-century Palestine and that the New Testament presents his teachings accurately.[23]

When liberal scholars proved unwilling to do battle over important intellectual matters, Machen accused theological modernism of anti-intellectualism. In *What Is Faith?* (1925) his purpose is to direct attention to the primacy of the intellect in religion and to break down the "false and disastrous" distinction between knowledge and faith. In short, Machen shows that Christian faith depends upon knowledge and includes certain assertions about historical and metaphysical reality that cannot be sheltered from scholarly investigation. Faith is at the most basic level an act of trust that requires knowledge about the object of faith. Knowledge about God, Christ, and the human condition is essential for genuine faith. Theology is thus integral to Christianity. Throughout the book Machen extols the virtues of theological and biblical study. In fact, he believed that church membership should be restricted to believers with an adequate knowledge of the Christian faith. Though this kind of knowledge will not in itself make one a Christian, requiring it would help redress the modern

tendency to divorce faith from knowledge.[24]

Machen was especially critical of the tendency in liberal circles—and, for that matter, among evangelicals also—to stress religious experience at the expense of theology.[25] In fact, liberalism was for Machen just one example of a lamentable intellectual decline in American society. Ignorance of the Bible among seminary students and theological naivete on the part of many clergy were additional instances of the woeful ignorance of the modern church. Machen attributed this problem in part to the decline of teaching and preaching within the churches and to the demise of the home as an educational institution. But the ultimate source of theological and biblical ignorance was the elevation of religious experience over formal theology. People no longer cared about doctrine or the content of their Bibles, Machen believed, because ministers were telling them that theology and the Bible are merely symbolic expressions of a deeper religious experience. Though he acknowledged that the theologians and philosophers responsible for this conception were by no means hostile to intellectual endeavor, they had, by depreciating the intellect and exalting the feelings instead, helped cause the church's intellectual decline.

Ecclesiastical Struggles

Machen's criticism of liberalism led directly to involvement in church politics. Indeed, throughout the last ten years of his life his scholarly output virtually dried up as he increasingly devoted more time, energy, and resources to Presbyterian affairs. As a professor at Princeton, Machen was always at a disadvantage in denominational

23. Ibid., 219, 384.

24. J. Gresham Machen, *What Is Faith?* (New York: Macmillan, 1925), 26, 49, 98–102, 157, 159.

25. Ibid., 15–45. For Machen's criticisms of evangelicals see J. Gresham Machen, "The Relation of Religion to Science and Philosophy," review of *Christianity at the Cross Roads*, by Edgar Young Mullins, *Princeton Theological Review* 24 (Jan. 1926): 38–66.

proceedings. Preachers, whether the conservative Clarence Macartney or the liberal Harry Emerson Fosdick, tended to be more popular than academics and therefore more likely to garner support. Furthermore, Princeton Seminary was somewhat isolated from the centers of Presbyterian power in Philadelphia and New York. Consequently, while Machen was popular through his writings and press coverage, he did not have a well-organized constituency to mobilize in church proceedings.

Machen's criticism of Protestant liberalism in *Christianity and Liberalism* grew out of his commitment to Presbyterian confessionalism and polity. In the early 1920s Protestant church leaders from various mainline denominations had proposed a plan for a union of the major Protestant communions in a consolidated church not unlike the United Church of Canada, which was formed in 1925. Machen opposed such proposals because, on the one hand, they made efficiency and social service the goals of church affairs, aims that fostered rather than resisted the increasing centralization of American life. More importantly, on the other hand, plans for church union were rooted in an indifference to theology that stemmed from liberal Protestant ideas about religious knowledge. Union would be achieved, Machen thought, not because Protestants had come to a common understanding of the gospel and the mission of the church, but because they agreed that such matters were no longer important. His opposition to liberalism, then, was as much a desire to preserve a distinct Presbyterian witness as it was to defend the Bible's historical reliability.[26]

Machen held that the church's primary task was to bear witness to Christ. As proof he cited the risen Christ's instructions to his followers, "Ye shall be my witnesses." The theological and historical character of the gospel meant that the church's task was primarily one of proclamation. In the specific case of the Presbyterian church, the Westminster Confession of Faith and the denomination's constitution dictated the content of the witnessing to be done by Presbyterian clergy. In fact, Presbyterian ordination vows put explicit limits upon what could be taught in Presbyterian pulpits and printed in denominational publications. In their oath of subscription Presbyterian ministers and elders affirmed that the Bible was the Word of God, "the only infallible rule of faith and practice," and that the Westminster Confession set forth "the system of doctrine taught in the Holy Scriptures." Machen believed that Presbyterian leaders who had once solemnly subscribed to these propositions were being dishonest if they thereafter decried the confession's theology as outdated or taught that the Bible was merely a collection of inspirational writings. All evangelical churches, for that matter, were committed by their constitutions to a particular creed. This commitment also restricted the church's financial resources. The Presbyterian church was obligated to use its funds to propagate the gospel as taught in the Bible and the Westminster Confession. To use those funds for any other purpose was a violation of trust.[27]

Liberal Presbyterian ministers had broken trust by denying and contradicting from their pulpits the very creed that they had affirmed in their ordination vows. Often they did not speak against the church's theology directly, but referred to the Westminster Confession as merely an expression of a deeper Christian experience. Still, for the sake of intellectual honesty, liberalism had to be purged from the church. Machen conceded that not everyone would agree that creeds are valuable. But whether the Westminster Confession is desirable for Presbyterians was not at issue here, since the denomination was bound by its consti-

26. J. Gresham Machen, "The Proposed Plan of Union," *Presbyterian* 90 (June 10, 1920): 8–9; and "The Second Declaration of the Council on Organic Union," *Presbyterian* 91 (March 17, 1921): 8, 26.

27. J. Gresham Machen, "The Parting of the Ways," *Presbyterian* 94 (April 1924): 7; Machen, *Christianity and Liberalism*, 163–66.

tution to that particular creed. Rather, the issue was whether a minister or church official was being faithful to his ordination vows. If a man preached and acted in accordance with the church's credal basis, then he could hold special office; if not, he had no business acting in an official capacity in the denomination.[28]

Machen's arguments were convincing to many conservatives but failed to gain the assent of the entire spectrum of evangelicals within the Presbyterian church. Some churchmen saw liberalism as certainly problematic, but largely an isolated phenomenon. The majority of the church, they believed, was still loyal to historical Christianity, so drastic measures were not needed. Moderate evangelicals such as Charles Erdman, professor of practical theology at Princeton Seminary, and Robert Speer, a prominent denominational executive and spokesman for Presbyterian missions, agreed that liberalism was a significant departure from the historic faith, but did not see the manifestations of it that Machen did. Machen's inability to convince these important and popular church leaders significantly diminished conservative chances for success.[29]

Machen tried to heighten the level of concern by developing the idea of the corporate witness of the church.[30] This notion was already present in his understanding of the church's credal basis. The Westminster Confession guaranteed that the Presbyterian church spoke uniformly through its many voices. This idea of the church's corporate witness became clearer as Machen pleaded with other conservatives to champion doctrinal regularity throughout the denomination. The church's witness was not individual but collective. When a man occupied a pulpit of the Presbyterian church, he spoke for the denomination and had to be in agreement with its confession and constitution. The notion of corporate witness also meant that the individual church members were responsible for denominational affairs. Presbyterians were not to rest content with the soundness of their own minister or their own congregation. Since the church's constitution regarded every preacher as a representative of the whole body and gave ecclesiastical courts the right to remove any who departed from denominational teaching, every church member had a vital responsibility for what was done in each pulpit and "still more plainly" for what was done by the denomination's agencies and boards. To give up that responsibility was to acquiesce in a corporate witness that was false.

Machen's conception of the visible church shows the influence of Southern Presbyterianism, a distinctive teaching of which was the spirituality of the church.[31] Machen echoed this idea when he made sharp distinctions between the spiritual and physical, the eternal and temporal aspects of human existence. According to Machen, the church's functions and tasks were strictly spiritual. Its responsibilities were to preach the Word, administer the sacraments, and nurture believers' sanctification; they did not include cultural or social duties. Machen found precedent for this view in the Westminster Confession (31.4), which said that synods and councils should concern themselves only with ecclesiastical, not civil, affairs. Of course, this principle did not prevent individual Christians from pursuing cultural and political matters. Machen himself held strong political convictions and joined organizations to promote his views. Rather, the principle meant that the church in its corporate capacity, whether at the denominational or congregational level, should not stray from its proper tasks.

28. Machen, "Parting of the Ways," 7–8.
29. See Bradley J. Longfield, *The Presbyterian Controversy* (New York: Oxford University Press, 1991).
30. Machen, "Parting of the Ways," 8.
31. See Ernest Trice Thompson, *The Spirituality of the Church: A Distinctive Doctrine of the Presbyterian Church in the United States* (Richmond: John Knox, 1961).

Machen forcefully expressed this same idea late in his career before a gathering of the American Academy of Political and Social Science. In an address called "The Responsibility of the Church in Our New Age," he spelled out the church's positive tasks: the church was to be "radically doctrinal," "radically intolerant," and "radically ethical."[32] Here we have a restatement of Machen's idea that the primary task of the church is to bear witness. The thrust of the address, however, was the limitations upon the church. Machen specified what the political and social scientists ought not expect from it. First of all, "you cannot expect from [the church] any cooperation with non-Christian religion or with a non-Christian program of ethical culture." There was no such thing, he insisted, "as a universally valid fund of religious principles" upon which particular religions could build. Second, it was improper to look to the church for "any official pronouncements upon the political or social questions of the day." Third, "cooperation with the state in anything involving the use of force" would be invalid because the church's weapons against evil are "spiritual, not carnal." The responsibility of the church in the new age, then, according to Machen, was the same as it always had been: "to testify that this world is lost in sin; that the span of human life—nay the length of human history—is an infinitesimal island in the awful depths of eternity; that there is a mysterious, holy, living God . . . infinitely beyond all; that He has revealed Himself to us in His Word and offered us communion with Himself through Jesus Christ the Lord." This task is unchanging and absolutely essential because it imparts "a treasure compared with which all the kingdoms of the earth—nay, all the wonders of the starry heavens—were as the dust of the earth."

The principle of the spirituality of the church had a distinctly American ring—dis-

tinguishing between spiritual and temporal affairs comported well with American notions about the separation of church and state. The legal implications of this separation of civil and ecclesiastical powers were fully evident in Machen's contractual conception of the church. Just as the Constitution of the United States obligates the American government to uphold freedom and take the form of a representative democracy, so, Machen argued, the constitution of the Presbyterian church commits its members to a particular system of theology and church polity.

Machen's insistence on separating spiritual from civil affairs meant that while he was committed to an intolerant church, he also defended religious liberty and cultural pluralism. Rather than conceiving of the state as a means for implementing and enforcing Christian norms and values, Machen thought that the state's chief business was to protect individuals, families, and other private associations from government interference. He noted that the state is an "involuntary organization; a man is forced to be a member of it whether he will or no." It would therefore be "an interference with liberty for the state to prescribe any one type of opinion" for its citizens.[33] Accordingly, Machen took exception to the government's attempts to regulate private education and to set the number of hours that children could work. These were matters for parents to decide; the state must not paternalistically require all families to conform to one standard.[34]

Machen was particularly zealous in his defense of civil liberties because of their close relationship to religious freedom. In fact, he often argued that the kind of intolerance he exhibited in the Presbyterian church was not only compatible with, but predicated upon civil liberty. Within the involuntary association of the state, he pointed out, individuals have the freedom to form organizations dedicated to a partic-

32. J. Gresham Machen, "The Responsibility of the Church in Our New Age," in *What Is Christianity?* 272–87.

33. Machen, *Christianity and Liberalism*, 168.
34. Ibid., 10–16.

ular purpose. The church is just one example. It is composed of a number of persons who agree upon a certain message about Christ and desire to unite in the propagation of that message. Because no one is forced by legal means to join the church, the principle of religious liberty is not violated by requiring ministers and church officials to assent to certain theological views.

Machen applied similar logic to the family and the school, two institutions that he thought were fundamental to nurturing Christian faith. Indeed, he thought civil liberties were so important for preserving a Christian witness that he defended the rights of non-Christians to found schools and rear children in a manner consistent with their religious heritage. Religious liberty, he maintained, should be extended not just to Protestants, but to all religions. Once the state has the power to decide which religions (or even opinions) are acceptable, it might decide that Christianity is not tolerable.[35]

If the principle of religious freedom means that the state may not interfere in religious affairs, it follows that religious bodies should not interfere in public matters. Two examples show how Machen applied this argument. One was the Eighteenth Amendment, which forbade the manufacture and sale of alcohol. When the Presbyterian church took up the issue of whether it should endorse Prohibition, Machen cast a negative vote. By involving itself in such political matters he thought the church would be losing sight of its proper function. Machen also opposed Bible reading and prayer in public schools because these practices violated the liberties of non-Christians.[36]

Machen's primary objection to Christian interference in public matters was that such activity compromised the message of the gospel. For instance, when many educa-

tors argued that Bible reading in primary and secondary schools would reinforce American notions about good and evil, he countered that the central theme of Scripture, and indeed the core of Christianity, is redemption: "To create the impression that other things in the Bible contain any hope for humanity apart from [grace] is to contradict the Bible at its root." He did not mean that schools should not enforce some kind of morality. But efforts to ground that morality upon the Bible must be avoided. A secular moral education, Machen admitted, is by no means sufficient, "for the only true grounding of morality is found in the revealed will of God."[37] Indeed, if a secularized education is, as seems likely, necessary, it is a "necessary evil."[38] But at least it avoids the greater harm of confusing the Bible's central teaching. By contrast, Bible reading in public schools runs the danger of removing from the Christian understanding of virtue and morality various essential considerations such as human depravity and divine grace.

The Northern Presbyterians, who had enjoyed a prominent place in American society, were ill prepared to follow Machen's views on the church and culture. As a result the last ten years of his life were filled with bitter battles to preserve the Calvinistic identity of the Presbyterian church. Between 1927 and 1929 he fought reorganizational efforts that took conservatives from a majority to a minority position within the faculty and administration of Princeton Seminary. When Machen lost that battle in 1929, he helped to form Westminster Seminary in Philadelphia. Then in 1933 Machen pleaded with the Presbyterian church to oppose an interdenominational report that endorsed liberal views on foreign missions. His defeat on that measure led to the establishment of the Independent Board for

---

35. Ibid., 168; see also 13–14 n. 2.

36. For an example of Machen's reasoning see "The Necessity of the Christian School," in *What Is Christianity?* 288–303.

37. J. Gresham Machen, "Reforming the Government Schools," in *Education, Christianity, and the State*, ed. John W. Robbins (Jefferson, Md.: Trinity Foundation, 1987), 64.

38. Ibid., 63.

Presbyterian Foreign Missions, an agency designed to support conservatives. For the Presbyterian church this was the proverbial last straw. Machen was ordered to give up his membership on the Independent Board. When he refused, he was tried for violating his ordination vows and resisting the lawful authority of the church. Finally, in 1936, Machen was expelled from the Presbyterian church. Within weeks Machen helped to found the Presbyterian Church of America. Sadly, he died only six months later while trying to rally support at a small church in Bismarck, North Dakota; and within a few years the fledgling denomination split into the Orthodox Presbyterian Church and the Bible Presbyterian Church.

Throughout these struggles, Machen's interpretation of what had driven him to found a new church was that the mainline Presbyterian church had compromised its corporate witness. The question was not whether its institutions had officially embraced liberalism. Machen readily conceded that there were still some conservatives in the mission field and pulpits. Rather, the issue was whether the institutions of the Presbyterian church had taken a clear and vigorous stand for the Calvinistic theology of the Westminster Confession against liberalism. In Machen's view, they most certainly had not.

Machen's views on the relation between church and society alienated most Presbyterians and were an important factor in the Presbyterian controversies. His conception of the church meant that rather than being a dominant institution, it was to represent only one viewpoint within the marketplace of ideas in America. Indeed, Machen blamed the privileged position of Protestantism within America for the demise of conservative Christian beliefs. In order to maintain their established position within a culture growing increasingly pluralistic, mainstream Protestant churches, he thought, had accommodated viewpoints that undermined the gospel. For Machen, the church had to be intolerant to retain its identity; and if intolerant, it could not provide leadership for a culture that encouraged religious pluralism. To be sure, Machen hoped that the church would grow and that Christians would someday outnumber unbelievers in America. Still, he held that the church's authority extended only to the faithful; it could not set the cultural norms for non-Christians.

Some historians have looked at Machen's ecclesiastical struggles and his leadership of a small, marginal denomination as a tragic ending to what had been a splendid academic career. Concurring with this view, even some evangelical historians have speculated that Machen's battles with the mainline Presbyterian church may not have been worth the effort, and that by founding the Presbyterian Church of America Machen cut himself off from the larger culture. To be sure, the influence of the new denomination and Westminster Seminary has been negligible within recent American Protestantism. But by founding these institutions Machen helped to preserve a tradition that otherwise might have become extinct. While Machen's scholarship has inspired a number of evangelical theologians and biblical scholars, his greatest legacy was to preserve an institutional witness to the conservative Presbyterian theology and scholarship he had defended so diligently.

Secondary Sources

Longfield, Bradley J. *The Presbyterian Controversy: Fundamentalists, Modernists, and Moderates.* New York: Oxford University Press, 1991.

Noll, Mark A. *Between Faith and Criticism: Evangelicals, Scholarship, and the Bible in America.* San Francisco: Harper and Row, 1986.

_____, ed. *The Princeton Theology 1812–1921: Scripture, Science, and Theological Method from Archibald Alexander to Benjamin Warfield.* Grand Rapids: Baker, 1983.

Stonehouse, Ned B. *J. Gresham Machen: A Biographical Memoir.* Grand Rapids: Eerdmans, 1954.

Henry C. Thiessen

Walter A. Elwell

Henry Clarence Thiessen was born of German immigrant parents, Cornelius and Helena (Kroeker) Thiessen, on October 20, 1883, in the rural town of Henderson, Nebraska. He was brought up in a conservative Mennonite home where both German and English were spoken. At the age of seventeen he experienced a profound conversion that would eventually reshape his entire life. Having spent three years quietly studying and preparing for a career in education, he taught in a public school in rural Nebraska from 1903 to 1905. In 1904 he married Anna Buller, who encouraged him in his work, but urged him to consider the calling of God that he himself had talked about. In 1906, accepting in faith that God wanted him to enter the ministry, he enrolled at Fort Wayne Bible School. Those were difficult years financially, but Henry acquitted himself well.

Upon graduation in 1909, Thiessen pastored the Missionary Church of Pandora, Ohio, where he learned what it means to put Christian principles into practice on a daily basis. He also learned that human effort, in the end, amounts to very little, and that only the grace of God can sustain one in any long-term way. This conclusion was reinforced for him by the frightful experiences of the First World War, as his parents' native land engaged in a near-suicidal conflict that dragged on for four long years. His own inherent pacifist instincts caused him to recoil from what he saw and to shift his focus from hoping for improvement in the historical situation through human effort to awaiting divine intervention in the form of the second coming of Christ. During this troubled period the doctrine of a secret rapture of the church, as outlined in the recently published Scofield Reference Bible (1909), was becoming more popular in America. This doctrine of a pretribulation rapture was to become a major force in Thiessen's later life, although the dispensationalism that underlies it never played a decisive role in his thinking.

Another factor that caused Thiessen to lean more heavily upon the Lord than upon himself was his physical health, which was never very good. He suffered from asthma his entire life and was often incapacitated by it. He never complained nor allowed it to interfere with his work. Nonetheless, the asthma made his life very difficult and taught him what it means to have God's strength perfected in human weakness.

Early Work on the Second Coming of Christ

Teaching was never far from Thiessen's mind; even during his seven years as a pastor he continued to develop his understanding of theology. In 1916 he returned to Fort Wayne Bible School to become an instructor in Bible; and in 1919, as a consequence of his administrative skills and natural leadership qualities, he was appointed principal, a position he held until 1923. Sometime between 1916 and 1919, while Thiessen was editing the German-language journal *Botschafter des Heils,* he wrote a treatise entitled *Kurze Studien über das zweite Kommen des Herrn* (*Brief Studies on the Second Coming of the Lord*). C. W. Oyer, his predecessor as principal, called it the best book in the German language on the subject of the second coming, and even more boldly stated that nothing better could be found in English.

The first of Thiessen's published works, *Kurze Studien* deals with a theme that was to occupy his thinking throughout his active ministry. He begins with five reasons why every believer should study the subject of Christ's return: (1) it is frequently mentioned in Scripture; (2) it is a key to understanding God's Word; (3) erroneous views abound; (4) it can have a practical influence on our lives; and (5) awareness of it will enable us to fulfil God's plan for this age.[1]

Before expounding on the two-part coming of Christ—coming for his saints and coming with his saints—Thiessen presents a standard dispensationalist scheme comprising seven periods.[2] He calls the first period Innocence; lasting from creation to the fall, it is described in Genesis 1–3. The second period, Conscience, is described in Genesis 4–7. It covers the time between the expulsion from the Garden of Eden to the flood (1,656 years). The third period Thiessen calls The Rule Of Men. Lasting for 427 years, it is described in Genesis 8–11 and ends with the Tower of Babel. The fourth period, Promise, lasted for 430 years, beginning with the call of Abraham and ending with the exodus from Egypt; it is described in Genesis 12–Exodus 11. The fifth period, Law, which lasted for 1,521 years, is described from Exodus 12 to Acts 1. Regarding the sixth period, which is called Grace, Thiessen says: "Between the 69th and 70th week [see Dan. 9:24–27] there is a great parenthesis, comprising the time of the Church of Christ. It is the time in which we now live."[3] This period is treated in Acts 2 to Revelation 3. The seventh and final period is called The Time When God Will Rule the Earth In Righteousness; described in Revelation 20, it will last 1,000 years. Following the seventh period a new heaven and a new earth will properly introduce the eternal order.

At the end of the book Thiessen included a typical dispensational chart, but it contradicts his text and shows that he had not thought the system through very well. On the chart he has dispensation six ending in the middle of the tribulation, three-and-a-half years after the rapture of the church, with dispensation seven, the millennium, beginning at that point, that is, in the middle of the tribulation and three-and-a-half years before Christ's return with his saints. Thiessen did this, supposedly, to avoid inserting another dispensation (the seven-year tribulation) in between periods six and

1. Henry C. Thiessen, *Kurze Studien über das zweite Kommen des Herrn* (Fort Wayne: Association Book Department, Bible Training School, n.d.), 7–13.

2. Ibid., 14–29.
3. Ibid., 23.

seven. He apparently did not fully realize what was entailed in his labeling the age of Grace "a great parenthesis." It must, in fact, be a parenthesis dividing dispensation five into two parts: the 1,521 years that ended in Acts 1 and the seven-year tribulation. This allows the age of Grace to end with the rapture and the millennium to begin with Christ's coming with his saints, as Thiessen says elsewhere. Following this line would have ironed out his theoretical difficulties.

The reason for the confusion is that the precise nature of the dispensations was never a particular interest of Thiessen's. Even though he was to write frequently on the second coming of Christ, he never grounded his theory of the pretribulation rapture in the dispensational system. In fact, he mentioned the system only one other time in all his literary career, some thirty years later, and then almost incidentally in a discussion of soteriology, where he says:

> He who works in an orderly way in nature has not left the salvation of man to haphazard and uncertain experimentation: Scripture shows us that He has a definite plan of salvation. This plan includes the means by which salvation is to be provided, the objectives that are to be realized, the persons that are to benefit by it, the conditions on which it is to be available, and the agents and means by which it is to be applied. It may be added that He has only one plan and that all must be saved in the same way, if they are to be saved at all, whether they be uncivilized or civilized, immoral or moral, whether living in the Old Testament dispensation or in the present age.

He then outlines God's method of salvation in the various dispensations:

1. In the Past
   (1) The Edenic Period
   (2) The Ante-Diluvian Period
   (3) The Post-Diluvian Period
   (4) The Patriarchal Period
   (5) The Period of Mosaic Law

2. In the Present
3. In the Future[4]

We should observe here that a notable and characteristic feature of Thiessen's discussion of the second coming is his stress upon the need for personal conversion to Christ and the ethical requirements that belief in Christ's return imposes upon us.[5] He was never interested in the subject for sensationalistic reasons.

Graduate Work on the Holy Spirit

Thiessen's experience at the Fort Wayne Bible School convinced him that if he wanted to continue teaching and writing, he needed both more training and the academic credibility that advanced study would provide him; so he spent the next six years pursuing further degrees. From 1923 to 1925 he studied at Northern Baptist Theological Seminary, where he received a Th.B. in 1925. While teaching at Northern Baptist in 1925–26, he began taking courses at Northwestern University, where he received a belated A.B. degree in 1927. He could now pursue a graduate degree at Northern Baptist, where he received a B.D. in 1928. A momentous decision on Thiessen's part then took him to Southern Baptist Theological Seminary where, studying with A. T. Robertson and Edgar Young Mullins, he earned his Ph.D. in 1929.

Thiessen wrote his dissertation on "The Holy Spirit in the Epistle to the Romans." In the introduction he explains his interest in the subject:

> The writer's interest in this doctrine goes back to three things in his life. In the first place, a godly grandmother gave him valuable instruction as to the Holy Spirit at the time of his conversion, when he was but seventeen years old. This made an impression on him. In the second place, after sev-

4. Henry C. Thiessen, *Introductory Lectures in Systematic Theology* (Grand Rapids: Eerdmans, 1949), 277–82.

5. Thiessen, *Kurze Studien*, 27–28, 59–60, 95.

eral years of Christian life he saw the need and the privilege of a fuller yielding to the Spirit. This resulted in a life of greater blessing and usefulness. And in the third place, during a period of fourteen years in the ministry, both as a pastor and as teacher in a theological institution, he was thrown together with some Christian friends who, in his opinion, went beyond the teaching of the Scriptures in their interpretation of certain aspects of the work of the Spirit. This led him to study the subject for himself and to come to his own conclusions as to some of the important phases of the Spirit's work. To this day his interest in the "ever present, truest Friend" continues, and he feels that because of such a practical contact with this truth his own life has been enriched.[6]

Working through the Book of Romans, Thiessen examines the names of the Holy Spirit, the actions of the Spirit in the life of the believer, the specific ministries of the Spirit, and the role of the Spirit in the life of Christ and in the resurrection at the end of this age. It is a good study, thoroughly conversant with the literature of the day, well argued, and nicely written.[7]

In his dissertation Thiessen presents six arguments regarding the work of the Holy Spirit: (1) it is complementary to the experience of justification; (2) it begins in an act

6. Henry C. Thiessen, "The Holy Spirit in the Epistle to the Romans," Ph.D. diss., Southern Baptist Theological Seminary, 1929, pp. iv–v.

7. In a typed note to his examiners Thiessen said: "Of the 97 books listed in my Bibliography I have read 86 in their entirety—all but the Commentaries on Romans by Meyer, Parry (Cambridge Greek Testament), and Denney (Expositor's Greek Testament), which I have merely consulted, and the Bible Encyclopaedias, Lexicons, and Concordances, which I have used as one uses such works of reference. I have also consulted a number of other books not here listed, as the footnotes in the thesis will show, which I do not consider important enough to include in a Bibliography." In view of Thiessen's excellent knowledge of German, it is curious that only one of the ninety-seven books listed in the bibliography is in German, namely, F. A. Philippi's *Commentar über den Brief Pauli an die Römer.* Moreover, it is quoted only once in the dissertation (p. 153).

and continues in a process; (3) it is both general and special (i.e., it relates to salvation as such as well as prepares the believer for particular kinds of Christian work); (4) it is ennobling and assuring; (5) it proceeds from the personal to the social; and (6) it embraces both the present and the future.[8] To receive the person of the Holy Spirit, continues Thiessen, we must be willing to allow him into our life, to put to death the practices of the body, and to walk according to his direction.[9]

It is clear from reading the dissertation that, in addition to the nature of the Spirit's work in our lives, Thiessen had two specific issues he wanted to deal with. The first was those liberal theories that said that Paul drew upon Greek thought, the mystery religions, and various other pagan ideas when he explained the personal, divine nature of the Holy Spirit. Thiessen's first chapter is a meticulous examination of those theories that would discredit Paul. It concludes that Paul's teaching was strictly a matter of divine revelation:

We have given much time and space to this review of the possible sources for Paul's teaching on the Holy Spirit, but the present-day claims that our Apostle is greatly indebted to one or more of them have made it necessary. In conclusion we may say that there is little or nothing to prove that such claims are true, excepting only the influence of Old Testament and early Christian teaching. In the light of his claims that he received his gospel by direct revelation and not even from the earlier apostles (Gal. 1:11, 12, 15–20; 2:1–14), we must be careful not to make him dependent upon any man or group of men. It is certainly unfair to him to assume that a chance similarity of expression between him and certain pagan religious or philosophical writings (when the meanings are so different) proves he borrowed from these writings. We, at any rate, shall accept Paul as knowing where he received

8. Thiessen, "Holy Spirit," 161–67.
9. Ibid., 171–76.

his teaching and so as setting before us the authoritative message of God.[10]

The second issue that Thiessen deals with, and to which he would return later, is the nature of the charismatic gifts. A comprehensive section entitled "Fruit and Gifts" concludes with a generally negative assessment of the possibility of exercising these gifts today:

> It is not quite clear whether a gift once received might again be withdrawn or was permanent for life. Paul says that prophecies and knowledge *katargēthēsontai* and tongues *pausontai* (1 Cor. 13:8); but it is hard to decide whether he means during the life time of the individual, or when a man passes from time into eternity, or in the course of the history of the Church. We know, of course, that there was a gradual cessation of the more miraculous *charismata* and Paul may have meant to say that that would be the case. Undoubtedly there is a real sense in which believers are still endowed with divine gifts; but it is not clear that Paul teaches that the more miraculous *charismata* would continue. He himself exercised several of them (1 Cor. 14:18, 19) and the Corinthians came "behind in no gift" (1 Cor. 1:7); but these historical facts cannot be interpreted as samples of what God wanted His people to have during this entire age.[11]

Work at Evangelical Theological College

Upon receiving his doctorate from Southern Baptist, Thiessen became the dean of Evangel University College of Theology in New Jersey, staying there for two years (1929–31). He was then appointed professor of New Testament literature and exegesis at Evangelical Theological College (later Dallas Theological

Seminary), where he taught from 1931 to 1935. During the second semester of the 1934–35 school year, Thiessen compiled a collection of student essays written under his direction. Entitled "Exegetical Essays in the Pastoral Epistles," this compilation, which was never published, takes a conservative line on such disparate subjects as appropriate women's apparel, elders and bishops, and the grace of God.

Because of his earlier editorial experience, Thiessen quickly became a subeditor of *Bibliotheca Sacra*, a publication of the school. Representing the Department of New Testament Greek and Literature, he wrote five articles for the journal. The first was "Should New Testament Greek Be 'Required' in Our Ministerial Training Courses?" Thiessen's strong feeling that it should is evident in his question, "Would it not be true today . . . that if teachers of theological truth returned to the exposition of the Scriptures from the original languages the foundations of modernism would soon be undermined and the way prepared for a great spiritual awakening?"[12]

The second article was "The Parable of the Nobleman and the Earthly Kingdom." In it Thiessen returned to one of his favorite themes, the second coming of Christ. In summing up he says: "We see, then, that the Parable of the Nobleman teaches that we should look for an earthly kingdom, that this kingdom will be set up when Christ returns, that His faithful servants will at that time receive a place on the throne with him, and that the unfaithful will lose even that which they seem to have."[13] He adds a characteristically ethical note by urging that we carry on till Christ comes, so that we may hear his word, "Well done!"

The next three articles constitute a four-part series entitled "Will the Church Pass

---

10. Ibid., 42.

11. Ibid., 125. In his discussion of the spiritual gifts Thiessen shows virtually no acquaintance with writings supporting a contrary opinion. One wonders how his advisors would have allowed this in a Ph.D. dissertation.

12. Henry C. Thiessen, "Should New Testament Greek Be 'Required' in Our Ministerial Training Courses?" *Bibliotheca Sacra* 91 (Jan. 1934): 45.

13. Henry C. Thiessen, "The Parable of the Nobleman and the Earthly Kingdom," *Bibliotheca Sacra* 91 (April 1934): 190.

through the Tribulation?"[14] In the first part Thiessen argues that the tribulation is not simply generalized persecution and martyrdom, but a special seven-year period that is yet to come. He bases his argument on Sir Robert Anderson's *Coming Prince,* which had worked out an explanation of the seventy weeks of Daniel that was congenial to Thiessen's interpretation.

Part two defines the church as "the whole company of God's people in this age"; it is not to be confused with Israel or even designated a spiritual Israel.[15] Thiessen closes this section with the rhetorical question, "Will any or all of those who are truly regenerated and alive when the time comes be obliged to pass through that awful period?"[16] The answer is, of course, no.

Part three begins with Robert Cameron's complaint that the theory of a pretribulation rapture is of recent origin, so Thiessen proposes to examine the church fathers on the subject. Instead of proving his point that pretribulationism was the view of the ancient church, Thiessen winds up somewhat inconclusively:

> Though on the whole the testimony of the Fathers is somewhat inconsistent, we seem to have in the Shepherd of Hermas a fairly clear indication of the fact that there were those who believed that the Church would be taken away before that period of judgment begins. In the light of the evidence we have presented, it is too much to say that there is "no hint of any approach to such a belief" in the Christian literature "from Polycarp down, until the strange utterances given out in the Church of Edward Irving," as Cameron maintains.[17]

14. Henry C. Thiessen, "Will the Church Pass through the Tribulation?" *Bibliotheca Sacra* 92 (Jan.–March 1935): 39–54; (April–June 1935): 187–205; (July–Sept. 1935): 292–314.
15. Ibid., 53.
16. Ibid., 54.
17. Ibid., 196.

In part four Thiessen turns from the writings of humans to the Word of God: "We come [now] to sure foundations. No matter how vaguely men may have expounded it, the revelation of God standeth sure."[18] Thiessen proceeds to marshal various scriptural arguments to show that the church will not go through the tribulation. The promise made to the church in Philadelphia that it would be kept from the hour of trial (Rev. 3:10) heads the list. Significantly, Thiessen views the church in Philadelphia as a symbol of the church of the present age:

> The characteristics of these churches [in Rev. 2–3] fit chronologically into their respective places in the history of the Church. The Church in Ephesus corresponds to the Apostolic Church. The Church in Smyrna finds its counterpart in the Martyr Church of the second and third centuries. The Church in Pergamos represents the State Church, beginning with Constantine and continuing to the end. The Church in Thyatira has the features of the Papal Church, beginning with Gregory the Great and continuing to the end. The Church in Sardis pictures the Reformation Church, beginning with the sixteenth century. The Church in Philadelphia sets forth the characteristics of the Missionary Church, beginning with the rise of modern missions under William Carey. And the Church in Laodicea portrays the Apostate Church of the last days. . . .
>
> If we accept this interpretation of these Letters, then we have here important teaching as to the time of the Rapture. It is clear that we are now in the Philadelphia period of the Church's history. The Laodicean Church is evidently the apostate part of Christendom, taking on more and more definite form in our day. On the basis of these facts we may say that while the Philadelphia Church is promised escape from the Tribulation,

18. Ibid., 196–97.

the Laodicean Church will be rejected by Christ and pass into that period.[19]

The series concludes with a characteristically moral exhortation in the light of Christ's second coming:

We may, then, comfort one another with the thought that our Lord may come at any moment! The "blessed hope" is not some distant prospect that can have little practical meaning for any but those who live during the Tribulation, or even then only for the few who have some prospect of escaping martyrdom under the Beast: It is a present possibility that cheers and sustains and purifies the godly.[20]

Work at Wheaton College

Upon leaving Evangelical Theological College in 1935, Thiessen went to Wheaton College (Illinois), where he was appointed associate professor of Bible and philosophy. The next year he was made a full professor and named chairman of the department; he also received an honorary D.D. from Northern Baptist Theological Seminary.

About this time Wheaton published a small work of Thiessen's entitled *The Work of the Holy Spirit*, with an introductory outline provided by J. Oliver Buswell, Jr., Wheaton's president. The purpose of the volume was to develop a noncharismatic interpretation of the baptism of the Holy Spirit and to encourage walking in the Spirit as the only way to lead a successful Christian life. Thiessen also wrote an extensive review, *The Concordant Version of the Sacred Scriptures: How Should We Regard It?* that was published by Loizeaux Brothers. This is a well-done, rather technical work rejecting the new translation on the basis of grammar, lexicology, text-critical eccentricities, bias, and, most particularly, heterodox doctrine. Specifically, the Concordant Version lacks proper

teachings on regeneration and the Trinity and denies eternal punishment.

In 1938 Wheaton announced the establishment of a seminary-level training course, offering both the Th.B. and the M.A. in theology. Thiessen was named director of the program. This was to become the Wheaton College Graduate School.

Having for several years lectured at churches and Bible conferences across the country on Christ's second coming, Thiessen received many requests for a compact statement on that subject. So he adapted his earlier articles from *Bibliotheca Sacra*, and in 1940 Zondervan published the result as *Will the Church Pass through the Tribulation?* In the introduction Harry A. Ironside, who was then pastor of the Moody Memorial Church in Chicago, observes that Thiessen's argument is "presented so plainly and so clearly . . . [that] a careful reading of it will be used of God to deliver many from the confusing idea of the Post-Tribulation Rapture."[21] In 1940 Zondervan also published a collection of Wheaton chapel talks entitled *Not by Bread Alone* and edited by Carl F. H. Henry. Thiessen's contribution, "The Unanswerable Question," clearly revealed his pastoral and evangelistic heart.[22] The "unanswerable question" is Hebrews 2:3, "How shall we escape, if we neglect so great salvation?" In his talk Thiessen made an impassioned plea for his hearers to come to faith in Christ as Lord and Savior.

Thiessen wrote his last articles for *Bibliotheca Sacra* in 1941. Continuing his interest in eschatological matters, but also going back to his days in graduate school by focusing on Romans, he examines in a two-part series "The Place of Israel in the Scheme of Redemption as Set Forth in Ro-

19. Ibid., 199–200.
20. Ibid., 314.

21. Henry C. Thiessen, *Will the Church Pass through the Tribulation?* (Grand Rapids: Zondervan, 1940), 2.
22. Henry C. Thiessen, "The Unanswerable Question," in *Not by Bread Alone*, ed. Carl F. H. Henry (Grand Rapids: Zondervan, 1940), 35–42.

mans 9–11."[23] He is concerned with the perplexing question of Israel's rejection by God and Paul's understanding of it. After discussing the nature, justice, cause, and extent of Israel's rejection, Thiessen goes on to find some positive significance in it. He argues that the divine rejection of Israel was designed by God to facilitate the spread of the gospel among the Gentiles, to stir Israel to emulate their conversion, and to admonish the Gentiles to humility and faithfulness.[24] On the difficult question of what "all Israel shall be saved" means in Romans 11:26, Thiessen rejects the idea that Paul has in view every Israelite, the remnant according to the election of grace, or every Israelite living when Christ returns. Rather, it is "only the [Israelite] nation that is left after these purging judgments [i.e., the events of the great tribulation] that will be saved."[25]

The issue of suffering had always exercised Thiessen, not only because of his own health problems, but also because of the obvious difficulties that God's people go through in this world. He had lived through the First World War and now saw his nation plunged into yet another conflict that threatened to engulf the globe. So in 1942 he wrote *Why Do the Righteous Suffer?* To answer that question he looks at the life of Job in the Old Testament. He concludes that the reasons for the afflictions of Job were to clarify his vision of God, to lead him to repentance, to correct erroneous views as to the afflictions of God's people, and to enrich the sufferer spiritually. Thiessen comments: "Ofttimes we cannot be brought into . . . consciousness of God in our lives apart from afflictions. . . . Let us, therefore, welcome the training of God in the school of suffering in order that we may become qualified for

the greatest possible spiritual prosperity."[26] It is characteristic of Thiessen's humility that not once does he mention the agonies that he himself had gone through.

Major Works

Introduction to the New Testament

The first of Thiessen's two major works, *Introduction to the New Testament,* was published in 1943. It was the outgrowth of classes taught at Evangelical Theological College and Wheaton. Thoroughly conservative in all the positions it espouses, it "makes no claims to originality beyond that of incorporating the new discoveries into the conservative position."[27] Thiessen acknowledges his debt to Henry Alford, George Salmon, B. F. Westcott, J. B. Lightfoot, Theodor Zahn, Alfred Plummer, R. J. Knowling, W. M. Ramsay, R. D. Shaw, Frederic Kenyon, and A. T. Robertson. One may judge this scholar by the academic company he keeps.

Thiessen divides the book into two unequal parts. Part I, the relatively small General Introduction, covers the canon, the materials and methods of textual criticism, and the doctrine of inspiration. Part II, the Special Introduction, covers the Synoptic Problem, the Synoptic Gospels, John and Acts, the Pauline Letters, the General Letters, Hebrews, and the Apocalypse.

In Part I, which is quite well informed, Thiessen adopts, in essence, the theories of Westcott and F. J. A. Hort, as modified by Kenyon and Burnett Streeter.[28] His approach is apologetic rather than academic, however, and he concludes his textual discussions with the oft-quoted words of Westcott and Hort:

> "If comparative trivialities, such as changes of order, the insertion or omis-

23. Henry C. Thiessen, "The Place of Israel in the Scheme of Redemption as Set Forth in Romans 9–11," *Bibliotheca Sacra* 98 (Jan.–March 1941): 78–91; (April–June 1941): 203–17.

24. Ibid., 206–12.

25. Ibid., 214.

26. Henry C. Thiessen, *Why Do the Righteous Suffer?* (Findlay, Ohio: Fundamental Truth, 1942), 35, 40.

27. Henry C. Thiessen, *Introduction to the New Testament* (Grand Rapids: Eerdmans, 1943), vii.

28. Ibid., 70–75.

sion of the article with proper names, and the like, are set aside, the words in our opinion still subject to doubt can hardly amount to more than a thousandth part of the whole New Testament." This would be a total of little more than a half page of the Greek Testament from which this statement is taken. Truly, this is not very much![29]

In discussing inspiration, Thiessen accepts the definition of Louis Gaussen: "that inexplicable power which the divine Spirit put forth of old on the authors of Holy Scripture, in order to their guidance even in the employment of the words they used, and to preserve them alike from all error and from all omission."[30] Thiessen makes three comments on this definition. First, he says that the exact mode of inspiration is unknown:

> The Holy Spirit wrought in the hearts and minds of the authors, but we cannot say exactly what He did, except that He guided them in the production of their works. The Spirit's revelation to the heart and His illumination of the mind to understand truth were, no doubt, often starting points for the Spirit's guidance in the writing of the books. At times the Spirit probably dictated the very words that were to be used; but that can scarcely have been His usual method, for the various authors of Scripture display distinct grammatical and stylistic differences, which could hardly have been the case if all had been directly dictated by the Spirit. It is best, we believe, to leave the question of the mode of inspiration unsettled and to insist merely that the Holy Spirit guided the authors of Holy Scriptures in the writing of the Word of God.[31]

Second, inspiration is verbal; the Holy Spirit "guided the writers to choose such words to express His message as were normal to their style and vocabulary and yet

were the very words in which He wanted it expressed."[32] Third, only the original autographs of Scripture are inspired. Thiessen then offers some proofs of inspiration and a refutation of various erroneous theories.

In Part II the sections on the Synoptic Problem and the Synoptic Gospels show the most work and originality, although Thiessen is careful to stay firmly within the conservative camp. After struggling with various modern views, he sets forth what he feels to be an adequate position on the Synoptic Problem:

> As contrasted with these other views, the true view gives primary consideration to the divine aspect in the composition of the Synoptics. It grants that the authors may have used "sources" for some of the materials in the Gospels but holds that they used them under the guidance and control of the Holy Spirit. This means that sometimes they used materials that had come to them from the immediate apostles of our Lord, and in the case of Matthew, materials that had come from his own observation and experience; that at other times they probably adopted parts of the oral tradition concerning the life and work of Christ that had come to their notice; that at still other times they appropriated a part or all of an account that was already in circulation in writing; but that over and above all the Holy Spirit quickened their memories as to the things which they had heard and seen, and guided them in the selections they made and in the editing and arranging of the materials. It is in this way that each one of the three produced in a most natural way an independent and verbally inspired account of the life of Christ. . . . [So] why not return to the belief in a verbally inspired record?[33]

The reader will note that the work of the Holy Spirit is paramount in Thiessen's understanding of the nature of the Gospels. By contrast, the naturalism of the

29. Ibid., 77.
30. Ibid., 79.
31. Ibid., 79–80.

32. Ibid., 80.
33. Ibid., 121–22, 128.

various modern theories is their undoing. A simple return to belief in God and the verbally inspired nature of the Scriptures will solve most, if not all, of the supposed problems and thus do away with skepticism regarding the truth of the Gospel material.

Introductory Lectures in Systematic Theology

In 1946, Thiessen's failing health compelled him to move to California, where he became head of the Theology Department at the Los Angeles Baptist Theological Seminary; but the pressures of work there were too much for him, so he soon retired completely. He died on July 25, 1947. Before dying he pleaded with the Lord to spare him long enough to finish his second major work, *Introductory Lectures in Systematic Theology*. But with only about one-third of the book completed, he realized that the end was near. One of the last entries in his diary is the comment that, at last, he is reconciled to going home to be with the Lord, if that is God's will.

Introductory Lectures began life in 1939 as a syllabus printed by Wheaton College; it gradually grew over the years. After Thiessen died in 1947, his wife asked his brother John to complete the project. He did so, carefully going over all of Henry's papers; and *Introductory Lectures* was published in October of 1949.

It is difficult to categorize Thiessen's theology because it is essentially eclectic. It could be described as a moderately Reformed, moderately dispensational, Baptistic evangelicalism of a practical, pastoral sort. The lectures rest on the premise that theology is possible because God has revealed himself in a general and a special way. General revelation is found in nature, history, and conscience—"it is addressed to all intelligent creatures generally and is accessible to all; it has for its object the supplying of the natural need of the man and the persuasion of the soul to seek after

the true God."[34] On the basis of the general revelation it is possible to prove that God exists. The traditional arguments from cosmology, teleology, ontology, morality, and congruity corroborate our innate belief in God. We may conclude that "there is a personal, extra-mundane, ethical, and self-revealing God."[35] Special revelation is to be found in miracles, prophecy, Jesus Christ, and the Scriptures, where we have "the verbally inspired Word of God."[36]

God, for Thiessen, has both essence and attributes. In essence he is spiritual (i.e., incorporeal, invisible, alive, personal), self-existent, immense (beyond space), and eternal (being the cause of time, God is himself free from all succession of time and possesses simultaneously his total duration). God's attributes, which Thiessen divides into nonmoral and moral, are omnipresence, omniscience, omnipotence, immortality, holiness, justice, goodness, and truth. Omniscience, Thiessen says, means "that He knows Himself and all other things, whether they be actual or merely possible, whether they be past, present, or future, and that He knows them perfectly and from all eternity. He knows things immediately, simultaneously, exhaustively and truly. He also knows the best ways to attain His desired ends."[37] A trinitarian, Thiessen also believes in the absolute equality of the Father, Son, and Holy Spirit.

The decrees of God, Thiessen points out, are the foundation for all God's actions:

They are not, as some erroneously suppose, inconsistent with free agency; they do not take away all motives for human exertion; and they do not make God the Author of sin. We believe that the decrees of God are His eternal purpose (in a real

34. Thiessen, *Introductory Lectures*, 32.
35. Ibid., 63.
36. Ibid., 107.
37. Ibid., 124.

sense all things are embraced in one purpose) or purposes, based on His most wise and holy counsel, whereby He freely and unchangeably, for His own glory, ordained, either efficaciously or permissively, all that comes to pass.[38]

God's decrees include prevenient grace, which Thiessen defines in Arminian fashion: "We believe that the common grace of God restores to the sinner the ability to make a favorable response to God. In other words, we hold that God, in His grace, makes it possible for all men to be saved."[39] On the other hand, election is of "all those who He foreknew would respond positively to prevenient grace."[40]

Creation was by divine fiat and *ex nihilo*. Thiessen accepts in large measure the gap theory as outlined by George Pember in *Earth's Earliest Ages*. This theory postulates that Genesis 1:1 speaks of the original creation; there followed a long period of time that ended with the fall of Satan and a judgment of the earth (Gen. 1:2); the world was then reconstructed in six twenty-four-hour days (Gen. 1:3–2:4). Thiessen accepts the idea of a very old earth, rejects theistic evolution, and admits that the age-day theory (i.e., the notion that the "days" of Gen. 1 may be epochs rather than twenty-four-hour periods) may be correct.[41] Thiessen believes in a direct creation of humankind, a historical Adam and Eve, a dichotomy of human nature (we are composed of body and soul), traducianism, a literal fall, and total depravity. He accepts the personality of Satan and the existence of angels and demons, who he thinks are the souls of the departed pre-Adamites looking for a place to rest (Pember's theory again).

Thiessen believes in the preexistence of Christ, his literal incarnation, his true humanity and deity, and his bodily resurrection and ascension. Jesus' death was vicarious, a satisfaction for sin, a ransom, and for all the world. Thiessen rejects the accident, martyr, moral-influence, governmental, and commercial theories of the atonement.

We are saved not by works, but by faith, which unites us to Christ and is the foundation for the imputation of his righteousness to us. Sanctification is both an act and a process; it does not produce sinless perfection. Once believers are saved, they can "never totally fall away from the state of grace into which they have been brought, nor fail to return from their backsliding in the end."[42]

The church is not Judaism improved, but was founded at Pentecost. It is both local and universal and consists of true believers only. It has organization and two ordinances (not sacraments), baptism and the Lord's Supper, ordinance being defined as "a visible sign of the saving truth of the Christian faith."[43] Baptism is for believers only, and the Lord's Supper is a memorial to the death of Christ.

The end of the present age will begin with a rapture of the church, followed by a seven-year great tribulation, the return of Christ to earth, a millennium, the final judgments, and the establishment of a new heaven, a new earth, and the New Jerusalem, the eternal dwelling of the church. Hell is the eternal destiny of Satan, his angels, and the unbelievers, where they will suffer forever in their rejection of God.

Thiessen's influence is largely the result of his two major works, *Introduction to the New Testament* and *Introductory Lectures in Systematic Theology*. The *Introduction to the New Testament* is still extensively used throughout the English-speaking world; in fact, the twenty-second printing was released in 1989. Similarly, the *Introductory Lectures in Systematic Theology* had gone through eighteen printings by

38. Ibid., 147.
39. Ibid., 155.
40. Ibid., 156–57, 344–45.
41. Ibid., 160–72, 195, 201.

42. Ibid., 385.
43. Ibid., 403–37; the quote is from p. 422.

1979, when a revised edition was issued; within a decade the revision had gone through nine printings.[44] Thiessen's *Lectures* has been translated into Portuguese, Indonesian, Korean, and French, and an English-language Philippine edition also exists. The strength of the *Lectures* lies in its strongly biblical basis (the Scripture index extends to thirty-seven pages), its excellent organization, and its understand-

ability.[45] It is a good place to start one's theological journey, as so many have found out; and if one chooses to go on from there, one could do no better than travel on in Thiessen's spirit of simplicity in the presence of God, humility, and profound faith in Christ.

---

44. Henry C. Thiessen, *Lectures in Systematic Theology*, rev. by Vernon D. Doerksen (Grand Rapids: Eerdmans, 1979). Though it is not our purpose to review Doerksen's work, it must be said that in places significant alterations were made in Thiessen's point of view, some of which he would have rejected entirely. The chapters on the decrees (ch. 10) and on election and vocation (ch. 28) are cases in point. When Doerksen says, "Some hold that God, in his foreknowledge, perceives what each man will do in response to his call, and elects men to salvation in harmony with his knowledge of their choice of him. This view, however, seems to run contrary to the biblical doctrine of the sovereignty of God as it relates to salvation. . . . For God to foreknow is for God to choose. His foreknowledge is his choice" (p. 258), he is rejecting Thiessen's view of election in a book that purports to have been written by Thiessen. The revision of the chapter on creation (ch. 11) is too brief and inconclusive to be of much help; Thiessen himself would not have objected except, perhaps, for the removal of his "Pemberisms." In other places Thiessen's already forceful presentation has been strengthened. He would, for instance,

have been quite happy with the material on eschatology (Part VIII). It is a shame that Doerksen has not addressed one of the real weaknesses of Thiessen's book—the total lack of interaction with contemporary nonevangelical thought. See Charles C. Ryrie, review of *Lectures in Systematic Theology*, by Henry C. Thiessen, *Christianity Today*, 29 May 1981, pp. 50–51; Richard Klann, review of *Lectures in Systematic Theology*, by Henry C. Thiessen, *Concordia Journal* 7.3 (May 1981): 131–32.

45. In his attempt to make theology more readable, Thiessen made excellent use of the more technical evangelical thinkers who preceded him. He quotes Augustus H. Strong 78 times, Charles Hodge 49 times, and William G. T. Shedd 40 times. Others are quoted far less extensively: George P. Fisher is used 15 times, William Evans 11 times (the same as John Calvin), Henry B. Smith 9 times, and John Miley 6 times. It is interesting that Lewis Sperry Chafer is quoted only twice, both times from *Major Bible Themes* (1926). On the debit side, Thiessen knew very little about and apparently was not interested in contemporary theologians whose views were not roughly in accord with his own. Thus there is very little interaction with the work of Karl Barth, Dietrich Bonhoeffer, and Emil Brunner.

Cornelius Van Til

John M. Frame

Cornelius Van Til was born on May 3, 1895, in Grootegast, the Netherlands, the sixth son of Ite Van Til, a dairy farmer, and his wife Klazina.[1] At the age of ten Cornelius moved with his family to Highland, Indiana. He picked up English quickly and spoke thereafter with very little trace of an accent.

The first of his family to receive a formal higher education, Van Til in 1914 entered Calvin Preparatory School in Grand Rapids, where he remained to study at Calvin College and at Calvin Theological Seminary. These institutions were all schools of Van Til's denomination, the Christian Reformed Church, which was made up mostly of Dutch immigrants like himself. But after his first year of seminary, Van Til transferred to Princeton Theological Seminary. In those days, Princeton was an orthodox Calvinistic school, as was Calvin, and there was much mutual respect between the two; but Princeton's roots were in American Presbyterianism rather than in the Dutch Reformed tradition represented by Calvin.

While in seminary, Van Til was also admitted to Princeton University as a graduate student in philosophy, working on a doctorate as he completed his seminary course.[2] In 1925 he completed a Th.M. at the seminary and married his childhood sweetheart, Rena Klooster; in 1927 he completed a Ph.D. at the university.

Influences

During his years in the Dutch Reformed community, Van Til became very im-

1. The biographical information in this article is (except for some items of personal knowledge) taken from William White, Jr., *Van Til: Defender of the Faith* (Nashville: Thomas Nelson, 1979). This book is an excellent introduction to Van Til's life and character, but it has weaknesses, especially in explaining his thought; see John M. Frame, review of *Van Til: Defender of the Faith,* by William White, Jr., *Westminster Theological Journal* 42.1 (Fall 1979): 198–203.

2. Princeton University and Princeton Seminary have always been distinct institutions.

pressed with the great Dutch church leaders Abraham Kuyper and Herman Bavinck. Kuyper was a Renaissance man: scholar, university founder, politician (briefly prime minister of the Netherlands), newspaper editor. With boundless energy and intellectual creativity, he sought to claim all areas of human life for the lordship of Christ. Bavinck, his colleague and follower, focused more narrowly on the discipline of systematic theology and produced a monumental four-volume *Reformed Dogmatics*.[3] The work of Klaas Schilder, a more recent Dutch thinker, also commanded Van Til's deep respect and interest.

Van Til arrived in Princeton too late to study with B. B. Warfield, arguably the greatest theological scholar America has produced, who had died in 1921; but Warfield's name was legendary during Van Til's student days, and Van Til respected him deeply, as well as Warfield's predecessor, the great Princeton theologian of the previous century, Charles Hodge. While at the seminary, Van Til became a close friend of Professor Geerhardus Vos, like himself a Dutch immigrant who had left Grand Rapids for Princeton. Vos brought to Princeton the discipline of "biblical theology," which sought to understand Scripture as a history of redemption. Van Til himself was more philosophically than exegetically inclined, but one can find echoes of Vos in Van Til's writings.[4] Van Til's preaching and much of his classroom teaching also contained a great deal of biblical theology; he would, for instance, trace the human epistemological predicament from the Garden of Eden to the judgments of Revelation.

The philosophical influences upon Van Til are a bit harder to define. At Calvin his most famous teacher was W. Harry

Jellema, described in my hearing by a well-known non-Christian philosopher as "the best teacher of philosophy in the United States." Jellema himself had studied with the Harvard idealist Josiah Royce, and may have motivated Van Til to study idealism at Princeton. Van Til's dissertation advisor at Princeton University was Archibald A. Bowman, whose sympathies also were with idealism and with the developing personalist movement. As did James Orr, with whose writings Van Til's apologetics shows some affinity, Van Til made liberal use of the idealist vocabulary (the philosophical use of the term *presupposition* originated in idealism). Nonetheless, Van Til always insisted that he rejected the substantive content of idealism, which identified the creator with the creature and made them subject to one another within an impersonal universe.

The most important philosophical influences on Van Til were distinctively Christian rather than idealist. Kuyper himself had urged that all human thought be governed by a Christian worldview derived from Scripture. To Kuyper, this worldview was antithetical to every secular ideology, whether philosophical, political, economic, aesthetic, or whatever. Kuyper's disciples sought to bring the Christian worldview to bear on politics, education, and journalism; naturally, some sought to express it in philosophy as well. Thus in the 1920s Herman Dooyeweerd, D. H. Theodoor Vollenhoven, and others in the Netherlands founded a school of thought called the "philosophy of the idea of law." It is unclear whether this school influenced the initial formulations of Van Til's apologetic, or whether he had developed his approach before his contact with the Dutch philosophy. Certainly there are many similarities, but also important differences. At any rate, Van Til wrote favorably about the early work of the Dutch school; and they, in turn, named Van Til as an editor of their journal, *Philosophia Reformata*. Though Van Til later became critical of this group, he was always aware of

---

3. Only a large part of volume 2 has been translated into English—Herman Bavinck, *The Doctrine of God*, trans. and ed. William Hendriksen (Grand Rapids: Baker, 1977).

4. See especially Cornelius Van Til, *Common Grace and the Gospel* (Nutley, N.J.: Presbyterian and Reformed, 1964) and *Christian Theistic Ethics* (Philadelphia: Westminster Theological Seminary, 1958).

the developments among them. Surely, then, in a broad sense at least, we must list the Dooyeweerdian school as one significant influence on Van Til's thought.

Career

After his graduation in 1927, Van Til spent one year as the pastor of the Christian Reformed Church in Spring Lake, Michigan, a work which he deeply enjoyed. He took a leave of absence from the pastorate to teach apologetics at Princeton Seminary during the academic year 1928–29. When the seminary offered him the chair of apologetics (in effect, a full professorship) at the end of that period, Van Til turned down the offer and returned to Spring Lake. He was strongly inclined to remain in the pastorate, and in addition he did not wish to cooperate in the reorganization of Princeton Seminary which had been mandated that spring by the General Assembly of the Presbyterian Church in the U.S.A. The reorganization was intended to purge the seminary's historic stand for orthodox Calvinism and make the school more representative of "all the points of view found in the church." To be included were the points of view of the thirteen hundred ministers who in 1924 had signed the notorious Auburn Affirmation, which declared the doctrines of biblical inspiration, the virgin birth of Christ, his substitutionary atonement, his bodily resurrection, and literal second coming to be humanly formulated theories; hence, ministerial candidates need not be required to subscribe to them.

However, there were those in the Presbyterian Church in the U.S.A. who sought to fight against the unbelief growing throughout the denomination and the church at large. The most notable of these was J. Gresham Machen, a teacher of New Testament at Princeton Seminary. Van Til did not study under Machen but knew him well and admired his scholarship, his ability to articulate the truth, and his stand for orthodox doctrine. Machen must be added to our list of men who influenced Van Til, for al-

most everything Van Til wrote and taught reflects Machen's theme that orthodoxy is indispensable to a Christian profession.[5] The great doctrines of the faith are not human inventions, but the teachings of God himself to us in his Word. One cannot claim to be a Christian while rejecting the teachings of Christ in Scripture. Indeed, Van Til went one step beyond Machen, seeking to show that orthodox Christian doctrine is, in one sense, necessary for any rational thought and conduct (see pp. 164, 166).

In response to the reorganizing of Princeton Seminary, Machen with other faculty members (Robert Dick Wilson, Oswald T. Allis) determined to start a new seminary that would be independent of the General Assembly's control and would continue to give students orthodox instruction in the tradition of Warfield, Vos, and Hodge. Younger men, R. B. Kuiper, Ned B. Stonehouse, Allan MacRae, and Paul Woolley, were added to the faculty; and Machen was eager to obtain Van Til's services in the area of apologetics. Van Til was extremely reluctant to leave Spring Lake, but after much correspondence and personal visits by Allis, Stonehouse, and Machen himself, Van Til, several days before opening exercises, accepted the offer. Westminster Theological Seminary opened its doors in Philadelphia in the fall of 1929, and Van Til remained on the faculty there until his retirement in 1972.

In 1936, Machen and several others were suspended from the ministry of the Presbyterian Church in the U.S.A. for their unwillingness to resign from an independent mission board which Machen had founded. The independent board represented conservative dissatisfaction with the official mission board, which tolerated among its missionaries liberal teaching along the lines of the Auburn Affirmation. Machen and the others did not accept this church discipline; among other irregularities, the ecclesiasti-

5. In my judgment, Machen's *Christianity and Liberalism* (New York: Macmillan, 1923) remains to this day the best presentation of this theme.

cal court had not permitted Machen to make a scriptural case for his conduct. So Machen and 130 other ministers founded a new denomination, originally called the Presbyterian Church of America,[6] but later forced to change its name under legal threat. Eventually the body called itself the Orthodox Presbyterian Church. In sympathy with Machen, Van Til transferred his membership from the Christian Reformed Church to the Orthodox Presbyterian Church, where he remained until his death in 1987.[7]

Publications

Van Til's first book, *The New Modernism*, caused a storm.[8] In it he attacked the idea that Karl Barth and Emil Brunner were basically Reformed evangelicals. As he elsewhere expressed his conclusion, "Barth simply does not believe the Christ of the Scripture at all."[9]

Van Til's second book tackled the subject of *Common Grace*.[10] *The Defense of the Faith* followed in 1955, the first complete public presentation of his distinctive apologetic system.[11] Incorporating much of his basic unpublished syllabus *Apologetics*, it included answers to his critics. For after

6. This should not be confused with the Presbyterian Church *in* America, which was founded in 1973 and still bears that name.

7. Van Til's Christian Reformed colleague at Westminster, R. B. Kuiper, also joined the Orthodox Presbyterian Church in 1936, but he returned to the Christian Reformed Church later when he became president of Calvin Seminary.

8. Cornelius Van Til, *The New Modernism* (Philadelphia: Presbyterian and Reformed, 1946).

9. Cornelius Van Til, *A Christian Theory of Knowledge* (Philadelphia: Presbyterian and Reformed, 1969), 229.

10. Cornelius Van Til, *Common Grace* (Philadelphia: Presbyterian and Reformed, 1947). This volume was later reissued as the first section of *Common Grace and the Gospel* (1964).

11. Cornelius Van Til, *The Defense of the Faith* (Philadelphia: Presbyterian and Reformed, 1955). A revised and abridged edition was issued in 1963. Unless there is indication to the contrary, future references to this work have the 1963 edition in view.

Van Til had taught at Calvin Seminary for one semester in 1952, a number of articles attacking his positions appeared in the *Calvin Forum*. James Daane, a Christian Reformed minister, wrote a whole volume critical of Van Til, *A Theology of Grace*.[12] Earlier, J. Oliver Buswell had written a very negative review of Van Til's *Common Grace* in his publication *The Bible Today*. Van Til addressed both Buswell and the Daane–*Calvin Forum* group in *The Defense of the Faith*. In 1963, the book was released in an abridged form that left out most of the debate between Van Til and his critics.

In 1962, Van Til published his second major critique of Barth, *Christianity and Barthianism* (the title intentionally reminiscent of Machen's *Christianity and Liberalism*).[13] *A Christian Theory of Knowledge* appeared in 1969. A somewhat expanded version of the syllabus of the same name, it incorporated some of the debate between Van Til and his critics that had been left out of the second edition of *The Defense of the Faith*.

In the late 1960s and 1970s, Van Til seems to have lost much of his reserve about publishing. A great many books came out in rapid succession: *Is God Dead? The Confession of 1967, Christ and the Jews, The Sovereignty of Grace, The New Hermeneutic, The New Synthesis Theology of the Netherlands, The God of Hope*. Most of these are fairly minor works, less important, at least, to the understanding of Van Til's thought than are some of his more basic syllabi.

Of those books still considered unpublished syllabi, some are among Van Til's most important writings: *An Introduction to Systematic Theology, Christian-Theistic Evidences, Christian Theistic Ethics*. His original syllabus, dating to 1929, was rereleased in the 1970s as *A Survey of Chris-*

12. James Daane, *A Theology of Grace* (Grand Rapids: Eerdmans, 1954).

13. Cornelius Van Til, *Christianity and Barthianism* (Philadelphia: Presbyterian and Reformed, 1962).

tian Epistemology—still an unpublished syllabus.[14]

Van Til also published a great many articles and reviews.[15] Of his many pamphlets, *Why I Believe in God* deserves special notice.[16] Perhaps the only writing Van Til actually directed toward unbelievers, it raises more questions than it answers, but it is well worth reading, for it contains some of the best writing Van Til ever did.

Teaching Style

Van Til quickly developed the reputation of having a brilliant mind with an encyclopedic knowledge of philosophy and theology. Personally, he was gracious and charming, with a sometimes wild sense of humor. He was said to be like the apostle Paul in that his writings were weighty and powerful, but his physical presence meek (2 Cor. 10:10). He spent as much time with simple people as with brilliant intellectuals. He would regularly visit sick friends in the hospital and minister to others in the hospital rooms, engaging them in conversation and prayer. He was generous with his time and resources—often willing to preach in little struggling churches and nursing homes, or supplying correspondents with some of his syllabi at his own expense.

As to his communication skills, perhaps the jury is still out. His preaching was very eloquent and challenging; in some ways it was better than his teaching. His teaching method was to assign readings in some of his unpublished syllabi and in the writings of others, and then to conduct a class dis-

14. This "unpublished" business was something of a joke among students. The books were, in fact, available to all; they were sold by mail-order companies and in bookstores. Still, Van Til remained rather modest about these syllabi and insisted on labeling them "unpublished."

15. For a complete bibliography of Van Til's works up to 1971, see *Jerusalem and Athens*, ed. E. R. Geehan (Nutley, N.J.: Presbyterian and Reformed, 1971), 492–98.

16. Cornelius Van Til, *Why I Believe in God* (Philadelphia: Committee on Christian Education, Orthodox Presbyterian Church, 1966).

cussion punctuated by ad hoc lectures on various topics which happened to come up. The discussion proceeded fast, too fast for many of the students, for they had no philosophical (and little theological) background. Van Til would write names and concepts on the board, usually just the first few letters of each word; at times the pace was dizzying. He rarely defined his concepts precisely. When students asked for definitions or tried to reduce his arguments to a logical sequence, Van Til usually resisted. What he did in such cases was to back up and start over, using essentially the same language he had used before. He seemed to think that regular repetition of certain ideas would result in their entering the students' minds by a kind of osmosis.

Van Til did have a great knack for illustrations and slogans—reducing complex ideas to homely, familiar dimensions. His lifelong love of farming revealed itself in stories about chickens and cows. Or consider some of his similes describing the unbeliever. The unbeliever's mind is like a buzz saw that works very efficiently but in the wrong direction.[17] The unbeliever who tries to explain the universe as the product of sheer chance is like a man made of water who tries to climb out of the water on a ladder made of water.[18] The unbeliever is prejudiced about everything, like a man with yellow glasses cemented to his face—"all is yellow to the jaundiced eye."[19] Students tended to latch on to these illustrations and short formulations (e.g., "the point of contact is deep within the natural man")[20] and would begin to feel that they had understood Van Til. Unfortunately, too often that understanding was rudimentary at best and erroneous at worst. Van Til himself was quite aware that there is only so much that one can learn through slogans and illustrations; eventually there must be careful analysis. (Thus he told us that term papers

17. Van Til, *Defense*, 74.
18. Ibid., 102.
19. Ibid., 77, 231.
20. Ibid., 94.

which merely repeated his slogans and illustrations without careful analysis would be graded no higher than "C.") But teaching the process of analysis was not Van Til's gift. Therefore even today there are many—both friends and enemies of Van Til's ideas—who have extremely confused notions of what he actually taught.[21]

Thus his modest reluctance to publish may not have been without basis. His books and syllabi contain some of the same problems: the force of his bold, exciting summaries, illustrations, and exhortation is weakened by inadequate definition, analysis, and argument. This reflects, to some extent, deficiency in communication skills, but also—and perhaps more significantly—Van Til's isolation.

Van Til always was something of an outsider in the theological, philosophical, and apologetic discussions of his day. A Dutchman teaching in a distinctively American environment, a rejecter of mainstream liberal theology who sought to excel as a theologian and philosopher, a Christian apologist who rejected virtually the entire tradition of apologetics as it had been practiced since the second century. He often spoke of the isolation of the Reformed faith, even as he made strongly negative comments about Roman Catholic, Arminian, and "less consistent Calvinist" theology. His negativity naturally led to more isolation. Rarely did Van Til engage in dialogue with other positions; rather, his style was confrontation.

Van Til's language, too, contributed to his isolation. Unlike most of the popular apologists, he used a great many technical philosophical and theological expressions, often inadequately defined and analyzed; even his homely illustrations could not compensate for his daunting style. Beyond this, his philosophical vocabulary was not the kind easily understood by other philosophers. Van Til's philosophical background was idealist, and increasingly during his career the philosophical climate turned away from idealism. In America, the newer movements were various forms of language analysis, which took great pride in their clarity, sharp definitions, and minute analysis of individual propositions—not the skills for which Van Til was known. And his theological language was often very technical as well. Though he could preach the gospel very simply to children and to the childlike, he preferred in his teaching to focus upon the more difficult areas of theological debate. He was not, like C. S. Lewis, a defender of "Mere Christianity." He intended to defend the entire Reformed faith down to the smallest detail.

Another facet of Van Til's isolation is that he was a brilliant philosopher in a denomination where, for most of his career, no one else was capable of discussing matters at his level (except, perhaps, Gordon H. Clark for a time; but Clark's presence meant more confrontation, not dialogue).[22] Nor was Van Til challenged by book and journal editors, for most of his articles were published in-house by the seminary's own *Westminster Theological Journal*, and his

---

21. Almost all of the published criticism of Van Til falls into this category. That includes most of the negative articles in *Jerusalem and Athens*, ed. Geehan, as well as R. C. Sproul, John H. Gerstner, and Arthur Lindsley, *Classical Apologetics* (Grand Rapids: Zondervan, 1984); see John M. Frame, review of *Classical Apologetics*, by R. C. Sproul et al., *Westminster Theological Journal* 47.2 (Fall 1985): 279–99. The same must be said of those who published critiques in the 1950s—Buswell, Daane, and the *Calvin Forum* group. As for misunderstandings by Van Til's friends, see Jim Halsey, "A Preliminary Critique," *Westminster Theological Journal* 39.1 (Fall 1976): 120–36, and the reply in John M. Frame, *Doctrine of the Knowledge of God* (Phillipsburg, N.J.: Presbyterian and Reformed, 1987), esp. 38–39, 51–52. Also note Frame, review of *Van Til*, by William White, Jr., and the interchange with White and others in *Journey* 3.2 (March–April 1988): 9–11; 3.4–5 (July–Oct. 1988): 45–46; and 4.1 (Jan.–Feb. 1989): 14–15, 22–23.

22. Space does not permit a full discussion here of this controversy within the Orthodox Presbyterian Church. See Frame, *Knowledge of God*, 21–40. Neither Van Til nor Clark was at his best in the debate, and the controversy (on rather technical philosophical matters which few actually understood) detracted much from the work of the gospel in the little denomination and at Westminster Seminary.

books were published by Presbyterian and Reformed, which was equally uncritical of him.

Such isolation may sometimes be necessary for the free development of important and controversial theological ideas. However, it creates obvious difficulties. For one thing, an isolated thinker has little opportunity to influence theology and the church at large. Thus Van Til is still not taken seriously by many people who ought to be very interested in what he had to say (e.g., the new Reformed-epistemology movement of Alvin Plantinga and Nicholas Wolterstorff).

Another result of the isolation was that Van Til was not effectively challenged during his career to define his terms, to explain the logical structure of his arguments, to examine his ambiguities. That kind of analysis now falls to others. Some years ago I reviewed a book that was friendly to Van Til, but that frequently misunderstood his ideas. I concluded with an exhortation that we supporters of Van Til set higher standards for ourselves. Van Til himself (then retired) wrote a note commending those sentiments, even though he was aware that they could lead to some negative conclusions about his teaching. Often he seemed to flee from such analysis; but at some level he probably knew that he had missed something by not having experienced the benefits of iron sharpening iron (Prov. 27:17) or of a multitude of counselors (Prov. 11:14; 15:22; 24:6).

Epistemology

The Essence of Knowledge

Nevertheless, for all of Van Til's weaknesses he is an important thinker indeed—perhaps the most important Christian thinker since John Calvin. That statement (coming from a not uncritical disciple) may at first seem extreme. To appreciate it, one must come to understand Van Til's contribution to contemporary theology.

Now to say that Van Til is the most important Christian thinker since Calvin is not to say that he is the most comprehensive thinker, or the clearest. Certainly it is not to say (as some of his more fanatical followers assume) that he is beyond criticism. Nor is it to say that he has had a greater impact on present-day Christian thought than has anybody else; indeed, his isolation continues, and his influence remains small. It is, rather, to say that he has made the Christian community aware of the only epistemology that is appropriate for it, thus laying a necessary foundation for all subsequent Christian reflection.

In describing his theory of knowledge, Van Til wrote, "Now the basic structure of my thought is very simple,"[23] and in essence it is. It is, one might say, the opposite of the secular philosopher Immanuel Kant's view and of the modern thought that follows his lead. Although Kant professed a kind of theism and an admiration for Jesus, he was clearly far from orthodox Christianity. Indeed, his major book on religion (*Religion within the Limits of Reason Alone*) has as its chief theme that the human mind must never subject itself to any authority beyond itself. Kant radically rejected the idea of authoritative revelation from God and asserted the autonomy of the human mind perhaps more clearly than had ever been done before (though secular philosophers had always maintained this notion). The human mind is to be its own supreme authority, its own criterion of truth and right.

In other works Kant argues that what makes our experience intelligible is largely, perhaps entirely, our own minds. We do not know what the world is really like; we know only how it appears to us, and how it appears to us is largely what we make it out to be. Thus not only is the human mind its own ultimate authority, but it also replaces God as the intelligent planner and creator of the experienced universe. Kant also regarded the human mind as the author of its own moral standards.

23. Van Til, *Defense*, 1955 ed., 23.

Kant is widely regarded as the most important philosopher of the modern period, for he showed the modern human, the secular, would-be-autonomous individual, what one would have to believe about knowledge and the world in order to be consistent with this presumed autonomy. In other words, he made the modern secular human epistemologically self-conscious. If modern individuals are not to bow to God, they must bow before themselves, and be Kantians.

If Kant taught secular unbelievers the essentials of their (until then subconscious) theory of knowledge, Van Til did the same for the Christian. While Kant said that we must completely avoid bowing before an external authority, Van Til taught that the only way to find truth is to bow before God's authoritative Scripture. This is Van Til's distinctive contribution to modern theology. Because of Van Til, we can at last define the essential philosophical differences between the Christian and the non-Christian worldviews.

For Van Til, God is the Creator, the world is his creature. Over and over again in class Van Til would draw two circles on the blackboard: a large circle representing God and a smaller circle below representing the creation. He insisted that Christianity has a "two-circle" worldview, as opposed to the "one-circle" worldview of secular thought. Secular thought makes all reality equal. If there is a god, he is equal to the world. But in Christianity God is the supreme Creator and therefore the supreme authority over all human thought. Kant told us to ignore the demands of any alleged revelation external to ourselves. Van Til tells us that the very essence of knowledge is to bring our thoughts into agreement with God's revealed Word.

Thinking God's thoughts after him is to be the rule not only in narrowly religious matters, but in every sphere of human life. (Here Van Til displays his Kuyperian heritage.) Studies in history, science, psychology, sociology, literary criticism; human activities such as business, sports, family life, worship, politics—every thought must be brought captive to the obedience of Christ (2 Cor. 10:5). Van Til supported Christian schools, for he considered it of first importance that children be taught all subjects from a biblical point of view. Not that Scripture teaches the details of plumbing or auto repair, but that it "speaks of everything" at least in general terms.[24] It teaches the fundamental values that must govern even gardening and boat maintenance.

The essence of Van Til's message is that God calls us to "presuppose" him in all our thinking.[25] This means that we must regard his revealed truth as more important and more certain than any other, and find in it the norms or criteria that all other knowledge must meet. No Christian can find fault with this message. Yet all of us must admit that we need to take it more seriously. So often what passes for Christian thought is secular ideas dressed up with a few biblical quotes taken out of context. We need to be far more conscious of Christ's lordship over all, so that (injurious though this may be to our pride) we will be more interested in what God's Word says than in what any secular thinker has to say.

The Effects of the Fall on Knowledge

Complications begin to set in when Van Til attempts to take into account the fall of humankind in Adam and the doctrine of sin. According to that biblical teaching, we are from conception (Ps. 51:5) guilty of Adam's first sin and bearers of a sinful nature (Rom. 3:10–18). In the Reformed doctrine of total depravity, fallen humans are wicked in all thoughts, words, and deeds (Gen. 6:5; 8:21; Isa. 64:6). Only the saving grace of

24. Van Til, *Defense*, 8.
25. Van Til is often called a "presuppositionalist." Unlike Gordon Clark, Van Til rarely used that term to describe himself. When he did, it was in deference to someone else's description of him (e.g., J. Oliver Buswell—see Van Til, *Christian Theory of Knowledge*, 276; see also 258). Furthermore, as far as I know, Van Til himself never defined "presupposition."

God in Jesus Christ can enable us to do anything good. Therefore those without Christian faith are utterly unable to please God (Rom. 8:7–8).

The fall means that all our decisions and actions are directed against God rather than motivated by the desire to glorify him. Thinking is one of those actions. Just as there is godly thinking, trying to think God's thoughts after him, so, as a consequence of the fall, there is universal ungodly thinking, rejecting God's revelation and seeking to oppose his plan for us. Hence the biblical antithesis between the wisdom of the world and the wisdom of God (the Book of Proverbs; 1 Cor. 1:18–2:16).

Van Til is fond of quoting the description of unbelievers that is found in Romans 1. He emphasizes that because of the clarity of God's revelation (vv. 18–20) unbelievers know God (vv. 20–21). However, they reject, in some sense, the knowledge they have. They do not glorify God or give thanks (v. 21), but become fools (v. 22) and exchange the glory of God for idolatry (v. 23), leading to even worse moral degradation (vv. 24, 26–31). So they have exchanged the truth for a lie (v. 25). Nevertheless, they continue to know God's law (v. 32), and that increases their responsibility.

Unbelievers, then, know God (Rom. 1:21), but in some sense do not know God (1 Cor. 2:14). They reject the knowledge they have. This paradox makes it difficult to characterize the unbelievers' mentality fully. Van Til, somewhat uncharacteristically, admits that this is a "very complicated" matter, a "difficult point."[26] Perhaps he should have left it at that. But he goes on to characterize unbelievers in various ways which are neither adequate to the biblical data nor consistent with one another.

Van Til often seems to insist that the unbeliever has no true knowledge at all, and thus there can be nothing on which the be-liever can and should agree with the unbeliever:

> The natural man cannot will to do God's will. He cannot even know what the good is.
>
> It will be quite impossible to find a common area of knowledge between believers and unbelievers unless there is agreement between them as to the nature of man himself. But there is no such agreement.
>
> But without the light of Christianity it is as little possible for man to have the correct view about himself and the world as it is to have the true view about God.[27]

This is a frequent theme in Van Til. If it were really true, it would seem that there can be no communication between believer and unbeliever, no common ground for apologetic discussion, and it would be impossible to maintain the apostle Paul's conviction that the unbeliever still knows God in some sense. Elsewhere, however, Van Til vehemently rejects the apparent meaning of these statements: "[I have] never denied that the unbeliever has true knowledge," he says with some sense of frustration.[28]

At this point the reader may well be thoroughly perplexed and ask, What kind of knowledge do unbelievers then have? Often Van Til characterizes their knowledge as "formal."[29] That is to say, unbelievers formulate sentences that sound true, but whose meaning differs from the usual in such a way that they are actually rendered false. That, however, would not normally be considered a form of knowledge, but an odd sort of ignorance. Doubtless, unbelievers sometimes engage in such language distortion as part of their rebellion against God, but surely not everything they say has this character. When unbelievers say,

---

26. Van Til, *Defense*, 50; Cornelius Van Til, *Introduction to Systematic Theology* (Nutley, N.J.: Presbyterian and Reformed, 1974), 25–26, 78.

27. Van Til, *Defense*, 54, 67, 73. I have about fifty more quotations to this effect in my notes! And they are taken from only six of his books.

28. Van Til, *Defense*, 1955 ed., 285.

29. Van Til, *Defense*, 59, 74, 77, 106, 206, etc.

"Washington is the capital of the United States," they certainly are not talking about Peoria. Besides, Van Til himself often characterizes unbelieving thought as true in more than a formal sense. He describes idealist ethics as "lofty"[30] and Plato's god as "noble."[31] He insists, too, that unbelievers' knowledge is not a mere potentiality but actual.[32] This would not be the case if their knowledge were purely formal.

Van Til describes the unbelievers' knowledge in many other ways. It is, for instance, a merely intellectual understanding without a moral stance.[33] But elsewhere he admits that this is an artificial distinction, for we cannot separate our logical powers from our moral powers.[34] He says sometimes that unbelievers are wrong on basics but often right on incidentals,[35] but then he also says that unbelievers (like the devils in James 2:19) can confess God and even accept an argument for his existence[36]—hardly incidental matters. Sometimes he suggests that the unbelievers' knowledge is subconscious,[37] but that sounds more like Sigmund Freud than Van Til. Besides, Van Til warns us elsewhere not to make too much of the distinction between unconscious and self-conscious action.[38] Clearly in Scripture devils and unbelievers consciously make true statements.

Van Til's most characteristic explanation is that unbelievers disagree with believers most often when they are "epistemologically self-conscious," that is, when they are most aware of trying to formulate and act out the implications of their unbelief.[39] This is true as a general empirical observation, but there is no biblical principle that

30. Ibid., 63.
31. Van Til, *Introduction,* 107.
32. Van Til, *Defense,* 156.
33. Ibid., 17, 301.
34. Van Til, *Introduction,* 92.
35. Van Til, *Defense,* 83; *Introduction,* 32.
36. Van Til, *Defense,* 175; *Introduction,* 197.
37. Van Til, *Defense,* 98; see also 94, 173, 231.
38. Van Til, *Introduction,* 90.
39. Van Til, *Common Grace and the Gospel,* 5, 84, 151.

requires us to accept it as some kind of rigid mathematical proportion. For all of Satan's epistemological self-consciousness, he does manage occasionally to utter true statements—for his own purposes, of course.

It is difficult to make sense out of all this. Clearly we need to go back to the drawing board. The solution may be something like this: The depravity of unbelievers leads them to use their knowledge against God, but it does not always or necessarily lead them to make false statements as such. Often, of course, unbelief will result in false beliefs and statements; but it may also result in a misuse of true ones. Of course, to rebel in this way against a God who is known to have all power and infinite love is in itself an unintelligent act; thus depravity always does affect the intellect, as Van Til says. But the concrete effects are not at all as evident to us or as predictable as Van Til sometimes seems to think. Accordingly, Christian apologists do not need to be embarrassed when they find themselves agreeing with unbelievers about something. Contrary to Van Til, a biblical apologetic need not exclude common notions or ideas, but may legitimately draw conclusions from them.

Apologetics

Traditionally, apologists have developed their defense of Christianity in two steps: (1) a philosophical argument (or arguments) for the existence of God; and (2) historical arguments for the truth of the New Testament, which usually focus on prophecy and miracle (especially the resurrection of Christ). Both these steps have presupposed some common ground between the apologist and the unbeliever. Arguments for the existence of God typically require initial agreement on the meaning of terms like "cause," "purpose," and "being." The historical arguments usually require some initial agreement on what is historically possible or probable.

Van Til objects to this traditional approach because it assumes common notions between believer and unbeliever. As we have seen, that criticism is flawed. But Van Til has further objections: (1) the traditional method seems to assume that we can understand the meaning of "cause," "purpose," and "being" without presupposing God; and (2) at best it yields only a god who is in some degree possible or probable, not the God of Scripture who is the standard of all possibility.

Objection (1) seems to be gratuitous. An apologist using the traditional method may very well presuppose that God is the author of cause and purpose, and that they are unintelligible apart from him; indeed, the apologist may be using the traditional arguments to establish that very belief. But having that presupposition in no way prevents the apologist from discussing "cause" before discussing God. As for objection (2), Van Til does teach that the evidence for God is "absolutely valid" rather than "merely probable."[40] But he also admits that our formulation of the argument may not be as cogent as the evidence itself.[41] To say that the argument is "merely probable" is not to say that the evidence for God is "merely probable"; rather, it is to confess honestly that our argument has not attained the level of cogency which God has placed in the evidence itself. Argument and evidence must be more carefully distinguished.

What does Van Til propose to put in the place of the traditional method? Sometimes he suggests a "presuppositional" form of the traditional method: (1) formulate proofs for the existence of God in which the theistic presuppositions regarding "cause," "purpose," and "being" are set forth explicitly;[42] and then (2) present historical arguments using the biblical criteria for historical possibility, probability, and truth.[43] The circularity involved in invoking biblical criteria to prove their own validity is really the same circularity involved in any argument for a supreme criterion of truth, whether in Christianity or rationalism or some other worldview. To prove that human reason is the supreme authority, we must use human reason; in order to prove that God's revelation is supreme, we must appeal to God's revelation. If the unbeliever objects to accepting our biblical criteria, we will use them anyway, just as we would reason with mental patients who have constructed their own dreamworld. In that case we do not reason on the basis of their false worldview, nor on some neutral position, but on the basis of our own worldview, which we know to be true.

More often, Van Til suggests an indirect method in which the believer accepts the unbeliever's position for argument's sake in order to show that no intelligible thought is possible on the presuppositions of unbelief.[44] He proves that thesis by showing that the only genuine alternatives to Christianity are (1) systems of logic which seek to unify reality, but cannot account for everything in the real world; and (2) the view that attributes everything to pure chance, which destroys the possibility of any unity or rational explanation. Van Til observes that unbelief necessarily drives people in one of these two directions, or to an unstable compromise between them. By contrast, the unique doctrine of the Trinity (God and therefore the world are equally one *and* many) keeps Christians from the dilemma of having to choose (1) or (2). He uses many ingenious examples from the history of philosophy and theology to buttress this point. We have much to learn from Van Til, but must reject the claim that his suggested method must replace everything that was done by the more traditional apologists. Rather, we should focus on his development of an epistemology that can

40. Van Til, *Defense*, 103–4.
41. Van Til, *Defense*, 200; *Christian Theory of Knowledge*, 289.
42. Van Til, *Defense*, 201; *Introduction*, 199.
43. Van Til, *Defense*, 202, 207; *Introduction*, 147.
44. Van Til, *Defense*, 100; *Christian Theory of Knowledge*, 18.

serve as a basis for what the traditional apologists have sought to do.[45]

Much more can be said about Van Til's contributions: his analysis of modern philosophy, science, and theology, as well as the peculiar emphases in his work as a systematic theologian (e.g., common grace as "earlier grace," God as three persons and one person, Reformed theology as what must be true if God is to be God). But space does not permit.

Legacy

Van Til's ideas are being taught by various individuals and groups today. The "theonomists" or Christian reconstructionists (e.g., Rousas J. Rushdoony) are thoroughgoing Van Tillians in their epistemology. Van Til himself never accepted their thesis that the details of the Old Testament law are to be applied to contemporary civil governments, but he did appreciate their support. Among them, Greg L. Bahnsen especially perpetuates Van Til's interests, emphases, and distinctive methods. Some, such as Gary North, have mounted criticisms of Van Til's amillennial eschatology, even though Van Til himself had almost no interest in the subject.[46]

Francis Schaeffer studied both with Van Til and with J. Oliver Buswell, and his apologetics incorporated elements from both. His emphasis on the Trinity as the solution to the "one and many" problem, for example, came from Van Til, as did much of his critique of culture. The L'Abri community continues, therefore, to perpetuate much of Van Til's work, even though Van Til himself was highly critical of Schaeffer.

Robert D. Knudsen, Van Til's immediate successor at Westminster Seminary, is a Dooyeweerdian who maintains a number of Van Tillian emphases, including Van Til's high doctrine of Scripture. William Edgar, who also teaches apologetics there, is influenced by both Van Til and Schaeffer.

For some reason, most of those today who know Van Til's work are either totally opposed to him or uncritically devoted to him (lambasting anyone they think is not a simon-pure Van Tillian).[47] The failure of Van Til to encourage critical analysis of his work may lie behind this phenomenon. It is our hope that the evaluation of his thought will from now on rest with critical disciples rather than with the debunkers or slavish followers.

45. Van Til characterizes his own work this way in *Defense*, 146.

46. Van Til's *Common Grace and the Gospel* does develop a theory that wickedness becomes worse and worse over the course of history. Like North, I do not find this theory to be biblical.

47. For examples see *Journey* 3.2 (March–April 1988): 9–11; 3.4–5 (July–Oct. 1988): 45–46; and 4.1 (Jan.–Feb. 1989): 14–15, 22–23.

John Murray

Sinclair B. Ferguson

John Murray's life spanned the first three-quarters of the twentieth century. Born on October 14, 1898, and reared on a croft near Bonar Bridge in the Highlands of Scotland, he "drank in godliness with his mother's milk" (to use words from John Calvin of which he would have approved). His father, Alexander Murray, a member of the Free Presbyterian Church of Scotland, set before him a lasting example of true Christian manhood. Following his father's death in 1942, John wrote: "There were few men in the Highlands of Scotland whose life and memory were surrounded by such fragrance, and whose life of consistent godliness claimed such veneration and respect. To be his son is a great privilege but also a tremendous responsibility."[1] Alexander Murray was the embodiment of the catechetical teaching John received in childhood, especially the principle that "to glorify God and enjoy him for ever" is the chief end of man.

Educated locally at Bonar Bridge Primary School and then at Dornoch Academy, John Murray enlisted towards the end of World War I (April 1917) in the Royal

Highlanders (Black Watch). Serving in France in 1918, he was struck by shrapnel during the last German offensive and permanently lost sight in his right eye. Honorably discharged, he entered the University of Glasgow the following year and graduated with an M.A. in 1923.

Murray's desire was to enter the ministry of his own denomination. The Free Presbyterian Church did not maintain a theological seminary, but used the old tutorial method of ministerial training. Happily for the Christian church at large, Murray's tutor was the wise and able Donald Beaton of Wick, who, recognizing his new student's academic prowess, made the very unusual suggestion that he be sent to Princeton Theological Seminary with a view to future service as a theological tutor in the Free Presbyterian Church.

1. Iain H. Murray, *The Life of John Murray* (Edinburgh: Banner of Truth Trust, 1984), 82.

Thus Murray enrolled at Princeton in 1924, doubtless without a clue as to the way in which the seminary's impending crisis would affect his whole future. The older emphases on Reformed orthodoxy and experiential piety exemplified in Charles Hodge and B. B. Warfield no longer stood unquestioned in the wider seminary constituency. Indeed, J. Gresham Machen had written that Old Princeton had died with Warfield in 1921. Nevertheless, the presence of Caspar Wistar Hodge, Oswald T. Allis, Geerhardus Vos, and Machen on the faculty must have thrilled the young Scot, even if Machen's recently published *Christianity and Liberalism* (1923) already hinted at the division that would soon take place.

Murray was an outstanding student. The *Princeton Seminary Bulletin* would later say, "Few students have maintained as high a level of scholarship as did Mr. Murray during his seminary course." He graduated in 1927 and returned to Scotland, still with the expectation of entering the pastoral ministry.

The way ahead was, however, blocked by a disagreement over the use of public transport on the Lord's Day. Murray did not believe that his church had the right to bar from the Lord's Table anyone who used public transport in order to attend worship on Sunday. So, instead of proceeding to ordination, he took advantage of the Gelston-Winthrop Scholarship he had been awarded at Princeton to do postgraduate study at New College, Edinburgh. While there, he received an invitation from Caspar Wistar Hodge to serve on the faculty at Princeton. This he agreed to do for the year 1929–30, little realizing that by the time of his arrival Machen, Allis, Robert Dick Wilson, and soon Cornelius Van Til, along with some fifty students, would have begun Westminster Theological Seminary in Philadelphia, determined to maintain the biblical orthodoxy of the Old Princeton tradition. (The fact that the neo-orthodox Emil Brunner would later come as a guest professor to succeed Hodge and then be invited to remain permanently simply confirmed the conviction that a theological drift was under way.)

The following year (1930) Murray himself moved to Westminster, where he was to spend the greater part of the rest of his life as a professor of systematic theology, first in the seminary's midcity location on property owned by Allis (a stark contrast to the Scottish croft!), and thereafter in the pleasant surroundings of the suburban campus on the northern outskirts of Philadelphia. Here he stood with Machen following his dismissal from the Presbyterian ministry and assisted him in both his private and public ministries. One of Machen's last acts before dying suddenly on January 1, 1937, was to send his younger colleague a telegram alluding to a topic which they had discussed at length and on which Murray's thinking had profoundly influenced him. It read: "I'm so thankful for the active obedience of Christ. No hope without it."[2]

Murray now committed himself to the Orthodox Presbyterian Church, which Machen had been instrumental in founding, and was ordained in 1937. His evangelistic concern found expression in his service as chairman of the Committee for the Propagation of the Reformed Faith in New England and his decade-long work as secretary of the Committee of Local Evangelism. The same concern led him to conduct Bible studies on board ship whenever he traveled between the United States and his home country.

As a professor Murray employed (and was deeply committed to) the lecture method. While he deplored self-assurance, in his final report to the seminary's accrediting association (perhaps with a view to anticipated criticism of his old-fashioned pedagogy, which allowed little time for questions and class discussion), he hinted that if his lectures, which reflected thirty years of teaching experience, were not already answering his students' questions,

2. Ibid., 64.

169

their questions were possibly not worth asking! He believed that the lecture method helped students to feel the weight and authority of biblical doctrine, and that the exercise of thinking and writing that was involved in recording notes aided the process of learning.

Murray's students remember the sense of *gravitas* which characterized his presence in the lecture room, yet both his prayers and his teaching were also marked by a rich and lively verbal animation. While, no doubt, his piety and manner might have seemed austere, even severe to some, no one who knew him failed to recognize what could only be called a serious joy and an energy for the gospel which commanded both respect and admiration. The affection in which he was held is perhaps best illustrated by the answer which new students always received when they inquired which was the glass eye—"It's the one that has a twinkle."

John Murray's influence on his students was profound, particularly his model of combining exegetical care with biblico-theological insights in expounding systematic theology. His wider ministry, largely in writing, may be dated from the 1950s, when a steady stream of influential works flowed from his pen. It was characteristic of his reticence that his publications date from his sixth and seventh decades. Several of these works remain standard studies and required reading in their field.

A bachelor throughout the whole of his seminary ministry, in 1966 Murray was heard to say on the Westminster campus (no doubt to the astonishment of some of his hearers, for more than one reason!): "If I marry in the next year, I will be younger than my grandfather was at his marriage." And this was precisely what he did, marrying a longtime friend, Valerie Knowlton, who had been a student at Westminster in the 1950s. Having earned a doctorate at Harvard, she became a professor of anatomy at the Woman's Medical College of Pennsylvania. Settling in Scotland on the family croft, they had two children, the second of whom was to survive her father by only a few months.

On his retirement and return to Scotland in 1966, Murray was free to engage in an extensive speaking ministry throughout the United Kingdom. He served as a speaker in churches, at Inter-Varsity gatherings, and perhaps most notably in a regular ministry at the increasingly significant Leicester Ministers Conference, which was organized by the Banner of Truth Trust, of which he was a trustee.

In his last years, Murray was asked to take pastoral oversight of the Free Church of Scotland congregation at Ardgay, some two miles from his home. Thus, to his great joy, at the end of his life came a taste of the work which in earlier years he had assumed would dominate the whole of it. Now an internationally respected theologian and author, he found his highest joy in expounding God's Word to the congregation of some two dozen people who gathered with him on the Lord's Day.

In 1975, cancer was diagnosed. According to his biographer, Murray bore his terminal illness with Christian grace and with the qualities which had marked his long Christian life:

> We do not know how many copies of the Greek New Testament John Murray wore out—he left several in that condition among his books—but in the last one which he used he had written inside the covers in the closing weeks of his life:

> O Lord, all that I do desire
> is still before thine eye,
> And of my heart the secret groans
> not hidden are from thee.[3]

He died in faith on May 8, 1975. As Cornelius Van Til, his colleague of thirty years, was later to comment, "Humble boldness marked John's every doing."

3. Ibid., 156. The stanza quoted is the Scottish Metrical Psalter rendering of Ps. 38:9.

A Systematic and Biblical Theologian

John Murray came to be widely regarded as one of the most significant orthodox Reformed theologians of his generation in the English-speaking world. Reared, as we have seen, in the Calvinistic theology and piety which flourished in the Reformed congregations of Highland Scotland, he had a profound sense of the majesty of God, human depravity, and the glories of the person and work of Christ. From childhood he had been taught to think both biblically and systematically about these truths. At Princeton, under Hodge, Machen, and particularly Geerhardus Vos (who had himself taught dogmatic theology prior to his appointment as Princeton's first professor of biblical theology),[4] these skills had been fine-tuned to prepare him to make important contributions to the exposition, defense, and development of the Reformed faith. Indebted to the theology of Calvin (in which he was an expert) and to the Puritan tradition, best represented by John Owen, Murray's work is reminiscent of both: it marries theology with spirituality in such a way that the latter suffuses the former and is not merely an addendum to it; and it combines careful scholarly exegesis with a theological systematizing which advances the understanding of Christian truth. Evidence of this is his commentary on Romans, which, at least in length and period of preparation, is his magnum opus.

Like Warfield, whom he so admired, Murray's contribution lies in his exposition of and insight into aspects of theology, elements in the individual loci, rather than in a lengthy systematic presentation of the whole. Doubtless his respect for Charles Hodge and his three-volume *Systematic Theology*, and the fact that Warfield himself had not produced such a work, made Mur-

ray reluctant to engage in that task himself. In retrospect, we may also note that in some respects Murray represents a transition in the method of Reformed systematics, highlighting the role of biblical theology and demonstrating its applications rather than producing a comprehensive treatise. This new emphasis is evident both in the amount of exegetical work in which he engaged as he forged doctrine and in his understanding of the nature and task of systematic theology.

While Murray (apparently to his regret)[5] did not give extensive attention to questions of prolegomena and methodology, he did publish two seminal essays in 1963 in the *Westminster Theological Journal* (of which he had been a founding editor in 1938). Here he crystalized the core of his thinking: "The task of systematic theology is to set forth in orderly and coherent manner the truth respecting God and his relations to men and the world. This truth is derived from the data of revelation."[6] This meant not only that theology, when interpreting the universe, must regard the general revelation as well as the special inscripturated revelation as normative, but also that systematic theology, with its logical method, must be informed by biblical theology, which deals with the same data (special revelation), but from the standpoint of the historical. Here Murray's guiding light was the Dutch-American Geerhardus Vos, who had taught him at Princeton and whom he later described as "the most penetrating exegete it has been my privilege to know."

In many ways Vos had been ahead of his time in his pioneering work in biblical theology and especially in his appreciation of the significance of the eschatological for understanding the apostolic message. Vos

4. See Richard B. Gaffin, Jr., ed., *Redemptive History and Biblical Interpretation: The Shorter Writings of Geerhardus Vos* (Phillipsburg, N.J.: Presbyterian and Reformed, 1980), ix–xxiii.

5. I owe this information to Murray's colleague Robert D. Knudsen, professor of apologetics at Westminster Seminary.

6. John Murray, *The Collected Writings of John Murray*, 4 vols. (Edinburgh: Banner of Truth Trust, 1976–83), 4:1. For the convenience of the reader, citations from Murray are, wherever possible, taken from this collection.

had emphasized the epochal character of the overall structure of special revelation, and the principles of continuity, accumulation, and advance that are evident therein. Systematic theology needed to take note of and be informed by this. Thus Murray argued that systematic theology is rooted in biblical exegesis, but also that "biblical theology is regulative of exegesis. It coordinates and synthesizes the whole witness of Scripture in the various topics with which it deals."[7] Murray's approach to every theological locus and issue was determined by these principles. Though he was well aware of the advances in the area of the history of ideas, his own contributions, when not specifically historical-theological in character, were heavily freighted with biblical exegesis and theology. It is noteworthy that when Ned B. Stonehouse, the first editor of the New International Commentary series, allotted the volume on Romans, he approached John Murray, who so obviously possessed the necessary exegetical tools and skills.

The Biblical Doctrine of Scripture

Against this background it is not surprising that Murray gave special attention to the unfolding of the biblical doctrine of Scripture, rejecting the neo-orthodox supposition that Scripture is not itself the Word of God, but only *becomes* so by the special action of God when it is heard or read. Scripture, in the neo-orthodox view, was simply the witness to the Word of God. Following Warfield's weighty defense of the orthodox doctrine of inspiration and authority, Murray contended against the theory of limited inspiration as well as the romantic notion of inspiration, and for "the view entertained of Scripture by our Lord and his apostles."[8] On the basis of passages such as 2 Timothy 3:16 and 2 Peter 1:16–21

he argued that all the revelation that God inspires reflects his own qualities of reliability. That this was Jesus' view Murray demonstrated by referring to such passages as Matthew 26:53–54; Luke 24:25–27; and John 10:33–36, which he saw as evidence of our Lord's "attitude of meticulous acceptance and reverence."[9]

While Murray recognized that, technically, the New Testament references he cited have the Old Testament canon in view, he employed a threefold argument to confirm the equal applicability of plenary inspiration to the New Testament: (1) the greater glory of the New Testament required a no less plenary and real inspiration for the New than for the Old; (2) the New Testament writers give evidence of a consciousness of divine authority (e.g., 1 Cor. 2:10–13; 14:37–38; 2 Thess. 3:12–14); and (3) the New Testament writers refer to other parts of the New Testament in the same way they refer to the Old (e.g., 2 Pet. 3:15–16).

Reject these considerations, and the view of biblical authority which is implied by them, Murray argued, and it becomes logically impossible to appeal to the Scripture as reliably authoritative on other subjects. If it is fallible in its teaching on its own nature, it cannot be relied on when it speaks of the nature of things (or people) other than itself. Note that Murray did not say that Scripture would therefore be useless, but simply that it would no longer be reliable.[10] He insisted that Scripture must provide its own guidelines for the way in which its infallibility or inerrancy (terms he regarded as theologically synonymous) is to be understood: "artificial and pedantic canons of errancy or inerrancy" he resisted:

We may not impose upon the Bible our own standards of truthfulness or our own notions of right and wrong. It is easy for proponents of inerrancy to set up certain canons of inerrancy which are arbitrarily

7. Ibid., 4:19.
8. Ibid., 4:42–43. Significantly, Murray devoted his inaugural lecture as professor of systematic theology (Nov. 16, 1939) to the topic of inspiration.

9. Ibid., 4:47.
10. Ibid., 4:56.

conceived and which prejudice the whole question from the outset. And it is still easier for the opponents of inerrancy to set up certain criteria in terms of which the Bible could readily be shown to be in error. Both attempts must be resisted. This is just saying that we must think of inerrancy concretely and our criterion of inerrancy must be divested of the *a priori* and often mechanical notions with which it is associated in the minds of many people, particularly those who are hostile to the doctrine.[11]

The "jot and tittle" inerrancy of which Jesus speaks (Matt. 5:18), Murray added, needs to be understood aright: "He is not speaking of jot and tittle inspiration in abstraction, for the simple reason that what represents a jot is no longer a jot if it exists in abstraction. . . . Jesus is thinking of jot and tittle in construction and combination with relevant words, clauses and phrases."[12] Thus, Murray contends, "it is not with words in abstraction that we are concerned, but with words in relationship."[13] Careful exegesis done in the light of biblical theology will alone determine what inerrancy means *in concreto*.

Murray further argued that the doctrine of inerrancy is a continuation of and consistent with the teaching of the Reformers and especially Calvin. One of the great controversies evoked by the neo-orthodoxy which had encroached on twentieth-century Presbyterianism was the question of the degree to which seventeenth-century Protestant orthodoxy had continued the teaching of Calvin. If Reformed orthodoxy was a distortion at this point, it, of course, could no longer claim to be a true heir of the Reformation. Here, in expounding Calvin, the exegetical care and mastery of the text which marked Murray's exposition of Scripture stood him in good stead. Over against the contentions of Charles A. Briggs and others that Calvin, Luther, and other

Reformers recognized errors in the Scriptures,[14] Murray denied that this was Calvin's position either in general or on particular details. Calvin did indeed speak of "mistakes" in regard to the text of Scripture; but, as Murray was able to demonstrate, in such cases the Reformer had in view the matter of textual transmission, not accuracy of content. Calvin also fully recognized the difficulties and even apparent tensions within Scripture. Sometimes Murray regarded the Genevan Reformer's resolutions of these problems as "ill advised."[15] But the very manner in which Calvin sought such resolutions was, as Murray recognized, an indication of his conviction of Scripture's inerrancy.

Continuity with Calvin is also evident in Murray's view of the Holy Spirit's role in attesting Scripture. Contrary to neo-orthodoxy, Murray, with Calvin, argued that the internal testimony of the Spirit does not give authority to Scripture, but witnesses to the authority Scripture already inherently possesses. The Spirit does not affect Scripture, but those who read and hear it. The difference between these two positions Murray regarded as "the most important cleavage within Protestantism today."[16] Against the view that it is "the ever-recurring act of God that is the authority-constituting fact," Murray argued that Scripture's authority rests on its God-breathed quality, on its divine authorship. This is a finished activity, of which the Spirit's ongoing testimony convinces our darkened minds. Here Murray stood in the great tradition of Calvin and Owen, applying to the threat which he saw emerging to biblical Christianity in his own day the biblical

11. Ibid., 4:26.
12. Ibid., 4:25.
13. Ibid., 4:28.

14. For Briggs's contention see ibid., 4:159; Briggs has, of course, been followed by Calvin scholars since his day, but by no means do all Calvin experts subscribe to his position. Indeed, Murray's view also enjoys a good deal of support.
15. Murray, *Collected Writings*, 4:175.
16. John Murray, "The Attestation of Scripture," in *The Infallible Word*, ed. Ned B. Stonehouse and Paul Woolley, 3d rev. ed. (Philadelphia: Presbyterian and Reformed, 1967), 43.

teaching they had recognized and utilized in their day.

In connection with the doctrine of Scripture (and indeed all doctrines), Murray stressed that theology is a creaturely activity. When we have stretched our intellectual powers to their capacity, our heightened understanding of revelation discloses as well our limitations. Our inability to solve all the problems connected with the doctrine of Scripture must be viewed in this light. Here the knowability and the incomprehensibility of God, the former a divine attribute, the latter essentially a limiting concept, coalesce. For Murray, standing on the high tower of revelation, the realization of our inadequacy led primarily to adoring worship. The very nature of Scripture served as a reminder that God is God:

> It must be freely admitted that there are difficulties connected with the doctrine of Biblical infallibility. . . . The conscientious student has . . . great difficulty sometimes in resolving problems raised by apparent contradictions. . . .
>
> It might seem that this confession of . . . inability to resolve seeming discrepancy is not compatible with faith in Scripture as infallible. This is, however, at the best, very superficial judgment. There is no doctrine of our Christian faith that does not confront us with unresolved difficulties here in this world, and the difficulties become all the greater just as we get nearer to the center. It is in connection with the most transcendent mysteries of our faith that the difficulties multiply. The person who thinks he has resolved all the difficulties surrounding our established faith in the Trinity has probably no faith in the Triune God. The person who encounters no unresolved mystery in the incarnation of the Son of God and his death on Calvary's tree has not yet learned the meaning of 1 Timothy 3:16. Yet these unanswered questions are not incompatible with unshaken faith in the Triune God and in Jesus Christ, the incarnate Son. The questions are often perplexing. But they are more often the questions of adoring

wonder rather than the questions of painful perplexity.

So there should be no surprise if faith in God's inerrant Word should be quite consonant with unresolved questions and difficulties with regard to the content of this faith.[17]

Theological Monographs

The Covenant of Grace

Reformed theology is covenantal in character. Indeed, according to Warfield covenant theology is the "architectonic principle" of the Westminster Confession. This is the theology in which Murray had been nourished since childhood. It is not surprising, therefore, that he would explore the biblical and historical materials which undergird it.

Murray's 1954 publication *The Covenant of Grace* bore the subtitle *A Biblico-Theological Study*, which indeed it was. In it he traced the nature of the divine covenants in Scripture, distancing himself in the process from the tendency in scholastic Reformed theology to define "covenant" as a compact or agreement, and arguing instead that in Scripture a covenant is "a sovereign administration of grace and promise."[18] In view of the present-day interest in the scriptural concept of covenant, it may be difficult for the coming generation of students to appreciate the degree to which this slim monograph proved to be a significant landmark. For two decades it served as the basic evangelical work on the doctrine of the covenant. In its own way it set a new standard for the use of biblical theology in systematic theology.

Murray's exposition was innovative in several ways. His starting point was not a comparison with the compacts or contracts

---

17. Ibid., 7–8.
18. John Murray, *The Covenant of Grace* (London: Tyndale, 1954), 30. It is of interest that the biblical and historical doctrine of the covenant had been the subject of Vos's rectoral address at the Theological School of the Christian Reformed Church (now Calvin Seminary); see Gaffin, ed., *Redemptive History*, 234–67.

of seventeenth-century mercantilism, but the biblical use of the term *berith* ("covenant"). Accordingly, he insisted that the highly charged question of whether the covenant was conditional or unconditional could not be resolved "without a reorientation in terms of a revised definition of the Biblical concept of covenant."[19] Furthermore, his view that in Scripture a covenant is essentially redemptive in nature inevitably raised the question of whether Reformed orthodoxy's description of the relationship between God and Adam as covenantal is accurate. Murray's response was to reject the term "covenant of works."

The Imputation of Adam's Sin

While rejecting the classic Reformed terminology, preferring the expression "Adamic administration" to "covenant of works," Murray nevertheless held firmly to the classic doctrine that the sin of Adam was imputed to all of his posterity. This issue had figured largely in American Presbyterianism, and had been a topic of special interest to the Hodges. Murray in fact took Caspar Wistar Hodge's course on the doctrine of imputation and would himself address the subject directly during a sabbatical leave in 1955 and 1956. The fruit of his studies appeared in 1956 and 1957 in a series of articles in the *Westminster Theological Journal*. These were later published as *The Imputation of Adam's Sin*.[20]

Against the background of previous debate and discussion, Murray set forward his own understanding of Romans 5:12–21. This passage, he argued, requires the doctrine of the immediate imputation of Adam's sin to all of his posterity. Murray offered four proofs: (1) the immediate conjunction of the sin of Adam and the death of all (vv. 12, 15, 17); (2) the immedi-

ate conjunction of the sin of Adam and the condemnation of all (vv. 16, 18); (3) the immediate conjunction of the sin of Adam and the sin of all (vv. 12, 19); and (4) the nature of the analogy between Christ and Adam.

The Imputation of Adam's Sin, which in some respects espouses a view somewhat different from that of Charles Hodge, is generally recognized as Murray's most difficult work. The reason is not the abstruseness of his style, but the depth to which he penetrates the logic of the Pauline teaching in Romans 5, so alien to the twentieth-century Western mind, and therefore not amenable to easy analysis. The essence of Paul's teaching lies in two of its emphases: on the one hand, the plight of sinful humanity, and, on the other, the nature of the atonement (which is actually the reversal of what took place in Adam). Murray is deeply sensitive to the fact that Romans 5:12–21 highlights the latter. He recognizes that the passage sheds light not only on atonement as obedience, but also on the inseparability of justification and sanctification, for both are based on union with Christ—a point that Murray stresses elsewhere (see p. 177).

Redemption—Accomplished and Applied

The emphasis of Reformed theology on divine sovereignty in salvation is often attributed exclusively to the nature of its doctrine of God. But to do so is to ignore the crucial factor of anthropology. Like Calvin, Murray recognized that divine sovereignty in salvation is necessitated by the nature and effect of human sin. Since in Adam we are spiritually dead and altogether incapable of spiritual good, we can neither achieve salvation through obedience, nor come to faith by a decision of our own will in its natural condition. Here Murray concurred heartily with the Westminster Confession that "man, by his fall into a state of sin, hath wholly lost all ability of will to any spiritual good accompanying salvation" (9.3).

To be sure, Murray believed that fallen humans possess the power of *alternative*

---

19. Murray, *Collected Writings*, 4:217.
20. John Murray, *The Imputation of Adam's Sin* (Grand Rapids: Eerdmans, 1959). This material may have been prepared in conjunction with the first volume of his commentary on Romans, which appeared the following year.

choice (i.e., they are able to choose between A and B). He vigorously contested, however, the view common in nineteenth- and twentieth-century evangelicalism that *with respect to salvation* the human will is free in the sense of possessing the power of contrary choice (i.e., free to choose the spiritually good rather than the spiritually evil). Murray's point is that, in whatever we choose, we are "under an unholy necessity of sinning."[21] Inability to choose spiritual good is not a denial of free agency, Murray argued, but rather the tragic form free agency takes in sinners. We act in keeping with our character and without any compulsion from the outside. Such is our depraved nature that we are necessarily incapable of willing that which pleases God or of willing in a manner that pleases him. Therefore, we are dependent on the sovereign activity of God not only for the objective provision of redemption, but also for its subjective reception.

To expound what is central to these themes, Murray penned his most popular and widely read study, *Redemption—Accomplished and Applied.* Here he distilled his understanding of the work of Christ and its implications. While it has been commonplace to employ the concepts of sacrifice, propitiation, reconciliation, and redemption in expounding the work of Christ, Murray believed that the concept of *obedience* "supplies us with an inclusive category in terms of which the atoning work of Christ may be viewed."[22] Obedience points to "the capacity in which Christ discharged all phases of his atoning work."[23] Tracing this motif back to Isaiah 53, Murray throughout the New Testament detected references to Christ's obedience, not least in Romans 5:12–21, which specifically contrasts his

obedience with Adam's disobedience. This obedience may conveniently be viewed as both active and passive, so long as we understand that no part of obedience is merely passive. Rather, the formula points to both what he achieved and what he suffered. He obeyed both by fulfilling the law and by accepting its sanctions against the sins of those for whom he died.

Murray was particularly anxious to bring to the fore the biblical teaching on the progressiveness of Christ's obedience, an aspect where he thought orthodoxy had been weak. The concept of learning obedience through suffering (Heb. 5:8) implies such progress, from the perfect boyhood obedience of Jesus to the climactic adult obedience of his death on the cross (Phil. 2:8). This safeguards the biblical emphasis on what Murray calls "corresponding degrees of complacency on the Father's part."[24] In Luke's terms, Christ grew in favor with God (2:52). This personal relationship between the Father and Son must be emphasized if the nature of the incarnation and Christ's obedience is to be fully appreciated:

> Obedience . . . is not something that may be conceived of artificially or abstractedly. It is obedience that enlisted all the resources of his perfect humanity, obedience that resided in his person, and obedience of which he is ever the perfect embodiment. . . . And we become the beneficiaries of it, indeed the partakers of it, by union with him. It is this that serves to advertise the significance of that which is the central truth of all soteriology, namely, union and communion with Christ.[25]

Further reference must be made to the centrality of the theme of union with Christ, but no exposition of Murray's understanding of the work of Christ would be complete without some mention of his convictions about the extent of the atonement. On this issue Murray held to the clas-

---

21. Murray, *Collected Writings*, 2:64.

22. John Murray, *Redemption—Accomplished and Applied* (Grand Rapids: Eerdmans, 1955; London: Banner of Truth, 1961), 24 (citations are from the 1961 ed.). This work was a development of a series of articles that appeared in the *Presbyterian Guardian* in 1952–54.

23. Murray, *Collected Writings*, 2:151.

24. Ibid., 2:153.

25. Murray, *Redemption*, 24; see also idem, *Collected Writings*, 2:161.

sic Reformed teaching, which was by no means popular among his academic peers or in evangelicalism generally. He averred that Christ died specifically for the salvation of the elect. Though numerous benefits flow to the world in general from Christ's work, he bore God's wrath against sin to redeem specific persons.[26]

Unless we hold to full-orbed universalism, Murray argued, we are bound to hold to some limitations in the purpose, accomplishment, or application of the atonement. If its purpose were universal, then its efficacy must be limited; for if some perish for whom Christ died, the atonement made for them cannot have been efficacious. Reformed theology has always objected to this view on the grounds that it disrupts the harmonious purpose and power of the Trinity; the Father, Son, and Spirit are rendered incapable of accomplishing exactly the same ends. Murray was anxious to safeguard what he saw as the biblical emphasis on the efficacy of Christ's work and the honor of the Triune God.

Murray did not base his view on autonomous logical or theological arguments, but appealed to a wide variety of textual and exegetical considerations. He argued, for example, that expressions like "world" and "all" rarely imply an all-inclusive universalism. Further, the New Testament's teaching on the work of Christ consistently stresses its efficacy: Christ actually redeems, reconciles, and propitiates. Efficacy is written into the nature of the atonement.[27] Murray found his strongest evidence in John 10:7–29, where Jesus teaches that he will die for his sheep, who are carefully distinguished from those who are not his sheep.[28]

Murray was aware of the standard objection to such teaching: it enervates evangelism and dismembers the gospel. How can we preach the gospel if we cannot tell people indiscriminately that Christ died for them? Unlike those who raised this objection, Murray, from the preaching he had heard since childhood, had come to the understanding that the doctrines of election and particular redemption present no barrier to the full preaching of the gospel in faithful New Testament terms. He pointed out that the phrase "Christ died for you," which many of his contemporaries regarded as so essential to the proclamation of the gospel, was not part of the New Testament language of proclamation! They erroneously identified the mode in which the gospel had come to be presented as the way in which it had in fact been expounded by the apostles. It is not, however, the benefits of Christ that are offered in the gospel, but Christ himself; the warrant for faith is not "Christ died for you," but Christ's promise to be the Savior of those who come to him.[29] Thus Murray sought to obviate hyper-Calvinism on the one hand and Arminianism on the other.[30] It must be said that hearing him preach would have dispelled any notion that his understanding of the biblical teaching was a barrier to impassioned proclamation of the gospel.

We have already noted that, in Murray's view, union with Christ is "the central truth of the whole doctrine of salvation."[31] In union with Christ not only do we enter into the grace of justification through his obedience (Rom. 5), but we simultaneously participate in sanctification (Rom. 6). In contrast to both Lutheran theology and popular evangelicalism, where justification dominates and sanctification serves as a

---

26. See Murray, *Redemption*, 59–75; idem, *Collected Writings*, 1:59–85, 4:106–12.

27. This was precisely the point at issue in fellow Scotsman John McLeod Campbell's *Nature of the Atonement* (1856), which argued against the evangelical interpretation of the atonement as penal substitution. If this were the nature of the atonement, its efficacy would by necessity be limited to the elect. Campbell therefore felt compelled to deny the classic Reformed teaching and to revise completely the doctrine of the nature of the atonement.

28. Murray, *Collected Writings*, 1:74.

29. Ibid., 1:82.

30. See John Murray, "The Message of Evangelism," in *Collected Writings*, 1:124–32, esp. 130–32.

31. Murray, *Redemption*, 170.

codicil confirming or advancing its reality, for Murray justification and sanctification are inseparably linked to one another because both are the effect of union with Christ. Indeed, when we recognize that they are different dimensions of the Christian's existence (technically, justification is an *act* of God in our behalf, sanctification a *work* of God upon our lives), we may say that justification and sanctification begin simultaneously, both being part of the one eschatological reality of our union with Christ.

Here again Murray captured and echoed Calvin's finest emphases.[32] But in one respect at least he advanced the Reformer's thought, providing what was probably the most lucid English-language exposition of Romans 6 to date.[33] The union with Christ which lies at the foundation of justification also means, wrote Murray, that we have died to sin and have been raised to newness of life in him. In fact, the New Testament perspective of sanctification is not so much that it is an ongoing process, but an already accomplished reality, a decisive breach with the dominion of sin and an entry into the reign of grace. For this concept Murray coined the expression "definitive sanctification." But far from suggesting that the Christian is therefore free from the struggle with sin (a perfectionist view), he recognized and stressed the biblical teaching that the Christian is to wage war on sin from the position of strength in Christ. The church's failure to grasp this point Murray saw as the source of great ethical weakness:

We are far too ready to give heed to what we deem to be the hard, empirical facts of Christian profession, and we have erased the clear line of demarcation which Scripture defines. As a result we have lost our vision of the high calling of God in Christ Jesus. Our ethic has lost its dynamic and we have become conformed to this world.

32. See John Calvin, *Institutes of the Christian Religion*, 3.1.1; and also his commentary on Rom. 8:13.
33. John Murray, *Principles of Conduct* (Grand Rapids: Eerdmans, 1957), 202–21; idem, *Collected Writings*, 2:277–93.

We know not the power of death to sin in the death of Christ, and we are not able to bear the rigour of the liberty of redemptive emancipation. "We died to sin": the glory of Christ's accomplishment and the guarantee of the Christian ethic are bound up with that doctrine. If we live in sin we have not died to it, and if we have not died to it we are not Christ's. If we died to sin we no longer live in it, for "we who are such as have died to sin, how shall we still live in it?" (Romans 6:2).[34]

Murray saw a further implication of union with Christ, one of great significance for the whole ethos of the Christian life: union with Christ brings with it, as its highest benediction and "the apex of redemptive grace and privilege," adoption by God.[35] By the twentieth century this doctrine had fallen into desuetude in evangelical thought. In the pristine theology of Calvin it had been a dominant motif, although never treated as a distinctive locus or given a separate chapter in his *Institutes*. The English Puritan theologians tended to treat the topic of adoption similarly, although it was given specific exposition in the Westminster Confession (12) and fine treatment by such authors as John Owen and Thomas Watson. But, perhaps through the influence of Francis Turretin on later Reformed thought, it fell into decline and was viewed as no more than the positive aspect of justification. Furthermore, the emphasis of liberal theology on the universal fatherhood of God and brotherhood of man considerably weakened the force of the evangelical exposition regarding the benefits of being adopted by God as a concomitant of salvation.

By contrast, under the influence of the Westminster Confession and Catechisms, Murray refused to regard adoption "as simply an aspect of justification or as another way of stating the privilege conferred by regeneration. It is," he argued, "much more than either or both of these acts of

34. Murray, *Principles of Conduct*, 205.
35. Murray, *Collected Writings*, 2:233.

grace."[36] While adoption is a judicial act, it points to the Christian's being sustained in a relationship to God which transcends justification. The Christian is an adopted child of God, and thereby becomes heir to all the privileges of the family of God. This determines the whole ethos of the Christian life, and reflects particularly on the character of Christian obedience, which is thereby rendered filial rather than servile. Adoption, Murray wrote with feeling, "staggers imagination because of its amazing condescension and love. The Spirit alone could be the seal of it on our hearts."[37]

Ethical Writings

One final area of Murray's theology must be mentioned, namely, his long-standing interest in the Christian ethic. This emerged in a series of six articles on divorce which were published in the *Westminster Theological Journal* from 1946 to 1949 and appeared in book form in 1953. With his characteristic care Murray worked through the biblical teaching stage by stage. His view was that divorce is legitimate on only two grounds: adultery and desertion of a believer by an unbeliever. In both cases he believed Scripture teaches that the wronged party is free to marry again. The book concludes with a series of case studies in which Murray seeks to apply the biblical teaching. It is noteworthy that, in keeping with his recognition of the limits of systematic theology, Murray concludes in one case study that "we are not able to answer [concerning the legitimacy of remarriage] dogmatically one way or the other."[38] On the other hand, contemporary society evinces so much legal confusion in this general area that the church should give serious consid-eration to recognizing divorce on biblical grounds.

In 1955 Murray gave the Payton Lectures at Fuller Theological Seminary; these were published in expanded form in 1957 under the title *Principles of Conduct*. Here the same exegetical concern already displayed in the volume on divorce is evident. But Murray now spells out his agenda more deliberately:

> One of the main purposes of the lectures and of this volume is to seek to show the basic unity and continuity of the biblical ethic. I have attempted to apply to the ethic of Scripture something of the biblico-theological method, understanding "Biblical Theology" in the sense defined by Geerhardus Vos as "that branch of Exegetical Theology which deals with the process of the self-revelation of God deposited in the Bible."[39]

In identifying with Vos, Murray deliberately distanced himself from the brand of biblical theology that had been characteristic of the history-of-religions school as well as from the much-vaunted biblical-theology movement of his own times. His position was that "the presentation given in the Scripture is the true transcript of what the history of revelation and redemption really was. The unity which we find in the Bible reflects the organic unity of the process of divine revelation of which the Bible itself is the depository."[40] In particular, Murray treated Genesis 1–3 as a historical record with remarkable implications for a biblico-theological understanding of the Christian ethic.

Adhering to a characteristically Reformed view of God's covenant, Murray sees the Decalogue as essentially built on God's original design for creation. The commandments are expressed negatively because they are set in the context of human depravity. Furthermore, Murray argues in detail that Old Testament and New

36. Murray, *Redemption*, 132.
37. Ibid., 134.
38. John Murray, *Divorce* (Philadelphia: Committee on Christian Education, Orthodox Presbyterian Church, 1953; Philadelphia: Presbyterian and Reformed, 1961), 115.
39. Murray, *Principles of Conduct*, 7.
40. Ibid., 8–9.

Testament, grace and law, law and love, cannot be regarded as antithetical. In Scripture they are complementary and indeed essential to one another. A study of the creation ordinances is therefore foundational to a proper understanding of the Christian ethic. These ordinances, as set forth in the opening chapters of Genesis, are marriage and family life, labor, and the Sabbath day. In addition, Murray sees the sanctity of life and of truth adumbrated in the creation narrative.

Murray's exposition, rigorous in detail and replete with exegetical and theological insight, is particularly trenchant in discussing law and grace. Here his commitment to the principle that biblical theology yields insight in particular exegesis produces a rich harvest. A notable instance is his comment on Paul's statement in Romans 6:14 that Christians are not under law but under grace:

> A good deal of the misconception pertaining to the relation of the law to the believer springs from a biblico-theological error of much broader proportions than a misinterpretation of Paul's statement in Romans 6:14. It is the misinterpretation of the Mosaic economy and covenant in relation to the new covenant. . . . The demand for obedience in the Mosaic covenant is principially identical with the same demand under the gospel. . . . Obedience belongs here no more "to the legal sphere of merit" than in the new covenant.[41]

The Mosaic economy, Murray is here contending, is itself an expression of grace. Consistently throughout Scripture the claims of law and the specific commands of God, which are rooted in his character, are motivated and effected in us by grace. Moreover, appealing to John 14:15 ("If ye love me, keep my commandments," KJV) and Deuteronomy 6:5 ("Thou shalt love the LORD thy God . . . ," KJV), Murray argues that law and love, far from being antitheti-

cal, are harmonious. Love itself is in fact a command of God! Thus all forms of antinomianism (including situation ethics, as he was later to demonstrate)[42] fail to meet basic biblical considerations. The law for Murray is not simply an academic matter; it is spiritually vital: "It is only myopia that prevents us from seeing this, and when there is a persistent animosity to the notion of keeping commandments the only conclusion is that there is either gross ignorance or malignant opposition to the testimony of Jesus."[43]

Following a fine chapter on "The Dynamic of the Biblical Ethic," in which he sets forward in some detail the import of union with Christ and gives hints of the concept of "definitive sanctification," Murray concludes his ethical studies, significantly, with a chapter on the fear of God, which he characterizes as "the soul of godliness . . . the sum of piety,"[44] and the fruit of the indwelling of the Spirit of Christ, who himself was endued with the Spirit of the fear of the Lord (Isa. 11:2–3). The ethical integrity which Murray sees the church summoned to by the biblical teaching he has expounded "is grounded in and is the fruit of the fear of God."[45] This fear is twofold: "the dread or terror of the Lord and . . . reverential awe"—terror in view of our sinfulness set in the light of his holiness; awe in the sense of filial reverence, which takes its origin not from our sinfulness, but from God's inherent glory.[46] It is this reverential awe which Murray considers the soul of godliness. Deterioration here is evidence of spiritual decline and the root of an inevitable moral collapse, because it is the truest expression of that God-consciousness which lies at the heart of seriously committed holiness of life. Murray is at his most eloquent when describing this

---

42. John Murray, "Situation Ethics," *Banner of Truth* 226 (July 1982): 7–16.
43. Murray, *Principles of Conduct*, 182.
44. Ibid., 229.
45. Ibid., 230.
46. Ibid., 233.

41. Ibid., 195, 200.

fear of God, putting into words the very piety which others saw in his life:

> The fear of God could be nothing less than the soul of rectitude. It is the apprehension of God's glory that constrains the fear of his name. It is that same glory that commands our totality commitment to him, totality trust and obedience. The fear of God is but the reflex in our consciousness of the transcendent perfection which alone could warrant and demand the totality of our commitment to him.[47]

Principles of Conduct abundantly realizes Murray's stated goal: to demonstrate "how fruitful ethical studies conducted along this line can be and how in this field, as well as in others, we may discover the organic unity and continuity of divine revelation."[48] But this volume does more—it shows John Murray to have been a theologian who *felt* what he believed.

Much more could be written about Murray's other works: his seven-hundred-page exposition of Romans as well as his studies on such subjects as the theology of Calvin and baptism.[49] He liked to think of himself and his contributions to the Christian church as embodying an old saying: a dwarf seated on the shoulders of a giant is able to see farther than the giant can. As one of the community of saints called to press farther on into the unfolding riches of the grace of God in the gospel, he sat on the shoulders of giant theologians, especially those in the Augustinian tradition like Calvin and Owen. Among North Americans, Jonathan Edwards, the Hodges, Warfield, and, of course, the unsung Geerhardus Vos were his theological fathers. Reared on a Scottish Highland croft and serving Christ far from home, John Murray proved to be their worthy heir.

Primary Sources

Murray, John. *Calvin on Scripture and Divine Sovereignty.* Grand Rapids: Baker, 1960.

———. *Christian Baptism.* Philadelphia: Committee on Christian Education, Orthodox Presbyterian Church, 1952. Reprint. Grand Rapids: Baker, n.d.

———. *The Collected Writings of John Murray.* 4 vols. Edinburgh: Banner of Truth Trust, 1976–83. (For a bibliography of Murray's writings see 4:361–75.)

———. *The Covenant of Grace.* London: Tyndale, 1954.

———. *Divorce.* Philadelphia: Committee on Christian Education, Orthodox Presbyterian Church, 1953. Reprint. Philadelphia: Presbyterian and Reformed, 1961.

———. *The Epistle to the Romans.* 2 vols. Grand Rapids: Eerdmans, 1960, 1965.

———. *The Imputation of Adam's Sin.* Grand Rapids: Eerdmans, 1959.

———. *Principles of Conduct.* Grand Rapids: Eerdmans, 1957.

———. *Redemption—Accomplished and Applied.* Grand Rapids: Eerdmans, 1955. London: Banner of Truth, 1961.

Secondary Source

Murray, Iain H. *The Life of John Murray.* Edinburgh: Banner of Truth Trust, 1984.

47. Ibid., 242.
48. Ibid., 7.
49. John Murray, *The Epistle to the Romans,* 2 vols. (Grand Rapids: Eerdmans, 1960, 1965); idem, *Calvin on Scripture and Divine Sovereignty* (Grand Rapids: Baker, 1960) = *Collected Writings,* 4:158–204; idem, *Christian Baptism* (Philadelphia: Committee on Christian Education, Orthodox Presbyterian Church, 1952; Grand Rapids: Baker, n.d.).

Gordon H. Clark

Ronald H. Nash

Few have defended the cause of biblical Christianity in the twentieth century with as much skill and determination as did Gordon H. Clark. As Carl F. H. Henry has pointed out, "Among articulate Christian philosophers on the American scene, none has addressed the broad sweep of contemporary concerns from an evangelical Protestant view more comprehensively than Gordon H. Clark."[1]

It is important to realize that much of Clark's significant work was done when American fundamentalism was at its lowest point—the years between 1930 and 1950. It is also important to realize that American evangelicalism was lifted out of that situation largely through the efforts of Clark and theologians like Carl Henry and Edward John Carnell, who had their first introduction to philosophy in Clark's courses at Wheaton College. After J. Gresham Machen died (1937), Clark made it a chief concern to champion the set of core beliefs that eventually came to serve as the foundation of evangelical scholarship in the 1950s.

While much of American fundamentalism was abandoning serious scholarship and retreating into what often appeared to be pious irrationalism, Clark was busy establishing his reputation as a philosopher to be reckoned with. While many fundamentalists[2] turned away from science and philosophy, Clark was asserting that Christian theism had absolutely nothing to fear from truth in any field. Instead of adopting the superpietistic subjectivism that led many

1. Carl F. H. Henry, "A Wide and Deep Swath," in *The Philosophy of Gordon H. Clark*, ed. Ronald H. Nash, 2d ed. (Jefferson, Md.: Trinity Foundation, 1992), 11.

2. Both Clark and Machen had some aversion to the term *fundamentalist*. But during the strange decades prior to the end of World War II, Clark did occasionally use the word. It was only after the war that "evangelical" and "fundamentalist" came to apply to different groups of people. See Ronald H. Nash, *The New Evangelicalism* (Grand Rapids: Zondervan, 1963); idem, *Evangelicals in America* (Nashville: Abingdon, 1987).

fundamentalists to eschew the laws of logic, Clark insisted that faith and reason are not antithetic. On the contrary, one enemy that biblical Christians should fear is a faith that is divorced from reason.

Life

Gordon Haddon Clark was born on August 31, 1902, in Philadelphia. His father, David Sanders Clark, had studied at Princeton Theological Seminary and in Scotland before assuming a fifty-year tenure as pastor of Bethel Presbyterian Church in Philadelphia.[3] The elder Clark was also an author; his works included *The Message from Patmos* and *A Syllabus of Systematic Theology*, which went through three editions. During his adolescent years in the parsonage, Gordon spent much time in his father's library of fifteen hundred books. Among the works he studied were John Laidlaw's *Bible Doctrine of Man*, James Orr's *Christian View of God and the World*, and John Calvin's *Institutes*, as well as the writings of B. B. Warfield and A. A. Hodge.

After graduating from the University of Pennsylvania in 1924, where he majored in French and was elected to Phi Beta Kappa, Clark began graduate studies in philosophy at the same school. During his years as a graduate student he began to teach philosophy, a career that continued at the University of Pennsylvania until 1936. Clark received his Ph.D. in 1929, having written a dissertation titled "Empedocles and Anaxagoras in Aristotle's *De Anima*."

On March 27, 1929, Clark married Ruth Schmidt. Their two daughters were born in 1936 and 1941. Also during 1929 Clark was ordained a ruling elder at Bethel Presbyterian Church. During the early years of the Depression, Clark was busy in other ways. He helped Machen organize what eventually became the Orthodox Presbyterian Church. From 1929 to 1936, in addition to his philosophy courses at the University of

Pennsylvania, Clark taught part-time at Reformed Episcopal Seminary in Philadelphia.

It is noteworthy that most of Clark's publications prior to 1952 were articles in secular philosophy journals or books issued by secular companies. This is in stark contrast to other evangelical scholars of the time, who, if they published at all, limited their work to fundamentalist publishers. Clark's first book, *Readings in Ethics*, was issued in 1931.[4] Edited in collaboration with Thomas V. Smith of the University of Chicago, it became a widely used text and went through several editions. Other books followed in 1940 and 1941.[5] While Clark did publish a few articles for evangelical magazines like *Moody Monthly* and more-serious evangelical periodicals like the *Evangelical Quarterly* and the *Westminster Theological Journal*, the bulk of his published articles and reviews prior to the 1950s appeared in scholarly journals such as the *New Scholasticism* and the *Philosophical Review*.[6] These studies reflect his continuing interest in ancient philosophy, especially the thought of Plotinus.

Clark's first book for a distinctly Christian audience was *A Christian Philosophy of Education*.[7] This work is an early statement of convictions that reappear in Clark's later writings; for example, the importance of approaching education (or any significant issue) from the perspective of a specific worldview, the clear superiority of the Christian worldview over its competitors,

---

3. Bethel Presbyterian Church was affiliated with the Reformed Presbyterians.

4. Gordon H. Clark and Thomas V. Smith, eds., *Readings in Ethics* (New York: F. S. Crofts, 1931).

5. Gordon H. Clark, ed., *Selections from Hellenistic Philosophy* (New York: F. S. Crofts, 1940); Seymour G. Martin, Gordon H. Clark, Francis P. Clarke, and Chester T. Ruddick, *A History of Philosophy* (New York: F. S. Crofts, 1941).

6. There are two bibliographies of Clark's publications. The one at the end of *Gordon H. Clark: Personal Recollections*, ed. John W. Robbins (Jefferson, Md.: Trinity Foundation, 1989) is alphabetical. A chronological bibliography appears at the end of *Philosophy of Gordon H. Clark*, ed. Nash.

7. Gordon H. Clark, *A Christian Philosophy of Education* (Grand Rapids: Eerdmans, 1946).

and the critical role that divine special revelation plays in providing the content of the Christian worldview.

By the time Clark's *Christian Philosophy of Education* appeared in 1946, a great deal had happened to him personally and professionally. In the fall of 1936, Clark left the University of Pennsylvania and assumed a position as associate professor of philosophy at Wheaton College, located about an hour's drive west of downtown Chicago. According to Carl Henry, a major reason for the move was Clark's desire to influence future generations of evangelical leaders. Clark, Henry states, "was fully aware that the modernist assault on Christian theism rested on speculative premises that could be countered effectively, and he was interested in preparing a generation of Christian scholars for serious intellectual engagement."[8]

During the seven years he taught at Wheaton, Clark's students included a number of young men who would become major figures in the renaissance of evangelical scholarship that followed World War II. These students included Henry, Carnell, and Paul King Jewett, all of whom became professors at Fuller Theological Seminary. They also included Edmund Clowney and Clair Davis, who served at Westminster Theological Seminary in Philadelphia. Even Billy Graham took at least one of Clark's courses.[9]

Unfortunately, there was at least one element of Clark's theological position that was unwelcome during his years on the Wheaton faculty, namely, his rather rigorous form of Calvinism. Henry reports that Clark's refusal to compromise his Calvinism led to dissension on the Wheaton campus (critics claimed that his Calvinism was blunting Wheaton's emphasis upon evange-

lism and missions) and finally to Clark's resignation in 1943.[10]

Clark's departure from Wheaton imposed a number of difficulties upon him and his family. It would be a year and a half before he accepted another academic post, this time as chairman of the small philosophy department at Butler University in Indianapolis. During the time between his leaving Wheaton and the start of his tenure at Butler in January 1945, Clark was ordained as a teaching elder by the Philadelphia Presbytery of the Orthodox Presbyterian Church. Unfortunately, this event also marked the beginning of a four-year controversy (1944–48) between Clark and Cornelius Van Til of Westminster Theological Seminary. Van Til and others fought Clark's standing in the Orthodox Presbyterian Church on the ground that Clark's philosophical views were inconsistent with important tenets of Reformed theology (see pp. 187–88).[11]

The years following Clark's move to Butler proved fruitful, even though he no longer had much access to students like those he had known at Wheaton, who combined interests in evangelical orthodoxy and in the history of philosophy. In 1951, he delivered the Payton Lectures at Fuller Theological Seminary, where several of his Wheaton students were now professors. These lectures were published in 1952 as *A Christian View of Men and Things*, a title that was reminiscent of books he had first encountered

8. Henry, "Wide and Deep Swath," 15.
9. For an intriguing account of what studying at Wheaton was like in the years just prior to World War II, see Carl F. H. Henry, *Confessions of a Theologian* (Waco: Word, 1986), ch. 5.

10. Henry, "Wide and Deep Swath," 16.
11. For an account of the Clark–Van Til debate that stresses broad issues, see Mark A. Noll and Cassandra Niemczyk, "Evangelicals and the Self-consciously Reformed," in *The Variety of American Evangelicalism*, ed. Donald W. Dayton and Robert K. Johnston (Knoxville: University of Tennessee Press, 1991), ch. 12. Following Clark's vindication in 1948, it was understandable that he left the Orthodox Presbyterian Church. He affiliated with the United Presbyterian Church until its 1958 merger with the predominantly liberal Presbyterian Church in the U.S.A. Clark then joined the Reformed Presbyterian Church, which in 1965 merged with the Evangelical Presbyterian Church to become the Reformed Presbyterian Church, Evangelical Synod.

in his father's library.[12] Clark criticized non-Christian theories of history, politics, ethics, and science from the unique perspective of the Christian worldview. The role of reason as a test of truth and the baneful consequences of rational inconsistency are emphases pervading *A Christian View*. The book ends with valuable chapters on religion and epistemology. The former contains a critical evaluation of the personalism of Edgar Sheffield Brightman, with its concept of a finite god. Clark's chapter on epistemology contains attacks on skepticism, relativism, and empiricism as either logically self-destructive or heedless of the various possible sources of human knowledge. Clark's own alternative to these inadequate theories of knowledge turned out to be a major restatement of views first systematized in the writings of Augustine.[13]

Clark's next two books were published in 1956 and 1957. *What Presbyterians Believe* is an enlightening exposition and uncompromising defense of the Westminster Confession.[14] *Thales to Dewey* soon became a widely used text in courses in the history of philosophy.[15] The book combines highly

original analysis and potent criticism of major figures. By contrasting secular thought's rejection of divinely revealed truth with the far more adequate biblical worldview, the book also serves as an indirect apologetic for the Christian faith.

As the editor of *Christianity Today*, Carl Henry frequently called on Clark for articles and book reviews. Between 1956 and 1967, Clark's byline appeared at least thirteen times. In the late 1960s, Clark was elected president of the Evangelical Theological Society. Twenty years earlier, he had been a founding member of the society and had helped to draft its statement of belief. In 1966, the philosophy department of Wheaton College invited Clark to be the featured lecturer at its annual fall conference. His three lectures later appeared in the festschrift *The Philosophy of Gordon H. Clark*.[16]

When Clark retired from Butler University in the spring of 1973, he briefly considered the possibility of joining the philosophy department at Western Kentucky University. He finally declined, citing as his reason the unpleasant prospect of packing and moving away from his Indianapolis home. But in the fall of 1974, Clark and his wife did move to Rising Fawn, Georgia, where he joined the faculty of Covenant College on Lookout Mountain. By all accounts, Clark's return to a distinctively evangelical college was a rewarding time, for both him and the fortunate students of the little college on the mountain. But tragedy struck when Clark's wife died on July 28, 1977. As a result, Clark eventually had to move out of his home on the mountain and spend his remaining days at Covenant College as a lodger in the homes of others.

Clark was eighty-one years old when he retired from Covenant College in 1983. During the previous fourteen years, he had taught summer courses at Sangre de Cristo Seminary in Westcliffe, Colorado, a school

12. Gordon H. Clark, *A Christian View of Men and Things* (Grand Rapids: Eerdmans, 1952; Jefferson, Md.: Trinity Foundation, 1991). I have in mind John Laidlaw's *Bible Doctrine of Man* and James Orr's *Christian View of God and the World, As Centring in the Incarnation.*

13. Clark himself never elaborated on the extent to which his theory of knowledge reflected the work of Augustine. Perhaps one reason for this was the fact that Augustine's epistemology had become obscure through centuries of misinterpretation. For a critical evaluation of these misreadings of Augustine and an exposition that reveals the points of contact between Clark and the bishop of Hippo, see Ronald H. Nash, *The Light of the Mind: St. Augustine's Theory of Knowledge* (Lexington: University Press of Kentucky, 1969). Clark offered many valuable comments during the writing of this work.

14. Gordon H. Clark, *What Presbyterians Believe* (Philadelphia: Presbyterian and Reformed, 1956)—this book was reissued in 1965 under the title *What Do Presbyterians Believe?*

15. Gordon H. Clark, *Thales to Dewey* (Boston: Houghton Mifflin, 1957; Jefferson, Md.: Trinity Foundation, 1990).

16. *The Philosophy of Gordon H. Clark*, ed. Ronald H. Nash (Philadelphia: Presbyterian and Reformed, 1968; 2d ed., Jefferson, Md.: Trinity Foundation, 1992), chs. 2–4.

operated by his son-in-law Dwight Zeller. Clark loved the Colorado mountains. It was fitting that he was buried near Westcliffe following his death there on April 9, 1985.

The Knowability of God

The knowability of God is a dominant motif in all of Clark's work. This theme, then, provides a convenient way of organizing and presenting many other aspects of his thought.

One of the best ways to investigate such a theme is to contrast it with the opposite viewpoint. In this case, an enormous range of modern thinkers occupy the other side of the line. The vast majority of nonevangelical thinkers since Immanuel Kant have maintained that human beings cannot have cognitive knowledge about God. While God, in their view, may be present in mystical experience (which yields no information or cognitive content) or in personal encounter, he is unknowable to the human mind.

Kant, the eighteenth-century German philosopher, lent enormous support to the belief that God is unknowable. Kant's system in effect erected a wall between the world as it appears to humans (the phenomenal world) and the world as it really is (the noumenal world). Human knowledge is restricted to the phenomenal world, the world as it is perceived by the senses and then shaped by the mind. Knowledge of any reality lying beyond the wall separating phenomena and noumena is forever unattainable. This means that human reason cannot penetrate the secrets of ultimate reality. Answers to the most basic questions of theology and metaphysics lie beyond the boundaries of human knowledge. Since God is not a subject of human experience, and since the human categories that make knowledge possible cannot be extended to transcendent reality, God is both unknown and unknowable.[17]

Kant's rejection of the possibility of cognitive knowledge about God was taken up by a succession of thinkers, including Friedrich Schleiermacher and Albrecht Ritschl, both of whom became major sources of Protestant liberalism.[18] While the neo-orthodox theologians who came on the scene after World War I saw their work as an antidote to the subjectivism of liberalism, they also rejected any possibility of human knowledge about God. Their view of special revelation had no room for propositional truth or cognitive knowledge.[19]

These modern Christian agnostics denied the possibility of human knowledge about God on three grounds:

1. *The nature of human knowledge.* This was Kant's position, which many even in the twentieth century continued to follow.
2. *The nature of God.* Some modern thinkers so exaggerated the transcendence of God (the "Wholly Other") that he could not possibly be an object of human knowledge. Ironically, this view found a home in some evangelical circles as a result of the influence of Cornelius Van Til.[20]
3. *The nature of human language.* Here human language was thought to be incapable of serving as an adequate carrier of information about God.

Considering humans unable to understand whatever God might attempt to say to them, many modern thinkers reinterpreted the human relationship to God as having nothing to do with the reception of information. It was explained instead as an inward personal experience with God. While no evangelical should deny the importance of an encounter with the living God, we

---

17. For more detail see Ronald H. Nash, *The Word of God and the Mind of Man* (Grand Rapids: Zondervan, 1982).

18. Ibid., ch. 2.

19. Exceptions among twentieth-century nonevangelical theologians are almost nonexistent. One of the few may be the later Karl Barth. See Nash, *Word of God*, chs. 3–4.

20. Nash, *Word of God*, ch. 9.

should beware the consequences of divorcing the experience of God from cognitive knowledge about him. Following Clark's lead in this matter, a small circle of evangelical thinkers challenged this type of Christian agnosticism. The most ambitious effort in this regard has been Carl Henry's six-volume *God, Revelation and Authority*.[21]

The evangelical counterattack refuted each of the three grounds of theological agnosticism, namely, the arguments based respectively on the nature of human knowledge, the nature of God, and the nature of human language. The position inspired by Clark's work marked a return to a major tradition of historic Christianity—affirmation of both an intelligible revelation from a rational, personal God and divinely given human ability to know the transcendent God through the medium of true propositions. Thus Clark's defense of the knowability of God has essential links to the other issues we will explore in this essay, namely, the relation between divine and human logic, the rationalism-empiricism debate, and the superiority of the Christian worldview.

The Relation between Divine and Human Logic

Much modern theology is tainted by a distrust of or contempt for such principles of logic as the law of noncontradiction (i.e., A is not non-A). Large numbers of fundamentalists and evangelicals who ought to know better promote and preach versions of irrationalism; they claim, for example, that faith has no intrinsic relationship to reason. Some Christian pietists urge the faithful to believe that God's logic and human logic are different somehow.

Clark correctly countered such claims by warning that down this path lies nothing but skepticism. "Truth is the same for God

and man," he argued.[22] After all, if God has the truth and we have something that differs from what God knows, then one thing is clear: we do not possess truth! If there is absolutely no point of contact between the divine logic and so-called human logic, then what passes as human reasoning can never be valid. And, of course, if this were so, then the putative reasoning of those who insist that there is a distinction between the divine and human logic cannot be valid![23]

Basic to the Christian worldview, Clark insisted, is the presupposition that human beings are created in the image of God. And essential to this image is a rationality that reflects the rationality of God's own mind. The New Testament and the early church fathers point to a similarity between the rational structure of the human mind and the rational structure of the mind of God. It is possible for the human *logos* ("mind") to know the divine *Logos* because God created us with the ability to think his thoughts after him. The laws of reason are the same for him and us.

It was Clark's views on this subject that sparked the controversy between him and Cornelius Van Til in the mid-1940s.[24] Van Til insisted that there is a qualitative difference between God's knowledge and the knowledge attainable by humans. What we can know and what God knows are qualitatively different. According to Van Til, our knowledge is always analogical of the divine knowledge. Although we can think God's thoughts after him, this must always be understood to mean that God's knowledge and ours do not coincide at a single

21. Carl F. H. Henry, *God, Revelation and Authority*, 6 vols. (Waco: Word, 1976–83). Similar concerns are apparent in Nash, *Word of God*.

22. Gordon H. Clark, "Wheaton Lecture II: The Axiom of Revelation," in *Philosophy of Gordon H. Clark*, ed. Nash, 76.

23. For an elaboration and defense of this claim, see Nash, *Word of God*, ch. 9.

24. For the substance of this controversy see Fred H. Klooster, *The Incomprehensibility of God in the Orthodox Presbyterian Conflict* (Franeker: T. Wever, 1951). The reader should be warned that Klooster's account reflects Van Til's side of the controversy.

point. A proposition cannot mean the same thing to God and us.

Clark disagreed. He was convinced that Van Til's position leads to skepticism. But while denying the alleged qualitative difference between human and divine knowledge, Clark did not deny the incomprehensibility of God, as had been charged against him in the debate. Nor did Clark say there are no differences between God's and our knowledge.[25] His formal answer to the charges included four points:

1. The essence of God's being is incomprehensible to man except as God reveals truths concerning his own nature; 2. The manner of God's knowing, an eternal intuition, is impossible for man; 3. Man can never know exhaustively and completely God's knowledge of any truth in all its relationships and implications; because every truth has an infinite number of relationships and implications and since each of these implications in turn has other infinite implications, these must ever, even in heaven, remain inexhaustible for man; 4. But . . . the doctrine of the incomprehensibility of God does not mean that a proposition, e.g., two times two are four, has one meaning for man and a qualitatively different meaning for God, or that some truth is conceptual and other truth is non-conceptual in nature.[26]

Arguing that Van Til's position entails skepticism, Clark pointed out that "if God knows all truths and knows the correct meaning of every proposition, and if no proposition means to man what it means to God, so that God's knowledge and man's knowledge do not coincide at any single point, it follows by rigorous necessity that man can have no truth at all. This conclusion is quite opposite to the views of Calvin (*Institutes* II, ii, 12–15), and undermines all Christianity."[27] At another time Clark noted that "if God has the truth and if man has only an analogy, it follows that he [man] does not have truth."[28] Of course, Clark acknowledged, the Bible "says God's thoughts are not our thoughts and his ways are not our ways. But is it good exegesis to say that this means his logic, his arithmetic, his truth are not ours? If this were so, what would the consequences be? It would mean not only that our additions and subtractions are all wrong, but also that all our thoughts, in history as well as in arithmetic, are all wrong. . . . To avoid such nonsense, which of course is a denial of the divine image . . . we must insist that truth is the same for God and man."[29] If Christians follow Van Til and deny all coincidence between God's mind and the human mind, we are left not only without any knowledge of God, but without any knowledge at all.

Rationalism or Empiricism?

Many Christian thinkers find empiricism attractive as they seek to work out the details of the Christian worldview. Clark took exception to any such approach and argued instead for a Christian rationalism along the lines first developed by Augustine.

Empiricism is the belief that all human knowledge arises from sense experience. Classical empiricists frequently compared the human mind at birth to a *tabula rasa*, a blank tablet. Humans possess no innate or inborn ideas or knowledge. The slate is clean. As they grow and develop, the senses

25. See Gordon H. Clark, "The Bible as Truth," *Bibliotheca Sacra* 114 (April 1957): 163; this essay was reprinted in Gordon H. Clark, *God's Hammer: The Bible and Its Critics*, 2d rev. ed. (Jefferson, Md.: Trinity Foundation, 1987), 24–38.

26. Gordon H. Clark et al., "The Answer to a Complaint against Several Actions and Decisions of the Presbytery of Philadelphia Taken in a Special Meeting Held on July 7, 1944," 9–10. Clark took pains to point out that the precise wording of this reply (which he and four others submitted to counter Van Til's complaint), and especially of point 3, was that of Floyd Hamilton. Clark had to accept the wording to satisfy his coauthors.

27. Gordon H. Clark, "Apologetics," in *Contemporary Evangelical Thought*, ed. Carl F. H. Henry (Grand Rapids: Baker, 1968), 159.

28. Clark, "The Bible as Truth," 164.

29. Clark, "Wheaton Lecture II," 76.

supply the mind with an ever-increasing stock of information. According to this model, all human knowledge results from what the mind does with the data supplied through the senses.

Classical rationalists countered by arguing that the human mind at birth is not a blank tablet. If we were not born with at least some innate ideas or forms of thought or categories, knowledge would be impossible. The impotence of empiricism is especially evident in the case of human knowledge of universal and necessary truth. Of course, many things in the world are contingent in the sense that they could have been otherwise. The typewriter used in writing this article happens to be brown, but it could have been red. Whether it is brown or red is a purely contingent feature of reality. But it is necessarily the case that the typewriter could not have been brown all over and red all over at the same time and in the same sense. The necessary truth that a typewriter that is brown all over cannot at the same time be red all over is not learned through sense experience. Sense experience may be able to report what is the case at a particular time. But sense experience is incapable of grasping what must be the case at all times. Sensation is impotent in the area of necessary and universal truth. Empiricism is, then, a grossly inadequate account of human knowledge.[30]

Empiricism cannot justify the most important kinds of human knowledge. For example, the truths of mathematics and geometry are not derivable from sense experience; the validity of logical reasoning is independent of experience. Each human experience of the world presupposes an *a priori* understanding of causality, space, and time. The question then is, Whence come these *a priori* organizing principles of human thought? Since, Clark contends, a blank mind cannot know, indeed is no

mind at all, we must turn in our quest for an adequate theory of knowledge to some form of apriorism.

The most famous modern version of apriorism, of course, is that of Immanuel Kant. But Clark correctly dismisses Kant's position as inadequate.[31] For one thing, Kant never explained how and why all human minds possess the same *a priori* forms of thought. Clark goes beyond Kant in holding that God has implanted the *a priori* human aptitudes for knowing and harmonized them with the laws of nature. Clark argues that an essential element of the image of God in human beings is a rationality that reflects the rationality of God's own mind. So much for the irrational claim that God's logic and human logic are different. Clark's view also effectively counters those who would argue that human language can never be an adequate carrier of divinely revealed truth. As Clark explains, language is God's gift to facilitate communion and communication on both the divine-human and human-human levels. And, as we have seen, God has also implanted in us the organizing principles of thought, which lies behind language as its necessary condition. Communication of information is possible, therefore, because we who use language are enlightened by the divine *Logos;* that is, we are in possession of certain innate ideas that reflect God's mind.[32]

Clark's line of argument in all this effectively challenges the three grounds upon which theological agnostics have denied the possibility of human knowledge about God, namely, that either the nature of God or the nature of human knowledge or problems associated with human language make knowledge of God impossible. There is nothing, Clark declares, in the nature of the divine transcendence that precludes the possibility of our knowing the mind of God.

---

30. There is not enough space here to consider in any detail Clark's many objections to empiricism. The interested reader might consult Clark, *Thales to Dewey*, 278–84, 357–94; idem, *Christian View*, 303–12.

31. See Clark, *Christian View*, 312–16; Ronald H. Nash, "Gordon Clark's Theory of Knowledge," in *Philosophy of Gordon H. Clark*, 141–47.

32. For details of this theory of language, see Nash, *Word of God*, ch. 11.

There is nothing irrational or illogical about the content of divine revelation. The Christian God is not the Unknown God of ancient Athens or modern Marburg. He is a God who created us as creatures capable of knowing his mind and will, and who has made information about his mind and will available in revealed truths.

Neither the nature of God nor the nature of human knowledge and language rules out the possibility of the human mind's attaining cognitive knowledge of the Word of God. Not only is divine special revelation in the form of true propositions possible, it is necessary if humans are to break free from their hopeless efforts to achieve knowledge about any of the truly important issues. The bankruptcy of all such human efforts apart from God's gracious revelation is one important thesis of Clark's *Thales to Dewey*.

The Superiority of the Christian Worldview

One of the books Clark encountered in his father's library was James Orr's *Christian View of God and the World*. While specific allusions are hard to find, it is clear that Orr's work was instrumental in getting Clark to think about Christianity and the other major systems of thought as worldviews. It is a mistake, Clark believed, to debate the relative merits of Christianity and its competitors on this or that single issue. The proper approach to apologetics is to assume or to presuppose that God exists and has revealed himself in the canonical Scriptures, infer the general content of the Christian worldview from the Bible, and then argue for its superiority vis-à-vis any competing worldview.

Every conflict between worldviews can ultimately be traced back to opposing first principles. When faced with a choice between antithetic first principles, we should choose the one which, when applied to the whole of reality, will give us the most coherent picture of the world. Clark maintains that "it would be impossible to have two self-consistent, mutually contradictory phi-

losophies. A false statement, so it is said, will always, if pursued far enough, imply its own falsity."[33]

But, Clark asks, what do we do if two first principles appear to be more or less self-consistent? This situation might well develop, for only someone with omniscience can apply the test for truth with complete success. Clark states that in such a situation we must choose that system which is more self-consistent, which more adequately satisfies the test of coherence. In Clark's opinion, that system will be Christian theism, though he admits that there will be problems:

> The theistic view of the world faces difficulties. There are questions to which Christianity seems to give an inadequate answer or none at all. But does anyone claim that pragmatism or realism or idealism gives adequate answers to all questions? Is humanism or naturalism free of difficulty? There has been an immense amount, not merely of inadequacy but of inconsistency in some of the greatest philosophers. . . . But if one system can provide plausible solutions to many problems while another leaves too many questions unanswered, if one system tends less to skepticism and gives more meaning to life, if one world view is consistent while others are self-contradictory, who can deny us, since we must choose, the right to choose the more promising first principle?[34]

The position we have just summarized certainly leaves the impression that Clark is recommending that the basic Christian presupposition be treated like any scientific hypothesis and be verified inductively. But this apparently inductive approach to the biblical worldview is totally rejected in Clark's Wheaton Lectures, where he insists on a rigid deductive approach.[35] He treats much like a geometrical axiom his basic

33. Clark, *Christian View*, 30.
34. Ibid., 34.
35. *Philosophy of Gordon H. Clark*, ed. Nash, chs. 2–4.

presupposition that God has revealed truth about himself in the canonical Scriptures. Clark then limits knowledge to deductions that can be made from the Bible.

It has been suggested that Clark's deductive presuppositionalism was a marked shift from what he held, say, at the time he wrote *A Christian View of Men and Things*.[36] The claim of such a shift in Clark's thinking remains problematic and is open to the counterargument that the deductive position was always implicit in his earlier writings.[37] Whatever the case, Clark's deductive version of presuppositionalism has disappointed some in that it limits human knowledge exclusively to the propositions contained in the Bible and propositions deducible therefrom. Obviously, such a position fails to account for all kinds of things that humans claim to know. That one's children exist, for example, can be known with surety, even if it cannot be deduced from the Bible. Evidently, Clark's use of the word *knowledge* is very idiosyncratic.[38]

But Clark's position on this issue should not detract from his magnificent accomplishments. Among them is his insistence that Truth at the level of the divine mind is a complete and total system. There is an "Omniscient Mind whose thought is systematic truth."[39] Since God exists and is omniscient, Clark continues,

we may infer that all problems and all solutions fit one another like pieces of a marvelous mosaic. The macrocosmic world with its microcosmic but thoughtful inhabitant [humans] will not be a fortuitous aggregation of unrelated elements. Instead of a series of disconnected proposi-

tions, truth will be a rational system, a logically ordered series, somewhat like geometry with its theorems and axioms, its implications and presuppositions. Each part will derive its significance from the whole. Christianity therefore has, or, one may even say, Christianity *is* a comprehensive view of all things: it takes the world, both material and spiritual, to be an ordered system. Consequently, if Christianity is to be defended against the objections of other philosophies, the only adequate method will be comprehensive.[40]

The importance of thinking of Christianity as a total world-and-life view should be obvious. But, Clark quickly adds, it does not follow that "a man must know everything in order to know anything. . . . To apprehend an intricate and beautiful mosaic, we must see it as a whole; and the parts are properly explained only in terms of the whole; but it does not follow that a perception of the pieces and some fragmentary information is impossible without full appreciation."[41]

Evaluation

There are some aspects of Clark's thought that would trouble almost any reader. Most of them are elements of his metaphysics that he seldom made explicit, in particular, his advocacy of what some would regard as an extreme type of idealism that seems to reduce all of reality to sets of propositions existing in the mind of God.[42] Since Clark thought it prudent not to expound such views in print, there is little point in trying to pursue a trail that he himself refused to mark.

It would also be a serious mistake to allow the troubling aspects in Clark's position to draw attention away from his major con-

36. See Nash, "Gordon Clark's Theory of Knowledge," in *Philosophy of Gordon H. Clark*, ch. 5.
37. Mary M. Crumpacker, "Clark's Axiom: Something New?" *Journal of the Evangelical Theological Society* 32 (1989): 355–65.
38. For more on this issue see Ronald H. Nash, *Faith and Reason* (Grand Rapids: Zondervan, 1988), 60–61.
39. Clark, *Christian View*, 24.
40. Ibid., 24–25.
41. Ibid., 25–26.
42. Nothing in this sentence is meant to suggest that Clark's view on this point is necessarily wrong. When students of philosophy have exhausted the other alternatives, they may turn to a position somewhat like his. Nonetheless, his view, initially at least, will prove difficult for many.

tributions to contemporary Christian thought. There is much that modern philosophers and theologians can learn from him: (1) the epistemological bankruptcy of philosophical and religious empiricism; (2) the indispensability of divine revelation to human knowledge; (3) the inevitable shortcomings of any attempt to remove the cognitive and propositional element from the content of divine special revelation; (4) the necessity of refusing to separate faith from reason, whether the impetus to do so be a humanistic attack on the legitimacy of faith, an existentialist critique of reason, or a Thomistic attempt to segregate the two into different realms of human knowledge; and (5) the continuing vitality and relevance of Calvinistic theology as formulated in the Westminster Confession of Faith.

Perhaps Clark's greatest legacy is his reminder that reason and logic have cosmic significance in the Christian worldview. Reason is intrinsically related to God. The law of noncontradiction is valid because the universe is the creation of a rational God. The rational world (the creation) is knowable because it is the objectification of the eternal thoughts of a rational God. And the mind of God can be known by the human *logos* because God has created us capable of such knowledge and has revealed propositional truth about himself in the canonical Scriptures.

Anyone who thoroughly studies such major works as *Thales to Dewey* and *A Christian View of Men and Things* will re-alize that Clark's devotion to truth and wisdom is not one whit less than his devotion to the Triune God. This is not surprising, for Clark carried with him the Augustinian conviction that to know truth is to know God since God is truth. If the Christian church were to adopt and stress Clark's understanding of the role of reason, truth, and propositional revelation in the Christian worldview, some of the serious theological errors of the twentieth century would be avoided in the future.[43]

Secondary Sources

Henry, Carl F. H. *God, Revelation and Authority.* 6 vols. Waco: Word, 1976–83.

Nash, Ronald H. *Faith and Reason: Searching for a Rational Faith.* Grand Rapids: Zondervan, 1988.

_____. *The Light of the Mind: St. Augustine's Theory of Knowledge.* Lexington: University Press of Kentucky, 1969.

_____. *The New Evangelicalism.* Grand Rapids: Zondervan, 1963.

_____. *The Word of God and the Mind of Man.* Grand Rapids: Zondervan, 1982.

_____, ed. *The Philosophy of Gordon H. Clark.* Philadelphia: Presbyterian and Reformed, 1968. 2d ed. Jefferson, Md.: Trinity Foundation, 1992.

Robbins, John W., ed. *Gordon H. Clark: Personal Recollections.* Jefferson, Md.: Trinity Foundation, 1989.

43. The author wishes to thank Carl Henry and John Robbins for reading early versions of this essay and offering many helpful comments.

G. C. Berkouwer

Gary L. Watts

One of the most engaging and prolific evangelical theologians of the twentieth century is G. C. (Gerrit Cornelis) Berkouwer. His style is dialogical and practical rather than philosophical and abstract, and a lively sense of curiosity pervades his writing. Though the discussions tend to be comprehensive and lengthy, which may make entrance to his dogmatic studies difficult at first, a reasonable effort will yield dividends well worth the investment. For though Berkouwer was unreservedly committed to a reflective and informed theology, and was thoroughly steeped in the theological and intellectual history of the Reformed tradition, he never for a moment lost sight of theology's need to focus on the practical concerns of the Christian life.

Berkouwer was born on June 8, 1903, in Amsterdam and was raised in a devoutly Reformed home.[1] He began his theological studies in 1922 at the Free University of Amsterdam during a time of turbulence and transition in his denomination, the Reformed Churches in the Netherlands.[2] The overwhelming influence of the Dutch politician and theologian Abraham Kuyper, who had died in 1920, was slowly beginning to wane. Kuyper had been the dominant figure in the formation of both the Free University and the Reformed Churches in the Netherlands, and had initiated an all-out battle against the encroachment of theological modernism. While Kuyper was willing to dialogue to a degree with different theological perspectives and to give them a hearing at the Free University, he felt that they should always be clearly contrasted

1. See George Puchinger, ed., *Gesprekken over Rome-Reformatie* (Delft: W. D. Meinema, 1965), 299; and Lewis B. Smedes, "G. C. Berkouwer," in *Creative Minds in Contemporary Theology*, ed. Philip Edgcumbe Hughes (Grand Rapids: Eerdmans, 1966), 63–98.

2. The Reformed Churches in the Netherlands (Gereformeerde Kerken in Nederland) is to be distinguished from the Netherlands Reformed Church (Nederlandse Hervormde Kerk), from which it had broken off during the time of Abraham Kuyper.

with conservative Calvinism, which he considered the correct view. Both in his politics and in his theology Kuyper's approach was polemical and embodied the conviction that "strength lies in isolation."[3]

In 1902 Herman Bavinck had succeeded Kuyper as professor of systematic theology at the Free University (a position Bavinck held until his death the year before Berkouwer's matriculation), and a new approach began to emerge. While also sharply opposed to liberalism and its antisupernaturalistic stance, the Leiden-trained Bavinck, desiring to demonstrate the catholicity of the Christian faith, urged dialogue. Concerning this change Berkouwer would later write, "The influence of Abraham Kuyper was no longer as powerful as it had once been. . . . Without denying the necessity of polemics, people wondered whether they ought not be carried on more carefully and more modestly. And on this point, a subtle difference between Bavinck and Kuyper began to show itself."[4] Berkouwer's early theological production exhibits the tension between these two approaches. And while Berkouwer finally demonstrates a much closer affinity to Bavinck than to Kuyper, in his early period there is a strongly polemical and defensive element.

In the early 1920s the tides of change were not limited to Berkouwer's own denomination; the waves of dialectical theology were breaking across Europe. Publication of the second edition of Karl Barth's commentary on Romans in 1922 had enormous impact on the theological world. Berkouwer and other students at the Free University struggled to trace the implications of this new perspective, which laid such a heavy emphasis upon the object of faith, the free and holy God. This movement away from the anthropocentric and subjective theology of the nineteenth and early twentieth centuries seemed to many evangelical theologians to hold promise. Yet the student Berkouwer wondered if the pendulum had not swung too far, and if the emphasis on the freedom of God had not become an arbitrariness which left the believer's faith no room for certainty.[5]

Early Writings

We must view Berkouwer's early publications against this background of theological ferment. In his doctoral dissertation, *Geloof en openbaring in de nieuwere Duitsche theologie* ("Faith and Revelation in Recent German Theology"), published in 1932, Berkouwer takes a firm stand against all theology which would allow the object of faith to be defined by the believing subject. Here we find a strongly polemical, Kuyperian reaction against subjective modernism and its undermining of the authority of Scripture. He attacks Albrecht Ritschl for allowing the needs of humanity to determine what is and what is not revelation, and Ernst Troeltsch for allowing psychological, transcendental principles to play a similar role. Such approaches lead to a subjectivity which undermines the independence of God's revelation.[6] Berkouwer asks, "How is it possible, when one does not accept the absolute authority of Holy Scripture as norm, to eliminate the productivity of the subject and to avoid the subjectivizing of the norm?"[7] The view with which Berkouwer contrasts these theologies is a firm commitment to the absolute authority of Scripture. Scripture accepted in its entirety as God's revelation is the necessary independent object over against which faith can remain purely receptive and nondeterminative.

3. This was a guiding principle of Kuyper's Anti-Revolutionary party. See Frank Vandenberg, *Abraham Kuyper* (Grand Rapids: Eerdmans, 1960), 72.

4. G. C. Berkouwer, *A Half Century of Theology*, trans. Lewis B. Smedes (Grand Rapids: Eerdmans, 1977), 12.

5. Ibid., 45.

6. G. C. Berkouwer, *Geloof en openbaring in de nieuwere Duitsche theologie* (Utrecht: Kemink, 1932), 66, 75.

7. Ibid., 236.

In the same volume Berkouwer is equally critical of those theologians who lay too much emphasis on the object of revelation. Berkouwer argues that in order to avoid subjectivity Barth turns the tables. God, who is usually considered the *object* of religious knowledge, becomes the *subject,* since God and his Word cannot be made into objects of human knowledge at will. In theory Berkouwer does not object to this idea. Indeed, within his own theological tradition Kuyper and Bavinck had both maintained a similar view.[8] The problem is the particular consequences which Barth derived therefrom. While Kuyper and Bavinck found no contradiction between God's freedom and an infallible Scripture, for Barth the absolute freedom of God allowed no such formal guarantee. Thus Barth refused to identify the Word of God directly with Scripture. It is this which Berkouwer opposes: "Herein all continuity between God and man is abolished. For in no way at all can man now have at his disposal God and his revelation."[9]

Berkouwer continues his criticism in the 1937 book entitled *Karl Barth,* where he expresses the fear that Barth's view ultimately leads to nominalism. Comparing Barth to William of Occam, Berkouwer points out that while Occam stressed the absolute freedom and sovereign will of God, the uncertainty evoked by this emphasis was checked by the authority of the church. In Barth's theology, however, the hidden reality of God is "no longer compensated by Church authority, tradition, or Holy Scripture."[10]

To navigate between the Scylla of humanistic subjectivism and the Charybdis of nominalistic objectivism, Berkouwer formulated a mediating concept: faith is not a creative, determinative power, but the human "correlate" of divine revelation. This term enabled Berkouwer to define the rela-

tionship between subject and object: while all creativity must lie on the side of the object of faith, this object cannot be so removed from the subject that the subject cannot "possess" it in any sense. For Berkouwer the one and only confession which protected both requirements of this "correlation" was the *absolute authority of the Word of God.* Recognizing Scripture in its entirety as God's unique, independent revelation avoids subjectivism. It also avoids nominalistic objectivism, because we can know with certainty that in Scripture we possess the very Word of God.

Berkouwer's emphasis upon Scripture as the Word of God led him quite naturally to the question of its relationship to scientific criticism. His 1938 publication *Het probleem der Schriftkritiek (The Problem of Scripture Criticism)* carefully works out his early position on this relationship. Here again he assumes a defensive and polemical posture and launches an all-out attack against higher criticism in all forms. Not only does he oppose the practice of criticism, but the attitude which drives it: "Scripture-critical thought does not have to do merely with several discoveries of historical inquiry, but with a specific attitude and method with far-reaching consequences."[11] In this early work Berkouwer stands against any and all attempts to synthesize critical study and dogmatics, and allows no room for a distinction between "radical and more moderate" criticism.[12]

Berkouwer observes that the critical attitude toward Scripture is supported by the view that revelation must always be a living personal encounter between God and individuals. If this is the case, we cannot identify the Bible with revelation, for doing so would substitute a dead intellectual assent for a living personal trust. Once again Berkouwer has Barth in mind. He notes that Barth views the Bible as containing both a historical dimension and a dimension of

---

8. Ibid., 205.
9. Ibid., 207.
10. G. C. Berkouwer, *Karl Barth* (Kampen: J. H. Kok, 1937), 82.

11. G. C. Berkouwer, *Het probleem der Schriftkritiek* (Kampen: J. H. Kok, 1938), 62.
12. Ibid., 60–61.

faith. Since revelation is present only in the dimension of faith, there can be no direct identification between Holy Scripture, which is a historical document, and the living Word of God. The Bible is a "witness" to revelation, but the witnesses are fallible men. Through this witness the church can hear the voice of the Lord. But it is only by the miracle of the Holy Spirit that one finds the revelation of God in this human witness. Berkouwer argues that this separation between the Word of God and the words of Holy Scripture leaves the door open for all forms of scriptural criticism.[13]

Against this background, Berkouwer outlines his own early view concerning the authority and interpretation of Scripture. Scripture can and should be identified with the Word of God. This is not merely a formal intellectual recognition with certain logical consequences. Rather, it is a confession of personal confidence in the Scripture and willingness to subject oneself to its unique authority. The danger of Scripture criticism is that it does not recognize the need to subject itself to the authority of Scripture. The temptation not to recognize this authority is, of course, present not only with critical inquiry, but "with the simple reading of Scripture, and with exegesis and with dogmatic reflection over the Word of God, and must be resisted over the *whole* line."[14]

But while Berkouwer rejects criticism in all its forms, he is careful to point out the "organic" nature of the inspiration of Scripture, a term previously used by Bavinck. The divine does "take the human into its service," and therefore the personalities, cultures, and worldviews of the writers of Scripture are evident.[15] However, this does not affect the reliability of their reporting. Phenomenological language may be employed, such as "the rising of the sun," but the historicity of the events described is not thereby impugned.

Along this line, Berkouwer holds to a literalism that extends down to the details of the first chapters of Genesis. He does not claim, however, that an orthodox view of scriptural authority necessarily demands so literal an interpretation. Rather, he proposes the principle (which also plays an important role in his later writing) that a decision on such a matter must never be "from the side of scientific results, but a decision of the Holy Scripture itself."[16] Any decision concerning the interpretation or historical accuracy of a scriptural account ought to arise from internal evidence rather than from some outside source. However, and this is crucial, a scientific result may quite legitimately serve as an occasion for further reflection on the meaning of a passage of Scripture, as long as it does not "lead to a conclusion which cannot arise *from Scripture itself.*"[17]

Berkouwer readily admits that "the *purpose* of the writing of history in Holy Scripture is wholly other than that of science."[18] But this specific purpose affects merely the choice and grouping of materials; it does not result in a distortion of the facts. And while we may not ever be able to determine the exact grounds upon which the selection was made, we can be sure that the material is historical.[19]

Thus in his early writings Berkouwer held to an almost literalistic interpretation of Scripture, a very strict doctrine of infallibility. However, following Kuyper and Bavinck, he did not arrive at his position on the basis of any kind of rational proof. That is, he did not argue that his particular understanding of scriptural authority was delineated in Scripture itself, or that it was a logical derivation from Scripture's divine nature. Rather, Berkouwer seems to have been driven at this point by an "all or nothing" dilemma and by a desire to avoid any form of dualism between the human and

13. Ibid., 30–34.
14. Ibid., 306.
15. Ibid., 326.

16. Ibid., 274.
17. Ibid.
18. Ibid., 341.
19. Ibid., 346.

the divine elements in Scripture.[20] If one were to grant to human criticism the right to judge the accuracy of scriptural revelation at any point, no matter how insignificant, then Scripture's objective authority would crumble. In that event, the only two options left would be to detach the kerygma from history altogether or to arbitrarily guard the historicity of certain crucial accounts. Finding both of these options unacceptable and continuing to avoid a rationalistic basis for his view, Berkouwer would in his later work come up with a somewhat different solution to the "all or nothing" dilemma (see p. 203).

Studies in Dogmatics

In 1945 Berkouwer assumed the chair of dogmatics at the Free University, and shortly afterward began his dogmatic work in earnest. In accord with his developing conversational and nonsystematic style, he produced not a single systematic theology or dogmatics, but a series of monographs dedicated to particular doctrinal issues. The series, which ultimately extended to fourteen volumes in English translation, is one of the most prodigious projects of evangelical theology in the twentieth century.

In the period which intervened between his theological studies and his assumption of the chair of dogmatics at the Free University, Berkouwer served as a pastor first in the northern province of Friesland and later in a suburb of Amsterdam. It is clear that practical pastoral concerns helped to shape his later work. Influential as well was the catastrophic experience of the Second World War, which is reflected in Berkouwer's growing emphasis on the need to bring theology to bear upon the real, existential problems of life. In *Wereldoorlog en theologie* ("World War and Theology"), an address given in October of 1945 at the Free University, he stated that such cataclysmic events constrain us to focus on the reality of God's presence in our lives and remind us

that "the Word of God never desires to lead us to an empty systematic which does not touch concrete life."[21] From this point on, Berkouwer's theology moved further and further from the isolationist and polemical stance of Kuyper. He turned willingly from separatism toward dialogue, particularly with Barthian theology and with the Roman Catholic Church, and from philosophical abstraction toward the concrete content of Christian faith.

The Three Volumes on Faith

With the initiation of his dogmatic series, Berkouwer took his concept of the correlation between faith and revelation and focused it on specific biblical content. The object of faith was no longer the abstract idea of revelation, but the living grace of God, and thus the correlation was now between faith and grace. The specific relationship between the believer's faith and God's grace is worked out in the three volumes *Faith and Justification, Faith and Sanctification,* and *Faith and Perseverance.*

As in his earlier work, here Berkouwer remains committed to the view of faith as purely receptive rather than creative. It is clear, then, that the correlation between faith and grace is not symmetrical. Justification must not be conceived of as a corporate act—part performed by the grace of God, part by our faith: "It is not as though justification flows from two springs, God's declaration and man's faith. It is faith that recognizes and accepts the exclusiveness of God's salvation."[22]

Every step along the path of the Christian life is guided by faith, the asymmetrical human correlate of God's gracious activity. This is just as true of the Christian experiences of sanctification and perseverance as it is of justification. Therefore, Berkouwer objects to any understanding of the Chris-

20. Ibid., 74–107, 324, 348.

21. G. C. Berkouwer, *Wereldoorlog en theologie* (Kampen: J. H. Kok, 1945), 41.
22. G. C. Berkouwer, *Faith and Justification,* trans. Lewis B. Smedes (Grand Rapids: Eerdmans, 1954), 18.

tian life which would make justification by faith the initial point of a purely human process. Rather, he points out in *Faith and Sanctification* that "the '*sola fide*' of justification made it possible, once for all, to regard justification and sanctification as almost identical acts of God, operative, in concentric circles of increasing radius, on the plane of individual human life."[23] Sanctification is not a corollary or afterword of human faith, but an act of God received in faith. So it is also with the doctrine of the perseverance of the saints. There is no automatic guarantee that one's past justification will lead to a firm continuance in the faith, nor is there any way to prove perseverance. Rather, certainty that one will persevere arises from faith in the enduring strength of God's grace. Perseverance is a confession of gratitude and praise which cannot exist apart from such faith.[24]

Perhaps the single most important contribution of these three volumes is Berkouwer's insight that the Christian life (*ordo salutis*) should not be conceived of as a straight line, but as a wheel with faith as the spokes: "Salvation in Christ—this is the center from which the lines are drawn to every point of the *way of salvation*. The lines themselves may be called faith. They connect every step on the way of salvation to salvation in Christ."[25] One can see from this model that life in Christ is never separated from the faith which connects it to God's grace. The hub of the wheel is God's gracious salvation in Christ; it must not be out of view for a moment. Faith is the human experience by which the believer at the various points of the Christian life always remains connected to this center.

As Berkouwer's concept of the object of faith turned from abstract revelation to the specific content of Christian doctrine, he also began to define the faith of the subject more carefully. He noted that biblical faith is not a neutral concept which is only later clarified in relation to this or that particular object. Faith in God and faith in one's friend are not two species of the same genus. Rather, biblical faith is uniquely defined by its object. Here we see Berkouwer's growing appreciation for Barth's perspective. While earlier he had criticized Barth for emphasizing the action of God to the extent that it completely enveloped the human act of faith, he now stated approvingly, "In his [Barth's] thought, too, there is a forceful insistence on defining faith by its object."[26] This careful listening which allowed Berkouwer to constantly reevaluate the theology of his partners in dialogue would continue to surface for the remainder of his career.

Rejection of Reason as the Road to Faith

Throughout his dogmatic series Berkouwer contends that faith as the human correlate of God's grace is neither creative nor meritorious, but completely receptive. Therefore, faith cannot be spoken of in isolation as a human power, for as such it would be empty, meaningless, and even irreligious. It always directs our focus away from itself and toward the grace of God. Here alone it is given content and substance. Therefore, faith and grace must be held in the closest connection. If a child walks off a tabletop into the waiting arms of her father, we might remark, "Look how much she trusts her father." But in that trust her eyes are never once taken off her father. The trust exists only because of the father's being there. God's grace is a constant presence. Human faith is a humble admission of our need of and reliance upon that grace.

Viewed in this way, faith can never be identified with intellectual assent: "Faith

23. G. C. Berkouwer, *Faith and Sanctification*, trans. John Vriend (Grand Rapids: Eerdmans, 1952), 27–28.

24. G. C. Berkouwer, *Faith and Perseverance*, trans. Robert D. Knudsen (Grand Rapids: Eerdmans, 1958), 205–8.

25. Berkouwer, *Faith and Justification*, 29.

26. Ibid., 174.

does not place a man before a certain number of accepted truths which he intellectually assents to; faith thrusts him, as a sinner, before God's holiness."[27] Therefore, in agreement with a theological tradition from Augustine through John Calvin to the Dutch Calvinist theologians Kuyper and Bavinck, Berkouwer rejects human reason as the means by which we attain Christian faith. He is not here denying that there is a certain rationality to Christian faith. Christianity is not inherently paradoxical, and one may certainly elucidate the connections between its various tenets. But faith is not a pot of gold to be found at the end of reason's rainbow. Berkouwer offers at least four arguments for his rejection of reason as the road to faith.

First of all, human reason is fallible and limited. Philosophical arguments are convincing only to certain people at certain periods of time. Such arguments offer only probable answers, and probability is no substitute for certainty. Furthermore, arguments for belief in God are always blunted by the presence of powerful arguments against it, such as the problem of evil. In *The Providence of God* Berkouwer examines a variety of human attempts at theodicy. But in his view each of these attempts to use reason to justify the ways of God fails. There is no solution along these lines, because "to be logical, we must either make God the author of sin or, to save God from this stigma, set the world loose from Him and His rule."[28] Berkouwer views these attempts at rationalistic theodicy as grounded in our deep desire not to accept responsibility for our sin. Either we try to place the blame elsewhere through a dualistic theology, or we try to lessen the seriousness of our evil, as in the harmonistic theodicy of Gottfried von Leibniz. Berkouwer concludes that "the problem of theod-

icy is insoluble outside of a faith that knows the limits of human reason."[29]

Second, viewing reason as faith's anchor tends to separate the unified act of faith into two parts. First comes the assent to the intellectual argument, and then later comes trust in Christ. Berkouwer does not deny that faith in Christ involves intellectual acceptance of both philosophical and historical assertions. But a problem arises when this intellectual assent is isolated from the commitment which follows, for they are two aspects of a unified response to the message of the gospel. And while we will surely ask questions about historical matters if, upon hearing the message, we are pierced to the heart and respond in repentance and acceptance, Berkouwer points out that the answers to those questions will arise from our faith rather than serve as its basis.

Third, Berkouwer contends that people simply do not come to faith by means of rational argument. Throughout all of his work Berkouwer is adamant that theology must touch people where they live. Theologians ought not to spin theories that do not take into account the issues with which people are struggling.[30] No one ever came to faith by devising a rationalistic basis for it. "The closer he may seem to have come in his search for proof, the further away he actually walked. He may hear the message of Christ, but he wishes first to examine it. He hears that Christ first asks his question, but he demands that his own questions be answered first. But as he puts his questions to the fore, Christ's question is tabled."[31]

The conviction that saving faith is based on historical research or logical argumentation implies that the ordinary believer cannot have any real trust. But Berkouwer suspects that even those who are involved in scholarly historical research do not really proceed as if their faith were more or

27. Ibid., 183.
28. G. C. Berkouwer, *The Providence of God*, trans. Lewis B. Smedes (Grand Rapids: Eerdmans, 1952), 257–58.

29. Ibid., 266.
30. Berkouwer, *Faith and Justification*, 9.
31. G. C. Berkouwer, "The Temptation of Relativism," *Christianity Today*, 14 October 1957, p. 7.

less suspended until they obtain the proper historical evidence. Rather, their search for a historical mooring is begun on the basis of an already existent faith.[32]

Finally, the most emphatic argument which Berkouwer offers for his rejection of reason as a basis for faith is the total corruption entailed by the fall. Here Berkouwer appeals both to Scripture and to the Reformed tradition of total depravity. In *Man: The Image of God* he argues that the image of God in humanity cannot be found in one specific part of the person, but must be understood as the whole person in relation to God.[33] Thus the corruption of the image extends to the whole person. Examination of what the Scripture has to say about our human state prior to receiving Christ reveals that the effects of sin are so grave and absolutely radical in their extent that humanity is actually described as dead. No part of the human psyche escapes contamination: "There is no limit or boundary within human nature beyond which we can find some last human reserve untouched by sin; it is man himself who is totally corrupt."[34]

However, the corruption of human reason by sin does not imply for Berkouwer that the fallen race has lost the ability to think logically. Rather, this corruption manifests itself in the connection between the heart and the understanding. Human beings may be able to follow the rules of logic, but they are not logic machines that can reason in complete isolation. They are an intricate combination of will, understanding, and emotions; and here sin will always play an influential role.

Having dethroned reason as guarantor of faith, Berkouwer replaces it with the Reformed concept of the inner testimony of the Holy Spirit. God's message to us in Scripture "does not wait until it has re-

ceived an unconditional guarantee from elsewhere on the basis of an instance outside of revelation," but our acceptance of it is the result "of the irresistible power of the work of the Spirit."[35] For Berkouwer faith in divine revelation arises under the guidance of the Holy Spirit. We cannot rely upon the tradition of the church, the conclusions of a logical argument, or any other outside guarantor. As we read the Scripture and come face to face with God's revelation, the Holy Spirit witnesses to our hearts and makes us certain that we have heard the truth.

Given Berkouwer's rejection of reason as a basis for faith and his similarity to Barth in defining faith by its object, one might expect to find in Berkouwer, as one finds in Barth, a radical reaction to natural theology and general revelation. However, Berkouwer takes a different approach. He denies the possibility of a natural theology built upon logical principles, but accepts the concept of general revelation. In *General Revelation* he notes that "only by distinguishing between general revelation and natural theology can we do justice to the message of Scripture."[36]

Berkouwer points out that Scripture witnesses repeatedly to the general revelation present in creation. But it also draws a distinction between the fact of general revelation and our ability to recognize it. Here Berkouwer relies on Calvin's image of the spectacles which are necessary if we are to see God's revelation. Revelation has been given, but because of our blindness we are not able to recognize it. Thus Berkouwer defends general revelation as a biblical concept, while being careful to deny to human beings in their natural state any possibility of arriving at true knowledge of God by means of this revelation. Rejecting such concepts as Bavinck's universal feeling of dependence, he stresses instead that "understanding, and seeing, and hearing, is

32. Berkouwer, *Half Century*, 167.
33. G. C. Berkouwer, *Man: The Image of God*, trans. Dirk W. Jellema (Grand Rapids: Eerdmans, 1962), 117.
34. Ibid., 135.

35. G. C. Berkouwer, *General Revelation* (Grand Rapids: Eerdmans, 1955), 88.
36. Ibid., 153.

possible only in the communion with him, in the enlightening of the eyes by the salvation of God, and by the Word of the Lord."[37]

In Barth's harsh reaction against natural theology, which takes general revelation in its sweep, Berkouwer sees the use of an *a priori* philosophical scheme. He points out that Barth's concept of revelation in Jesus Christ alone forces him to isolate himself from the history of exegesis of Romans 1, and to deny the knowledge of God which Paul attributes to the heathen. For Berkouwer this is an overreaction which obscures the clear statements of Scripture. He refers to Barth's system as "Christo-logic" and a "schematizing" of Scripture.[38]

But Barth's dismissal of general revelation was far from the only place where Berkouwer opposed "schematizing." His focus on faith as noncreative reception of God's revelation, along with his strong stand against rationalistic theology, led him to speak out adamantly against any type of theological speculation which seeks to go beyond the words of Scripture itself. He decried both speculation which interprets Scripture by use of *a priori* philosophical schemes and *a posteriori* speculative procedures which draw out philosophical implications that go far beyond what is actually stated in Scripture.

Berkouwer cites as an example of *a priori* speculation the various attempts to impose on the biblical view of human nature a dualistic anthropology which divides human beings into spiritual soul and material body. Such efforts lead to unwarranted speculation concerning immortality and the nature of the soul; they tend to assert an independent immortality of the soul which does not square with the scriptural data. Berkouwer counters "that Scripture does not call our attention to a natural immortality to be concluded from the nature and structure of the soul as an anthropological given involving essential indestructibil-

ity."[39] Further, he questions the legitimacy of the controversy between the creationist and traducianist views of the soul, since "nowhere in Scripture is the origin of the soul spoken of as a separate theme."[40]

Nowhere is Berkouwer's concern about the danger of *a posteriori* speculation that takes scriptural statements to logical extremes more clear than in his volume on *Divine Election*. He opens his first chapter, "The Boundaries of Reflection," with the monitory reminder "that in the history of the Church and theology all kinds of speculations and deviations have occurred."[41] He is particularly concerned that the doctrine of election not be turned into a theory of determinism. While the Bible presents election as a theme intended to bring comfort, speculative theories turn it into doctrine which is threatening and harmful to congregations.

This whole problem takes on a specific focus when Berkouwer discusses election and rejection (double predestination). He first emphasizes that the context of every scriptural reference to election is a doxology or hymn of praise for the salvation of God. He then asks whether the concept of rejection, which the church has at times confessed, finds its "origin in the logical conclusion that election implies rejection or . . . in the testimony of Scripture itself."[42] He concludes that the former seems to be the case. Whenever the church has adopted a determinism based on the concept of causality, it must view election and rejection as parallel situations: if God is the cause of election, then logically he must be the cause of rejection as well. This reasoning is not supported by Scripture, however: "Scripture repeatedly speaks of God's rejection as a divine answer in history, as a reaction to man's sin and disobedience, not as

---

37. Ibid., 131–32.
38. Ibid., 109.
39. Berkouwer, *Man*, 248.
40. Ibid., 295.
41. G. C. Berkouwer, *Divine Election*, trans. Hugo Bekker (Grand Rapids: Eerdmans, 1960), 7.
42. Ibid., 173.

its cause."[43] Whereas Scripture tells us that God elected us before the foundation of the world and is the true cause and author of our salvation, it never says that God is the author of our sin. Scripture does not present rejection as God's eternal decision, but "as a reactive deed, a holy, divine answer to the sin of man."[44] Berkouwer's stance against speculation regarding election led to one of his most helpful and instructive contributions to dogmatic theology: a clear and biblically grounded view of election which rejects the distorted symmetry of double predestination while maintaining a vital and scriptural witness to God's sovereignty.

Berkouwer's reasons for battling theological speculation in its various forms are clear. First, such speculation can easily lead to an obscuring of the text so that we do not see exactly what revelation has to say. Second, the process of speculation is harmful to the person in the pew, because straightforward statements of Scripture can be interpreted by a philosophical system to say the opposite of their commonsense meaning. This takes the Bible away from the average Christian, and thus distorts its purpose. Behind many of these speculative schemes lies humanity's sinful desire to know more than we have been told or perhaps even to justify ourselves before God.

In accordance with his principle of not speculating beyond the bounds of Scripture, Berkouwer was quite willing to admit that there are limitations to the human understanding of the divine. He employed two terms throughout his dogmatic series in order to emphasize this limitation. In contrast to a perfect understanding of revelation, which would result in intellectual assent, he emphasized the "mystery" of a revelation that cannot be fully comprehended, which results in a "confession" of faith with praise. Scripture contains mysteries beyond human comprehension; and

confession, wherever one does not fully understand, simply accepts what has been revealed by God.

This willingness to accept mystery and not to limit Scripture by the canon of human reason is nowhere more evident than in Berkouwer's writing concerning the person and work of Christ. In the face of many twentieth-century attempts to explain the incarnation in rational terms, or to explain it away, Berkouwer stresses that we cannot pretend to solve the mystery of Christ's person.[45] Indeed, "there is no stronger defense against speculation than the confession of this Lord as he comes to us in the revelation of God. Here speculation succumbs before the faith which overcomes the world."[46] In contrast to a theologian like Wolfhart Pannenberg, who feels that the scriptural witness to the substitutionary death of Christ can be accepted only if it can be explained in terms of a thoroughly modern anthropology, Berkouwer is satisfied to state that "the doctrine of substitution is based squarely on the teaching of Scripture."[47] Acceptance of Scripture's teaching on this issue, as on other crucial issues, is not a matter of intellectual persuasion, for "only by the power of the Holy Spirit can [the] protests against substitution be conquered in the joyful accepting of this gift, namely, the forgiveness of sins."[48]

A Biblically Informed Faith Grounded in the Spirit's Witness

Over against a theology built on human speculation and rational argument, Berkouwer relentlessly defended a biblically informed theology founded upon the witness of the Holy Spirit. Rather than appealing to a philosophical system, he called believers to listen carefully to the Word of God.

43. Ibid., 183.
44. Ibid., 184.

45. G. C. Berkouwer, *The Person of Christ*, trans. John Vriend (Grand Rapids: Eerdmans, 1954), 249.
46. Ibid., 363.
47. G. C. Berkouwer, *The Work of Christ*, trans. Cornelius Lambregtse (Grand Rapids: Eerdmans, 1965), 309.
48. Ibid., 311.

Throughout his career he remained unswervingly committed to the Reformed principle of *sola Scriptura*. Scripture in every case must be the final authority for theology. It is in this area that Berkouwer raised his most serious complaint against Roman Catholic theology. In his *Conflict with Rome*, the Dutch edition of which was published in 1945, he pointed out that the Roman Catholic dependence on two sources of authority—Scripture and tradition—often relegates Scripture to the background.[49] Berkouwer later viewed the developments of the Second Vatican Council as promising because they indicated a shift away from the reliance on two authorities. Nonetheless, he wrote in *The Second Vatican Council and the New Catholicism* that the central problem still remained. For whenever church tradition serves to guarantee the interpretation of Scripture, it acts as an *a priori* authority which bypasses the need for living faith.[50]

But with his rejection of the Catholic notion of dual authorities, Berkouwer did not turn to a naive individualism for the interpretation of Scripture. He remained a committed confessional theologian. In almost every theological discussion one finds references to the various Reformed confessions: the Heidelberg Catechism, the Belgic Confession, the Canons of Dort, the Gallic Confession, the Westminster Confession. These confessions are an important part of theology and, next to Scripture, represent most clearly the faith of the church. Nonetheless, we ought ever bear in mind that they are only a reflection and must in the end yield to the witness of Scripture itself.[51]

But though this commitment to Scripture pervades Berkouwer's work from beginning to end, there is undeniably a development in his understanding of the nature of Scripture. In his earliest writing he had tried to construct a defensive bulwark against the encroachment of any and all biblical criticism; if one point were conceded, all might be lost. But in 1949, with the beginning of his dogmatic series, it became clear that Berkouwer intended to work out a new understanding that faith involves more than a formal acceptance of an infallible Bible. The faith aroused by the Holy Spirit has one central focus—salvation in Christ—which is identical with the focus of the apostolic witness found in Scripture. Keeping one's eye on this focus reduces the problems that have arisen as a result of the particular historical contexts in which the apostolic witness was delivered. For while the different historical situations evoked a variety of expressions, they all witness to the same message of salvation. Because his object of faith was no longer revelation in the abstract, but the concrete message of salvation in Christ, Berkouwer could now see various levels in Scripture that his earlier work had not recognized. Real historical situations had determined the way in which the gospel was presented; the result was varying levels of profundity in Scripture. What is important, however, is that their message is *essentially* the same.

By concentrating on the central focus of Scripture, Berkouwer was able to move beyond the "all or nothing" dilemma which had so dominated his earlier thought. Since only the message of salvation is essential, there is no reason to be preoccupied with the way in which it is presented, or to deny the influence of historical factors. We need not, as in kerygmatic theology, detach the apostolic preaching from the historical Jesus, nor, on the other hand, regard the Gospels as a scientific biography of Jesus. Their message, their purpose, is to speak of the Christ: "The historical record may have been strongly influenced by its kerygmatic purpose, but the final purpose of the gospel

49. G. C. Berkouwer, *The Conflict with Rome*, trans. H. de Jongste and David H. Freeman (Philadelphia: Presbyterian and Reformed, 1957), 32.

50. G. C. Berkouwer, *The Second Vatican Council and the New Catholicism*, trans. Lewis B. Smedes (Grand Rapids: Eerdmans, 1965), 137–38.

51. Berkouwer, *Faith and Justification*, 40; idem, *Person*, 91.

nonetheless is to demonstrate the truthfulness of what has been said of the Christ."[52]

For Berkouwer this emphasis on the central focus implies that Scripture should not be atomized. If we keep our eyes on the purpose of Scripture, we will not be sidetracked looking for independent information on other subjects:

> After all, theology as a science does not command some sort of special methodology which can reach that which other sciences, dealing with aspects of man's nature, cannot reach. . . . It has often been thought that this was indeed the case, and theologians have thought to find specific "data" which they could force the various sciences dealing with man to accept. In this way, a conflict arose between theology and the growing sciences dealing with man (such as psychology)—much in the same way that conflicts broke out when theologians made Scripture into a source of data regarding the natural sciences (physics, etc.). But such an interpretation does not realize that the real *scopus,* the real concern of revelation, is not the furnishing of such bits of information.[53]

This view received its clearest formulation in *Holy Scripture,* where Berkouwer carefully develops his insight concerning the central message of Scripture. The gospel is this message. The canon itself developed around it. That is, the first books to be accepted focused on salvation in Christ, and the later books were adopted because they adhered to this theme. Therefore, there is ultimately no distinction between the Bible and its message. There may be a center and a periphery, but it all witnesses to Jesus Christ. We are drawn to the central message of gracious salvation, and from there our trust moves out to the periphery of Scripture, which is always understood in relation to its center.

The Holy Spirit is a witness in and through the very words of Scripture which

bear this message of salvation. His testimony is not a guarantee of a formally inerrant book, but a convicting and convincing power regarding the content of Scripture. Thus authority is not granted to the Bible irrespective of its content, but is inextricably connected to the central message it carries.[54] The Spirit does not testify to the trustworthiness of the Bible before we read it and encounter the gospel:

> The *testimonium* does not supply an *a priori* certainty regarding Scripture, which afterwards is supplemented with and through its message. . . . The Spirit's witness begins by binding us to the center of Scripture, namely, Jesus Christ. The extent of this authority is of no significance at first. Only by degrees does Scripture begin to fascinate us by its organic composition in a gradual assimilation process regarding its content and its message.[55]

The Spirit evokes faith in connection with the experience of God's grace in the act of justification. One cannot know the witness of the Spirit to Scripture apart from an encounter with the central message of justification and salvation through Christ. Thus Berkouwer can approvingly quote Bavinck's statement that "our belief in Scripture decreases and increases together with our trust in Christ."[56]

The common phrase "the truth hurts" can help us comprehend Berkouwer's understanding of the witness of the Spirit. When someone says something critical about us, there is at times a tiny twinge of conscience deep inside which tells us that the truth has been spoken. Now that twinge does not come just before the other person speaks, so that we know beforehand that whatever is said next is going to be true. But it comes upon our actually hearing the statement, in connection with our giving ear to the words and grasping their mean-

---

52. Berkouwer, *Person,* 35.
53. Berkouwer, *Man,* 29–30.

54. G. C. Berkouwer, *Holy Scripture,* trans. and ed. Jack B. Rogers (Grand Rapids: Eerdmans, 1975), 32.
55. Ibid., 44–45.
56. Ibid., 44.

ing. In like manner, before we actually turn to the pages of God's Word, we receive no guarantee that here we will discover truth. Yet as we read the message we know it is true; this is no mere twinge of conscience, but the conviction of the Holy Spirit.

For Berkouwer this reliance upon the witness of the Spirit does not lead to subjectivism or pneumatic exegesis. The message to which the Spirit testifies comes to us in meaningful human language. By reading the actual words of the text and going through the normal process of human understanding, we come into contact with the gospel message, are convicted of sin, and experience God's grace and forgiveness. Along this path we also come to a confession of confidence in the authority of Scripture. From this starting point our confidence stretches across the many and varied witnesses contained in the Bible. But at every point the authority and infallibility of Scripture are to be seen in relation to the central message.

Berkouwer also found that his focus upon Scripture's central message guarded against the dualistic division between the Word of God and the Bible which he had seen in Barth's theology. There is no need to separate the Word of God from the actual words of Scripture, as if the Bible contains or becomes God's Word, but cannot be God's Word. The whole Bible is God's Word. We must be mindful, however, that the words in it are also human words, and therefore we must always interpret them in the light of Scripture's purpose.[57]

With the authority of Scripture firmly grounded in the Spirit's witness, we need no longer defend that authority by artificial human standards. If we encounter in the Gospels two accounts of the same event which differ in minor detail, we need not ask how this squares with modern standards of history. Rather, we should ask how these accounts serve the purpose of witnessing to salvation in Jesus Christ. It may

well be that minute accuracy is in no way the point of the accounts, in which case the detail provided does not reflect upon their reliability.[58]

Therefore, in contrast with his earlier view, Berkouwer is now willing to see certain aspects of the creation narrative as related to the polemical situation of Israel. But we must also note that Berkouwer still insists that Scripture should be judged only on its own grounds and not by external standards. In his earliest works Berkouwer had argued that science could become the "occasion" for a new understanding of Scripture, as long as that understanding was based on internal considerations, and not merely on external evidence. Now, in explaining his new exegesis of Genesis, he declares that "indeed, scientific research as an 'occasion' did play a role. But it cannot be stated that this occasion and the exegesis are in clear conflict with each other."[59]

Scientific research into the cosmologies of ancient Israel's contemporaries or into the origins of the earth might serve as occasion for further reflection as to what certain biblical imagery was intended to convey. But scientific results must never be allowed to contradict Scripture. They may be used only to make us ask whether we have truly allowed Scripture to speak or whether we have misconstrued its message. With regard to scientific research as an occasion for a new interpretation of the first chapters of Genesis Berkouwer says, "One asked himself whether the story itself might not contain various indications of [a] possibility [other than the literal interpretation of every detail], namely that the reality of creation as a good and beneficent act of God and the fall and guilt of man were spoken about in the form of a 'clothing' or 'imagery.'"[60] Thus Berkouwer's reevaluation is not to be understood as a capitulation to science, but as an interpretation based on a

57. Ibid., 184.

58. Ibid., 244–52.
59. Ibid., 295.
60. G. C. Berkouwer, *De Heilige Schrift*, 2 vols. (Kampen: J. H. Kok, 1967), 2:314–15.

closer examination of the Scripture itself, which was in turn occasioned by the results of scientific research.

In this way Berkouwer sought to overcome the "all or nothing" dilemma regarding Scripture's reliability. True, there is a time-bound structure to Scripture; the authors were not lifted out of their historical setting nor granted more knowledge of science and history than were their contemporaries. But this does not imply that one must sift out the human from the divine so that we are left with a dualistic concept of Scripture. For, as Berkouwer points out, all the human words are also God's words, and they are to be interpreted in the light of their divine purpose of witnessing to Christ.

Contributions and Influence

It is too early to determine the extent of Berkouwer's influence within evangelical theology. But his contributions to the ongoing theological discussion are clear at several points. Berkouwer once described Bavinck as "a model of how theology could be done with commitment to the truth combined with openness to problems, and carefulness in judgments against others."[61] This statement is certainly no less true of Berkouwer himself. He saw dialogue as crucial. "The alternative," he noted, "is *monologue*. And monologists are usually people who are afraid to let the gospel lead them into a genuine encounter with others."[62] The history of evangelical theology has often been marred by separatism, mistrust, and misunderstanding. In contrast, Berkouwer dedicated himself to open and honest dialogue, and worked hard to avoid reducing the theology of others to simplistic philosophical schemata.

That this approach can provide a workable model for future theologians is more than wishful thinking, for it has already opened meaningful conversation between Berkouwer's own evangelical and Re-

formed position and two principal partners in dialogue, the Roman Catholic Church and the dialectical theology of Karl Barth. From early on Berkouwer had engaged in debate with Roman Catholic theology concerning matters of authority. Though he strongly defended the Reformed position, he refused to stereotype the views of Roman Catholicism, and always had an eye out for movement and growth in it. In 1957, two years before Pope John XXIII's unexpected initiation of the Second Vatican Council, Berkouwer published *Nieuwe perspectieven in de controverse Rome-Reformatie* (*New Perspectives on the Controversy between Rome and the Reformation*), in which he demonstrated his acute awareness of the changes which were brewing within the Catholic church.[63] He was a Protestant observer at the council, and of his book *The Second Vatican Council and the New Catholicism* F. Haarsma, a Dutch Catholic professor, stated, "I consider that with this book he has really gone through the wrestling of the Council. He was totally involved. It affected his very heart. He suffered with us and rejoiced with us."[64] Berkouwer's most recent work, *Zoeken en vinden: Herinneringen en ervaringen* (*Seeking and Finding: Remembrances and Experiences*), published in 1989, also devotes a chapter to the ongoing discussion with the Catholic church.[65]

Berkouwer's continuing conversation with Barth's theology reflects a similar openness. His early book, *Karl Barth*, was so thoroughly critical that the only positive remark Barth made was that it had a nice cover. But Berkouwer's *Triumph of Grace in the Theology of Karl Barth* demonstrated such care to understand Barth's theological concerns that Barth himself referred to it as

61. Berkouwer, *Half Century*, 18.
62. Berkouwer, *Second Vatican Council*, 29.

63. G. C. Berkouwer, *Nieuwe perspectieven in de controverse Rome-Reformatie* (Amsterdam: Noord-Hollandscher, 1957).
64. F. Haarsma, interview recorded in *Gesprekken*, ed. Puchinger, 289–90.
65. G. C. Berkouwer, *Zoeken en vinden: Herinneringen en ervaringen* (Kampen: Kok, 1989).

a "great book."[66] And in his reflections on his career as recorded in *A Half Century of Theology*, Berkouwer devoted an entire chapter to analyzing the influential voice of Karl Barth.[67]

In addition to open dialogue, Berkouwer offers a model of a thoroughly biblical yet nonspeculative theological orientation. As Berkouwer refused to reduce the theology of others to simplistic terms, so he strove in his own theology not to be guided by predetermined philosophical principles, but to turn again and again with open ears to the Word of God. For the reader of Berkouwer's theology this is at the same time frustrating and refreshing. His shying away from systematizing makes it difficult to summarize in a few lines the major thrusts of his dogmatic studies, but it also provides the key for understanding what lies at their center point: an unquenchable desire to hear the voice of God without human *a prioris*. It is also for this reason that one searches Berkouwer's writings in vain for any explicit hermeneutic or philosophical prolegomena. His approach, however, is not a naive one which denies the influence of human prejudgment and preunderstanding, but a conscious refusal to grant them formal status alongside God's revelation.

This approach has been especially helpful in the continuing evangelical discussion concerning the authority of Holy Scripture. Berkouwer was concerned to defend the authority of Scripture on its own terms, without first predetermining the precise shape this authority should take. Recognizing that the Bible is God's book, we must, he declared, refrain from dictating the exact nature of its contents. Berkouwer's focus on the central message and the need to interpret all parts of Scripture in relation to

the single purpose of witnessing to Christ allowed him to make room for a variety of historical witnesses, each playing a particular role in clarifying the gospel of salvation. Thus Berkouwer steered a middle course between the neo-orthodox refusal to identify Scripture with the Word of God and a Warfieldian concept of scientific inerrancy.

But perhaps Berkouwer's most important contribution is his constant reminder that within the theological endeavor Christian faith must retain its receptive nature, since faith can never be other than the human correlate of God's gracious revelation. Therefore, as Berkouwer himself demonstrated so clearly, theology must always be willing and determined to listen: to the person in the pew, to the voice of the church in the confessions, to other Christian theologies, but above all to the ever-renewed voice of the Word of God.

Primary Sources

Berkouwer, G. C. *The Conflict with Rome.* Translated by H. de Jongste and David H. Freeman. Philadelphia: Presbyterian and Reformed, 1957.

_____. *A Half Century of Theology.* Translated by Lewis B. Smedes. Grand Rapids: Eerdmans, 1977.

_____. *Modern Uncertainty and Christian Faith.* Grand Rapids: Eerdmans, 1953.

_____. *Recent Developments in Roman Catholic Thought.* Translated by J. J. Lamberts. Grand Rapids: Eerdmans, 1958.

_____. *The Second Vatican Council and the New Catholicism.* Translated by Lewis B. Smedes. Grand Rapids: Eerdmans, 1965.

_____. *Studies in Dogmatics.* 14 vols. Grand Rapids: Eerdmans, 1952–76. Vol. 1, *Faith and Sanctification*, 1952; vol. 2, *The Providence of God*, 1952; vol. 3, *Faith and Justification*, 1954; vol. 4, *The Person of Christ*, 1954; vol. 5, *General Revelation*, 1955; vol. 6, *Faith and Perseverance*, 1958; vol. 7, *Divine Election*, 1960; vol. 8, *Man: The Image of God*, 1962; vol. 9, *The Work of Christ*, 1965; vol. 10, *The Sacraments*, 1969; vol. 11, *Sin*, 1971; vol. 12, *The Return of Christ*, 1972; vol. 13, *Holy Scripture*, 1975; vol. 14, *The Church*, 1976.

66. G. C. Berkouwer, *The Triumph of Grace in the Theology of Karl Barth*, trans. Harry R. Boer (Grand Rapids: Eerdmans, 1956); Karl Barth, *Church Dogmatics*, vol. 4, part 2, *The Doctrine of Reconciliation*, trans. Geoffrey W. Bromiley (Edinburgh: T. and T. Clark, 1958), xii.

67. Berkouwer, *Half Century*, 39–74.

_____. *The Triumph of Grace in the Theology of Karl Barth.* Translated by Harry R. Boer. Grand Rapids: Eerdmans, 1956.

Secondary Sources

Collord, Paul. "The Problem of Authority for Dogmatics in G. C. Berkouwer." Ph.D. diss., State University of Iowa, 1964.

Puchinger, George, ed. *Gesprekken over Rome-Reformatie.* Delft: W. D. Meinema, 1965.

Rogers, Jack B., and Donald K. McKim. *The Authority and Interpretation of Scripture.* San Francisco: Harper and Row, 1979.

Smedes, Lewis B. "G. C. Berkouwer." In *Creative Minds in Contemporary Theology,* edited by Philip Edgcumbe Hughes, 63–98. Grand Rapids: Eerdmans, 1966.

Vandenberg, Frank. *Abraham Kuyper.* Grand Rapids: Eerdmans, 1960.

Watts, Gary L. "The Theological Method of G. C. Berkouwer." Ph.D. diss., Fuller Theological Seminary, 1981.

Charles W. Carter

Charles R. Wilson

On May 14, 1905, Charles W. Carter was born in Southport, Indiana, just outside Indianapolis. More than eighty years later, he is presently scholar in residence at Indiana Wesleyan University. From an inauspicious beginning, he became a recognized religion scholar with a world vision, an astute professor who engaged more than twelve thousand students in scholarly endeavor, and a competent author of some twenty books on religion, philosophy, theology, ethics, and world missions.

Carter's first eighteen years gave little indication as to the direction of his life. They were marked by relative poverty and minimal opportunity for achievement, and life had little real meaning. He was nonreligious, illiterate regarding prayer and the Bible, and heedless of parental restraint and moral accountability.

After reaching the age of eighteen, Carter began to realize that his lifestyle was breaking to pieces on the hard edges of reality. On occasions he wondered if life were worthwhile. In later reflection upon his teen years, he wrote that he was like a wanderer in the great "Sahara Desert, with nothing but sandy waste stretching out before me."[1] But then in 1923 he experienced the great divide of his life. During a city-wide evangelistic meeting in the Methodist Episcopal Church of Brookings, South Dakota, he was converted to the Christian faith.

Carter's conversion changed the course of his life and thought. He experienced a remarkable opening of himself to the supernatural. This opening of himself involved a personal acknowledgment of and commitment to God as he is revealed in Jesus Christ and the Scriptures. Another result of Carter's conversion was an intense missionary concern to proclaim the Christian gos-

1. Charles W. Carter, *Missionaries Extraordinary: The Life and Labors of Charles and Elizabeth Carter* (N.p.: Charles W. Carter, 1982), 13.

209

pel. Within a year, he was preaching as opportunities occurred. He soon came to a clear inner conviction that he was called by God to dedicate his entire life to preaching the gospel of Jesus Christ. Realizing his need for training and education, he enrolled in Dakota Wesleyan University.

While at the university Carter was introduced to the theory of naturalistic evolution. During the 1920s many students were enamored of this theory, but Carter viewed it as a clear contradiction of the Bible. He was confused and enveloped in spiritual darkness that threatened to engulf even his reason. After months of severe struggle, in earnestness of spirit he opened his Bible and began reading the Genesis story. As he read, the light of Scripture broke upon him. A deep assurance came to him regarding the integrity and authority of the Bible and its account of origins. He resumed his university studies with a great calm in his soul. That assurance remained with him, for, as he wrote in 1982, "Nor has this humanistic theory of evolution ever shaken my faith since that day."[2]

In 1925, in order to prepare himself to preach, Carter enrolled in God's Bible School and Training Home. The education which he received there was greatly enhanced by the extracurricular requirements of preaching at city missions and doing personal evangelism among the poor and underprivileged of Cincinnati. The Bible-school training, together with its concomitants of preaching and personal evangelism, brought Carter a widening consciousness of the need for evangelism in other lands. He declared himself willing to go anywhere in the world for the sake of the gospel.

In 1928, after completing Bible school and being commissioned for missionary service by the Wesleyan Methodist Mission Board, Carter set sail with his young bride Elizabeth for a three-year term in Sierra Leone. Following this term of service, he enrolled in Marion College (now Indiana Wesleyan University), where he received the A.B. and Th.B. He took additional work at Winona Lake School of Theology, receiving the Th.M. in the summer of 1933.

Carter returned to Sierra Leone in 1934 to serve as principal and professor at the Clarke Memorial Biblical Seminary. These responsibilities whetted his interest in learning. While missionary service, preaching, and evangelism had been continuing imperatives in his life, he now acknowledged a deep yearning for Christian scholarship as well.

The Carters' service in Sierra Leone ended in 1945. Returning to the United States, Charles was offered a professorship at Marion College. This precipitated an intensive period of teaching as well as graduate study. From 1946 to 1957, he taught courses in missions, cultural anthropology, the Bible (especially the Book of Acts and the Epistles of Paul), and philosophy. During this time, he received the B.D. degree from Asbury Theological Seminary, and the M.A. and Th.M. degrees from Butler University.

In 1959 Carter joined the faculty of Taylor University, where he remained until 1971, adding ethics to the courses he had taught at Marion. In 1968 he was awarded an honorary D.D. by Asbury. During his 1969 sabbatical from Taylor, he served as a lecturer and missionary-evangelist in the countries of Taiwan, the Philippines, Japan, and India.

Amid all the teaching and all the traveling, Carter's life remained totally "directed toward spreading the Gospel of Christ throughout the world."[3] Thus, along with his extensive scholarly endeavors, he retained fidelity to his call to preach. Accordingly, he fulfilled the requirements for the office of elder in the Wesleyan Methodist Church and was ordained in 1934. Thereafter, preaching played an even greater role in his life. For he would never forget that, as

2. Ibid., 19.

3. Ibid., viii.

a consequent of his conversion, he had also received a divine call to proclaim the gospel.

Carter spent the years 1972–74 on Taiwan, teaching courses in Christian ethics, philosophy of religion, and theology at China Evangelical Seminary in Taipei and the Oriental Missionary Society Bible College in Taichung. This was a major opportunity to present in cross-cultural ministry the claims of the gospel of Christ. From 1974 to 1991 he once again taught at Marion College (Indiana Wesleyan), where he continues at present as scholar in residence.

A Contemporary Wesleyan Perspective on Theology

In the preface to *Contemporary Wesleyan Theology*, Carter articulates clearly his mature view of the authority of the Bible: "The divine revelation in the Judeo-Christian Scriptures is the plenary-dynamic, inspired, authoritative record of God's nature and will for mankind, and thus is absolute and infallible in itself."[4] Buttressed by such confidence in the authority of the Bible as the Word of God, his development of theological truths has proved to be biblical in substance and Wesleyan in methodology.

It may be helpful here to concisely describe the method John Wesley used to formulate doctrines for his Methodist societies in eighteenth-century Great Britain. He endeavored to develop a doctrinal consensus by assembling the clergymen and lay preachers who were assisting in the Methodist movement. These so-called conferences, the first of which was held in 1744, provided for open discussions. When Wesley's position regarding the particular doctrine under consideration was challenged, he would make his primary appeal to the Bible. However, recognizing the fact that appeal to the Bible alone rarely settles doctrinal controversies, he would then appeal

to Christian tradition, then to reason and logical coherence, and finally to Christian experience. Albert C. Outler summarizes Wesley's system of proof: "We can see in Wesley a distinctive theological *method*, with Scripture as its pre-eminent norm but interfaced with tradition, reason and Christian experience as dynamic and interactive aids in the interpretation of the Word of God in Scripture."[5]

Along with his distinctive method Wesley urged that theological discussion, like all human endeavors, be conducted in a spirit of love. This is made especially clear in his sermon entitled "Catholic Spirit," which begins, "It is allowed even by those who do not pay this great debt, that love is due to all mankind. . . . All men approve of this; but do all men practise it? Daily experience shows the contrary. . . . The two grand, general hinderances are, First, that they cannot all think alike; and, in consequence of this, Secondly, they cannot all walk alike."[6] Wesley uses the term *catholic* in the finest sense of that word, to refer to a person with an all-embracing love: "His heart is enlarged toward all mankind, those he knows and those he does not; he embraces with strong and cordial affection, neighbours and strangers, friends and enemies. This is catholic or universal love. And he that has this is of a catholic spirit."[7] Wesley encourages Christians who have differing, even irreconcilable theological opinions, to cultivate such a spirit: "I do not mean, 'Be of my opinion.' You need not: I do not expect or desire it. Neither do I mean, 'I will be of your opinion.' I cannot. . . . Keep you your opinion: I mine; and that as steadily as ever. You need not even endeavour to come over to me, or bring me over to you. . . . Let all opinions alone on

4. *A Contemporary Wesleyan Theology*, ed. Charles W. Carter, 2 vols. (Grand Rapids: Francis Asbury [Zondervan], 1983), 1:12.

5. Albert C. Outler, "The Wesleyan Quadrilateral in Wesley," *Wesleyan Theological Journal* 20.1 (Spring 1985): 9.

6. John Wesley, "Catholic Spirit," in *The Works of John Wesley*, 14 vols. (Kansas City, Mo.: Beacon Hill, 1979), 5:492–93.

7. Ibid., 503.

one side and the other: Only 'give me thine hand.'"[8] Theological opinion must not divide Christians, for they are called to love one another. There is an important distinction to be made here between divinely revealed truth and humanly devised opinion. Wesley recognized that the catholic spirit of love is an essential part of God's absolute truth, while the intellectual propensity to affirm theological opinions is strictly a human, and therefore fallible, endeavor.

Contemporary Wesleyan Theology, of which Carter is the general editor, epitomizes the Wesleyan methodology and a catholic spirit. Twenty-three theologians representing seven Wesleyan denominations contributed to this work, which aims at bringing the Wesleyan perspective to bear on contemporary Christian thought. Under Carter's editorial leadership, the project as a whole relies basically on the authority of Scripture as it covers various biblical, systematic, and practical aspects of theology.

Carter sets the general tone for *Contemporary Wesleyan Theology* in the preface, where he observes that "theology is man's rational understanding and interpretation of the absolute revelation and is thus necessarily relative to time and human culture."[9] It is obvious to him that God reveals while we merely theologize. God's revelation is complete and final; human theology is incomplete and finite. Carter explains that because theology is necessarily limited in apprehending revelation, the contributors to the project have, in a catholic spirit, been open to other views: "Although the authors are basically Wesleyan orientated in their theological persuasions, they are not narrow or constricted in their religious views or interpretations. They do not hesitate to investigate and appropriate the best from all theological scholarship that serves to illuminate and enforce the truth of God's divinely revealed Word."[10]

Having in the preface affirmed the authority of the Bible and acknowledged the limitations of theology, Carter also contributes to the text proper a strong theology of missions. He views the Bible as mandating the evangelization of the whole world. The epitome of the divine mandate is the Great Commission (Matt. 28:18–20). In a penetrating analysis Carter notes that this mandate rests on universal divine authority ("all authority"), is universal in scope ("all the nations"), enjoins disciples to complete obedience ("teaching them to observe all that I have commanded you"), and offers comforting assurance ("I am with you always").[11]

A Missionary Extraordinary

The Carters personify the implementation of the Great Commission. For many years they were involved in missionary endeavors. An account of their experiences in many lands is entitled *Missionaries Extraordinary*, a unique designation that in no way should be interpreted as implying superiority. Rather, it simply means "out of the ordinary" in the sense that many of their activities are not usually thought of as missionary activities. Not only have they been missionaries—they have been pastors and evangelists; they have been involved in the areas of health care and administration; there has been college and seminary teaching, as well as lecturing and writing. All of these endeavors give evidence of the impact which the divine mandate to take the gospel to the whole world has had on the Carters. Their lives of faithful obedience to God's Word bear witness to the sufficiency of his grace.

Carter has given special attention to the relation between the Old Testament and the divine mandate in the Great Commission. On the basis of the authority of the Bible, he rejects naturalistic evolution, for the Genesis account clearly affirms that the human race was created in the image of

8. Ibid., 499.
9. *Contemporary Wesleyan Theology*, ed. Carter, 1:12.
10. Ibid.

11. Ibid., 2:648–49.

God. With the fall, however, as recorded in Genesis 3, they became alienated from him. God in his love undertook to deal with this estrangement of his creation. Only divine efficacy was adequate to bring about reconciliation. God's plan for the reconciliation of humanity involved both Old Testament Israel and the incarnation of his own Son. Carter stresses that the purpose of Israel's election was to make known to all nations God's redemptive design involving the coming Messiah. Here Carter utilizes Johannes Blauw's distinction between the general direction of God's universal redemptive purpose to be accomplished through Israel and that of his purpose to be accomplished through Christ. The redemption accomplished through Israel was centripetal; that accomplished through Christ is centrifugal.[12] Through Israel the nations were to be drawn to God by beholding her faithfulness to him. Now that Christ has accomplished redemption, however, believing disciples are instead sent out into all the world.

Another tenet of Carter's missiology is that the contemporary ecumenical and evangelical views of the missionary task should be brought together. The ecumenical view is that the Bible emphasizes social and political liberation; the evangelical view is that the biblical mandate sets priority on personal repentance and salvation. How, then, should we view the missionary task of the twentieth century and beyond? Carter suggests that "ultimately there ought to be a way to bring the two sides of the debate together. Looking to a common authority in the Word, preaching salvation in Jesus Christ, and being dedicated to evangelizing the world should not preclude the possibility of identifying with people who suffer unreasonable economic, social, and political oppression."[13]

12. Ibid., 2:635.
13. Ibid., 2:680.

A Dynamic Approach to the Subject of the Holy Spirit

A theological truth which has been a subject of keen interest to Carter over the years is the Holy Spirit. A number of factors have served to produce and nourish this interest. First, during his missionary service in Africa, and later in South America, Mexico, and the Far East, he had occasion to witness unusual manifestations and activities of the Holy Spirit, including powerful spiritual awakenings and revivals. Second, his college and seminary teaching for many years focused on the Book of Acts, with its emphasis on the Holy Spirit at work through the apostles. Third, he dug even deeper into the subject when along with Ralph Earle he coauthored a major commentary on *The Acts of the Apostles* (1959).

In 1974 Carter's definitive work on the Holy Spirit, *The Person and Ministry of the Holy Spirit: A Wesleyan Perspective*, was published. The immediate circumstances behind this volume are worth noting. In the decade of the seventies there was a surge of interest in the Holy Spirit. In response a three-volume publishing project was proposed: three different authors were selected to represent, respectively, the Calvinist, the Pentecostal, and the Wesleyan view of the Holy Spirit. Carter's contribution to the project was a biblical study of the Holy Spirit from Genesis to Revelation. In Genesis we find the Holy Spirit already active in the creation of the universe, and particularly in the creation of humanity. And in Revelation the Spirit issues the final invitation to salvation in Christ: "The Spirit and the bride say, 'Come'" (Rev. 22:17 NASB).

Carter's Wesleyan orientation is evident in the preface of the book, where he points out that the Bible emphasizes the activity of the Holy Spirit. Therefore, Carter's study will be dynamic in its emphasis; that is, it will concentrate on the activity of the Holy Spirit in revealing God, the great divine plan, and the provision of redemption.[14] This dynamic emphasis avoids the theoretical, or speculative, approach that seeks to conceptualize the Holy Spirit. The dynamic approach focuses on the practical and the concrete. Here Carter cites John Wesley as his model: "It is a well-known fact that John Wesley was a *dynamic* rather than a systematic theologian. He was practical rather than speculative."[15] Wesley's emphasis on dynamic truth resulted in the moral and spiritual transformation of eighteenth-century Great Britain, a phenomenon that spread to North America and launched a missionary movement into virtually all the world.

The role of the Holy Spirit in the Book of Acts is one of Carter's main themes. In dealing with what happened on the day of Pentecost, when believers were baptized with the Holy Spirit, Carter frankly acknowledges that there are wide theological differences. Among evangelicals there are the Reformed, the Pentecostal, and the Wesleyan points of view. As a Wesleyan, Carter interprets the baptism with the Holy Spirit in terms of practical experience. The believers on the day of Pentecost experienced sanctification, the power and cleansing of the Spirit. This is the way God demonstrates his power and purity in the life of every believer, not only those who were present on the day of Pentecost, but believers of every generation. The baptism with the Holy Spirit is a sanctifying experience which is subsequent to the experience of regeneration. It is not, however, the end of the work of the Holy Spirit in believers. Romans 8 unfolds the continuing dynamic of the Holy Spirit in the life of the regenerate and sanctified believer.

It is significant for Carter that the baptism of the Holy Spirit on the day of Pentecost is entwined with the Great Commission given by Jesus Christ (Matt. 28:18–20; Acts 1:8). The witnessing of the disciples in response to the Great Commission did not begin until they were baptized with the Holy Spirit. On that occasion a divine miracle occurred in order that witnessing could take place. The "tongues" that were spoken by the disciples were various languages distinctly and intelligently uttered. Every member of the throng assembled in Jerusalem heard in his or her own language the disciples preaching and witnessing concerning the resurrection and lordship of Jesus Christ. Carter draws twelve conclusions regarding what happened on the day of Pentecost:

1. The miracle was wrought by the Holy Spirit.
2. It directly affected the disciples' speaking rather than the multitude's hearing.
3. It was necessary because of the presence of many nationalities.
4. The disciples' speech was intelligible to the multitude.
5. The languages were used by God to bring repentance.
6. Three thousand repented.
7. The conversion of so many attests to the genuineness of the miracle.
8. Acts 2 gives the most definitive account of the gift of tongues—here it is basically a vehicle for evangelization and a token of the universality of the Christian gospel.
9. Paul's discussion of speaking in tongues (1 Cor. 12–14) is in harmony with Luke's definitive presentation in Acts.
10. The gift of tongues in Acts 2 was for evangelistic purposes rather than for personal edification.
11. Peter's sermon centered on Jesus Christ rather than on speaking in tongues.
12. The divine gift of languages in Jerusalem on the day of Pentecost signified the beginning of the universal missionary program of the gospel as it is set forth by Christ in Acts 1:8.[16]

14. Charles W. Carter, *The Person and Ministry of the Holy Spirit: A Wesleyan Perspective* (Grand Rapids: Baker, 1974), 8.

15. Ibid.

16. Ibid., 216–19.

Carter's dynamic approach to the subject offers us a timely opportunity to rediscover the relevance of the Holy Spirit in our day. Whoever accepts the biblical account has far-reaching possibilities here and now through the Holy Spirit. He is given to all who believe in Jesus Christ for salvation. He makes life a matter of God's possibilities rather than human incapacities, God's promises rather than human anxieties, and God's presence rather than human plans and programs. The words of Zechariah, the prophet of old, are relevant for us, "Not by might nor by power, but by My Spirit, says the LORD of hosts" (Zech. 4:6 NASB).

A Wesleyan Approach to Ethics

Related to Carter's interest in the Holy Spirit as the dynamic for living the Christian life is his concern for an adequate dynamic for Christian ethics. This personal concern together with his awareness of a growing interest in ethical issues in recent decades was instrumental in the decision to collaborate with R. Duane Thompson in writing *The Biblical Ethic of Love*. In contrast to contemporary views of all ethical issues as relative and situational, Carter's view is absolute: "It is the position of the authors of this work that the Judeo-Christian faith offers an absolute ethical standard of altruistic love, motivated by the just and righteous God of the Bible who is Himself love, and who is revealed in the Holy Scriptures and taught and exemplified by His Son Jesus Christ."[17]

Like Wesley, Carter maintains that Christian ethics is founded upon and expresses the inner experience of a Christian. Paul describes that experience in Romans 5:5: "The love of God has been poured out within our hearts through the Holy Spirit who was given to us" (NASB). Setting forth the absolute Christian norm in ethics, Wesley says, "The Christian rule of right and wrong is the word of God, the writings of the Old and New Testament; . . . this being the whole and sole outward rule whereby [the Christian's] conscience is to be directed in all things."[18] Carter has confidence in this approach because eighteenth-century Great Britain was morally transformed by the dynamic ethic of the movement begun with Wesley. There is similar hope for the twentieth century if we accept God's revelation and give allegiance to the norm of moral righteousness and integrity manifested in the life and teaching of Jesus Christ.

Carter points out that there is an enabling power to help us put our good resolutions and worthy insights into practice. The good news is that the Holy Spirit has come. He is the objective dynamic that exerts moral power in the life of the Christian. The Holy Spirit is the hope for the ethical crisis of today.

In addition to a personal ethic, Carter speaks of a Christian social ethic. The Christian's moral relation to the state and to the family must reflect the vertical relationship which the Christian has with God. On this topic Carter draws principally from the ethical teachings Jesus lays down in the Gospels and Paul's application of these principles to practical Christian living. The essence of Paul's ethic is well summarized in Romans 13: the Christian political ethic (vv. 1–7); the Christian social ethic of mutual love (vv. 8–10); and the Christian personal ethic of righteous and holy living (vv. 11–14).[19] Carter insists that all successful moral reform moves from the personal area to the social, and not vice versa.[20]

A Wesleyan Eschatology

Carter has also given a Wesleyan perspective on eschatology. In *Life's Lordship over Death: A Study of Immortality and the*

---

17. Charles W. Carter and R. Duane Thompson, *The Biblical Ethic of Love* (New York: Peter Lang, 1990), ix–x.

18. John Wesley, "The Witness of Our Own Spirit," in *Works of John Wesley*, 5:136.

19. Carter and Thompson, *Biblical Ethic*, 138.

20. Ibid., 132.

Hereafter from a Wesleyan Perspective, he seeks to convey a solid Christian optimism and hope regarding the future. He states this aim in the preface: "If this book inspires in the minds and lives of the readers a renewed degree of optimism and hope for humanity and the universe in the outworking of God's redemptive plan through Jesus Christ, that will be the author's greatest reward."[21]

As Carter views the contemporary scene, he finds two extreme perceptions regarding the future. On the one hand, there is depressing pessimism; on the other hand, there is naive optimism. Carter offers a mediating perception, namely, a Christian realism as set forth by Paul in Romans 8:28: "We know that God causes all things to work together for good to those who love God, to those who are called according to His purpose" (NASB). Carter's mediating position unflinchingly reckons with the death-dealing effects of the fall, Satan, and sin; yet it also affirms that God is working out his redemptive plan for the final restoration of humankind and the created order. Paul provides some insight regarding the scope and content of the divine plan: "For the anxious longing of the creation waits eagerly for the revealing of the sons of God. For the creation was subjected to futility, not of its own will, but because of Him who subjected it, in hope that the creation itself also will be set free from its slavery to corruption into the freedom of the glory of the children of God" (Rom. 8:19–21 NASB).

It is Carter's view that immortality of the Christian's soul begins at conversion; thus the death of the body has no real effect.[22] Jesus Christ is the sole source of the Christian's immortality. He imparts the very life of God. "The life of Christ is an infinite divine energy which transcends all forms of empirical and sensible manifestations. It is God's life in Christ imparted by the Spirit to the true believer."[23] This immortality is characterized by a spiritual body, unending duration, freedom from sin and evil, personal identity and consciousness, and endless growth and development in God's grace. Carter takes great pains in analyzing the word *zōē,* which in the Greek New Testament denotes Christian immortality as qualitatively transcendent to the present mortal life. The term is used, especially by John, to set forth the life that comes by the new birth.

Associated with the discussion of the immortality of the soul is a consideration of heaven and its characteristics. For Carter, God and heaven are inseparable. The relation is indissoluble. Heaven is where God is. The very character of God constitutes heaven. When we are in right relationship with God, who is loving and just, we enjoy God's presence, and that is the essence of heaven. When we are not in right relationship with God, we experience God's justice, and that is the essence of hell.

As to the location of heaven, Carter seeks to avoid two extreme and erroneous views. First is the dualistic view of heaven and earth: there is a strict dichotomy between the present evil world of this realm below and God's holy world above. We currently live in the world below, which is wholly dominated by Satan, yet we look forward to the time when we will go home to heaven. Then the present creation will be completely destroyed. Carter asserts, "This is not the clear teaching of the Bible."[24]

Second is the immanentistic view, with advocates such as Rudolf Bultmann, Paul Tillich, and Harvey Cox. God and heaven are not transcendent to the present world order. God and heaven are not "out there." Rather, they are wholly immanent in the universe.

Dualism and immanentism are invalid explanations as to where heaven is. Dualism overemphasizes transcendence, locating heaven somewhere "out there." Imma-

21. Charles W. Carter, *Life's Lordship over Death: A Study of Immortality and the Hereafter from a Wesleyan Perspective* (Indianapolis: Wesley, 1988), xvi.

22. Ibid., 71.

23. Ibid., 86.

24. Ibid., 95.

nentism denies transcendence, locating heaven "here," within the present creation. Over against dualism and immanentism, Carter finds his position best expressed in the second stanza of an old evangelical song by C. F. Butler, "Where Jesus Is, 'Tis Heaven":

> Once Heaven seemed a far-off place,
> Till Jesus showed His smiling face;
> Now it's begun within my soul,
> 'Twill last while endless ages roll.

Heaven is both the experience of God's presence here and now by those who are redeemed and their hope of God's presence in the sweet by-and-by. There is a continuity between the present experience and the future hope. In the present, heaven has begun; in the future, heaven will continue forever. Secure in this truth, Carter closes his book on a note of indomitable Christian realism as well as vibrant expectation: "Thus in the final consummation of God's redemptive provision in Christ there will be demonstrated 'Life's Lordship over Death,' the God-given life that overcomes death forever."[25]

Evaluation

Charles Carter has contributed substantially to evangelical Christian life and thought. His varied activities—preaching, evangelizing, teaching, writing—have been in obedience to God and his call. Accepting the authority of the Bible, he has studied it with intense faithfulness and intelligent insight. He has consistently acknowledged that the Bible, as the Word of God, is the sufficient guide for redemption and sanctification.

Throughout his studies of the Bible, Carter has maintained an emphasis on practicality and applicability. While downplaying the theoretical and speculative elements in theology, he has made them serviceable to the practical. This approach, he

believes, is in keeping with the revealed truth of the Bible and the interpretive efforts of John Wesley. Carter's emphasis upon the enabling dynamic of theology has given his contributions a distinctive persuasiveness and power.

Carter has espoused Arminian and Wesleyan views in a manner worthy of note. His irenic and conciliatory approach is to be commended. It should also be noted that his intercultural experiences of many years have contributed to a worldwide outlook. His practicality has kept him in touch with real people of all ages and many cultures. He is sympathetic with those in the midst of trials, and he rejoices with those who experience triumphs.

Though Carter did not develop a comprehensive system of Christian thought, he has been a prolific writer on theological themes. Holding to the Bible as authoritative and trustworthy, he has been in the vanguard of efforts to provide a contemporary Wesleyan viewpoint in theology. He has fostered the Wesleyan spirit by encouraging open theological discussions. Relevant here is the distinction between divinely revealed truth, such as the importance of displaying a catholic spirit of love, and humanly devised opinions. That a catholic spirit has priority over the intellectual propensity to assert an opinion is part of the Wesleyan perspective and has been a guiding principle for Carter throughout his life and work.

Another effort to which Carter has been committed is the upholding of supernaturalism against the humanistic attempts to deny and even obliterate it as an option in worldviews. Again and again his contributions, both oral and written, have set forth compelling evidence and valid arguments in support of divine revelation. His most compelling point is that humanism has reduced us humans to the status of victims in the contemporary situation; however, supernaturalism offers us ultimate victory. Christian realism, affirming supernaturalism, proclaims, as was earlier noted, "We

25. Ibid., 115.

know that God causes all things to work together for good to those who love God, to those who are called according to His purpose" (Rom. 8:28 NASB).

Primary Sources

Carter, Charles W. *As They Prayed: Great Bible Prayers.* Salem, Ohio: Schmul, 1991.

_____. *A Half-Century of American Wesleyan Methodist Missions in West Africa.* Syracuse: Wesleyan Methodist Publishing Association, 1940.

_____. *Life's Lordship over Death: A Study of Immortality and the Hereafter from a Wesleyan Perspective.* Indianapolis: Wesley, 1988.

_____. *Missionaries Extraordinary: The Life and Labors of Charles and Elizabeth Carter.* N.p.: Charles W. Carter, 1982.

_____. *The Person and Ministry of the Holy Spirit: A Wesleyan Perspective.* Grand Rapids: Baker, 1974.

_____, and Ralph Earle. *The Acts of the Apostles.* Grand Rapids: Zondervan, 1959.

_____, and R. Duane Thompson. *The Biblical Ethic of Love.* New York: Peter Lang, 1990.

A Contemporary Wesleyan Theology. Edited by Charles W. Carter. 2 vols. Grand Rapids: Francis Asbury (Zondervan), 1983.

Wesleyan Bible Commentary. Edited by Charles W. Carter. 6 vols. Grand Rapids: Eerdmans, 1964–69.

Helmut Thielicke

C. George Fry

Helmut Thielicke was one of the giants of German theology in the twentieth century. Called the Lutheran Karl Barth and the German Athanasius, Thielicke has also been compared to such major preachers as W. M. Macgregor, Theodore Zahn, A. E. Garvie, A. J. Gossip, James Moffatt, and James S. Stewart.[1] Anglican divine Geoffrey Bromiley views Thielicke as an exponent of "a basic orthodoxy" who, amid a secular generation, engaged "in lively and thoughtful interaction with contemporary theological discussion."[2] As a minister whose career came to fruition during and after World War II, Thielicke has been hailed as a preacher for apocalyptic times whose teaching had a sense of eschatological urgency.[3] Many

have been attracted to his passion for social justice, labeling Thielicke the German Reinhold Niebuhr. Still others, impressed by his deeply felt compassion, have regarded him as a Johannine theologian whose preaching was rich in gospel proclamation, ethics, and apocalyptic vision. Rooted within the churchly tradition of German Lutheranism, Thielicke nevertheless took as a model the Baptist minister Charles Haddon Spurgeon, causing some to interpret his style as a synthesis of the State Church and the Free. For others, Thielicke's principal contribution was a free and creative theology of the Holy Spirit.

A Renaissance man of catholic interests, Thielicke cannot easily be placed within any of the usual divisions of theology. Ranging at will over the entire realm of religion, Thielicke was an exegete, church

1. John W. Doberstein, Translator's Note to *Christ and the Meaning of Life: A Book of Sermons and Meditations*, by Helmut Thielicke, trans. John W. Doberstein (New York: Harper, 1962), 7.

2. Geoffrey W. Bromiley, Editor's Preface to *Evangelical Faith*, by Helmut Thielicke, trans. Geoffrey W. Bromiley, 3 vols. (Grand Rapids: Eerdmans, 1974–82), 2:5.

3. Harold H. Zietlow, interview with author, Fort Wayne, 5 January 1992. Zietlow did postdoctoral work with Thielicke in the 1960s at the University of Hamburg. Several of the following characterizations of Thielicke are drawn from this interview.

historian, ethicist, systematician, and pastoral theologian.[4] For some this also means that Thielicke is impossible to label theologically. To that charge Thielicke himself replied, "My adversaries hung the title *conservative* around my neck in derision—I wear it with pride."[5] Perhaps it is safest to say that Helmut Thielicke was a universal man doing total theology from deeply held evangelical convictions, but addressing the ecumenical church.[6] A memorial summation in *Christianity Today* stated, "Though Thielicke takes positions that put him at odds with American evangelicals at some points, his work in ethics and systematic theology has shown him to be an innovative interpreter well within the mainstream of historic Christian faith."[7]

4. "Thielicke's published output is prodigious in scope and erudition," notes John W. Doberstein, Translator's Introduction to *The Waiting Father: Sermons on the Parables of Jesus*, by Helmut Thielicke, trans. John W. Doberstein (New York: Harper, 1959), 9.

5. Zietlow, interview.

6. The word *evangelical* has several meanings. In sixteenth-century Germany it meant Lutheran as opposed to Roman Catholic. In nineteenth-century Europe "evangelical" referred to the Low Church party within the Anglican church; it also denoted the United Church of Prussia, which brought Lutheran and Reformed Christians together in 1817. Sometimes within Lutheran usage "evangelical" means "gospel-based" as opposed to "law-oriented"; it refers to an ethic centered in grace rather than judgment. In twentieth-century America "evangelical" describes those Christians who hold to the authority of Scripture, the centrality of grace, and the necessity of personal conversion followed by sanctified living. As a Lutheran who worked often in union churches and relied heavily on the Word and a personal trust in Jesus, Thielicke was predictably "evangelical." After touring the United States in 1963, he mused, "People of all denominations and theological tendencies were apparently ready to listen to me. The liberals probably thought: He speaks in modern style, so he must be one of us; the Baptists said: He has written a book on Spurgeon, so he is close to us; the fundamentalists noted that my sermons were expositions of biblical texts and often included me in their ranks; and the Lutherans said: After all, he comes from Hamburg, *ergo*. . . ." (Helmut Thielicke, *Between Heaven and Earth: Conversations with American Christians*, trans. John W. Doberstein [New York: Harper and Row, 1965], xiv).

7. Roger Lundeen, "Helmut Thielicke Is Dead at 77," *Christianity Today*, 18 April 1986, p. 42.

Life

The Early Years

Helmut Thielicke's life spanned most of the twentieth century. Born in Wuppertal, Germany, on December 4, 1908, he was the son of the local rector, Reinhard T. Thielicke, and his wife Laura (Lore) Koehler. Thielicke died in Hamburg on March 5, 1986.[8] His was a traditional middle-class German upbringing, and Thielicke frequently recalled the joys of a childhood in imperial Germany when everything seemed secure. Typical is his recollection of a summer at camp when excess energy exploded into all kinds of mischief. For instance, a group of campers would play a game called "Here Comes the Holy Ghost"—covering themselves with sheets, they "descended upon innocent sleepers [and] had all kinds of fun when a small panic broke out in the dark room."[9]

Nurtured in the Lutheran faith, Thielicke could not recall a time when Jesus was not his Lord and Savior. This is not to imply that his faith was conventional. He had an intense sense of the supernatural and a conviction of Christ's personal guidance of the events of his life. Witness his own testimony regarding one of those events:

Some years ago I was paralyzed and medical science was unable to do anything further for me. At that time the head of a well-known university gave it as his opinion that I had only a few months to live. Then in these months—actually a short time before the doors were to close, as I was approaching the end in full consciousness of my condition—the news suddenly arrived that a new medicine had been discovered which could cure or at least keep within limits this illness, hitherto beyond control. This was the medicine that keeps me alive, and which at that time suddenly restored a

8. For biographical sketches see *Contemporary Authors: New Revision Series*, ed. Ann Evory (Detroit: Gale, 1984), 11:500–502; *Brockhaus Enzyklopädie*, 17th ed., s.v. "Thielicke, Helmut."

9. Thielicke, *Christ and the Meaning of Life*, 56.

doomed cripple and turned him into an able-bodied man.[10]

While this discovery came about quite naturally in the course of scientific research, Thielicke viewed it as a miracle: the Lord "disposed these chains of causality in such a way that they had to meet at this specific moment." Like John Wesley, who saw a particular purpose in his having been spared from the flames of the burning rectory when he was six years old, Thielicke preached that when one encounters Christ, one must leap or retreat.[11] "God is no piker," Thielicke declared. "He has said that he who comes to him will not be cast out. But you *must* come to him, you must beseech and besiege him."[12] For Thielicke, then, faith was existential, nurtured on one's encounter with Christ in Scripture.

An ardent reader of the Bible from childhood, one of Thielicke's favorite books was Job. Once, while traveling in the tropics, Thielicke reflected on the infinity of the inner structure of the Bible: "God opens up new dimensions for me every time I read it. Shall I ever sound it out?"[13] Having early on sensed God's direction in his life, he affirmed that "the Christian is and always will be an adventurer, who can never make long-range plans, but rather waits for God's decisions."[14]

Persuaded of the Spirit's guidance, Thielicke prepared for the ministry in typical German fashion, attending a number of universities—Greifswald, Marburg, and Bonn—and then taking two doctorates from Erlangen (a Ph.D. in 1931, a Th.D. in 1934). From 1936 until 1940 he taught at the University of Heidelberg and then in 1941 accepted ordination into the State Church, where he would invest his entire ministry. Believing that "we have not yet fully exploited the possibilities of the national church," Thielicke urged evangelicals not to abandon it. It was imperative to remain in the mixed churches, where there was a prime need for instruction and information. "Either the church will do its basic work and turn to the foundation of its faith," he declared, "or it will die." On the other hand, in words reminiscent of another major German theologian, C. F. W. Walther (spiritual father of the Lutheran Church–Missouri Synod), who felt convinced of the need to separate from the national church, Thielicke admitted, "The local rain of the gospel can easily pass and water more receptive fields. If I read the signs aright, we are close to midnight."[15]

Thielicke began his ministry in the twilight, if not at midnight. The land of Bach, Beethoven, Brahms, and Thomas Mann had produced Adolf Hitler and National Socialism. After the security of his childhood in the days of the Kaiser,[16] Thielicke came of age in a Germany faced with defeat in a world war, the shame of the imposed Treaty of Versailles, the instability of the Weimar Republic, the great inflation of 1923 followed by the temporary prosperity

10. Helmut Thielicke, *Man in God's World*, trans. John W. Doberstein (New York: Harper and Row, 1963), 101.

11. Helmut Thielicke, *I Believe: The Christian's Creed*, trans. John W. Doberstein and H. George Anderson (Philadelphia: Fortress, 1968), x.

12. Thielicke, *Waiting Father*, 192.

13. Helmut Thielicke, *African Diary: My Search for Understanding* (Waco: Word, 1974), 12.

14. Thielicke, *Between Heaven and Earth*, 6.

15. Helmut Thielicke, *The Hidden Question of God*, trans. Geoffrey W. Bromiley (Grand Rapids: Eerdmans, 1977), 31–33. Like many evangelicals in mixed or inclusive churches, Thielicke wrestled with the problem of pluralism: "If pluralism means variety of theological standpoints and practical emphases, then it can be the sign of a living organism whose members have different functions. In spite of the variety of functions there can then be knowledge of the common root and of common fellowship in one body. Without the common center, however, pluralism can be the mark of centrifugal disintegration" (p. 28).

16. Today we know that the security of the Second Reich (1871–1918) was not all that it seemed to be. See Robert K. Massie, *Dreadnought: Britain, Germany, and the Coming of the Great War* (New York: Random House, 1991). Massie regards the prewar decade as a prelude to the coming of Armageddon. Robert Asprey, *The German High Command at War: Hindenburg and Ludendorff Conduct World War I* (New York: Morrow, 1991), has given us some insight into the futility and cost of World War I.

of the late twenties, the collapse of the economy in 1929, a political impotence generated by the proliferation of parties, and the fear of the rise of communism. By the time Thielicke graduated from Erlangen, the "people clamored for the strong man, the apocalyptic redeemer figure." Into this context came the strong man who "knew how to dissemble. . . . One had to look very closely to see the cloven hoof beneath the angel's luminous robes."[17]

No force seemed able to stop the rise of Hitler. The military was trained to be non-political and to render obedience to their leader. Germans had a great respect for the state and a profound distrust of rebellion. The royal family had fled, and the old aristocracy was discredited. Democratic institutions were fragile and perceived as having been imposed by foreign powers. For Thielicke, however, the problem was ultimately theological: a spiritual failure had seized Germany. There was a false anthropology; humans were regarded in terms of their functional ability. Since they were but machines, the solution to all difficulties seemed to be to find the most efficient operator (*Führer*, Hitler's favorite title, literally means "conductor" or "driver," as in streetcar operator). The church, Thielicke was convinced, had failed to show that "the dignity of man rests not upon his functional ability, but rather upon the fact that God loves him, that he was dearly purchased, that Christ died for him, and that therefore he stands under the protection of God's eternal goodness."[18]

The German church was ill prepared to meet the crisis of National Socialism. Christianity in Germany was divided into four main communities: Roman Catholic, Lutheran, Reformed, and United (a merger of the Lutheran and Reformed traditions). Within the predominant Protestant population there had been a proliferation of theologies since the heyday of confessionalism in the sixteenth century.[19] The Age of the Baroque had seen the confessional churches polarized between orthodoxy (later called repristinationist theology) and Pietism (or experiential religion). During the German Enlightenment a widespread rationalism ("the rule of reason in matters religious") infected the elite of society. After the French Revolution and Napoleon a variety of reconstructionist efforts had been attempted, ranging from the romanticism of Friedrich Schleiermacher to the idealism of Georg Hegel. With the Industrial Revolution came the rise of nihilism and secularism and the effort by some, like Adolf von Harnack, to evolve a mediating and ethical liberalism. Prior to the Great War classical liberalism was probably the most popular brand of Protestantism in the universities. Karl Barth's *Römerbrief* in 1919 was a clarion call for a return to the canon, the confessions, the creeds, and the historic cultus. In response to Barth's biblical Christianity, a Confessing Church arose in Germany in the 1930s. It is with that church within the German church that Thielicke identified.[20]

17. See Helmut Thielicke, "Why the Holocaust?" *Christianity Today*, 27 January 1978, pp. 8–14, for a brilliant analysis of those times.

18. Ibid., 10–11. A classic contemporary report is William L. Shirer, *Berlin Diary: The Journal of a Foreign Correspondent, 1934–1941* (New York: Knopf, 1941); see also his monumental *Rise and Fall of the Third Reich* (New York: Simon and Schuster, 1960); and idem, *20th Century Journey: A Memoir of a Life and the Times*, vol. 2, *The Nightmare Years, 1930–1940* (Boston: Little, Brown, 1984).

19. For background see C. George Fry, ed., *The Age of Lutheran Orthodoxy, 1530–1648* (Fort Wayne: Concordia Theological Seminary Press, 1979); idem, *European Theology, 1648–1914* (Fort Wayne: Concordia Theological Seminary Press, 1976); idem, *Protestant Theology, 1914–1975* (Fort Wayne: Concordia Theological Seminary Press, 1977); C. George Fry and Duane W. H. Arnold, eds., *A Lutheran Reader* (Fort Wayne: Concordia Theological Seminary Press, 1982); and idem, *The Way, the Truth, and the Life: An Introduction to Lutheran Christianity* (Grand Rapids: Baker, 1982).

20. Erwin L. Lueker sees Thielicke as strongly influenced by Barth; see "Dogmatics," in *Lutheran Cyclopedia*, ed. Erwin L. Lueker, rev. ed. (St. Louis: Concordia, 1975), 242–44; see also Thielicke's penetrating study *Nihilism: Its Origin and Nature, with a Christian Answer*, trans. John W. Doberstein (New York: Harper, 1961).

Even in the worst of times a Christian, Thielicke believed, is to fulfil his role in the natural order of life. Indeed, Martin Luther had once remarked that even if he knew the Lord was returning on the morrow, he would plant a tree today. A chief element in the natural order of life for Lutherans is marriage and a family. On September 28, 1937, Helmut Thielicke married Marie-Luise Hermann. To this union were born four children—Wolfram, Berthold, Elisabeth, and Rainer. Thielicke's happiest times were spent with his family. Together with his children he loved to play with the family dogs and to go hunting, fishing, or mushrooming. In spite of the Nazi tyranny and then the terrors of the Second World War, the Thielickes developed a strong family life. Crucial to their sense of community were daily devotions, for Thielicke believed that the father is priest to his family. Next in importance to praying was reading; thus the children were read to for an hour almost every day.[21] Both mind and soul were nurtured in the Thielicke home. Thielicke had nothing but praise for any woman "who watches over the souls of children, who teaches them to pray and brings them up to be true men—true men because they stand before God—that woman is not only the guardian of the sphere of private life and the home; she is also one of the secret powers and means of the Kingdom of God that influence the public and thaw the ice of the godless systems with simple, insignificant-seeming grains of salt which are the eternal Word."[22] For Thielicke his home was a sanctuary and refuge as he carried on his ministry in very difficult times.

World War II

It was not at all evident in 1941 when Thielicke was ordained a Lutheran pastor that he would become one of Germany's most distinguished ministers, eventually

receiving the Great Cross of the Order of Merit as well as honorary doctorates from the universities of Heidelberg (1946), Glasgow (1956), and Waterloo, Canada (1974), and from Lenoir Rhyne College (1975), nor that for forty-five years he would serve both in the parish and in the university, including a term as president of the Conference of University Rectors for the German Federal Republic (1951). Although destined to become known as the most prominent of German Lutheran dogmaticians, Thielicke in 1940 was removed by the state from his initial teaching position at the University of Heidelberg. Thielicke later recalled with gratitude that his unemployment ended when "Bishop Theophil Wurm of the territorial church in Württemberg, who played a significant role in the confessing church, accepted the outlaw and provided me with a pastorate in the little town of Ravensburg in the extreme south of Germany. There the secret police imposed an injunction which proscribed my traveling or speaking anywhere else in the country. Only in the town itself was I permitted to preach. I had long since been forbidden to publish."[23]

For a while Thielicke was isolated like John on the isle of Patmos, and visions of the apocalypse became everyday reality. Writing from Ravensburg to a former student, a soldier soon to die in action, Thielicke reflected that events like terrors, wars, and natural catastrophes have never opened the way to God. "Not even the famous 'March of God through history' was noisy enough to force people to listen. It took more than that. . . . People finally began to listen and turn to God only when the prophets . . . empowered by the gift of God's Spirit, were there to 'interpret' that march and those events." Thielicke concluded, "The promise was attached to the Word of God, not to God's march."[24]

21. Thielicke, *Christ and the Meaning of Life*, 154.
22. Helmut Thielicke, *The Freedom of the Christian Man: A Christian Confrontation with the Secular Gods*, trans. John W. Doberstein (New York: Harper and Row, 1963), 215.

23. Helmut Thielicke, *Death and Life*, trans. Edward H. Schroeder (Philadelphia: Fortress, 1970), ix.
24. Ibid., xviii. The student was Hans Felix Hedderich, a doctoral candidate.

Exiled by the policies of the Third Reich, Thielicke found comfort solely in the Word of God. Emerging as an eloquent preacher of the Scriptures, he was called to head the Theological Office of the Church of Württemberg (1943–45) and was given permission by the Nazi authorities to deliver an evening lecture each week in the historic Stuttgart Cathedral. Thielicke knew that he "must prepare people for the terrible things that lay before them by giving them instruction—quite simply, just instruction in the mysteries of our faith."[25] For that purpose Thielicke turned to the *Enchiridion* or *Small Catechism* of Martin Luther. As he lectured on its five principal parts—the Ten Commandments, the Apostles' Creed, the Lord's Prayer, baptism, and the Lord's Supper— "evening after evening some three thousand persons gathered together: workers and businessmen, students and professors, soldiers and generals, Nazi functionaries (naturally in civilian clothes!) and Jews, Dutch compulsory laborers . . . and sometimes whole classes from the schools. It was an overwhelming time for me. Never since have I experienced such intense listening."[26]

Soon the massive air raids began. When the streetcars could no longer run, people "came on foot, often from many miles away, through the fields of ruins and rubble" even on dark and frightening winter evenings.[27] But then the cathedral itself was destroyed. Thielicke wrote, "I can still see the towering torch of this venerable house of God. . . . I stood there holding in my hand a key to a door that no longer existed."[28]

During such terrible times Luther's words rang true:

> Let goods and kindred go,
> This mortal life also;
> The body they may kill;
> God's truth abideth still,
> His kingdom is forever.

Hungering for the comfort of God's truth, Thielicke's dispersed audience demanded that he continue his series. Two meeting places out in the suburbs were located, but they were also destroyed. Then in even more distant Bad Cannstatt the fellowship reassembled and the series resumed. Because the Nazis refused him permission to place a regular advertisement, Thielicke simply ran the small notice, "Thursday, 8 P.M. T." The congregation gathered. "The hall was so overcrowded," Thielicke remembered, "that I was apprehensive of what might happen if an air-raid alarm occurred." When this actually happened at a subsequent meeting, Thielicke asked everybody to leave quietly for the bomb shelter. Then he gave the benediction while the organist played an evening hymn. One of the last to leave, Thielicke found the bomb shelter by the light of the flashing guns, but those inside refused to admit him. Persistently pounding on the door, he was finally pulled inside. The organist, however, had been killed.[29]

The lectures resumed and more than two hundred members of the audience took notes, each making at least ten copies to send to soldiers at the front. Later Thielicke learned that in this way "the eternal Word had been a comfort and a stay to them in the cold steppes of Russia or the desert sands of Egypt."[30]

By 1944 the impending collapse of the Third Reich was evident. The Anglo-American invasion of Normandy assured the oppressed that liberation was near. Concurrently, however, the failure of the German conspiracy to assassinate Hitler, in which the Confessing Church (including Thielicke) had been involved, guaranteed that the Nazis would fight to the bitter end.[31] Later Thielicke described the end of the war as a decisive moment, a potentially

25. Thielicke, *Man in God's World*, 8.
26. Ibid., 8–9.
27. Ibid., 9.
28. Ibid.
29. Ibid., 9–10.
30. Ibid., 10–11.
31. Because of his role in the plot, Thielicke narrowly escaped the gallows; see "Helmut Thielicke," *Christian Century*, 19–26 March 1986, p. 290.

precious and fruitful hour for the gospel. With the collapse of their country the Germans went through a tremendous shock and turned to the only surviving institution, the church, for answers. But "the Church at that time did not find the message for the hour." Failing to preach repentance and salvation, it offered instead "a proclamation of a collective guilt and a hysteria of self-accusation" which led to a psychological rather than theological understanding of recent German history. While there was a return to religion, there was no national revival, for "we seemed to be denied a prophetic awakening."[32]

The Postwar Years

The Second World War (1939–45) was the watershed of Thielicke's life. His initial thirty-seven years (1908–45) had been spent in preparation for ministry and in opposition to the Nazi tyranny. His remaining years would be invested in the theological and ethical reconstruction of German Christianity. For nine years, from 1945 to 1954, Thielicke would serve as a professor of systematic theology at Tübingen, acting as rector of the university in 1951. In 1954 there came a call to be the first dean of the theological faculty at the University of Hamburg as well as preacher at the historic St. Michael's Church. By the time of his retirement in 1974 Thielicke had a reputation

as a churchman on all levels—an effective parish pastor, an influential leader in the regional State Church, a national spokesman for German evangelicalism, a European Protestant recognized on both sides of the Iron Curtain, and a global interpreter of the faith, equally at home in North America, Black Africa, or East Asia.[33] To many who met him Thielicke seemed a unique blend of the confessional (Lutheran), evangelical, and ecumenical streams within world Christianity.[34]

Preaching

"The value of a dogmatics," Thielicke wrote, "depends on whether it can be preached."[35] He was convinced that preaching has primacy over theology.[36] In part that is because "our faith is greater than our theology."[37] It is also because "the primary decisions are reached in the preaching, where the active Word becomes Event."[38] Thus Thielicke's theology must be viewed as a theology of the pulpit. In an age when most German clerics regarded themselves as either university or church theolo-

---

32. Thielicke, "Why the Holocaust?" 12–13. This is not to deny that many individuals claimed the promises of faith. During the cleanup after one air raid, Thielicke was garbed in work clothes and all covered with grime. Not recognizing him, a woman asked where Pastor Thielicke was. When assured of his identity, she showed him her husband's cap and said, "This is all that was left of him. Only last Thursday I was with him attending your lecture, and I want to thank you for preparing him for his death." Then she quietly shook Thielicke's hand (Thielicke, *Man in God's World*, 10). On other occasions Thielicke gave catechism lessons to twenty boys from a Latin school who were manning an antiaircraft battery outside Stuttgart—"I walked out to visit them regularly and we sat down among the guns and talked about the 'last things'" (Helmut Thielicke, "But Man Fell on Earth," *Christianity Today*, 4 March 1977, p. 13).

33. Thielicke, *I Believe*, 231, records a remarkable yet typical incident: "Once, kneeling in the prairie sand of South-West Africa, I celebrated the Lord's Supper with some Herero tribesmen. They had never heard of our city, and I had known nothing of that remote bush country, 'where the deer and the antelope play.' Neither of us understood a single word of the other's language. But when I made the sign of the cross with my hand and pronounced the name 'Jesus' their dark faces lit up. We ate the same bread and drank from the same chalice, despite *Apartheid*. . . . Then the scales fell from my eyes. . . . I understood the miracle of the Church."

34. Americans especially noted this unique blend. Said one American admirer, "You have freed the fettered and bound the wandering spirits" (Thielicke, *Between Heaven and Earth*, xv).

35. Thielicke, *Evangelical Faith*, 1:378.

36. Helmut Thielicke, *How Modern Should Theology Be?* trans. H. George Anderson (Philadelphia: Fortress, 1969), 85. See also Helmut Thielicke, *Die Angst des heutigen Theologie Studenten von dem geistlichen Amt* (Tübingen: Mohr, 1967).

37. Thielicke, *Between Heaven and Earth*, 45.

38. Thielicke, *How Modern Should Theology Be?* 85.

gians, Thielicke was both. His American friend, admirer, and translator, John Doberstein, found this synthesis of the academy and the parish to be the key to Thielicke's theology:

> Here is a university professor, steeped in the lore and language of theology and philosophy, who, nevertheless, because of his closeness to life and his passionate concern to communicate to men in real life, can draw, without benefit of public relations techniques and high-powered promotional build-up, thousands of people, young and old, men and women, sophisticated students and ordinary shopworkers, filling the largest church in non-church-going Hamburg (capacity four thousand) on Sundays and again during the week.[39]

Though Thielicke was an effective teacher and scholar, his major contribution to theology was made as a preacher. Like the American Congregationalist, Washington Gladden, who remarked that nearly all of his forty books had originated from his preparation of sermons, so Thielicke could assert, accurately, that most of his publications resulted from his preaching labors. Comparing Thielicke's sermons to the Oxford movement's "Tracts for the Times" in terms of their impact on the contemporary church, Bromiley views Thielicke as one of the greatest German-language preachers since Luther.[40]

Thielicke preached in a wide variety of settings, from the parish church in Ravensburg to the great cathedral in Stuttgart, from open-air meetings on the African veldt to sedate college chapels in America. Perhaps he is most remembered for his innovative Saturday evening services at St. Michael's, the largest church in Hamburg. Writing in 1967, after a decade of preaching

from that pulpit, Thielicke spoke with love of the "green spire of Saint Michael's, towering high over the Elbe."[41] On the eve of each Sabbath a large and diverse congregation would assemble, some coming from distant suburbs, some walking from adjacent slums; some devout believers, others casual seekers; but the wonder was that between three and four thousand people came into the heart of what has been called the German Corinth to hear a professor preach. His power derived in part from his physical presence. Towering more than six feet three inches in height, Thielicke was an imposing figure when garbed in black robe and doughnut-shaped clerical collar. Doberstein was impressed with Thielicke's style, his "deep scholarly, Biblical, and theological mastery with strong, vividly colorful, pictorial utterance, eschewing the worn cliché and employing the stirring verb and the fascinating picture."[42] Bromiley noted his use of the apt quotation, the striking simile, the hymns of the church, and powerful illustrations from experience; equally impressive were his vividness, forceful arrangement, and awareness of the needs of real people, a characteristic that caused many to call him existential.[43] His rapid speaking, effective gestures, penetrating glance, and rich voice combined with his warm, personal, pastoral manner to make a Thielicke sermon an event.

Lutheran Elements

As a preacher, Thielicke combined elements of both the Lutheran and Free Church traditions. We can identify at least six distinctively Lutheran traits:

1. Thielicke's preaching was biblical. Textually based and exegetically developed, his sermons were expositions of specific passages. "The Bible," Thielicke believed,

39. Doberstein, Translator's Introduction to *The Waiting Father*, 7.

40. Geoffrey W. Bromiley, Introduction to *The Silence of God*, by Helmut Thielicke, trans. Geoffrey W. Bromiley (Grand Rapids: Eerdmans, 1962), v.

41. Thielicke, *I Believe*, xiv.

42. Doberstein, Translator's Note to *Christ and the Meaning of Life*, 7.

43. Bromiley, Introduction to *The Silence of God*, vi–vii.

"gives us an account of a living history, a living encounter of living men with the living God."[44] The personal Word, Christ, comes in the written Word, the Bible, through the articulated word, preaching, to become the saving word, conversion in the listener's heart. Here Thielicke held to the formal principle of the Lutheran Reformation: doctrine is derived from the Holy Scriptures and the pure Word of God. His sermons often followed the pericopes of the liturgical calendar or were presented as series, for instance, on the parables, temptations, or miracles of Christ, the petitions of the Lord's Prayer, or the first twelve chapters of Genesis.[45]

2. Thielicke's preaching was evangelical. Christ-centered and oriented toward the cross, his sermons stressed the atonement. Like Dwight L. Moody, the American lay evangelist, Thielicke felt that any sermon that did not make clear the way of salvation was a failure. Here Thielicke held to the material principle of the Lutheran Reformation: faith is the way of salvation, which is found only in Jesus Christ. If preaching is based on the Bible (*sola Scriptura*), its content will be Christ (*solus Christus*) and his grace (*sola gratia*) received by faith alone (*sola fide*). That content, once it is assimilated by the individual, must be shared. "We receive the liberating gift of forgiveness only if we pass it on immediately," said Thielicke.[46] A good example of the evangelical nature of Thielicke's preaching is his sermon on "The Joy of Repentance." He quoted Friedrich Rückert's verse with favor:

> In every man there lives an image
> Of what he ought to be.
> As long as he is not that image,
> He ne'er at rest will be.

Rest, continued Thielicke, can be found only through saving faith in Jesus.[47]

3. Thielicke's preaching was confessional. Bound by the three ecumenical creeds—the Apostles', the Nicene, and the Athanasian—and by the distinctive doctrines of the Evangelical Lutheran Church as stated in the Book of Concord (1580), Thielicke preached the faith of the church, not his own subjective opinions. Neither a repristinationist nor a reconstructionist, Thielicke was a dynamic teacher of historic Christianity. "The basic truths of the faith," he declared, "are obviously constant and unalterable."[48] The confessions help the minister distinguish between *Glaubensgrund* ("the foundation of faith") and *Glaubensgedanken* ("thoughts about faith," i.e., teachings that supplement, illustrate, or explain the fundamentals).[49] Creeds are road maps guiding the traveler safely

44. Thielicke, *Between Heaven and Earth*, 4.

45. Thielicke is best known in America for his sermons. Representative translations include *The Waiting Father* (sermons on the parables of Jesus); *Christ and the Meaning of Life; Our Heavenly Father: Sermons on the Lord's Prayer*, trans. John W. Doberstein (New York: Harper, 1960); *Between God and Satan* (sermons on the temptations of Christ), trans. C. C. Barber (Grand Rapids: Eerdmans, 1958); *How to Believe Again* (sermons for God-seekers), trans. H. George Anderson (Philadelphia: Fortress, 1972); *How the World Began: Man in the First Chapters of the Bible*, trans. John W. Doberstein (Philadelphia: Muhlenberg, 1961); *Out of the Depths*, trans. Geoffrey W. Bromiley (Grand Rapids: Eerdmans, 1962); *Life Can Begin Again: Sermons on the Sermon on the Mount*, trans. John W. Doberstein (Philadelphia: Fortress, 1963); *Being a Christian When the Chips Are Down*, trans. H. George Anderson (Philadelphia: Fortress, 1979); *The Five Brothers of the Rich Man*, trans. John W. Doberstein (London: Church Pastoral-Aid Society, 1962). A number of individual sermons are readily available in *Christianity Today*: "But Man Fell on Earth," *Christianity Today*, 4 March 1977, pp. 3–15; "How Can I Be Sure of the Risen Christ?" *Christianity Today*, 18 March 1983, pp. 14–17; "Deliver Us from Evil," *Christianity Today*, 9 November 1984, pp. 30–35; "The Mystery of Death," *Christianity Today*, 15 February 1985, pp. 20–25; "The Great Temptation," *Christianity Today*, 12 July 1985, pp. 26–31; "Why I Celebrate Christmas," *Christianity Today*, 9 December 1988, pp. 21–22.

46. Thielicke, *Christ and the Meaning of Life*, 82.

47. Ibid., 185.

48. Thielicke, *How Modern Should Theology Be?* 4.

49. Thielicke, *Between Heaven and Earth*, 65.

through the realm of religion. Accordingly, in the style of Lutheran preachers ever since the Reformation, Thielicke delivered series of sermons on the principal parts of the catechism and the Apostles' Creed.[50]

4. Thielicke's preaching was doctrinal. Preachers within the Lutheran tradition are expected to be theologians and to develop the major themes of the faith. "Systematic theology," wrote one Lutheran teacher, "is the highest form of theological science." That conviction informs classic Lutheran pulpit oratory. And indeed the distinctive doctrines of the Lutheran tradition were evident in Thielicke's sermons. He expounded on the ubiquity of the body of the ascended Christ (which makes his real presence possible in the mass), baptismal regeneration, the efficacy of the means of grace (Word and sacrament) even in the absence of saving faith (in such a context Christ comes as Judge, not Savior), and the division of God's Word into law and gospel. From the law comes accusation, driving one to repentance; from the gospel comes consolation, creating belief and trust in Christ.[51] There was no mistaking the fact that Thielicke was Lutheran.

5. Thielicke's preaching was intellectual. Lutheranism was born in a university, and it has remained a scholar's church. From the pulpit Thielicke did not hesitate to quote Konrad Lorenz, Gotthold Ephraim Lessing, Johann Wolfgang von Goethe (a must for a German Lutheran preacher), Georges Bernanos, Bertolt Brecht, Jean-Paul Sartre, Blaise Pascal, Martin Heidegger, Søren Kierkegaard, Plato and Aristotle, Alfred North Whitehead, and Albert Einstein, to give a small sample of the range in

his homilies. "Nothing in this world is alien to this preacher," noted one observer. A Thielicke sermon could include a reference to a James Dean movie, an off-Broadway play, or a recent space mission. It is evident that Thielicke was of the same mold as Albert Schweitzer, Immanuel Kant, Georg Hegel, and Gottfried Wilhelm Leibniz. To love God is also to worship him with the mind.

6. Thielicke's preaching was pastoral. While Lutherans use many terms for their clerics—"father," "minister," "preacher"—the favorite is "pastor." The Lutheran sermon is envisioned not simply as an individual exercise of the preacher, but as an expression of the congregational flock. As a priest representing his people, the pastor in the pulpit articulates their hopes and fears in the presence of the almighty God. For that reason Thielicke's sermons were rich in pastoral recollection. Typical is the following example:

> In a family I was visiting the twenty-five-year-old son was present. He was fast becoming a black sheep. He had been mixed up in many unsavory affairs and had almost broken his mother's heart. Yet suddenly he sat down at the piano and played some chorales from *St. Matthew's Passion*. He played these very movingly and it greatly touched me. His sister, however, angrily whispered in my ear, "What a hypocrite!" She obviously believed that by playing in this way the young man wanted to make a good impression on me as a theologian.
> But was he really a hypocrite? . . . [There was a real possibility that] the man who played this chorale was crying out for deliverance.[52]

Thielicke's interpretation of the young man's behavior reflects a pastor's heart obviously nurtured in the heritage of compassionate and forgiving spiritual care.

50. See, e.g., Thielicke, *I Believe*.
51. "The Law," noted Thielicke, "gives me self-knowledge by disclosing the gulf between what I ought to be according to my God-given destiny and what I am in fact" (this is the classic formula *lex semper accusat* ["the law always accuses"]). For Thielicke the law-gospel dialectic remained a fundamental issue between the two great Protestant confessions, Lutheranism and Calvinism, though it is today no reason for schism (Thielicke, *Evangelical Faith*, 2:185, 201, 203).

52. Thielicke, *Hidden Question of God*, 17–18.

Free-Church Elements

On the other hand, while Thielicke was identifiably Lutheran, he was also profoundly influenced by the Free Church tradition. This is evident in his book on preaching, *Encounter with Spurgeon*. Doberstein commented, "How piquant, how wonderful, how 'ecumenical,' that Helmut Thielicke, the highly educated German university professor and Lutheran theologian, should find such deep and warm kinship with Charles Haddon Spurgeon, the self-educated, Victorian Baptist preacher, who to this day remains a 'prince among preachers' in the English and American tradition."[53] Thielicke urged his students to read and imitate Spurgeon: "I am almost tempted to shout out to those who are serving the eternal Word as preachers . . . : Sell all that you have . . . and buy Spurgeon. . . . Let him be a Socrates who helps you to find your own way."[54] And what Thielicke advised his students, he practiced himself. There are at least four ways in which the impact of Free-Church Christianity on Thielicke's preaching is apparent:

1. Thielicke's preaching was devotional. He lamented that most German Lutheran "preaching is, to be sure, largely correct, exegetically 'legitimate,' workmanlike and tidy; but it is also remarkably dead and lacking in infectious power."[55] Spurgeon by contrast avoided the clerical mind and the code language of tradition. Plunging into the worldly context where people lived and into the Word of God where the Spirit hovered, he emerged with a dynamic message. Convinced that a number of preachers had failed because they took flight into the highly liturgical and ceremonial, Thielicke changed the format of his Saturday evening services at St. Michael's. A prayer-meeting quality was evident. Those who attended were impressed by Thielicke's creativity in public worship. The following prayer is representative of the liturgies that he authored:

> Stand by us, Lord, for night is coming,
>   and the day is drawing to a close.
> Stand by us, and by your whole church.
> Stand by us in the twilight of the day,
>   in the twilight of life,
>   and in the twilight of the world.
> Stand by us with your grace and goodness,
>   with your holy Word and Sacrament,
>   and with your comfort and blessing.
> Stand by us when we are overtaken
>   by the night of trouble and anxiety,
>   the night of doubt and despair,
>   and the night of bitter death.
> Stand by us and by all your faithful ones
>   now and forever.[56]

It is not surprising that parishioners described Thielicke's services as fresh, vibrant, intense, and energetic.

2. Thielicke's preaching was personal. He had no patience either with evangelicals who were "salvation engineers" or with those churchmen who were efficient bureaucrats. Preaching for him was not mechanical nor susceptible to technology. Spurgeon, he wrote, was effective because a never-ceasing supply flowed into him from

---

53. John W. Doberstein, Translator's Preface to *Encounter with Spurgeon*, by Helmut Thielicke, trans. John W. Doberstein (Philadelphia: Fortress, 1963), v.

54. Thielicke, *Encounter with Spurgeon*, 45.

55. Ibid., 2.

56. Thielicke, *How Modern Should Theology Be?* iii. Doberstein felt that the devotional quality of Thielicke's preaching was essential to his ability "to speak to modern man as a person in his peculiar predicament" (Doberstein, Translator's Introduction to *The Waiting Father*, 8). Thielicke scandalized some of the more conservative Lutherans when he stated: "I admit that reciting the Apostles' Creed in the service is somewhat of an annoyance to me. . . . I am somewhat troubled by the fact that the Apostles' Creed seems almost to diffuse an atmosphere of misunderstandings. . . . I am not very happy about the erecting of this super-steep wall of the Apostles' Creed in our services of worship, nor about the many who are hungry and thirsty, the people for whom the promises of faith were intended, but who suddenly grow faint and lapse into silence" (Thielicke, *I Believe*, xii). Some conservative Lutherans found such statements contradictory to his confessional vows. Thielicke was convinced, however, that public worship needed an evangelistic quality if it was to reach the post-Christian population of the secular modern age.

the channels of Holy Scripture. Possessed by the Word, Spurgeon's preaching was personal testimony. He shared with the public what was in his own soul: he was not a professional minister whose preaching was determined by what his congregation expected him to say in exchange for his wages. The man behind the robe always was evident, particularly in "a happy mental constitution" such as befits a minister. Like Spurgeon, Thielicke enjoyed "the blessed seasons of 'Easter laughter' in the church," recognizing that "laughter is always a form of engagement."[57] One is reminded of the American Episcopalian, Phillips Brooks, who contended that "preaching is truth conveyed through personality."

3. Thielicke's preaching was spiritual. "It's terrifying," he wrote, "to think that I could stand here and preach about things that are more important than food or drink."[58] Furthermore, "preaching encompasses a tremendously broad complex of procedures—ranging from prayer for the miracle of the Spirit through study of the text itself and the structuring of a sermon outline to the workmanlike mastery of effective speech."[59] Like Spurgeon, Thielicke was convinced that it is imperative for the preacher to avoid busyness and to be "immersed . . . in the quietness of prayer and meditation, receptively filling his mind and soul"; only after being recreated in those quiet hours should he go forth "to pour himself out without reserve."[60]

4. Thielicke's preaching was practical. Like Spurgeon, Thielicke believed that the preacher is an instrument (*Werkzeug*) of the

Word, of Christ's purpose to obtain, retain, and sustain members of the kingdom of God. For the saved, preaching is to provide power for sanctification, for daily growth in grace. For the lost, preaching is to be an invitation to salvation. Spurgeon was a "shepherd who was content to allow his robe—including his clerical robe—to be torn to tatters by thorns and sharp stones as he climbed after the lost sheep."[61] So intent was the Baptist pastor on saving souls that he "seemed . . . engaged more in training for a cross-country race than in liturgical exercises."[62] Following in Spurgeon's steps, Thielicke was called existential and evangelical because of his practical concern for saving souls.

Theology

Both in the pulpit and in the classroom, Thielicke was a theologian of wide-ranging interests, exploring such topics as ethics, the church and higher education, religion and politics, technology, popular recreation, and major philosophical systems.[63]

---

61. Ibid., 4.
62. Ibid., 41.
63. "The regard for truth," Thielicke asserted, "dare never become greater outside the church than it is in the church" (*Between Heaven and Earth*, 10). The catholicity of his writings is suggested by a list of representative titles: *Der Einzelne und der Apparat: Von der Freiheit des Menschen im technischen Zeitalter* (Hamburg: Furche, 1966); *The Doctor as Judge of Who Shall Live and Who Shall Die*, trans. H. George Anderson (Philadelphia: Fortress, 1976); *The Ethics of Sex*, trans. John W. Doberstein (New York: Harper and Row, 1964); *Die erzieherische Verantwortung der Universität: Grundfragen der Hochschulreform* (Tübingen: J. C. B. Mohr, 1952); *Die evangelische Kirche und die Politik: Ethisch-politischer Traktat über einige Zeitfragen* (Stuttgart: Evangelisches, 1953); *Fragen des Christentums an die moderne Welt: Untersuchungen zur geistigen und religiösen Krise des Abendlandes* (Tübingen: J. C. B. Mohr, 1948); *Mensch sein, Mensch werden: Entwurf einer christlichen Anthropologie* (Munich: Piper, 1976); *Theological Ethics*, trans. William H. Lazareth, 2 vols. (Philadelphia: Fortress, 1966, 1969); *The Trouble with the Church: A Call for Renewal*, trans. John W. Doberstein (New York: Harper and Row, 1965); *Offenbarung, Vernunft und Existenz: Studien zur Religionsphilosophie Lessings* (Gütersloh: G. Mohr, 1959); *Die*

---

57. Thielicke, *Encounter with Spurgeon*, 19–25. He noted in regard to a Spurgeon sermon: "Suddenly the Kingdom of God popped up not only in men's hearts but also in their diaphragms, laying hold upon even this part of nature." The preacher must be "a person, like ourselves, who lives with the message and has obviously tried it and found that one *can* live with it." Preaching is, then, a testimony (pp. 25, 32).
58. Thielicke, *How Modern Should Theology Be?* 8.
59. Thielicke, *Encounter with Spurgeon*, 2.
60. Ibid., 7.

More a situational than systematic theologian, addressing particular questions in particular contexts, he wrote with a sense of ardor, a feeling for order, and the gift of total candor. He served as a guest professor at Drew University and lectured at various other institutions, including Union Theological Seminary, Chicago Federated Theological Faculty, Princeton, and Heidelberg. Thielicke's thought, while subtle, complex, and subject to change over a period of four decades, can be summed up under three categories—revelation, redemption, and reconciliation.

Revelation

Within the Lutheran tradition there has been a basic dichotomy between philosophical and biblical theology. Philosophical theologians, like Paul Tillich, affirm the value of natural revelation, while biblical confessionalists, like Paul Althaus, assert that knowledge of God apart from Scripture is inadequate. Thielicke placed himself squarely in the biblical camp.

In a manner similar to Karl Barth, Thielicke saw problems in relying on natural law.[64] There was the danger of autonomy, for "rational man, like later existential man, wants to be sovereign in his own world. With the help of a process of projection, he thus makes God a function in his system of norms."[65] This, of course, becomes a form of idolatry. Furthermore,

nature in its indirectness is ambivalent. . . . It does not make God manifest. It envelops

him in mystery. . . . The same applies to the manifestation and concealment of God in history. Here again God is not set forth directly so that one can grasp him. The course of historical events as we see them is inscrutable. . . . [For that reason] we can speak of revelation in the strict sense only when the author of revelation manifests himself in, if we will, "absolute directness," i.e., only when he is identical with the mode of his manifestation. This holds true, however, only of his Word. God is his Word.[66]

This self-revelation comes in Christ, the canon, and proclamation. The personal Word, Christ, is the incarnate Word of history, the inscripturate Word of the Bible, the inculcated Word of preaching and the sacraments.

For Thielicke the Bible was the Word of God, the source and norm of all spiritual teaching and evangelical preaching. "In Holy Scriptures," he wrote, we have "the great acts and messages of God . . . proclaimed to us."[67] Through the Bible "God communicates this to us by calling men into his service, by attesting himself to them, and by dealing with them."[68] In the Bible God speaks "as a man speaks to his friend." Thielicke was not especially interested in the question of inspiration, however, confessing that he had no patience with "a fantastic idea of a heavenly cybernetics in which God was the guide of a process of automatic writing."[69] Addressing American fundamentalists, Thielicke asserted, "I am not primarily interested in the Bible at all. I am interested only in the Lord Jesus Christ. The Holy Scripture is only the ship in which he sleeps. And because he is sleeping in it, I am then also interested in the ship."[70]

As Thielicke was not concerned with concepts like infallibility and inerrancy, he was also not interested in the conflict of sci-

---

Schuld der Anderen: Ein Briefwechsel zwischen Helmut Thielicke und Hermann Diem (Göttingen: Vandenhoeck and Ruprecht, 1948); *Theologie der Anfechtung* (Tübingen: J. C. B. Mohr, 1949); *Sport und Humanität* (Tübingen: Wunderlich, 1967); "Reflections on Bultmann's Hermeneutic," *Expository Times* 67 (1956): 154–57, 175–77; and, with Leonhard Goppelt and Hans-Rudolf Muller-Schwefe, *The Easter Message Today: Three Essays* (New York: Nelson, 1964).

64. Douglas Sturm, "Natural Law," in *Encyclopedia of Religion*, ed. Mircea Eliade, 16 vols. (New York: Macmillan, 1987), 10:324.

65. Thielicke, *Evangelical Faith*, 2:18.

66. Ibid., 11–12.
67. Thielicke, *Between Heaven and Earth*, 3.
68. Ibid., 4.
69. Ibid., 6.
70. Ibid.

ence and religion. Thielicke was a theistic evolutionist who believed that the church makes a disastrous error when it forces one "to choose between a 'scientific' or 'biblical' view of creation"; this error Thielicke felt to be a by-product of the "error" of holding to "the doctrine of *verbal inspiration*,' which means the doctrine that every word of the Bible . . . is inspired."[71] With regard to creation he wrote: "I know that life on earth is millions of years old and that man also developed upward from animality in an unimaginably long process. . . . I can *either* ask where man came from biologically and receive the answer that he sprung from prehuman animal forms, *or* I can also ask *to what purpose* he is here, and what he was intended to be, what is the point of his existence."[72] Though accepting Darwinism, Thielicke believed that "the evolution of man still remains a *miracle*, a real *creation*."[73]

Redemption

A strong sense of the supernatural permeated Thielicke's theology. The miraculous was for him no issue, for "without miracles our prayers would simply become meaningless. Prayer would be degraded into a monologue."[74] Faith itself is the greatest of all miracles, wrought in the heart by the Holy Spirit.

In Thielicke's supernaturalism, the world is a place of intense struggle between God and the demonic. Evil is personal; the devil delights to throw into confusion and set at odds all that God has made.[75] The fall of Adam and Eve was also our fall, for we are constantly in the situation of wanting to be untrue to God and his purposes for this planet.[76] "The disobedience of man consists . . . in the fact that he wants to be *superman*. He wants to 'be like God.' He is

the notoriously Unbound One."[77] Violating the boundaries in which God has placed us, "we want *more* than the Lord has allowed to us. We want *more* success, *more* power, *more* money. . . . We no longer take any limits into account."[78] Unwilling to be what we were meant to be, we have fallen into death. "Man's mortality is rooted not in creation but in his fall from creation. Thus death is not of the created *order*; it is *dis*order [due to] man's fall from order."[79]

Jesus Christ has redeemed us from this death and disorder. True God and true man, he became incarnate to fulfil the offices of Priest, Prophet, and King for our salvation. The heart of the Christian revelation is the cross, for in the atonement Jesus paid the price of our sin. Thielicke subscribed to the various classic models of the cross.[80] The Passover metaphor is valid because the blood of Christ's sacrifice protects, expiates, and restores fellowship. The penal metaphor (based on Isa. 53) indicates that we have violated not just the law of God but the love of the Father. The political and military metaphor is also useful, for there was combat on Calvary between God and Satan, resulting in the defeat of the powers of darkness and the exaltation of Jesus as the exemplar of authentic humanity. The substitutionary model of the atonement was especially critical in Thielicke's theology. And as one firmly rooted within Lutheranism, he often gave prominence to the doctrine of satisfaction, as when he said: "How else can one understand the Cross of Calvary except that here God's holiness is in conflict with his grace: he does not simply pass over man's sin lightly, but rather throws himself into it, casts himself into the balance, by 'giving his only begotten Son.' Golgotha is a pain in God's heart. . . . This is a God overcoming himself, this

71. Thielicke, *Man in God's World*, 81.
72. Thielicke, *Christ and the Meaning of Life*, 159.
73. Thielicke, *Man in God's World*, 87.
74. Ibid., 103.
75. Ibid., 167.
76. Thielicke, *Between God and Satan*, 3.

77. Thielicke, "Mystery of Death," 22.
78. Ibid.
79. Thielicke, *Death and Life*, 1.
80. Thielicke, *Evangelical Faith*, 2:392–406. Thielicke's orthodox teachings on the Trinity and his Lutheran view of the sacraments are both anchored in his rich understanding of the theology of the cross.

is a struggle of God with himself. So emphatically is this the story of a living heart."[81] For students of church history it is clear that Thielicke worked within the framework of inherited soteriological teaching.

Reconciliation

The redemption purchased by Christ results in reconciliation. If asked, "When were you saved and reconciled with God?" Thielicke would have answered, "First, when Christ died on the cross. Second, when I was baptized. Third, daily, as I live in the faith. Finally, when Christ comes again."[82] As a preacher of the cross, Thielicke gave priority to the doctrine of justification. Perhaps that is to be expected of a Lutheran. But sanctification, or growth in grace, was also a major part of his theology. Morality, for him, was a personal and public response to God's gift. Believers produce good works, for everything in the life of the justified is declared good for Christ's sake. Always *simul justus et peccator* ("concurrently saint and sinner"), the Christian strives to please God by obeying the divine law, following the example of Christ, and witnessing to the unbelieving world. In so doing, the Christian expresses one's citizenship in the kingdom of God, appreciation for salvation, and expectation of the triumph of God at the end of time.[83]

For Thielicke the church, in its ministry of Word and sacrament, was the Spirit's vehicle for calling men and women to faith. An ethical realist, Thielicke had no anticipation that the kingdom of God would emerge within history through some kind of evolutionary process. Only the return of Christ in the second advent will result in the final triumph of goodness over evil and of the saints over Satan, sin, the world, and their lesser selves. In this interim age between the two advents of the Savior, the church has a ministry of faith (proclaiming and teaching), love (expressing care and concern through sacraments and philanthropy), and hope (prophetic expectation of the end). As the community of reconciliation, it is God's last and best effort for the human race prior to the dramatic end of history and the creation of a new heaven and a new earth.

Just as Thielicke's preaching style was eclectic, drawing abundantly from both Lutheranism and the Free Church, so, too, his theology was wide-ranging. A firm advocate of the Lutheran tradition, he explored its major elements with his own evangelical fervor. When we take into account as well his courageous leadership during the war years and in the subsequent reconstruction of German Christianity, there is no denying that Helmut Thielicke was one of the theological giants of our time.

81. Thielicke, *Between Heaven and Earth,* 5.
82. Zietlow, interview.
83. Ibid.

John F. Walvoord

John D. Hannah

John Flipse Walvoord was born on May 1, 1910, in Sheboygan, Wisconsin, the third and last child of John Garrett Walvoord and Mary Flipse Walvoord.[1] He benefited immensely from the security provided by a stable family that believed in education and religious training. John's father, though he entered high

1. Specific biographical sources are rather meager and often lack a critical perspective. Timothy G. Mink, "John F. Walvoord at Dallas Theological Seminary," Ph.D diss., North Texas State University, 1987, has some general insights, but is not creatively organized; the bibliography is helpful. Rudolf A. Renfer's "History of Dallas Theological Seminary," Ph.D. diss., University of Texas, 1959, provides some insight into the earliest years of Walvoord's career. Of the available periodical literature the most helpful articles include Donald K. Campbell, "Walvoord: A Tribute," *Kindred Spirit* 10 (Spring 1986): 5–7 (this material also appears in *Walvoord: A Tribute*, ed. Donald K. Campbell [Chicago: Moody, 1982], 7–12); Michael Fluent, "John F. Walvoord: Staunch Conservative Retires from Dallas Seminary," *Fundamentalist Journal* 5 (April 1986): 61–63; John A. Witmer, "'What Hath God Wrought'—Fifty Years of Dallas Theological Seminary. Part II. Building upon the Foundation," *Bibliotheca Sacra* 131 (Jan.–March 1974): 3–13; and "Q & A: An Interview with John F. Walvoord," *Fundamentalist Journal* 3 (Oct. 1984): 47–49.

school after his twentieth birthday, obtained a normal-school education that allowed him to become a teacher in the Horace Mann School in Sheboygan and, later, a principal. Eventually, he obtained a degree from the University of Wisconsin and served as a school superintendent.

The Christ-centered nature of the Walvoord home was evident even before John was born. Because of severe health problems, doctors had advised his mother to consider an abortion; however, a firm conviction that the Lord had given this child persuaded the parents to continue the pregnancy. Mary not only survived the pregnancy, but lived to be 102. The Walvoords were members of the First Presbyterian Church, where John's father served as an elder and Sunday-school superintendent. At the age of nine, John joined the church, having committed the Westminster Shorter Catechism to memory. Three years later he began to read the Bible daily, though, as he confesses, a true religious awakening had not occurred; the endeavor was motivated by a determination to attain righteousness through works.

In 1925 the family moved to Racine, where John's father became the principal of a junior high school. During high school not only did John excel in academics and athletics, but his religious training bore fruit in a profound personal attachment to the Christian faith. The family joined the Union Gospel Tabernacle, now the Racine Bible Church, a nondenominational, independent body. Having been impressed in Sheboygan by a retired Baptist minister who spoke to First Presbyterian's youth group in 1922, John had a year later answered an altar call and made a commitment to full-time Christian work. This appears, however, to have been more an evidence of the Spirit's wooing than of his redemptive work, because it was only after moving to Racine that John came to an evangelical conversion. While studying Galatians with a church group led by William McCarrell, who would later be among the founders of the Independent Fundamental Churches of America (1930), John came to an awareness of the full sufficiency of the free grace of Christ apart from any human endeavors. He cryptically commented, "If I was not saved before, I was saved then."[2]

In 1928 Walvoord entered Wheaton College, a private Christian liberal-arts institution under the presidency of J. Oliver Buswell, Jr. There Walvoord pursued a rigorous course of study, majoring in Greek and minoring in Latin, excelled in athletics (football and track), and was a member of the debate team which won the Illinois championship in 1930 and 1931. In addition, he was president of the college's Christian Endeavor and the missionary volunteer band (his desire to serve as a missionary in China or India likely sprang from this involvement). With some additional course work one summer at the University of Colorado, he was able to complete his undergraduate degree in 1931 with honors.

Because of his Presbyterian heritage, Walvoord considered taking graduate studies at Princeton Seminary, but then he turned in another direction. At about that time Lewis Sperry Chafer, president of the Evangelical Theological College (now Dallas Theological Seminary) and a cleric in the Presbyterian church, had come to speak at the Union Gospel Tabernacle and made a deep impression on Walvoord.[3] Further, Buswell, who had received a D.D. from the Evangelical Theological College in 1927 (Chafer had received the same degree from Wheaton the previous year) recommended the Dallas school over Princeton.[4] The theological affinity between Wheaton and the Evangelical Theological College (e.g., an aversion to both modernism and the fanatical fringe of evangelicalism known as fundamentalism,[5] a shared Presbyterian heri-

2. Fluent, "John F. Walvoord," 62.

3. For a discussion of Chafer and the Dallas Theological Seminary, see Renfer, "History"; and John D. Hannah, "The Social and Intellectual Origins of the Evangelical Theological College," Ph.D. diss., University of Texas at Dallas, 1988.

4. For Buswell's and Chafer's degrees see Hannah, "Social and Intellectual Origins," 358, 157.

5. Chafer and Buswell were exceedingly suspicious of the more strident wing of the evangelical-fundamentalist coalition as reflected in the World Christian Fundamentals Association (founded 1919) under the leadership of William B. Riley and J. Frank Norris. In reply to Buswell's inquiry about the Evangelical Theological College's relationship to the fundamentalist movement of the 1920s, Chafer stated: "I think you know quite well the attitude we hold. While we stand for all of the Fundamentals of the Word of God, we are not identified with the Fundamentalist Movement as such. I have not been in sympathy with the movement from its beginnings" (Chafer to Buswell, 14 Feb. 1930, Lewis Sperry Chafer Papers, Archives, Dallas Theological Seminary).

tage, premillennialism,[6] and the Keswick tradition),[7] as well as a summer program that the Evangelical Theological College conducted in Wheaton's facilities for a brief period, made Wheaton a conduit to Dallas at that time. Ten percent of the B.A. students who entered the Evangelical Theological College between 1924 and 1929 were from Wheaton; that figure increased to 35 percent between 1930 and 1935. Wheaton was by far the richest source of the seminary's entrants.[8]

Upon entering the Evangelical Theological College, a school with an eclectic heritage rooted in the Bible conference movement of the late nineteenth century (hence the unique stress on survey of the English Bible and the Keswick concept of progressive sanctification), Reformed understandings of soteriology that were in some respects shaped by Saumurian Calvinism,

6. A distancing of sorts between Chafer and Buswell did occur in the 1930s. John Murray of Westminster Seminary had argued that ancient premillennialism (a view that emphasized testamental continuity and a single people of God as opposed to testamental discontinuity and two forever distinct peoples of God—Israel and the church) had historical precedent, but modern premillennialism (i.e., dispensational premillennialism) did not. Buswell defended Murray's assertion: "Whereas I am ardently a premillennialist, my own personal views are quite extremely opposed to what is commonly called dispensationalism" (J. Oliver Buswell, Jr., "A Premillennialist's View," *Presbyterian Guardian*, 14 Nov. 1936, p. 46). To Chafer he wrote: "I have disagreed with you in regard to your interpretation of the dispensation of the law for over ten years. Now I am a premillennialist, and you are a premillennialist. My premillennial view is not identical with your view of the dispensation of the law. I defend the premillennial view. You are under attack from the enemies of premillennialism for points of doctrine which I personally do not accept" (Buswell to Chafer, 24 May 1937, J. Oliver Buswell, Jr., Papers, Archives, Dallas Theological Seminary).

7. For a discussion of the influence of the Keswick movement on this segment of evangelicalism, see George M. Marsden, *Fundamentalism and American Culture* (New York: Oxford University Press, 1980), 72–80; and Douglas W. Frank, *Less than Conquerors: How Evangelicals Entered the Twentieth Century* (Grand Rapids: Eerdmans, 1986), 103–66.

8. Hannah, "Social and Intellectual Origins," 269.

and Darbyite dispensationalism and modern premillennialism—a syncretism in tune with the heritage of the Union Gospel Tabernacle and Wheaton College (though Buswell rejected Chafer's dispensationalism)—Walvoord pursued a regular curriculum of seminary studies, graduating with both a Th.B. and a Th.M. degree in 1934.[9] He was particularly impressed in his training by Chafer, professor of systematic theology; Harry A. Ironside, a visiting professor of Bible who was of Brethren affiliation; and Henry Theissen, the Greek teacher who had arrived in 1931 and left for Wheaton College in 1935—the only Ph.D. on the faculty at that time. With missionary service in mind, Walvoord engaged himself in Christian ministry on the weekends and in the summers organized vacation Bible schools in rural areas of the Midwest. Having secured an application to serve with the China Inland Mission, a dream of his mother's for him, he sought God's guidance, but he met only silence; he turned to the possibility of a pastorate, but there was no sense of the Lord's leading.[10] Under Chafer's influence he made the decision to enter the doctoral program and assume the pastorate of the Rosen Heights Presbyterian Church in Fort Worth (now Northwest Bible Church). He completed the Th.D. degree in 1936 and then sought a pastorate in the Midwest.

At this point Chafer offered Walvoord a position as registrar and associate professor of systematic theology at Dallas Theological Seminary (the new name of the Evangelical Theological College).[11] Walvoord sensed the direction of God to accept that position and commuted from his pastorate in Fort Worth. Finding the registrar's office disorganized and records nearly nonexistent, he plunged himself into his duties; with an amazing combination of diligence

9. Witmer, "What Hath God Wrought," 4; for the syncretism at the school see Hannah, "Social and Intellectual Origins," 164–70, 189–93, 201–9.

10. Fluent, "John F. Walvoord," 63; Campbell, "Walvoord," 6.

11. Witmer, "What Hath God Wrought," 4.

and productivity, he excelled as a learned teacher, administrator, and pastor.

In 1939 Walvoord married Geraldine Lundgren of Geneva, Illinois, after an acquaintanceship that spanned seven years; the couple had four sons—John Edward, James Randall, Timothy, and Paul. In addition to a bewildering array of commitments, he served as moderator of the Fort Worth Presbytery twice and as permanent clerk for ten years. He also began classes at Texas Christian University and was granted an A.M. degree in philosophy in 1945. He had wrestled with the possibility of seeking a two-year leave of absence from Dallas to pursue a Ph.D. degree in philosophy at Princeton University; however, the strain of federally mandated year-round classes during the war years made Chafer reluctant to lose his services.

Chafer's declining health, as evidenced by heart problems, limited his labors, making it clear that he could no longer single-handedly direct the institution. The solution was to bring his protégé into a more prominent role, though Walvoord already had numerous duties, including serving as the secretary of the faculty (1940–45). While continuing with his responsibilities in the Department of Systematic Theology, he became assistant to the president in 1945. The function of the new position was far beyond that of an assistant; in addition to assuming oversight of a mountain of institutional correspondence, he served as chairman of the faculty and director of publicity. He also took over an increasing portion of Chafer's ministry at Bible conferences.[12]

The death of Chafer on August 22, 1952, left the institution bereft of its first and only president. This was a crucial period, for the seminary was in the midst of its first building project since 1929. Walvoord was appointed president of the seminary and promoted to professor of systematic theology.[13] He was installed formally in February 1953 at the dedication of Chafer Chapel.[14] Because of the increasing burdens of his seminary duties, he had resigned from the Rosen Heights Presbyterian Church in 1950. He subsequently joined the Independent Fundamental Churches of America, leaving the Presbyterian Church in the United States.[15] Taking over the leadership of the seminary from a man who had enjoyed an enormous reputation in the ranks of dispensational premillennialists, and who had occupied the presidency for twenty-eight years, required courage and strength. Walvoord would lead the school as president for thirty-three years, retiring from the post to accept emeritus status as chancellor in 1986. He had served on its faculty for fifty years.[16] In those years of pressing presidential duties, he emerged as a foremost scholar and writer in the field of eschatological studies. He was recognized for his achievements by both a D.D. degree from Wheaton College in 1960 and a Litt.D. from Liberty Baptist Seminary in 1984.

Presidency of Dallas Theological Seminary

The contribution of John Walvoord as a theologian cannot be separated from either the institution he directed and defined for over three decades or his large scholarly output following John Nelson Darby, James Hall Brookes, C. I. Scofield, and Lewis Sperry Chafer in the defense and delineation of dispensational premillennialism.

---

12. "Dr. Charles A. Nash Appointed Registrar," *Dallas Theological Seminary Bulletin* 21 (July–Sept. 1945): 2; Mink, "John F. Walvoord," 75–109.

13. "Board of Incorporate Members Unanimously Elects Dr. John F. Walvoord President of Seminary," *Dallas Theological Seminary Bulletin* 28 (Nov.–Dec. 1952): 2.

14. "Seminary Combines Inauguration of President with Dedication of Chafer Chapel," *Dallas Theological Seminary Bulletin* 29 (Jan.–Feb. 1953): 2.

15. Mink, "John F. Walvoord," 159.

16. Campbell, "Walvoord," 5; *Walvoord*, ed. Campbell, 7.

The seminary emerged in the context of the theological and social trauma that polarized several of the Northern denominations at the turn of the present century. Deeply rooted in the reactionary Bible conference movement of the previous decades, the school was the fulfilment of Chafer's aspirations.[17] An Ohioan of Presbyterian affiliation, Chafer had traveled extensively, beginning in the 1890s, as an evangelist's assistant, then as an evangelist, and eventually as a popular Bible teacher.[18] The theological features of the school deeply reflect the religious experience of its founder, as well as one particular substratum of the evangelicalism of that day.[19]

Through his travels, often with Scofield, and conversations with numerous pastors and colleagues, Chafer had become convinced that an entirely new departure was needed in ministerial training.[20] The standard theological curriculum had three glaring deficiencies: failure to provide an inten-

sive study of each book of the Bible,[21] to foster the spiritual development of each student (particularly through the principles and interpretative insights associated with the Keswick and Northfield conferences), and to teach dispensationalism and premillennialism, which he felt provided singular insights for understanding and unfolding the simple, clear teachings of Scripture.[22] In essence Dallas Seminary sought to institutionalize the theological distinctives of the Bible conference movement; it was convinced that the theological malaise of the day could be remedied by biblically informed teachers.[23] An early announcement alerted prospective students that "the college has been established to meet a direct demand and to fill a widespread need because of its peculiar aims, one dominant feature of which is the thorough training in the Scriptures with special reference to expository preaching and teaching."[24] This, Chafer averred, was the best defense of historical Christianity.

As Walvoord succeeded Chafer, he was committed to continuing the basic emphases of the school. He commented, "I tried not to change much. . . . In the beginning

---

17. Walvoord has commented: "The seminary was really a carryover from the Bible institute movement, with emphasis on Bible content. Chafer's goal was to raise this to the seminary level and produce teachers who could go back to the Bible institute and train others. So many of the Bible teachers in that era were self-trained men and Chafer felt the need for gaining respectability in the teaching of the Bible. Of course his ambition was realized in the early days of the seminary when about 25 percent of our graduates went back to teaching.

"Today the percentages are a little lower, but certainly the numbers are just as high. Many Bible colleges and Evangelical seminaries insist on a Dallas-trained man when looking for faculty. There is hardly a Bible college of any size that has not one or more of our Dallas men on the faculty. At least a hundred of our men are either deans or presidents of schools of this sort. The number one reason for this is we give them the content of the Bible and interpret the Bible literally from a premillennial perspective" ("Q and A," 47).

18. Hannah, "Social and Intellectual Origins," 72–144.

19. Ibid., 182–92; see also Rollin T. Chafer, "Some Distinctive Features of the Evangelical Theological College," *Evangelical Theological College Bulletin* 2 (Nov. 1925): 6–13.

20. Lewis Sperry Chafer, "A New Departure in Theological Training," *Our Hope* 34 (Jan. 1928): 432.

21. Lewis Sperry Chafer, "Effective Ministerial Training," *Evangelical Theological College Bulletin* 1 (May 1925): 10–11.

22. This point is immensely important to grasp if we are to understand the seminary and its second president; dispensational premillennialism (i.e., modern dispensationalism) was the grid through which the Bible was to be interpreted. To truly know the Bible, to be an accurate teacher of it, one had to embrace this perspective with regard to every book of the Bible; see Hannah, "Social and Intellectual Origins," 187–88. For recent discussions of the rise of dispensational premillennialism, see Ernest R. Sandeen, *The Roots of Fundamentalism: British and American Millenarianism, 1800–1930* (Chicago: University of Chicago Press, 1970); and Timothy P. Weber, *Living in the Shadow of the Second Coming: American Premillennialism, 1875–1982*, rev. and enlarged ed. (Grand Rapids: Zondervan, 1983).

23. "The Opening Exercises," *Evangelical Theological College Bulletin* 1 (Jan. 1925): 13–14.

24. Quoted in "Dr. John F. Walvoord on the Distinctives of Dallas Seminary," *Kindred Spirit* 4 (Fall 1980): 5.

we really concentrated on keeping stability, maintaining the educational distinctives."[25] Yet at the same time it was necessary to organize for the future. Chafer's years at the helm had been dominated by the Great Depression and World War II. "Times had changed," Walvoord would later recall. "We were in the post-war boom. Previously the Depression had made survival the goal. It was time to move ahead." And the Walvoord years did evidence enormous changes in the institution.[26]

The most pressing immediate need was the financial plight of the school. Almost from its inception the seminary had faced financial shortfalls, even though there were annual deliverances.[27] The new president was able, by instituting some simple measures such as telling the school's donors of its needs and charging a modest tuition, to balance the budget, pay off the debt, and launch into an aggressive building program that would transform the campus.[28] At his inauguration in 1953, Chafer Chapel, the first new building since 1929, was dedicated. The Walvoord administration witnessed an almost continuous acquisition of properties and more buildings. Mosher Library was completed in 1960, and a large residence hall, a former YWCA near the campus, was secured in 1969. In the 1970s new buildings, the Todd Building in 1972 and Academic II in 1974, literally refocused the seminary to face toward Live Oak Street. The Timothy Walvoord Building, a student union, completed the main campus in 1982.[29] What had started out as two structures along a single street has now become seven major academic buildings encompassing an entire city block. There are also various apartments and offices in the immediate environs. The immense growth of the campus was in direct response to an enormous era of growth in the student population. From a student body of 281 in 1953, the size of the school rose to 1,647 in the spring of 1986. Particularly impressive is the fact that the school was able to post financial surpluses during the era of huge growth.[30]

In addition to the campus and student body, the faculty grew substantially, reaching an apex of seventy-one in 1986. This is indicative of the educational progress during Walvoord's tenure. Perhaps the most important accomplishment of the school, and most indicative of its direction, was the acquisition in 1969 of accreditation by the Southern Association of Colleges and Secondary Schools.[31] Two new departments were added to the school: the Department of Christian Education (1958) and the Department of World Missions (1963).[32] The 1970s witnessed an explosion of academic programs. In 1972 a summer program was instituted, and in 1974 a winter term was added so that classes would be conducted year-round.[33] In that year two further changes were effected. First, the board approved the first new degree program since 1931. The new program, the master of arts in biblical studies, was a two-year course that waived the traditional language requirements. Second, women were admitted into this program, the first time they were permitted student status.[34] (By 1986 women were permitted to enter most of the school's degree programs.) Also, a lay institute taught by students was started as an evening program. In 1980 a program leading to the D.Min. degree was inaugurated; subsequently, several additional M.A. programs were introduced (e.g.,

25. Ibid.
26. Hannah, "Social and Intellectual Origins," 273–317.
27. Mink, "John F. Walvoord," 71.
28. Witmer, "What Hath God Wrought," 8–9.
29. Ibid., 3–4; "Report of the President to the Board of Incorporate Members of Dallas Theological Seminary," 1986–87, p. 1.

30. "Report of the President," 1986–87, p. 1.
31. Witmer, "What Hath God Wrought," 11.
32. Ibid.
33. "Report of the President to the Board of Incorporate Members of Dallas Theological Seminary," 1975, p. 5; Mink, "John F. Walvoord," 276.
34. "Report of the President," 1975, p. 6.

cross-cultural ministries, Christian education).[35]

As president of Dallas Seminary, Walvoord proved to be a man of vision who projected the aura of confidence and stability. In the words of Howard Hendricks, a long-time faculty member: "I think Dr. Walvoord's educational philosophy has been one of vision. He has articulated a vision for the future that was lacking in 1952. He has built one of the stronger teams in terms of the faculty that I have seen in any Christian school. He built a base of continuity in terms of faculty that is almost unheard of. And he was committed to quality."[36] In comparing the three presidents, it might be argued that Chafer was a visionary who felt an acute need for an exclusively premillenarian, dispensationalist school; he established the first such institution in the country. Walvoord brought it from financial distress to numerical and academic prominence; while maintaining Chafer's vision, he equipped the seminary to prepare pastors, leaders, and teachers for a narrow segment of American evangelicalism.[37] The administration of Donald Campbell (1986–) has sought to position the school to become a

voice in a wider spectrum of the evangelical movement. Chafer gave birth to the school, Walvoord made it into a world-class institution, and Campbell has sought to bring it into the center of American Christianity.

Scholarly Contribution

In addition to directing the most prominent dispensationalist school in the country for over three decades, Walvoord has emerged as an eminent scholar in the realm of prophetical and eschatological studies.[38] Admittedly, his interests have been almost entirely apologetic and polemic as he attempted to define the school's distinctive theology and defend it as a biblically warranted interpretation of Scripture. John Witmer has written of him, "Already nationally known as a theologian and Bible teacher when elected President of Dallas

35. "New Degree to Be Offered," *Kindred Spirit* 3 (Fall 1979): 12b; "Report of the President to the Board of Incorporate Members of Dallas Theological Seminary," 22–23 October 1987, pp. 7–8.

36. Quoted in Mink, "John F. Walvoord," 322.

37. The *Dallas Morning News*, 26 July 1992, J11, referred to Walvoord as "the grand old man of fundamentalism." Such a statement could be misleading if one does not realize that the term *fundamentalism* has changed in nuance in this century. In the early decades the term was a synonym for the evangelical-conservative coalition that responded to the rise of the modernist movement in theology. This coalition, as George Marsden has defined it, was a broad group that found cohesion in hostility to liberalism and in a shared view of Scripture. The coalition was, however, shattered in the 1930s and 1940s. From theological divisions in the 1930s (e.g., modern premillennialism precluded affiliation with the Reformed tradition) and sociological and theological dissension in the 1940s and 1950s emerged the separatist or nondenominational movement. The term *fundamentalism* came to be used of this subsegment of American evangelicalism.

If Walvoord is to be labeled a fundamentalist, it must be recognized that the term signifies a broad spectrum of ideologies and practices, and that he speaks for but a segment of it. To say that he is the grand old man of fundamentalism is at best an overstatement. He saw Dallas Seminary as serving a narrow segment of the conservative movement in America. It catered to the theological Right (i.e., the "real" fundamentalists), which was characterized by separatist and legalistic preoccupations. This group eschewed the progressive evangelical movement on the theological Left as becoming soft on the inerrancy of Scripture. It also held to a domino theory of theology that began with premillennial dispensationalism. For concise discussions of the current polarities within evangelicalism see *The Evangelicals: What They Believe, Who They Are, Where They Are Changing*, ed. David F. Wells and John D. Woodbridge (Nashville: Abingdon, 1975); Donald G. Bloesch, *The Future of Evangelical Christianity: A Call For Unity amid Diversity*, 2d rev. ed. (Colorado Springs: Helmers and Howard, 1988); and *Evangelicalism and Modern America*, ed. George M. Marsden (Grand Rapids: Eerdmans, 1984).

38. In the context of the mounting international crisis with Iraq, which caused interest in prophecy and the sales of the revised edition of Walvoord's *Armageddon, Oil and the Middle East Crisis* (Grand Rapids: Zondervan, 1990) to soar, a front-page article ("Armageddon") in the *Chicago Tribune*, 14 October 1990, referred to Walvoord as "the king of prophecy." This is a not so subtle evidence of his stature among scholars and writers in this field.

Seminary, Dr. Walvoord has increasingly grown through the years of his administration as a leading world spokesman for biblical Christianity."[39] In addition to his growing prominence through ministry at various Bible conferences and churches, his stature in the modern premillennialist movement is evidenced by his service on the committee of scholars that produced the New Scofield Reference Bible in 1967, a revision of Scofield's work of 1909 and 1917.[40] Far more important in the defense of modern dispensationalism (a more precise designation would be classical or traditional modern dispensationalism), however, has been his personal literary output.

Along with the presidency of the seminary, the editorship of *Bibliotheca Sacra* became one of Walvoord's responsibilities.[41]

For thirty-three years (1952–85), amidst huge administrative duties, he directed the journal in the defense of evangelical theology in general and dispensational premillennialism in particular.[42] He contributed a total of 127 articles.[43] Between 1937 and 1970 he contributed 93 articles, including 57 on eschatological issues, 18 on Christology, 7 on soteriology, and 6 on pneumatology. Between 1971 and 1980 he wrote 28 articles, 23 on eschatological themes and 5 on pneumatology. Finally, between 1981 and 1990 he prepared 6 articles, 5 on eschatology and 1 on pneumatology. Of the 127 articles, 85 were on eschatological themes. Accordingly, Campbell notes, "His subject is biblical eschatology, his field of specialization and expertise."[44]

Further, Walvoord has authored nineteen books: *The Doctrine of the Holy Spirit* (1943; revised in 1954 and 1958); *The Return of the Lord* (1955); *The Thessalonian Epistles* (1956); *The Rapture Question* (1957; revised in 1979); *The Millennial Kingdom* (1959); *To Live Is Christ: An Exposition of the Epistle of Paul to the Philippians* (1961; reissued in 1971 as *Philippians: Triumph in Christ); Israel in Prophecy* (1962); *The Church in Prophecy* (1964); *The Nations in Prophecy* (1967; the last three were published together in 1988 as *Israel, the Nations, and the Church in Prophecy); Truth for Today* (1963); *The Revelation of Jesus Christ* (1966); *Jesus Christ Our Lord* (1969); *Daniel, the Key to Prophetic Revelation* (1971); *The Holy Spirit at Work Today* (1973); *Matthew: Thy Kingdom Come* (1974); *Armageddon, Oil and the Middle East Crisis* (1974; revised in 1990); *The Blessed Hope and the Tribulation* (1976); *The Prophecy Knowledge Handbook* (1990); and *Major Bible Prophecies* (1991). He has

39. Witmer, "What Hath God Wrought," 9–10.
40. Revisions that the new edition makes in Scofield's notes are instructive for students interested in the recent developments in dispensationalism. For example, in the note on Matthew 3:2 Scofield listed three aspects of the kingdom of heaven: (1) the kingdom that was at hand in Christ's day, though it was rejected and postponed; (2) the present mystery form; and (3) the physical fulfilment to be realized in the future millennial reign. The committee of scholars kept this note essentially intact, but with one rather remarkable alteration. Reference to 2 Samuel 7:12–16 (the Davidic covenant) was moved from category (2) to category (3). The committee sought to argue that the Davidic covenant has only a future fulfilment, whereas Scofield had suggested that there is a present fulfilment in the reign of David's greater Son. Similarly, in contrast to the classical dispensationalists, progressive dispensationalists maintain that the Davidic covenant is being fulfilled in the church today. For a discussion of recent changes in dispensationalism see *Dispensationalism, Israel and the Church: The Search for Definition,* ed. Craig A. Blaising and Darrell L. Bock (Grand Rapids: Zondervan, 1992); Craig A. Blaising, "Development of Dispensationalism by Contemporary Dispensationalists," *Bibliotheca Sacra* 145 (July–Sept. 1988): 254–80; Robert L. Saucy, "Contemporary Dispensational Thought," *TSF Bulletin* 7 (March–April 1984): 10–11.
41. For a discussion of this journal see John Henry Bennetch, "The Biography of *Bibliotheca Sacra*," *Bibliotheca Sacra* 100 (Jan.–March 1943): 8–30; Arnold D. Ehlert, "Editorial," *Bibliotheca Sacra* 98 (Jan.–March 1941): 5–6; John A. Witmer, "'What Hath God Wrought'—Fifty Years of Dallas Theological Sem-

inary. Part I. God's Man and His Dream," *Bibliotheca Sacra* 130 (Oct.–Dec. 1973): 301.
42. "Changing of the Guard," *Bibliotheca Sacra* 142 (Oct.–Dec. 1985): 291.
43. *An Analytical Index to BIBLIOTHECA SACRA* (1934–70): 183–85; (1971–80): 44–46; (1981–90): 85.
44. Campbell, "Walvoord," 7.

also edited several works: *Inspiration and Interpretation* (1957); *Major Bible Themes* (1974—a revision of Chafer's 1926 volume by the same title); *The Bib Sac Reader* (1983—a collection of articles that had appeared in the journal between 1934 and 1983); *The Bible Knowledge Commentary* (1983—a two-volume work by the seminary faculty); and *Systematic Theology* (1988—a two-volume abridgment of Chafer's eight-volume 1947–48 publication).

Our survey makes it quite evident where Walvoord invested his literary energies: "The titles of the writings indicate the emphasis of Dr. Walvoord's thought and teaching. He has been an ardent exponent of the premillennial and dispensational system of theology."[45] A friend has made an ironic, insightful comment on his work and its reception by American evangelicalism in general: "He never got the credit in my judgment for the thinker he is. In certain circles he has, but . . . the evangelical world at large—the world that thinks of itself as theologians— has never given him the credit he deserved. . . . When he was forty years old [when he was about to become president of the seminary], if he had addressed himself purely as a theologian, he might have done what no other man has ever done as a dispensationalist, and that is make Dispensationalism respectable [to the evangelical theologians]."[46]

Dispensational Premillennialism

A perusal of Walvoord's writings makes it clear that his major focus was not upon modern dispensationalism as a system, but upon its eschatological implications. He accepted the theological structure that dispensationalists impose upon the Bible (e.g., literal interpretation, progressive revelation, discontinuity between the covenants,[47] and

45. *Walvoord*, ed. Campbell, 11.
46. Quoted in Mink, "John F. Walvoord," 316.
47. See John F. Walvoord, *The Prophecy Knowledge Handbook* (Wheaton, Ill.: Victor, 1990), 12—"The Bible progressively reveals the truth of God in such a way that changes are recognized as the contrast be-

a sharp contrast between Israel and the church). Embracing the tenets of modern premillennialism, as derived from Chafer (who in turn had been heavily influenced by Scofield) and cogently expressed by Charles Ryrie,[48] Walvoord specifically delineated the prophetical details of that system.

Integral to Walvoord's understanding of Scripture, as well as to classic dispensationalism as a whole, is the concept of two distinct peoples of God with two distinct programs having two distinct destinies. Also integral is the assumption of the literal integrity of Scripture, which entails the crucial concept that prophecy is not fulfilled figuratively; when a promise is given and later fulfilled in Scripture, it always comes to pass literally and specifically (i.e., the fulfilment directly involves the very people to whom the promise was originally given).[49] The two distinct peoples having two separate destinies are Israel and the church (a people neither Jew nor Gentile, but a new entity in Christ). The covenantal promises made to Israel (the Abrahamic, Davidic, and new covenants) are yet to be fulfilled; in the meantime, Israel has been scattered among the Gentiles because of her disobedience. On the basis of his concept of prophetic fulfilment Walvoord concludes that there is to be a future for ethnic Israel:

1. It is obvious that Israel has not possessed the land permanently.

tween Mosaic Law and the present age of grace. Late revelation may replace earlier revelation as a standard of faith without contradicting it."
48. Charles C. Ryrie, *Dispensationalism Today* (Chicago: Moody, 1965), 22–47, 86–109.
49. For a discussion of Walvoord's interpretative assumptions see Walvoord, *Prophecy Knowledge Handbook*, 9–17. He also notes (p. 14) that "many prophecies of Scripture were fulfilled shortly after their revelation. At least half of the prophecies of the Bible have already been fulfilled literally. Such fulfillment confirms the fact that unfulfilled prophecy will also be literally fulfilled as one can anticipate from fulfillment of prophecy already achieved. Fulfilled prophecy is an important guide in interpreting prophecy unfulfilled and generally confirms the concept of literal interpretation of prophecy" (see also pp. 648–763).

2. The prophets clearly promise that Israel will be regathered from the third dispersion and be in her land during the millennial kingdom.

3. It is evident that the promises given to Israel will not be fulfilled by the church or the Gentiles.

4. So the promise must be fulfilled by the physical seed of Jacob in keeping with the Abrahamic covenant.[50]

The church age, which commenced on the day of Pentecost (Acts 2), is distinct from God's program for Israel. It is an era in which the fulfilment of God's promises to the nation Israel has been postponed. God in this era is provoking Israel to jealousy by turning to the Gentiles; in a sense unknown or unanticipated in the Old Testament Scriptures, the present era is an age of grace for non-Jews.

Walvoord's distinction between Israel and the church has recently been modified in at least one respect. In his earlier writings Walvoord struggled with the relation between the church and the new covenant given to Israel (Jer. 31; Heb. 8) and concluded with Chafer that there must be two new covenants.[51] More recently, he has come to Scofield's position that there is but one new covenant with two separate fulfilments.[52] With regard to the Davidic covenant (2 Sam. 7), however, Walvoord, in contrast to Scofield and the progressive dispensationalists, is unwilling to see a fulfilment in the church.[53] While he is willing to grant that "the Bible does refer to a form of the Kingdom in the present age," it must not be confused with or allowed to denigrate the future fulfilment.[54]

God's interim program for the peoples of the earth (i.e., the church) will end with the rapture of the church. Inasmuch as various historical events suggest that what is to occur after the rapture, namely, Christ's second coming *with* his saints, is near, it is logical to infer that Christ's coming *for* his saints is imminent.[55] This distinction between the two aspects of the second coming, a distinction that is built on the assumption of two peoples and two programs of God, is crucial in Walvoord's schematization.[56]

Once the rapture of the church has taken place, God will turn to his people Israel and bring to literal fulfilment the Old Testament promise of a land, a seed (Christ reigning), and universal blessing. However, unrepentant Israel must be brought to this happy state of millennial blessing through judgment—the great tribulation. The chronological framework for these events is found in Daniel 9:24–27, where the prophet predicts a "seventy week" era for Israel. According to Walvoord, and dispensationalists generally, sixty-nine of those "weeks" were historically fulfilled during the period from Nehemiah's rebuilding of Jerusalem to the death of Christ. A pivotal "week" (seven years), however, remains.[57] This will be a time of judgment; it will conclude the "times of the Gentiles," a term that refers to Israel in the Diaspora (i.e., from the Babylonian captivity to the second coming).

In Walvoord's view, a central part of the scriptural revelation is its "careful explanation of the second coming of Jesus Christ. Many predictions were made about the important events that will occur before Christ's second coming. When these events are placed in their proper order, the result

50. John F. Walvoord, *Major Bible Prophecies* (Grand Rapids: Zondervan, 1991), 95.

51. John F. Walvoord, "The New Covenant with Israel," *Bibliotheca Sacra* 103 (Jan.–March 1946): 27; 110 (July–Sept. 1953): 193–205.

52. Walvoord, *Major Bible Prophecies*, 188–91.

53. Ibid., 108–9; see also n. 40.

54. John F. Walvoord, "The Kingdom of God in the New Testament," *Bibliotheca Sacra* 139 (Oct.–Dec. 1982): 310.

55. Walvoord, *Major Bible Prophecies*, 229–48, 265–304; idem, *Prophecy Knowledge Handbook*, 481–83.

56. John F. Walvoord, *What We Believe: Discovering the Truths of Scripture* (Grand Rapids: Discovery House, 1990), 143–57.

57. Walvoord, *Major Bible Prophecies*, 165–75; idem, *Prophecy Knowledge Handbook*, 248–59; idem, *What We Believe*, 165–66.

is a prophetic calendar of what soon may happen in the world."[58] And, indeed, signs of the second coming as well as precursors of the great tribulation are already evident in history. Walvoord believes that the world is on the brink of a ten-nation confederacy, a revival of the Roman Empire ("the Roman Empire has never had the ending predicted in Scripture").[59] A world demagogue, the Antichrist, will also emerge, as will an oppressive world religion.[60] According to the prophetic timetable, Israel will make a pact with the revived Roman Empire, a coalition of nations from Western Europe. The nation Israel will be invaded by Russia, a nonaligned power (the king of the north, the prince of Rosh), and be utterly destroyed.[61] This, Walvoord suggests, may catapult the ruler of the ten nations into unrivaled power in the middle of the great tribulation and inaugurate huge judgments against the earth in the latter half of that catastrophic period.[62]

The great tribulation will end in a final conflagration, the battle of Armageddon; Christ will return in glory to Mount Zion in an act of divine judgment on the nations.[63] This is the second coming of Christ. "A utopian world will follow."[64] Christ will inaugurate a literal kingdom upon the earth. The essential purpose of this millennial age will be to fulfil the covenantal promises to Israel. Says Walvoord, "The Millennium will be the occasion of the final restoration of Israel."[65] At the conclusion of this era, the final judgment of humankind will take place before the great white throne. This will be followed by the creation of the new heavens and new earth, the final abode of the redeemed.[66] Although Walvoord is clear that there are two separate peoples of God with two distinct programs, he is not so clear as to how their eternal destinies will differ. Thus the new Jerusalem, while identified distinctly as the city of the bride (the church), "nevertheless includes in its boundaries the saints of all ages and the holy angels."[67]

We have seen that the contribution of John F. Walvoord to the evangelical movement in America and beyond has been twofold. As an industrious visionary president, he used enormous energy to bring a small, debt-encumbered seminary to its current status as a large, prosperous, world-class institution. As a scholar and writer he sought to preserve and advance the heritage of the Bible conference movement as it was represented in a number of Bible institutes and the school of postgraduate education established by his mentor and predecessor. In the former task he was eminently successful; in the latter—the defense of dispensational premillennialism—he was less so. He himself has suggested that his interpretive viewpoint has not attracted the sympathies of the broad spectrum of evangelical scholars.[68] This, however, should not disguise the fact that he is an accomplished scholar whose writings are highly regarded in the evangelical subculture to which he belongs.

58. Walvoord, *Armageddon*, 13.

59. Walvoord, *Major Bible Prophecies*, 313.

60. Walvoord, *Major Bible Prophecies*, 312–27; idem, *What We Believe*, 164–71; idem, *Armageddon*, 109–62.

61. Walvoord, *Major Bible Prophecies*, 328–37.

62. Walvoord, *Major Bible Prophecies*, 337, 346–53; idem, *What We Believe*, 167–68; idem, *Armageddon*, 163–75.

63. Walvoord, *Major Bible Prophecies*, 354–75; idem, *What We Believe*, 175–83; idem, *Armageddon*, 177–99.

64. Walvoord, *Armageddon*, 199.

65. Walvoord, *Major Bible Prophecies*, 391; see also 389–406; idem, *What We Believe*, 183–89.

66. Walvoord, *Major Bible Prophecies*, 407–28; idem, *What We Believe*, 195–98.

67. Walvoord, *Major Bible Prophecies*, 415.

68. "Q and A," 47–48.

Francis Schaeffer

Colin Duriez

It was in London in the fall of 1966 that I first heard Francis Schaeffer. Rapidly sketching diagrams on a chalkboard, he spoke compassionately of the development of the modern person's "line of despair" as classical philosophy had come to a dead end. The choice was between taking a leap of faith and viewing the human condition as futile, unless. . . . His American voice was slightly high-pitched, his expression (as *Time Magazine* once dubbed it) sad-faced, and his attire unusual. Yet the content of his lectures, full of unfamiliar references and concepts, gripped the heart and mind. Those lectures, repeated at the end of that year for an Inter-Varsity conference, were the basis of his *Escape from Reason* (1968), which traces from the time of Thomas Aquinas and his natural theology what Schaeffer's associate Hans Rookmaaker called the death of a culture.

After Schaeffer left the Inter-Varsity conference in the British Midlands, one of the leaders found his box of chalks and dubbed it "cosmic chalk," leading to the expression "Francis Schaeffer's cosmic chalk and talk." In a sense this captures the man. In his passionate concern for truth—no, not just truth, but "true truth"—he ranged not only through the world today and yesterday, but

also through the universe. His preferred medium was talk—conversation, whether with an individual or with a large group of people. He had the uncanny knack of addressing an individual personally, even if one was sitting with several hundred other people. His tapes, books, and films are best seen as embodiments of his conversation or table talk.

Schaeffer's quaint expression "true truth" is typical of the penetrating style he employed to communicate. He invented terms and images that seemed rough wood, and yet allowed his message to get through. He was conscious that evangelicals talk about truth rather as Martha talked about the resurrection—it did not really apply to her dead brother right now. But truth for Schaeffer went right back to the God behind all created reality, a God who is there and not silent. If God is there, then there are answers to the deep human questions. If he is not, there are no answers. There is no point in waiting at the train station if no train is coming. Truth must lead to spiritual reality.

Schaeffer unashamedly viewed truth as a system coherently expressed in the reliable words of Scripture. Though truth is never merely intellectual and theoretical, he nevertheless demonstrated its intellectual force in the areas of epistemology, metaphysics, and morals. He also demonstrated briefly that truth can be expressed in a theoretical system, yet he saw it more fundamentally as encompassing all areas of human life, such as the presuppositional, the devotional, and the cultural, as well as law, politics, and personal relationships. True spirituality involves the totalitarian rule of Christ over all of life. Schaeffer spoke about this in an interview: "I was one of the first evangelical writers to speak of the meaning of Christianity in music, art, philosophy, and such things. As time went on, and I emphasized increasingly the Lordship of Christ, it became obvious that the battlefields were not only the cultural and intellectual ones, but also in the area of law."[1] The lordship of Christ was to become the integration point of Schaeffer's theology.

To return to the personal note introduced at the beginning of this article: When I first heard Francis Schaeffer, I was on my way to two years' evangelistic work with university students in Istanbul. Schaeffer's words worked their way into my mind, and the next summer I spent several weeks at the L'Abri community in Switzerland. As we talked, he sensed the depths of my inward struggles in trying to find my place in the Christian life. While convinced of biblical truth and authority, I yet felt deeply dissatisfied on a personal level. The fact that most people in the world were both suffering in the here and now and lost forever (two hells, not one!) gave me great anguish.

Walking up a mountain road, Schaeffer simply pointed out to me the biblical view of the person and spirituality—that we are meant to be creative and to be involved as Christians in the *whole* of life. He also convinced me that the fall of Adam and Eve as an actual event in history is the key to some of the deepest questions. I can still remember the penny dropping, as I suddenly understood. Here was the meaning of human life. The implications of human choice go on forever and ever. This was the beginning of a great—though far from easy—liberation.

The purpose of relating this example is to emphasize that Schaeffer's work and writing always centered on the personal. Many of my friends at that time also had their lives touched by him, and by the community of L'Abri, which made incarnate his convictions. Feeling for the individual and the touch of a healing community were for him the ultimate apologetic for the true truth of the Christian faith. Each one was helped in a very individual way. To state this is not hagiography, but fact.[2]

It is well known that Schaeffer saw himself first of all as an evangelist (despite a publisher's blurb labeling him "theologian and philosopher, foremost evangelical thinker of our day"). His apologetics was shaped in this context and hence was person-centered.[3] He felt that if the God revealed in the Bible truly exists, is really there, then the most important of all facts is a person. Personality is at the center of reality. And if Christians really believe that, they are obliged to value the people they encounter. I had the sense—and I know my friends did—that Schaeffer valued us first and foremost as people bearing God's im-

1. Colin Duriez, "Francis Schaeffer—Facing Up to the Central Questions," *Third Way* 4.1 (Dec. 1980): 5.

2. See, e.g., the autobiography by Sylvester Jacobs, *Born Black* (London: Hodder and Stoughton, 1977); for a photographic account of L'Abri in Switzerland, see idem, *Portrait of a Shelter* (Downers Grove, Ill.: Inter-Varsity, 1973).

3. This person-centered approach, so appropriate to our postmodern world, has been taken up by Alister E. McGrath, *Bridge-Building: Effective Christian Apologetics* (Leicester, Eng.: Inter-Varsity, 1992).

age. Most of his writings grew out of his conversations and discussions with people who turned up at L'Abri, his home high in the Swiss Alps.

Intermediate between his writings and those encounters were his lectures and table talk, which he at first only reluctantly allowed to be put on audiotape. Eventually well over a thousand hours of lectures, discussions, and talks were recorded. Those of us who were students at L'Abri listened to his high-pitched voice through headphones for many hours, assiduously taking notes. Many students also prepared seminar papers, called Farel House papers after the study area named for the great Reformer. I remember sitting one sunny day in a Swiss meadow and nervously reading through a paper which I was to give that evening. I feared that my essay, which tried to show that fantasy and imagination can be forms of true knowledge, would be torn to pieces by the analytic mind of the great thinker, who valued reason so highly. To my surprise (and looking back, I see the many faults in my paper) he warmly and kindly endorsed its direction. Later, I came to appreciate the extent of his encouragement of the arts as a vital and strategic Christian activity.

If we are to capture the essence of Francis Schaeffer, it is important to understand his impact on individuals and on movements such as the recent awakening to the arts that is being experienced by many Christians. It is also necessary to sketch his life and the formation of the L'Abri community. Concentrating only on his books (and possibly films and taped lectures) does not give a complete picture. He acknowledged, for example, that one could come away from his books with a negative view of the arts. This is because his books have a prophetic function of pointing out the sorrow and pain at the heart of modern culture, and the despair that has come about through communal as well as individual rebellion against God. On the other hand, those who knew and studied under Schaef-

fer were often inspired to intense involvement in the arts. Hence the necessity of going beyond his books.

It is also important to remember that Schaeffer's eventually voluminous writings evolved from personal conversations. He has had his critics, some of them very kind, some of them uncertain about his broad strokes, some uncharitable.[4] It is inevitable that publication on so massive a scale will be critically scrutinized. Any criticism, however, needs to bear in mind what the evangelist and apologist was doing. Only in this way can the true depth of his scholarship and wisdom be appreciated. Scholarship does not consist only of specialized and highly technical writing. Schaeffer was a man of the broad sweep and the generalization, rather like C. S. Lewis's popular theology and even some of his literary criticism. This is how J. I. Packer sees Schaeffer.[5] And Os Guinness once pointed out that the greatest thing about Francis Schaeffer was Francis Schaeffer.[6] What, then, was his history?

Background

Francis Schaeffer was the child of working-class parents of German ancestry.[7] He was born on January 30, 1912, in Germantown, Pennsylvania. Nearly three years later, on November 3, 1914, his future wife, Edith Seville, was born in China of missionary parents. As a child he helped his father in his duties as a caretaker, which included carpentry. Not surprisingly, Francis chose

4. For a cross section of criticism that takes Schaeffer's work very seriously, see *Reflections on Francis Schaeffer*, ed. Ronald W. Ruegsegger (Grand Rapids: Zondervan, 1986).

5. See the forewords in *Reflections*, ed. Ruegsegger, and Francis A. Schaeffer, *Francis A. Schaeffer Trilogy* (Westchester, Ill.: Crossway, 1990).

6. Memorial service for Francis Schaeffer, All Souls Church, Langham Place, London, 25 July 1984.

7. For information on Schaeffer's background and life see Edith Schaeffer, *The Tapestry* (Waco: Word, 1981); Christopher Catherwood, *Five Evangelical Leaders* (Wheaton, Ill.: Harold Shaw, 1985); and *Reflections*, ed. Ruegsegger.

woodwork and technical drawing as his main subjects when he started high school.

By the age of seventeen, young Schaeffer was working part-time on a fish wagon. He later admitted to having "barely made it" in high school.[8] But a dramatic change took place in his intellectual development when he taught English to a Russian count. The count learned English by reading a book on Greek philosophy. Schaeffer had read some philosophy in high school, but this particular book opened his mind. A churchgoer (though the church he attended was liberal) he started to read the Bible alongside Ovid. He later observed: "The United States when I was young through the Twenties and Thirties showed basically a Christian consensus. It was, of course, poorly applied in certain areas, such as race or compassionate use of accumulated wealth."[9] In his reading of the Bible he was surprised to find answers to the deep philosophical questions he had begun to ask. The dawning excitement never was to leave him. After a six-month period of reading through the Bible he committed himself to Christ and the Christian faith. By September of 1930, which was the year of his high-school graduation, he was able to jot in his diary that "all truth is from the Bible."[10]

After high school Schaeffer enrolled at the Drexel Institute as an engineering student. He was in a dilemma, however, for he felt an unmistakable calling from God to be a pastor. His parents wanted him to be a craftsman like his father, but by the end of the year he persuaded them that his life should dramatically change course.

The fall of the next year found Schaeffer at Hampden-Sydney College in southern Virginia. As he studied for the ministry, there were various indications of the unusual quality of his character: the way in which he faced bullying, his participation in a Sunday school for black people in the

vicinity, and his service as president of the Student Christian Association.

The year after starting at Hampden-Sydney, Francis Schaeffer met Edith Seville at the First Presbyterian Church of Germantown. In her he discovered an ally against liberal attacks upon the integrity of Scripture. In 1935, after he graduated magna cum laude, the two cast their fortunes together in marriage. Edith's culture and refinement perfectly complemented his concern with personal relationships, which was forged by his working-class background, but was also a unique part of his temperament. The two together shaped the later work of L'Abri, and Edith's books added to the overall impact of Francis's writings. In the first ten years of their marriage three daughters were born.

Schaeffer entered Westminster Theological Seminary in September 1935. The lecturers at that period included Cornelius Van Til, J. Gresham Machen, and John Murray. Van Til and Allan MacRae of the Biblical Theological Seminary, he would later recall, particularly stirred his intellectual thought.[11]

When Machen's growing controversy with the Presbyterian Church in the U.S.A. led to his being expelled from the ministry, Schaeffer and several others, including Carl McIntire, felt compelled to separate from the denomination as well. This led to the founding of Faith Theological Seminary in Wilmington under Allan MacRae. Schaeffer moved from Westminster to Faith to complete his studies, in 1938 becoming the first minister of the newly organized Bible Presbyterian Church. He was based in Grove City, Pennsylvania. In 1941 he moved to a church in Chester, Pennsylvania, where he identified with the many working-class members of his congregation, both city and country folk.

Reflecting on this period of theological and ecclesiastical turmoil, the Schaeffers in later life were not happy with some of the

---

8. Philip Yancey, *Open Windows* (Westchester, Ill.: Crossway, 1982), 115.

9. Ibid., 127.

10. Catherwood, *Five Evangelical Leaders*, 112.

11. Yancey, *Open Windows*, 116.

decisions made in early career, particularly regarding the issue of separation. They came to see that truth (both in theory and in relationships with fellow Christians) is more foundational than maintaining ecclesiastical separation. The horizons of their future work began to open up when the Schaeffer family moved to St. Louis in 1943, where they began an organization called Children for Christ. At first it was intended to help the local Bible Presbyterian Church reach out to the children of St. Louis, but the movement eventually spread to other churches and then other denominations (though, at that time, the Schaeffers were still separatist). This seemingly small evangelistic outreach to children was the stimulus which led Francis and Edith to Europe in the crucial years following the Second World War. When Francis expressed interest in the state of youth work and of the church's confrontation with theological liberalism in Europe, his denomination's mission board authorized him to make a fact-finding tour in 1947, a tour which changed his life, and which was eventually to change the lives of countless others throughout Europe and the world.

The Call of Europe

The young pastor, then in his mid-thirties, spent three months traveling, first around France, then visiting Geneva and Lausanne in Switzerland, before making his way up to Oslo for a young people's convention. His conviction that evangelicals must separate themselves from liberalism and its embodiment in the spreading ecumenical movement intensified. He was inspired by many European evangelicals he met, including Ole Hallesby in Norway and Martyn Lloyd-Jones in Britain. All the time, the conviction was growing in his heart that God was calling him to serve Europe in some way, however small.

When Schaeffer returned to the United States, his mission board asked him if he would go to the Netherlands to prepare for an international conference in Amsterdam in August of 1948. Thus it happened that in February 1948 the nomadic existence of the Schaeffer family began, as they set sail for Europe.

In Amsterdam Francis Schaeffer met a serious young Dutchman named Hans Rookmaaker, who was gathering what was to become one of the largest jazz collections in Europe. On discovering that Schaeffer was an American, Rookmaaker approached him for a quick chat about black music. The two of them ended up talking to 4 A.M., mainly about modern art. This was the start of a long and deeply significant friendship. Not surprisingly, it began with a conversation, like so much in Francis Schaeffer's life. The two men were shaped and enriched by each other's ideas and biblical understanding. Both had been converted largely by reading through the Bible with philosophical questions in mind. Rookmaaker's questions had been sharpened by his agony over the fate of Jewish people, including a close friend, in occupied Holland. Later he and his wife Anky became members of L'Abri Fellowship, leading its distinctive work in the Netherlands.

L'Abri was not even a dream in 1948, but the spiritual unity between the two men was real. Many years later, in his inaugural lecture in the chair of art history at the Free University in Amsterdam, Rookmaaker paid public tribute to his friend:

> It seems to me a token, not only of our friendship but also of our spiritual unity, that you have come from Switzerland for this occasion. Since the first time we met, in 1948, we have had many long talks about faith, philosophy, reality, art, the modern world and their mutual relations. I owe very much to these discussions, which have helped to shape my thoughts on these subjects. I want to express my deep gratitude, and consider it a great honour and joy to be a member of L'Abri Fellowship.[12]

12. See Hans R. Rookmaaker, *Art and the Public Today*, 2d ed. (Huémoz-sur-Ollon, Switz.: L'Abri Fellowship, 1969).

In a subsequent interview Rookmaaker again spoke of the tangible unity that bore so much fruit:

> It was in 1948 that I met Schaeffer. . . . I was a bit dissatisfied with Dutch Christianity, which I felt was in some cases below what it should be, particularly on the level of personal faith and way of walking with the Lord. On the other hand, I feel that Anglo-Saxon Christianity really lacks the intellectual insight we have developed in Holland. In a way, what Dr. Schaeffer and I have tried to do is to fuse the two things, to make them into something new.[13]

In the next few years the family settled in Switzerland, their son Franky was born, and Francis and Edith kept busy working with children and warning evangelical churches about liberalism and the more subtle threat of neo-orthodoxy, specifically as embodied in the theology of Karl Barth. Barthianism was a particular problem because of the attractiveness of his thought, especially his attacks upon theological liberalism. To depict the dangers of neo-orthodoxy, Schaeffer focused on the historical context of religious existentialism. At about the same time the husband-and-wife team created Sunday-school material that was based on the Gospel of Luke and later published as *Everybody Can Know*.[14]

The Crisis

In the *Sunday School Times* of June 16 and June 23, 1951, Francis Schaeffer published an article on "The Secret of Power and Enjoyment of the Lord: The Need for Both Purity and Love in the Christian Life." The opening words reflect deep spiritual struggle:

> What is the secret of power? Certainly, as we consider Christianity today—true,

Bible-believing Christianity—we must be impressed by the fact that there is not the consistent power that there has been in certain periods of the past. The same thing is also true of the enjoyment of the Lord. In our day, life is such that, while Christians do many things to serve the Lord, it is obvious from our faces and our conversations that few enjoy Him.

These heartfelt words go back to the previous winter, when he had paced up and down in his hayloft in the Swiss village of Champéry when the weather was wet, and walked the countryside when it was dry, re-examining the basis of his faith and commitment to the Lord. His goal was a true evangelical spirituality that was obedient to Scripture and did not neglect the work of the Holy Spirit. He emerged as committed as ever to a systematic theology, but also convinced of the need for moment-by-moment dependence upon Christ, a truly existential dimension to faith. Without a present reality, he felt, an orthodox theology does not lead to power and enjoyment of the Lord.

Schaeffer's profound spiritual struggles in 1951 led to not only the *Sunday School Times* articles, but also his book *True Spirituality*, which was not published until 1971.[15] This volume was shaped from a series of talks originally given in 1953 at a Bible camp in the United States. They were honed and re-presented in Switzerland after L'Abri had started. They were given again in the United States in 1963, and at L'Abri in 1964, at which time they reached their final form. Actually, the book was based on transcriptions of audiotapes of the L'Abri lectures, tapes students at L'Abri were encouraged to listen to alongside their studies of Christianity and culture.

Schaeffer always believed that without this deep struggle to find reality in the Christian life the work of L'Abri would never have started. There were several test-

13. Colin Duriez, "Interview with H. R. Rookmaaker," *Crusade*, April 1972.

14. Francis A. Schaeffer and Edith Schaeffer, *Everybody Can Know* (Wheaton, Ill.: Tyndale, 1973).

15. Francis A. Schaeffer, *True Spirituality* (Wheaton, Ill.: Tyndale, 1971).

ing years, however, before it was inaugurated in 1955, and the Schaeffers cast off their links with their mission board. They were on their own—unless God was real.

The Genesis of L'Abri

Francis and Edith Schaeffer were prepared to continue their dual work of reaching post-Christian children—European children who had had no opportunity to hear the gospel—and of alerting evangelical churches throughout Europe to the dangers of theological liberalism and neo-orthodoxy. Over the seven years between their arrival in Switzerland as nomads and their settling in the Alpine village of Huémoz-sur-Ollon, where L'Abri became based, however, a new factor had gradually entered their lives. Boarding-school children, mainly girls, of many nationalities came to attend their worship services and, more importantly, to raise questions about the Christian faith. At first the services were in the Schaeffers' home, but then they were allowed to utilize an abandoned Protestant church (they lived in a Roman Catholic canton). The discussions took on increasing importance, leading to a realization of the need for a work like L'Abri, even though buried in the rural Alps! Years later, Schaeffer confessed, "I was amazed in those discussions to find that I could answer those girls' questions in a way that a lot of them actually became interested."[16]

By word of mouth, the news spread to college and university students that there was a place in the Alps where one could get honest answers to life's deepest questions. Schaeffer was basically content to continue carefully and compassionately listening and then giving answers to the small groups of students who became, during their stay, part of the Schaeffers' home. Though sometimes he felt frustrated, he believed that God would work on the seeds he and Edith planted. They had the joy of seeing some students praying to Christ for salvation. In

the early days there was no thought of books, or films, or even audiotapes of conversations and discussions. The development from tapes to books to films was a gradual, almost reluctant process.

What led to the fact that by 1968 over one thousand hours of audiotape, covering such themes as true spirituality, the books of Romans and Revelation, the Westminster Confession, and various cultural issues, had been recorded? Schaeffer himself explained in 1980:

> When I was working at L'Abri in the early days, I really expected just to be talking one to one. I never intended even to make tapes, and the tape programme just opened up. It's rather ironic now.
>
> Somebody sent us a tape recorder and I said, "I'll never use it. It'll kill the spontaneity of the conversation." The tape recorder must have been in our office for at least six months. Then, one Saturday night, down in Les Melezes living room, we had a really bang up conversation going with some Smith College girls. One of our workers came up and said to Edith, "It's a shame this isn't being recorded; it'll be lost. If you'll just make a lot of noise serving tea, I'll hide the microphone in the flowers." I noticed some kind of confusion, and wondered what was going on. When I found out later that the conversation had been recorded, I must say I was furious. I felt this was unfair to those girls; they thought it was a private conversation. Then to my amazement every one of the girls was delighted, and bought copies of the tape to take home, not only for themselves, but for their friends. This opened the tape programme: it was as simple as that.[17]

A turning point in the development of L'Abri was the founding of a similar work in England in 1958, after Francis had given lectures in Oxford and elsewhere in Britain. That work was eventually to be led by Ranald Macaulay, who married the Schaef-

16. Quoted in Yancey, *Open Windows,* 105.

17. Duriez, "Francis Schaeffer," 5.

fers' second daughter, Susan. The establishment of an English L'Abri was symbolic of the deep influence Schaeffer was to have on a generation of British evangelicals. In particular, he forged warm and significant links with Inter-Varsity Fellowship (the British equivalent of Inter-Varsity Christian Fellowship). He also took a deep interest in what was happening both on the British theological scene and in British culture, especially when its rock music began to have a worldwide influence.

Major Writings

Escape from Reason

Like the long-term community-based work of L'Abri in Switzerland, speaking tours of British and American universities and colleges gradually became a pattern in Francis Schaeffer's life. It was out of these tours that the books most frequently associated with him were born.

Apart from a few booklets—*Basic Bible Studies, Empire Builder for Boys* (1946), and *Empire Builder for Girls* (1946)—Francis Schaeffer's first published book was *Escape from Reason*.[18] Like the tape program, the book program came into being without conscious planning, but because of demand. In fact, most of Schaeffer's now voluminous writings are based on transcripts of talks captured on audiotape. The evolution of *Escape from Reason* is typical.

Fall 1966—London. Lectures tracing the despair of modern humanity from a medieval dualism of nature and grace are given to young people embarking on a mission program under Operation Mobilisation. The same series of lectures, which has already been given at the Free University of Amsterdam, is filmed by a lecturer at Indiana University for use with students in the United States.

New Year 1967—The Midlands. Schaeffer is guest speaker at the annual confer-

ence of the Graduates Fellowship, which is part of Inter-Varsity Fellowship. He gives three talks, all of which overrun his allotted time by a half hour or more. He is asked to give one more talk, the chairman being given orders to get him to finish on time for the meal which follows—in vain. The talks, however, make an indelible impact on the audience, including a number of future evangelical leaders.

April 1967. Oliver Barclay, the general secretary of Inter-Varsity Fellowship, hands over to Geraint Fielder, one of the staff workers, a transcript of the tapes of the lectures Schaeffer gave at the conference. Fielder agrees to consider whether the material warrants publication. He spends the next two weeks editing it and then meets with Schaeffer at the English L'Abri (then in Ealing, London) to discuss the project.

June 15, 1967. Schaeffer writes to Fielder, thanking him for all the work he has put into editing. An even more appreciative letter, dated August 14, whimsically wishes that Fielder was at L'Abri in Switzerland to work on more taped material.

March 1968. Publication of *Escape from Reason*.

Upon revising *Escape from Reason* not long before his death from cancer, Schaeffer reaffirmed its continuing topicality. In fact, he felt that it was more topical in 1980 than when it was first published.

The preface to *Escape from Reason* explains why Schaeffer, in analyzing the trends in modern thought, begins deep in the Middle Ages with Thomas Aquinas. Such an analysis, he points out, should be concerned with both philosophy and history. By investigating the historical background, we can discover the "unchanging truth in a changing world."

Because of Aquinas's accommodation to the intellectual tradition of Greece and Rome, asserts Schaeffer, Christian thinking was seriously weakened. In particular, Thomas allowed human thinking an autonomy from biblical revelation. This auton-

---

18. Francis A. Schaeffer, *Escape from Reason* (Downers Grove, Ill.: Inter-Varsity, 1968).

omy was not in the proper sense of free, dignified human thought, but in the sense of rationalism. As a result, in some areas of reality knowledge was viewed as beginning with the human mind rather than depending totally upon biblical revelation.

When Thomas allowed the human mind to begin from itself, albeit in a limited way, there were serious consequences for the issue of nature and grace, which was a frame of reference throughout the later Middle Ages and beyond. "Nature," in Schaeffer's words, "began to eat up grace." Grace was the realm of universals and of absolute principles. In the Greco-Roman scheme universals determined reality, and nature was essentially unimportant. In Christian thinking, however, nature exists in its own right. Observing that it is glorifying to God to explore nature, Aquinas helped the process which led to modern science. However, the new emphasis on nature in conjunction with even a limited autonomy of the human mind had the result that knowledge now focused on particulars and eventually was unable to attain universals.[19] Schaeffer graphically and movingly demonstrates this dilemma in the person of Leonardo da Vinci. Unlike the distinctively modern person, Leonardo never relinquished the hope of a unified field of knowledge encompassing nature and grace, particulars and universals, quantities and qualities, fact and meaning.

The next stage in the development of modern consciousness, according to Schaeffer, was a paradigm shift from nature and grace to nature and freedom. Between these worlds of discourse there was still continuity, however. Most importantly, philosophers, scientists, and artists continued to seek a unified field of knowledge. On the negative side, they also worked within the framework let in by Aquinas: instead of

depending totally on the biblical revelation, where God discloses truth about both himself and his creation, including the identity of the human being, knowledge began with the human mind. In addition, there was increasing tension between human freedom and the conception of the human being as a mechanism describable in terms of natural laws.

Parallel to this period was the Protestant Reformation.[20] This development was free of the dilemmas of the nature-freedom paradigm, even though its dependence on biblical revelation was far from perfect. Nevertheless, it introduced into society and culture insights about nature and the human being which resulted in tangible blessings which reverberate to our day: the principles of democratic government, the growth of scientific knowledge and technology, enormous advances in health care, a strong legal base which protects the weak and powerless, a richness in the arts and language, and so on.

The final step in the development of modernity is described by Schaeffer as an absolute discontinuity with the past. There was a paradigm shift like no other (except perhaps in the East millennia ago). Here the vanguard thinkers abandoned the human quest for a unified field of knowledge. The realm that in the past had been labeled grace or freedom was put beyond the categories of rationality. All that gives meaning to the world and to the human being was seen as lying outside of rational investigation, now identified with scientific knowledge. Universals no longer obeyed what Schaeffer called "classical rationality." They were no longer subject to basic logic such as the law of noncontradiction, nor were they to be understood in causal terms.

There was, however, at the same time a significant continuity with the past. The modern consciousness was still humanistic

---

19. Michael Polanyi, *Personal Knowledge* (Chicago: University of Chicago Press, 1974), points out the dramatic consequences of this kind of reductionism. He argues that to avoid loss of meaning, particulars should be indwelt rather than focused on.

20. For a more extensive discussion see Francis A. Schaeffer, *How Should We Then Live?* (Old Tappan, N.J.: Revell, 1976).

in the sense of believing that humans begin from themselves in knowing and in defining reality. Thus there was now open revolt against the idea that true knowledge is totally dependent upon biblical revelation.

The leap into nonrational meaning centered, for Schaeffer, in the giant figures of the philosophers Georg Hegel and Søren Kierkegaard. The remainder of *Escape from Reason* traces the chronological, geographical, and social spread of the new way of thinking, a way of thinking that, in C. S. Lewis's phrase, divides modern people from "Old Western Man."[21]

Schaeffer describes the methodology of the old rationality as antithesis: A is true in contrast to non-A. God is there in contrast to his not being there. Beauty is in contrast to ugliness. Evil and cruelty are in contrast to goodness. Murder, theft, and similar deeds are wrong. The deliberate killing of an unborn child is an evil, and ignoring such an act is a sin of omission. Such judgments are foreign to the new way of thinking.

Escape from Reason provides the frame for much of Schaeffer's lifework as a pastor, apologist, and latterly a campaigner for human rights. His work should be seen in this context rather than that of academic philosophy, theology, or even the politics of the American Right. Not surprisingly, his little book, which reads like an intellectual slide-show, has provoked criticisms which also apply to some of his other publications. Some have disputed his thumbnail sketches of great historical figures. This is particularly true of his portrayals of Aquinas and Kierkegaard.[22] It should be borne

in mind that there is room for honest differences of interpretation of such figures. It is plausible to see, as Schaeffer does, Kierkegaard as the father of both religious and secular existentialism. The interpretation of Aquinas is also plausible. If Aquinas did open the floodgate of rationalistic knowledge, we need not conclude that much or even most of his work is not valuable nor distinctly Christian. The key issue here perhaps is the causal relationship between significant individuals and historical changes. It may be that figures like Aquinas and Kierkegaard were not first movers, so to speak, but articulated the spirit of their times, their thinking and creativity patterned by a paradigm or world model that was either dominant or coming into existence. If this is so, we should be able to cite contemporaries whose thinking was similar to that of Aquinas or Kierkegaard. It may also be that hindsight leads us to see meanings in their work of which they themselves were not fully conscious, and from which they may even have recoiled had they been.

Schaeffer is in line with many scholars, however, in seeing Aquinas and Kierkegaard as radically innovative. The philosopher Herman Dooyeweerd's analysis of the "ground-motives" of form-matter, nature-grace, and nature-freedom backs up Schaeffer's sketch of Aquinas.[23] Schaeffer's portrait also fits, in spirit, with C. S. Lewis's understanding of the period:

> The recovery of Aristotle's text dates from the second half of the twelfth century: the dominance of his doctrine soon followed.

---

21. See C. S. Lewis, *"De descriptione temporum,"* in C. S. Lewis, *Selected Literary Essays,* ed. Walter Hooper (New York: Cambridge University Press, 1969), 1–14. Lewis identified the shift into modern consciousness with the rise of the "machine archetype," which was associated with a myth of progress. Unlike Schaeffer, Lewis's emphasis is more on the sociology of knowledge and world models than on ideas.

22. See *Reflections,* ed. Ruegsegger, 112–15, 118–20; and Norman L. Geisler, *Thomas Aquinas: An Evangelical Appraisal* (Grand Rapids: Baker, 1991), 61.

23. Herman Dooyeweerd, *A New Critique of Theoretical Thought,* 4 vols. (Philadelphia: Presbyterian and Reformed, 1953–58), 1:36, 180–81; idem, *The Roots of Western Culture* (Toronto: Wedge, 1979), ch. 5; and L. Kalsbeek, *Contours of a Christian Philosophy* (Toronto: Wedge, 1975), 144. Indeed, Schaeffer has been charged with employing Dooyeweerd's analysis without acknowledgment. However, Schaeffer owed no debt to Dooyeweerd except for a single unnamed article on nature and grace (Francis A. Schaeffer, letter to Colin Duriez, 16 June 1972).

Aristotle is, before all, the philosopher of divisions. His effect on his greatest disciple [Aquinas], as M. Gilson has traced it, was to dig new chasms between God and the world, between human knowledge and reality, between faith and reason. Heaven began, under this dispensation, to seem farther off. The danger of Pantheism grew less: the danger of mechanical Deism came a step nearer. It is almost as if the first, faint shadow of Descartes, or even of "our present discontents" had fallen across the scene.[24]

The God Who Is There

Another essential book in Schaeffer's corpus was in preparation before and published soon after *Escape from Reason*. This book—*The God Who Is There*—was really his first venture into deliberate publication.[25] He had been as reluctant about going into print as he had been about being recorded on audiotape. He himself explained how *The God Who Is There* came about:

As I lectured in very many places, in Britain, Germany and the USA, I gradually developed a basic lecture, "Speaking historic Christianity into the 20th century world." When I gave it at Wheaton College, Illinois, they asked if they could put it out as a small xeroxed book. I said, "Well, only for your students, because I don't want published books." When I saw that, however, and read it over, I realised I had a responsibility to publish. It became *The God Who Is There*.[26]

This seminal book was originally released in what the British publisher informally described to Schaeffer as their "egghead series." Though the initial pressrun was low, the book was soon reprinted several times and later issued in a more popular format.

24. C. S. Lewis, *The Allegory of Love* (New York: Oxford University Press, 1958), 88. For more on the medieval world model see idem, *The Discarded Image* (New York: Cambridge University Press, 1964).
25. Francis A. Schaeffer, *The God Who Is There* (London: Hodder and Stoughton; Chicago: Inter-Varsity, 1968).
26. Duriez, "Francis Schaeffer," 6.

The God Who Is There picks up on the thesis of *Escape from Reason*, tracing the origins of the modern relativism in knowledge and morals to an abandonment of the perennial human search for a unified field of knowledge. All that gives meaning to human beings and their society and culture is relegated to the realm of the mystical and nonrational. Schaeffer ascribes to the period of Hegel and Kierkegaard the notion that a leap of faith is necessary if we are to find any meaning in human life. He then traces the steps by which this mentality eventually spread to every part of society and culture. He emphasizes as well the role that modern theology has played in promoting relativism and the mystical leap. The problem is particularly insidious because the new theology uses orthodox Christian terminology, conveying the impression of rational content and categories that in fact are increasingly absent. Friedrich Nietzsche's declaration of the death of God has proven to be prophetic.

Because the modern person is typically "below the line of despair," we have to rethink Christian apologetics and evangelism. Classical apologetics fails to communicate because it is built on the old methodology of antithesis. It was once meaningful to speak of God's existing (as opposed to his not existing), of sin, of the finished work of Christ; this, however, is no longer the case. We must now begin by recognizing that Christian belief is in fact radical in our day and how it differs from the new theology. If, for example, we say that the Bible is true even though its portrayal of historical events is full of errors of fact, we are speaking with the voice of the new theology, of modernity, not of biblical Christianity. Schaeffer goes on to demonstrate a person-centered apologetics which will have bite in our day. We have to combine obedience to the written words of Scripture with a demonstrable godly reality in our own lives and in our relations with others. Focus on personality and the individual is the ultimate apologetic for the

Christian faith. Each human being is confronted with the form of the real universe and the reality of one's own humanness. Only Christian faith is at home with these fundamental realities. Non-Christian systems actually divide the individual internally, because they pull one away from these basic realities.

Schaeffer's unshakable realism allows him to steer a path between extreme presuppositionalism and evidentialism or foundationalism in apologetics. Although Christianity is a system, a fact for which no apologies need be made, it is also a historic faith. It is therefore in this respect open to verification. If Christ did not rise from the dead at an actual time in history, our faith is in vain. But what, then, is the role of presuppositions? Schaeffer explains: "I do believe that presuppositions are crucial. . . . From my way of looking at them, presuppositions are not accepted by you unconsciously, as a prior condition to your first move of thought. For me, the proper way to get at it is that, if you are a thinking person, you decide what set of presuppositions are going to lead to the answers to the questions."[27]

He Is There and He Is Not Silent

Underlying both *Escape from Reason* and *The God Who Is There* was a concern for the issue of knowledge. Schaeffer had demonstrated that shifting approaches to knowledge in the recent and far-off history of the West had had dramatic consequences for how we live (and die). He turned once again to this matter in *He Is There and He Is Not Silent* (1972), arguing that only the historic Christian faith gives adequate answers in the fundamental areas of metaphysics, morals, and epistemology.[28] In each of these areas he posits that God's existence and communication to us are "necessary." If he is not there, or if he is there but is silent, then there are no answers to the big

human questions in these areas. These questions are particularly acute for modern people, which is why Schaeffer was so concerned, as a pastor and apologist, to express the exciting answers to be found in a biblical Christianity.

He Is There and He Is Not Silent, inevitably, is popular philosophy as well as popular theology. Yet Schaeffer does not write as a philosopher. That is not his intention. In fact, this book is the furthest he went in philosophical debate, and he had no wish to go further. Consequently, there may be difficulties for the reader. For instance, Schaeffer's use of the term *necessity* is not the standard philosophical use (i.e., the opposite of "contingency"). By the "necessity" of historic Christianity he means that without God's existence and communication there are no answers to the fundamental human questions. His analysis of Western cultural themes in previous books had demonstrated the lack of answers outside of biblical Christianity, resulting in the despair of modern humans. Though God's existence and communication answer these questions, Christianity stands or falls as truth on the basis of historical events such as the death and resurrection of a first-century Palestinian called Jesus.

Schaeffer was the author of over twenty books and booklets in total. Two of them were coauthored, one with Edith and the other with the distinguished pediatric surgeon C. Everett Koop.[29] There is some overlap in material, but all the publications have been usefully gathered together and thematically arranged in *The Complete Works of Francis A. Schaeffer*.[30] Though ill from cancer, he was able to revise his books for this compilation. Most importantly, he

27. Ibid., 8.
28. Francis A. Schaeffer, *He Is There and He Is Not Silent* (Wheaton, Ill.: Tyndale, 1972).
29. Schaeffer and Schaeffer, *Everybody Can Know*; Francis A. Schaeffer and C. Everett Koop, *Whatever Happened to the Human Race?* (Old Tappan, N.J.: Revell, 1979).
30. Francis A. Schaeffer, *The Complete Works of Francis A. Schaeffer*, 5 vols. (Westchester, Ill.: Crossway, 1982).

rewrote a section on his apologetic method for the new edition of *The God Who Is There* (Appendix A). The core books of the corpus, the first of which was not published until he was fifty-six, are the trilogy *Escape from Reason*, *The God Who Is There*, and *He Is There and He Is Not Silent*. It is essential, however, to read *True Spirituality* to get to the heartbeat of his theology. Also worthy of special mention is *Pollution and the Death of Man*, a pioneering statement of proper evangelical concern for the environment, for nature our "fair sister."[31]

The Final Phase

Schaeffer's realism—his concern for the practice of truth in his generation—inevitably led him to defend the rights of the unborn child, the weak, and the elderly. His theology was that of the lordship of Christ over every area of life—the womb as well as the university seminar room. This prolife stance received special emphasis only after his move into filmmaking, into what he would have called general culture. Just as he had been persuaded first to record talks and discussions, and then to publish books, so was he eventually persuaded of the value of films. The idea came from his son Franky, though in 1966 the *Escape from Reason* lectures had been recorded on film. He explained how the *How Should We Then Live?* film series came about:

As the books came out and sold so well—millions, in 25 languages—the next thing was that Franky came to me and said, "Dad, you're saying something that most people aren't saying. In order to give what you're saying a wide hearing, would you do a film?" This was a brand new idea, and I was very reticent. The more I thought and prayed about it, the more I realised that, rather than being a discontinuity, a film is very much a continuity with writing books. Quite frankly, also, I had seen Kenneth Clark's *Civilisation*, and felt that he

was totally unfair, especially in the "Reformation" episode, so I wanted to counter that in some way.[32]

Parallel to the film series was a large-format hardback book of the same name. Especially written rather than based upon tapes, *How Should We Then Live?* is one of Schaeffer's finest books. Its portrayal of the history of art (necessarily selective) was written in consultation with Hans Rookmaaker. Other consultants were used for other areas, for example, music. The basic thesis of *Escape from Reason* was greatly expanded, with the historical sweep now going right back to Roman times.

Schaeffer spoke at various seminars where the film series was shown, a pattern which anticipated the more controversial series *Whatever Happened to the Human Race?* the project in which Koop collaborated. Their concern was the widespread increase in abortion on demand, and the concomitant peril of a likely spread of euthanasia. Schaeffer and Koop attributed this development to a monolithic acceptance of moral and epistemological relativism in the West. The tangible blessings that had accrued to society from Christian insights into human nature were rapidly being eroded by the new humanism. The film series and the book of the same name emphasized the historic nature of the Christian truth-claims.

While filming the new series, Schaeffer learned that he had cancer of the lymph system. Only immediate medical action saved his life, and thereafter frequent courses of chemotherapy were necessary. The shadow of death intensified his concern to do what he could to try to reverse the horrific trend of easy abortion, resulting in the deaths of millions of unborn children. As one British evangelist put it, "One of the most dangerous places to be today is in your mother's womb."

Joining the prolife lobby identified Schaeffer with America's religious Right,

31. Francis A. Schaeffer, *Pollution and the Death of Man* (Wheaton, Ill.: Tyndale, 1970).

32. Duriez, "Francis Schaeffer," 6.

which was able to exercise considerable political clout during the Reagan era. The German magazine *Der Spiegel* described him as "the philosopher of the Moral Majority." His book *A Christian Manifesto* dismayed some of his most loyal followers by advocating civil disobedience in intolerable circumstances. Some undiscerning readers, it was felt, could easily see him as advocating civil religion. In aligning with the religious Right, however, Schaeffer was in fact simply trying to put into practice his concept of cobelligerency. For the prolife issue transcends political wings. In the United Kingdom, for example, one of the best-known prolife members of Parliament belongs to the centrist Liberal Democratic party. Cobelligerency in social action now replaced Schaeffer's separatism, which he had abandoned in 1951 during his struggles over true spirituality.

At the close of his life, Schaeffer was involved not only in the prolife controversy, but in a distinctive stand in the "battle for the Bible." It has been claimed that his activity in this area, including his helping to found the International Council on Biblical Inerrancy (1977), was his separatism reemerging.[33] But for Schaeffer the battle lines were not drawn around the inerrancy of Scripture as such. Such a position could be held coldly, without love. Rather, for him, the watershed issue was *obeying* the Bible.

Thus Schaeffer's stance on inerrancy does not mean that we have to read the Bible in a wooden, uneducated way. It is true that where it touches on the cosmos, that is, where it puts a control on scientific investigation by imparting true knowledge about nature, there are absolute limits; but within those limits there is enormous freedom. The very honesty of his approach in *Genesis in Space and Time* frees him from the restrictions of young-earth creationism, though he is undoubtedly a creationist.[34] In

his view, evangelical scientists who speculate that the physical part of our being may have been created by God through biological evolution are free at least to hypothesize and investigate. On the other hand, Schaeffer emphasizes that modern science was founded on the presuppositions so clearly set forth in early Genesis. And he courageously defines the absolute limits. For example, without the actual sin of a real first man and woman in history there is no explanation of the problem of evil. Without it our present world is morally normal rather than abnormal, and therefore God's judgment of the world is either meaningless or arbitrary.

The open nature of Schaeffer's inerrantist view of the Bible is demonstrated in his stance on eschatology. Though he was a thoroughgoing premillennialist, he treated this position as of secondary rather than of primary importance. His relations with fellow Christians were unaffected by disagreements about the millennium. The absolute limit in this case was the biblical teaching that Christ will return on an actual day in the future, though we do not know the timing in advance.

Here we must leave the life and work of Francis Schaeffer, a figure as indelibly part of today's evangelical consciousness as when he died in May 1984. L'Abri continues in several countries, including the United States, Britain, the Netherlands, and Switzerland. In all of them, the personal and communal elements are still the focal concerns. The work is a quiet one, despite the media spotlight's having been on Schaeffer in his closing years.

Great changes in the lives of numerous Christians throughout the world began with a conversation with Francis Schaeffer. His books are still best read as a conversation. But though their prose is generally rough-and-ready, they are shot through with vivid analogies and figures: the upper and lower story, the universe and two chairs, the fish developing lungs in an air-

33. This point has been argued by Forrest Baird in *Reflections*, ed. Ruegsegger, 64.

34. Francis A. Schaeffer, *Genesis in Space and Time* (Downers Grove, Ill.: Inter-Varsity, 1972).

less universe, the line of despair. The books continue to challenge Christian and non-Christian alike with both the full meaning of biblical truth and penetrating insight into the modern world, a world which grips us all in its spell. Perhaps the best summation of Schaeffer's contributions is a remark made at a gathering at an evangelical college where various criticisms of his approach to culture were being raised: "Say what you will, just remember that without Francis Schaeffer, most evangelicals would not even be in a discussion like this."[35]

Primary Sources

Schaeffer, Francis A. *The Complete Works of Francis A. Schaeffer.* 5 vols. Westchester, Ill.: Crossway, 1982.

_____. *The Letters of Francis A. Schaeffer.* Edited by Lane T. Dennis. Westchester, Ill.: Crossway, 1986.

35. Stephen Board, "The Rise of Francis Schaeffer," *Eternity* 28.6 (June 1977): 59.

_____, and Edith Schaeffer. *Everybody Can Know.* Wheaton, Ill.: Tyndale, 1973.

Secondary Sources

Catherwood, Christopher. *Five Evangelical Leaders.* Wheaton, Ill.: Harold Shaw, 1985.

Duriez, Colin. "Francis Schaeffer—Facing Up to the Central Questions." *Third Way* 4.1 (Dec. 1980): 5–8.

Francis Schaeffer: Portraits of the Man and His Work. Edited by Lane T. Dennis. Westchester, Ill.: Crossway, 1986.

Morris, Thomas V. *Francis Schaeffer's Apologetics: A Critique.* Chicago: Moody, 1976.

Reflections on Francis Schaeffer. Edited by Ronald W. Ruegsegger. Grand Rapids: Zondervan, 1986.

Schaeffer, Edith. *L'Abri.* Wheaton, Ill.: Tyndale, 1969.

_____. *The Tapestry.* Waco: Word, 1981.

Yancey, Philip. *Open Windows.* Westchester, Ill.: Crossway, 1982.

Carl F. H. Henry

Richard A. Purdy

Carl Ferdinand Howard Henry was born in New York City on January 22, 1913, the first of the eight children of German immigrants Karl F. Heinrich and Johanna Vaethroeder. Raised on a small Long Island farm, young Carl, by his junior year in high school, was able to type eighty-five words per minute.[1] This skill, among others, secured reporting and editorial assignments during the Depression years, at first with local weeklies and then with larger newspapers like the *New York Herald Tribune* and the *New York Daily News*.

In the summer of 1933, Henry was converted to personal faith in Christ. Two years later, he enrolled in Wheaton College's undergraduate philosophy program, studying under department chairman Gordon H. Clark. In 1938 Henry began graduate studies in theology at both Northern Baptist Theological Seminary and Wheaton, during which time he met his wife-to-be, Helga Bender, in a typing class he was teaching. They married in 1941, the year in which Henry completed his B.D. from Northern and his M.A. from Wheaton and was or-

dained in the Baptist ministry. He received a Th.D. from Northern in May 1942 and shortly afterwards was added to its full-time faculty.

In 1947 Henry left Northern, joining Edward John Carnell in doctoral studies under personalist philosopher Edgar S. Brightman at Boston University. The two obtained Ph.D.s in 1949. Also in 1947 Henry, Charles Fuller, Harold Ockenga (pastor of Park Street Church, Boston), Wilbur Smith, and Everett Harrison shared the vision of establishing an evangelical seminary in California. Fuller's father had left a considerable estate, and with the availability of property in Pasadena and Ockenga's willingness to become president, Fuller Theological Seminary opened in September of 1947. In 1950 Henry pur-

1. Carl F. H. Henry, *Confessions of a Theologian* (Waco: Word, 1986), 30.

260

chased a home in Pasadena and began teaching theology full-time at Fuller.

In 1955 the magazine *Christianity Today* was founded for the purpose of addressing theologically oriented liberal clergy. Henry was approached by financier J. Howard Pew of Sun Oil and Billy Graham's father-in-law, L. Nelson Bell, about the possibility of becoming editor. Taking a leave of absence from his position at Fuller, Henry joined the staff and commuted every other month from his California residence to the magazine's headquarters in Washington, D.C., one-and-a-half blocks from the White House.

The next year Henry renewed his editorship, extended his leave from Fuller, and relocated his home to Arlington, Virginia. The board of *Christianity Today* kept pushing Henry for a permanent commitment, but he, with others, had several concerns, predominantly the recurring efforts to change the magazine's character from an intellectual journal for clergy to a lay publication.[2] Added to this, Bell's appointment as executive editor combined with his board status, Henry believed, was destabilizing to editorial autonomy.[3] And long work hours were beginning to take their toll. Partly from fatigue but also from the desire to become more fully acquainted with theological trends, Henry took a full-year sabbatical in 1963, traveling through Africa, the Middle East, and Europe.[4] In Europe he interviewed many liberal and conservative theologians, distilling significant trends in Continental theology for publication.

In 1968 Henry resigned from *Christianity Today*. Top management had become chary of their editor's long-term vocational preferences and stipulated lifelong commitment in his renewal contract.[5] Henry opted for management's counteroffer to appoint him editor-at-large. During his aggressive

leadership *Christianity Today* had advanced from an initial 15,000 paying subscribers in 1956 to 154,000.[6]

In September 1968 Henry departed for Cambridge University, committing a half year of research to a volume on epistemology and another half year to a volume on ontology. The title of this projected series, *God, Revelation and Authority*, reflected his belief that all talk about God is merely conjectural if God has not revealed himself.[7] Following this extended research Henry commenced a professorship at Eastern Baptist Theological Seminary. But Eastern's stance on the issue of biblical errors and the evolving ambiguity of the term *evangelical* induced Henry to withdraw from the school at the close of the 1973–74 academic year.

At the other end of the spectrum, Henry took issue with radical fundamentalists when Harold Lindsell's *Battle for the Bible* was published in 1976. Shortly after its release, some prominent theologians categorized those evangelicals who denied inerrancy as "false evangelicals" (Henry preferred the term *inconsistent*).[8] Henry believed that the new categorization would further confuse perceptions of "evangelicalism." At *Christianity Today* he had frequently enlisted the literary creativity of esteemed Christian scholars like F. F. Bruce and G. C. Berkouwer, who were now subsumed under the new label.[9]

Disconcerted by ongoing evangelical disunity, Henry continued to work within the inerrantist camp. In 1974 he was invited by Stan Mooneyham to become lecturer-at-large for World Vision International, a position he held through 1986. This global ministry enabled Henry to write, lecture, and preach at influential seminaries and universities throughout Africa, Europe, and Asia, in addition to the United States. From

2. Ibid., 182.
3. Ibid., 183.
4. Ibid., 196 (ch. 11 is titled "A Workaholic's Sabbatical").
5. Ibid., 282.

6. Ibid., 163, 286. The initial number was announced at a prepublication news conference.
7. Ibid., 304–5.
8. Ibid., 365.
9. Ibid.

1974 to the present Henry has also been a visiting professor at Trinity Evangelical Divinity School; and since 1990 he has served as lecturer-at-large with Prison Fellowship Ministries.

The First Task of Apologetics: Refutation of Nonbiblical Alternatives

Grounding his epistemology in revelation, Henry states that since Christianity makes claims to universal truth, the Christian apologist must (1) adduce criteria for verifying truth and (2) "show that non-Biblical alternatives are futile," a project which, he says, "will encompass all . . . eras of cultural experience and call them to account."[10] Nonbiblical alternatives are futile because they are logically inconsistent. There is ultimately one comprehensive system, one set of axioms and consistent deductions which constitute the mind of God.[11] The task of apologetics, therefore, is twofold: (1) to investigate and expose inconsistency in contrary positions, and (2) to demonstrate the consistency of the axioms of Christian revelation.[12]

Henry concedes that the task of apologetics is a tedious project and that there is "no final achievement" of it in current theology, so the apologist must with eternal patience strive to approximate the mind of God.[13] But Henry applauds Gordon H. Clark for laying a superb foundation. "To no contemporary," he says in the opening chapter of *God, Revelation and Authority*, "do I owe a profounder debt. . . . I have considered him the peer of evangelical philosophers in identifying the logical inconsisten-

cies that beset nonevangelical alternatives and in exhibiting the intellectual superiority of Christian theism."[14]

All proof—even the proof of logic—presupposes logic.[15] There are not several logics, as some have ventured, but only "one logic to which all propositions are answerable."[16] Apart from rational consistency the unbeliever, Henry insists, cannot recognize the superiority of Christian claims over those of competing religions and philosophies. Christian apologetics yields "persuasive rational evidence" that, while not compelling belief, calls one into accountability.[17] Moreover, the effort to find logical consistency in the data of, for example, history, science, psychology, and ethics, yields a broad, impressive coherence (a "subordinate test for truth") that supports the Christian faith.[18] Without demeaning the necessity of regeneration, Henry ties the success of his apagogic method (i.e., defending Christianity by logically refuting the alternatives) to the image of God in humans, which, though fallen, retains its logical nature.[19]

Refutation of Naturalism

Henry alludes constantly to naturalism, the view that nature "is not only real . . . [but] ultimate," a premise he considers to be "the central postulate of the modern mind"; this view includes, among other elements, implicit denial of the supernatural.[20] The claim by some that science requires naturalism is somewhat surreptitious, Henry responds, since the premise

10. Carl F. H. Henry, *God, Revelation and Authority*, 6 vols. (Waco: Word, 1976–83), 1:228, 224, 234, 215.

11. Ibid., 1:227; "the more orderly and logical that exposition [of theology] is, the nearer the expositor will be to the mind of God in his revelation" (pp. 240–41).

12. Ibid., 1:241.

13. Ibid., 1:240; "we do not indeed have a theology of Glory" (p. 241).

14. Ibid., 1:10.

15. Ibid., 1:223.

16. Ibid., 3:385.

17. Ibid., 1:234.

18. Ibid., 1:232.

19. Ibid., 2:130; see also 1:357–60. Henry says elsewhere: "All man needs to know God as he truly is, is God's intelligible disclosure and rational concepts that qualify man—on the basis of the imago Dei—to comprehend the content of God's logically ordered revelation" (4:119).

20. Carl F. H. Henry, *Christian Personal Ethics* (Grand Rapids: Eerdmans, 1957), 23; idem, *The Drift of Western Thought* (Grand Rapids: Eerdmans, 1951), 41.

that nature alone is real is not a given, and nothing in physical observation or scientific methodology yields it.[21] Nevertheless, while an idealistic philosophy of science is equally tenable, naturalism persists as "the prevailing philosophy of science."[22]

A cardinal tenet of naturalism is that everything is subordinate to space-time processes. But this tenet is not self-evident, and naturalism is plagued with similarly questionable inferences at every turn, according to Henry. In fact, the basic premise that nature alone is real is as vacuous of meaning as it is empirically nonverifiable. In substantial agreement with Immanuel Kant, Henry observes that the terms *real* and *exist,* being "predicates of everything, . . . distinguish nothing."[23] Since dreams, hallucinations, and lies are all real, to say that nature is real does not explain nature nor disclose whether it is something outside ourselves (objective) or within our minds (subjective). Similarly, the naturalistic notion that everything changes entails a contradiction—"the unchanging dogma that all norms are changing."[24] And, quoting Thomas Kuhn, Henry agrees that there are no neutral observations. Indeed, contemporary physicists have admitted that atomic minutiae like quarks and gluons are not "observed facts," but inferences or interpretations.[25]

With Clark, Henry holds that induction is a fallacious methodology, since no number of empirical instances from yesterday can establish a general theory for yesterday, today, or tomorrow. Only exhaustive induction justifies a law.[26] Among so-called laws

originally underwritten but subsequently dropped by scientists are causality and uniformity. When describing the turbulence of natural processes, today's scientist focuses instead on their correlation (as did David Hume) or discontinuity (Werner Heisenberg). Henry approvingly cites Kuhn's analysis of what happens when the scientific light, so to speak, goes on. At the point of discovery, the scientist transcends methodology. The discovery comes from intuition or divine revelation, not science. The key to the new knowledge is detached creativity, not induction from raw data.[27]

Valid deduction as frequently eludes the scientist, according to Henry. Light, for example, is sometimes thought of as a wave, sometimes as a particle; it all depends upon which theory is the starting point. But while it is one thing to deduce a particular entity from a scientific theory, it is quite another to deduce a general philosophy therefrom. Henry observes that the more general the philosophy, the further removed it is from the scientific data. Determinism (genetic or environmental) and indeterminism, for example, cannot be deduced from physical observation.[28]

With God excluded, the scientist is prone to "reduce everything including the human self to quantifiable, mathematical formulas that swallow up the personal in the impersonal."[29] But those formulas are customarily nonlinear, leading Henry to several conclusions: "tentativity is the essence of [the scientist's] methodology"; the scientist focuses on how something works rather than on the more important questions of what, why, and who; equations do not so much describe the performance of nature as the physicist's mode of operation in the laboratory; and science is generally involved in a "subjective world," an "abstraction" of "useful symbols" yielding "highly refined opin-

21. Carl F. H. Henry, *Giving a Reason for Our Hope* (Boston: Wilde, 1949), 26; idem, *Notes on the Doctrine of God* (Boston: Wilde, 1949), 27.

22. Carl F. H. Henry, *Answers for the Now Generation* (Chicago: Moody, 1949), 31.

23. Henry, *God, Revelation and Authority,* 1:252.

24. Henry, *Drift,* 66 n. 24.

25. Henry, *God, Revelation and Authority,* 1:178; the reference is to Thomas S. Kuhn, *The Structure of Scientific Revolutions* (Chicago: University of Chicago Press, 1962).

26. Henry, *God, Revelation and Authority,* 1:174, 263.

27. Ibid., 1:176.

28. Ibid., 1:175.

29. Carl F. H. Henry, *New Strides of Faith* (Chicago: Moody, 1972), 18.

ion, but not really knowledge."[30] Whether or not science is good or valuable depends upon whether there are objective goods or values.[31] Since quantitative methodologies do not yield qualitative propositions, science must reach beyond itself for a metaphysical base to differentiate good from bad, right from wrong, value from worthlessness.

In the early 1920s, a small group of philosophers from Vienna connected meaningfulness with empirical verification. Logical positivism, as their system was called, held that inasmuch as a proposition like "God is love" is not empirically verifiable, it is not so much false as meaningless. The veracity of the statement never becomes a consideration because it is prejudged as inconsequential.

Opposing this viewpoint, Henry first insists that meaning must be known prior to verification.[32] For example, if we do not know in advance what the statement "that tree is green" means, we do not know what to verify. More pointedly, logical positivists must first know the meaning of their major premise that "empirical verification is the criterion for meaning" before they can determine its truth or falsity. If they use empirical verification to establish the meaning of this theorem, they are reasoning in a circle.

Secondly, Henry contends that "the truth or falsity of a statement does not determine its meaningfulness."[33] The sentence "there is a good surfing beach on the moon" is meaningful before empirical verification, even if highly improbable. The point is that verification relates to truth and falsity, not to meaning. On positivist premises, sym-

bolic equations, algebraic and geometric statements, and all the data of past history, Henry correctly assesses, are prejudged as meaningless.[34] In the end, he rightly dismisses logical positivism as "self-defeating and self-destructive," a noncontender.[35]

Henry's perspective on the limits of naturalism should be self-evident at this point. Progress is not, as naturalism suggests, an empirical datum; indeed, twentieth-century depravity is hard empirical evidence against nineteenth-century optimism. The evolutionary theory also implies that explanation and truth are emerging along with everything else. But unless something is exempted from space-time processes, Henry notes, historical progress is indefinable.[36]

Furthermore, naturalism can contribute nothing more than a self-destructive pluralism to ethics and religion. It does not resolve the recurring tensions in ethics between egoism and altruism, pain and pleasure, reward and duty. History yields rather contradictory opinions of right and wrong. For us to know the ought requires an authority higher than ourselves. In addition, the brevity of life together with the possibility of existential annihilation destroys any teleological justification for ethics.[37]

Just as naturalism cannot resolve contradictory ethical opinions, it multiplies religions and even the definitions of "religion." Under naturalism, "religion is a nebulous concept," containing not so much as a single universal thread or element.[38] Indeed, it cannot even be defined as "the worship of a divine being," for that would exclude Buddhism.

In rejecting naturalism Henry also rejects Aquinas's theistic proofs. The tail end of arguments that begin with a finite world,

30. Carl F. H. Henry, "Science and Religion," in *Contemporary Evangelical Thought*, ed. Carl F. H. Henry (Grand Rapids: Baker, 1968), 261, 273; Henry, *God, Revelation and Authority*, 1:274–75; and Carl F. H. Henry, "Evangelicals Shape Philosophy of Science," *Christianity Today*, 6 July 1959, p. 32.

31. Carl F. H. Henry, "Modern Science and Values," *Asbury Seminarian* 4.3 (Fall 1949): 91.

32. Henry, *God, Revelation and Authority*, 1:104.

33. Ibid., 1:103.

34. Ibid., 1:104–11.

35. Ibid., 110.

36. Carl F. H. Henry, *Remaking the Modern Mind* (Grand Rapids: Eerdmans, 1946), 142–48, 165–67.

37. Henry, *Christian Personal Ethics*, 26–90.

38. Henry, *New Strides*, 43.

he states, is "a finite god at best," possibly schizophrenic, but certainly not single-minded or holy; that god might be a present correlator, but surely not a past creator or cause. An infinite string of gods and an eternal universe are equally valid conclusions from empirical data. Empirical evidence for creation *ex nihilo* is ruled out by definition. In regard to the theory that creation originated with a big bang, which is not an equivalent concept, Henry reiterates Hume's argument that what people call causality in the natural realm is merely a misreading of temporal sequences.[39]

Likewise dismissed is historical verification of Christianity, resting as it does on nonempirical premises such as the integrity and reliability of the apostles. Moreover, even if God were to show his color and shape, we would have no written guarantee that he would retain these qualities.[40]

Henry concludes his analysis of naturalism with two observations about the relationship between Christianity and science. First, because naturalism cannot legislate past, present, or future possibilities, science cannot judge the legitimacy of miraculous events.[41] There are, therefore, no valid scientific objections to Christianity. Second, the metaphysical base for the regularity required for scientific inquiry can be found in the Bible, but is not observed in nature.[42]

Refutation of Subjectivism

Subjectivism is another position that has frequently occupied Henry's attention. He charges Immanuel Kant's subjectivization of rational categories with being the impetus behind the irrationality found in modern existential and dialectical thought. Prior to Kant, there was "no uniform determination of the a priori [i.e., presupposi-

tions]."[43] There were, however, two general types, philosophical and theological. The two agreed formally that (1) the world of flux, from which Heraclitus had concluded that one never steps into the same river twice, was transcended by an unchanging, eternal, invisible, supernatural, mental realm; and that (2) this realm was logically prior to knowledge; that is, it was itself the object of thought. For Plato, this was a world of transcendent Ideas; in the Hebrew-Christian tradition, the unchanging realm was a God of personality, intelligence, and will. Henry refers to the personality and intelligence as philosophical transcendent *a priori*.

The pre-Kantians differed, and the primary tensions between their ideas (e.g., between permanence and change, or between the one and the many) remained unsynthesized. But there was significant agreement that the world was objective. With René Descartes's *Cogito, ergo sum* ("I think, therefore I am"), however, there came a turning point toward rational subjectivization.[44] Kant pointed out that since existence is not a predicate, Descartes's famous line does not escape subjectivity; indeed, the sentence reduces to the tautology "I, therefore I."

Kant agreed with Hume that empirical data yield only sequences and that causes (necessities) are inferences beyond the data. If cause, he reasoned, cannot be derived from empirical data, then either it originates in the mind or knowledge is impossible. Kant concluded that the *a priori* that regulate knowledge, formerly thought to be objects (even worlds), are actually internal categories—forms of space and time that are prior to sense perception, and ideas of unity, cause, and universality that are prior to cognition—operating on some ir-

---

39. Henry, *God, Revelation and Authority*, 2:106–18; *Remaking*, 202–3.
40. Henry, *God, Revelation and Authority*, 1:158, 267.
41. Ibid., 1:256, 271.
42. So Christianity is "more the mother than the avowed enemy of modern Science" (Henry, *Drift*, 44).

43. Henry, *God, Revelation and Authority*, 1:280.
44. After Descartes's *Cogito*, "the relation of subject and object arises as the primary issue of epistemology. . . . The conflict between the subjective and the objective, innate ideas and external images, becomes permanent" (Henry, *God, Revelation and Authority*, 1:303).

rational given. The aftermath of Kant's conclusion was that there was no longer a rational base for believing that space, time, and cause are objective. Kant eventually multiplied his regulative categories, which Henry labels philosophical transcendent *a priori*, to the point where he had reasoned his way back to a Platonic world. But unlike Plato, Kant denied that this noumenal world of things-in-themselves (or things-as-they-really-are) can ever be an object of knowledge.

Kant's hypothesis of a noumenal world was just that, a hypothesis. Subsequent thinkers validly observed that his epistemology, if consistent, would preclude an objective noumenal world: since the noumena were unknowable, Kant could not prove they were objective. Although he spoke of the noumena, inconsistently, as "causing" phenomena, in the end he located the noumena in the mind.[45] Henry points out that while Kant posited a "pre-established harmony" as the basis of his categories, without the biblical perspective of a Creator and a divine image in humans he could offer no valid reasons why such a harmony should exist.[46] Moreover, because he defined knowledge as a synthesis between the precognitive forms and sensory content, Kant could not explain how or why the categories could be known at all.

It was not long before Kant's thought influenced both philosophy and theology. The overwhelming effect on theology, according to Henry, was a return to intuitionalism, the view that objects are not essential to religious knowledge.[47] What had formerly been considered objective carriers of revelation, truth, and history were now considered to be myths, indefinable symbols or codes, anthropomorphic representations of the supernatural. To obtain literal truths, these symbols had to be decoded or demythologized—by theologians no less. From myths, it was believed, one could derive useful truths of universal human experience. Thus the *a priori* shifted from an objective world to subjective experience.

The demythologization process led to disagreements over what the symbols represented, whether they were essential or nonessential, and to what extent they constituted the biblical revelation.[48] No guidelines were given for distinguishing the mythical from nonmythical elements or for safeguarding the historical Christ from being "enmythologized." Although propositions do contain symbols, Henry points out that there is no valid move from myth to truth.[49] Seeing the demythologizing process as endless, he concludes that the term *myth* became "a 'tramp' word of uncertain identity and even contradictory nuances."[50]

Kant's detachment of history from metaphysics, Martin Heidegger's concept of ontological discontinuities between the present and the past, and Albert Schweitzer's *Quest of the Historical Jesus*, which cast doubt on the historical reliability of the Gospels, all combined to further obliterate the line between subjectivity and objectivity, moving religious experience inevitably beyond myth and symbol to transpropositional, transhistorical encounter. Knowing God through revealed truths or history was superseded by an alleged Person-to-person encounter that transcended rational categories completely. This perspective-altering event was the essence of dialectical (neo-orthodox) theology.[51]

Henry equates the apropositional encounter with bumping into something in the dark. According to the dialectical theologians, the infinite qualitative difference between God and humans prohibits conceptualizing both the God with whom one collides and the collision itself. Thus it matters little whether religious sentences are

---

45. Henry, *God, Revelation and Authority*, 1:390–92.

46. Ibid., 1:358.

47. Ibid., 1:273–74.

48. Ibid., 1:59.

49. Ibid., 3:152.

50. Ibid., 1:59.

51. Ibid., 3:282–83.

logical or illogical. True revelation is paradoxical, above and beyond words, addressed to the will, not the intellect. God does not inform, he commands.

Henry cuts deeply into the irrational assumptions of dialectical theology. He begins by pointing out that the biblical God commands repentance and that repentance means a change of mind. Further, dialectical theology supplies no logical criterion for distinguishing self-consciousness from God-consciousness, the temporal "i" from the eternal Thou.[52] He adds that "it makes little difference whether one calls the confronting subject God or the transcendental ego [a term Kant used for the higher self in humans]."[53] Nor is it certain that one is confronting a single Thou rather than an It or any one (or several) of the multitudinous gods of competing religions.[54] Lacking propositional truths, one does not know who or what is being encountered.

Regrettably, the *Heilsgeschichte* school and Wolfhart Pannenberg, who, to their credit, emphasize historical revelation, have been ineffective in reestablishing the objectivity of truth. And so, still detached from propositional truths, isolated biblical events remain "irruptive intrusions . . . inexplicable and meaningless."[55] Thus, Rudolf Bultmann was unable to convert Heidegger's disciples, who disapproved of the effort to derive meaningful theology from the discontinuous data of history.[56] The dialectical theologians continued to allow for the creativity of the human knower in the revelation event, since no reason could be assigned for an exclusive treatment of biblical propositions against competing claims to revelation.

Henry predictably rejects the historical schools' concept of eschatological verification, which views the past and present not as absolute, but merely as relative to the future. In such a scheme, dogmatics is subject to all the skepticism of naturalistic historiography, faith resting upon "the shifting tides of historical consensus."[57] When all is said and done, events in themselves do not speak, they just show.

The Second Task of Apologetics: Defense of the Axioms of Christian Revelation

Propositional Revelation

Implicit in all that has been said about Henry's reactions to naturalism and subjectivism is his rationale for the proposition, the biblical sentence, as the basic unit of revelation. Dismissing as nonsense the evolutionary theory that word meanings derive from sounds, he maintains that words have identities that originate not in empirical noise, but in the set of propositions where they are used. Even in ordinary discourse a word carries an implicit negation; for example, a "cat" is, among other things, a "not-dog." If this were not true, if "cat" meant "dog," words might carry so much meaning as to make communication impossible. Were there an infinite number of definitions for each term, every sentence would mean the same thing, and hence would have no meaning at all. Completely open concepts destroy the very possibility of communication.[58]

Isolated words, though they have specific meanings, are neither true nor false. Truth and falsity, rather, attach to propositions; and propositions, to be fully understood, obtain meaning from a universe of discourse (Henry here concurs with Ludwig Wittgenstein and Willard Quine).[59] The final frontier, of course, is a monologue from the mind of God. That part of his omniscience that he chooses to reveal is clear, rational, and true knowledge. Contrary

52. Ibid., 3:281.
53. Henry, *Christian Personal Ethics,* 138.
54. Henry, *God, Revelation and Authority,* 2:289; 3:281.
55. Carl F. H. Henry, *The Protestant Dilemma* (Grand Rapids: Eerdmans, 1949), 95.
56. Henry, *God, Revelation and Authority,* 2:284.

57. Ibid., 2:304.
58. Ibid., 3:223–327.
59. Ibid., 3:302, 389, 394–95; 4:106.

to Donald Bloesch and Norman Geisler, who view revelation as analogical, Henry asserts that sentences from God are univocally expressed; that is, God does not tell us what he is like, he tells us what he is. To deny univocal predication, Henry says, is fatal to theology. God is no more "sort of omniscient" than he is "both holy and unholy."[60]

Nonpropositional revelation, by contrast, is unintelligible, unverifiable, and hence unable to convey the factuality and meaning of biblical events. So we must give priority to propositional revelation. The true definitions of God, sin, and grace are given in the propositions of the Bible, the Word of God.

The Bible—Authoritative, Inspired, Infallible, Inerrant

Henry insists that "the first claim to be made about the Bible is not its inerrancy nor its inspiration but its authority."[61] The history of Israel and the church reveals that Scripture, once it had been delivered by prophet or apostle, was recognized as authoritative truth immediately—not at the end of a lengthy redaction process.[62] No one among the prophets, Christ himself, the apostles, or the church consciously differentiated between temporally authoritative cultural elements and permanently binding transcultural elements.[63]

Although inerrancy is the "governing epistemological axiom" of Christian doctrine and the "evangelical heritage, the historic commitment of the Christian church," it is inspiration, according to Henry, that guarantees the factuality of biblical events.[64] He defines inspiration as that "supernatural influence upon divinely chosen prophets and apostles whereby the Spirit of God assures the truth and trustworthiness of their oral and written procla-

mation."[65] Neither external dictation nor internal frenzy, inspiration is predominantly a relationship between the Holy Spirit and the writings, not the writers. It is limited to the full ("plenary") original autographs of the Old and New Testament.[66]

In contrast to inspiration, the Spirit's illumination of believers does not create new truth or understanding. He neither "alters nor expands the truth of revelation"; rather, he "repeat[s] the grammatical sense of Scripture."[67] He "promotes theological comprehension" and "creates new attitudes."[68] Henry emphasizes that "the new birth is not prerequisite to the knowledge of God," which every human already possesses by virtue of the image of God within.[69] Illumination, therefore, is not the perspective-altering event posited by neo-orthodox (dialectical) theology.

Infallibility presupposes inerrancy, but is not its equivalent. The copies of the original biblical texts are not error-free; on the other hand, they also are not error-prone.[70] The copies, Henry says, "reliably and authoritatively communicate the truth and purposes of God to man" for the primary purpose of redemption.[71] In adjudging their faithfulness to the originals, Henry contends that it is not correct to apply the standards of twentieth-century mathematics to the phenomenological statements of the biblical era, inasmuch as the Bible did accommodate cultural idioms.[72]

If the originals were not inerrant, Henry maintains, textual criticism would be fruitless. Only on the assumption that the original text is inerrant is there validity to the commission of the textual critic, which is to investigate (1) the coextension between the copies and the assumed inerrant text and (2) the original, intended meaning of the

60. Ibid., 4:118, 365.
61. Ibid., 4:27.
62. Ibid., 4:432, 439, 442.
63. Ibid., 4:126, 255.
64. Ibid., 4:367.

65. Ibid., 4:129.
66. Ibid., 4:143.
67. Ibid., 4:282.
68. Ibid., 4:273.
69. Ibid., 1:229.
70. Ibid., 4:220 n. l.
71. Ibid., 4:246.
72. Ibid., 4:201–2.

authors.[73] The criticism that no one has exhibited errorless originals is countered by the fact that no one has produced errant originals either.[74]

Although archaeological finds have repeatedly undermined critical theories, modern biblical criticism's "redefinition . . . [of inspiration] in nonconceptual categories" has had a destructive impact.[75] Insisting that "the doctrine of the Bible controls all other doctrines of the Christian faith," Henry deplores as "hermeneutical nihilism" all functional, historical, and dialectical theories of revelation.[76] Functions and encounters do not differentiate truth claims. The Bible as propositional revelation is the Christian's *a priori*.

The Doctrine of God

Henry's primary theology consists of apologetic responses to both secular objections and issues raised within the evangelical camp. Many issues emerge from speculations concerning the nature of God; indeed, "the concept of God is determinative for all other concepts."[77] We will look briefly at Henry's comments on (1) God's timeless immutability, (2) his triune nature, and (3) his sovereignty over moral evil.

1. In the past several years, evangelicals have debated whether God's eternal nature should be viewed as timeless or temporal. Henry summarizes the philosophical backdrop, tracing the conflict to Parmenides, who rejected the concept of change (becoming), and Heraclitus, who rejected the concept of permanence (being). Paul Tillich's changeless Being Itself to some degree represents Parmenidean thought in contemporary theology. Process theologians like Alfred North Whitehead and Schubert Ogden have offered a synthetic solution in the form of a god composed of both timeless (primordial) and temporal (consequent) poles.

In Henry's view, neither Tillich's attributeless Being nor process theology's bipolar god is evangelically acceptable.[78] Biblical statements of God's coming and going are not references to his internal features, but anthropomorphic expressions of his relationship to creation. "God," Henry says, "does not 'come to himself'—far less 'come to self-consciousness'" in some evolutionary way.[79] Additionally, God's becoming is properly restricted to the incarnation; and while there are "procession elements" (i.e., begetting and proceeding) between the members of the Trinity, these do not qualify as temporal.[80]

Henry states that mainstream Christian orthodoxy has consistently inferred from Scripture (1) that God, being perfect, cannot change absolutely except to something inferior, and therefore must be timelessly eternal; and (2) that God created time concomitantly with the universe—all this in spite of what Henry acknowledges is a mere handful of references and an evident lack of systematic expression in the Bible.[81] He does contend, however, against theologians like Boethius, who describe omniscience as an "everlasting now." Although it is true that God knows all things simultaneously, his decree logically differentiates the now from the not-nows, which are the past and the future, definitional distinctions which are necessary preconditions of history.[82] Even God does not at this moment know the past as the now, he knows it as the past. On the other hand, timelessness is compatible with

73. Ibid., 4:416.
74. Ibid., 4:208.
75. Ibid., 4:75.
76. Carl F. H. Henry, *Frontiers in Modern Theology* (Chicago: Moody, 1966), 138.
77. Henry, *Remaking*, 175.
78. Henry, *God, Revelation and Authority*, 5:50.
79. Ibid., 5:53.
80. Ibid., 5:62.
81. Ibid., 5:239–64. Henry says elsewhere, "If perfect, [God] can change [only] for the worse, and hence he will not change himself nor can he be compelled to change by anything outside himself" (p. 304). The attempt to combine immutability with any sort of change, Henry concludes, is "a feat as difficult as riding two horses moving in opposite directions" (p. 288).
82. Ibid., 5:270–76.

the statement "God foreknows prior to creation." In any case, God's knowledge is not contingent upon temporal experience, but upon his timeless decree. Thus, Henry distinguishes a knowledge *"of* succession" from a knowledge *"in* succession."[83]

Henry adds that while synthesis of divine immutability and a once-for-all act like creation is difficult for us, it is not impossible. It will be helpful to keep in mind (1) the logical consistency between an eternal cause and a temporal effect (here Henry follows Aquinas),[84] and (2) the legitimate predication of timeless (we might also say "infinite," though Henry believes the term is nebulous)[85] omnipotence with reference to the internal relationships between the Father, Son, and Spirit, namely, the Father's generation of the Son and procession of the Spirit. This substitutes for Origen's conjectural solution that creation is coeternal and the equally inventive hypothesis that omnipotence began with creation, both views presupposing that omnipotence is a relation with an external object (a predicate) rather than an internal attribute.[86]

To solve another difficulty, Henry observes that the biblical references to God's temporal repentance (e.g., Jon. 3:10) are as anthropomorphic as are spatial references to bodily parts (e.g., God's arm). Such language must be subordinated to the language that affirms that God in himself does not repent (e.g., 1 Sam. 15:29).[87]

2. The doctrine of the Trinity, Henry declares, "contributes significantly to resolving the vexing problem of the one and the many."[88] But objections to this doctrine reign among unbelievers. One objection, that the Trinity is contradictory, is easily refuted—the persons are not three and one in the same sense, "not 3x = 1x but rather 3x in 1y."[89] The formula is indeed complex but not contradictory.

Further obfuscation has resulted from the use of confusing terms like (1) the Greek *hypostasis* ("that which lies beneath"), which implies some Aristotelian substance or stuff underlying the trinitarian members; (2) the Greek *ousia* ("being"), which Tillich, following Parmenides, utilized to represent God as transcending personality; and (3) the Latin term *persona*, which, belied by its English equivalent, has the root meaning of "mask." Stressing that the term *essence* is not used in the Bible, Henry declares that it signifies no more than the set of God's attributes. There is, accordingly, no underlying undefined "stuff," only attributes (internal perfections) and predicates (relationships to creation).[90] Though none of this, however complicated, is contradictory or contrary to personality, Henry concludes his analysis of the Trinity with a bit of mystery, approvingly quoting from Augustine's *De trinitate:* "We say . . . three persons, not that we would say this, but that we would not be silent . . . not because Scripture does so, but because Scripture does not forbid" (5.9; 7.4).

3. From the standpoint of apologetics, the ethically threatening dilemma of God's sovereignty over moral evil is far prior to questions concerning the content of personal and social ethics. Atheists jump at this allegedly legitimate obstacle to faith; believers more often run away. Not Henry.

Gordon Clark, Henry's Calvinist tutor, resolves the problem by definition, arguing that God is "ex-lex," that is, outside or above the law he imposes on humans. Since there is no God above God, and since humans are hardly in a position to legislate, there is no law that tells God what he should or should not do. Humans, on the other hand, are responsible, not because they are free, but because God sovereignly imposes accountability on them.[91]

In several instances, Henry appears to agree with his mentor. Any option is prefer-

---

83. Ibid., 5:276–77.
84. Ibid., 5:263.
85. Ibid., 5:219–34.
86. Ibid., 5:314.
87. Ibid., 5:304.
88. Ibid., 5:168.
89. Ibid., 5:165.

90. Ibid., 5:183–84, 203; 186.
91. Gordon H. Clark, *Religion, Reason and Revelation* (Philadelphia: Presbyterian and Reformed, 1961), 239–41.

able, he says, to the view that sin lies beyond the purposes of God. He agrees that "God's willing of sin is not itself sin," and that "the foreordination of an evil act is not itself evil."[92] Commenting on the Dead Sea Scrolls' version of Isaiah 45:6–7 (which declares that God creates *ra*ᶜ, a term used in Gen. 6:5 for moral evil), Henry says, "God can be an ultimate cause of evil, as orthodox theism conceives him, without himself being an aspect of evil. . . . Since the distinction between good and evil is grounded in God's will, the sovereign God in some sense creates sin. But to say that God commits sin is unthinkable, for Scripture throughout depicts sin as abhorrent to him."[93]

In other places, Henry argues his case by refuting some popular theological notions. On the basis of God's perfections, he affirms that this world is the only possible world, rather than merely the best of several possible ones.[94] He parts company with those who appeal to foreknowledge to resolve the problem, for "given the view of God's timeless eternity, the distinction between foreknowledge and divine foreordination falls away."[95] He contends that the theory that accountability requires freedom merely concedes secular humanism's insistence on human autonomy over and against God, and that responsibility does not demand that we have the power of contrary choice.[96] And he believes that the fashionable notions of class predestination, universalism, and a permissive divine will are unscriptural and illogical.[97]

Henry is clear that God in his sovereignty over moral evil does not force anyone to sin. Rather, God's decree makes human moral agency possible. Taking note of the "capacity of Adamic nature to obey God before the fall," Henry states that after the fall

God "himself effectuates no acts as sinful." In general accord with Louis Berkhof, Henry says that God "does not work in man 'both to will and to do,' when man goes contrary to His revealed will." And he endorses the Belgic Confession and Canons of Dort, which "expressly deny that God is the cause of sin and unbelief."[98] This may seem at odds with his earlier assertions, but, in the manner of Clark's appeal to equivocal relationships to the same law, Henry speaks of different motives within the same act. He says, for example, that "God need not will [the acts that] he wills for the reasons others may will them."[99] The same act may involve a sinful human motive and a good divine motive (Gen. 50:20).

Henry's Writings

Missions and Evangelism

Henry's very first publication, *A Doorway to Heaven* (1942), is the story of Chicago's Pacific Garden Mission.[100] The book went through twelve editions. A year later, Henry published his Th.D. dissertation under the title *Successful Church Publicity: A Guidebook for Christian Publicists*.[101] This work contrasts the biblical good news with secular news.

Apologetics

Henry's efforts in apologetics began in 1946 with *Remaking the Modern Mind* (actually, modern mindlessness is what he had in mind), in which he criticized the subrational temperament of contemporary existentialism.

Four medium-length publications appeared in 1949: *Giving a Reason for Our Hope*, a transcript of question-and-answer

92. Henry, *God, Revelation and Authority*, 5:283, 315.
93. Ibid., 6:294.
94. Ibid., 6:272–73.
95. Ibid., 5:284.
96. Ibid., 6:79–84.
97. Ibid., 6:85; 6:277–79; 6:86, 295.
98. Ibid., 6:84–86.
99. Ibid., 5:315.
100. Carl F. H. Henry, *A Doorway to Heaven* (Grand Rapids: Zondervan, 1942). Founded in 1877, the rescue mission provides food, clothing, and shelter.
101. Carl F. H. Henry, *Successful Church Publicity: A Guidebook for Christian Publicists* (Grand Rapids: Zondervan, 1943).

sessions with students at the First Baptist Church of Hollywood; *Notes on the Doctrine of God*, a collection of materials used in a college-age Sunday-school class at Immanuel Baptist Church in Pasadena; *The Protestant Dilemma*, a follow-up volume to *Remaking the Modern Mind;* and *Answers for the Now Generation*. In these volumes Henry contrasts the biblical and evolutionary concepts of time, attacks liberal assumptions (e.g., the perfectibility of humanity) that have collapsed under the weight of twentieth-century depravity, and presents alternatives of faith that are open to the modern unbeliever.

Henry's excellent summary of *Fifty Years of Protestant Theology* (1950), a volume covering German, British, French, and American thinkers, opens with a discussion of the philosophical assumptions that prevailed at the end of the nineteenth century and then turns to the dialectical response of the twentieth.[102]

In *Personal Idealism and Strong's Theology* (1951), Henry discusses the influence of Hermann Lotze's and Borden Parker Bowne's ethical monism on the theology of Augustus Hopkins Strong.[103]

Henry notes that *The Drift of Western Thought* (his W. B. Riley Memorial Lectures at Northwestern, published in 1951) is toward naturalism, including the notions of human animality, the subjectivity and relativity of moral distinctions, and the overall transcendence of meaningless time and change. This work emphasizes that the conceptual continuity between the Old and New Testaments is a strong argument for Christianity.

Frontiers in Modern Theology (1966) is a summary of the transition, confusion, and options in European theology as Rudolf Bultmann's ten-year regnancy came to an end in a bitter revolt against demythologization. Henry highlights the general weakness of positions that are independent of dogma.

The first two volumes of Henry's magnum opus, *God, Revelation and Authority*, appeared in 1976. Volume 1 is an epistemological attack on existential and dialectical theologies. Volume 2 discusses various theses on divine revelation; the subjects include God's transcendence and his names. Volumes 3 and 4, published in 1979, continue with the incarnation, the Logos, propositional revelation, the Bible, and the Holy Spirit. Volume 5 (1982) and volume 6 (1983) discuss the doctrine of God, his attributes, and the working out of his plan—from creation to redemption through final judgment.

American Orthodoxy in a Declining Culture

In *The Uneasy Conscience of Modern Fundamentalism* (1948), Henry attacks fundamentalism's intolerant and antischolastic temperament and castigates the movement for its apathy toward social ethics.[104]

According to Henry, the *Evangelical Responsibility in Contemporary Theology* (his Wilkinson Lectures at Northern Baptist Theological Seminary, published in 1957) is to restore unity after the destructive influences of modernism, ecumenism, fundamentalism, and neo-orthodoxy have run their courses.[105]

In *The God Who Shows Himself* (1966), Henry queries the theory that ecumenism leads to unity, a postulate, he says, that is yet to be proven. He also impugns the detachment of Christian doctrine and ethics from public education, because this feature

---

102. Carl F. H. Henry, *Fifty Years of Protestant Theology* (Boston: Wilde, 1950).

103. Carl F. H. Henry, *Personal Idealism and Strong's Theology* (Wheaton, Ill.: Van Kampen, 1951); this is actually Henry's Ph.D. dissertation, "The Influence of Personalistic Idealism on the Theology of Augustus Hopkins Strong." Strong felt that the new emphasis on divine immanence was a theological gain (see also Henry, *Fifty Years*, 22–23).

104. Carl F. H. Henry, *The Uneasy Conscience of Modern Fundamentalism* (Grand Rapids: Eerdmans, 1948).

105. Carl F. H. Henry, *Evangelical Responsibility in Contemporary Theology* (Grand Rapids: Eerdmans, 1957).

of the separation of church and state can lead only to moral decline.[106]

Evangelicals at the Brink of Crisis (1967) aims at evangelical unity, without which Christianity could by the year 2000 become "a wilderness cult in a secular society with no more public significance than the ancient Essenes in their Dead Sea caves."[107] Similar warnings are echoed in *Faith at the Frontiers* (1969), in which Henry calls for a theological initiative that will shatter the complacency of a self-confident unregenerated conscience operating, to its own detriment, without transcendent justice.[108]

A Plea for Evangelical Demonstration (1971) expresses regret that "American Protestant orthodoxy has produced no unified social ethics or program of evangelical social action." Henry calls the church to "enunciate the revealed will of God" concerning social justice.[109] Again in *New Strides of Faith* (1972) he notes that "by failing to transcend their isolation and independency, evangelical Christians have virtually forfeited a golden opportunity to shape the religious outlook of the twentieth century."[110] He restates the need for a unity that will transcend counterproductive denominational plurality.

Henry's *Evangelicals in Search of Identity* (1976) was not well received since it touched a sensitive nerve, the conflicts and ambiguities within evangelicalism. He once more laments that evangelicalism has been "painfully weak in shaping American national conscience."[111]

The Christian Mindset in a Secular Society: Promoting Evangelical Renewal & National Righteousness (1984) assesses continuing American trends—naturalism, secular humanism, communist and capitalist materialism, the evangelical disregard for social concerns, brute savagery, shortcomings in democracy, the media's virtual denial of the supernatural, and the overall lethargy toward truth and morals. Evangelicals, he observes, have produced "no articulate philosophy of political involvement."[112]

Christian Countermoves in a Decadent Culture (1986) calls for a comprehensive Christian thrust against humanist teachings. "All the modern gods [e.g., power and wealth]," Henry insists, "are sick and dying." The root of the problem is that "ours is the first generation in history to attempt to build a culture on naturalistic relativism."[113]

Conversations with Carl Henry: Christianity for Today (1986), *Twilight of a Great Civilization* (1988), and *Toward a Recovery of Christian Belief* (1990) continue his dire predictions for American culture in the light of contemporary immorality.[114] Henry argues that apart from a renewed metaphysical anchor moral relativism will displace the skeletal remains of American humanism in a short time.

Ethics

In *Christian Personal Ethics* (1957) Henry contrasts the source and universally valid content of Christian ethics with various speculative systems. He takes into con-

106. Carl F. H. Henry, *The God Who Shows Himself* (Waco: Word, 1966).

107. Carl F. H. Henry, *Evangelicals at the Brink of Crisis* (Waco: Word, 1967), 111.

108. Carl F. H. Henry, *Faith at the Frontiers* (Chicago: Moody, 1969).

109. Carl F. H. Henry, *A Plea for Evangelical Demonstration* (Grand Rapids: Baker, 1971), 22, 103.

110. Henry, *New Strides,* 52.

111. Carl F. H. Henry, *Evangelicals in Search of Identity* (Waco: Word, 1976), 42. This volume is a reprint of ten successive essays that appeared in *Christianity Today.*

112. Carl F. H. Henry, *The Christian Mindset in a Secular Society: Promoting Evangelical Renewal & National Righteousness* (Portland: Multnomah, 1984), 98.

113. Carl F. H. Henry, *Christian Countermoves in a Decadent Culture* (Portland: Multnomah, 1986), 107, 35.

114. Carl F. H. Henry, *Conversations with Carl Henry: Christianity for Today* (Lewiston, N.Y.: Edwin Mellen, 1986); idem, *Twilight of a Great Civilization* (Westchester, Ill.: Crossway, 1988); idem, *Toward a Recovery of Christian Belief* (Wheaton, Ill.: Crossway, 1990).

sideration the fall and redemptive history from personal regeneration to the final judgment.

Aspects of Christian Social Ethics (1964) accents the legitimate but limited authority of government to restrain evil; this authority is invested in government by the God in whom "righteousness and benevolence are equally ultimate."[115] The church should both transform society with the gospel and expound basic biblical principles of social justice and duty. There is no religious sanction for any one particular form of government, nor is there a Christian position on every specific social issue. But revolution is never an option for the believer, who must trust divine providence in the context of injustice.

Miscellaneous Works

Henry's *Glimpses of a Sacred Land,* published in 1953, is his memoirs of a 1951 tour to the Holy Land.

Confessions of a Theologian (1986) is Henry's autobiography, a candid review of his personal history. Also touched upon are his regret over opportunities lost by evangelicals and his vision for the future.

Carl Henry at His Best: A Lifetime of Quotable Thoughts (1990) is an outstanding synopsis of Henry's views, introduced by Charles Colson and carefully categorized.

In addition to the books we have summarized and seven hundred articles, which could not possibly be listed here, Henry has edited and contributed essays to *Contemporary Evangelical Thought* (1957); *Revelation and the Bible* (1958); *The Biblical Expositor* (1960); *Basic Christian Doctrines* (1962); *Christian Faith and Modern Theology* (1964); *Jesus of Nazareth, Saviour and Lord* (1966); *One Race, One Gospel, One Task* (1966); *Fundamentals of the Faith* (1969); *Baker's Dictionary of Christian Ethics* (1973); *Quest for Reality: Christianity and the Counter Culture* (1973); and *Horizons of*

115. Carl F. H. Henry, *Aspects of Christian Social Ethics* (Grand Rapids: Eerdmans, 1964), 146.

Science: Christian Scholars Speak Out (1978).

Influence

It would be difficult to overstate Henry's impact. Through his work with *Christianity Today,* World Vision International, and Prison Fellowship Ministries he has influenced theologians, evangelists, political leaders, and laypersons throughout the world. Among the other organizations with which Henry is affiliated is the National Association of Evangelicals. Shortly after its establishment in 1942, Henry served as public-relations coordinator, literary-book editor, and then board member. At its ninth annual convention he arranged a special forum in Chicago to deal with such issues as labor and race relations. When a commission on social ethics was set up in 1952, Henry served as cochairman.

Among Henry's other credits are service on the editorial committee (1949) and then as president (1968–69) of the Evangelical Theological Society (he himself had been the first to suggest the society's name). In 1966 Henry was elected chairman of the Berlin World Congress on Evangelism, a meeting of twelve hundred evangelists from a hundred nations. And in 1971 he served as program chairman of the Jerusalem Conference, a three-day discussion of eschatology attended by fourteen hundred evangelical Christians. From 1971 to 1974 he was president of the board of the Institute for Advanced Christian Studies, which had been founded in 1966 to fund writing that promotes the Christian worldview.

A measure of the impact of Henry's own writing is the fact that only six months after publication the first two volumes of *God, Revelation and Authority* went into their second printing. They tied for first place in *Eternity Magazine*'s annual survey to determine the best books in the religious field. Upon completion of the six-volume set, Henry received an honorary D.D. from Gordon-Conwell Theological Seminary, and the Evangelical Christian Publishers Association presented him with their Gold Medallion Award in the theology-and-doctrine category. For this work Henry received written commendations from President Jimmy Carter and Richard C. Ostling, religion editor at *Time Magazine*, who called Henry "the leading theologian of the nation's growing evangelical flank."

In 1977 Henry was instrumental in founding the Council for Biblical Inerrancy, an organization established to temper the fundamentalist mood and renew credibility for inerrantists. A further tribute came when Bob E. Patterson included Henry in his Makers of the Modern Theological Mind series.[116] Patterson called Henry "the prime interpreter of evangelical theology."

Henry's professorships at Northern Baptist, Fuller, and Eastern have already been mentioned. He also served as dean at Fuller and as visiting professor of theology at Wheaton College, Gordon Divinity School, and Trinity Evangelical Divinity School. He has been a member of the board of Gordon College (1962–68), the Ethics and Public Policy Center (1980), Prison Fellowship Ministries (1981–), and the Institute on Religion and Democracy (1982–). He was also cochairman of the Evangelical Affirmations Conference in 1989.

On the international scene Henry has lectured at the Japan School of Theology, the Asian Center for Theological Studies and Mission (Seoul), Korea Baptist Theo-

logical Seminary, the Asian Theological Seminary in the Philippines, China Graduate School of Technology, China Evangelical Seminary, and several schools in India. He has corresponded with and interviewed the leading conservative and liberal theologians in Europe. In the summer of 1969, Henry accompanied his longtime friend Billy Graham on tour and spoke to pastors in Germany and Switzerland. He has preached in South America, Africa, the Middle East, and throughout Eastern Europe.

In addition to his two earned doctoral degrees, Henry has been awarded six honorary doctorates, the Freedoms Foundation Award twice (1954, 1966), and the Faith and Freedom Award from the Religious Heritage of America (1975). A member of numerous theological, philosophical, and literary societies, he is listed in the *Dictionary of American Philosophers*, the *Dictionary of American Scholars*, *Who's Who in America*, *Who's Who in American Education*, *Who's Who in Religion*, and *Who's Who in the World*. At the time of this writing, Henry has been the subject of eight master's theses and ten doctoral dissertations written from a variety of theological persuasions. Special honors include establishment of the Carl F. H. Henry Manuscript Collection at Syracuse University and the Carl F. H. Henry Study and Resource Center at Trinity Evangelical Divinity School. Surely there can be no doubt that Henry has a secure standing among the leading evangelical theologians of our day.

116. Bob E. Patterson, *Carl F. H. Henry* (Waco: Word, 1983).

Anthony Hoekema

Cornelis P. Venema

Anthony Andrew Hoekema was born in Drachten, the Netherlands, in 1913 and emigrated with his family to the United States in 1923. He was raised in a Christian Reformed home and nurtured in the confessions of the Dutch Reformed churches (the Heidelberg Catechism, the Belgic Confession, and the Canons of Dort). The influence of his training in the Reformed tradition continued throughout his life and ministry and decisively shaped his later theological method and position.

Hoekema distinguished himself as a student at a young age and was attracted to the fields of psychology and theology. He studied at Calvin College (A.B., 1936), the denominational school of the Christian Reformed Church, and at the University of Michigan (A.M. in psychology, 1937). He then engaged in theological study at Calvin Theological Seminary (Th.B., 1942), Princeton Theological Seminary (1942–44; Th.D., 1953), and Cambridge University (1965–66 and 1973–74).

Before teaching theology, Hoekema served several Christian Reformed churches as a minister of the Word and sacrament. Ordained in 1944, he served as pastor of

Twelfth Street Christian Reformed Church of Grand Rapids, Michigan (1944–50); Bethel Christian Reformed Church of Paterson, New Jersey (1950–54); and Alger Park Christian Reformed Church of Grand Rapids (1954–56).

Having served a brief stint as an instructor in psychology, English, and speech at Calvin College in 1939–41, Hoekema embarked upon a lifetime of teaching theology when he was appointed as a lecturer in dogmatics at Calvin Theological Seminary in 1955. From 1956 to 1958 he served as a professor of Bible at Calvin College, and then in 1958 he was promoted to the position of professor of systematic theology at the seminary, where he continued to teach until his retirement in 1978.

Even this brief glimpse at Hoekema's background and lifework as a preacher and teacher tells a considerable story about his devotion to the ministry of the Word of God and his commitment to the confessional tradition of the Reformed churches. Hoekema would not likely be characterized as a "creative" or "innovative" thinker, to employ the terms so often used to compliment modern theologians, though sometimes to cover a tendency to stray from the moorings of historic, orthodox Christian faith. He was content to work faithfully from within the hermeneutical framework set by the Reformed church's confessional response to the Scriptures.

To say that Hoekema was not an innovator is not to suggest that he was a traditionalist who simply sought a repristination of the Reformed faith and confession. His writings and teaching were marked by a fresh reading and exegesis of the Scriptures, and a critical rethinking of the old answers to questions still pressing. Furthermore, they were characterized by a contemporaneity in that Hoekema constantly interacted with recent theological developments. His writings also manifested a biblically ecumenical spirit that recognized the Christian church in general and contemporary culture as the proper context for theological reflection. He was particularly anxious to introduce the distinctives of Reformed theology to the larger evangelical community of North America. His participation in many of the debates within North American evangelicalism testified to his affinity with the tenets of the evangelical faith, albeit with a distinctively Reformed accent.

Early Interests and Writings

It is instructive to observe that Hoekema's early theological interests and writings were prophetic of his later interests and writings. Most of the topics to which he would address himself in the mature phase of his theological work had been anticipated in his early career.

Hoekema's lifelong fascination with the doctrine of the human person in relation to God was evident not only in his study of psychology at the University of Michigan, but also in his early concentration upon the classical Reformed understanding of the covenant of grace. In his doctoral dissertation, "Herman Bavinck's Doctrine of the Covenant," and in several of his first essays, Hoekema expounded a doctrine of the covenant which simultaneously emphasized the sovereign grace of God and his covenant partner's obligation to respond to that grace in faith and repentance.[1] Hoekema sought to develop within the contours of the Reformed view of God's sovereign grace, expressed most emphatically in its doctrine of predestination, the understanding that our humanity is truly realized only in fellowship with God.[2] In this respect his whole endeavor might be interpreted as a systematic development of John Calvin's well-known dictum that "nearly all the wisdom we possess, that is to say, true and sound wisdom, consists of two parts: the knowledge of God and of ourselves."[3]

In a significant and representative article, "The Centrality of the Covenant of Grace," Hoekema enunciated the impor-

1. Anthony A. Hoekema, "Herman Bavinck's Doctrine of the Covenant," Th.D. diss., Princeton Theological Seminary, 1953; idem, "The Centrality of the Covenant of Grace," *Reformed Journal* 5 (Dec. 1955): 3–5; idem, "Covenantal Evangelism," *Banner* 90 (1955): 1510–11, 1526; idem, "Covenant Consciousness—Does It Occupy a Central Place in Our Denominational Program?" *Banner* 91 (1956): 1350–51.

2. It should be noted that Hoekema nowhere contested the main lines of the historic Reformed view of predestination and election. He resisted, however, any inferences from this doctrine which would undercut human responsibility or treat the operation of God's grace in Christ in mechanical or impersonal terms. For his view of election see Anthony A. Hoekema, "Predestination and Evangelism," *Banner* 86 (1951): 391; idem, "The Sovereignty of God Principle," *Banner* 94 (May 22, 1959): 9, 21; idem, "Needed: A New Translation of the Canons of Dort," *Calvin Theological Journal* 3 (1968): 41–47; and idem, "A New English Translation of the Canons of Dort," *Calvin Theological Journal* 3 (1968): 133–61.

3. John Calvin, *Institutes of the Christian Religion*, ed. John T. McNeill (Philadelphia: Westminster, 1960), 1.1.1.

tance of this covenant for the development of a Christian anthropology. He began by noting that the Reformed tradition has usually been understood to take its starting point from the sovereignty of God, and consequently has often been criticized for its failure to accentuate the responsibility of humankind. In reply to this criticism, Hoekema argued that, particularly in its development of the covenant of grace, the Reformed tradition had held in proper balance the sovereignty of God and the responsibility of humankind:

> Without for a moment denying that the sovereignty of God is the fundamental principle of Calvinism, I should like to point out that in the doctrine of the covenant of grace, properly understood, we have precisely that emphasis on the sovereignty of God, but in addition an emphasis on the responsibility of man. It is, in fact, one of the beauties of the doctrine of the covenant that it gives equal emphasis to both of these aspects of Biblical truth.[4]

The virtue of this doctrine, according to Hoekema, is its emphasis upon the mutuality of the relationship which God graciously establishes between himself and his people. God's covenant partner is not forced or compelled to respond to his gracious initiative; rather, the covenant emphasizes "reciprocal love" between God and his people, and their moral need to respond to God's grace "freely, willingly, lovingly."[5]

What especially attracted Hoekema to the Reformed understanding of the cov-

enant was the place it gives to humanity's free and reciprocal response to God's grace. The covenant of grace provides a framework for a covenantal anthropology. It is not surprising, therefore, to find Hoekema following up his early writings on the covenant with an important essay on G. C. Berkouwer's view of the image of God.[6] This essay delineates a number of themes which would become commonplace in Hoekema's later works.

Hoekema agreed with Berkouwer that, in the face of a renewed interest in humankind and the realities of human existence, the need for a biblical anthropology had become especially pressing. Existentialism, together with a more realistic assessment of humanity's ability to make the right choices, had provided an opportunity for renewed reflection upon the biblical teaching that man is a creature who was made in God's image but who has turned in disobedience from his Creator.[7] Missing from most contemporary anthropologies, however, was the understanding that "relatedness to God" is "constitutive of man's being."[8]

Hoekema's assessment of Berkouwer's view of the image of God was generally positive. A number of themes in Berkouwer's study were judged to be significant contributions to the articulation of a biblical doctrine of humanity. Many of these same themes were to become an integral part of Hoekema's mature understanding of the image of God: the insistence that we cannot begin to understand anything of man's true nature apart from his inescapable related-

4. Hoekema, "Centrality," 3.

5. Ibid., 4. Hoekema's views on the covenant of grace and human responsibility before God are reflected as well in two subsequent articles: Anthony A. Hoekema, "Calvin's Doctrine of the Covenant of Grace," *Reformed Review* 15 (1962): 1–12; and idem, "The Covenant of Grace in Calvin's Teaching," *Calvin Theological Journal* 2 (1967): 133–61. In the former article Hoekema insists that "an understanding of Calvin's teaching on the covenant gives one a more balanced picture of his theology than can be obtained from a study of his teaching on divine predestination alone" (pp. 11–12).

6. Anthony A. Hoekema, "Berkouwer on the Image of God," *Reformed Journal* 8 (May 1958): 19–21; 8 (June 1958): 11–14.

7. Hoekema was convinced that existentialism was a significant indicator of a pronounced and lively interest in anthropology, to which Christian theology had to address itself; see Anthony A. Hoekema, "Sören Kierkegaard—A Tremendous Influence in Contemporary Thought," *Banner* 92 (Sept. 6, 1957): 9; 92 (Sept. 13, 1957): 9.

8. Hoekema, "Berkouwer on the Image," *Reformed Journal* 8 (May 1958): 19.

ness to God, his Creator and Redeemer; the balanced view of the depravity of humankind in their sin and the restraint upon that depravity by God's common grace; and the dynamic definition of the image of God in the redeemed person as a growing conformity to Christ in true knowledge, righteousness, and holiness.[9]

Though Hoekema never gave sustained attention to the encyclopedic issue of theology as a science and its distinctive object and methods, there is an article from his early period which provides an indication of his approach.[10] In this article Hoekema summarized and evaluated a recent paper of the Wheaton College departments of Bible and philosophy on the subject of the inspiration of the Bible. Hoekema's article is worthy of notice as a statement of his intention to develop his theology upon the basis of scriptural authority.

Hoekema began his evaluation by characterizing the Wheaton paper as an excellent statement of the divine inspiration of the Bible. It fully accorded with the historic Reformed view of the plenary and verbal inspiration of the Scriptures, avoiding the theory of mechanical dictation while also repudiating the neo-orthodox view that the Bible is only a fallible witness to God's revelation. The Wheaton statement rightly emphasized that the Scriptures are the only possible basis for any true knowledge of God.

Nonetheless, after approving the basic thrust, Hoekema proceeded to register minor objections to some aspects of the Wheaton statement and to criticize a major flaw in its defense of biblical inspiration. According to Hoekema, the paper was, if anything, too weak in its response to historical criticism and neo-orthodoxy. The report should have differentiated more carefully between "historical research" and "historical criticism," thereby promoting

the canons of grammatical-historical exegesis without falling prey to a critical investigation of the Scriptures which contradicts their inspiration and consequent authority. Furthermore, the paper insufficiently addressed itself to neo-orthodoxy's denial of the complete reliability of the inspired texts. It did not clearly assert that those who stray significantly from the orthodox view of scriptural inspiration often imperil their subscription to the cardinal doctrines of Christian orthodoxy.

Remarkably, Hoekema distanced himself from one prominent feature of the Wheaton document. In his judgment the statement ascribed too great a role to rational evidences in authenticating the biblical texts. Appealing to the historic Reformed emphasis on the internal testimony of the Holy Spirit, he maintained that God alone is able to confirm his Word to us. According to Hoekema, we are unable to discern the things of the Spirit apart from the Spirit's own working in our hearts, making us receptive and submissive to the Word. The only "reasonable" standpoint for us to take in response to the speech of our Creator is a believing submission worked in us by the Spirit of regeneration. Were we to proceed alternatively on the foundation of rational evidences, as the Wheaton statement suggested, we would then "build the superstructure of our faith on a foundation of human reason, instead of on the absolute and final authority of God."[11]

It is clear that in his brief review of the Wheaton paper Hoekema embraced the historic doctrine of scriptural infallibility and inerrancy which has played such an important role in the development of evangelicalism in North America. Though he never addressed himself to the issue in a programmatic way, one might say that this doctrine was the presupposition from which he proceeded in all of his theological writings.

9. Ibid., *Reformed Journal* 8 (June 1958): 13–14.
10. Anthony A. Hoekema, "An Evaluation of 'The Wheaton Position on Inspiration,'" *Torch and Trumpet* 7 (Oct. 1957): 12–15.

11. Ibid., 15.

Particular Issues

The Major Cults

After his early efforts to formulate a biblical anthropology, Hoekema entered into a fruitful period of teaching and writing in which he produced a number of well-received studies, some of which have become standard works in their field. Throughout this period Hoekema displayed a lively interest in theological and ecclesiastical developments, particularly within North American evangelicalism. Many of his studies demonstrate a remarkable ability to engage in irenic debate without distorting the viewpoints or impugning the motives of those with whom he differed. Hoekema pursued all of this work in a spirit of unwavering submission to the authority of the written Word and with an unflagging appreciation for the Reformed confessions.

During his years of teaching at Calvin Seminary, Hoekema addressed in succession three important issues: the major cults in North America, the phenomena of Pentecostalism and Neo-Pentecostalism, and the Christian's self-image. *The Four Major Cults* is a study of Christian Science, Jehovah's Witnesses, Mormonism, and Seventh-Day Adventism, all of which developed within and helped to shape the religious landscape of North America. Arising out of a seminary course, the book addresses the cults primarily in terms of their distinctive teachings on the major topics of Christian theology. Hoekema begins each exposition with a brief history of the cult and then discusses its specific position on the main topics customarily considered in systematic theology.

Though *The Four Major Cults* is somewhat dated, in view of the remarkable growth of and changes in these cults, it continues to provide the single most comprehensive theological assessment of them. One of its controversial features was Hoekema's insistence that Seventh-Day Adventism be designated a cult. For in its historic teaching and practice Adventism fulfilled what Hoekema regarded as the necessary and sufficient conditions for identifying a group as a cult: an extrascriptural source of authority; denial of the doctrine of justification by grace alone; devaluation of Christ's person and work; self-designation of the group as the exclusive community of the saved; and a self-assigned decisive role in the unfolding of God's purpose for the end times.[12] Accordingly, Hoekema concluded that Adventism had a status comparable to that of Christian Science, Jehovah's Witnesses, and Mormonism.

Pentecostalism

After his consideration of the cults, Hoekema turned to a subject which was to interest him throughout the remainder of his life—the emergence of a number of Pentecostal churches and the growth of the Neo-Pentecostal movement. Here Hoekema's interest focused more closely upon the Protestant Christian community, where Pentecostalism, for all its strengths, represented what he was convinced was a departure from the biblical norms.

Hoekema's evaluation of Pentecostalism followed a pattern evident in many of his writings—a fair statement of the teaching with which he differed, acknowledgment of its contribution, correction of its distortions of traditional Christian practice, and evaluation in the light of biblical and confessional standards. He expressed his intentions in the preface to *What about Tongue-Speaking?* his first book-length treatment of Pentecostalism:

> I should like to make clear at the outset that I am very grateful for what God is accomplishing through Christians of Pentecostal persuasion, particularly on the mission fields of the world. I look upon Pentecostals and Neo-Pentecostals as brothers in Christ, and therefore what I shall be saying about their views on the tongues question I shall be saying in a spirit of Christian love. I should like to have my Pentecostal friends consider this

12. Anthony A. Hoekema, *The Four Major Cults* (Grand Rapids: Eerdmans, 1963), 373–403.

book a kind of theological conversation with them, with the purpose of arriving at a better understanding of what God's Word teaches about the subject under discussion.[13]

In a subsequent study, *Holy Spirit Baptism*, Hoekema addressed more particularly the phenomenon of Neo-Pentecostalism and its peculiar teaching of a postconversion second blessing, usually termed "baptism in" or "with" the Holy Spirit.

Hoekema began *What about Tongue-Speaking?* by carefully tracing the phenomenon of glossolalia from the early Montanist movement through the recent development of Neo-Pentecostalism. He then explained why the Pentecostal movement put so much emphasis on tongue-speaking. Recognizing that there is a variety of viewpoints within the movement, Hoekema nonetheless concluded that "with possible exceptions, the dominant position of Neo-Pentecostalism on the significance of glossolalia is the same as that of the Pentecostals: tongue-speaking is the necessary evidence that one has received the baptism of the Spirit."[14] In the Pentecostal understanding, glossolalia is a necessary initial evidence of Spirit baptism and therefore is to be sought by all believers who wish to have confirmed their baptism in the Spirit.

Following his survey of the history of tongue-speaking and his explanation of its prominence within Pentecostalism, Hoekema proceeded to subject the movement to biblical and theological scrutiny. He argued that the New Testament references to baptism with the Holy Spirit ordinarily designate the historic event of Pentecost; they do not designate a separate experience of an individual's being baptized in the Spirit after conversion. He also maintained that 1 Corinthians 12:13, a text which associates the word *baptize* with the Holy Spirit and is often cited as teaching a postconversion

Spirit baptism, describes "the regeneration of all believers that is symbolized by water baptism, and does not picture a 'second work of grace' or a 'second infilling with the Spirit' or a 'second blessing' subsequent to and distinct from regeneration."[15] Furthermore, Hoekema considered 1 Corinthians 12–14 to teach that glossolalia has some value, but that this value is "carefully circumscribed":

> One certainly does not get the impression from these chapters that tongue-speaking is the *sine qua non* of mature Christianity—the gift which is indispensable for vibrant personal devotions, warm and fervent intercession, or full-orbed victorious Christian living. The predominant impression one receives from a careful study of these chapters is rather that if one is seeking the very best gifts, he will probably not seek glossolalia.[16]

In considering the biblical teaching on tongue-speaking, Hoekema carefully adhered to the Reformed hermeneutical principles of comparing Scripture with Scripture and distinguishing between historical and doctrinal texts. He concluded that the New Testament teaches a Spirit baptism which occurred at Pentecost as an event of dispensational or epochal significance for all of subsequent redemptive history. What occurred at Pentecost was a unique, nonrepeatable outpouring of the Spirit which affects every believer who is incorporated into the body of Christ. There is, then, a primary hermeneutical error in the view of glossolalia as a postconversion initial evidence of Spirit baptism today. The error consists in failure to read the accounts in Acts in terms of redemptive history. Furthermore, in adjudicating an issue like tongue-speaking, the New Testament Epistles should have precedence, since they are doctrinal in character rather than historical. One of the root errors of Pentecostal-

---

13. Anthony A. Hoekema, *What about Tongue-Speaking?* (Grand Rapids: Eerdmans, 1966), 5.

14. Ibid., 48.

15. Ibid., 62–63.

16. Ibid., 100–101.

ism is its confusion of the *historia salutis,* the history of salvation, including the unique event of Pentecost, with the *ordo salutis,* the application of salvation in the life of the individual believer.

In his theological evaluation of tongue-speaking, Hoekema strongly criticized certain Pentecostal beliefs which he found objectionable and unsubstantiated by Scripture. Six such theological tenets in particular were singled out for critical scrutiny: that all the miraculous gifts of the Spirit are still present in the church today; that every believer ought to seek a special, postconversion Spirit baptism; that spiritual blessings invariably entail physical evidence or confirmation; that the person and work of Christ may be subordinated to the Spirit; that there are two qualitatively distinct categories of believers, those who have and those who have not been baptized in the Spirit; and that only in the twentieth century has the church been adequately empowered and gifted by the Spirit for the work of ministry.[17]

Despite these considerable theological deficiencies in Pentecostalism, Hoekema concluded his study of the movement with a chapter entitled "What We Can Learn from the Tongue-Speaking Movement." Hoekema regarded as inadequate a wholesale rejection that failed to recognize the merits of Pentecostalism and its correction of genuine defects in the life of the church. For example, Hoekema credited Pentecostalism with restoring a proper understanding of the Spirit's person and work as absolutely indispensable to the church's ministry. He also judged its recognition of the emotional needs of believers to be a needed corrective to the sometimes overly intellectualized and barren form of Christian practice and worship found in many traditional churches. Pentecostalism raised anew an emphasis upon worship as a congregational offering of praise to the Lord, and often revitalized the role and fervency

of prayer in the lives of believers. Pentecostalism also reawakened interest in the missionary task of the church and the priesthood of all believers, gifted as they are for the work of ministering to the needs of fellow members in Christ.

Hoekema's biblical and theological evaluation, though often sharp and penetrating in its objections to some of the distinctive teachings and practices of Pentecostalism, was also balanced and sensitive in recognizing its praiseworthy features. The conclusion to his second book on Pentecostalism, *Holy Spirit Baptism,* well captures his overall assessment of the movement:

> We may sum up as follows: Believers do not need to seek a post-conversion "baptism in the Spirit," but they do need to be continually filled with the Spirit who dwells within. Let us then enter into the fulness of our heritage as children of God. Let us experience the full richness of union with Christ. Let us see ourselves, not just as depraved sinners, but as new creatures in Christ. Let us grasp by faith the infinite resources we have in Christ. Let us daily be filled with the Spirit, and let our lives reflect the radiancy of that Spirit. May God grant us all increasingly to know the love of Christ which passes knowledge, and to be filled with all the fulness of God.[18]

The Christian's Self-Image

In the assessment of Pentecostalism that we have just quoted, there is a phrase which invites consideration of the third subject to which Hoekema addressed himself during the mature phase of his theological writing, a subject for which he has become well known. When Hoekema spoke of the need for Christians to see themselves "not just as depraved sinners, but as new creatures in Christ," he gave expression to one of the more controversial and innovative features of his theology. This recalled his early interest in formulating a Christian anthropology, to which he returned in 1975 with the

17. Ibid., 103–23.

18. Anthony A. Hoekema, *Holy Spirit Baptism* (Grand Rapids: Eerdmans, 1972), 93.

publication of *The Christian Looks at Himself.* The thesis of this study was born out of a lengthy process of evaluating the traditional Reformed approach to anthropology and bringing a theological understanding of the human person into conversation with the perspectives of modern psychology. In the preface, Hoekema noted that the "topic of the Christian self-image has a particular fascination for me because of my interest in both psychology and theology."[19] Written on the foundation of his earlier studies of the covenant and a paper on the Christian self-image given at the 1971 convention of the Christian Association for Psychological Studies, *The Christian Looks at Himself* represented something of a departure from the main lines of Reformed and evangelical anthropologies.

Hoekema contended that the traditional Christian doctrine of humanity often militated against the development of a positive self-image. Employing the term *self-image* to designate the way in which we regard ourselves or conceive of our own worth, Hoekema observed that conservative evangelical Christians often had a negative self-image. Given preaching which accented sin and misery, hymns which highlighted the unworthiness of the sinner in the presence of God, and a theology which emphasized the fall into sin and its consequences more than the doctrine of creation and redemption through Christ, the evangelical community had "been writing our continuing sinfulness in capital letters, and our newness in Christ in small letters."[20]

Hoekema found the antidote for this malady in a revived emphasis upon the biblical doctrine of humankind's creation in the image of God and the Spirit's renewal of that image through the work of Christ. He was convinced that the resources for the cultivation of a positive and psychologically constructive self-image lay in the tenets of the classical Christian doctrines of creation and redemption. Without resorting to the humanistic presuppositions so pervasive in modern psychology, it was possible, he believed, to develop a Christian understanding of the self which would work against a negative and destructive self-image: "It is not a question of *either* the Christian faith *or* a positive self-image. Rather, when the Christian faith is accepted in its totality, that faith brings with it a predominantly positive self-image."[21]

Hoekema developed his thesis by re-evaluating the biblical view of sin and grace and its implications for the Christian self-image. Taking the apostle Paul as a paradigm, he noted that the apostle, whom no one could accuse of minimizing or downplaying the reality and power of sin in human life, had a surprisingly robust self-image. This self-image was founded upon the marvel of God's sovereign grace in Christ, a grace more than equal to the circumstance of human sin. Thus "Paul, despite his deep sense of sin, had a positive self-image. He saw himself as a person upon whom God had showered His grace, whom God had enabled and was still enabling to live a fruitful life for Christ, and whom God so continued to fill with His Spirit that his life could be an example to others."[22]

Hoekema acknowledged that the Scriptures deepen our awareness of our sin and guilt; they do not treat the ugly reality of sin in a facile manner. But the Scriptures also teach that the power and reality of God's work in Christ through the Spirit are greater than the power and reality of our sin! They teach us to look at ourselves preeminently in terms of *what we are in Christ and not what we were by nature.* Thus a biblically sensitive self-image is oriented to what the grace of God in Christ is accomplishing in us; this becomes the point of departure for a new and positive Christian self-image.

One of the striking aspects of Hoekema's argument is his move away from the his-

19. Anthony A. Hoekema, *The Christian Looks at Himself* (Grand Rapids: Eerdmans, 1975), 10.

20. Ibid., 18.

21. Ibid., 23.

22. Ibid., 30.

toric Reformed reading of Romans 7. Romans 7:13–25 had been traditionally understood to be a description of the regenerate person's constant and unremitting struggle with the remaining power of sin. Hoekema, on the contrary, took the position that Romans 7 is a description of an unregenerate individual "who is trying to fight sin through the law alone, apart from the strength of the Holy Spirit."[23] Romans 7, then, is not describing the Christian life as a kind of dialectic between sin and grace, disobedience and obedience. Nor does Romans 7 support a "negative" or pessimistic assessment of the progress and advance of the Christian in sanctification and renewal. In defense of this exegesis, Hoekema adduced a number of textual and contextual factors, arguing that, were the apostle Paul describing the regenerate person in Romans 7, it would not comport well with his descriptions elsewhere of the Spirit's triumph over the flesh in the lives of those who are new creatures in Christ.

Major Theological Studies

Eschatology

In addition to addressing particular issues from a biblical and Reformed standpoint, Hoekema made a lasting contribution to evangelicalism with three major theological studies, the last of which was published posthumously in 1989. Each of these studies evinced the qualities of Hoekema's earlier theological writing—a careful and fresh reading of the biblical texts, sensitivity and loyalty to the historic Reformed confessions, and a self-conscious contemporaneity in which the questions pressing today were forthrightly addressed.

In the first of these theological studies, *The Bible and the Future*, Hoekema turned to a subject to which he had earlier paid some attention—the biblical teaching on the future or eschatology. Already in his *Four Major Cults* and in his contribution to a symposium in which evangelicals dis-

cussed differing millennial views, Hoekema had been a capable defender of the classic amillennialist position.[24] And now *The Bible and the Future* treated the whole range of topics traditionally considered under the rubric of eschatology; it included extensive interaction with recent developments in biblical eschatology and the evangelical debates on the subject of the millennium.

Hoekema set up a dichotomy between inaugurated eschatology and future eschatology. By "inaugurated eschatology" he meant those aspects of the biblical promises for the future which have been partially fulfilled and realized in the redemptive accomplishments of Christ and the postascension outpouring of the Spirit at Pentecost. Hoekema noted that traditional discussions have tended to treat inaugurated eschatology as a kind of postscript largely unrelated to the main topics of theology. These discussions have been insufficiently aware of the pervasively eschatological character of biblical revelation, oriented as it is to the working out of God's redemptive purposes in history and to the consummation of those purposes at the end of time. At the outset of his study, therefore, Hoekema asserted that "to understand biblical eschatology, we must see it as an integral aspect of all of biblical revelation. Eschatology must not be thought of as something which is found in, say, such Bible books as Daniel and Revelation, but as dominating and permeating the entire message of the Bible."[25] Indeed, in the gospel we have a prolepsis of the ultimate consummation of God's redemptive purposes in the new heavens and earth. There are, then, an "already" and a "not yet" with respect to the presence of the kingdom of God in history.

23. Ibid., 62.

24. Anthony A. Hoekema, "Amillennialism," in *The Meaning of the Millennium: Four Views,* ed. Robert G. Clouse (Downers Grove, Ill.: Inter-Varsity, 1977), 155–87.

25. Anthony A. Hoekema, *The Bible and the Future* (Grand Rapids: Eerdmans, 1979), 3.

After having provided a summary account of the biblical teaching concerning inaugurated eschatology, Hoekema gave more sustained attention to future eschatology, those aspects of the Bible's teaching about the future which pertain to the events still to come in the fulfilment of God's work of redemption. Here Hoekema followed the classical order of treatment, dealing first with the subject of individual eschatology (physical death, immortality, the intermediate state) and then with the subject of general eschatology (expectation of the parousia, the signs of the times, the second coming of Christ, the millennium, the resurrection of the body, the final judgment, and the final state).

Since Hoekema's discussion of the millennium was one of the more controversial features of his eschatology and affords a good sampling of his position, it will be profitable to review his argument briefly here. Hoekema, recognizing the misleading nature of the term *amillennialism*,[26] argued for the view that the millennium mentioned in Revelation 20:4–6 is a present reality, the reign of the souls of deceased believers with Christ in heaven during the period of the proclamation of the gospel. Because the millennium is now and contemporaneous with the entire period between Christ's ascension and his second coming, we ought to understand the second coming of Christ to involve not two phases but only one. Christ's second coming will consummate the course of redemptive history and inaugurate the final state.

Hoekema argued that Revelation 20 must be approached from within the framework of the Book of Revelation as a whole. Following the interpretation of William Hendriksen, Hoekema understood the book to contain seven major sections, each of which parallels the others and depicts the circumstance of the church and the world from the time of Christ's first coming to his second coming.[27] According to this view, which is known as progressive parallelism, these parallel sections succeed one another in a progressive manner, so that there is a discernible eschatological development from the first to the last, with an increasing emphasis upon the final victory of Christ.

Taking Revelation 20 as one of the parallel sections providing a comprehensive description of the course of redemptive history between Christ's first and second comings, Hoekema did not interpret the reference to "a thousand years" as a literal period of one thousand years, but as a period of indeterminate length and a symbol of completeness.[28] The binding of Satan mentioned in Revelation 20 must be interpreted in terms of the parallels in the Gospels which speak of the gospel age as a period in which the Good News will spread to the ends of the earth and the nations will be discipled. During the course of the spread of the gospel, Satan is bound in the sense that he is rendered incapable of deceiving the nations or preventing the gathering of God's people into the church. Hoekema further argued that the reference in Revelation 20 to the martyrs who come to life and reign with Christ for a thousand years designates their present reign with Christ in heaven. It does not refer to a literal bodily resurrection to be distinguished from a subsequent resurrection of others after a period of one thousand years. Thus, interpreting Revelation 20 by analogy with the whole of scriptural teaching (*tota Scriptura*), Hoekema concluded that the millennium is the present period of redemptive history in which Christ's work of gathering the nations through his Word and Spirit is being successfully prosecuted.

In Hoekema's defense of classical amillennial eschatology, it is evident that a

26. While the term suggests that there is "no millennium," amillennialists do not deny the reality of the millennium; rather, their identification of it is different from that of the classic premillennialist or dispensationalist (Hoekema, *Bible and the Future*, 173–74).

27. See William Hendriksen, *More than Conquerors* (Grand Rapids: Baker, 1940).

28. Hoekema, *Bible and the Future*, 227.

number of distinctive Reformed emphases are enunciated. For Hoekema classical premillennialism, and especially dispensationalism, broke the unity between the Old and the New Testaments in the progressive unfolding and realization of the covenant of grace. Only in an amillennial eschatology is it possible to do justice to the biblical emphasis upon the presence and centrality of the kingdom of God in history, now and in the future. Amillennialism is not unduly optimistic about the prospects of that kingdom in the present (compare postmillennialism), nor does it relegate the kingdom to a future millennium exclusively. Amillennial eschatology provides a basis for a biblical realism about the course of redemptive history in the present and the future. Hoekema also answered the common complaint of dispensationalists that amillennialism provides no place for the concrete fulfilment of the biblical promises concerning the future coming of God's kingdom on earth. It does so, Hoekema insisted, by emphasizing that the consummation of the kingdom of God at Christ's return will inaugurate new heavens and a new earth in which all of these promises will be realized.

The Doctrine of Humanity

The second of Hoekema's major theological studies, *Created in God's Image*, addressed the topic with which he began his theological writing and to which, as we have seen, he often returned—the doctrine of humanity.[29] In this comprehensive statement Hoekema reiterated his conviction that the biblical doctrine of man is especially important in the modern theological context.

In a fashion reminiscent of his earlier treatment of the doctrine of the covenant and its significance for biblical anthropology, Hoekema introduced *Created in God's Image* by emphasizing the biblical view of man as a created person. There is a dual emphasis here. On the one hand, man is a

creature, wholly dependent on God, the Creator. On the other hand, man is a person, a being uniquely capable of making decisions and establishing goals. However paradoxical or inconsistent these emphases may appear, they together constitute something of the mystery of human nature. Hoekema even suggested that these separate emphases may well account for the divergence historically between the Arminian and Calvinist views of salvation—the former stressing the personhood of man, the latter the creatureliness of man.

After setting forth the conception of man as a created person, Hoekema took up the central biblical metaphor of man as the image of God. Hoekema understood this metaphor to describe that creaturely likeness or analogy that we bear to God in our own person, in our relations with others, and in our being called and endowed to exercise dominion over the creation. Though this image has been distorted and perverted by the fall into sin, it has not been entirely lost or eradicated. In the course of the history of redemption, we see the image of God in all its perfection in Jesus Christ alone. All who by faith are joined to him and sanctified by his Spirit are being restored to the true knowledge, righteousness, and holiness entailed in the image of God. The image of God must be understood, therefore, in the light of the history of redemption. First created in God's image, man finds that this image, though retained in part, has been seriously corrupted and distorted by the fall. Only through Christ's work by the Spirit is the image of God renewed in us, a process which will issue in total conformity to Christ when God's work of redemption is completed.

In the course of his development of a biblical anthropology, Hoekema not only returned to a number of themes elaborated earlier in his review of Berkouwer's *Man: The Image of God*, but also clarified some aspects of his own position which had been criticized by others. For example, he sought to clarify his conviction that we need to re-

29. Anthony A. Hoekema, *Created in God's Image* (Grand Rapids: Eerdmans, 1986).

tain the classical distinction between the image of God in a "broader" or "structural" sense (what man is) and a "narrower" or "functional" sense (what man does). The image of God, Hoekema maintained, involves both the structural dimensions of human nature (those capacities of reason, moral choice, and the like that distinguish man from the other creatures) and the functional dimensions (those acts of reason, choice, and the like that produce growth in and express true knowledge, righteousness, and holiness).

Hoekema also clarified his previous writing on the Christian's positive self-image by distancing himself from some of the unbiblical emphases on self-love and self-esteem that are found in evangelical contexts. For Hoekema, the terms *self-love* and *self-esteem*, though they were becoming more and more popular in contemporary Christian literature and preaching, were suspect, since they tended toward self-worship and an unholy pride in one's own person. We should rather speak of a Christian's self-image, remembering that we are what we are by virtue of God's having created and renewed us by grace alone. The Christian self-image boasts not in ourselves, but in what we have become by grace, glorying not in our own works, but in the fruit of Christ's work in us.

Soteriology

The third of Hoekema's major theological studies, *Saved by Grace,* constituted a fitting conclusion to his lifelong work as a Reformed theologian. Since we cannot rightly know ourselves apart from recognition of our relatedness to God, not only as Creator but also as Redeemer, the subject of God's grace in the salvation of his people was, for Hoekema, the center of the Christian view of humanity. Accordingly, in the opening chapters of his final study he provided a general orientation to soteriology, considering such questions as the propriety and usefulness of *ordo salutis* ("order of salvation") as a theological construct, the role of the Holy Spirit in the application of Christ's saving work, and the central importance of the believer's union with Christ.

In a revealing introductory chapter, Hoekema acknowledged that his theological standpoint was Reformed and that this entailed a number of distinctive emphases: the decisiveness of the sovereign grace of God in the salvation of the sinner; God's eternal decree of election as the source of his saving work; the particularity or definiteness of the saving work of God in Christ, both in its provision and in its application; the preeminence of the Holy Spirit as the one who sovereignly ministers Christ's saving work in us. Salvation is wholly, from its inception to its conclusion, a work of God's sovereign and free grace. Hoekema characteristically added, however, that this grace does not obliterate or remove the obligation to respond in faith and repentance to the work of the Spirit. In Reformed theology, salvation is God's work and our task, however paradoxical this may seem to us. "We must believe," declared Hoekema, "that both sides of these apparently contradictory sets of thoughts are true, since the Bible teaches both."[30]

Hoekema, in his discussion of the *ordo salutis,* presented a mediating position. On the one hand, he rejected John Murray's argument that a definite *ordo salutis* can be deduced from scriptural givens and logical considerations. And on the other hand, Hoekema was not content with G. C. Berkouwer's suggestion that, in viewing the Word and faith as correlates, we need speak only of the "way of salvation." Hoekema maintained that we should think of *ordo salutis* as a description of the one work of God's saving grace, which comprises a variety of aspects. These aspects are to be understood as facets of the single work of salvation, conceptually distinct but not chronologically successive (as if they followed each other in strict temporal order). Consisting of both punctiliar acts (e.g., jus-

30. Anthony A. Hoekema, *Saved by Grace* (Grand Rapids: Eerdmans, 1989), 5.

tification) and progressive operations (e.g., sanctification) which bear a particular relation to one another, they are distinct integral parts of the one basic process of salvation. Thus Hoekema also opposed those recent forms of *ordo salutis* which incorporate a second blessing or postconversion participation in the fulness of the Spirit. Here he had in view those soteriologies which include the Wesleyan teaching of Christian perfection or entire sanctification, the Pentecostal concept of baptism in the Spirit, and the distinction between carnal and spiritual Christians which is found in some evangelical contexts.

After having considered the difficult question of the *ordo salutis*, Hoekema addressed the equally difficult question of the role of the Holy Spirit in the process of the believer's salvation. Noting the Westminster Confession of Faith's affirmation that the Spirit is the "only efficient agent in the application of redemption," Hoekema argued that the Spirit's role is essentially to unite us with Christ. By the Spirit's working through the Word of the gospel, we are joined with Christ and made to partake of all his saving benefits.

Following the approach already set forth in his earlier studies, *What about Tongue-Speaking?* and *Holy Spirit Baptism*, Hoekema maintained the historic and classical position of Reformed theology that some of the gifts of the Spirit operative in the Apostolic Era are not to be expected as a regular and normative feature of the life of the church today. Those gifts which were given to authenticate the message of Christ and his apostles in the unique foundational epoch of the New Testament church (e.g., tongues, prophesyings, miracles of healing) are no longer integral to the continuing edification of the church, built as it is upon the foundation laid once for all by the apostles. Once again Hoekema, though he acknowledged the continued and sometimes special working of the Spirit subsequent to conversion, repudiated the Neo-Pentecostal doctrine of baptism in the Holy Spirit with its assumption of a qualitatively new post-conversion working of the Spirit that is given to some, though not all, believers.

The remainder of *Saved by Grace* treated the various aspects of the *ordo salutis*: the gospel call, effectual calling, regeneration, conversion, repentance, faith, justification, sanctification, perseverance. Developing his previous assertion that the chief work of the Holy Spirit in the application of salvation is to unite us with Christ, Hoekema explicated the *ordo salutis* by discussing various aspects of this union, beginning with its roots in the eternal and gracious election of God's people in Christ, moving to its basis in the saving work of Christ in behalf of his people, and finally turning to our actual union with Christ in regeneration, faith, sanctification, and the like. These various aspects of the *ordo salutis* are different ways of describing the implications of union with Christ. In joining with him we are given new life from the dead (regeneration), a new status (justification), a new direction (conversion), a new holiness (sanctification), and a new persistence (perseverance).

With *Saved by Grace* Hoekema completed a lifetime of theological reflection and thought. Like his previous studies, it is a model of clarity of expression, fresh exegesis of the biblical text, contemporaneity, and rootedness in the Reformed confessional tradition. It well exemplifies his lifelong effort to provide a contemporary statement of the biblical and Reformed faith, one which answers new questions without being faddish or facile. The heart of that faith was, for Hoekema, the biblical message of God's free gift of salvation in Christ. Only in the context of a believing response to God's gracious initiative in Christ are we able to understand ourselves aright—as sinners saved by grace alone. The theological anthropology with which Hoekema was concerned throughout his life finds its resolution in understanding God's gracious covenantal initiative in Christ.

Hoekema's contribution to evangelical thought lies in the depth of his biblical insight and respect for the confessional tradition of the Reformed churches. Rather than following the pattern of so much contemporary theology, going from crisis to crisis and approaching the text of Scripture without the discipline of the church's confessions, Hoekema's theological reflection displayed a breadth of biblical and confessional knowledge which enabled him to address contemporary issues fruitfully and to make further progress in understanding. In so doing he sought to guard himself against two dangers incipient in evangelicalism—approaching the biblical text without the guidance of the church's previous reflection upon Scripture, and being content to re-pristinate the past without freshly addressing the present context. For Hoekema these dangers could best be avoided by addressing the present upon the basis of the wealth of the church's confessions and a renewed engagement with the whole of Scripture (*tota Scriptura*).

Bernard Ramm

Kevin J. Vanhoozer

Bernard Ramm was born in Butte, Montana on August 1, 1916. As a young boy, he was introduced to atomic theory, relativity, and chemistry by a Russian engineer, the father of one of his playmates. Ramm attributed his enduring scientific interest to this early exposure. He became a Christian in the summer between high school and university through his brother, John Bernard Ramm. After earning a B.A. from the University of Washington in 1938, he attended the Eastern Baptist Theological Seminary in Philadelphia, where he won the Middler's Scholarship Prize and the Church History Prize. In his last year of seminary he also took graduate courses in philosophy at the University of Pennsylvania.

For much of the 1940s Ramm was both student and teacher. He obtained his M.A. in philosophy at the University of Southern California in 1947, and in 1950 he received his Ph.D. from the same institution, his dissertation being entitled "An Investigation of Some Recent Efforts to Justify Metaphysical Statements from Science with Special Reference to Physics." During this time Ramm served a short stint as pastor of Lake Street Baptist Church in Glendale, California, before becoming a professor of biblical

languages at the Los Angeles Baptist Theological Seminary (1944–45) and then head of the Department of Philosophy and Apologetics at the Bible Institute of Los Angeles (1945–51). In 1948 he was the midyear lecturer at Western Baptist Theological Seminary, where he delivered the talks that eventually became his first published work, *Problems in Christian Apologetics* (1949).

The beginnings of the evangelical movement as distinct from fundamentalism also took place during the 1940s. Ramm had become a Christian in the last years of the fundamentalist-modernist debates, which opposed a literalistic understanding of the Bible to a critical one, and a supernaturalistic view of the world to a naturalistic one. As a young Christian, Ramm was warned to read only safe books in order not to catch the theological disease called modernism.

In reflecting on this time, Ramm admitted that it was tempting "to live one's theological life within the confines of a small fort with very high walls."[1] But throughout most of his career, he did not build such walls, but actually marched round them. In his teaching and writing, he strove to bring evangelical theology into the sphere of free and open discourse with the modern world. How does Ezekiel measure up to Albert Einstein? Jeremiah to Carl Jung? From the outset, he was committed to giving intellectual respectability to conservative orthodox theology, rather than simply pulling up the drawbridge and refusing to dialogue with the modern world, as was the tendency of the fundamentalists.

Ramm's natural dialogue partners in the 1940s were fundamentalists and modernists. As he sought a middle way between these opposing positions—the one almost idolatrously devoted to the Bible and thus disdainful of the valid discoveries of modern science, and the other so fascinated with the modern worldview that it no longer heard the Word of God in the Bible— he discovered in the 1950s the works of two twentieth-century theologians—the Dutch Calvinist Abraham Kuyper and the Swiss neo-orthodox Karl Barth—who were to have a lasting influence on his thought. In the preface to his *Special Revelation and the Word of God* Ramm wrote, "My indebtedness to Abraham Kuyper's *Principles of Sacred Theology* is evident on almost every page. Long before the emergence of either fundamentalism or neo-orthodoxy he avoided the extremes of which both would later be guilty."[2] Fundamentalism suffers from an incipient bibliolatry, and neo-orthodoxy, another major alternative to the fundamentalist-liberal dichotomy, tends to depreciate the cognitive aspect of revelation. To put it another way, fundamentalism forgets that the Bible is a book of salvation, and neo-orthodoxy forgets that the Bible communicates knowledge of God. Ramm considered Kuyper to be the greatest Reformed theologian between John Calvin and Barth. With regard to the doctrines of inspiration and revelation, Ramm wrote, "Kuyper was far more profound, far more philosophically minded, far more culturally oriented than the [other] orthodox authors I had read. . . . Kuyper provided a small but important bridge to Barth. . . . Time and time again I found parallels between Barth's thought and Kuyper's."[3]

Though Ramm had chanced upon a volume by Barth in the 1940s, he had to postpone any serious engagement with Barth until after the completion of his doctoral studies in 1950. During his years as associate professor of philosophy at Bethel College and Seminary in St. Paul (1951–54) and as director of graduate studies in religion at Baylor University (1954–59), he began a daily reading of Barth's *Church Dogmatics* and his shorter writings according to a set schedule. Ramm decided that of all the contemporary theologians Barth was doing the best job of relating historic Reformed theology to modern biblical criticism. Consequently, Ramm chose to spend a sabbatical year (1957–58) in Basel, Switzerland, where he faithfully attended the Saturday-afternoon English-language seminars held in Barth's home. Ramm came with a list of questions and took notes on Barth's replies. These literary and personal encounters with Barth materially changed some of the ways in which Ramm thought, lectured, and wrote about theology. The first material change stemmed from Barth's exhortation to be fearless in theology—if God's Word is in Scripture, who can stand against it? In a flash of insight, Ramm took this exhortation to heart and grasped its implications. It helped liberate him from the fortress mentality of fundamentalism, which

---

1. Bernard Ramm, "Helps from Karl Barth," in Donald K. McKim, ed., *How Karl Barth Changed My Mind* (Grand Rapids: Eerdmans, 1986), 121.

2. Bernard Ramm, *Special Revelation and the Word of God* (Grand Rapids: Eerdmans, 1961), 7.

3. Bernard Ramm, *After Fundamentalism: The Future of Evangelical Theology* (San Francisco: Harper and Row, 1983), 9.

continued doggedly to resist the siege of modern learning. His apologetic strategy had to be revised; referring to his work prior to 1957, he spoke of "the futility and intellectual bankruptcy of my former strategy."[4] We may need, therefore, to speak of a turn in Ramm's theological development, occurring sometime after 1957. The second material impact on Ramm's thinking was Barth's great respect for historical theology. Ramm contrasted this with his earlier pietistic attitude (another holdover from fundamentalism), which tended to rely on the individual's present experience of the Holy Spirit rather than on the Spirit's guidance of saints past. Ramm applauded Barth's stretching the term *ecumenical* to include one's predecessors in the theological dialogue. The third help from Barth concerned the way in which he correlated biblical criticism with biblical inspiration and authority (see p. 304).

From 1959 to 1986 Ramm continued to teach evangelical and ecumenical theology at a succession of Baptist institutions: at California Baptist Theological Seminary (1959–74), at Eastern Baptist Theological Seminary (1974–77), and lastly as Pearl Rawlings Hamilton Professor of Christian Theology at the American Baptist Seminary of the West (1978–86). In 1961–62 he gave the Clarence Edward Macartney Lectures at Whitworth College in Spokane, Washington, which were published as *The Christian College in the Twentieth Century* (1963). In 1963 he was an American Baptist delegate to the Faith and Order Conference in Montreal. In addition to his seminary teaching, he was involved almost every summer from 1955 to 1978 in training leaders for Young Life, and he also worked with World Vision teams in India, Indonesia, Japan, and Argentina. On December 31, 1986, at the age of seventy, he retired from the American Baptist Seminary of the West, an occasion marked by dinners and a special commendation at the 1987 commencement. A vic-

tim of Parkinson's disease, he died on August 11, 1992, in Laguna Hills, California.

Bernard Ramm must be considered one of the foremost American evangelical theologians of the twentieth century. Only Carl F. H. Henry's works are comparable in quantity and quality. Ramm authored some twenty books, including several textbooks, as well as about one hundred articles and reviews in the fields of apologetics, hermeneutics, theology, and ethics. Together with Henry, he helped shape the intellectual contours of American evangelicalism in the wake of the fundamentalist-modernist split. In a particularly fertile twelve-year period (1949–61), Ramm produced no fewer than eight important books, including textbooks that for over a generation represented the best of evangelical thinking on the relationship between science and theology, apologetics, and hermeneutics. His books have been translated into Spanish, Japanese, Korean, and Serbian. Despite his firm commitment to Baptist institutions, he was a spokesman for an evangelical theology that was orthodox and ecumenical, more concerned to stress his Protestantism than his particular denomination.[5] He also helped shape evangelical opinion as consulting editor of and frequent contributor to *Eternity* and *Christianity Today*.

Ramm's thought continues to be discussed by evangelical theologians, particularly in the wake of his 1983 work, *After Fundamentalism: The Future of Evangelical Theology*, in which he commends the theological method of Karl Barth to evangelicals. From his first work to his last, Ramm tried to stake out a postfundamentalist position that would at once be faithful to the Reformation and the Word of God while at the same time interacting honestly with modern learning. This endeavor has proven

4. Ramm, "Helps," 121.

5. It is noteworthy that the adjectives *Protestant* and *Christian* occur in the titles of several of his early works. Ramm believed that the Reformed faith is the truest expression of the Christian religion (see his *The God Who Makes a Difference: A Christian Appeal to Reason* [Waco: Word, 1972]).

to be most significant: the evangelical-theology division of the American Academy of Religion devoted its November 1990 session to a discussion of the theme "Bernard Ramm and the Continuing Agenda of Evangelical Theology." The papers there presented focused on the relationship between science and theology and on the nature of theological method. A month later, the National Association of Baptist Professors of Religion published a *festschrift* both to honor Ramm's thought and to assess its abiding significance.[6] This work includes tributes to Ramm as well as studies of various aspects of his thought and a complete bibliography. Ramm's theological method has also been the subject of a Ph.D. dissertation.[7]

Apologetic Writings

There is a division of labor within Christian theology: the theologian states and structures the faith into a system of belief; the apologist verifies it. In the space of five years (1949–54) Ramm authored four textbooks that touched on different aspects of apologetics, that branch of theology particularly concerned with defending the faith and replying to objections. In *Protestant Christian Evidences* (1953), he is concerned with demonstrating the factuality of Christianity for those whose faith needs intellectual buttressing. What kinds of evidences, he asks, are sufficient for such a task? Ramm here relies on material facts (e.g., documents), supernatural facts (e.g., events that can be explained only by invoking the category of the supernatural), and experiential facts (e.g., the transforming power of regeneration) to argue for the truth of Christianity and the Christian Scriptures. Accordingly, *Protestant Christian Evidences* is full of familiar arguments for the super-

natural character of the Bible; for example, fulfilled prophecies, miracles, and the resurrection. Ramm then uses the supernatural character of the Bible to verify Christianity: Inspiration is "the only adequate hypothesis to account for the Bible. Christianity stands verified by a supernatural book."[8]

Ramm's work in the philosophy of science shaped one of his central theses, namely, that arguments about evidences always involve metaphysical assumptions, often unstated, about the nature of reality. We cannot even say, "Jesus is my Savior," without committing ourselves to a position with metaphysical implications. Ramm contends that evidences for Christianity are correctly understood and used only if one's metaphysical position is theistic. Other metaphysical systems, say, materialism or naturalism, emphasize material facts and conceive them too strictly. Science does have validity, but only within limits; science may try to reduce qualities to quantities, but it has no right to apply this method to all forms of human experience. For instance, it is metaphysics, not science, that decides whether or not the immaterial and supernatural exist. The real question is, What metaphysical view, what view of the universe, will establish the rights of science within its own sphere yet permit or recognize a supernatural dimension as well? In arguing that naturalism is a metaphysical rather than a scientific position, Ramm made a point that is worth repeating today. He argued that naturalism ("all is Nature") is inadequate to explain the totality of human experience: consciousness is more than brain activity, and morality is more than physical stimulus. This is not to say that the Christian must be antiscience; on the contrary, Ramm contended that Nature is known aright and science works aright only on the basis of Christian theism—the

---

6. See *Perspectives in Religious Studies* 17 (Winter 1990): 5–101.

7. David Miller, "The Theological System of Bernard Ramm," Ph.D. diss., Southwestern Baptist Theological Seminary, 1982.

8. Bernard Ramm, *Protestant Christian Evidences: A Textbook of the Evidences of the Truthfulness of the Christian Faith for Conservative Protestants* (Chicago: Moody, 1953), 249.

belief that there is a supreme personal God distinct from but related to the created world.

Ramm wrote *The Christian View of Science and Scripture* (1954) in order to rehabilitate the noble tradition of learned evangelicals who have taken great care to learn the facts of science and Scripture. This noble tradition had been buried by fundamentalist bibliolatry, a reflex product of fear rather than faith. God wrote both the Bible and the book of Nature—why then should we tear asunder what God has put together? The fundamentalist who insists that Scripture is right and science is wrong "makes the words of God and the work of God clash," for the two books of God must ultimately tell the *same* story.[9] *The Christian View of Science and Scripture* is an intelligent and impassioned plea for an approach that creates harmony between modern learning and the Bible. Until recently, Ramm's book was the standard evangelical text on the subject. George Marsden recounts Billy Graham's high opinion of the view of inspiration it set forth. Graham suggested in a letter to Harold Lindsell that Ramm's approach to Scripture was more in line with the aims of the new evangelical movement than was that of Carl Henry, whom he initially feared to be too fundamentalistic! Despite Graham's warm reception, however, many conservative Christians were worried about Ramm's suggestion that inspiration need not imply accuracy in scientific detail. These fears were fueled by passages that seemed to allow a certain measure of biological evolution, albeit theistically directed. By the summer of 1955, according to Marsden, "Ramm's book had indeed caused the largest stir in fundamentalism since the RSV controversy."[10]

True to his conviction that the usefulness of evidences ultimately depends on philosophies, Ramm deals in the first part of *The Christian View of Science and Scripture* with general issues pertaining to the philosophy of science and theology, and in the second part with apparent conflicts between specific sciences—astronomy, geology, biology, anthropology—and Scripture. Not ad hoc arguments, but a proper philosophy of Nature is necessary if Scripture and science are to agree on the facts and how to interpret them: "The evangelical always fought the battle on too narrow a strip. He argued over the authenticity of this or that bone . . . this or that detail in geology."[11] What Ramm worked for, and achieved, in *The Christian View of Science and Scripture* is an overarching integrative strategy which specifies the principle governing the relation of biblical and scientific data. Crucial in this endeavor is recognition of the proper limits to each enterprise. Theologians must be careful not to identify Christianity with any one scientific worldview. Scientists, for their part, must likewise be careful not to identify science with any one philosophical worldview.

When it speaks of natural things, biblical language is popular, not scientific. Scripture describes things the way they appear to the ordinary observer and does not theorize as to their actual nature: "Gen. 1 does not defend Aristotle or Ptolemy or Copernicus or Newton or Einstein or Milne."[12] Moreover, the language of the Bible comes to us dressed in the cultural forms of the day. However, the theological truths embedded in these outmoded cultural categories are inspired. God is Creator, whether we picture creation as did the ancient Babylonians or as did Einstein. How do we tell what in the biblical language is cultural and what transcends culture? What is to stop us, say, from throwing the doctrine of vicarious atonement out with the cultural image of

9. Bernard Ramm, *The Christian View of Science and Scripture* (Grand Rapids: Eerdmans, 1954), 23.

10. George M. Marsden, *Reforming Fundamentalism: Fuller Seminary and the New Evangelicalism* (Grand Rapids: Eerdmans, 1987), 158–59.

11. Ramm, *Science and Scripture*, 22.

12. Ibid., 48. Ramm calls biblical language phenomenal and nonpostulational.

sacrifice? Ramm recognized the difficulties involved and suggested that what is directly theological is also transcultural. But as Nancey Murphy pointed out in her address to the evangelical-theology division of the American Academy of Religion, the cultural and the transcultural are not always so easily distinguished; for example, is a dichotomous view of the constitutional makeup of human beings natural or theological?

Though the Bible does not theorize, it does have a view of Nature. What is Nature? Nature is the creation of an almighty God, and can be explained by reference not only to the mechanical laws which describe its present working, but also to the ultimate ends for which it was made. The Bible views God not as First Cause, but as "World-Ground." The latter designation is far richer, for it embraces God as Sustainer and Provider and Goal as well as First Cause. From a theistic point of view, the laws of Nature express the will of God. With Kuyper, Ramm suggests that it is the role of the Holy Spirit to lead the creature to its destiny and to cause it to develop according to its innate character. The Spirit is the hidden intelligence in Nature who directs the acorn to become an oak and the human person to reflect the image of God. The Spirit is the divine entelechy in Nature, the presence and power which leads creation towards its appointed end, its ultimate purpose—the glory of God. Ramm's name for this Christian philosophy of Nature is "progressive creationism." Ramm follows Augustine in distinguishing an original creation *ex nihilo* and a subsequent formation in which matter has form imposed upon it. Ramm believes that the formation of creation was a progressive operation, not a punctiliar fiat. If dry land appeared, it was the Spirit who set the laws of geology in motion to produce it. The Spirit fulfilled the command of God by working in Nature through a temporal process. Ramm bristled at the suggestion that progressive creationism weakens or questions divine omnipotence. God spoke, and it was so—but this says nothing about

how long it took. So where fundamentalists asserted fiat creationism, and modern science asserted naturalistic evolution, Ramm blazed a third way: progressive creation through natural law.

Ramm applied his ideas concerning the nature of biblical language and progressive creationism to problems that arise when Scripture confronts the findings of modern astronomy, geology, biology, and anthropology. With regard to astronomy, the biblical accounts are remarkably free from the usual astrological and mythological elements that characterize other ancient Near Eastern documents. The celestial bodies were not deified, but were considered servants of the divine will: "The lesson which the Hebrews learned from the stars was not any theory, such as the Copernican, but rather the faithfulness of God."[13] But surely science and Scripture conflict when it comes to the Genesis account of a six-day creation of the universe and human beings? The burden of *The Christian View of Science and Scripture* is to argue (1) that not all evangelicals believe that human beings were created in 4004 B.C., (2) that many believe the universe to be billions of years old, and (3) that consequently some form of evolution, theistically conceived, may be compatible with Christian faith. Again Ramm insists that the Genesis account, like the rest of biblical language, is neither literal science nor ancient mythology, but a purified, nontheoretical literary vehicle for conveying the revelation of God. Some may take a naive literalistic view of the Genesis account and conclude, with James Ussher and John Lightfoot, that creation took place the week of October 18 to 24, 4004 B.C., but this is to fly in the face of modern geological evidence. For Ramm, Genesis is not about geology but theology. Its intent is to prohibit idolatrous views of the universe and to evoke from human beings the worship that belongs to God the Creator. The six days are not to be construed as chronological, as if

13. Ibid., 96.

each paragraph in Genesis 1 corresponds to a geological epoch, but as pictorial and theological. This is not to relegate theology to the backseat of cosmological discussion. On the contrary, both geology and theology have something to contribute: Genesis is about the First Cause, and geology is about the secondary causes which God used to form the earth.

What position should evangelicals adopt with regard to biology? Does accepting the facts of modern biology mean bowing the knee before Charles Darwin? Here Ramm urges evangelicals to develop a philosophy of biology. Darwin's evolutionary theory interpreted the facts from the perspective of a naturalistic philosophy. But these same facts may also be interpreted from the perspective of a supernaturalistic philosophy that takes divine creation seriously. Indeed, divine creation may account for more facts than Darwin could. For instance, Ramm argues that the conditions necessary for any life at all on earth are so complex that it is virtually impossible to think of them as occurring by chance. Progressive creationism, which attributes the order in the universe to the entelechy or guidance of the Holy Spirit, explains much that the theory of evolution explains and much that the theory of evolution does not. Furthermore, if true, evolutionary theory is true only of biology and not of cosmology—evolution cannot explain the ultimate origin of the universe. Is evolution contrary to Scripture? Ramm suggests the following litmus test: a scientific theory is anti-Christian only when it denies something in the Christian philosophy of Nature, that is, only when it denies one of the basic theological principles of faith. If evolution is viewed as a secondary cause (i.e., as an instrument of the Holy Spirit), it can be tolerated by Christianity. But the theory which best accounts for all the evidence is, in Ramm's opinion, progressive creationism. Progressive creationism allows for both a series of divine creative acts and a temporal process whereby the Holy Spirit, making use of secondary causes, guides to their appointed end the events set in motion by divine fiat.

Ramm was not only a practitioner, but also a theoretician of Christian apologetics, as is evident in his *Varieties of Christian Apologetics*.[14] How can we demonstrate Christian truth and the knowledge of God? Is this best done with a geometric proof, a probability statement, a poem? What role does philosophy play in attaining knowledge of God? How does human sinfulness affect our knowledge of God? What is the relation of faith to reason? Ramm points out three major approaches to these questions. The first type of apologetic system stresses the uniqueness of the Christian experience of grace. Blaise Pascal and Søren Kierkegaard are characteristic of this approach, which values an ineffable personal experience over rational understanding and persuasion. Thomas Aquinas is the best representative of the second type of apologetic, which holds that reason is competent to attain knowledge of God through studying the world and human nature. The third type of Christian apologetic builds on special revelation and is represented by Augustine, Calvin, and Kuyper. These three types correspond, roughly, to the theologies of neo-orthodoxy, Roman Catholicism, and the evangelicalism represented by Ramm himself. What Augustine, Calvin, Kuyper, and Ramm share is a conviction that fallen human beings (and fallen human reason) are unable to achieve knowledge of God without a gracious divine illumination. Special revelation is necessary!

Trilogy on Divine Revelation

Studying the structure of divine revelation meant turning from apologetics, the

14. Bernard Ramm, *Varieties of Christian Apologetics: An Introduction to the Christian Philosophy of Religion* (Grand Rapids: Baker, 1962). This is a revision of an earlier work, *Types of Apologetic Systems* (Wheaton, Ill.: Van Kampen, 1953). Ramm rewrote the introductory essay and replaced chapters on Edward John Carnell and Cornelius Van Til with chapters on Calvin and Kuyper.

verification of the Christian belief system, to systematic theology—its construction. In this area Ramm produced a noteworthy trilogy comprising *The Pattern of Religious Authority* (1957), *The Witness of the Spirit* (1959), and *Special Revelation and the Word of God* (1961). Because divergent views on the nature of special revelation lie at the heart of many major differences in theology, Ramm was persuaded that exploring the issue at length would lead to a better grasp of evangelical theology vis-à-vis the alternatives. In each volume he was careful to speak of the structure of the particular doctrine under consideration. That is, he was concerned to find the central principle of each doctrine and the pattern employed to concretely express and apply it.

Few would contest the principle that God is the final authority in religion—but what does this mean? How does God express his authority? Through the Roman Catholic Church? through the best human philosophies? through religious experience? through the Hebrew and Christian Scriptures? In *The Pattern of Religious Authority* Ramm notes that Augustine correlated authority with revelation. God expresses his authority by divine self-revelation. As in the other sciences, so too in theology the object to be investigated has authority. But in theology, knowledge of the object—God—can be conveyed to the human subject only by means of revelation. Experience and reason may be modes of apprehending authority, but authority rests in what is apprehended, not in the instrument of apprehension. The historic Protestant principle recognizes the Holy Spirit speaking in the Scriptures as the primary religious authority, and so stands opposed to liberal Protestantism's emphasis on the authority of experience and Roman Catholicism's emphasis on the authority of tradition. At the same time, Ramm objects to the abbreviated Protestant principle that states, "The Bible and only the Bible is the religion of Protestants." The true Protestant principle recognizes both an objective divine revelation (inspired Scripture) and a subjective divine witness (the Holy Spirit).[15]

Just how damaging is the abbreviated Protestant principle? Is it possible that well-meaning conservatives, with their doctrine of inerrancy, have substituted a paper pope for the living one? For Ramm the decisive refutation of the abbreviated Protestant principle is the phenomenon of cults. Many cults appeal to the Bible as their authority. Do they, then, have the right principle of authority but an improper hermeneutic? No, they do not have the right principle of authority. For they largely ignore the biblical focus on the primary human need, salvation in Jesus Christ: "Christ is the supreme object of the witness of the Spirit, and Christ is the supreme content of the Scriptures. The Spirit who bears His chief witness to Christ also inspired the Scriptures. The Scriptures are inspired by the Spirit and they witness supremely to Christ, the personal Word of God. Such is the pattern of authority, and the three elements of it must be held in proper relationship. The cultist fails to keep the person and work of Jesus Christ central."[16] Ramm believed that evangelicalism, born in the wake of the fundamentalist-modernist controversy over Scripture, was in danger of lapsing into the abbreviated Protestant principle. It was largely for this reason that he chose as the theme of his next book *The Witness of the Spirit*—a doctrine which Ramm thought had almost disappeared from evangelical theology.

In making the *testimonium* of the Spirit—his internal witness that persuades us that the Scripture is God's Word—part of the structure of religious authority, Ramm believed he was being true to the Reformers, and to the structure of revelation itself. Martin Luther and John Calvin insisted,

---

15. Ramm offers three pages of documentation showing that the abbreviated Protestant principle is a departure from the historic Reformation confessions—Bernard Ramm, *The Pattern of Religious Authority* (Grand Rapids: Eerdmans, 1957), 30–33.

16. Ibid., 37.

against Roman Catholicism, that only the Holy Spirit, not the church, can authorize the Scriptures. Neither tradition, nor reason, nor experience, but only Word and Spirit together are sufficient to persuade men and women that the Bible is the Word of God. Against the enthusiasts Calvin argued that the Spirit is a witness to a content (the Word), not a communication in himself. The Spirit's primary role is to witness to the Word of God, not to provide a substitute for it. An inordinate concern with the person of the Holy Spirit (Ramm here mentions Pentecostalism) leads one to overlook the Spirit's witness to Christ and thus to "build a temple where Scripture permits only a tent."[17]

Revelation always comes in this double structure—objective truth (Word) and subjective illumination (Spirit). The nature of the inner witness of the Spirit is such that it presupposes an objective revelation. "Illumination" refers to the Spirit's enabling persons blinded by sin to see clearly the truth and divinity of God's Word. Thus it is incorrect to charge the doctrine of the *testimonium* with subjectivism. Such a charge, Ramm argues, ignores the basic structure of the Spirit's work as it is described in Scripture and by Calvin. There can be no witness without that to which the witness points: "The *testimonium* is an illumination and a persuasion. It is not an impartation of knowledge. . . . It would lose its character as a witness if it were an impartation of knowledge."[18] The Spirit enables us to see what is already there: the majesty and perfection of Scripture, and the truth of its gospel message. This also means that there could be no internal witness of the Spirit without the prior redemptive work of Jesus Christ. The *testimonium* therefore presupposes both an objective revelation and a historical redemption.

Jesus Christ is the Word of God, but this Word can be received only through the ministry of the Spirit. With regard to the structure of revelation, then, Ramm concurs with Barth's trinitarian understanding: God gives his Word and sends his Spirit to witness to and minister his Word. Furthermore, the sending of the Word and of the Spirit to witness to him represents a redemptive act, for the witness of the Spirit produces knowledge of God, which is more than a cognitive increase. To know and to be able to affirm that "Jesus is Lord" is an effect not merely of intellectual illumination, but also of spiritual regeneration: "The true knowledge of God is gained with a teacher and a grammar, the Holy Spirit and the Sacred Writings."[19] The Spirit's primary witness is to the gospel of Jesus Christ.[20] Ramm's christocentric treatment of the *testimonium* leads him to resist once more abbreviated Protestantism. Reliance on the Bible alone, he declares, might lead to biblicism or to theological rationalism and so displace, albeit unintentionally, the Holy Spirit. Ramm argues that the Reformers anchored the witness of the Spirit to Christology and to soteriology. Ramm asserts, with Kuyper, that Pentecost is the crowning salvific event, for it reveals subjectively in individuals the grace of God revealed objectively in history.

Why should contemporary evangelical theology be concerned about the doctrine of the *testimonium?* Ramm maintains that a recovery of the *testimonium* is necessary if evangelicals wish to avoid the excesses of both Protestant liberalism and fundamentalism. Though liberal theologians rightly linked religious experience to the Spirit of God, they erred in their analysis of the structure of the *testimonium*. Ramm concurs with Barth's assessment: religious lib-

---

17. Bernard Ramm, *The Witness of the Spirit: An Essay on the Contemporary Relevance of the Internal Witness of the Holy Spirit* (Grand Rapids: Eerdmans, 1959), 30 n. 1.
18. Ibid., 93.

19. Ibid., 64.
20. Ramm acknowledges that by logical extension the Spirit witnesses to the entire biblical canon, inasmuch as the rest of the New Testament is related to the Gospels and the Old Testament is related to the New Testament (*Witness*, 69).

eralism hears only humans talking to themselves. A closer analysis of the structure of the *testimonium* shows, as we have seen, that the witness of the Spirit presupposes objective revelation. If there is no Word of God, there can be no *testimonium*.

Does fundamentalism do any better? Once again the problem with fundamentalism is its abbreviated or narrowed understanding of the Christian faith. In its debate with modernism "fundamentalism was so concerned to defend the inspiration of the Scriptures against all liberals outside the camp . . . that it lost track of the more comprehensive doctrine of revelation."[21] The same concern to uphold the divinity of Scripture led fundamentalists to overlook the Bible's instrumental character. But the divinity of Scripture consists in more than its being without error—after all, many noninspired texts can attain that status. No, what makes Scripture divine is its wholly reliable witness to Christ—a witness which has both revelatory and redemptive significance. Calvin and Reformed orthodoxy (when not affected by scholasticism) insisted upon the instrumental character of Scripture, that is, its function of making one wise unto salvation. Calvin said that the Word without the Spirit is "only a clang which disturbs the air and strikes our ear, but does not press into our hearts."[22] It is the message, not the magic, of the Bible which makes it a fit instrument of divine revelation. Fundamentalism, for its part, "ended up with a sacramental view of Sacred Scripture, a kind of *ex opere operato* of the printed word."[23] This was the theological support for its doctrine of inerrancy that claimed scientific accuracy for the Scriptures.

To distinguish itself from fundamentalism as well as from liberalism and neo-orthodoxy, evangelical theology must focus on the doctrine of revelation. This subject is also central to the debate about the nature

and scope of biblical authority: has God spoken, and if so, where and in what way? In addition, the doctrine of revelation is vital to the Christian scheme of theology, because God and his gracious saving activity can be known only if he himself communicates this knowledge. Ramm makes these points in the culmination of his trilogy on revelation, *Special Revelation and the Word of God*. "*Revelation is the autobiography of God*. . . . It is that knowledge *about* God which is *from* God."[24] In order to speak to specific persons in concrete situations, special revelation comes "clothed" in the "costume" (e.g., the language) and "custom" (e.g., the culture) of the day. A revelation not so clothed in the language and culture of the day would be unintelligible and would communicate nothing. Thus the "cosmic-anthropic" principle that we saw in Ramm's apologetic writings reappears in his doctrine of revelation. Here the principle signifies that God condescends to human beings and accommodates his message by taking on worldly or human forms. For example, God speaks Hebrew and Greek, uses historical events, and in the incarnation takes a human body which can hunger and thirst. However, Ramm insists that we really do know God through this mediated revelation.

One point in particular should be noted about the modality of speech. Language brings the culture of the speaker along with it; what writers say reflects the society and the time in which they live. Moreover, the biblical writers used the literary forms that were common in their day. We must not assume that biblical discourse conforms to our twentieth-century standards of historiography: "Much harm has been done to Scripture by those within and without the Church by assuming that all statements in the Bible are on the same logical level, on which level they are either true or false. How untrue this is to oratory and literature!"[25] It is important not only for herme-

---

21. Ramm, *Witness*, 124.
22. John Calvin, *Institutes of the Christian Religion*, 4.14.8.
23. Ramm, *Witness*, 125.

24. Ramm, *Special Revelation*, 17.
25. Ibid., 68.

neutics, but also for apologetics and theology, to recognize that divine revelation is mediated through a variety of literary forms—forms which make sense and truth claims according to the rules of diverse literary genres. Evangelicals should not read the Bible as a collection of heavenly sayings from Chairman God.

Though words are essential for recognizing certain historical events as divine revelation, Ramm is careful to assign logical priority to revelation as historical event. There is a word from God only because there is something to be said, and what God imparts in special revelation is not mere information, but a word of life, a saving message, a gospel. Word and Event must be held together as closely as Word and Spirit: "A revelatory word separated from the redeeming event is an abstraction; a saving event separated from the interpreting word is opaque."[26] Jesus Christ—the Word made flesh—is the substance of revelation. To forget this truth is to slip into a form of abbreviated Protestantism, which falls short of the gospel: "The temptation of biblicism is that it can speak of the inspiration of the Scriptures *apart from* the Lord they enshrine."[27] The evangelical, according to Ramm, should recognize that the intention of special revelation is to restore fallen persons to a saving knowledge of God. With Kuyper, Ramm says that the Bible is the God-given instrument used by the Holy Spirit to lead sinners to Christ. This consistent focus on the gospel of Jesus Christ distinguishes the evangelical from the fundamentalist's preoccupation with biblical inspiration as an end in itself.[28]

26. Ibid., 82.
27. Ibid., 117.
28. Kern Robert Trembath, *Evangelical Theories of Biblical Inspiration: A Review and Proposal* (New York: Oxford University Press, 1987), 57–64, argues that Ramm's functional or instrumental understanding of inspiration leads him to identify inspiration with the *testimonium*. Ramm would then be saying that inspiration is in the readers rather than in the writers of Scripture.

Ramm proceeds to make two observations about the structure of special revelation. First, the structure of revelation entails both an activity and a product. The activity—speaking—is preserved in writing. Scripture is thus a product of divine revelation. Second, knowledge of God is revelation's raison d'être. Revelation communicates a knowledge of God which originates with God himself (archetypal knowledge). What is given through the modality of special revelation, on the other hand, is ectypal knowledge of God, which Ramm defines as that part of God's own archetypal knowledge that he wants us to know. Knowledge of God must come from revelation; no matter how exalted or exciting the human experience, it never carries us beyond the human. Without special revelation "the theologian will be like an alchemist, for he will attempt to convert the lead of religious experience into the gold of the knowledge of God."[29] On the other hand, given special revelation, the theologian's task is to sort out systematically the knowledge of God it conveys. Ramm's advice on the use of philosophy for this endeavor, hidden in a footnote, is worth repeating: "The theologian must learn to take *all philosophies* seriously for he does not know which one God may use in the furtherance of the study of theology; and he must learn to take *none* seriously or else he has surrendered the autonomy of special revelation."[30]

Ramm suggests that biblical translations are legitimate products of revelation. Revelation is not bound to Hebrew or Greek, for language is a modality of revelation, not the product. It is the church's responsibility to make God's revelation known among all the nations; the church is not to hold the Scripture in custody as a bank holds a deposit in its vaults. Rather, the church is to make the Bible available in other languages. Here hard questions await: how much of the message belongs to its original culture? what is the significance of the sacrificial im-

29. Ramm, *Special Revelation*, 142.
30. Ibid., n. 5.

agery used to describe the cross? what is Ezekiel really talking about? The church's stewardship of the Bible means that it must interpret the Scriptures. Ramm believed that this issue merited an entire book—*Protestant Biblical Interpretation.*

Hermeneutics

Originally issued in 1950, *Protestant Biblical Interpretation* was revised three times in the next twenty years, in part because Ramm believed that how to interpret the Bible is as important an issue in the twentieth century as it was during the Reformation. To say we rely on the inner witness of the Spirit does not eliminate the need for sound hermeneutics. For how can we know that it is really the Holy Spirit speaking, except from evidence that shows a given interpretation to be the legitimate meaning of the words? Ramm's task, then, was to exhibit the structure of Protestant interpretation, which he identifies as the literal system of hermeneutics, whose architects were the Reformers. Indeed, Ramm observes that "there was a *hermeneutical Reformation* which preceded the ecclesiastical Reformation."[31]

Just as *The Christian View of Science and Scripture* argues that evangelicals need not adopt an antiscience attitude, so here Ramm argues that evangelicals need not be anticriticism. If evolutionary theory is one of the gains in modern science, so biblical criticism is one of the gains of modern historiography. Ramm acknowledges the challenge to evangelicals: can one believe in an inspired Scripture *and* use historical-critical methods to uncover its meaning, as one would with other texts that display the signs of their times? Ramm is convinced that one can, for the goal of biblical interpretation is not to show that the Bible speaks truly about astronomy, geology, and biology, but rather to edify. Biblical interpretation should make us wise unto salvation, not science. The cosmic-anthropic

principle of revelation has hermeneutical significance too. The *form* of revelation is adapted or accommodated to the language and culture of the day, but not so revelation's content: "We are tempted to say that revelation is present in Scripture *in, with,* and *under* the cultural so that the purely cultural is never made revelational, yet the revelation cannot be isolated from its cultural form."[32]

Two theological assumptions underlie the way Protestants interpret Scripture. First, Protestants affirm the perspicuity or clarity of Scripture. External or grammatical clarity means that an interpreter who follows the laws of language and literature can discover the meaning of the text. Internal clarity, on the other hand, signifies that the Spirit works in the mind and heart, enabling the interpreter to see the meaning of Scripture as God's own truth. Second, Protestants affirm the unity of Scripture. Their catchwords "analogy of faith" and "Scripture interprets Scripture" mean that the more difficult portions should be seen in the light of the clearer parts; for underneath the diverse linguistic, literary, and cultural forms of expression, there is a fundamental unity of content. Just what this unity consists in is hard to state. Is it the formal conceptual unity of a coherent system of truth, as the Westminster Confession of Faith suggests, or is it a christological unity which reduces every doctrine to the doctrine of Christ, as Ramm believes Barth maintained? Ramm's work represents an attempt to combine the best of both approaches.

Proceeding on theological assumptions alone does not guarantee hermeneutical success. The interpreter of Scripture must also be a philologist—a "lover of words." The meaning of a text is to be determined by studying its words and grammar as well as its historical, cultural, and literary contexts. "The true philological spirit, or critical spirit, or scholarly spirit, in Biblical interpretation has as its goal to discover the

---

31. Bernard Ramm, *Protestant Biblical Interpretation,* 3d rev. ed. (Grand Rapids: Baker, 1970), 52.

32. Ibid., 160.

original meaning and intention of the text."[33] This was the goal of the Reformers, especially of Calvin, who had been trained as a humanist to work with the original languages.

Reformation exegesis was oriented to the literal sense, that is, the sense communicated by words in their ordinary usage. Ramm is quick to point out that the literal method is not "letterism," an approach which is insensitive to nuances, wordplays, metaphors, and the like, and which might be more accurately described as "*un*lettered." Only an interpretation which seeks to preserve the grammatical, historical, and literary sense of the text (viz., the literal interpretation) can effectively guard against exegetical abuse of Scripture. Philology—the love and respect of words in context—acts as a control on Protestant biblical interpretation. Ramm's related remarks on genre anticipated the recent literary interest in the Scriptures. All of Scripture is expressed in some kind of literary genre. This insight constitutes a major hermeneutical manifesto: before asking whether a text is true or false, we must determine what kind of text it is. Some evangelicals, in their haste to defend the entire truth of the Bible, have ignored this fundamental interpretive principle. Indeed, many of the debates between evangelicals in the 1970s and 1980s turned on this very maxim. Ramm asserts unequivocally that there is no inherent harm in a literary genre. A genre is simply a means of communication. The danger comes only when one fails to recognize what kind of communication is involved. Ramm's philological principle—respect the ordinary use of words in their literary context or genre— was at work already in his *Christian View of Science and Scripture*. That book was the result of a conclusion about the genre of Genesis—it is not science, but phenomenal, nontheoretical language about the cosmos and its origin. Indeed, Ramm's major con-

tribution in apologetics and hermeneutics alike may be located just here, in his distinction between the literal method of evangelicals and the literalism of fundamentalists: "It must be made clear that the mainline Reformation scholarship . . . has no part with that kind of Biblical interpretation that runs roughshod over literary genre and interprets Scripture with a grinding literalism."[34]

Postfundamentalist Evangelicalism: The Union of Sacred and Secular Science

Evangelical theology gains its identity not only from its differences with fundamentalism, but also from its historic heritage and its place in the contemporary theological debate. Ramm plots the evangelical position with respect to both past and present in his *Handbook of Contemporary Theology* (1966) and *Evangelical Heritage: A Study in Historical Theology* (1973), where he defines evangelical Christianity as "that version of Christianity which places the priority of the Word and Act of God over the faith, response, or experiences of men."[35] Evangelicals belong to both the rational West and the Reformation. The dialogue between evangelicals and neo-orthodoxy is particularly important for Ramm because both groups claim to be the legitimate heirs of the Reformers.

For much of the 1960s and 1970s, Ramm treated neo-orthodoxy as a competitive system distinguished by its redefinition of the structure of divine revelation. Revelation is a dynamic concept for neo-orthodoxy. Revelation is not in words but rather in the event wherein God encounters human beings. By the "Word of God" the neo-orthodox mean "God Himself in the act of

33. Ibid., 115.

34. Ibid., 146. With regard to fundamentalist eschatology Ramm adds that "it is the lack of any real appreciation of literary genre that forces Fundamentalists to make such absurd assertions about future events."

35. Bernard Ramm, *The Evangelical Heritage: A Study in Historical Theology* (Waco: Word, 1973), 13.

self-revelation."[36] This act of self-revelation occurs when God addresses and encounters us through the mediation of the Bible. Barth's view of the Bible makes it a normative witness to Christ, but not an infallible text on such nonchristological topics as science and history. "All historical and orthodox forms of *inspiration* are denied. . . . God's speech is not words (orthodox view) but is *His personal presence.*"[37] Ramm differs from the neo-orthodox theologians at this point. With Calvin he attributes a certain majesty to Scripture. Scripture is the inspired document which preserves special revelation and thus participates in the structure of revelation itself.[38] Ramm maintains that only an inspired, true Word is an adequate object of the Spirit's witness. The neo-orthodox version of the *testimonium* is faulty, for their doctrine of inspiration does not render Scripture suitable for use as an instrument of the Spirit. Ramm further argues that revelation can be said to be true only if there is some propositional content: "Is it not strange alchemy which can transmute truths of revelation out of a truthless revelation?"[39] For Ramm, revelation is both a meeting and a knowing of God. "How a nonpropositional revelation gives rise to a *valid* propositional witness is the unsolved problem of neo-orthodoxy. It is our prediction that when neo-orthodoxy passes from the evangelistic stage to the critical stage a 'propositional wing' will develop."[40]

Despite Ramm's stated reservations, one reviewer of *The Evangelical Heritage* found Ramm moving to a position of conservative neo-orthodoxy. For Ramm there observed

that while some evangelicals branded Karl Barth a new modernist, and others hailed him as an evangelical neo-orthodox, he would adopt a third approach—critical dialogue with Barth in order to sift out the good from the bad. Ramm had discovered several valuable aspects to neo-orthodox theology, including its attack on liberalism, its summons to Scripture as the authority for theology, and its appreciation of the tradition of the Reformers. Ten years later, Ramm published an even more positive assessment of neo-orthodoxy or, more specifically, of the theology of Karl Barth. *After Fundamentalism: The Future of Evangelical Theology* (1983) was called a "major publishing event." Colin Gunton wrote in the *Expository Times* that "the book may well succeed in breaking new ground in theology, bringing evangelicals more into the centre of contemporary debate, for the greater health of all sides."[41] This was precisely Ramm's aim: postfundamentalist evangelical theology willing to learn from modernity without succumbing to its spell. For evangelical theology was somewhat warped from the outset, the misshapen offspring of a polemical debate between fundamentalists and liberals. It is in need of a new paradigm, and a critical dialogue with Karl Barth is the tonic Ramm prescribes in his *After Fundamentalism.*

Can evangelicalism recover the Reformation heritage in such a way as to survive the legitimate criticisms of the Enlightenment and flourish in the modern world? While fundamentalists seek to shield themselves from the Enlightenment, the evangelical believes that it cannot be undone and, indeed, must in some areas be appropriated. "The evangelical knows that he can only be a contemporary man. He cannot undo the genuine progress in science, technology, and learning in general. Any retreat to a safe past in theological literature is a failure of nerve to live in the present."[42] There must

36. Ramm, *Pattern*, 93.

37. Ramm, *Protestant Biblical Interpretation*, 71.

38. Bernard Ramm, *A Handbook of Contemporary Theology* (Grand Rapids: Eerdmans, 1966), 137–38. Though Barth calls Scripture a witness to revelation rather than revelation itself, Ramm argues that this makes Scripture part of the structure of revelation. Ramm would prefer Barth to say that revelation is polydimensional, and that one of its dimensions is Scripture.

39. Ramm, *Special Revelation*, 151.

40. Ramm, *Protestant Biblical Interpretation*, 165.

41. Colin Gunton, review of *After Fundamentalism*, by Bernard Ramm, *Expository Times* 94 (1983): 250.

42. Ramm, *Evangelical Heritage*, 140.

be a way to be both a modern person and a biblical Christian. The great theological challenge in the wake of the Enlightenment is to preserve the intellectual integrity of evangelical faith. Ramm was concerned that neither he nor other evangelicals had a systematic method of interacting with modern knowledge. Both liberalism and fundamentalism represent extreme reactions to the Enlightenment: liberals capitulate to the Enlightenment and thus betray biblical faith; fundamentalists are guilty of obscurantism insofar as they turn their back on modern learning. Barth, on the other hand, is both child and critic of the Enlightenment and is thus able to come to terms with modern learning and historic Reformed theology. Ramm devotes several chapters of *After Fundamentalism* to Barth's approach to matters as diverse as preaching, apologetics, ethics, revelation, and Scripture, and concludes in every case that Barth's theological method is the most adequate for evangelicals. One of the main contributions of the book is Ramm's own careful reading of Karl Barth, a reading that includes some significant reservations. Ramm expresses the hope that his evenhanded presentation of Barth's theology will counteract earlier evangelical appraisals, which were usually too negative and too neat.

Ramm's aim was to get Barth into proper focus. He did so by concentrating on the key to unlocking Barth's system, the doctrine of revelation. The Word of God—God revealing himself—is never under human control, but is always a gracious gift. Reason can receive but never achieve knowledge of God, which is available only in Jesus Christ. The crucial point for our purposes here is that Barth draws a distinction between the Word of God (divine revelation) and Scripture. Many evangelicals do not have a theological principle for dealing with the human elements of Scripture, but make desultory attempts to resolve one textual problem after the other. Barth, however, acknowledges the human elements of Scripture (and thus the appropriateness of

biblical criticism) while simultaneously maintaining the Bible's theological integrity as a witness to revelation: "The Word of God exists 'in, with, and under' the culturally conditioned text."[43] The language and culture of the Bible are fully human (and so fair game for critical study), but the content—the gospel of Jesus Christ—has come to humanity from God. The infallible Word is "in" the fallible words. To use one of Barth's favorite images, the Word of God comes to us through errant human words just as the risen Christ passed through locked doors. The miracle of verbal inspiration is that Jesus Christ comes to men and women through the texts of the Christian Scriptures. Ramm approves Barth's christological principle: it is the content of Christianity, not a formal theory of revelation or inspiration, which makes Christianity believable. On the formal level, there is nothing to distinguish the Christian view of biblical inspiration from, say, the Islamic view of the Koran. Thus Ramm asserts, contradicting some earlier remarks, "The Christian faith cannot be established solely on a high view for revelation and inspiration. The best apologetics for Holy Scripture for modern people is the Christological content."[44] He goes on to suggest that the christological principle allows one to distinguish the transcultural from the merely cultural in Scripture.

In 1985 Ramm published two works of constructive theology, *An Evangelical Christology* and *Offense to Reason: The Theology of Sin*.[45] Donald Bloesch immediately judged the latter to be Ramm's magnum opus. It is indeed a fitting summation of Ramm's career, combining as it does aspects of apologetics, hermeneutics, historical theology, and theology's dialogue with the sciences. Written in the wake of *After Fundamentalism*, *Offense to Reason* may be

43. Ramm, *After Fundamentalism*, 47.
44. Ibid., 132.
45. Bernard Ramm, *An Evangelical Christology* (Nashville: Nelson, 1985); idem, *Offense to Reason: The Theology of Sin* (San Francisco: Harper and Row, 1985).

viewed as a possible model for a new chapter in evangelical theology. We may well wonder to what extent it conforms to the guidelines for the future of evangelical theology which he gave in *The Evangelical Heritage*. There Ramm encouraged evangelical theologians to pursue both "sacred" and "secular" science, and in the end to show them to constitute an organic unity. *Offense to Reason* is Ramm's attempt to correlate contemporary culture and science with the historic Christian faith. Surely the doctrine of original sin, an "offense" to modern thinkers, constitutes the supreme test case for Ramm's goal of making the historic Reformed faith intellectually respectable in a post-Enlightenment context. Ramm's approach takes its inspiration from Pascal: the doctrine of original sin may be beyond our ability to explain, but without it we remain incomprehensible to ourselves. Ramm considers a host of thinkers, Christians and non-Christians alike, as well as a host of disciplines, and concludes that the doctrine of original sin more adequately accounts for the history of humanity than does any alternative hypothesis. None of the secular alternatives—whether that of Immanuel Kant, Sigmund Freud, Karl Marx, or B. F. Skinner—better accounts for the universality of human evil. Having entered into a critical dialogue with the secular sciences (especially modern psychology), Ramm comes to the conclusion that the Christian doctrine of sin gives the most comprehensive and satisfying explanation of personal and social ills.

What of sacred science and Ramm's attempt to formulate a biblical view of sin? Here he follows G. C. Berkouwer's biblical *a priori* that God is neither the cause nor author of sin as well as Barth's conviction that sin can be understood only from the perspective of the cross—from the perspective of the gospel rather than the law. Ramm is perhaps never more dialectical than in his attempt to state the meaning of Romans 5:12–21, a text which he deems the most difficult in the entire New Testament. Ramm relies extensively on Barth at this point, though he mentions his "predicament" of not knowing whether Barth is saying something old in a new way or whether he is introducing something entirely new. He follows Barth in classifying Genesis 2–3 as a literary saga. The story of Adam and Eve is a divinely inspired literary reconstruction of prehistorical events. As such, the theology of the account is narrative rather than propositional in nature: "Theology by narration means that the generic or type is more important than the individual or person."[46] Adam is, apparently, both a generic figure who stands for the entire human race and an individual person at the origin of Israel's history. Adam is the code name of the person who connects universal history with Hebrew history. Neither Genesis 3 nor Romans 5 intends to give an explanation of *how* and *when* the human race fell. The theological point, the revelatory truth, is *that* humanity is fallen. Perhaps there were humanlike creatures before Adam, as modern anthropology holds. Genesis does not, in Ramm's opinion, intend to address the question of the antiquity of the human race. But regardless of how and when the human race came to be, Genesis declares it fallen. Ramm's dialectical strategy is strained to the limit when he suggests that the actions of generic Adam, the figure in the Genesis narrative, "represent" datable historical events, as a courtroom reenactment of a crime represents the actual crime itself. Ramm does not explain the exact nature of this representative relationship. Nevertheless, he does argue convincingly that Christian doctrine remains humanity's best hope for understanding the human condition.

Evaluation

Clark Pinnock calls Ramm a "quintessential postfundamentalist theologian";[47] an-

46. Ramm, *Offense to Reason*, 70.
47. Clark H. Pinnock, "Bernard Ramm: Postfundamentalist Coming to Terms with Modernity," *Perspectives in Religious Studies* 17 (Winter 1990): 15.

other reviewer describes him as a "conservative neo-orthodox theologian." The life and career of Bernard Ramm paralleled to some extent the life and varieties of evangelicalism. Ramm himself defined "evangelicalism" as "the historic Christian faith as reflected in the great creeds of the ancient Church, and in the spirit and writings of the Reformers."[48] He helped shape evangelical theology in the 1950s with his textbooks on apologetics and hermeneutics. His last works are less textbooks which state final positions than they are exploratory monographs which raise questions and point in new directions. Throughout his career he struggled to be a theologian sensitive to the cultural and intellectual issues of his day and faithful to the biblical and orthodox faith, proving time and again in apologetics, hermeneutics, and theology to be a thinker of the avant-garde rather than the rear guard.[49]

Ramm offers concrete guidelines for the future of evangelical theology. Evangelicals must be students of Scripture and students of contemporary culture and ideas. Evangelicals must also know the inner structure of evangelical theology, which bases its human reflections upon divine revelation. To repeat a quotation we cited earlier: the theologian whose foundation is other than divine revelation "will be like an alchemist, for he will attempt to convert the lead of religious experience into the gold of the knowledge of God."[50] Ramm here borrows Abraham Kuyper's figure of special revelation as a gold mine, with knowledge of God as the gold, and comments: "The historical, literary, and especially poetic character of much of Scripture demands Kuyper's

analogy of the gold mine. . . . Only by a careful mining and smelting do we arrive at the knowledge of God in this book."[51] Like Kuyper, Ramm puts revelation at the center of his theology, Scripture at the center of his doctrine of revelation, Christ in the center of Scripture, and the Spirit alongside the Word. Judged by his own criteria, Ramm excelled both in the school of sacred science and in the school of secular science. And though not everything he touched turned to gold, his was the work of the diligent miner rather than the impetuous alchemist. There is much that is worthwhile for evangelical theology in Ramm's textbooks and explorations alike. Neither Midas nor alchemist, Ramm spent a lifetime working in the mines, digging into and uncovering the inner structure of Scripture and Reformed tradition. Evangelicals are only now beginning to mine Ramm's theology for the wealth it contains, as is attested by the 1990 session of the American Academy of Religion and the festschrift.

Ramm thought that Barth had grasped the inner structure of evangelical theology in a way that made it a relevant and viable option in the modern world. Barth's way of correlating biblical criticism and divine revelation, inspiration, and authority represents the best modern attempt to unify science and Scripture. And yet, more mining remains to be done. In one of his last publications, Ramm expressed his hope that "in the future someone will put Barth's thesis together in a more convincing way."[52] Ramm was not that person; evangelicalism must wait for another. Ramm's function and significance resemble the biblical figure who is the namesake of his denomination. Like John the Baptist, Bernard Ramm pointed to Christ and prepared a way for evangelical theology to go forward.

---

48. Ramm, *Science and Scripture*, 9.

49. In the early 1970s, for example, he wrote: "It is my conviction that the next impetus to rethink our evangelical doctrines of inspiration and revelation is going to come from the modern communications theory" (*Evangelical Heritage*, 163).

50. Ramm, *Special Revelation*, 142.

51. Ibid., 155–56.

52. Ramm, "Helps from Karl Barth," 125.

J. Rodman Williams

Stanley M. Burgess

John Rodman Williams was born on August 21, 1918, in Clyde, North Carolina, the son of John Rodman and Odessa Lee (Medford) Williams. In 1939 he received an A.B. from Davidson College, where he had been Phi Beta Kappa. He then earned his B.D. (1943) and Th.M. (1944) at Union Theological Seminary in Virginia, and was ordained in the Presbyterian Church in the United States (1943). He served as a chaplain in the Marine Corps from 1944 to 1946. In 1954 he earned a Ph.D. in philosophy of religion and ethics at Columbia University and Union Theological Seminary (N.Y.).

Williams married Johanna Servaas in 1949, and they have three children. He was appointed associate professor of philosophy at Beloit College, where he taught until 1952. Subsequently he served as pastor of the First Presbyterian Church of Rockford, Illinois (1952–59), and as professor of systematic theology at Austin Presbyterian Seminary (1959–72).

From 1965 onwards, Williams has been active in the charismatic movement. He was an early president of the International Presbyterian Charismatic Communion, a participant for several years in the Vatican-Pentecostal dialogue, and the organizer of several conferences for leaders of the charismatic movement in Europe. Representing Pentecostalism, he served as a member of the Faith and Order Commission of the World Council of Churches. In 1972 he helped to set up and became president of Melodyland School of Theology in Anaheim, California—an experimental undergraduate and graduate school committed to charismatic and ecumenical principles as well as the evangelical tradition. In 1985 Williams served as president of the Society for Pentecostal Studies. Currently he is professor of theology at the School of Biblical Studies at Regent University (formerly CBN University) in Virginia Beach, Virginia.[1]

1. For further biographical data see *Dictionary of American Scholars*, 8th ed., or *Who's Who in American Religion*, 3d ed., s.v. "Williams, John Rodman."

Williams's early publications are in marked contrast to those written after 1965. For example, a series of devotionals written for *Thy Will, My Will* in 1956 shows interest in the person and work of the Holy Spirit, but not from a charismatic perspective.[2] There is no emphasis on reception of the Spirit or on spiritual gifting. The lesson to be learned from Acts 2:4 is simply the importance of speaking the truth about Christ and of being led by the Holy Spirit into all truth. But Williams does point out the need for greater power in Christian living, which he links to the intervention of the divine Spirit: "God wants to break through into the lives of people. . . . Pray earnestly that God's Holy Spirit may 'come upon you' so that He may make your witness effective." Repentance and God's forgiveness are seen as preconditions for such power.

Williams's other early writings reveal a variety of interests, including the ecumenical movement, worship styles, and the relationship of existentialism to the Christian church.[3] In his book *Contemporary Existentialism and Christian Faith*, Williams examines the thought of, among others, Jean-Paul Sartre, Martin Heidegger, Karl Jaspers, Paul Tillich, and Rudolf Bultmann. He acknowledges that existentialism shares many features with the Christian faith: (1) emphasis on truth as an inward experience; (2) the view that humankind is unique; (3) recognition that belief in God is not easy for many people today; and (4) a concern to probe the human condition of deep anxiety

and a desire to meet it constructively. On the negative side, he finds much in existentialism to criticize: (1) the belief that truth and existence center in humankind; (2) the teaching that the degree of belief or disbelief in God makes little difference; (3) the acceptance of anxiety as a condition written into the very structure of the human being; and (4) the absence of any valid goal in life other than self-fulfilment. Williams found it necessary in this volume to come to grips with those basic questions about Christian faith which had been raised in his studies under Paul Tillich at Union Theological Seminary (N.Y.). In so doing, he prepared himself for the next, and most important step, in his theological formation.

The great watershed in Williams's career was his entry into the charismatic movement in November 1965. The crisis came with a Pentecostal-like experience during which he spoke in an unknown language. In a letter written to Brick Bradford in 1970, Williams states that during Thanksgiving week of 1965 he sensed "in an overwhelming way the tremendous reality of the Holy Spirit."[4] A growing feeling of emptiness and impotence, which had led to some months of seeking and praying, came to an end when God graciously answered his pleas and filled him with the Holy Spirit. "It was 'joy unspeakable,' reality amazing, upsurge of 'heavenly language'—glory! I *received* my baptism in the Holy Spirit."

In another example of the great change in his life Williams reports that at one time he could see no value in the gift of tongues.[5] Indeed, the whole matter was a bit repugnant to his sensibilities. However, there came a time when all this suddenly changed. One day, while he was repeating the opening words of Psalm 103, "Bless the

2. J. Rodman Williams, "The Holy Spirit," *Thy Will, My Will* (Board of Christian Education, Presbyterian Church in the United States), April–June 1956, pp. 61–74.

3. J. Rodman Williams, "Am I a Protestant? Am I Also a Catholic?" *Adult Uniform Lesson* (Board of Christian Education, Presbyterian Church in the United States) 60.2 (April–June 1962): 1–6; idem, "Can Protestants and Roman Catholics Get Together?" *Presbyterian Survey* 52 (Oct. 1962): 10–13; idem, "A Theological Critique of Some Contemporary Trends in Worship," *Austin Seminary Bulletin*, June 1960, pp. 48–57; idem, *Contemporary Existentialism and Christian Faith* (Englewood Cliffs, N.J.: Prentice-Hall, 1965).

4. J. Rodman Williams, "Have You Received the Baptism of the Holy Spirit?" open letter to Brick Bradford, editor of the "Newsletter of the Charismatic Communion of Presbyterian Ministers," January 1970.

5. J. Rodman Williams, "Why Speak in Tongues?" *New Covenant*, January 1978, pp. 14–16.

LORD, O my soul; and all that is within me, bless his holy name! Bless the LORD, O my soul, and forget not all his benefits" (RSV), he experienced a sudden desire to praise God with all that was within him, to break forth in heavenly blessing. He reports that immediately thereafter "came the gift of a new tongue, a spiritual language—an unexpected, even shocking event."

This experience changed Williams as a person and as a scholar. He came to identify with the emerging charismatic movement, and soon became part of its leadership. With but very few exceptions, his professional work thereafter has centered on the person and work of the Holy Spirit, with special attention to spiritual gifts. The capstone of his writings is a three-volume systematic theology for charismatics that is entitled *Renewal Theology.*[6] His understanding of God is less a matter of church dogma, or even of scriptural teaching, than it is "the summons to a life of Triune existence—life lived in the reality of God as Father, Son, and Holy Spirit."[7] For Williams, the most important happening in the church today is the rediscovery of the Pentecostal reality, that is, the coming of God's Holy Spirit in power to the believing individual and community.[8]

The Reception of the Holy Spirit

Like so many other charismatics with roots in a sacramental tradition, Williams had to come to grips with the issue of when an individual receives the Holy Spirit. In a 1969 paper, he examines the position of the church fathers and of John Calvin on the relationship between the initial act of faith and the reception of the Holy Spirit.[9] He notes that in general the early Fathers recognize a chronological separation between initial faith and the reception of the divine Spirit. They do not view baptism, but a subsequent act—the laying on of hands or chrismation—as the event in which the Spirit is conferred. In addition, many of the Fathers mention the multiplicity of spiritual gifts, which are generally seen as consequent to the reception of the Spirit. Nothing is received, however, without faith. Moreover, the Fathers acknowledge that not all who are baptized are ready to receive the Holy Spirit. There needs to be a "walk in the newness of life to receive the new wine." The church fathers also understand that the Holy Spirit is present and active in the believer prior to the reception of the Spirit.

Like the early church fathers, John Calvin believed that, however closely related, initial faith and the reception of the Holy Spirit are not to be identified as the same event. Unlike the Fathers, however, Calvin did not recognize a reception of the Spirit for such purposes as perfecting, illuminating, and fulfilling. This, to Calvin, seemed to represent a detraction from the work of the Spirit in initial faith. Like the early church, Calvin held the singular gifts of the Spirit to be highly significant, but in contradistinction to the Fathers, he claimed that God withdrew these gifts permanently after the first proclamation of the gospel. These spiritual gifts Calvin identified with the reception of the Holy Spirit. Since the gifts have been withdrawn, all practices that have to do with the reception of the Spirit are vain and empty.

In his 1970 letter to Brick Bradford, Williams asserts that the believer is baptized in the Spirit at the time of water baptism, but that this baptism in the Spirit is often appropriated or experienced later. He refers to this later experience as *receiving* the bap-

6. J. Rodman Williams, *Renewal Theology,* 3 vols. (Grand Rapids: Zondervan, 1988–). Volume 1 deals with God, the world, and redemption. Volume 2 treats salvation, the Holy Spirit, and Christian living. Volume 3 will be concerned with the church, the kingdom, and last things.

7. J. Rodman Williams, *The Pentecostal Reality* (Plainfield, N.J.: Logos International, 1972), 108.

8. Ibid., 4–6.

9. J. Rodman Williams, "The Holy Spirit in the Early Church and in Calvin's Theology" (paper written for the Permanent Theological Committee of the Presbyterian Church in the United States, 1969).

tism in the Spirit.[10] By 1971, however, his terminology had changed somewhat. In *The Era of the Spirit* he discusses the period between the *coming* of the indwelling Spirit in water baptism and the subsequent *filling* of the Spirit—a period in the Christian life that in no way is to be seen as substandard.[11] In addition, he now suggests that water baptism and the laying on of hands are sacramental actions that may or may not be accompanied by the gift of the Spirit.

At the 1972 meeting of the Society for Pentecostal Studies, Williams presented a paper entitled "Pentecostal Theology: A Neo-Pentecostal Viewpoint."[12] Here he suggests that Pentecostalism "is right in not binding conversion-regeneration and Spirit-baptism to particular sacramental actions." Spirit baptism is not an addition to one's becoming a Christian, but the climactic moment of entrance into Christian life. It is not to be identified with redemption, but with the gift of God's presence and power. The two, while belonging together in the totality of Christian initiation, often are separated in their actual occurrence. This may be understood from the perspective of Christian initiation as a process involving both forgiveness of sins (redemption) and the gift of the Holy Spirit. Thus it is not proper to speak of Christians and Spirit-baptized Christians, but only of persons in process of Christian initiation. In some cases at baptism there is little or no active and personal faith on the part of the recipient—as, for example, in the case of infant baptism. While the reality is at hand, the fulfilment (or the full expression of what baptism signifies and conveys) may not yet have occurred.

By 1980 the evolution of Williams's concept of Spirit baptism had brought him even closer to Pentecostal thinking. In *The Gift of the Holy Spirit Today* he states that water baptism is neither a precondition nor a channel for the gift of the Spirit, nor is the work of the Holy Spirit in baptism the gift of the Spirit.[13] And in his 1985 presidential address to the Society for Pentecostal Studies, Williams asserted that the gift of the Holy Spirit is a distinct and unique action of God, so it cannot be viewed as simply a release or an actualization of what is already there.[14] He now finds suspect any viewpoint which minimizes the necessity of a special event or experience through which the gift may flourish.

Williams teaches that the gift of the Spirit is a direct fulfilment of the promise of God, and comes from the exalted Jesus. This gift follows upon the completion of God's redeeming work in the believer through Christ. It is bestowed in abundance, with suddenness and forcefulness, and according to divine sovereignty upon those who believe in Jesus Christ and faithfully wait with expectancy for the gift. The divine Spirit takes possession of a person or community, enveloping them with his presence and power. This envelopment is best described as "being baptized"—being pervaded or filled. The event of the Spirit is basically a community happening. It often comes about when people are gathered for worship and fellowship.[15]

The central purpose for the gift of the Holy Spirit is the empowerment of believers to witness, to be channels for the radical transformation of human existence, to prophesy, and to perform mighty works (signs and wonders, including healings and the casting out of demons).[16] In addition, the Spirit seals those who receive Christ, thus certifying to the world and giving as-

10. Williams, "Have You Received," 1–2.

11. J. Rodman Williams, *The Era of the Spirit* (Plainfield, N.J.: Logos International, 1971).

12. J. Rodman Williams, "Pentecostal Theology: A Neo-Pentecostal Viewpoint," in Russell P. Spittler, ed., *Perspectives on the New Pentecostalism* (Grand Rapids: Baker, 1976), 76–85.

13. J. Rodman Williams, *The Gift of the Holy Spirit Today* (Plainfield, N.J.: Logos International, 1980).

14. J. Rodman Williams, "Pentecostal/Charismatic Theology" (presidential address delivered at the 15th annual meeting of the Society for Pentecostal Studies, Nov. 1985).

15. Williams, *Pentecostal Reality*, 16.

16. Williams, *Gift*, 1–3, 7–9, 11–20, 43–84, 105–7, 116–18; idem, *Renewal Theology*, 2:243–63.

surance to believers that they are saved and accepted by God. The Spirit also guides disciples into all truth.[17]

In the early church the primary response to receiving the Holy Spirit was praise. The effects or results of the gift of the Holy Spirit in today's church are an extraordinary sense of the reality of God, fulness of joy, an assurance of God's act of salvation, boldness in speech and action, deepening of fellowship, and a continuing praise of God.[18]

The Gifts of the Holy Spirit

The Holy Spirit, who is bestowed by Jesus Christ, confers other gifts in turn. Like most Pentecostals and charismatics, Williams focuses primarily on the list in 1 Corinthians 12:8–10; there is relatively little mention of similar lists in Romans 12; Ephesians 4; 1 Peter 4; and Isaiah 11:2 (the last-mentioned being the list emphasized by the church historically).[19] The gifts or charismata listed in 1 Corinthians are understood to represent a profound opening up of the range of spiritual manifestations.

All spiritual gifts derive from the exalted Jesus and come to those who affirm in the Spirit that "Jesus is Lord." Each and every person in the community is given a manifestation of the Spirit; the charismata are not intended to be the possessions of a spiritual elite. All of the spiritual gifts are needed for the proper and full functioning of the body. If only one gift is missing or not functioning, the body is sorely handi-

capped. But when each person performs his or her Spirit-given role, the body of Christ is both able to function normally and to be built up in faith and ministry.

While the gifts are varied, they are all manifestations of the Holy Spirit. Notwithstanding the identification of the gifts with the Spirit, all members of the Trinity are at work in each. And in all spiritual gifts there also is a human involvement: the Spirit expresses himself in and through human activity.

Of course, the bestowal of spiritual gifts leaves the door open for human abuse. Williams is careful to point out that spiritual gifts are intended for ministry throughout the body of believers, not for individual enhancement. Proper zeal for the gifts pays no heed to one's own needs, wishes, or pleasure. All the gifts must be exercised in love, or else they are noisy, abrasive, and virtually worthless. Any exercise of a gift of the Spirit that does not result in edification of the body is inappropriate and out of order. But, Williams warns, the church should not overreact to abuse of spiritual gifts by forgetting or neglecting them, for they are divine manifestations.[20]

Mental Gifts

On the basis of 1 Corinthians 12:7–10 Williams states that the Spirit's presence is expressed in nine spiritual gifts. He sees a close connection between the first two—the word of wisdom and the word of knowledge—and the last two, various kinds of tongues and the interpretation of tongues. The first two are word (*logos*) gifts; the last two deal with tongues. In between are five other gifts. Williams reacts negatively to any alteration in Paul's sequencing—a practice of numerous Pentecostal and charismatic writers who prefer three groups with three gifts in each; for example, (1) the word of wisdom, the word of knowledge, distinguishing of spirits; (2) prophecy, tongues, interpretation of tongues; and (3) faith, gifts of healing, miracles.

17. Williams, *Renewal Theology*, 2:237–42, 263–68.

18. Williams, *Gift*, 27–29, 123–50; idem, *Renewal Theology*, 2:307–19.

19. For a discussion of the history of spiritual gifts within the church, both Western and Eastern, see Stanley M. Burgess, *The Spirit and the Church: Antiquity* (Peabody, Mass.: Hendrickson, 1984), and *The Holy Spirit: Eastern Christian Traditions* (Peabody, Mass.: Hendrickson, 1989). Two summary chapters are included in Stanley M. Burgess, Gary B. McGee, and Patrick H. Alexander, eds., *Dictionary of Pentecostal and Charismatic Movements* (Grand Rapids: Zondervan, 1988), 417–44.

20. Williams, *Renewal Theology*, 2:323–46.

The word of wisdom and the word of knowledge are not expressions of ordinary wisdom and knowledge, but result from divine illumination. They are gifts that involve speaking; what is spoken is the actual gift. The word of wisdom is in some way an explication of the mystery of God that centers in Christ Jesus, whom Paul refers to as "our wisdom" (1 Cor. 1:30). What happens here is that the Holy Spirit searches the divine depths and increasingly makes them known. Such wisdom is primarily and most profoundly Jesus Christ, in whom are hidden all treasures of wisdom and knowledge. Every word of wisdom will be in complete agreement with the written testimony of Scripture. Indeed, a word of wisdom under the Spirit's illumination can bring a true apprehension of the scriptural meaning. But it will not add any new truth beyond Scripture. Williams suggests that this spiritual gift is particularly needed in the preaching ministry or proclamation of the church.[21]

The word of knowledge grows out of an awareness of the wide range of blessings that God has bestowed on his children in Jesus Christ. It is an utterance of truth in Spirit-taught words about God's blessings, inspired instruction that occurs within the gathered community. It is the teaching, rather than the teacher (the person who speaks to the community), that is the actual gift. The word of knowledge may involve mutual teaching and admonishment, but is much more. It is the oral communication of inspired knowledge that edifies the body of believers. Though the word of wisdom is a gift bestowed on preachers, and the word of knowledge on local teachers, neither preaching nor teaching as such is a manifestation of the Spirit.[22]

Extramental Gifts

The gift of faith refers to a special impartation of faith that is for the common good; it is to be differentiated from both saving faith and the faith that is a fruit of the

Spirit. The gift of faith is the first in Paul's list in 1 Corinthians 12 that is not essentially mental. Unlike the word of wisdom and the word of knowledge, the gift of faith, together with the following four gifts, is extramental ("outside the mind"). It often provides an immediate context for the exercise of the two gifts that follow: gifts of healing and the working of miracles. The gift of faith is variously apportioned to individuals within the body and can lead to extraordinary effects. In this connection, Williams warns against confusing the gift of faith with the so-called word-of-faith teaching, which insists that we can put God to work for us by making a positive confession, thereby overarching divine sovereignty with human control.[23] Word-of-faith teaching has little to do with the gift of faith, and is generally human- rather than God-centered.[24]

Gifts of healing also are bestowed by the Spirit on specific individuals within the community of believers. Contrary to the popular perception of a faith healer, however, the person who receives this spiritual blessing does not directly perform healings, but only transmits the gift. Because human life is not free from all sickness, an individual may be a genuine channel for gifts of healing, and yet a particular healing will not occur. Nevertheless, these gifts should be sought after. Williams is especially direct in his condemnation of those who hold that the gifts of healing were intended only for New Testament times and are no longer operational.[25]

The working of miracles (or powers) is another gift apportioned by the Spirit to selected individuals. Miracles comprise all demonstrations of supernatural power, including those mentioned by Jesus as he sent out the apostles: "Preach as you go, saying, 'The kingdom of heaven is at hand.' Heal the

21. Ibid., 2:349–54.
22. Ibid., 2:348–58.

23. For more information see Leonard Lovett, "Positive Confession Theology," in Burgess et al., *Dictionary*, 718–20.
24. Williams, *Renewal Theology*, 2:358–67.
25. Ibid., 2:367–75.

sick, raise the dead, cleanse lepers, cast out demons" (Matt. 10:7–8 RSV). Paul himself as an apostle had healed the sick, cast out demons, and raised the dead. This gifting is for those who believe in Christ, who expect miracles today, and who step out in faith to accomplish that which is beyond normal human expectation. There must be a need that only a miracle can remedy, and there also must be a genuine compassion on the part of the one ministering to that need.

Miracles, Williams stresses, are not magic; they are not to be associated with exhibitionism, and they cannot be programed. Signs and wonders, especially physical healings and the casting out of demons or evil spirits, are proof to people that something extraordinary is going on.[26] Because he anticipates the final coming of the kingdom, Williams expects increased miraculous activity in the immediate future. Such supernatural activity will herald the coming of the kingdom in power and glory.[27]

Among spiritual gifts, prophecy is especially to be valued, for it has great power to edify believers and to bring to conviction any unbelievers who might be present.[28] Paul encouraged the Corinthians to "earnestly desire the spiritual gifts, especially that you may prophesy" (1 Cor. 14:1 RSV). While this gift is an individual distribution by the Holy Spirit, it is available to all. Whenever the Spirit is outpoured, the result is that people without distinction of sex or class are able to prophesy. They are gifted by the Spirit on a particular occasion to speak forth prophetically. This does not mean that a person who occasionally prophesies holds the office of prophet. According to Williams, the term *prophet* in New Testament usage refers to those who in association with the apostles laid the foundation of the church (1 Cor. 12:28; Eph. 2:20; 3:5; 4:11; Rev. 18:20).

Prophecy is built upon revelation. A person prophesies because God has revealed something, a message he wants that particular individual to declare. Prophecy is not a prepared message, for the revelation immediately issues in speech. Prophetic words are spontaneous and divinely inspired.

Prophecy has been called a miracle in the form of speech. It is much more a forthtelling than a foretelling. It speaks to the present situation of the people within the congregation. Of course, a word of prophecy may very well have a future aspect, but it is not primarily predictive.

Prophecy may confirm, but never by itself directs. We may believe that God is leading in a certain direction, and then a prophecy occurs that confirms it. On the other hand, Williams warns, predictive or directional prophecy can undermine a person's relationship to God, and possibly lead to other disastrous results. Such prophecy is to be strongly guarded against.

According to Paul, the purpose of the gift of prophecy is to upbuild, to exhort, and to console (1 Cor. 14:3). This threefold purpose of prophecy speaks to a wide range of needs in the gathered assembly. Clearly, prophecy is intended primarily for believers. However, a side effect often is the drawing of unbelievers and outsiders to Christ through the heart searching and conviction that prophecy evokes.

Once prophetic utterance has been delivered, it is necessary for the gathered community to weigh what has been said. This consists in testing both the human vehicle and the utterance itself. Williams suggests five tests: (1) any prophecy that breathes a spirit foreign to Christ cannot be accepted; (2) true prophecy always will be harmonious with Scripture; (3) true prophecy edifies or builds up the community (judgmental or negative prophecy is suspect); (4) true prophecy finds consent and agreement in the minds and hearts of others within the community; and (5) true prophecy glorifies God, not humans. Prophecy that meets these tests should be allowed to proceed in

26. Williams, *Gift*, 57–72; idem, *Era of the Spirit*, 20.
27. Williams, *Renewal Theology*, 2:375–80.
28. Williams, *Gift*, 50–57.

an orderly manner, without disruption or interruption.[29]

The gift of distinguishing (or discerning) spirits is also conferred by the Holy Spirit on selected individuals for the common good. Distinguishing spirits is possible only through the Spirit of God, who illuminates a particular individual. The gift serves to discern the specific spirit at work in any expression or activity within the Christian community. For example, it enables one to perceive the spirit at work in an individual who is prophesying. Inner feelings and motivations are perceived. In the process there is a piercing through the outer façade to the inner spirit. Or the Holy Spirit may enable one to perceive a spiritual problem that lies at the root of a human ailment. But the illumination itself does not resolve the problem. There must be follow-up ministry to the newly perceived need. This may entail simply a word of encouragement, or it may take the form of correction.

A critically important function of the gift of discernment is the perception of demonic spirits. Williams contends that where the Holy Spirit is at work, often the counterforce of evil spirits also is present. This can be particularly true in the case of prophetic utterance. Pleasant and soothing words are not always from God. There also are occasions when what appears to be divine is actually a satanic counterfeit. Finally, if good or angelic spirits are sent to minister to believers, then it can be expected that they may likewise be recognized by a special gift of the Holy Spirit.[30]

Supramental Gifts

The final two spiritual gifts listed in 1 Corinthians 12—various kinds of tongues and the interpretation of tongues—belong together. These twin gifts are so intimate that the first is not to function without the second. They are unique in that they have no scriptural precedent before the coming of the Holy Spirit at Pentecost. Williams sug-

gests that this may be the reason that they are listed last by Paul. The gifts of tongues and interpretation also are unique in that they are supramental, operating "beyond the mind." This contrasts with the first two gifts, which are mental, and the next five, which are extramental.

The gift of tongues is not "the ability to speak in different kinds of tongues," as the 1978 edition of the New International Version renders it; nor is the gift that of "ecstatic utterance," as the New English Bible translates. "Ability" suggests some human capacity, whereas the gift is essentially the Spirit's function. "Ecstatic utterance" implies irrational and highly charged emotional speech, whereas the gift is suprarational speech and not simply emotional expression. The Holy Spirit provides the language, taking control of the human apparatus—mouth, tongue, and vocal cords. This is not to suggest that the divine Spirit forces such speech to occur, for there is no divine seizure. Rather, the person freely does the speaking, and the Spirit graciously provides the language. Furthermore, speaking in tongues is not irrational or nonsensical utterance, but has intelligible content. The very fact that interpretation is expected to follow is evidence of intelligibility.[31]

As with most spiritual gifts, the various kinds of tongues (or ministry tongues) are not distributed by the Holy Spirit to all (1 Cor. 12:11, 30). On this point Williams differs with most Pentecostals. He distinguishes the gift of tongues from the glossolalia manifested by all present in the upper room at the time of the coming of the Holy Spirit (Acts 2:4). He also excludes from the gift of tongues those "glossolalic" utterances that accompany the ongoing life of prayer and praise. In devotional context, all believers may speak in tongues.[32] But ministry tongues are exercised only by those who have received the gift of various kinds of tongues. Williams's point is that a person

---

29. Williams, *Renewal Theology*, 2:380–88.
30. Ibid., 2:388–94.

31. Ibid., 2:220–22.
32. Williams, *Gift*, 38–41; idem, *Renewal Theology*, 2:397–98.

may regularly speak or even sing in tongues, but only rarely, if ever, experience the gift of tongues.

Those who are gifted with various kinds of tongues must use them within the gathered community for the common good. As with other spiritual gifts, tongues are not to be exercised for personal gain or elite standing in the charismatic community.

That Paul refers to "various kinds of tongues" suggests that they are not always of the same character. From accounts of the phenomena at Jerusalem and Caesarea, Williams concludes that glossolalia may involve transcendent praise of God. What we have here, then, are not, as they have sometimes been designated, "missionary tongues," equipping each of the disciples to go forth with a particular language so he could witness to a specific nation or people. Paul also describes speaking in tongues as uttering mysteries (1 Cor. 14:2). Prayer in the Spirit may entail a deep communication with God that goes beyond ordinary speech into the utterance of divine mysteries; the Holy Spirit speaks through the human spirit the things of God. Speaking in tongues may also be the offering up of prayers of supplication to God. Here the Spirit enables the believer to reach a deeper and fuller level of prayer life. Finally, tongues may be an eschatological sign—an indication of the last days (Acts 2:17).[33]

Each variety of glossolalia is a supreme communication with God and a significant means of self-edification. But speaking in tongues also is intended as a sign to unbelievers (1 Cor. 14:22), preparing the way for faith (as at Pentecost). Williams suggests that tongues may have a kind of shock effect that leads to inquiry and even to an openness to the gospel. But when the "unspiritual man" does not accept such gifts of the Spirit of God—when they are foolishness to him (1 Cor. 2:14)—he stands under divine judgment.

Williams recognizes a difficulty in harmonizing what appears to be the utterance of foreign languages at Pentecost and the later instances of glossolalia, which are unknown tongues (transcendent praise) needing interpretation.[34] He reasons that at Pentecost the assembled faithful spoke in "other tongues," which the Holy Spirit immediately translated into the many languages of the attending multitude. There were two miracles: one of speech and the other of hearing. He concludes that the tongues spoken at Pentecost and thereafter were not foreign languages, but pneumatic or transcendent speech.[35]

Williams recognizes that the church tends towards two extremes on the exercise of tongues. He insists that both are to be avoided. First, the church at large today gives no place at all to tongues. Williams asserts, however, that the gift of tongues is one of the Spirit's manifestations for the common good and hence must have a regular place in the ongoing ministry of the church. Paul says as much: "When you assemble, each one has a psalm, has a teaching, has a revelation, has a tongue, has an interpretation" (1 Cor. 14:26 NASB). The second extreme is that of the first-century Corinthian congregation and some modern Pentecostal and charismatic groups who exaggerate the place of tongues. It is imperative, according to Williams, that tongues have a proper but not all-important place.

Paul explicitly insists that ministry tongues be exercised in an orderly fashion, with "only two or at most three" utterances in an assembly, and these in turn (1 Cor. 14:27). Williams concurs, adding, "Propriety and fittingness are to be the hallmark of things in the assembly. . . . This is truly an important message to the church of Corinth and to the church of any time and place."[36]

It is Williams's historical judgment that glossolalia did not cease with the apostles, but has continued, along with all the other

---

33. Williams, *Renewal Theology*, 2:225–36.

34. Williams, *Gift*, 29–31.
35. Williams, *Renewal Theology*, 2:215.
36. Ibid., 2:394–402; the quotation is from p. 402.

spiritual gifts, down to our own day. Here he cites Eddie Ensley's identification of a long-standing Roman Catholic tradition of intense spontaneous worship that transcended the ordinary. This "jubilation" undoubtedly included tongue-speaking.[37] Furthermore, Williams argues that, for the individual Christian, speaking in tongues is intended to be a continuing experience beyond the initial reception of the Holy Spirit.[38] In other words, glossolalia is intended historically for all of the Christian Era, and individually for as long as the Christian continues to live in the Spirit.

Williams directly addresses the issue of whether tongue-speaking is the initial evidence of reception of the Spirit (baptism in/with/of the Holy Spirit)—a foundational doctrine for most Pentecostals. He observes that in all the biblical accounts where glossolalia is specifically mentioned (in Jerusalem, Caesarea, and Ephesus) or clearly implied (in Samaria), it is proper to say that glossolalia was the primary evidence for the Spirit's reception.[39] But he adds that "tongues are not constitutive of the gift of the Spirit." Rather, they "are declarative, namely, that the gift has been received."[40]

The final spiritual gift listed by Paul in 1 Corinthians 12 is interpretation of tongues. Williams informs his readers that, like the other charismata, this is an individual gift or manifestation of the Holy Spirit, not to be exercised by all Christians at all times. Further, this gift is not interpretation in general (e.g., of Scripture), but is limited to interpretation of glossolalia.

Though in a known language, the interpretation of tongues is a supramental operation of the Holy Spirit. It is not based upon a rational comprehension of what the tongue-speaking has declared. The inter-

pretation comes from a realm beyond the human mind. Unlike translating a foreign language into the vernacular, no human ability is required. The interpretation may be a word-for-word translation, but usually is directed more to the meaning of the utterance. Thus an interpretation may be lengthier or shorter than the tongue-speaking. The significance of interpretation is that it makes known the content of the message in tongues. Only through interpretation can the congregation know whether the glossolalic utterance is an offering of praise to God (Acts 2:11), a supplication or intercession, or a mystery (1 Cor. 14:2) which may be a specific message from God to the corporate body or to a given individual.

Since tongues are to be spoken "each in turn" (1 Cor. 14:27), interpretation should follow in turn after each utterance. But while there may be two or three tongues, only one person will be gifted by the Holy Spirit to interpret on each occasion. The interpretation of glossolalia is so important that Paul directs those who speak in a tongue to pray that they might interpret also (1 Cor. 14:13). If there is no interpreter present, the individual speakers should keep quiet and talk only to themselves and to God (1 Cor. 14:28). Williams asserts that the problem at Corinth was not tongue-speaking per se, but doing so out of order and then failing to interpret. Without interpretation, prophecy is the greater gift. But with interpretation, tongue-speaking is equal to prophecy (1 Cor. 14:5).[41]

Spiritual Gifts in Relation to Spiritual Fruits and Scripture

Williams makes a clear distinction between gifts of the Spirit and spiritual fruits as listed in Galatians 5:22–23. Although there are nine gifts and nine fruits, Williams argues that they are totally different in character. He understands spiritual gifts to be immediate self-expressions of the Spirit that occur through human instruments

---

37. See J. Rodman Williams, Preface to *Sounds of Wonder: A Popular History of Speaking in Tongues in the Catholic Tradition,* by Eddie Ensley (New York: Paulist, 1977), x–xii; see also Williams, *Gift,* 41–42.

38. Williams, *Renewal Theology,* 2:216–20.

39. Ibid., 2:211–12; Williams, *Gift,* 36–41.

40. Williams, *Gift,* 37.

41. Williams, *Renewal Theology,* 2:402–9.

open to his movement, while spiritual fruits take time to develop and are found only in individuals maturing in their Christian lives.

Williams agrees with the charge that many charismatics give insufficient devotion to the spiritual fruits and holy living—exhibiting carnality while exercising the charismata; and he points out that this is not unlike the Corinthians to whom Paul wrote. Williams asserts that the most dynamic movement of the Spirit in the church is his release of sanctifying power, his breaking through into the totality of the self. In short, "it is the making operational of sanctification."[42] Williams admits that there is a real need today among charismatics for many of the Pauline admonitions. At the same time, he insists that this is no reason to forget the spiritual gifts, because they alone are the manifestation of the Holy Spirit.[43]

Because of the emphasis placed by modern Pentecostals and charismatics on spiritual gifts, Williams has been careful to define the relative importance of the charismata and Scripture. Fearing that he was being misinterpreted on this issue, in 1977 he wrote an article addressing the authority of Scripture.[44] He affirmed the absolute priority of Scripture over contemporary experience. The Scriptures are God's authoritative Word in a way that no modern prophecy or revelation can possibly be. The Scriptures are God-breathed (2 Tim. 3:16) and therefore completely trustworthy, whereas all contemporary utterance—such as prophecy—is subject to evaluation by those who hear it. A revelation that does not agree with Scripture, or claims to bring to light a new spiritual truth not given in Scripture, is no revelation at all.

Having said this, however, Williams affirmed that God did not cease to reveal himself with the closing of the New Testament canon. He does continue to speak today. The evangelical recognizes that true preaching is far more than a recitation of Scripture; it entails speaking God's living word to the contemporary situation. In the process, "the Spirit as the living God moves through and beyond the records of past witness." The charismatic says essentially the same thing, although including additional avenues beyond preaching, such as prophecy and interpreted tongues.

In several of his writings, Williams suggests that participants in the charismatic movement actually show a higher regard for the authority of God's written Word than do many of their critics. For charismatics, Scripture takes on new life, meaning, and authority. They experience inward confirmation of scriptural normativity. The Bible, then, is authoritative not merely as an accepted external norm, but as a self-vindicating reality. On the other hand, many evangelicals, for all their talk, do not really accept the full authority of Holy Scripture. They relegate to past history or in other ways downplay the significance of passages dealing with the outpouring and gifts of the Spirit. In so doing, Williams argues, they deny Scripture's full normativity and settle for a limited view of the Bible's authority.

The Permanence of Spiritual Gifts

Williams firmly opposes Protestant "cessationism," the view that God stopped speaking through certain spiritual gifts (especially prophecy and tongues) with the passing of the Apostolic Era or with the establishment of the New Testament canon. For him, all spiritual gifts are extraordinary, supernatural, and *permanent*.[45] Before reading Eddie Ensley's *Sounds of Wonder* (1977), however, Williams seems to

---

42. Williams, *Era of the Spirit*, 42–43. Williams in fact devotes an entire chapter of *Renewal Theology* to the subject of sanctification, which he recognizes as one of the primary works of the Holy Spirit (2:83–117).

43. Williams, *Renewal Theology*, 2:330–31.

44. J. Rodman Williams, "The Authority of Scripture and the Charismatic Movement," *Logos* 7.3 (May–June 1977): 31.

45. J. Rodman Williams, "Charismatic Movement," in *Evangelical Dictionary of Theology*, ed. Walter A. Elwell (Grand Rapids: Baker, 1984), 208.

have accepted the traditional Pentecostal view that spiritual gifts were especially common only in the first century A.D. and in the twentieth century with the Pentecostal-charismatic renewals.

According to the traditional Pentecostal perspective, the eighteen hundred years between the first and twentieth centuries saw a reduction in the church's experience of the Holy Spirit and charismata, as increased officialism, institutionalism, and sacerdotalism served to dim spiritual vitality.[46] The Middle Ages, for example, saw minimal spiritual vigor, with little record of the Holy Spirit's coming to anoint and to empower. It is true that leaders of the Protestant Reformation did address the role of the Spirit in inspiring Scripture, in making faith possible, and in bringing about regeneration, union with Christ, and sanctification. But there was insufficient recognition of the extraordinary and unique event of the coming of the Holy Spirit and the importance of spiritual gifts. Those who did place emphasis on spiritual vitality were derided as *Schwärmer* ("enthusiasts"). The Quakers recaptured many elements of the New Testament view of the Holy Spirit, but their concept of the Inner Light represented him as a resident fact of all human lives which needs only to be recognized and elicited.

John Wesley went beyond the Reformation in his concern for entire sanctification or Christian perfection, a work of the Holy Spirit. He also went beyond John Calvin in envisioning the possibility of some future restoration of the extraordinary gifts, but did not seem to view this as very consequential. In the Holiness movement, a continuation of Wesleyan theology, it became common to speak of the second experience of sanctification as Spirit baptism. With the growth of revivalism in the later nineteenth century came an emphasis on Spirit baptism as a second experience with endowment of power. However, Williams argued that it was only with the rise of the Pente-

costal movement at the beginning of the twentieth century and with the subsequent charismatic renewal that there was a recovery of the primitive dynamism of the Holy Spirit.

Once he had read Ensley's *Sounds of Wonder*, Williams began to speak of the Holy Spirit's ongoing activity throughout Christian history. As we saw earlier, Ensley identified in Roman Catholicism a long tradition of jubilation, singing and praying in the realm of the Spirit. Jubilation also entailed anticipation of the miraculous, especially of extraordinary healings. Ensley recognized three phases in the tradition of jubilation. First, the period from about the fourth through the eighth centuries was characterized by much spontaneity in worship, improvised songs, clapping of hands, and even spiritual dance. During the second period, the ninth century until the sixteenth, spontaneous jubilation was no longer an expected part of worship, but continued in the lives of saints and mystics, as well as among many ordinary believers. From the sixteenth century onwards, the tradition of jubilation was almost completely forgotten as growing formalism replaced deeper spiritual experiences. Finally, at Vatican II a new concern for spirituality arose.

Williams finds Ensley's history of Catholic charismatic spirituality pregnant with meaning for the modern charismatic renewal. He now recognizes an ongoing charismatic tradition in the Catholic church for the first sixteen centuries of the Christian Era; this tradition then faded for both Catholics and Protestants until the twentieth century. Williams views the contemporary charismatic movement as a rebirth of this earlier historical tradition, for the two share the same deep and searching spirituality. It is clear that throughout history hungry hearts have yearned for a greater experience of God's immanent presence, and he has responded.

46. This position is expressed in Williams, *Pentecostal Reality* (1972).

Contributions

J. Rodman Williams has become both a major proponent and theologian of the contemporary charismatic renewal.[47] He points to the benefits that this movement has had within historic churches:

1. Recovery of a dynamic sense of the reality of the Christian faith
2. Renewal of the community of believers as a fellowship (*koinōnia*) of the Holy Spirit
3. Manifestation of a wide range of spiritual gifts, especially those discussed in 1 Corinthians 12–14
4. The renewing experience of baptism in the Holy Spirit, often accompanied by tongues
5. Reemergence of a spiritual unity that transcends denominational barriers
6. Rediscovery of dynamic Christian witness
7. Revitalization of an eschatological perspective[48]

In explaining the renewed concern with the end times, Williams stresses the role of the Holy Spirit in intensifying believers' yearning for Christ to return, for effective proclamation of the gospel to all nations until the parousia, for the courage and wisdom needed to face whatever persecution may come, and for the power to cope with demonic spirits. The outpouring of the Holy Spirit is a sign of the ushering in of the last days. The Spirit also sanctifies or prepares the believer for the coming of the Lord. And when the parousia occurs, the Holy Spirit will raise the mortal bodies of the faithful to eternal incorruptibility.[49]

Because of numerous misconceptions and controversies that have surrounded the modern Pentecostal and charismatic renewals, and because of the need for people of the Spirit to find common grounds, Williams has given considerable attention to various perspectives on the Holy Spirit: evangelical, Pentecostal, sacramental, mystical, and "renewalist." Evangelicals generally believe that all truly converted or born-again Christians are Spirit-baptized. Pentecostals, on the other hand, contend that there are both Christians and Spirit-baptized Christians, and that Spirit baptism is subsequent to regeneration. Sacramentalists see Spirit baptism as occurring at the moment of water baptism or confirmation. This position has been viewed by evangelicals and Pentecostalists as, in effect, a nominal Christianity. Sacramentalists who believe that the gift of the Holy Spirit occurs in confirmation do share with Pentecostals the view that Spirit baptism is distinct from regeneration.[50] The mystic assumes that unity with the divine Spirit can occur with or without the mediation of Jesus Christ; the only requirements are meditation and a stripping away of artificial barriers. Thus, all talk about the work of Jesus Christ in redemption as being necessary to the reception of the Spirit is out of place to the mystic. Renewalists seek restoration of some golden age of the church, but often with little or no emphasis on either the gift of the Holy Spirit or spiritual gifts.[51]

For the benefit of those who are confused by these various views, Williams attempts to synthesize the evangelical, Pentecostal, and sacramental. One of his suggestions is to think of Spirit baptism as an aspect of Christian initiation. This would eliminate any need to speak in terms of Christians and Spirit-baptized Christians. Both categories can best be understood as persons in process of Christian initiation.[52]

---

47. For a defense of the modern charismatic movement, with its relevance to the broader church, see Williams, *Era of the Spirit*, 9–38.

48. J. Rodman Williams, "A Profile of the Charismatic Movement," *Christianity Today*, 28 February 1975, p. 9.

49. J. Rodman Williams, "The Holy Spirit and Eschatology," *Pneuma* 3.2 (Fall 1981): 54–58.

50. Williams, "Pentecostal Theology," 77–85.

51. Williams, *Gift*, 151–52.

52. Williams, "Pentecostal Theology," 82–83.

One of the strong points of Williams's writings is his willingness to address controversial topics. These include homosexuality, which he clearly states is not a viable Christian lifestyle;[53] eternal security, which is consistent with the Westminster Confession, but is not to be viewed as infallible assurance for all true believers;[54] and snake handling, which he views as presumptuous rather than miraculous.[55] He insists that there is no teaching of baptismal regeneration in the Bible.[56] As a Presbyterian, he also addresses the issue of predestination. He concludes that there are two destinations, but not two predestinations. Christ came to save, not to condemn.[57] Williams rejects including the *filioque* clause in Western creeds, reasoning that while the Holy Spirit is sent from the Son and the Father (John 14:26), the procession of the Spirit is from the Father alone (John 15:26).[58] He argues strongly for supernatural healing, while chastising those who reject medical measures.[59] And, as we have seen, he challenges the presumption of the word-of-faith teaching that "you can write your own ticket with God."[60]

While Williams is a leader and one of the most prominent thinkers in the charismatic movement, it should not be assumed that he is a one-issue theologian. In his three-volume *Renewal Theology*, Williams deals systematically with the full range of Christian truth, including such topics as angels, the effects of sin, the incarnation, and Christian living. But each of these is treated from the charismatic perspective. For example, he discusses in considerable detail the role of the Holy Spirit in inspiring Holy Writ, and then in illuminating scriptural

passages for the reader. In similar fashion, he asserts that the climactic blessing of the exalted Lord is the gift of the Holy Spirit,[61] and that the indwelling of Christ in the believer is identical with the indwelling of the Holy Spirit.[62]

Essentially, what Williams has done is to reintroduce the person and role of the Holy Spirit into every Christian question and issue. Long neglected by Western churches, the divine Third Person had become, so to speak, the dark side of the moon, the forgotten Paraclete.[63] However, twentieth-century Pentecostal and charismatic movements have sparked a renewed emphasis on the Holy Spirit. It could hardly have been expected that systematic theologies from this new perspective would surface immediately. Indeed, the very idea of a theology from a Pentecostal-charismatic viewpoint seems somewhat paradoxical. Pentecostals and charismatics have been characterized as experiential, emotional, and subjective, while theology is reasonable and objective. But systematic theology and the Pentecostal-charismatic message are not mutually exclusive. Numerous classical Pentecostals have attempted systematic theologies, although they have tended to fall short of being comprehensive. What Williams has provided is the first truly all-inclusive theology from the Pentecostal-charismatic perspective.

But Williams's contribution reaches beyond his writings. He has come to serve as an exemplar for Pentecostals and charismatics who are coming to recognize that it is entirely proper to ask penetrating questions about one's experiences as well as one's faith and tradition. Because of scholars like J. Rodman Williams, reflective thought no longer seems out of place to those who pursue a life in the Spirit.

53. Williams, *Renewal Theology*, 2:99 n. 74. According to Williams, the Holy Spirit provides purification from the abomination of homosexuality (p. 252).

54. Ibid., 2:267 n. 114.

55. Ibid., 2:377 n. 142.

56. Ibid., 2:38–39.

57. Ibid., 2:21.

58. Ibid., 1:93 n. 35.

59. Ibid., 2:372–73.

60. Ibid., 2:365–66.

61. Ibid., 1:412.

62. Ibid., 2:32.

63. Eastern Christianity always has placed a high emphasis on the Holy Spirit; see Burgess, *Holy Spirit*.

Edward John Carnell

Gordon R. Lewis

D estined to become one of the leaders in the rise of evangelicalism in the twentieth century, Edward John Carnell was born in 1919 in Antigo, Wisconsin.[1] He was the son of a Baptist pastor who had come to the United States from England and studied two years at Moody Bible Institute. Though a confirmed fundamentalist, Herbert Carnell deplored the acrimonious debates between fundamentalists and liberals in the meetings of the Northern Baptist Convention.

Educational Influences

After an unimpressive record in high school, Edward Carnell enrolled at Wheaton College (1937–41), where his academic abilities were awakened by a professor of philosophy, Gordon H. Clark. In his *Introduction to Christian Apologetics*, Carnell would later acknowledge "an incalculable indebtedness to his former professor, Dr. Gordon Haddon Clark of Butler University, whose spiritual kindness, fatherly interest, and academic patience made the convictions which stimulated the penning of this volume possible."[2] Clark defended Christianity primarily by exhibiting its logical consistency and displaying the contradictions in other systems. Although Carnell also included empirical and existential data among the criteria of truth (see p. 327), he never abandoned Clark's emphasis on the law of noncontradiction.

During his Th.B. and Th.M. studies at Westminster Theological Seminary (1941–44), Carnell came under the influence of Cornelius Van Til. In his *Introduction to Christian Apologetics* Carnell also paid tribute to Van Til's stress on trinitarianism as the solution to the philosophical problem

1. For details of Carnell's early life, see Rudolph Nelson, *The Making and Unmaking of an Evangelical Mind: The Case of Edward Carnell* (New York: Cambridge University Press, 1987), 16–27.

2. Edward John Carnell, *Introduction to Christian Apologetics* (Grand Rapids: Eerdmans, 1948), 9.

of the one and the many.[3] In addition, Van Til had pointed out to him the impact that presuppositions have upon all of our thought about experience. But Carnell could not agree that these presuppositions are too ultimate for critical examination and testing. Rather, Carnell considered them hypotheses to be either verified or falsified by evidence. In content his logical starting point was identical with Van Til's—the God of the Bible. But the view that Carnell simply followed in the stream of Dutch presuppositionalists that include Van Til, Abraham Kuyper, and Herman Dooyeweerd does not adequately take into consideration the distinction he drew between untestable presuppositions and hypotheses that can be verified.[4]

As a student at Westminster, Carnell was also influenced by the writings of its cofounder, New Testament scholar J. Gresham Machen. Carnell echoed Machen's affirmation that "at no point is faith independent of the knowledge upon which it is logically based."[5] And with Machen he indicted the Hegelian rationalists for Procrusteanizing and geometrizing reality. He noted, for example, that Ferdinand Christian Baur, "on the basis of his Hegelian philosophy, with its 'thesis, antithesis, and synthesis,' expected to find a conflict in the apostolic age with a gradual compromise and settlement. And he found that phenomenon surely enough—in defiance of the facts, but in agreement with his philosophy."[6] Carnell also agreed with Machen

that "the great weapon with which the disciples of Jesus set out to conquer the world was not a mere comprehension of eternal principles; it was an historical message, an account of something that had recently happened, it was the message, 'He is risen.'"[7]

Carnell's writings also reflect his study of philosopher-theologian James Orr. Carnell quotes Orr that, flowing from God, who is himself truth, the system of meaning in the Bible "has a character, coherence, and unity of its own, and stands in sharp contrast with counter theories and speculations. . . . [It] has the stamp of reason and reality upon itself, and can amply justify itself at the bar both of history and of experience."[8] Quoting Orr again, Carnell notes that "a religion based on feeling is the vaguest, most unreliable, most unstable of all things. A strong, stable, religious life can be built on no other ground than that of intelligent conviction."[9] Carnell likewise agrees with Orr that skepticism becomes irresistible "when one leaves the doctrine that Christ is God for a mediating position."[10] And with Orr he concurs that the issue of miracles is not of this or that particular miracle. Far more crucial matters are at stake here: Is there a supernatural being? If so, does that being govern the world and relate to humans? Who is Christ? How can we obtain redemption? Is there a hereafter? "It is these larger questions that have to be settled first, and then the question of particular miracles will fall into its proper place."[11] Humans, Carnell points out, "*will* think on those deep problems which lie at the root of

3. Ibid., 41 n. 23; Carnell observes that "unity in God is no more fundamental than diversity and diversity in God is no more fundamental than unity."

4. For the view that Carnell was a traditional presuppositionalist, see Kenneth C. Harper, "Edward John Carnell: An Evaluation of His Apologetics," *Journal of the Evangelical Theological Society* 20 (1977): 144. For a full comparison of Carnell and Van Til, see Gordon R. Lewis, "Van Til and Carnell," in *Jerusalem and Athens*, ed. E. R. Geehan (Nutley, N.J.: Presbyterian and Reformed, 1971), 349–61. For Van Til's "Response," see pp. 361–68.

5. Carnell, *Introduction*, 82; cf. J. Gresham Machen, *What Is Faith?* (New York: Macmillan, 1925), 94.

6. Carnell, *Introduction*, 82; cf. Machen, *What Is Faith?* 63.

7. Carnell, *Introduction*, 114; cf. p. 121; and J. Gresham Machen, *Christianity and Liberalism* (New York: Macmillan, 1923), 28–29.

8. Carnell, *Introduction*, 108; cf. James Orr, *The Christian View of God and the World* (Grand Rapids: Eerdmans, 1948), 16.

9. Carnell, *Introduction*, 81; cf. Orr, *Christian View*, 20.

10. Carnell, *Introduction*, 111; cf. Orr, *Christian View*, Lecture II.

11. Carnell, *Introduction*, 244; cf. Orr, *Christian View*, 10–11.

religious belief—on the nature of God, His character, His relations to the world and men, sin, the means of deliverance from it, the end to which all things are moving,— and if Christianity does not give them an answer, suited to their deeper and more reflective moods, they will simply put it aside as inadequate for their needs."[12]

While doing graduate work at Harvard University (1944–48), Carnell interacted at length with the existentialism of Reinhold Niebuhr. Having learned much from Niebuhr's realistic view of sin's pervasiveness, he later noted, for example, that fundamentalism "exempts itself from the limits that original sin places on history; it wages holy wars without acknowledging the elements of pride and personal interest that prompt the call to battle."[13] Carnell differed, however, with Niebuhr's assumption of an infinite qualitative distinction between God and humans, maintaining that God created the human mind to think (at least in part) his thoughts after him. So Carnell opposed Niebuhr's contention that there is no univocal point between God and humanity such as the law of noncontradiction. Carnell also opposed Niebuhr's belief that an irresolvable dialectic between time and eternity renders all seemingly logical and literal biblical teaching symbolic. "Having given the lion's share in his epistemology to [an inward] empiricism," Carnell wrote, "Niebuhr cannot avoid skepticism within the natural law. Everything is provisional and tentative."[14] In the end Niebuhr is left with "an absolute relativism."[15] Carnell concluded, *The evangelical says that inward experience is to be explained in terms of the Biblical revelation, whereas existentialism says that the Biblical revelation is to be explained in terms of our inward experience."[16]*

It was from another influential professor at Harvard in 1944, D. Elton Trueblood, that Carnell adopted his verificational approach—integrating his varied logical, empirical, and existential emphases in hypothetical (if . . . , then . . .) sequences. Although Trueblood noted what he interpreted as emotional difficulties and narrow dogmatism, Carnell was open enough to learn from him.[17] Trueblood's *Logic of Belief* is the source of Carnell's observation that inner personal experience of God sustains one not merely temporarily, as do drugs, but through both bright and dark hours.[18] Carnell also utilizes Trueblood's statement that "if all evil, whether moral, natural or intellectual, is truly illusory, we are foolish indeed to fight it; it would be far preferable to forget it."[19] And citing Trueblood's *Predicament of Modern Man*, Carnell observes, "Man is an animal who is peculiarly in need of something to buttress and to guide his spiritual life. Without this, the very capacities that make him a little lower than the angels lead to his destruction. The beasts do not need a philosophy or a religion, but man does."[20] Carnell also uses Trueblood's argument in *Philosophy of Religion* (a later version of *The Logic of Belief*) that *if* God exists, *then* we can make sense of several lines of evidence stemming from our subjective human experience as well as from external observation. Carnell's own hypothetical starting point is not mere theism ("if God exists"), but the Triune God disclosed in the Jesus of history and in the inspired teaching of Scripture, and most frequently referred to as simply "the God

12. Carnell, *Introduction*, 278; cf. Orr, *Christian View*, 21.
13. Edward John Carnell, *The Case for Orthodox Theology* (Philadelphia: Westminster, 1959), 114.
14. Edward John Carnell, *The Theology of Reinhold Niebuhr* (Grand Rapids: Eerdmans, 1951), 131.
15. Ibid., 130.
16. Ibid., 138.
17. Trueblood's assessment is part of Carnell's permanent Harvard file (Nelson, *Making*, 60).
18. Carnell, *Introduction*, 75.
19. Ibid., 286; cf. D. Elton Trueblood, *The Logic of Belief* (New York: Harper, 1942), 286.
20. Carnell, *Introduction*, 228; cf. D. Elton Trueblood, *The Predicament of Modern Man* (New York: Harper, 1944), 17.

who has revealed Himself in Scripture" or "the God of the Bible."[21]

Carnell learned much at Boston University (1945–49) from empirical philosopher Edgar S. Brightman; for example, a theologian cannot ignore the hard data of sensory observation. Utilizing Brightman's evaluation of various criteria of truth, Carnell argued that consistency "tells us in general that all things must stand together; it does not tell us specifically how, or where, or why they are to stand."[22] Like Brightman, Carnell insisted that religious emotion, if worthy, must conform to truth, and not truth to religious emotion.[23] In addition, philosophy is interested in everything in the universe that in any way enters into human experience.[24] Carnell quoted Brightman, "In any event one's starting point is not decisive in philosophical investigation. The main thing is to include the whole range of relevant experience before we are through."[25] Parting ways with Brightman, however, Carnell vigorously opposed his case for a finite God and his denial of God's absoluteness.[26]

During his graduate studies Carnell furthered his existentialist interests through study of the writings of Søren Kierkegaard. In fact, Carnell's dissertation at Boston University considered "The Problem of Verification in Søren Kierkegaard" (1949). Carnell appreciated many of Kierkegaard's emphases, especially the individual's total dependence on God in humility, thankfulness, and love:

> Kierkegaard developed the meaning of Christian love with a profundity, thoroughness, and biblical accuracy which, it is no exaggeration to say, surpassed all

previous efforts. . . . He was convinced—and rightly so—that far too many ethicists were quagmired in legalism . . . that love is the fulfillment of the law, and that the ethical self falls short of its duties until it performs works of love. . . . The term "existential" may strike some as nothing but a sign of academic pomposity, but it actually signifies that the *spiritual being* of a person has no reality apart from works of love.[27]

In contrast to all the strengths Carnell found in Kierkegaard, he continued to find epistemological weakness. Kierkegaard offered "a very inadequate relation between the Christian religion and public evidences. . . . Although Kierkegaard said many fine things about faith, he was rather disappointing when he attempted to define the relation between faith and public evidences."[28] Whereas Kierkegaard claimed that certainty and passion do not go together, Carnell maintained that "as far as the state of certainty is concerned, *the one and only issue is the sufficiency of the evidences. All else is beside the point. . . . Sufficiency is simply a characteristic of evidences on which we are willing to act."[29] This statement from Carnell's last publication reflected his continuing concern that one's opinions in philosophy and theology fit the facts, that is, be well informed.

Did Carnell radically change his apologetic later in life? Although his later publications emphasize existential values more than do his earlier books, they are consistent with his earlier studies. In his *Introduction to Christian Apologetics* (1948), the facts or givens include internal existentialist data as well as external empirical data. And his *Christian Commitment* (1957) emphasizes the law of noncontradiction and the sufficiency of the evidence.[30] Interpret-

21. Carnell, *Introduction*, 101.
22. Ibid., 59; cf. Edgar S. Brightman, *An Introduction to Philosophy* (New York: Holt, 1925), 60.
23. Carnell, *Introduction*, 82.
24. Ibid., 95; cf. Brightman, *Introduction*, 4.
25. Carnell, *Introduction*, 123; cf. Edgar S. Brightman, *A Philosophy of Religion* (New York: Prentice-Hall, 1940), 343.
26. Carnell, *Introduction*, 288, 298; cf. Brightman, *Philosophy*, 313–14.

27. Edward John Carnell, *The Burden of Søren Kierkegaard* (Grand Rapids: Eerdmans, 1965), 166–68.
28. Ibid., 169.
29. Ibid., 170.
30. Edward John Carnell, *Christian Commitment: An Apologetic* (New York: Macmillan, 1957), 38–42, 77–78, 114.

ers of Carnell who claim that he radically changed his approach in later years do not do justice to either the variety in his graduate work on Niebuhr and Kierkegaard or his continued interest to the end of his life in verifying hypotheses.[31] In *Christian Commitment,* one of his later works, he wrote, "Christianity is true because its major elements are consistent with one another and with the broad facts of history and nature."[32]

Early Success

During his graduate studies in theology and philosophy at Harvard and Boston universities, Carnell taught philosophy and apologetics at Gordon College and philosophy of religion at Gordon Divinity School. As one of his students at Gordon College in those years, I took all the courses I could from the stimulating young professor. The brilliant scholar punctuated his lectures with stories of his dialogues with empiricists and existentialists at the universities. He challenged students fresh from pietistic homes and churches to formulate a defense of their faith in the God of the Bible. Carnell's account of a visit to the Mother Church of Christian Science was unforgettable. "The fervent testimonies of healings," he said, "outdid many of the testimony meetings in evangelical churches. But the fervency of testimonies and the changed lives did not of themselves show that Christian Science is true." Experienced healings did not free the belief system from contradictions and discrepancies with fact.

While teaching and completing two doctorates in theology and philosophy, Carnell found time to write *An Introduction to Christian Apologetics.* It won a $5,000 prize from the publisher. Not yet thirty years of age, with one earned doctorate, nearly an-

other, and a prize-winning book to his credit, Carnell was invited to teach at the new Fuller Theological Seminary.

Carnell arrived in Pasadena in September 1948, excited about teaching both philosophical apologetics and systematic theology. Ahead of his times, he published *Television, Servant or Master?* in 1950. In 1951 a revision of his Harvard dissertation, *The Theology of Reinhold Niebuhr,* came out. This was followed in 1952 by *A Philosophy of the Christian Religion,* a substantial work on values.

From 1954 to 1959 Carnell gave up teaching theology and writing major books to serve as president of Fuller Seminary. Under his leadership it achieved accreditation. Robert Rankin, a member of the accreditation team of the American Theological Schools, said, "The accomplishments of the Seminary are sound measurements, I believe, of the distinguished leadership which Dr. Carnell gave to it during those formative years of his Presidency."[33]

Verificational Method

Carnell's most significant scholarly contribution was his method of reasoning to determine the truth when one is faced with contradictory interpretations or claims. His method of justifying beliefs integrates the emphases of Clark on logic, Van Til on presuppositions, Machen on historical facts, Brightman on empirical givens, and existentialists like Niebuhr and Kierkegaard on internal data. Carnell's "if . . . , then . . ." verificational approach acknowledges that there is subjectivity in every decision about the ultimately real and good. But it also finds that some convictions are better informed than others. The more coherent and viable proposals have greater probability than do the others.

Carnell was acutely aware that minds torn asunder by contradictory claims regarding such ultimate concerns as God, Christ, and the Bible cannot commit them-

31. John A. Sims, *Edward John Carnell: Defender of the Faith* (Washington, D.C.: University Press of America, 1979), contrasts "Carnell the Rationalist" (ch. 3) with "Carnell in Transition" (ch. 4) and "The Mature Carnell" (ch. 5).

32. Carnell, *Christian Commitment,* 286.

33. Cited by Nelson, *Making,* 97.

selves authentically to God's kingdom. Nor can these contradictory claims upon our loyalties be finally resolved by appeals to authority. For the authorities at Rome, Mecca, Salt Lake City, and Benares contradict one another. Appeals to self-authenticating religious experience and intuition are not the answer either, for they also result in contradictions. One must choose between contradictory claims on other grounds.[34]

By what method of reasoning, then, can contradictory claims be resolved? Carnell carefully considered and rejected deductive, inductive, and mystical approaches. Deductive reasoning from assumed premises, axioms, or presuppositions to conclusions that are logically true is useful only if the premises are in fact true. If the proponents of particular religious claims merely assume the truth of their basic premises, their reasoning is circular.

A purely inductive method of reasoning is equally unfit for the task. It assumes that the mind is a tabula rasa that observes empirical phenomena and then infers general conclusions with various degrees of probability. Total objectivity, however, seems impossible in religion as in other fields. Our controlled observations are extremely hampered by limitations of time, space, energy, and funding. Furthermore, an inductive method can neither confirm nor disconfirm the universal statements entailed in Christian faith; for example, that all people ought to respect the rights of others. A purely empirical approach can never completely confirm God's sovereignty over all. Hence Carnell does not utilize the usual inductive arguments for God's existence.[35]

The mystical method assumes that religious knowledge is a matter of immediate experiential acquaintance. Carnell acknowledges that mystical experiences and personal encounters do provide important data. Unfortunately, however, the experiences do not interpret themselves. Natural-

ists explain them as the intellect's being overwhelmed by emotions. Monists regard them as a realization of fusion with the cosmos. And theists may speak of a Person-to-person encounter with a living God distinct from the world but active in it. Only critical discernment determines whether an immediate experience is introverted, narcissistic self-worship, a consciousness of fusion with Mother Nature, a personal awareness of the Creator, or a selling of one's soul to the devil. Without discernment we cannot distinguish authentic from counterfeit religious experiences.

Having rejected the deductive, inductive, and mystical approaches to settling conflicting truth claims about the ultimate subject-object of worship, Carnell proposed a verificational method of reasoning. The logical starting point of this critical method is not unexamined presuppositions, supposedly objective observations, or immediate religious experiences, but interpretive hypotheses that may be either confirmed or disconfirmed. Thus Carnell meticulously examined the hypothesis that the Triune God of the Bible exists. *If* he exists, reasoned Carnell, *then* we should be able to make sense of life logically, factually, and existentially. Rudolph Nelson refers to Carnell as a presuppositionalist who "comes close" to writing 359 pages "begging the question."[36] But Nelson fails to comprehend the difference between untestable presuppositions and hypotheses that can be confirmed or falsified. Carnell's method is neither presuppositional nor circular. It calls for an openness that will consider any hypothesis and follow the evidence where it leads.

Is there, Carnell asks, common ground with unbelievers? Or are religious issues too ultimate and emotively explosive for productive cognitive evaluation? Is it possible to consider with a high degree of philosophical fairness issues with such deep, po-

---

34. Carnell, *Introduction*, 45–64.
35. Ibid., 122–51.

36. Rudolph Nelson, "Fundamentalism at Harvard: The Case of Edward John Carnell," *Quarterly Review* 2.2 (Summer 1982): 95.

larizing loyalties? Carnell finds a basis for dialogue with different cultures and philosophies in an analysis of what makes human experience meaningful. This initial step provides the ground rules for his verificational procedure. Analysis of what makes human experience meaningful is not inductive or deductive inference from experience to something outside it. Neither is it simply a phenomenological description of our experiences. Rather, it is a reflective evaluation of the various elements already present in our experience. This cannot be done by proxy through what we hear from others. It is one's own unique experience that one analyzes.[37]

Carnell's analysis of what makes human experience meaningful provided several points of contact with non-Christians. These points of contact are featured in a number of his apologetic works: (1) respect for the inherent worth and rights of others—a valuing of other persons above all else (*A Philosophy of the Christian Religion*); (2) relationships characterized by justice, consideration, and love (*Christian Commitment*); and (3) care about the psychological well-being of others (*The Kingdom of Love and the Pride of Life*).[38] Other points of contact, however different initial worldviews may be, include (4) intellectual honesty and humble acknowledgment of relevant evidence; and (5) communication in a way that others can follow, that is, without intellectual hypocrisy or self-contradiction (*Introduction to Christian Apologetics*). These universal points of contact enable finite, fallen humans in a pluralistic world to live and learn productively, and to move beyond mere opinions to increasingly well-informed, correctable opinions, and eventually to well-founded, true opinions.

On the basis of the common ground identified by his analysis of what makes human experience meaningful, Carnell observed that there are certain normative standards by which to test claims about ultimate moral and religious realities. Anyone's starting points may be tested by three basic criteria of truth: (1) logical noncontradiction, (2) empirical adequacy, and (3) existential (ethical, axiological, and psychological) viability. Carnell often summed up these elements as "systematic consistency." A true or well-founded option is without contradiction and fits the facts empirically (externally) and existentially (internally).[39] One using Carnell's method of justifying beliefs will accept the hypothesis that provides the most coherent account of both areas of relevant data. Attainment of the ideal of complete knowledge is not possible, but one will accept as more probable the worldview with fewest difficulties and the greatest coherence and viability.

While reason plays a necessary role in Carnell's verificational method, it is not sufficient. Carnell did not find this issue easy. And no reader ought to imagine it so. In Carnell's perspective of faith and reason, which is Augustinian rather than Thomistic, the ultimate object of religious faith remains unseen, but the signs indicating its reality are seen. Their actuality and significance can be either confirmed or disconfirmed. Thus, reason (*scientia*) precedes faith in testing conflicting claims. When a view is confirmed, it is seen to be adequate, and we have good cause to believe in its invisible referent. In this way faith in the God who personally relates is established, and we can then make wise choices according to his eternal wisdom (*sapientia*) in all areas of life.[40]

Another indication that Carnell's apologetic is more in the tradition of Augustine than of Aquinas is that he defends orthodox or evangelical Christianity, not mere theism. In defending belief in the God of Jesus Christ and of the Bible he includes more

---

37. Carnell, *Christian Commitment*, 44–46.

38. Edward John Carnell, *The Kingdom of Love and the Pride of Life* (Grand Rapids: Eerdmans, 1960), 6.

39. Carnell, *Introduction*, 56–64.

40. For development of this Augustinian view see Gordon R. Lewis, "Faith and Reason in the Thought of St. Augustine," Ph.D. diss., Syracuse University, 1959.

theology than traditional arguments for the existence of God. Carnell emphasizes trinitarianism, the incarnation, scriptural authority, illumination, and existential works of love. Further, it is not the case that reason functions alone for part of the way and is then followed by a leap of faith.[41] Rather, reason distinguishes what to believe and why; belief in the reality designated then leads to a commitment; this faith in turn leads to the desire for more knowledge. Knowledge and faith lead to each other in a kind of Augustinian chain reaction.[42]

The basis of faith, according to Carnell, is knowledge of what is to be believed and why one is to believe that and not something else. Who cannot see that knowledge precedes belief? But faith is more than knowledge. Knowledge, to be sure, is a necessary prerequisite; and faith is based on the sufficiency of the evidence. But faith is whole-souled trust in God's Word as true.[43] More than knowledge is needed, therefore. The Spirit must overcome opposing desires and stubborn, pride-filled wills. The Spirit's task is not to create new revelation or new evidence, but to secure response to the evidence publicly available.[44] Faith guided by truth away from idols to the God who relates evokes emotional responses. A new convert joyfully sings, "O happy day, when Jesus washed my sins away!" But such "feelings are only as secure as the system of truth which fortifies them. . . . Truth establishes feelings; feelings do not establish truth."[45]

Ontologically, the outcome of Carnell's critical epistemology is a critical realism. A mature use of his verificational method moves toward a nondisillusioning sense of reality. Critical realism in the study of what is real (metaphysics) is not to be confused with a naive realism, a commonsense realism, nor idealism. Against idealism, critical realism retains the belief of naive and commonsense realism in independent things and states of affairs. On the other hand, the fact that, say, the statue of David in Florence can be seen from different angles does not mean that our knowledge is nothing but varied perspectives. The variety of perspectives (indeed, the same individual may have different perspectives at different times and in different situations) calls for a critical discernment. A critical method is indispensable if we are to confirm or dismiss partial beliefs about elephants, persons, events, and God. Whether derived from common sense, sensory observation, rational analysis, or mystical intuition, our perspectives are limited. Hence we must always be open to considering additional elements of truth.[46]

In brief, as responsible students of the God-originated Word we must justify our proposed interpretations by showing that they coherently fit the relevant literary, grammatical, historical, and contextual evidence. Similarly, as responsible observers of the God-governed world we must justify our interpretations thereof by showing that they without contradiction account for the relevant data we receive not only physically (through the five senses), but also morally, psychologically, and experientially. By using Carnell's comprehensive verificational method and three basic criteria of truth students of human experience and of Scripture can successfully evaluate contradictory claims about reality.

---

41. Carnell throughout his life deplored the tendency to divorce faith and reason. See his "On Faith and Reason," in *The Case for Biblical Christianity*, ed. Ronald H. Nash (Grand Rapids: Eerdmans, 1969), 48–57.

42. Carnell quotes Augustine's characterization of faith as "reason with assent" (*Introduction*, 69); also, "the mind, by natural endowment from the Creator, enjoys immediate apprehension of those standards which make our search for the true, the good, and the beautiful meaningful" (p. 152).

43. Carnell, *Introduction*, 66.

44. Ibid., 65–88.

45. Ibid., 87–88.

46. For a more thorough exposition of Carnell's major apologetic works, see Gordon R. Lewis, *Testing Christianity's Truth Claims* (Lanham, Md.: University Press of America, 1990), chs. 7–10.

Carnell was himself one of the first evangelicals to be heard across theological and philosophical lines. Neo-orthodox theologian William Hordern regarded Carnell's work "a major attempt to converse with modern philosophy and nonconservative theology. Carnell served warning that the new conservative was no longer content to hide in an intellectual ghetto. He was prepared to march out into the modern world and meet it on its own terms."[47] And John Stackhouse called Carnell an "archetypal evangelical [who] foreswore the claustrophobic security of the fundamentalist bedroom. He apparently never paused at the doorway, but he boldly strode out into that marketplace to learn as well as to teach. Those who wish to call themselves 'evangelical' today might well ask themselves, 'Who follows in his train?'"[48] For those who adopt Carnell's methodology will be able to enter into discussion with nonconservative Christian theologians and with non-Christians.

The Issue of Biblical Inerrancy

In his first book, Carnell maintained that religious revelation is derived from the canon of Scripture, which is plenarily inspired.[49] By "inspired" he meant that the authors were "moved by the Holy Spirit to write down only what God approved."[50] He concluded his chapter on "The Problem of Biblical Criticism" with the affirmation that "Christianity knows no contradiction of its radicals," but that there will be "the perpetual presence of minor difficulties."[51] While some of Carnell's interpreters think that he moved away from this early position, David Fraser says, "Careful examina-

tion of his writings makes this doubtful. It appears rather that he refined his understanding of [inspiration] so as to face more honestly the inductive difficulties of the Bible without shifting from a basic conviction of complete trustworthiness."[52]

Rudolph Nelson has proposed that the issue of biblical inerrancy was a major source of tension throughout Carnell's life. Carnell was

> burdened with the dead weight of Clarkean rationalism and an anachronistic theology inextricably tied to an inerrant Bible. . . . [He not only] never achieved the happy harmony of head and heart but . . . found intolerable (unconsciously perhaps) his failure to do so. . . . He was too imbued with the constraints of rationalism ever to be comfortable with Kierkegaardian existentialism and too inward ever to be content with Clarkean rationalism. He could not jettison the one in favor of the other.[53]

In *The Case for Orthodox Theology* Carnell did classify as orthodox the view that the formal inerrant record contains errant historical detail, but he did not espouse that position. Similarly, with the purpose of defending all who were orthodox (but not necessarily fundamentalist), Carnell included James Orr's approach to inspiration as well as the Princeton Theology. The intramural debate between Orr and B. B. Warfield, he said, "had not been successfully terminated."[54] Nelson's view that this issue was a major source of Carnell's psychological unrest is belied by Carnell's subsequent statement:

> Orthodoxy may never officially decide whether the Holy Spirit corrected the documents from which the Chronicler drew his information. But this resolution does not affect the theology of the church, for Paul received his theology directly from

47. William Hordern, *A Layman's Guide to Protestant Theology* (New York: Macmillan, 1960), 67.

48. John G. Stackhouse, Jr., "Who Follows in His Train? Edward John Carnell as a Model for Evangelical Theology," *Crux* 21.2 (June 1985): 24.

49. Carnell, *Introduction*, ch. 12; see also pp. 58, 60–66, 110, 355.

50. Ibid., 191 n. 1.

51. Ibid., 209–10.

52. David A. Fraser, "A Reasonable Faith: The Apologetic of Edward John Carnell," *Studia Biblica et Theologica* 5.2 (Oct. 1975): 57.

53. Nelson, *Making*, 226–27.

54. Carnell, *Case for Orthodox Theology*, 109.

Jesus Christ (Gal. 1:11–12). He did not draw on existing documents. . . . Orthodoxy's intramural debate on inspiration in no way disturbs the truth of the gospel, and to think that it does is cultic.[55]

In his introductory course in logic, Carnell distinguished sentences as verbal vehicles from the propositional meanings they convey. Applying this basic logical distinction, I have argued, and I think he would, that truth or errorlessness is a quality of the Bible's propositional assertions or meanings, whereas infallibility or effectiveness is a quality of the Bible's sentences.[56] Robert Price suggests that Carnell and other neo-evangelical leaders were moving toward a merely conceptual view of inspiration.[57] But Carnell affirmed both the truth of the Bible's conceptual teaching and its effectiveness as a verbal communication, for God's truth disclosed accomplishes its purpose.

While engaging in dialogue with Karl Barth in Chicago in 1962, Carnell mentioned that he, too, faced difficulties with historical detail. For this attempt to identify with Barth and his failure to challenge Barth when he was given the opportunity, Carnell was attacked by fundamentalists—with some justification. But, as Carl Henry recalls, he later "reaffirmed his belief in inerrancy and indicated that he considered Barth's reply unsatisfactory." Indeed, Carnell insisted that "evangelical Christianity should not jettison the doctrine of inerrancy."[58]

Carnell's position on inerrancy is also made clear in a letter written to *Christianity Today* the year before he died:

Warfield clearly perceived that a Christian has no more right to construct a doctrine of biblical authority out of deference to the (presumed) inductive difficulties in the Bible, than he has to construct a doctrine of salvation out of deference to the (actual) difficulties which arise whenever one tries to discover the hidden logic in such events as (a) the Son of God's assumption of human nature, or (b) the Son of God's offering up of this human nature as a vicarious atonement for sin. . . .

We are free to reject the doctrine of the Bible's view of itself, of course, but if we do so we are demolishing the procedure by which we determine the substance of *any* Christian doctrine.[59]

Furthermore, at the time of his death Carnell had affirmed in the introduction to a book he was writing on the Bible that the view of "Biblical inerrancy . . . in my finite judgment is correct." Henry concludes, "If we inquire about Nelson's preferred alternative, we are left pretty much with a bag of wind. . . . To his dying day, Carnell would have fought the imaginative proposals that Nelson postulates. Many quotations Nelson cites by way of implicit criticism of Carnell's positions are akin to those that Carnell would have wrestled and pinned to the mat."[60] Historian George Marsden acknowledges that for Carnell "the inerrancy issue remained a source of constant strain."[61] But Carnell as an academician would have well handled the strain involved. The roots of Carnell's major anxieties must be sought elsewhere.

55. Ibid., 111.
56. Gordon R. Lewis, "What Does Infallibility Mean?" *Journal of the Evangelical Theological Society* 6 (1963): 18–27; reprinted in Ronald Youngblood, ed., *Evangelicals and Inerrancy* (Nashville: Nelson, 1984), 35–48.
57. Robert M. Price, "Neo-Evangelicals and Scripture: A Forgotten Period of Ferment," *Christian Scholar's Review* 15.4 (1986): 315–30.
58. Carl F. H. Henry, "A Victim of Inerrancy?" *Christianity Today*, 21 April 1989, p. 51.

59. Edward John Carnell, "The Penny or the Cake," *Christianity Today*, 14 October 1966, p. 23.
60. Henry, "Victim," 51.
61. George M. Marsden, *Reforming Fundamentalism: Fuller Seminary and the New Evangelicalism* (Grand Rapids: Eerdmans, 1987), 208. Jerry H. Gill's review of Marsden's work also focuses on the issue of whether "inerrancy" applies only to matters of faith and practice or signifies that the Bible is without error of any kind (*Journal of the American Academy of Religion* 58.1 [Spring 1990]: 132).

Personal Struggles

In *The Making and Unmaking of an Evangelical Mind* Nelson sees Carnell's life as a parallel to his own experience of breaking away from evangelicalism. Nelson writes, "By the time Carnell died in 1967, I was beyond the point where his books [on apologetics] could have changed the course of my life. For about this time I was forced to acknowledge that for some twenty years my own faith had been suffering a steady process of erosion."[62] Finally, Nelson's faith was chipped away down to the core, and he was "through playing intellectual games." Then, he says, "I cut all my ties with creedal and institutional Christianity."[63]

Do Nelson's struggles with the view that the Bible is inerrant and historic Christianity is true really parallel Carnell's experience? The indications that Carnell's faith unraveled are very tenuous and circumstantial: offhand remarks he made while working in the dining hall as a student at Wheaton College, the comments of friends, and his need for medication and counseling. Indeed, Nelson undermines the credibility of his own thesis: "Admittedly, we can find little evidence of ideological uncertainty in [Carnell's] published writings. . . . I have no illusions that the Edward Carnell who has emerged in this book is an objective factual reproduction of the real thing. . . . He is rather a Carnell that I have had a part in creating."[64] Reviewing Nelson's book on Carnell, John Stackhouse observed a pervasive background assumption that Carnell's revealed religion is false. But "Nelson needs to *demonstrate* how Carnell's reasoning—or how evangelicalism itself—falls short. And this he finally fails to do. . . . The author's assertion and limited evidence that evangelicalism was an intellectual and spiritual cul-de-sac for Carnell—and, much more, that it is for *everyone*—cannot take the place of a proper demonstration of this crucial point in his interpretation."[65]

How then are we to explain Carnell's internal struggles? Carnell's anxieties stemmed from several factors other than uncertainty about the truth of the Bible's basic tenets.

1. Having identified himself as a fundamentalist in his early years, Carnell struggled with issues related to fundamentalist legalism, negativism, and separatism. He was awakened out of dogmatic slumber to realize that possession of truth does not mean possession of virtue! Sanctification requires also an existential repentance, faith, and love. Carnell commented, "I know that much of this will sound elementary to outsiders. But to one reared in the tyrannical legalism of fundamentalism, the recovery of a genuine theology of grace is no insignificant feat. The feat calls for a generous outlay of intellectual honesty and personal integrity."[66]

2. Carnell's early successes probably occasioned unrealistic hopes for his entire career. By the age of thirty he had to his credit two earned doctorates, a prize-winning book, a record of outstanding teaching, and appointment to the Fuller Seminary faculty. At the age of thirty-five he became president of the seminary. The demands of administration did not allow him to keep up his impressive record. Carnell's experience reminds one of John Stuart Mill, whose private education gave him an advantage of a quarter of a century over his contemporaries. But it also contributed to a breakdown.[67]

3. A major source of Carnell's anxiety was his five years of administrative duties as president of Fuller, for which he himself

62. Nelson, *Making*, 5.
63. Ibid., 6.
64. Ibid., 11, 15.

65. John G. Stackhouse, Jr., review of *The Making and Unmaking of an Evangelical Mind*, by Rudolph Nelson, *Christian Century*, 3–10 February 1988, p. 131.
66. Edward John Carnell, "Orthodoxy: Cultic vs. Classical," in *Case for Biblical Christianity*, ed. Nash, 47.
67. John Stuart Mill, *Autobiography* (London: Oxford University Press, 1873), 26, 112–19.

said he had neither the time nor the inclination.

4. Personal attacks by fundamentalist leaders had traumatic effects. These attacks came not only on Carnell, but also on Fuller Seminary and radio preacher Charles E. Fuller. The income generated by the national radio broadcast (and so the seminary's income) was seriously curtailed. The first public attack on Carnell came for his use of the Revised Standard Version of the Bible, which was alleged to reflect liberal assumptions. Marsden reports: "In the midst of all this, Fuller called a moratorium on public faculty discussion of the RSV. E. J. Carnell later wrote that the bitter 'war of nerves' of the orthodox against him for defending the RSV was what first made him realize that 'orthodoxy suffered from a serious illness.' Having until then always thought of himself as a great champion of orthodoxy, Carnell began to examine whether he needed to purge himself of his own fundamentalist illness."[68]

Although able to relate fairly and lovingly to people who were on the Left of his position, Carnell found it increasingly difficult to respond in like manner to critics from the Right. Instead, he published a scathing attack categorizing them as "cultic." Bernard Ramm, in a review of *The Case for Orthodox Theology*, warned that Carnell's "treatment of the fundamentalists will call forth a very strong reaction from them, and I would remind the good author that the fundamentalists, for all the shortcomings they might have, are still members of the Church."[69]

5. Consider also the time and energy Carnell was compelled to devote to pursuits other than his beloved philosophy and theology. This driven scholar eventually declared, "All my free time must now, of necessity, go into ethics. I literally have hundreds of books and articles with which I must make peace—and soon."[70]

6. Carnell suffered mentally and physically from the side effects of the psychiatric treatment of the time. Seeking to combat lifelong depression and insomnia, he underwent numerous electroshock treatments and became a barbiturate addict.[71] "Victimized by heavy sedation and accompanying memory loss," the classroom presence of this onetime master teacher became "marked by concentration on personal problems, academic ineffectiveness, and dwindling student interest."[72]

Carnell never found the ivory tower in which theologians are alleged to spin out their theories. Theologians are fully human persons with both finite and fallen natures. Their special interests and commitments do not exempt philosophers of religion from responsibilities as parents, neighbors, citizens, administrators, fund-raisers, counselors, evangelists, pastors, and teachers.

Attributing Carnell's death to an unknown amount of barbiturates, the coroner concluded, "I find death undetermined whether accidental or suicidal." Without sufficient basis to rule the case a suicide, the more probable hypothesis is that Carnell had experienced difficulty in getting to sleep while anticipating the next day's lecture at a Roman Catholic institution. On the advice of his psychiatrist, Carnell's wife had customarily dispensed sleeping pills as needed because of his occasional unreliability in keeping track of the dosage.[73] Marsden concludes: "Carnell died as the result of acute depression that one way or another overwhelmed his rational control. He was in a state in which desperation could have obliterated normal categories of intention. If his death was in any sense willed, it

68. Marsden, *Reforming Fundamentalism*, 138; the allusion is to Edward John Carnell, in *How My Mind Has Changed*, ed. Harold E. Fey (Cleveland: Meridian, 1960), 91–93.

69. Bernard Ramm, "Sideswipes and Sidesteps," *Eternity* 10.9 (Sept. 1959): 40; see also Millard J. Erickson, *The New Evangelical Theology* (Westwood, N.J.: Revell, 1968), 207–8.

70. Edward John Carnell, letter to Don Weber, 19 September 1962; Nelson, *Making*, 114.

71. Henry, "Victim of Inerrancy?" 50.

72. Ibid., 51.

73. Nelson, *Making*, 119.

was not premeditated. It had none of the Carnell organization. The overdose was 'moderate,' and the room showed signs that the seizure was unexpected."[74]

Theology

Although some elements of Carnell's theology are evident in *The Theology of Reinhold Niebuhr*, the primary exposition of his doctrinal stance is *The Case for Orthodox Theology* (1959), written as part of a trilogy that also included William Hordern's *Case for a New Reformation Theology* and L. Harold DeWolf's *Case for Theology in Liberal Perspective*. Carnell's slender work explicitly discusses "Theology" in a single chapter (5) of twelve pages based on Paul's Epistle to the Romans. Here Carnell incisively states his views of human sinfulness, divine righteousness, justification, federal headship, sanctification, the unique Christian conflict, and adoption. The subjects of the other chapters are foundations, faith, authority, hermeneutics, proof, difficulties, perils, and the future.

The book contains much pungent material. Millard Erickson writes, "The chapter on 'difficulties' in Carnell's *Case* book, for instance, is one of the most candid pieces of self-criticism in all of theology."[75] Regarding him "as one of the more prolific and articulate apologists for biblical Christianity in our generation," Ronald Nash compiled and edited a number of Carnell's essays on theology, philosophy of religion, ethics, ecumenism, fundamentalism, separatism, and other topics of contemporary interest (*The Case for Biblical Christianity*). John Sims says, "Much of Carnell's contribution lay in the fact that his theology provided a balanced view of the subjective and objective aspects of revelation."[76]

At the beginning of *The Case for Orthodox Theology*, Carnell differentiates theology from apologetics: "Statement draws on theology; defense draws on apologetics."[77]

There follows a volume of incisive statements, many of which, unfortunately, are not well supported in terms of his own verificational approach to knowledge. For example, he declares, "The theology of orthodox theology is the theology of the Reformers, and the theology of the Reformers is the theology of the prophets and apostles."[78] Arminians might well demand some justification for this identification of orthodoxy with Reformed theology. One would have expected Carnell to consider the Reformed and Wesleyan-Arminian theologies hypotheses to be tested by the law of noncontradiction and by the facts, external and internal. Similarly, rather than considering orthodoxy and fundamentalism two hypotheses to be critically examined by the criteria of truth, Carnell simply denounces fundamentalism as a mentality divorced from the creeds of the church, seeking status by negation, and dominated by ideological thinking that is rigid, intolerant, and doctrinaire.[79]

As a writer of theology, Carnell effectively states his conclusions, but does not adequately disclose the data and method of reasoning by which he arrived at them. Had Carnell used his verificational method in his work on orthodox theology, he would have at least briefly traced lines of relevant evidence from the whole Bible in support of his assertions. But he limits himself to Romans as the ideal treatise in systematic theology, because it is not a corrective for any specific dissensions, heresies, or attacks on Paul's authority.

Ignoring as it did Carnell's own verificational method and criteria of truth, *The Case for Orthodox Theology* aroused controversy. A simple statement of theological conclusions without presenting a coherent basis for them naturally raises controversy. Wise students of theology, like those in other fields, justify the statements they make! Theological as well as philosophical knowledge is not mere opinion. It is not even true opinion. Knowledge in theology, as elsewhere, is *well-founded* true opinion.

74. Marsden, *Reforming Fundamentalism*, 258.
75. Erickson, *New Evangelical Theology*, 219.
76. Sims, *Carnell*, 147.
77. Carnell, *Case for Orthodox Theology*, 13.

78. Ibid., 127.
79. Ibid., 113–14, 117.

Why did Carnell not utilize his own method in *The Case for Orthodox Theology?* The limits of space may be part of the answer. He may not have regarded the givens of Scripture as evidence parallel to the givens of nature and history. It may be that if Carnell had not taken the presidency of Fuller and had taught theology through those years, he would have given more thought to theological methodology. He felt deeply his lack of opportunity to pursue theology more fully. After stepping down from the presidency and returning to life as a professor, he said in a note to his brother-in-law, "Remember I lost five years as president. I also lost the field I had prepared for—systematic theology."[80]

Influence

Carnell's methodological contribution to evangelical Christianity can be seen in a variety of fields. Some of the writers we will cite represent independent, parallel developments showing ways in which his method may be applied. But most show his impact directly.

In ethics a Carnell-like approach is used by Oliver Barclay. His reasoning is neither deductive nor inductive, he explains. Rather, it is "a whole Gestalt framework that is uniquely convincing as an explanation of the phenomena of life, both intellectual and experimental." The ethic of love given us ready-made in the Bible, Barclay argues, fits and explains human thinking and experience as nothing else does. Christian ethical hypotheses have a uniquely convincing explanatory value.[81]

In the sciences David Dye's *Faith and the Physical World: A Comprehensive View* rec-

ommends Carnell's works highly and shows how a Christian worldview consistently accounts for all the aspects of human life. Using a verificational approach, Dye concludes that physical reality exists, logic applies, and causality operates not deterministically, but probabilistically.[82]

Bernard Ramm supplied the factual confirmation of the Christian hypothesis in his *Protestant Christian Evidences,* arguing that by reason of its factuality Christianity is the religion which reflects reality.[83] Richard Purtill's *Reason to Believe* similarly seeks to show that Christianity not only is logically possible, but also fits known facts.[84]

For purposes of preevangelism Francis Schaeffer made use of a nontechnical version of Carnell's apologetic method. Schaeffer's reasoning was not that of a Van Tillian presuppositionalist, as Thomas Morris holds, nor of an evidentialist, as Robert Reymond maintains.[85] All reasoning is not either deductive or inductive.[86] A third way of reasoning beyond induction and deduction needs to be recognized in both Carnell and Schaeffer. It starts, not with allegedly objective empirical data impinging on a blank mind, nor with unchallengeable premises, but with hypotheses to be tested. Charles Peirce calls this process abduction: "Abduction is the means whereby hypotheses are

---

80. Carnell, letter to Weber; Nelson, *Making,* 226 n. 28.

81. Oliver R. Barclay, "The Nature of Christian Morality," in *Law, Morality and the Bible,* ed. Bruce Kaye and Gordon Wenham (Downers Grove, Ill.: Inter-Varsity, 1978), 128–29. For an evaluation of Carnell's use of Scripture in discussing such ethical values as self-acceptance and moral knowledge, justice, consideration, and love, see Kenneth W. Wozniak, *Ethics in the Thought of Edward John Carnell* (Lanham, Md.: University Press of America, 1963).

82. David L. Dye, *Faith and the Physical World: A Comprehensive View* (Grand Rapids: Eerdmans, 1966).

83. Bernard Ramm, *Protestant Christian Evidences* (Chicago: Moody, 1953), 16.

84. Richard L. Purtill, *Reason to Believe* (Grand Rapids: Eerdmans, 1974).

85. Thomas V. Morris, *Francis Schaeffer's Apologetics: A Critique* (Chicago: Moody, 1976); Robert L. Reymond, *The Justification of Knowledge* (Nutley, N.J.: Presbyterian and Reformed, 1976), 136–48.

86. In another example of this illicit either/or classification, Thom Notaro, *Van Til and the Use of Evidence* (Phillipsburg, N.J.: Presbyterian and Reformed, 1980), 13, lists various presuppositionalists and evidentialists and then names as "siding more or less with one or the other position: E. J. Carnell, Gordon Lewis, Bernard Ramm, John Gerstner, Francis Schaeffer, and Norman Geisler. . . . Though some of these figures are difficult to categorize, their contributions generally lend support to either a presuppositionalist or an evidentialist persuasion."

generated, moving from a particular case to a possible explanation of the case."[87] John Warwick Montgomery calls it "retroduction," holding that "scientific theories are conceptual Gestalts, built up retroductively through imaginative attempts to render phenomena intelligible."[88] Although Schaeffer's works do not cite sources, his apologetic method generally follows this third way of reasoning, Carnell's verificational approach.[89]

Os Guinness asks, "Can the truth claims of historic Christianity be verified? . . . Is there a God who is truly there, who speaks and who speaks clearly?"[90] In a manner reminiscent of Carnell's analysis, Guinness verifies the claim that there is a general revelation in nature and humanity by asking which view of humanity best accords with the way we must live if we are to be truly human. Which proposal provides a sufficient basis for living meaningfully?[91] Then he tests the claims of special revelation in Christ and the Bible: "If what the Bible says is true, it is open to scrutiny, to examination, to falsification; no one is asked to believe in it as anything other than credible."[92] Echoing Carnell's view of faith as "the resting of the mind on the sufficiency of the evidence," Guinness concludes that "the evidence for Christian truth is not exhaustive, but it is sufficient."[93]

We should also mention briefly a number of other apologists whose work is reminiscent of Carnell's. Colin Chapman's apologetic starts, not with the lowest common denominator of all views of Christianity, but with biblical Christianity: "God has revealed the truth about himself, the universe, and man. The truth he has revealed is open to verification."[94] Henry Close's *Reasons for Our Faith* is "dedicated to Edward John Carnell, Christian scholar, stimulating teacher, to whom I owe my interest in this subject."[95] Colin Brown's treatment of *Philosophy and the Christian Faith* suggests "a new type of natural theology" in which the Christian faith can be presented as a hypothesis. Christianity, he concludes, "suggests explanations for phenomena which are otherwise inexplicable. It makes sense of what at first seemed senseless. It gives wholeness to life which is missing in other views. This is so whether we look at the universe in general or at personal experience of life. . . . It [the Bible] does provide a key which gives coherence and meaning to life as a whole."[96] And Alan Richardson's method of determining the meaning of the New Testament as a whole is remarkably similar to Carnell's. Having mentioned a flat descriptive approach and an approach based on presuppositions, Richardson explains a third possibility:

The way in which one may attempt to state the theology of the NT (in this third sense) is by the framing of an hypothesis (whether consciously or unconsciously) and then testing it by continual checking with the NT documents and other relevant evidence from the period. This is in fact the way in which historical-critical interpretation is done nowadays in every field of historical reconstruction. It necessarily involves a personal or subjective element, but this is now seen to be unavoidable, as the illusion of scientific or presuppositionless history recedes. It does not, however, involve an absolute subjectivism or historical relativism, for the pursuit of history as

87. See William L. Reese, *Dictionary of Philosophy and Religion* (Atlantic Highlands, N.J.: Humanities, 1980), 1.

88. John Warwick Montgomery, *The Suicide of Christian Theology* (Minneapolis: Bethany Fellowship, 1970), 276.

89. Gordon R. Lewis, "Schaeffer's Apologetic Method," in *Reflections on Francis Schaeffer*, ed. Ronald W. Ruegsegger (Grand Rapids: Zondervan, 1986), 69–104.

90. Os Guinness, *The Dust of Death* (Downers Grove, Ill.: Inter-Varsity, 1973), 334.

91. Ibid., 352.

92. Ibid., 354.

93. Ibid., 359.

94. Colin G. Chapman, *Christianity on Trial* (Wheaton, Ill.: Tyndale, 1975), xii, 9.

95. Henry T. Close, *Reasons for Our Faith* (Richmond: John Knox, 1962).

96. Colin Brown, *Philosophy and the Christian Faith* (Chicago: Inter-Varsity, 1969), 265, 273–74.

humane science involves the conviction that one historical interpretation can be rationally shown to be better than another. Each hypothesis must be evaluated by the evidence available.[97]

Finally, Carnell's critical method has been influential in my own writing. In apologetics my *Testing Christianity's Truth Claims* compares six evangelical approaches and concludes that Carnell's incorporates the strengths of the others while avoiding their weaknesses.[98] An earlier work, *Decide for Yourself: A Theological Workbook*, attempts to apply his verificational method to various theological issues.[99] And my three-volume *Integrative Theology*, coauthored by Bruce Demarest, applies the method with greater thoroughness by following a six-step procedure:

1. Definition of the problem
2. Survey of the alternative hypotheses in historical and contemporary theology
3. A test of their ability to explain relevant data drawn from the primary sources of Christian theology, the Old and New Testaments
4. Proposal of a systematic formulation that integrates the strengths of those alternatives that have biblical support
5. Apologetic interaction with those that do not
6. Exploration of the relevance for life and ministry[100]

In this way historical, biblical, systematic, apologetic, and practical theology are integrated.

One of the chief advantages of the verificational method is that it provides a way to break out of hermeneutical circles. With due recognition of the presuppositions and subjectivity involved, biblical interpreters representing different positions can communicate by using Carnell's approach. Because there are several points of contact between them, they can break out of circular reasoning and accept those hypotheses with the highest measure of objective validity.[101] Another advantage of Carnell's method is that its criteria of truth are effective tests of alleged prophets and revelations today.[102] When the public media repeated the claim that transcendental meditation was compatible with Christian worship, I compared the two hypotheses on various counts: their spiritual leader, their views of the source and basic problem of humanity, their understanding of what it means to experience God.[103] Readers of *What Everyone Should Know about Transcendental Meditation* can judge for themselves whether the two hypotheses are consistent or contradictory.

Clearly, Carnell's verificational method is adaptable to numerous fields and issues because it is realistic in recognizing presuppositions and subjectivity. But its criteria of truth supply many checks on unwarranted religious claims and facilitate moving toward decision making with some degree of objective validity. The impact of Carnell's method of problem solving will continue to be felt as long as discerning people seek to

97. Alan Richardson, *A Dictionary of Christian Theology* (Philadelphia: Westminster, 1969), 229.

98. Lewis, *Testing Christianity's Truth Claims*, 296–339. This work compares Carnell's method with the approaches of J. Oliver Buswell, Jr., Stuart Hackett, Gordon Clark, Cornelius Van Til, and Warren Young. The early Clark Pinnock, John Warwick Montgomery, Norman Geisler, George Mavrodes, Arthur Holmes, Josh McDowell, and C. S. Lewis are examined in the appendix.

99. Gordon R. Lewis, *Decide for Yourself: A Theological Workbook* (Downers Grove, Ill.: Inter-Varsity, 1970).

100. Gordon R. Lewis and Bruce A. Demarest, *Integrative Theology*, 3 vols. (Grand Rapids: Zondervan, 1987–).

101. Gordon R. Lewis, "A Response to Presuppositions of Non-Evangelical Hermeneutics [by Millard J. Erickson]," in *Hermeneutics, Inerrancy, and the Bible: Papers from ICBI Summit II*, ed. Earl D. Radmacher and Robert D. Preus (Grand Rapids: Zondervan, 1984), 615–25.

102. Gordon R. Lewis, *Confronting the Cults* (Philadelphia: Presbyterian and Reformed, 1966), 43–58.

103. Gordon R. Lewis, *What Everyone Should Know about Transcendental Meditation* (Glendale, Calif.: Regal, 1975).

distinguish truth from error concerning upright living in the real world.

Primary Sources

Carnell, Edward John. *The Burden of Søren Kierkegaard*. Grand Rapids: Eerdmans, 1965.

_____. *The Case for Biblical Christianity*. Edited by Ronald H. Nash. Grand Rapids: Eerdmans, 1969.

_____. *The Case for Orthodox Theology*. Philadelphia: Westminster, 1959.

_____. *Christian Commitment: An Apologetic*. New York: Macmillan, 1957.

_____. "Fundamentalism." In *Handbook of Christian Theology*, edited by Marvin Halverson and Arthur A. Cohen, 142–43. New York: Meridian, 1958.

_____. "The Government of the Church." In *Basic Christian Doctrines*, edited by Carl F. H. Henry, 248–54. New York: Holt, Rinehart and Winston, 1962.

_____. *Introduction to Christian Apologetics*. Grand Rapids: Eerdmans, 1948.

_____. *The Kingdom of Love and the Pride of Life*. Grand Rapids: Eerdmans, 1960.

_____. "Niebuhr's Criteria of Verification." In *Reinhold Niebuhr: His Religious, Social, and Political Thought*, edited by Charles W. Kegley and Robert W. Bretall, 379–80. New York: Macmillan, 1956.

_____. *A Philosophy of the Christian Religion*. Grand Rapids: Eerdmans, 1952.

_____. "Reinhold Niebuhr's View of Scripture." In *Inspiration and Interpretation*, edited by John F. Walvoord, 239–52. Grand Rapids: Eerdmans, 1957.

_____. "The Son of God." In *Empirical Theology of Henry Nelson Wieman*, edited by Robert W. Bretall, 306–14. New York: Macmillan, 1963.

_____. *Television, Servant or Master?* Grand Rapids: Eerdmans, 1950.

_____. *The Theology of Reinhold Niebuhr*. Grand Rapids: Eerdmans, 1951.

Secondary Sources

Erickson, Millard J. *The New Evangelical Theology*. Westwood, N.J.: Revell, 1968.

Lewis, Gordon R. *Testing Christianity's Truth Claims*, chs. 7–10. Lanham, Md.: University Press of America, 1990.

Nash, Ronald H. *The New Evangelicalism*. Grand Rapids: Zondervan, 1963.

Nelson, Rudolph. *The Making and Unmaking of an Evangelical Mind: The Case of Edward Carnell*. New York: Cambridge University Press, 1987. For reviews of this controversial work see *Christianity Today*, 21 April 1989, pp. 50–51 (Carl F. H. Henry); *Eternity* 39.7/8 (July–Aug. 1988): 36–37 (Stephen Board); *Christian Century*, 3–10 February 1988, pp. 129–31 (John G. Stackhouse).

Ramm, Bernard. *Types of Apologetic Systems*, 210–36. Wheaton, Ill.: Van Kampen, 1953.

Sims, John A. *Edward John Carnell: Defender of the Faith*. Washington, D.C. University Press of America, 1979.

Wozniak, Kenneth W. *Ethics in the Thought of Edward John Carnell*. Lanham, Md.: University Press of America, 1983.

John R. W. Stott

Peter Williams

John Robert Walmsley Stott, the only son of a leading Harley Street physician, Sir Arnold Stott, was born on April 27, 1921. His father was "a scientific secularist," but his mother brought him up as "a devout Lutheran."[1] He went to the famous Rugby School, where in 1938 he had a conversion experience under the ministry of E. J. H. Nash ("Bash"). Nash, who had developed a remarkable ministry amongst public-school boys, nurtured the young Stott, writing to him at least once a week for five years.

Stott was an idealistic young man who went up to Trinity College, Cambridge, in 1939 as an "instinctive pacifist."[2] This was an unusual attitude for an evangelical in those days, though one also held by Bash. It led to a severe straining of Stott's relationship with his father, who was by now a major general in the Army Medical Service. For two years the elder Stott virtually refused to speak to his son. As a consequence, Bash became almost a surrogate father, subjecting the young man to severe and

ruthless criticism, but also shaping significantly his Christian understanding. Bash was no intellectual—indeed, he was rather anti-intellectual—and seems particularly to have feared and distrusted theology. But Stott had what he modestly calls "an enquiring mind," which led to a first class in modern languages in the first part of his degree and in theology in the second part.[3] That he opted for theology was significant of the direction of his mind, and perhaps significant too as an indication of a new direction within evangelicalism. Academic theology was, it seemed, no longer to be feared and sneered at; rather, there was a commitment to use the mind in the service of God. Somewhat surprisingly, Bash does

1. John Eddison, ed., *'Bash': A Study in Spiritual Power* (Basingstoke: Marshall, Morgan and Scott, 1983), 57.

2. Ibid., 59.

3. Christopher Catherwood, *Five Evangelical Leaders* (Wheaton, Ill.: Harold Shaw, 1985), 17.

not appear to have objected, possibly because he was confident of Stott's capacity and maturity.[4] Even at this stage Stott was concerned to bridge the enormous gap between most British evangelicals and the intellectual world. A measure of the divide is that evangelical students were still warned of the dangers of social action and involvement in politics. Such concerns seemed "a fatal distraction from the main job in hand."[5]

That John Stott was unusual was recognized even in this rather narrow milieu. The leaders of the Cambridge Inter-Collegiate Christian Union had the wisdom not to ask him to join their committee, thus affording him time for evangelism and pastoral work.[6] In 1945 he was ordained and became a curate in the parish in which he had been brought up, and to which he was to be attached for the whole of his ministry—All Souls, Langham Place. In 1950 he became rector. In 1970 he handed over much of the responsibility to Michael Baughen, and from 1975 he has held the title of rector emeritus.[7]

From that base Stott has exercised an enormously significant ministry. He was from the first a teacher and preacher of the highest quality, committed to the centrality of the Bible. Consequently, he concentrated on expository preaching. The church was strategically placed in central London, so Stott began to use, as a means of evangelism, a monthly "guest service," to which the congregation was encouraged to invite non-Christians. He also began in 1950 an annual training school to equip lay people for evangelism.[8] And in 1961 he set up the All Souls International Fellowship to develop work among the many students from overseas.[9]

Stott's international vision, however, already encompassed much more than this. In 1961 he was a major force in the foundation of the Evangelical Fellowship in the Anglican Communion. This body displayed the emerging Stott hallmarks: a clearly evangelical but nonconfrontational approach; practical aims—the bringing of Anglican evangelicals worldwide into a closer fellowship; and concern that the evangelical voice be heard and commended so that an increasing evangelical contribution might be made throughout the Anglican communion. To achieve these ends, a number of evangelical councils were established. In England this took the form of the Church of England Evangelical Council, which was inevitably under Stott's chairmanship. This group was to be of key importance over the next thirty years, first of all as a think tank, and then as a standing committee of the Anglican Evangelical Assembly (AEA).[10]

This well illustrates the international nature and extraparochial character of Stott's ministry, a feature established very early through his preaching, evangelism, and writing. A mission he led at Cambridge University in 1952 represented the re-emergence of a much more scholarly and theologically credible style of evangelism. His addresses on this occasion were the foundation for *Basic Christianity*, which was to become his most widely read book.[11] He was soon in very great demand as a preacher and evangelist, particularly in

4. Ibid., 18.

5. Oliver R. Barclay, *Whatever Happened to the Jesus Lane Lot?* (Leicester: Inter-Varsity, 1977), 119.

6. Ibid., 111.

7. David L. Edwards with John R. W. Stott, *Essentials: A Liberal-Evangelical Dialogue* (London: Hodder and Stoughton, 1988), 2.

8. Ibid., 8. Catherwood, *Five Evangelical Leaders*, 22, dates this to 1961.

9. Catherwood, *Five Evangelical Leaders*, 24.

10. Randle Manwaring, *From Controversy to Co-Existence: Evangelicals in the Church of England, 1914–1980* (New York: Cambridge University Press, 1985), 110.

11. John R. W. Stott, *Basic Christianity* (Grand Rapids: Eerdmans, 1958); see also Barclay, *Whatever Happened*, 126–27. *Basic Christianity* has been translated into thirty-six languages (see Martyn Eden and David F. Wells, eds., *The Gospel in the Modern World: A Tribute to John Stott* [Leicester: Inter-Varsity, 1991], 273).

university contexts. Even at this early stage he was recognized as a leader within evangelical Anglicanism, at any rate among the younger clergy. He had natural gifts of leadership, as evidenced, for example, by his having been head boy at Rugby.[12] Another mark of these gifts was his role in resurrecting the Eclectic Society (1955). Founded in 1783 by John Newton to bring evangelical clergy together, this organization had long been defunct. In its new shape it was confined to Anglican clergy under forty years of age and was, in its early days, composed mainly of "Bash" men with an Oxford or Cambridge background.[13] It soon became more broadly based, however, and under Stott's leadership provided a forum in which younger evangelicals could debate and explore issues outside the boundaries set up by their cautious elders, who were used to a much more defensive evangelicalism. The Eclectic Society was crucial in articulating new goals for evangelicalism and giving confidence to the emerging new leadership.

By the 1960s Stott's central role within British evangelical Anglicanism was plain. His intellectual and theological capacity, his powerful and effective preaching, his visionary planning, and his capacity to create new national and international structures to embody the vision have already been noted. There were other qualities which marked him out as a leader of stature. He was, in the words of David Edwards, "a man of God, able to draw others into God's presence." Though an intellectual, Stott gave "the spiritual and the moral priority over the intellectual."[14] To those with whom he disagreed he showed a spirit of humble love which enabled him to appeal across the disparate forces within evangelicalism and to shake off the image of intolerant negativism which had too often characterized British evangelicalism in the first half of the twentieth century. He was, moreover, open to the rethinking and reformulations which marked the radical 1960s. These reformulations were hugely significant to evangelical Anglicanism, and Scott was central in their evolution. This can be seen in a number of ways.

First, Stott gave decisive direction to Anglican evangelicals when there was a major difference of opinion at the National Evangelical Assembly in October 1966. The issue was whether evangelicals should secede from their denominations when they felt that orthodox doctrine had been compromised. The nonconformist evangelical leader Martyn Lloyd-Jones urged this course of action. Stott, who was in the chair, "with much nervousness and diffidence" argued that both history and Scripture were against Lloyd-Jones's views.[15] If Stott later came to feel that he had abused the role of the chair in speaking so plainly and emotionally, his views remained unaltered.[16] That there were few who followed Lloyd-Jones's powerful call was in large part due to Stott's influence.

Second, Stott was persuaded at some stage after the World Congress on Evangelism in Berlin in 1966 that the Great Commission included "social as well as evangelistic responsibility, unless we are to be guilty of distorting the words of Jesus."[17] This meant that a new ingredient—social action—was added to doctrinal, expository preaching, which had hitherto been his hallmark.[18] This new ingredient was to become increasingly central. Under his direction a series of annual lectures by specialists on various relevant subjects began in 1974. And in 1982 he founded the London Institute for Contemporary Christianity, an

12. Catherwood, *Five Evangelical Leaders*, 16.
13. Michael Saward, *The Anglican Church Today: Evangelicals on the Move* (London: Mowbray, 1987), 32.
14. Edwards, *Essentials*, 15–16.

15. Catherwood, *Five Evangelical Leaders*, 84.
16. Christopher Catherwood, ed., *Martyn Lloyd-Jones: Chosen by God* (Westchester, Ill.: Good News, 1986), 207.
17. John R. W. Stott, *Christian Mission in the Modern World*, 2d ed. (London: Falcon, 1977), 23.
18. Catherwood, *Five Evangelical Leaders*, 28.

action that a couple of years later led to a detailed study of some of the most intractable ethical and social problems of the time.[19]

Third, and related to the first two considerations, was Stott's role in the National Evangelical Anglican Congresses (Keele, 1967; Nottingham, 1977; and Caisters, 1988). It is universally recognized that Keele marked a watershed for English Anglican evangelicalism, and that Stott's role as chairman was decisive in enabling the younger evangelicals to have a major voice. The result was a statement which marked new directions: penitence for the individualism of the past; commitment to the present and future of the Church of England; renunciation of secession; endorsement of dialogue with other traditions; determination to work through the ethical implications of evangelical doctrines, "not only for the redemption of individuals but also for a reformation of society"; and making "a weekly celebration of the sacrament . . . the central corporate service of the church."[20] This was, judges Adrian Hastings, "one of the most important ecclesiastical documents not only of the sixties but of this century," for it "greatly altered the Evangelical sense of direction."[21] At Nottingham, Stott was still central and enunciated the concern of the congress to apply the "truthfulness of Scripture [to] complex contemporary questions"; at the same time he acknowledged with characteristic humility and realism that the main contributors were "sometimes less than sure" in their understanding of how this should happen.[22] If in the experiential, more self-consciously charismatic atmosphere of

Caisters he remained formally central, but in reality more peripheral than he had previously been, he had played a key role in the emergence of the annual Anglican Evangelical Assembly.

Fourth, Stott came to terms, though rather uneasily, with the charismatic movement. Having encountered the movement in its early manifestations in English Anglicanism through his curate Michael Harper, Stott disavowed it in 1964.[23] In the 1970s, however, he came to a practical rapprochement. Though his theological views did not change, he came to see that he had been "too negative" and "too reluctant to meet its leaders and talk with them."[24] His tempered acceptance of the movement was evidenced by his signing a joint statement of charismatic and noncharismatic English Anglican leaders in 1977.[25] Though the document did not achieve agreement in detail, it did indicate a great deal of goodwill and understanding, which was surely significant in preventing a greater fissure over the issue. Stott now acknowledged that the charismatic movement had been beneficial to many and was "a healthy challenge to all mediocre Christian living and all stuffy church life."[26] He seemed prepared to "suspend judgement" on some charismatic manifestations and experiences, provided that they did not entail anything contrary to Scripture and that they were "beneficial to the believer and edifying to the church."[27]

Meanwhile, freed in 1970 from the day-to-day duties of pastoring a church, Stott became an increasingly major figure on the stage of world evangelicalism and Christianity. He developed tools for his vision, which had long been far wider than the

19. John R. W. Stott, *Issues Facing Christians Today* (Basingstoke: Marshalls, 1984); in 1992 the institute was renamed Christian Impact.

20. Philip Crowe, ed., *Keele '67: The National Evangelical Anglican Congress Statement* (London: Falcon, 1967), 19ff.

21. Adrian Hastings, *A History of English Christianity, 1920–1985* (London: Collins, 1986), 554.

22. John R. W. Stott, ed., *Obeying Christ in a Changing World*, 3 vols. (Glasgow: Collins, 1977), 1:7.

23. David Bebbington, *Evangelicalism in Modern Britain: A History from the 1730s to the 1980s* (London: Unwin Hyman, 1989), 247.

24. John R. W. Stott, *Baptism and Fullness: The Work of the Holy Spirit Today*, 2d ed. (Downers Grove, Ill.: Inter-Varsity, 1976), 9.

25. "Gospel and Spirit," *Churchman* 91 (1977): 102–13.

26. Stott, *Baptism and Fullness*, 7.

27. Ibid., 73.

Church of England and indeed Anglicanism. The Langham Trust, which was set up in 1969, enabled Stott to travel widely, particularly in the Third World; it gave to potential Third World Christian leaders scholarships for doctoral work at British centers of academic excellence; and it provided funds for educational, medical, and social needs in the Third World.[28] In 1971 Stott created the Evangelical Literature Trust to distribute Christian literature in Third World and Eastern European countries. The initial funding came from Stott's book royalties, but in time came from many other sources. By 1990 books with a face value of £1.2 million were distributed.[29] All this was in addition to Stott's international initiatives through the Evangelical Fellowship in the Anglican Communion, which, in addition to strategic planning, played a substantial role in providing scholarships and distributing literature.[30]

Even more important has been Stott's role as a sort of unaccredited international ecclesiastical statesman. Sir Arnold Stott had wanted his son to join the diplomatic service—and with some reason, as John demonstrated when playing "the role of diplomat in many evangelical gatherings."[31] His most telling contribution was at the Lausanne Congress on World Evangelization (1974). Here was a stage where evangelicals were separated not only by national but also by church boundaries, where there were many who had withdrawn from traditional denominations because of perceived compromises, and who were deeply hostile

to the sort of ecumenical dialogue to which Keele had committed evangelical Anglicans. In this situation Stott was very influential as a theologian, speaker, president of the commission which produced the final draft of the Lausanne Covenant, and chairman of a follow-up committee, the Lausanne Theological and Education Group. It was, Hastings judges, because of him "that the Lausanne Covenant avoided a commitment to the verbal inspiration of Scripture, made social action a partner of evangelism, and stressed—instead of individual and undenominational evangelism—the collective responsibility of the visible Church." This was all the more remarkable, Hastings argues, as none of these positions was particularly congenial to mainline American evangelicals.[32] It is not possible at this stage in time and without access to Lausanne primary sources to assess the accuracy of this judgment. It has a general plausibility, though it will become clear that Stott's own view of Scripture is broadly that of conservative evangelicalism as defined in the Chicago Statement. Moreover, there were many other voices speaking urgently for the emphases which are said to have emerged thanks to him. It is certain, however, that he did have a key role in drafting the covenant. Christopher Catherwood's judgment that Stott bridged the divide between the traditionalists, who trusted him because of his commitment to evangelism and his "known devotion to the exposition of the Word of God," and the radicals, who respected him because of his "evident concern for the poor and oppressed," has an authentic ring to it.[33]

Stott so closely intertwines reflection and action that it is impossible to look at his theology without paying close attention to the context in which it has been hammered out. Though intellectually very gifted, he has never been motivated to be an academic. He is self-confessedly "by temperament an activist," and his work has been

---

28. In 1974 it established a sister charity in the United States, the Langham Foundation; similar developments subsequently took place in Canada (1978) and Australia (1979).

29. Through agreements with publishers and authors, the Evangelical Literature Trust can often purchase books at a price substantially below their face value.

30. At the time of this writing, it had given 117 scholarships, which have enabled foreign students, sponsored by their home churches, to pursue further theological study in Britain. Many of them now occupy key positions in those churches.

31. Catherwood, *Five Evangelical Leaders*, 20.

32. Hastings, *English Christianity*, 616.

33. Catherwood, *Five Evangelical Leaders*, 42.

driven by evangelistic, pastoral, and ethical concerns.[34] His books, then, have not pressed back the frontiers for theologians. They have, instead, sought to make the Scriptures accessible in a way which takes seriously but not slavishly the contribution of theologians; and recently, at any rate, they have sought to explore in some depth the biblical message for today's world. They mix passionate conviction with open-minded exploration, a deep conservatism in regard to the biblical text with a sometimes adventurous radicalism in relation to its application, and occasionally a surprisingly savage rejection of positions he regards as false with a generally irenic disposition towards those who hold them. Thus he combines the urgency of the evangelist, the conviction of the dogmatic theologian who is also a pastor, the generosity of a wide-ranging churchman who has discovered unexpected affinities with those he once took to be implacable opponents, some of the caution of an upper-middle-class English diplomat, much of the charm of an instinctive persuader, the considerable self-awareness of a person who is both brave and humble enough to acknowledge having much to repent of and much to learn, and the unself-conscious love that results from an unusually close relationship with the Lord. This is a most effective combination which has ensured that his books, articles, and contributions to conferences have been as popular with committed and serious evangelical church members as they have been largely ignored by most academic theologians.

Doctrine of Scripture

There is no doubt that the starting place for understanding Stott's theology must be his doctrine of Scripture. He most definitely does not subscribe to the theory of mechanical dictation; on the contrary, he is much concerned to stress that the "background, convictions and gifts [of the biblical authors] were fully and freely expressed

in what they said and wrote." But if God did not destroy their personality, "neither did their personality destroy God's inspiration."[35] He is the source of Scripture. It is therefore true and, to quote the Lausanne Covenant, "without error in all that it affirms."[36] In the end the clinching argument is Christ's attitude toward Scripture—inasmuch as "He endorsed the authority of Scripture, we are bound to conclude that His authority and Scripture's authority either stand or fall together."[37]

Stott is, however, determined not to be considered a fundamentalist. This is primarily because of fundamentalism's tendency toward the view that God actually dictated the Scriptures, which undermines the human element. The dictation theory insufficiently emphasizes the fact that the Bible is both a human and divine book. There is a "dual authorship."[38] Because it is human, the Bible must be studied critically. Consequently, Stott has no problems in principle with the approach of biblical criticism, though he may often disagree with its presuppositions and conclusions. While he defends the role of biblical criticism, he takes a very high view of the divine in Scripture and is prepared to align himself with the inerrantists, provided that the phrases "as originally given" and "as correctly interpreted" are inserted as qualifiers. At the same time, and this is typical of the breadth of the man, he is very anxious not to cause polarization with evangelicals who hold a somewhat less rigorous position.[39]

All this opens up the question of interpretation, which Stott clearly regards as of the very first importance. Here the dangers of dependency on reason or on tradition, rather than submission to biblical author-

34. Ibid., 24.

35. C. René Padilla, ed., *The New Face of Evangelicalism: An International Symposium on the Lausanne Covenant* (London: Hodder and Stoughton, 1976), 36.
36. Ibid., 37.
37. John R. W. Stott, *Understanding the Bible* (London: Scripture Union, 1972), 190.
38. Ibid., 185.
39. Edwards, *Essentials*, 95, 101.

ity, loom large for all—including evangelicals.[40] If there is a proper submission to its authority, then the power of the Bible will be released. That means reading the Bible expectantly and trusting to hear what it says rather than depending on extrabiblical visions and revelations.[41] It also means a commitment to expository preaching.[42]

This basic position of submission to the authority of Scripture has been unchanged throughout Stott's ministry. It was evident, for example, at Keele.[43] Where there has been significant movement is in the understanding of the importance of interpretation and in particular the role of culture. This does not seem to have been a dominant subject in his earlier works; rather we find an emphasis on the Holy Spirit's guidance to the individual combined with a rather grudging acknowledgment that the church must have a place provided that it does not undermine the Reformers' insistence on "the right of private judgment," and a commendation of the use of our "rational and critical powers."[44] After Lausanne the emphasis is increasingly that God uses "the cultural background of the biblical writers in order to convey through each a message appropriate to them as real people in real situations."[45] It is therefore crucially important to allow the various cultures to apprehend the Word which is particularly fitting for them. The gospel cannot be precisely packaged, but must be delivered with great sensitivity both to the leading of the Spirit and to the existential situation.[46] Accordingly, in the words of the Willowbank Report, which came out of the Lausanne committee chaired by Stott, "the church must be allowed to indigenize itself, and to 'celebrate, sing and dance' the

gospel in its own cultural medium."[47] At the same time he warns that this must not lead to provincialism that is adrift from the church and the rest of the world. Indeed, though his evangelical suspicion of tradition remains apparent, he does seem open to taking it seriously if it is understood as progressing and developing. He speaks, for example, of the continuing illumination of the Holy Spirit and its "progressively clarifying the church's mind on the great doctrines of Scripture"; he also implies that the twentieth-century church enjoys a richer heritage than did any previous generation.[48]

Emphasis on the Cross

If "we bow to the authority of Scripture because we bow to the authority of Christ," we make the cross the center of our Christian understanding, for it "stood at the centre of Jesus' own perspective."[49] Stott's weightiest book is devoted to this theme and, in particular, to the contention that the atonement is to be understood objectively.[50] In his explication he vigorously defends the concepts of substitution, satisfaction, and propitiation.[51] He views sin with the utmost seriousness, defining it as an active "refusing to acknowledge and obey [God] as our Creator and Lord."[52] It is an individual responsibility. We are morally responsible agents whose sin is incompatible with God's holiness.[53] Stott rejects as unproven C. H. Dodd's and Anthony Hanson's descriptions of God's wrath as imper-

40. Padilla, *New Face*, 39.
41. Ibid., 41.
42. Ibid., 42.
43. J. I. Packer, ed., *Guidelines: Anglican Evangelicals Face the Future* (London: Falcon, 1967), 42.
44. Stott, *Understanding*, 214, 212.
45. Padilla, *New Face*, 44–45.
46. Edwards, *Essentials*, 330.

47. Lausanne Committee for World Evangelization, "The Willowbank Report: Gospel and Culture," Lausanne Occasional Papers, no. 2 (Wheaton, Ill.: Lausanne Committee for World Evangelization, 1978), 26–27.
48. Padilla, *New Face*, 47.
49. Stott, *Understanding*, 203; John R. W. Stott, *The Cross of Christ* (Downers Grove, Ill.: Inter-Varsity, 1986), 25.
50. Stott, *Cross*, 9.
51. Ibid., 10.
52. Ibid., 90.
53. Ibid., 95, 102.

sonal.[54] Writing powerfully of the incompatibility of divine holiness and human sin, he suggests that a major contemporary problem is the failure to take sin seriously.[55] He quotes approvingly R. W. Dale's judgment: "It is partly because sin does not provoke our own wrath, that we do not believe that sin provokes the wrath of God."[56]

God's answer to sin was the atoning death of Christ, and the key to understanding what it achieved is substitution. Stott rejects any suggestion, however, that Christ appeased a wrathful God. Rather, God and Christ took "the initiative together to save sinners."[57] Thus our substitute is neither God alone, nor Christ alone, "but *God in Christ,* who was truly and fully both God and man, and who, on that account, was uniquely qualified to represent both God and man and to mediate between them."[58] This removes, Stott argues, any sense of immorality from substitutionary atonement, "since the substitute for the law-breakers is none other than the divine Lawmaker himself."[59] Yet Stott also contends that there was a moment of dereliction reflected in the cry, "My God, my God, why have you forsaken me?" (Mark 15:34 NIV). This was real separation, but a separation "voluntarily accepted by both the Father and the Son."[60] Substitution, then, is central to understanding the atonement, but it is a substitution in which God is totally involved. The cross "smashes to smithereens" any idea of God's enjoying the suffering of the world, for on the cross he himself entered into its suffering. "We are not to envisage Him on a deck-chair, but on a cross. The God who allows us to suffer, once suffered himself in Christ, and continues to suffer with us and for us today."[61] Stott of course uses other terms—propitiation, redemption, justification, reconciliation—but he argues that substitution is not a parallel to them, "but rather the foundation of them all, without which each lacks cogency."[62]

Not surprisingly, such an uncompromising defense of an unpopular doctrine has opened Stott to severe criticism. David Edwards, for example, asks why if substitution is the heart of the gospel, it is not so categorized in the Gospels.[63] Indeed, he declares that the idea of God's "sacrificing himself to himself [is] not only inexplicable but also incomprehensible."[64] Stott's reply is typical: gently pointing out a misrepresentation of what he had said (his actual words were, "God's satisfying himself by substituting himself for us"), he goes back to the biblical evidence and argues that only the concept of substitution satisfactorily explains it; all other attempts at explanation fail to provide "a radical enough remedy for my needs."[65] He thus contends that the concept of substitution is not meaningless.[66]

Emphasis on Preaching and Evangelism

Stott's emphasis on preaching and evangelism flows naturally from the cross: "The gospel is in essence the good news of Christ crucified," and it is ever the task of the preacher to bring the cross "out of the past and into the present."[67] Stott characterizes himself as "an impenitent believer in the indispensable necessity of preaching both for evangelism and for the healthy growth of the church."[68] Preaching is, in essence, "making known the Name of the Lord."[69] The con-

54. Ibid., 105.
55. Ibid., 108.
56. Ibid., 109.
57. Ibid., 151.
58. Ibid., 156.
59. Ibid., 159.
60. Ibid., 81.
61. Ibid., 329.

62. Ibid., 168.
63. Edwards, *Essentials,* 129, 139.
64. Ibid., 152.
65. Ibid., 166, 168.
66. Ibid., 166.
67. Ibid., 343.
68. John R. W. Stott, *I Believe in Preaching* (London: Hodder and Stoughton, 1982), 9.
69. Ibid., 82.

temporary disenchantment with preaching is the result of a loss of confidence in the gospel. There needs to be less concern for what modern individuals have to say to the church, and more concern for what the church has to say to them.[70] Stott has great confidence in the appeal of the Bible: "For whenever the Bible is truly and systematically expounded, God uses it to give his people the vision without which they perish."[71] This declaring of the truth of the Word is above all the task of the pastor.[72] Demanding much in the way of time, intellect, resources, and prayer, it must be followed by appropriate application.[73] Such commitment is demonstrated in Stott's joint editorship of The Bible Speaks Today series and in his personal contribution of six New Testament commentaries to it.

We have already suggested that Stott's recent writings give a greater emphasis to contemporary culture. He admits that his practice in the past was "to expound the biblical text and leave the application largely to the Holy Spirit."[74] He now speaks of throwing bridges across the "broad and deep divide of two thousand years of changing culture."[75] This means understanding both the ancient and the modern world. It also means making greater rather than fewer demands on congregations. Too often, he judges, people come to church "with their problems, and they leave with their problems. The sermon has not spoken to their need."[76] Stott's vision for preaching is underpinned by a fundamental conviction about human rationality. The intelligence of the congregation must not be underestimated:

My plea is that we treat them as real people with real questions; that we grapple in

our sermons with real issues; and that we build bridges into the real world in which they live and love, work and play, laugh and weep, struggle and suffer, grow old and die. We have to provoke them to think about their life in all its moods, to challenge them to make Jesus Christ the Lord of every area of it, and to demonstrate his contemporary relevance.[77]

In all this there is a recurring emphasis on recovering "the lost Christian mind."[78] Here the influence of Harry Blamires is evident.[79] Blamires had stressed the degree to which Christians have come to accept secular attitudes and have lost the framework of Christian presuppositions.[80] Stott pleads for a restoration of that framework, a balanced emphasis on creation, the fall, redemption, and the coming consummation. This can be achieved only by weekly preaching which features these teachings.

Emphasis on Social Issues

A natural extension of such preaching is to apply the Christian message to both personal ethics and sociopolitical issues. As far as general personal ethics are concerned, Stott is somewhat withering about the way some Christians have "pitifully trivialised" the real problems by an unhealthy concentration on insignificant matters relating to worldliness.[81] Such matters are microethics in comparison with the really significant issues that must be dealt with. The gospel has consequences for Christian behavior. These consequences must be spelled out in preaching; to do so is "neither legalism nor pharisaism but plain apostolic Christianity."[82]

Stott then moves on to social and political issues. These, too, should be dealt with—and from the pulpit. Stott is clear

70. Ibid., 89.
71. Ibid., 113.
72. Ibid., 120.
73. John R. W. Stott, *The Preacher's Portrait: Some New Testament Word Studies* (Grand Rapids: Eerdmans, 1961), 31.
74. Stott, *I Believe*, 141.
75. Ibid., 138.
76. Ibid., 145–46.

77. Ibid., 147.
78. Ibid., 170.
79. Catherwood, *Five Evangelical Leaders*, 28; Stott, *Issues*, 32ff.; Stott, *I Believe*, 170–73.
80. Stott, *Issues*, 33.
81. Stott, *I Believe*, 155.
82. Ibid., 158.

that, when taken together, several of the basic doctrines of Christianity (God is Creator, Lawgiver, Lord, and Judge; humans are of unique worth because they are made in God's image; Christ identifies with humankind and calls Christians to identify with others; salvation involves radical transformation; and the church should be at once distinct from the world and able to penetrate it for Christ) constitute "the biblical basis for mission, for both evangelistic and social responsibility. They lay upon us our obligation to be involved in the life of the world."[83] Because they do that, there is inevitably a responsibility on the preacher "to open up the biblical principles which relate to the problems of contemporary society, in such a way as to help everybody to develop a Christian judgment about them, and to inspire and encourage the opinion-formers and policy-makers in the congregation, who occupy influential positions in public life, to apply these biblical principles to their professional life."[84]

When sociopolitical issues are deeply controversial, they must not be ignored (the way of the coward) or presented in a partisan way (a misuse of the pulpit). Rather, the aim should be to enunciate the biblical principles in such a way that the preacher's own position is clear, but the congregation is given space to form their own opinions according to those principles.[85] There is a strong duty on the local church to develop "a prophetic ministry to proclaim the law of God and to teach justice . . . to be the conscience of the community . . . to help the [members of the church] develop a Christian mind, so that [they] may learn to think Christianly even about controversial questions."[86]

All this demands close and detailed work on the issues of the day, a task from which Stott does not shrink. His chosen style, which is wholly typical of his character, is "the strategy of 'persuasion' by argument."[87] In a non-Christian, pluralist society, this strategy, instead of laying down laws (whether biblical or any other kind) authoritatively, involves arguing "the intrinsic truth and value of a thing which is self-evident and therefore self-authenticating."[88] All humans have an inkling of God's law; arguments need to be deployed to show that its aim is one's own well-being and that of society.[89] Quite often these arguments will appeal to self-interest, but that is to be expected and is indeed necessary. Stott quotes William Temple approvingly: "The art of government in fact is the art of so ordering life that self-interest prompts what justice demands."[90] A realist about politics, Stott recognizes that those who are involved in public life will often have to use ad hominem arguments, "and in the policies they develop they will have to be content with reality."[91] Christians who live in democratic societies are particularly advantaged because democracy "reflects the balanced biblical view of man"; it is "the political expression of 'persuasion' by argument." Ideally, in calling for discussion, criticism, and compromise, democracy involves more people in decisions and is concerned with the interests of all rather than of a faction or a party.[92]

Stott remains hopeful about what can be achieved. While secular society succumbs to feelings of alienation and helplessness, many Christians, he laments, fall into line with a tendency to pessimism. For this pessimism they have neither historical nor biblical justification. In particular the doctrine of humanity's having been created in the

83. Stott, *Issues*, 25.
84. Stott, *I Believe*, 167.
85. Ibid., 171.
86. Lausanne Committee for World Evangelization, "The Grand Rapids Report: Evangelism and Social Responsibility: An Evangelical Commitment," Lausanne Occasional Papers, no. 21 (Exeter: Paternoster, 1982), 52.
87. Stott, *Issues*, 50.
88. Ibid., 51.
89. Ibid., 52.
90. Ibid., 57.
91. Ibid., 60.
92. Ibid., 59.

image of God gives grounds for hope: "The divine image . . . has not been obliterated . . . there are non-Christian people who have good marriages, non-Christian parents who bring their children up well, non-Christian industrialists who run factories on a just basis, and non-Christian doctors who still take the Hippocratic standards as their guide and are conscientious in the care of their patients."[93] Yet this is no argument to proceed as if the task were only to rouse people to some innate sense of God's law within their hearts. The doctrine of redemption is crucial here. There is a close relationship between evangelism and social responsibility.[94] In the end, societies which have begun to accept the gospel are more likely to demonstrate social justice.[95] Stott is confident that a tiny minority of Christians can achieve a great deal.

In relation to particular questions, Stott's approach is careful, fair, judicious, and extremely well briefed. Where the Bible speaks or appears to speak with clarity, his conclusions are always in tune with it, even if that means going against the contemporary grain—as with his views on women in the ministry. Where the Bible is not clear, his views can be quite radical. He is a nuclear pacifist. He is ecologically aware.[96] A supporter of global economic cooperation and an increased voice for workers, he also protests against cultural imperialism.[97]

It follows from all that has gone before that evangelism and social action are primary concerns for Stott. He eschews any view which makes either evangelism or social action the sole goal.[98] The Great Commission in its Johannine form is the linchpin: "As thou didst send me into the world, so I have sent them into the world" (John 17:18 RSV). Jesus was sent as both Savior

and servant in such a way that it is quite impossible "to separate his works from his words."[99] If Christians are sent in the same way, it follows that they must also serve.

Emphasis on Dialogue

Evangelism, Stott stresses, is an announcement of the Good News "irrespective of the results."[100] The Good News is of course that of Jesus—his death for our sins, his resurrection, the fact that he reigns "and has authority both to command repentance and faith, and to bestow forgiveness of sins and the gift of the Spirit on all those who repent, believe and are baptized."[101] Preaching is the major means of presenting the Good News, but Stott is open to dialogue with other faiths on the grounds that Jesus was "constantly addressing questions to his hearers' minds and consciences."[102] Dialogue, however, must ever be subordinate to proclamation which has conversion as its end.[103] Unacceptable is the type of dialogue emphasizing, as does the World Council of Churches on occasion, that Christ is present in non-Christian religions to the point where it seems that the non-Christian becomes "the bearer of Christ's message to the Christian."[104]

There is, of course, a sense in which Christ is present in non-Christians. Paul makes it clear that there is a universal knowledge of God which is sufficient to render all humans without excuse. And John speaks of the Logos's being in the world long before he actually came. Because of this presence, everyone "possesses some degree of light by his reason and conscience. And we should not hesitate to claim that everything good, beautiful and true, in all history and in all the earth, has come from Jesus Christ, even though men

93. Ibid., 64.
94. See Lausanne Committee, "Evangelism and Social Responsibility."
95. Stott, *Issues*, 70.
96. Ibid., 119.
97. Edwards, *Essentials*, 239–40.
98. Stott, *Christian Mission*, 16–17.

99. Ibid., 24.
100. Ibid., 38.
101. Ibid., 54.
102. Ibid., 61.
103. Ibid., 63.
104. Ibid., 66.

are ignorant of its origin."[105] Stott hastens to add that this is not a saving light. Humans have, however, sufficient light to be responsible for their rebellion against God, even though they have not heard of Christ. When pressed on the issue of their fate, Stott is neither wholly agnostic nor certain that they will inevitably perish. He cherishes the hope "that the majority of the human race will be saved," of course citing biblical support (Luke 13:29; 1 Tim. 2:4; 2 Pet. 3:9; Rev. 7: 9).[106]

Who is to carry out the task of ministry in the world? Stott emphasizes the lay role and acknowledges the influence of the charismatic movement in bringing it back to the center.[107] Yet he is clear that overseers or pastors remain necessary in churches of any size.[108] They will work in teams, and at least some are likely to be full-time.[109] On the other hand, Stott is uneasy with the concept of priesthood because he has been unable to find any support for it in the Bible. This has been noted by friendly critics such as George Carey and is in line with Stott's general uneasiness in discussing such issues as the sacraments, the church, and tradition.[110]

Clearly, Stott values the sacraments, though many of his references to them serve only to emphasize the primacy of the Word.[111] Equally clearly the church is central in Stott's thought; after all, it is "the creation of God by his Word."[112] Yet it would be quite difficult to work out an elaborate ecclesiology from Stott's writings. We do know from his differences with Lloyd-Jones that he does not believe in a pure church. Indeed, many of his references to the church come with a sad catalogue of how

far it has departed at various times from its Word-based center. And while he maintains that the beliefs of evangelicalism are "historic, mainline, trinitarian Christianity,"[113] he retains and values fellowship with many, such as Edwards, who find difficulties in the evangelical position. His primary concern, it would seem, has been to reform the church rather than to define its boundaries.

Stott has little sympathy with the value which many place on tradition. Though he does sometimes mention it favorably as a counter to excessive evangelical individualism, these references are always heavily couched with declarations that tradition does not possess the infallibility of Scripture.[114] More particularly, reliance on tradition ignores the Reformers' insistence on the right of private judgment.[115] It is, declares Stott, "the birthright of every child of God to learn his Father's voice speaking to him directly through Scripture."[116] Here there seems to be more than an echo of nineteenth-century evangelical apologetic against Tractarian excesses.

In contrast to Stott's position, Peter Toon has argued that the right of private judgment was more likely a seventeenth-century rather than a sixteenth-century concept.[117] Certainly the Reformers saw the Word as primary, and in theory it was possible for them to be forced into a position where they had to hold to the Word against the whole church.[118] In practice, however, when they disagreed with the contemporary church, they felt assured that they, rather than the contemporary church, were in tune with the traditions of the true

105. Ibid., 68.

106. Edwards, *Essentials*, 327–28.

107. Stott, *I Believe*, 116.

108. Ibid., 116–17.

109. Ibid., 121.

110. George Carey, "Reflections upon the Nature of Ministry and Priesthood in the Light of the Lima Report," *Anvil* 3 (1986): 19 n. 2.

111. Stott, *I Believe*, 114.

112. Ibid., 109.

113. Edwards, *Essentials*, 39.

114. Padilla, *New Face*, 47.

115. Ibid., 46; Stott, *Understanding*, 214; John R. W. Stott and Basil Meeking, eds., *The Evangelical–Roman Catholic Dialogue on Mission, 1977–1984* (Grand Rapids: Eerdmans, 1986), 22.

116. Stott, *Understanding*, 214.

117. Peter Toon, *Evangelical Theology, 1833–1856: A Response to Tractarianism* (Atlanta: John Knox, 1979), 136.

118. Paul D. L. Avis, *The Church in the Theology of the Reformers* (Atlanta: John Knox, 1981), 17.

church; and they certainly resisted the tendency of some of their followers towards valuing the judgment of the individual over that of the church with its long-held and deep understanding of the biblical revelation. It was the view of the Reformers that the Bible had primacy and was in continuity with much church tradition; accordingly, no individual plowman ignorant of the long and painful battles for doctrinal understanding should pit his judgment, however much apparently formed under Scripture, against that of the church.

It is perhaps significant that when Stott engages in dialogue with Roman Catholics, issues such as the sacraments, the church, and tradition do not seem to loom large. While there may be an emphasis in Stott on understanding Scripture within a community context,[119] the areas of meaningful dialogue seem to be biblical authority, mission, salvation, and the relationship between the gospel and culture. This is not surprising because it is in these areas that Stott's strengths lie.

A Practical Rapprochement with the Charismatic Movement

We have already noted that Stott came to a practical acceptance of the charismatic movement without abandoning his theological reservations. His fundamental objection was that Spirit baptism was regarded as an addition to the initial experience of salvation in Christ.[120] All Christians by definition have experienced Spirit baptism, though there is a constant need to be filled with the Spirit, for "the fullness of the Spirit is to be continuously appropriated by faith."[121] The chief evidence thereof will be one's moral life rather

than miraculous gifts, the Spirit's fruit rather than the Spirit's gifts, a desire for fellowship and worship rather than any particular dramatic manifestation.[122]

A problem with dramatic manifestations is that their origin and nature are not always clear. They may be demonic, they may be psychologically induced; on the other hand, they may be analogous to conversion experiences, or they may be an authentic deeper experience of God. He can come in varied and fresh ways appropriate to different personalities and thus fill his people with a love for him—Father, Son, and Holy Spirit.[123] Stott is concerned that these experiences not be stereotyped by a few zealous souls, for though God may sometimes grant such experiences, they are certainly not necessary to the Christian life.[124]

What is crucial to the Christian life is the fruit of spiritual growth. This demands discipline and personal endeavor and can be achieved only gradually. Nonetheless, special gifts are important for the diverse ministry of the church. They will be varied, more often in continuity than in discontinuity with one's natural gifts, and may occasionally be miraculous. Miraculous gifts will be quite rare, however, because by definition miracles are "a creative deviation from God's normal and natural ways of working."[125] Furthermore, miracles were intended to authenticate the four main vehicles of God's special revelation—the law, the prophets, the Lord, and the apostles—all of which lie in the past; there can therefore be no expectation of frequent miracles today.[126] In regard to contemporary manifestations Stott advocates open-minded inquiry. He reserves the word *prophet*, however, for those who had a role in God's special revelation before that revelation was completed, for this is the biblical understanding of the term. He also main-

119. Stott and Meeking, *Evangelical–Roman Catholic Dialogue*, 22.
120. David Neff and George K. Brushaber, "The Remaking of English Evangelicalism: Signs, Wonders, and Worries in the Land of Canterbury," *Christianity Today*, 5 February 1990, p. 26; Stott, *Baptism and Fullness*, 10.
121. Stott, *Baptism and Fullness*, 43–44, 54.

122. Ibid., 54–55.
123. Ibid., 66–67.
124. Ibid., 71.
125. Ibid., 96.
126. Ibid., 98.

tains that the New Testament tongues were communications in other languages rather than ecstatic utterances, and that there is no benefit to tongues without a translation.[127]

All this amounts to placing substantial question marks over the current charismatic movement. At the same time we have noted that Stott now acknowledges that the movement can bring blessing; clearly, he values its emphasis on the ministry of every member and indeed sees its protest against clericalism as one of the main factors in its growth.[128] In all of this discussion Stott reveals his commitment to Scripture, using all the powers of reason that God has given him, and yet we also see the fair-mindedness and graciousness which are his hallmark. Nonetheless, Stott's stance here, perhaps more than on any other issue, shows that he is more comfortable with the Puritan, Reformed tradition of evangelicalism than with Pietism, Keswick, and the charismatic movement. The former, in the shape that it has taken since the late eighteenth century, owes much to the Enlightenment; the latter, to the Romantic movement.[129] Stott is, in this sense, an "Enlightenment man"; that is, he takes reason and a belief in a God of order as his starting place. David Bebbington observes that Stott's career is evidence that evangelicalism has embraced rather than discarded the most admirable values of the Enlightenment, including "scientific investigation, hope for the future and humane reform"; indeed, "the career of John Stott is an enduring monument [to the principle that these] do not stand opposed to evangelical religion."[130] The assessment of Stott as an Enlightenment man also explains some of his problems with the experiential emphasis of the charismatic movement. It is surely highly significant

that Stott asserts, in the course of a discussion on tongues, that the biblical God "is a rational God and does not delight in irrationality or unintelligibility."[131]

Influence

John Stott is a rare combination of preacher, teacher, pastor, evangelist, church statesman and diplomat, strategic planner and creative administrator, theologian, and ambassador for Christ. He must surely be placed alongside Charles Simeon as one of the most positive, creative, and formative leaders of English Anglican evangelicalism during the last two hundred years. This influence has done much to create and nurture the present strength of evangelicalism within the Church of England. It is not surprising, then, that Edwards considers him to be "apart from William Temple . . . the most influential clergyman in the Church of England during the twentieth century."[132]

Assessing Stott's role in the worldwide church is more difficult. Manifestly, he has had great influence in the English-speaking world and those countries which have been evangelized by missionaries from that world. His inspiration and support of church leaders in less developed countries, combined with the immensely practical aid that he has organized (particularly, high-level theological study), may come to be regarded as one of his most enduring contributions. Because he decided not to be the official representative of a particular church, but a spokesman for worldwide evangelicalism, he has not had the decisive role in great international and ecumenical gatherings that might otherwise have been possible. On the other hand, his calls for a consistent reliance on biblical authority, a passionate commitment to evangelism, an engagement with the many-sided dilemmas in God's world, and

127. Ibid., 112–13.
128. Ibid., 104.
129. Bebbington, *Evangelicalism*, 50–55, 167–69.
130. Cited in Eden and Wells, *Gospel in the Modern World*, 78.

131. Stott, *Baptism and Fullness*, 113.
132. Edwards, *Essentials*, 1.

a careful creation of the structures necessary to draw evangelicals together and to effect practical policies have wielded considerable influence. In all this he has been a voice of authority, but also of calm, open, enlightened reason and common sense.

The true extent of Stott's long-term influence will be evident only when the future course of the charismatic movement becomes clear. Will it be absorbed into evangelicalism and the church at large, adding depth and richness, but not undermining fundamental convictions about authority, preaching, and the role of the Christian mind? Or will it, as Stott at times appears to fear, subvert most of the principles for which he has stood?[133] Nothing, however, can take away from his immediate impact. That a rather patrician upper-middle-class Englishman with a high view of biblical authority and a wholehearted commitment to godly reason and to careful organization has been such a mighty force in a world that is suspicious of inherited privilege, reluctant to acknowledge authority, inclined to be dismissive of structure, and more concerned to follow the immediate instincts of the heart than to engage in the hard work necessary for a true understanding of the Word and its implications for the world, is one of the modern miracles of the Lord.

---

133. See Neff and Brushaber, "Remaking," 26.

Primary Sources

Stott, John R. W. *Baptism and Fullness: The Work of the Holy Spirit Today.* 2d ed. Downers Grove, Ill.: Inter-Varsity, 1976.

_____. *Basic Christianity.* Grand Rapids: Eerdmans, 1958. Rev. ed. London: Inter-Varsity, 1971.

_____. *Christian Mission in the Modern World.* 2d ed. London: Falcon, 1977.

_____. *The Cross of Christ.* Downers Grove, Ill.: Inter-Varsity, 1986.

_____. "A Fresh Look at Ministry in the New Testament." *Proceedings of the Anglican Evangelical Assembly* 1 (1983): 19–33.

_____. *I Believe in Preaching.* London: Hodder and Stoughton, 1982.

_____. *Issues Facing Christians Today.* Basingstoke: Marshalls, 1984.

_____. *The Preacher's Portrait: Some New Testament Word Studies.* Grand Rapids: Eerdmans, 1961.

_____. *Understanding the Bible.* London: Scripture Union, 1972.

_____, and Basil Meeking, eds. *The Evangelical–Roman Catholic Dialogue on Mission, 1977–1984.* Grand Rapids: Eerdmans, 1986.

Secondary Sources

Catherwood, Christopher. *Five Evangelical Leaders.* Wheaton, Ill.: Harold Shaw, 1985.

Eden, Martyn, and David F. Wells, eds. *The Gospel in the Modern World: A Tribute to John Stott.* Leicester: Inter-Varsity, 1991.

Edwards, David L., with John R. W. Stott. *Essentials: A Liberal-Evangelical Dialogue.* London: Hodder and Stoughton, 1988.

Robert D. Preus

Kurt E. Marquart

Robert David Preus, Lutheran theologian, churchman, and seminary president, was born on October 16, 1924, in St. Paul, Minnesota, the youngest son of the then governor, Jacob ("Jake") A. O. Preus. It is above all to his parents, under God, that Robert Preus attributes both his love of theology as a living knowledge of God in Christ and his corresponding keen concern for the salvation of a lost humanity through faithful mission work.

Our opening remarks have already sketched Preus as, in broad terms, an evangelical. Perhaps a clarification is in order. We may distinguish at least three layers of meaning in the term *evangelical:* (1) The word was used of those who by virtue of the Reformation had rediscovered the gospel (evangel) of full and free salvation solely through faith in Jesus Christ.[1] (2) In nineteenth-century Germany "evangelical" denoted the Lutheran-Calvinist alliance against the growing influence of Roman Catholicism.[2] (3) In modern America "evangelical" generally denotes an interdenominational but basically Reformed

or Arminian conservatism regarding Christ and Holy Scripture. People who hold to this position stress "evangelistic" outreach in the style of, say, Billy Graham, and are often millennialist in orientation.

A glance at Preus's bibliography confirms that he qualifies as an evangelical in what amounts to an overlap of senses (1) and (3).[3] Along with an evident zeal for mis-

1. The Lutheran *Book of Concord*, ed. Theodore G. Tappert (Philadelphia: Muhlenberg, 1959), uses this sense of the word when it speaks of "Evangelical churches and schools" (p. 506).

2. An American transplant of this German usage appears in the title *Evangelical Catechism* (Minneapolis: Augsburg, 1982). Robert Preus castigated this catechism for equivocating not only on the traditional interconfessional differences (e.g., on the sacraments), but on all articles of faith, including such basics as the virgin birth, miracles, the atonement, the resurrection, the divinity of Christ, and the Trinity: "Nowhere in the entire book which is entitled the *Evangelical Catechism* are we told unequivocally what the Gospel is. How tragic! How utterly tragic!" (*Affirm* 9.8 [April 1983]: 7).

3. "Robert D. Preus: Bibliography," *Springfielder* 38.2 (Sept. 1974): 95–98; "Robert D. Preus: A Bibliography 1974–1984," *Concordia Theological Quarterly* 49.2–3 (April–July 1985): 83–85. *Concordia Theological Quarterly* is the continuation of the *Springfielder*.

sions, his work has focused largely on the central core of the gospel—the atonement and justification—and on biblical authority, including inerrancy. While it is true that the confessional, sacramental, churchly dimension associated with sense (1) does not ordinarily characterize sense (3), there have of late been signs that many Christians who are evangelicals in sense (3) are yearning for the wholeness of sense (1).[4] For Preus himself "evangelical" and "confessional" are as a matter of course not opposites but twins.[5]

Preus's life and ministry fall into three very distinct phases: (1) the early years (1924–1957); (2) professorship at Concordia Seminary in St. Louis (1957–1974); and (3) presidency of Concordia Seminary in Springfield (Ill.) and Fort Wayne (1974–1993). Of these the last two will for obvious reasons receive the major emphasis in the present overview. We will find that Preus's story is inextricably intertwined with that of the Lutheran Church–Missouri Synod in our time, and specifically that there are direct correlations between his St. Louis and Springfield–Fort Wayne periods, and the two major theological crises which confronted that church body during those years.

The Early Years

Robert Preus was the second son of Governor Jacob Preus and Idella Haugen Preus to survive infancy. Twin boys had been born in 1910, but lived only a few months. Robert's older brother Jacob ("Jack") was born in 1920. The newborn Robert and his brother Jack were both featured with their

father in the *Minneapolis Star* as a part of the 1924 Christmas Seal campaign. Having failed in his bid to succeed the late Senator Knute Nelson in Washington, D.C., the elder Preus retired from politics in 1925, when his second gubernatorial term was up. The family moved to Chicago in 1925, where Jake Preus devoted himself successfully to insurance work. He regarded his cofounding of the Lutheran Brotherhood insurance giant as the crowning achievement of his life.

Young Robert took both his primary and his secondary education in the public schools of his neighborhood. His father was a devout and loving man with intense moral convictions. Having himself scrupulously paid off debts for relatives who found themselves unable to do so, Jake Preus impressed upon his sons the absolute necessity of honest dealings. One incident particularly burnt itself into Robert's memory. Together with some friends young Robert, then nine years old, had stolen from the local Woolworth and then denied his guilt. Thereupon his father told him that his stealing and lying would have to be cured in reform school. The boy was told to pack a few belongings. After doing so, he was taken to the railway station and put on a train. Only at that point did the father relent and take his remorseful son home.

The Preuses numbered among their ancestors in Norway many clergymen, including a headmaster at the Cathedral School in Kristiansand. Herman Amberg Preus (1825–1894), Robert's great-grandfather, immigrated to the United States, where he helped to found the old Norwegian Lutheran Synod in 1853 and eventually became its president. His son, Christian Keyser Preus, became president of Luther College in Decorah, Iowa. When congratulated by a little celebration in front of his house upon his son Jake's inauguration as governor of Minnesota, Christian Preus replied that he was proud—but would have been even prouder had his son been or-

4. *The Orthodox Evangelicals*, ed. Robert Webber and Donald G. Bloesch (Nashville: Thomas Nelson, 1978).

5. In the first sentence of his foreword to Kurt E. Marquart, *Anatomy of an Explosion: A Theological Analysis of the Missouri Synod Conflict* (Grand Rapids: Baker, 1978), Preus characterizes the account that is to follow as "the story of a large, confessional church body gradually, almost imperceptibly but seemingly irrevocably, losing its evangelical and confessional character" (p. iii).

dained into the ministry![6] Both of the governor's sons did in fact become pastors, and he was immensely proud of both, writing to Robert in 1944: "Mother and I should be the happiest people in the world if we could raise such fine boys and their father is such a rascal."[7]

After graduating from Luther College with his B.A. degree, Robert entered Luther Theological Seminary in St. Paul, where his uncle Herman Preus served as a professor. This seminary, like Luther College, belonged to the Norwegian Lutheran Church of America, the large merger of 1917. A minority group with leanings toward the Lutheran Church–Missouri Synod had declined to join the merger and formed the Evangelical Lutheran Synod. Both Preus brothers found the seminary atmosphere oppressive, laden with theological compromise, evasion, and indifference. Shortly before graduation, Robert transferred to Bethany Lutheran Seminary, which the Evangelical Lutheran Synod had recently established in Mankato; and in 1947 he became its first graduate.

Ordained in October 1947, Robert Preus served congregations in Mayville, North Dakota, and Bygland, Minnesota, for two years. In 1948 he married Donna Rockman, and the couple were ultimately blessed with ten children and over forty grandchildren. In 1949 he entered the University of Minnesota for further academic work. He then went to the University of Edinburgh, where in 1952 he completed his first doctorate (Ph.D.).

After Edinburgh, Preus was called to the Evangelical Lutheran Synod's Harvard Street Church in Cambridge, Massachusetts. Three years later he accepted a call to serve three small congregations near Fosston, Minnesota. Then came a major change. In 1955 both Jack and Robert had supported the Evangelical Lutheran Synod's

suspension of relations with the Missouri Synod on account of the latter's developing liberalism. Later both brothers joined the Missouri Synod, Robert as instructor at Concordia Seminary in St. Louis (1957), and Jack at Concordia Seminary in Springfield (1958). Much has been made of this apparent about-face, as though it meant a surrender of theological integrity to practical church politics.[8] Subsequent history does not bear out this interpretation. The Preus brothers had changed not their theological principles, but their assessment of the Missouri Synod. It is one thing when youthful idealism is strangled by self-seeking; it is quite another when idealism ill informed is tempered by idealism better informed. A realistic and charitable assumption is that Jack and Robert Preus, upon better acquaintance with the Missouri Synod, decided that the situation there was not hopeless, and that their battle for evangelical, confessional orthodoxy might better be waged in the much larger Missouri Synod. Their move, then, was merely a tactical, not a strategic change. "A foolish consistency," wrote Ralph Waldo Emerson, "is the hobgoblin of little minds."

Professorship at Concordia Seminary (St. Louis)

There can be little doubt that Robert Preus was catapulted into his professorship at Concordia by the studies which culminated in the publication of his doctoral thesis, *The Inspiration of Scripture: A Study of the Theology of the Seventeenth Century Lutheran Dogmaticians.*[9] Nothing like this had been seen in conservative North American Lutheran circles for some time. The book was reissued by the publishing house of the Evangelical Lutheran Synod in 1957, the same year in which Preus was called to the

---

6. James E. Adams, *Preus of Missouri and the Great Lutheran Civil War* (New York: Harper and Row, 1977), 45–46. A number of other biographical details in this essay are also based on Adams's account.

7. Ibid., 53.

8. Adams, *Preus of Missouri*, tends in this direction; see, e.g., pp. 95ff.

9. Robert D. Preus, *The Inspiration of Scripture: A Study of the Theology of the Seventeenth Century Lutheran Dogmaticians* (London: Oliver and Boyd, 1955).

faculty of the Missouri Synod's flagship seminary in St. Louis.

The Lutheran Church–Missouri Synod had been founded in 1847 as the German Evangelical Lutheran Synod of Missouri, Ohio, and Other States. The two world wars no doubt shook the Missouri Synod out of its German ethnic cocoon sooner than would have been the case had the normal forces of gradual acculturation simply run their course. Bear in mind that apart from the Book of Concord (the Lutheran canon of creeds and confessions) itself, few of the standard Lutheran sources had been translated into English from the original Latin or German. The fifty-five-volume American edition of *Luther's Works* had only just begun to appear (1955). The clergy's rapid loss of competence in both German and Latin had made them dependent on English-language theological resources, which naturally did not reflect the distinctive character of the Lutheran Reformation. A classic identity crisis was in the making.

By 1957, when Robert Preus was called to St. Louis as an instructor in symbolics (creeds and confessions) and philosophy, theological ferment among the students there was well advanced, as can be seen from the student journal, the *Seminarian*. Soon the ferment spread to the faculty itself. A stale traditionalism was simply no match for the allurements of the new theologies from abroad, especially Barthianism. Clifford Nelson has captured the atmosphere well:

> Many of these men, who found their way into teaching positions in major colleges and seminaries of the Lutheran churches, including Concordia Seminary (St. Louis), had been exposed to contemporary biblical research (Dodd, Hoskyns, Wright, Albright, Bultmann, G. Bornkamm, von Rad, *et al.*); to contemporary theologians such as Nygren, Aulen, Barth, Brunner, Tillich, and the Niebuhrs; and to the Luther researches of Swedes, Germans, Englishmen, and Americans (notably Wilhelm Pauck and Roland Bainton). One re-

sult was that in the course of time students were exposed to a new brand of Lutheranism that was remarkably similar in all schools, whether in Chicago, Philadelphia, the Twin Cities, or St. Louis.[10]

Student unrest at St. Louis came to a head in a series of special presentations and discussions. "The chief questions of the students centered in the extent to which the Scriptures themselves and the Confessions of the Church teach a doctrine of Verbal Inspiration and what the function of that doctrine is."[11] Some of the faculty courageously attempted to hold the line in respect to biblical inspiration.

The new professor and the American edition of his book on inspiration arrived on campus together and made an immediate impact. Scholarly, yet personable and friendly, Preus was well liked by both students and colleagues, even by those who did not agree with his theological orthodoxy. His academic credentials and competence were such that he could not be dismissed as a blinkered establishment hack loyally passing on clichés uncritically inherited from the tribal elders. In this respect Preus resembled another outsider, John Warwick Montgomery, whose work was to appear meteorlike a decade later in the Missouri Synod's firmament.[12]

Preus's book on inspiration supplied welcome ammunition for the traditionalists, then very much on the defensive. The old inspiration doctrine was routinely ridiculed as a scholastic artifice contrived by seventeenth-century dogmaticians from pagan (Aristotelian) philosophical pedantries, and inflicted on the church contrary to the dynamic or Hebrew genius of the Bible and of an existentially reinterpreted Luther. It was

10. E. Clifford Nelson, *Lutheranism in North America, 1914–1970* (Minneapolis: Augsburg, 1972), 164–65.

11. Richard R. Caemmerer, ed., "Essays on the Inspiration of Scripture," *Concordia Theological Monthly* 25.10 (Oct. 1954): 298.

12. John Warwick Montgomery, *Crisis in Lutheran Theology*, 2 vols. (Grand Rapids: Baker, 1967).

of course much easier to bat about carica-
tures of the old divines than to study them.
The Preus volume actually engaged their
arguments in detail and at first hand. The
treatment was sympathetic, but by no
means uncritical. For instance, Preus judi-
ciously analyzes what might be meant by
the term "Lutheran scholasticism," and
grants some of the critics' charges while refuting others.[13] He grants, too, that the Ar-
istotelian-scholastic mode employed by the
old theologians sometimes misled even major figures like Johann Gerhard, David Hol-
laz, and Johann Baier into a rationalistic
departure from sound biblical doctrine, for
instance, on predestination.[14]

On the other hand, Preus defends the
seventeenth-century divines against the
popular charge that they taught a mechanical view of inspiration. Even the early Hermann Sasse was not immune from such
misunderstandings. In reply Preus shows
that Latin terms like *dictatio* do not have
the same narrow meanings as do their English derivatives. Also, "the troublesome
word *'dictatio'* cannot possibly have a
purely mechanical connotation, [for] the
dogmaticians speak of a *'dictatio rerum'* [a
dictation of things or subject matter; cf. *dictatio verborum*, a dictation of words]."[15]

All in all, the Preus volume effectively re-
habilitated the theological integrity of the
old inspiration dogma. Verbal inspiration,
inerrancy, and the sufficiency and clarity of
Holy Scripture were again shown to make
good sense within the continuity of orthodox Christian doctrine from biblical days
till the present. In his detailed treatment of
an obscure controversy—occasioned by
"the renegade Lutheran" Hermann Rath-
mann's divorcing the external biblical
Word from the power of the Holy Spirit—
Preus proves biblically and theologically
the indissoluble unity between Spirit and
Word, and thus the spiritual power of that
Word. It is no accident that Preus ventures

precisely in this context a critical reference
to Karl Barth's proclivity for downplaying
the merely external and earthly aspects of
the Bible.[16]

It goes without saying that Preus's book
and the influence afforded by his teaching
position in St. Louis did not settle the simmering controversy. Things had already
gone too far for that. Throughout the sixties
Concordia Seminary acquired more and
more young faculty members who were devoted to historical criticism, and were
therefore deaf to the claims of the historic
Christian doctrine of inspiration. Fearing
the advent of a less compliant synodical administration, the seminary in 1969 called to
its presidency John Tietjen, who was identified with the progressive forces. The
synod, however, in that same year, elected
Jack Preus as its president. Now the die was
cast. There followed the dramatic Seminex
episode, which has become the subject of
several books.[17] Robert Preus was of course
deeply involved at every stage. Early in
1972, when confronted with President Tietjen's claim that no one could competently
teach at the seminary "without using historical-critical methodology," Preus replied
publicly:

> When I joined this faculty the so-called
> historical-critical method was not em-
> ployed but generally rejected by this fac-
> ulty. A couple of exegetes might have advo-

13. Preus, *Inspiration*, xv.
14. Ibid., 211.
15. Ibid., 72–73.

16. Ibid., 182. Preus was to take on Barth in con-
siderable detail in a series of essays published in *Concordia Theological Monthly* 31.2, 3, 4, 10 (Feb., March,
April, Oct. 1960).
17. For a broad journalistic treatment see Adams,
Preus of Missouri. Two largely documentary volumes
are Marquart, *Anatomy of an Explosion;* and Board of
Control, Concordia Seminary, St. Louis, *Exodus from
Concordia: A Report on the 1974 Walkout* (St. Louis:
The Board, 1977). More-personal accounts are Frederick W. Danker, *No Room in the Brotherhood: The
Preus-Otten Purge of Missouri* (St. Louis: Clayton,
1977); and John H. Tietjen, *Memoirs in Exile: Confes-
sional Hope and Institutional Conflict* (Minneapolis:
Augsburg Fortress, 1990). For Robert Preus's empa-
thetic and magnanimous review of the latter see *Logia:
A Journal of Lutheran Theology* 1.1 (Oct. 1992): 74–78.

cated using certain aspects of it, but this was all. Now after fifteen years, during which the method has been quietly and gradually brought in, we are told that it is impossible to do exegesis at a seminary without using it.

I must respond that as a called teacher at Concordia Seminary, committed to the sacred Scriptures and the Lutheran Confessions, I cannot and will not use the historical-critical method as such for its false basic presuppositions and its false goals and conclusions. I have [said] this privately and publicly and in every possible forum, in joint faculty meetings and before the Council of Presidents, in my classes, in papers delivered throughout the Synod, in periodicals and books, and before our Board of Control. And I intend to do the same in the future in this school or anywhere else with the help of God.[18]

Meanwhile Synod President Jack Preus had just issued a "Statement of Scriptural and Confessional Principles," in which he showed the historical-critical ideology to be incompatible with the Scriptures and the Lutheran confessions. This document was intended to help the seminary's board of control evaluate the hundreds of pages of testimony that Preus's fact-finding committee had gathered from the faculty between December 1970 and March 1971. In September 1972 Preus published his "Report of the Synodical President to the Lutheran Church–Missouri Synod" (the so-called Blue Book), which, without revealing the identities of particular professors, gave copious extracts from their answers to various theological questions. President Preus concluded: "The case now lies before the church. . . . It is becoming increasingly clear that we have two theologies. With the influential position the Seminary holds in the church, its views will prevail unless the Synod directs otherwise and sees to it that its directives are implemented."

18. Cited in *Exodus from Concordia*, 33; Preus's remarks originally appeared in *Spectrum* (a Concordia Seminary student publication), 10 March 1972.

The synod decided the issue in 1973 at its New Orleans convention when it adopted as its own Jack Preus's "Statement of Scriptural and Confessional Principles." A separate, painstaking resolution dealt with the position held by the majority of the faculty (who were opposed by a minority of five, including Robert Preus). The majority's loose views of biblical authority and clarity, particularly in such matters as the "facticity of miracle accounts and their details; historicity of Adam and Eve as real persons; . . . predictive prophecies in the Old Testament which are in fact Messianic; [and] the doctrine of angels" were held to be "in fact false doctrine running counter to the Holy Scriptures, the Lutheran Confessions, and the synodical stance and for that reason 'cannot be tolerated in the church of God, much less be excused and defended'" (the concluding phrase comes directly from the Formula of Concord of 1577).

Amid much theatricality, including demonstrations, armbands, and impromptu sidewalk communion services before television cameras, the Tietjen party argued that the proposed resolution was theologically and procedurally improper. This effort was in vain. The majority at the convention supported the synod president and the old theology. In January 1974 Tietjen was suspended from the seminary presidency. A majority of the faculty and student body chose to declare a moratorium on classes. When the striking professors failed to return to work by a time stipulated by the board, they were relieved of their positions. The great majority now moved, again with maximum publicity from the media, to premises provided by St. Louis University, a Jesuit school. Thus was formed Concordia Seminary in Exile, or Seminex, which a few years later was absorbed by a number of other schools, including the Lutheran School of Theology at Chicago.

Meanwhile the Concordia campus retained only five professors. Of these Martin Scharlemann became acting president, and Robert Preus chairman of the Department of Historical Theology as well as acting registrar and academic dean. When, as a result of the enormous strains of confrontation and his new responsibilities, Scharlemann became ill, Preus had to take on the position of acting president. Although some had predicted gloom and doom, the institution recovered quickly and is today again flourishing. The judgment of Harold Lindsell, a former editor of *Christianity Today* and himself a Baptist, is worth quoting: "To the best of my knowledge the victory of orthodoxy in the Missouri Synod is the only case of its kind in twentieth-century American Christianity. . . . Perhaps the Missouri story will help evangelicals in other places as they wage their own battles for theological orthodoxy."[19] Preus in turn praised Lindsell for sounding the alarm: "History is repeating itself. What happened at the St. Louis seminary prior to 1974 is happening at Fuller Seminary today. And it is happening elsewhere among those who call themselves Evangelicals. . . . Harold Lindsell's book, *The Battle for the Bible* . . . was right on target as he analyzed what is going on in evangelical circles today."[20]

Personally, the St. Louis years were rich and rewarding ones. The last five of Preus's children were born there. In 1969 he earned his second doctorate, a D.Theol. from the University of Strasbourg. Out of his studies in France came *The Theology of Post-Reformation Lutheranism*, which established Preus as the leading English-language interpreter of the seventeenth-century Lutheran divines.[21] The well-known Swed-ish scholar Bengt Hägglund has paid a high tribute to this much underrated period: "With respect to its versatile comprehension of theological material and the breadth of its knowledge of the Bible, Lutheran orthodoxy marks the high point in the entire history of theology."[22]

In presenting the theology of the old divines, Preus avoids the false sort of objectivity which, without taking a personal stand, seeks only to dust off this or that quaint little detail. What he presents is in fact largely his own theology. The dogmaticians are criticized, to be sure—but also defended against later thinkers, such as Immanuel Kant, the positivists, and Karl Barth. While Preus stresses the originality and individuality of the classic post-Reformation teachers, he also makes clear their fundamental unity of approach and doctrine. In short, he views their theology not as a series of disconnected snapshots, but as a moving picture, that is, an organic whole.

Although Preus freely criticizes some of the later dogmaticians like Johann Baier and Johann Adam Osiander for their "excessive scholasticism," he at once goes on to argue that, contrary to the modern interpretation, there is "no theological cleavage between the period of the Reformation and the period of Lutheran orthodoxy." Indeed, the dogmaticians were as determined as Martin Luther not to allow to reason a *magisterial* (master's) or substantive role in theology. On the other hand, when "Luther spoke of killing and butchering reason, he never meant that God wanted us to be stupid or to think and talk nonsense; he was speaking of the abuse of reason in judging God's revelation." There is, in other words, a ministerial (servant's) use of reason, which seeks not to judge, but only to understand revealed truth.[23]

---

19. Harold Lindsell, *The Bible in the Balance* (Grand Rapids: Zondervan, 1979), 244.

20. Robert D. Preus, review of *Biblical Authority*, edited by Jack B. Rogers, in Lindsell, *Bible in the Balance*, 366.

21. Robert D. Preus, *The Theology of Post-Reformation Lutheranism*, 2 vols. (St. Louis: Concordia, 1970, 1972). Edward Farley, *Ecclesial Reflection: An Anatomy of Theological Method* (Philadelphia: Fortress, 1982), 121n, states that Preus's *Inspiration of Scripture* and *Theology of Post-Reformation Lutheranism* are, "on the Lutheran side, the fullest historical studies of the seventeenth-century theologians on Scripture."

22. Bengt Hägglund, *History of Theology*, trans. Gene J. Lund (St. Louis: Concordia, 1968), 303.

23. Preus, *Post-Reformation Lutheranism*, 1:41–42. Here is a prime illustration that the allegedly scholastic seventeenth-century divines made independent

Among the dogmaticians' notable contributions is their improvement on Thomas Aquinas in the matter of the existence of God. For example, Abraham Calov insists, against Aquinas, that God's existence is not merely a preamble to faith, but "that the very chief article of faith is that God is."[24] Yes, there are reasonable arguments for the existence of God (Rom. 1:20). But they produce philosophy, not faith or theology. Faith is "always based upon a special word or revelation of God." Anything else is mere human opinion or knowledge. "Calov assumes a complete distinction between the theory or opinion of a philosopher and the faith of a Christian. In spite of the fact that they speak of the same thing, faith and philosophy remain in two completely different and distinct categories." Remarkably similar was the conclusion of Etienne Gilson, the great modern interpreter of Thomas Aquinas: "This distinction of orders allows us to understand how the same intellect can know by reason the God of philosophy and know by faith the God of Moses, of Abraham, of Isaac, and of Jacob. . . . Philosophy knows that there exists a being that all call God, but no philosophy can suspect the existence of the God of Scripture."[25]

Preus devotes considerable space to the correct understanding of the very nature of theology, as this is argued first by Johann Gerhard, and then, at much greater length, by Abraham Calov. Theology, these teach-

ers insisted, is not a theoretical or speculative science, as Thomas and the scholastics had thought, but a practical, God-given, salvation-oriented skill or aptitude. It is like medicine, which is interested in anatomical and chemical facts not for their own sake, but for the sake of imparting healing to sick people. This practical nature of theology, with its total dependence on the divinely given Word and sacraments, has profound consequences. Preus thoroughly approves this view of theology: "To maintain the practical character of theology against all forms of theological dilettantism, speculation, scientism, and dead orthodoxy is the perennial task of evangelical theology."[26]

Presidency of Concordia Seminary (Springfield and Fort Wayne)

Robert Preus was to face the practical challenges of theology even more directly after September 15, 1974, the date of his inauguration as the thirteenth president of Concordia Theological Seminary in Springfield. *Time Magazine* commented: "Concordia Seminary of Springfield, Illinois, has an aggressive new president, the Rev. Robert D. Preus—Jack's brother and a conservative with impressive intellectual credentials."[27] Robert's programmatic inaugural address, based on the institution's name, established clear priorities: "Concordia" stands for true, uncompromised unity in regard to all of the articles of the biblical gospel as they are set out in the Book of Concord of 1580. "Theological" means that the divine truth must be the actual stuff of the curriculum; a mere lip service, while secularism is allowed to pervade and corrode all content, is not satisfactory. "Seminary," finally, im-

and creative use of Thomas Aquinas. Their distinction between magisterial and ministerial reason does justice to a crucial aspect of the Christian truth, which undifferentiated talk about faith and reason simply fails to capture (see the sympathetic exposition of Aquinas's view in Norman L. Geisler, *Thomas Aquinas: An Evangelical Appraisal* [Grand Rapids: Baker, 1991], 57–69). The old dogmaticians have left behind a monumental example of just what Geisler suggests needs to be done—pressing Aquinas's superb intellectual equipment into the service of biblical, Reformation theology.

24. Preus, *Post-Reformation Lutheranism*, 2:38.

25. Etienne Gilson, *The Philosopher and Theology*, trans. Cecile Gilson (New York: Random House, 1962), 81.

26. Preus, *Post-Reformation Lutheranism*, 1:194. Preus would later state: "God is not an idea or theory. He is the living Lord of heaven and earth, the Creator and Sustainer of all things, the Redeemer and Savior of all men. One cannot study theology without being caught up by it, changed, born again, without commitment, without faith" ("Inauguration Address," *Springfielder* 38.2 [Sept. 1974]: 93).

27. *Time Magazine*, 9 September 1974, p. 67.

plies the implanting and cultivation of spiritual life, not mere intellectualism or even moralism for that matter. "That is what we seek to inculcate here: total commitment, commitment to the highest and greatest work in all the world, ministry, the ministry of the Gospel, the ministry of reconciliation."[28]

Academically, the Springfield seminary had always played second fiddle to St. Louis. It was the "practical" seminary. Continuing the policy of his brother Jack, who had preceded him as president, Robert wished to upgrade the seminary's academic standing without giving up any of its practical, pastoral orientation. Already in his inaugural address he was able to announce the addition of a graduate school, which would grant the doctorate in ministry as well as master's degrees in sacred theology. Preus set out to build an academically and theologically strong faculty. In 1976 the seminary was moved to Fort Wayne, where it had been founded over a hundred years before. It now occupies the beautiful campus designed by Eero Saarinen in the mid-1950s.

The cause of missions was always close to Preus's heart. He served for years on the synodical board of missions, where he stressed concern for a global vision and sound theological underpinnings. Thanks largely to his energetic support, Concordia Seminary in St. Catharines, Ontario, was launched, and theological leadership provided for Lutheran mission work in Haiti. In the 1980s Fort Wayne added a Department of Missions and created centers for Hispanic studies and ministry to the deaf. By 1991 the doctorate in missiology was offered.

In 1974, the year of his inauguration as seminary president, Preus also attended the Lausanne Congress on World Evangelization. He was impressed by the large number of representatives from Africa and Asia. As for the Lausanne Covenant, he found the document to be "as good a statement as one could expect." Theologically, it fell somewhat short of the level of the Berlin Congress of 1966. Specifically, the "means of grace and baptism, as the Spirit's vehicle for evangelization, were simply ignored."[29]

Also occupying Preus's attention at this time was the simmering missiology debate that in 1968 had boiled over within the World Council of Churches. Thundered Donald McGavran, the founder of the Church Growth movement: "They do not believe that it makes an eternal difference whether men accept the Lord Jesus and are baptized in His name. They do not believe that in the Bible we have the authoritative, infallible Word of God. . . . Their theology allows them to take neither the Church nor the salvation of men's souls seriously."[30] McGavran's "they" of course included many mainstream Lutherans as well as the mission wing of Missouri's Seminex movement. It was in this context that Preus published, in 1975, a major essay on "The Confessions and the Mission of the Church."[31]

Contrary to fashionable notions of the day, Preus maintained that the church is a spiritual, not a political fellowship. Therefore "the work of the church is the work of the Spirit; and anything which is not clearly the Spirit's work is not the work of the church." The Spirit, Preus continued, gives faith and salvation only through the gospel and the sacraments. To be sure, works of

---

28. Preus, "Inauguration Address," 94.

29. Robert D. Preus, "Reflections on the International Congress on World Evangelization," *Affirm*, 14 November 1974, p. 6.

30. Donald A. McGavran, "Church Growth Strategy Continued," *International Review of Missions* 57 (July 1968): 339. See also *The Conciliar-Evangelical Debate: The Crucial Documents, 1964–1976*, ed. Donald A. McGavran (South Pasadena: William Carey Library, 1977); Harvey T. Hoekstra, *The World Council of Churches and the Demise of Evangelism* (Wheaton, Ill.: Tyndale, 1979); and Edward R. Norman, *Christianity and the World Order* (New York: Oxford University Press, 1979).

31. Robert D. Preus, "The Confessions and the Mission of the Church," *Springfielder* 39.1 (June 1975): 20–39.

love flow from saving faith. But there are good *"theological* reasons why our Confessions do not and really could not advocate corporate, institutional, ecclesiastical activity in the sphere of social and civil affairs, what we today would call social or political action."

Most basic here is the sharp distinction that the Bible and the Reformation make between God's two authorities or governments, the spiritual and the political. While Christians in their various callings are to serve God and their neighbors according to the Ten Commandments, and while the church is to proclaim these commandments to high and low alike, rulers included, "it is," concluded Preus on the basis of the Lutheran confessions, "as members of the church . . . who have their specific calling that rulers are given such counsel." Preus employed a similar argument in defending the confessions against the charge of being indifferent to missions. On the contrary, he contended, by freeing the gospel from dependence on works and from entanglements with Caesar, the Reformation liberated the church and her ministry "for mission in the true sense. . . . The passion for the Gospel is the passion for souls, and this is the essence of the spirit of mission."

Finally, Preus's article criticized as theologically vacuous and frivolous the "Report on Renewal in Mission" that was put forth by the Uppsala Assembly of the World Council (1968): "The urgency for proclaiming the Gospel is simply not apparent in the Uppsala Report. And this is inexcusable." While advocating ongoing substantive conversations, Preus saw no future for the present ecumenical movement as reflected in the "unevangelical and even heretical" approach of the report. "To identify with a great movement which so tragically buries the Gospel and misses the crucial mission of the church would constitute a compromise and denial of our understanding of the Gospel and the work of Christ's church."

Among the most fruitful of his intercon fessional endeavors was Preus's participa tion in the three summits of the Interna tional Council on Biblical Inerrancy (197 1982, 1986). These meetings brought t gether scholars from various background and the disciplined exchange and clarifica tion of ideas were obviously beneficial. Fo mal agreements were produced by the fir and second summits: "The Chicago Stat ment on Biblical Inerrancy" (1978) an "The Chicago Statement on Biblical He meneutics" (1982).[32] The third summit pr duced no formal statement, but dealt wit specific interpretations and applications t current social issues, where confession differences naturally played their part. Perhaps the most clearly Lutheran contr bution to these discussions is embodied Article II of the statement on hermeneutic "WE AFFIRM that as Christ is God an Man in one Person, so Scripture is, indiv ibly, God's Word in human language. W DENY that the humble, human form Scripture entails errancy any more than th humanity of Christ, even in His humilia tion, entails sin."[34]

In a similar vein we should note Preus contribution to the Conference on Biblic Inerrancy sponsored by the six seminarie of the Southern Baptist Convention (1987 His essay was criticized as one-sided by on respondent, and hailed by another as pa of "a monumental contribution to the evan gelical cause through both scholarship an statesmanship."[35]

32. For the statement on inerrancy see Lindse *Bible in the Balance*, 366–71; for the statement c hermeneutics see *Hermeneutics, Inerrancy, and the B ble: Papers from ICBI Summit II*, ed. Earl D. Radm cher and Robert D. Preus (Grand Rapids: Zonderva 1984), 881–87.

33. *Applying the Scriptures: Papers from ICBI Sun mit III*, ed. Kenneth S. Kantzer (Grand Rapid Zondervan, 1987). Preus's contribution, "The Livir God" (pp. 1–18), deals with soteriological and trinita ian matters.

34. *Hermeneutics*, ed. Radmacher and Preus, 88

35. *Proceedings of the Conference on Biblical I errancy, 1987* (Nashville: Broadman, 1987), 65.

In honor of Preus's sixtieth birthday, a festschrift was published by his friends and colleagues.[36] In addition to the local talent, there were contributions by distinguished confessional churchmen and scholars from Australia, Brazil, Germany, Great Britain, and Sweden. The volume paid tribute to Preus for having "striven to tip the balance in favor of theological rather than bureaucratic impulses in the shaping of pastoral training and preparation." This strength, generally appreciated by Preus's teaching colleagues, had its liabilities, however, and nearly proved to be his undoing. Bureaucracies are notoriously fond of safe, rule-driven behavior, and allergic to creative eruptions of substance. Church bureaucracies are no exception.

The catalyst for Preus's difficulties was the Church Growth movement. In an initial burst of enthusiasm reflecting Preus's concern for missions, the Fort Wayne faculty had petitioned the 1977 convention of the Missouri Synod to have each of its subdivisions or districts "make a thorough study of the Church Growth materials." What is more, the districts were to be urged to "organize, equip, and place into action all of the Church Growth principles as needed in the evangelization of our nation and the world under the norms of the Scriptures and the Lutheran Confessions." By the time of the 1986 synodical convention, however, the same faculty, while appreciating the "valuable lessons of common sense" to be learned from Church Growth, asked that "the Synod warn against the Arminian and charismatic nature of the church-growth movement."

This cooling of the initial enthusiasm for Church Growth was inevitable, given Preus's insistence on theological integrity as a necessary condition of all proper mission work. Ever anxious that the seminary be relevant to the church's practical needs,

36. Kurt E. Marquart, John R. Stephenson, and Bjarne W. Teigen, eds., *A Lively Legacy: Essays in Honor of Robert Preus* (Fort Wayne: Concordia Theological Seminary Press, 1985).

Preus organized a number of public dialogues in which Lutheran advocates of Church Growth played a part. These discussions did not defuse the developing theological tensions, but heightened them. The rift was between the practical men of action and the theologians. The former saw the latter as hopelessly impractical theorists out of touch with modern reality. The latter, in turn, thought that the former were uncritically imbibing theological content along with Church Growth methods. The Fort Wayne faculty became increasingly concerned that the churchly Lutheran heritage was being jettisoned in a vapid, and ultimately futile, flirtation with popular culture.

This debate over substance versus style or, in the context of missiology, gospel versus culture raised in acute form the wider question of the connection between confessional and evangelical. For Preus it had always been axiomatic that if the ancient creeds and the sixteenth-century confessions were truly faithful to the gospel, then one could not be evangelical without being confessional, and vice versa. He bristled at the idea that for the sake of a broad, popular appeal, the confessions might be sidelined into some safe preserve for cultural white elephants. A gospel so liberated from clear doctrinal content and contours would be an insipid mush unworthy of the noble name *evangelical*. There is no generic gospel apart from doctrinal specifics. The New Testament, he asserted, is controversial, not platitudinous.

From the beginning of his presidency Robert Preus had sought ways and means to raise the confessional consciousness of the future clergy. The aim was to counter the cultural predilections for the bland, the banal, and the inoffensive. After the move to Fort Wayne an annual Symposium on the Lutheran Confessions was begun. Here scholars and churchmen of widely different backgrounds could engage each other in the give-and-take of responsible academic debate. Other Preus creations include the

International Foundation for Lutheran Confessional Research and the Luther Academy, both dedicated to the pursuit of Reformation-related scholarship. The foundation is underwriting the Confessional Lutheran Dogmatics series, a projected eleven volumes being compiled under Preus's general editorship.

The renewed confessional awareness that developed particularly among the younger clergy of the Missouri Synod in the 1980s was not uniformly welcomed. It was on a collision course not only with the looser views of the remnants of the Seminex movement, but also with a conservative biblicism mixed with a missionary pragmatism that took its cue from the Church Growth movement. On the one hand, the confessionally minded resisted what they regarded as a slide into a generic Protestant pietism and emotionalism. The proexpansion forces, on the other hand, were impatient with what they took to be a stubborn clinging to ethnic trivia, which stood in the way of successful mass evangelism in the current American culture. Some administrative types took the view that if only the synod could rid itself of the confessional extremists as it had rid itself of the liberal ones in the 1970s, there would be peace at last.

The focus of the synodical tensions had changed from biblical authority to questions about the nature of the church, the ministry, and the confessions. In 1981 the synodical convention had accepted unchanged a resolution from the Preus-led Fort Wayne faculty which was highly critical of the more liberal members of the Lutheran Council in the U.S.A., namely, the American Lutheran Church and the Lutheran Church in America.[37] Nothing much

came of this resolution, and the Lutheran Council in the U.S.A. eventually disappeared with the formation of the new Evangelical Lutheran Church in America, which includes the American Lutheran Church and the Lutheran Church in America, but not the Lutheran Church–Missouri Synod. By 1989 the Fort Wayne seminary was warning its synodical convention that the Evangelical Lutheran Church in America, which ordained women and practiced interdenominational church fellowship, was really a union church and not confessionally Lutheran. The situation was said to "lend renewed urgency in our region of the world to the question: 'Will Lutheranism everywhere become merely a viewpoint within church bodies that are not in fact Lutheran?' (H. Sasse, We Confess the Church, 42)." No action was taken by the convention, since the synodical leadership sought friendly relations with the Evangelical Lutheran Church in America and muted all criticism.

The push for less restrictive practices came not only from the pro–Evangelical Lutheran Church in America forces, but also from those who were under the influence of Church Growth. The latter also demanded lay ministers in public worship, something which went completely against the grain of the confessional Lutheran understanding of the gospel ministry. At the same time bureaucratic pressures brought into question the old Lutheran doctrine of the permanency of the call into the ministry. Preus himself countered with a ringing defense of the old doctrine.[38]

---

37. The faculty drew attention to an essay in which a leading biblical scholar from the Lutheran Church in America had undermined the whole traditional Christology of the creeds. The faculty's proposal read: "Resolved, That the Synod hereby instruct its President to request the Division of Theological Studies [of the Lutheran Council in the U.S.A.] to place on the division's agenda as a matter of urgency a thorough dis-

cussion of the far-reaching implications of historical criticism, as practiced in U.S. Lutheranism, for: (a) the central Christological-Trinitarian core of the Gospel; (b) the very possibility of confessional subscription; and (c) the preamble of LCUSA's constitution, according to which the participating Lutheran church bodies . . . see in the three Ecumenical Creeds and in the Confessions of the Lutheran Church . . . a pure exposition of the Word of God."

38. Robert D. Preus, The Doctrine of the Call in the Confessions and Lutheran Orthodoxy, Luther Academy Monograph 1 (Fort Wayne: Luther Academy, 1991).

In short, while the Missouri Synod had faced a crisis in the 1970s over biblical authority, it faced in the 1980s a confessional crisis on the nature of the church and the ministry. Fort Wayne was of course by no means the only force for confessionalism. Strong confessional impulses emanated from the St. Louis seminary as well. Yet Preus came to embody this renewed confessional awareness in a special way. A shrewd observer remarked in a pan-Lutheran publication: "Robert Preus would eschew the label 'evangelical catholic,' but he did create and protect a climate on the Fort Wayne campus that fostered a strong confessional theology coupled with a respectable liturgical life."[39]

In view of Preus's worldwide reputation within confessional Lutheranism and beyond, there was considerable shock when he was against his wishes given honorable retirement by the seminary's board of regents in 1989. With the support of many friends, he decided to contest the decision in the church's court system; in the meantime he obtained the help of the civil courts in preventing the appointment of a permanent replacement. The case caused a good deal of turmoil in the Missouri Synod. In response to various defensive actions on Preus's part, the synod's top leadership (the so-called praesidium, consisting of the president and the five vice-presidents) accused him of conduct unbecoming a Christian, and had him removed from the clergy roster. The synod's highest tribunal, the commission on appeals, ultimately reinstated Preus as seminary president (in a 5 to 4 decision) and restored him to the clergy roster (by a vote of 9 to 0). Synodical officials refused to accept this outcome, and sought to bring the matter before the synod's 1992 convention in Pittsburgh. The convention narrowly (by a vote of 580 to 568) defeated the incumbent president, Ralph Bohlmann, and elected Alvin Barry instead. It also abolished the old adjudication-and-appeals system, replacing it with a new conflict-resolution procedure, which gives the impression of having been hastily improvised. The convention did, however, heed its bylaws in not reopening the Preus case. Instead it ratified an agreement according to which Preus was to remain president till May 1993 or a new president was chosen, whichever occurred first.[40] Meanwhile, a mutually acceptable administrator was to handle executive and academic affairs.

The outcome was, of course, a compromise. Yet Preus was essentially vindicated in that the final decision of the commission on appeals was left standing. He was permitted to spend the rest of his productive years doing what he loves best—teaching sacred theology and thus preparing men for the awesome work of stewards of the life-giving mysteries of God (1 Cor. 4:1).

This essay, which was read before the 1990 Symposium on the Lutheran Confessions, was printed and sent to all Missouri Synod congregations by Our Savior Church and School of Houston.

39. John T. Pless, "Previewing Missouri's Convention," *Forum Letter* 21.6 (June 29, 1992): 6.

40. In April 1993 David Schmiel was installed as the new president.

Charles C. Ryrie

Paul P. Enns

Charles Caldwell Ryrie was born on March 2, 1925, in St. Louis, Missouri, and spent his early years in Alton, Illinois. At the age of five he was led to faith in Christ by his father, a banker. Young Charles displayed academic prowess early, graduating from high school at the age of sixteen in January 1942. His father felt Charles needed further polish academically, so Charles enrolled in Stony Brook School on Long Island for one semester. Here young Ryrie became acquainted with headmaster Frank E. Gaebelein, son of Arno C. Gaebelein. Gaebelein had influenced Charles's older brother to attend Haverford College, a Quaker institution in suburban Philadelphia, and Charles followed his brother's path there. Attendance at regularly scheduled Quaker meetings with leaders like Rufus Jones and faculty member Douglas Steere was required at Haverford. During his college days in Philadelphia, Charles also went to hear the eloquent Donald Grey Barnhouse, pastor of the historic Tenth Presbyterian Church.

Ryrie majored in mathematics at Haverford, where he was elected to Phi Beta Kappa. He was intent on following family tradition by entering a banking career, but God had other plans for him. Through his maternal grandfather, who lived in the Ryrie household, Charles had earlier become acquainted with Lewis Sperry Chafer, one of the founders of the Evangelical Theological College, which later became Dallas Theological Seminary. The Chafers, both accomplished musicians, would sit at the piano in the Ryrie home and sing duets. The Lord was already working in Charles's heart in those days to lead him to become a prominent theologian and articulator of evangelicalism and dispensationalism. When Chafer came to Philadelphia for a speaking engagement, Charles made an appointment to meet with him. In a hotel on April 23, 1943, Chafer provided spiritual counsel, and Charles Ryrie dedicated his life to ministry for the Lord.

Despite the fact that Ryrie had not yet completed his college program, he applied to Dallas Theological Seminary, was accepted, and enrolled in the summer of 1944. After attending Dallas for two years he petitioned Haverford to grant him his diploma on the basis of his studies at Dallas. (Haverford had made similar allowances for medical students.) Haverford agreed, conferring the baccalaureate degree in June 1946; and Dallas Seminary awarded him a Th.M. in May 1947. His master's thesis researched "The Relation of the New Covenant to Premillennialism," undoubtedly laying the foundation for Ryrie's becoming a major spokesman for premillennialism.

That summer Ryrie's teaching career was launched at the Midwest Bible and Missionary Institute (which later became part of Calvary Bible College). Ryrie had his sights set on studying that fall under the renowned Carl F. H. Henry at Northern Baptist Theological Seminary, but when Henry left Northern to become a founding faculty member of Fuller Seminary in Pasadena, Ryrie found himself back at Dallas Seminary. In 1949 he graduated with high honors with a Th.D. degree; his dissertation was subsequently revised and published as *The Basis of the Premillennial Faith*.

In the fall of 1948 Ryrie had accepted an invitation to teach mathematics and Bible at Westmont College in Santa Barbara, but upon arriving he was appointed associate professor of Greek and Bible. A crisis occurred at Westmont in 1950 when the president was dismissed and the two-thirds of the faculty who attempted to force the board to reinstate him were told that their tendered resignations had been accepted! Ryrie's responsibilities increased immediately. In addition to teaching Greek and Bible he became dean of men and chairman of the Department of Biblical Studies and Philosophy.

But further studies abroad beckoned. Charles enrolled in the University of Edinburgh, completing the Ph.D. program in less than two years. There he studied under Matthew Black, J. H. S. Burleigh, Thomas Torrance, and James Stewart, scholars who were genuinely liberal and tolerant of other viewpoints. They gave Ryrie considerable help—and even listened to him preach his conservative theology. Edinburgh proved a stimulating experience for Ryrie and sharpened his skills as a scholar and theologian. His dissertation was subsequently published as *The Place of Women in the Church*.

In 1953 Ryrie returned to Dallas to teach systematic theology. In 1958 he was invited to serve as president of the historic Philadelphia College of Bible. Finding this position a pleasant, enjoyable experience, he particularly looked forward to the Friday chapel services at which he would address the students. Some of these messages were later published under the title *Making the Most of Life*. In 1962 he went back to Dallas to teach systematic theology and assume the post of dean of doctoral studies, where he remained until his retirement in 1983.

Amid his many responsibilities Ryrie found time to deliver lectures at Bethel Theological Seminary, Biola University, Cedarville College, and Moody Bible Institute. Similar commitments carried him to Europe, Israel, the lands of the apostle Paul, South Africa, Mexico, Central America, Haiti, Argentina, and Brazil. Two of his books (*The Miracles of Our Lord* and *So Great Salvation*) received the Gold Medallion Award from the Evangelical Christian Publishers Association. And for his theological acumen he was awarded an honorary Litt.D. by Liberty Baptist Theological Seminary.

A Master of Communication

In the classroom as well as on the printed page Ryrie has proved to be a master communicator. His classes would frequently assume an unorthodox pattern as he would focus on one student in particular and ask for a theological definition: "Give me a definition of the hypostatic union of Christ." After the student's definition, Ryrie would ask, "What did you omit?" And then, "Try again, and this time include all the important elements and remove any extraneous words." Back and forth the discussion continued until the student arrived at a precise and concise definition. It was an important lesson, not only in theology but in communication.

Ryrie's senior-level course in theology was no different. To solidify the students' thinking, he challenged them to defend their theological positions. Using Carl Henry's *Basic Christian Doctrines* as a launching pad, Ryrie created situations that forced the students to justify their own views and to demonstrate acquaintance with contemporary theology. The classes involved considerable debate and dialogue with the professor, frequently to the chagrin of the students!

Ryrie could communicate equally well in writing. Consider as proof the fact that some of his books have exceeded two hundred thousand copies in sales. One of his most recent works, *Basic Theology*, while a five-hundred-page compendium of his position, is not at all ponderous reading. It is an example of Ryrie's unusual ability to state profound theological doctrines concisely but in a highly lucid fashion. Looking for greater detail, some may assume that something has been omitted, but upon reading and reflecting, it becomes apparent that Ryrie has explained doctrine thoroughly without using any cumbersome or extraneous words.

But Ryrie's extensive writing ministry did not begin with theological tomes. His first published work was *Easy Object Lessons* (1949), which was followed by *Easy-to-Give Object Lessons* (1954). These volumes demonstrate not only Ryrie's ability in communication but also his versatility. Written for Sunday-school teachers and anyone else wishing to improve their instruction with catchy object lessons, Ryrie's simple and contemporary examples clarify basic biblical truths. Whether he was writing for Sunday-school teachers or reminding charismatics that they could not draw a distinction between being baptized "by" the Holy Spirit (1 Cor. 12:13) and "with" the Holy Spirit (Acts 1:5) since the same Greek phrase (*en pneumati*) is involved, the style was always the same: lucid, concise explanation. The early volumes set the standard in communication skills that were to characterize Ryrie's writings throughout the decades. And they no doubt reveal the reason for Ryrie's popularity—avoiding technical theological jargon, he wrote for ordinary readers, enabling them to comprehend important biblical and theological truth.

Ryrie's works also reflect theological and biblical acuity. In responding to the double-talk of those who affirm plenary verbal inspiration but deny inerrancy, Ryrie suggests that it has become necessary to say, "I believe in the verbal, plenary, infallible, unlimited inerrancy of the Bible."[1] And of those who affirm limited inerrancy Ryrie asks, "Why not 'limited errancy'? If the Bible has limitations on its inerrancy, then obviously it is errant, though not completely so. So limited inerrancy and limited errancy amount to the same thing. But why do the proponents of limited inerrancy not want to use the equivalent label 'limited errancy'? One cannot be sure of the answer, but it could hardly be denied that limited inerrancy is a much more palatable label."[2]

The sharpness of Ryrie's mind is equally evident in his response to proponents of the view that it is impossible to accept Christ as Savior without also making him the Lord of the whole of one's life. Ryrie points out, for example, that they acknowledge that a moment of failure does not invalidate the genuineness of the disciple's salvation. He then counters, "My immediate reaction to such a statement is to want to ask if two moments would? Or a week of defection, or a month, or a year? Or two? How serious a failure and for how long before we must conclude that such a person was in fact not saved?"[3] These are penetrating comments that

1. Charles C. Ryrie, *What You Should Know about Inerrancy* (Chicago: Moody, 1981), 17.
2. Ibid.
3. Charles C. Ryrie, *So Great Salvation* (Wheaton, Ill.: Victor, 1989), 48.

pierce the heart of the subject and unmask the problems in the view of his opponents.

One highly admirable trait in Ryrie's writing is his irenic spirit. In the foreword to Ryrie's *Dispensationalism Today* Frank Gaebelein remarks, "Although Dr. Ryrie has deep convictions about dispensationalism and the opposition to it, he has kept his temper and presented his case candidly and graciously. The last chapter is an eloquent and reasonable plea for tolerance." In concert with this remark, Warren Wiersbe comments in the foreword to Ryrie's *So Great Salvation*: "Dr. Ryrie writes with humility and compassion. He has not overreacted to what some extremists have written. Rather, he calmly and logically expounds the Word of God and seeks to bring clarity where there may be confusion, and gentleness where there may be harsh dogmatism. . . . He seeks to obey the words of 2 Timothy 2:24–25: 'And the Lord's bondservant must not be quarrelsome, but be kind to all, able to teach, patient when wronged, with gentleness correcting those who are in opposition.'" Doctrinal distinctives aside, a similar spirit by those holding contrary views would foster Christian unity.

The Basis of the Premillennial Faith

First published in 1953, unquestionably one of the most important books Ryrie authored is *The Basis of the Premillennial Faith*, which sets forth the foundation and system of premillennial interpretation. In this volume, which is a revision of his Th.D. dissertation, Ryrie seeks to demonstrate that "premillennialism is a system of Biblical truth. It is not merely an interpretation of one passage in the last book of the Bible."[4] That is, he seeks to dispel the notion that premillennialism is built solely on Revelation 20:4–6.

One of Ryrie's arguments is that premillennialism is the historic faith of the church. Quoting liberal theologian Adolf von Harnack and church historian Philip Schaff, Ryrie contends that the Apostolic Fathers believed in the premillennial return of Christ. He cites, among others, the Didache, Clement of Rome, the Shepherd of Hermas, Barnabas, and Ignatius of Antioch. Justin Martyr wrote, "There will be resurrection of the dead and a thousand years in Jerusalem, which will then be built, adorned, and enlarged as the prophets Ezekiel and Isaiah and others declare."[5] Tertullian declared, "A kingdom is promised to us upon the earth . . . it will be after the resurrection for a thousand years in the divinely-built city of Jerusalem." Ryrie concludes, "In the face of such overwhelming evidence, who can deny that premillennialism was the faith of the early church?"[6]

But there must be a basis for defending premillennialism, regardless of whether it was held by the early church. Ryrie posits that basis in a hermeneutical system that presupposes plenary verbal inspiration and interprets the Bible literally, carefully considering the grammar of a passage, its context, and its relationship to the rest of Scripture. Any spiritualizing of Scripture (which to Ryrie is the same as allegorizing) is to be rejected. Contrasting allegorical (amillennial) and literal (premillennial) interpretation, Ryrie argues that "allegorical interpretation fosters modernism."[7] On the other hand, "when the principles of literal interpretation both in regard to general and special hermeneutics are followed, the result is the premillennial system of doctrine."[8]

In interpreting the Bible literally, Ryrie focuses on the promises given to Abraham and David, which he contends have not been fulfilled, but will be at the return of Jesus Christ. For Ryrie, the Abrahamic covenant is the watershed between premillennialism and amillennialism. While amillennial theologians insist that the covenant

---

4. Charles C. Ryrie, *The Basis of the Premillennial Faith* (Neptune, N.J.: Loizeaux, 1953), 6.

5. Quoted in Ryrie, *Premillennial Faith,* 22.
6. Ibid., 23.
7. Ibid., 46.
8. Ibid., 47.

promises to Israel were conditional,[9] Ryrie asserts their unconditional nature. The promises God made to Abraham concerning a land, a posterity, and a blessing were unconditional and have never been fulfilled. The conclusion? "Israel is promised permanent possession of the land and permanent existence as a nation. This is based on the unconditional character of the covenant. Since the Church does not fulfill the national promises of the covenant, these promises await a future fulfillment by the nation Israel."[10]

No less important here is the Davidic covenant (2 Sam. 7:12–16), promising a posterity to David as well as an eternal throne and kingdom. Ryrie cites various Old Testament prophets (Isa. 9:6–7; Jer. 23:5–6; 30:8–9; 33:14–22; Ezek. 37:24–25; Dan. 7:13–14; Hos. 3:4–5; Amos 9:11; Zech. 14:4, 9) to show that a future earthly kingdom is in view. But was not the kingdom inaugurated at the first advent of Christ? Ryrie explains that the kingdom was indeed offered by Christ, but it was rejected by the Jewish people. That did not, however, abrogate the kingdom promises to the nation. In fact, promises given after Israel's rejection of the kingdom anticipate future fulfilment of the Davidic covenant (Matt. 25:1–13, 31–46; Acts 15:14–18). The church does not fulfil these promises. Instead, the Davidic covenant will someday find fulfilment on earth with the nation Israel, ruled by the personal presence of Messiah.[11]

A Versatile Theological Writer

Ryrie's theological versatility can be seen in two volumes published in the 1950s—*Neo-orthodoxy* (1956) and *Biblical Theology of the New Testament* (1959). Although *Neo-orthodoxy* is but sixty-two pages, the volume crystalizes the theology of Karl Barth, Emil Brunner, and H. Richard Niebuhr for the layperson—no small task indeed! What layperson would be prepared to tackle Barth's *Church Dogmatics* or his *Römerbrief*? In his summary critique Ryrie reminds the reader that "neo-orthodoxy is an attempt—and an unsuccessful one at that—to reinterpret traditional Christianity in such a way as to make it more acceptable to the so-called intellectual advance of the age."[12] In so doing, Ryrie argues, neo-orthodoxy accepts the tenets of higher criticism, labels the creation story a myth, teaches that the Bible is not the Word of God but only an errant witness to the Word (Christ), and suggests that whether Christ rose physically and bodily matters little. Ryrie concludes: "Original sin is the truest thing in the world, but the account of it in Genesis is only a story [in neo-orthodoxy]. The resurrection of Christ is the truest thing in the world, but the Gospel accounts of it are 'hopelessly garbled [in neo-orthodoxy].' Christ is the Bread of Life, but of course not one word of the Gospel of John is historical [in neo-orthodoxy]. Is it too strong a statement to say that neo-orthodoxy is a theological hoax?"[13]

In *Biblical Theology of the New Testament* Ryrie plowed new ground. Although biblical theology has become popular in the last several decades, Ryrie wrote before the subject began to interest conservatives (e.g., Donald Guthrie, *New Testament Theology*, 1981; Gerhard Hasel, *New Testament Theology*, 1977; George E. Ladd, *A Theology of the New Testament*, 1974; Leon Morris, *New Testament Theology*, 1986). Ryrie explains biblical theology as a systematization of theology that considers the historical circumstances and the progressiveness of revelation, but utilizes the Bible as its source. Accordingly, biblical theology must be exegetical—"historical-grammatical interpretation is the basis of all Biblical Theology."[14]

9. E.g., William E. Cox, *Amillennialism Today* (Philadelphia: Presbyterian and Reformed, 1966), 40–42.

10. Ryrie, *Premillennial Faith*, 74–75.

11. Charles C. Ryrie, *Basic Theology* (Wheaton, Ill.: Victor, 1986), 459–60.

12. Charles C. Ryrie, *Neo-orthodoxy* (Chicago: Moody, 1956), 50.

13. Ibid., 60.

14. Charles C. Ryrie, *Biblical Theology of the New Testament* (Chicago: Moody, 1959), 16.

An example of Ryrie's exegetical theology is his *Grace of God,* published in 1963. The subject intrigued Ryrie because "grace is the watershed that divides Roman Catholicism from Protestantism, Calvinism from Arminianism, modern liberalism from conservatism."[15] Ryrie traces the meaning of the Hebrew and Greek terms for "grace," and then proceeds to draw practical applications: How does one live under grace? What is legalism? What is liberty? These questions impinge on how people view the Christian life. Shall we live under a legalistic agenda? Can liberty turn into license? Ryrie identifies legalism as "an attitude. Although it involves code, motive, and power, it is basically an attitude. . . . A legalistic attitude is, of course, directed toward a given code. Its motivation is wrong, and its power is not that of the Spirit. . . . Legalism may be defined as a 'fleshly attitude which conforms to a code for the purpose of exalting self.'"[16] Christian liberty, on the other hand, is restricted by love, which is identified as doing the will of God. Christian liberty "brings to the believer the freedom to be a slave of righteousness (Rom. 6:18). Such liberty does not place a Christian in the position of being able to live as he pleases; it is not license. It does place him in the position of being able to live as God pleases, a freedom which he did not have as an unregenerate person."[17] These statements, written three decades ago, are an adequate answer to those critics who, troubled by Ryrie's view that it is possible to be saved without making Christ the Lord of one's life, accuse him of leading believers into license through his emphasis on grace.

Always one to simplify theology, making it accessible to laypersons, Ryrie has written, in addition to *The Grace of God,* several other volumes in Moody's Handbook of Bible Doctrine series. The concise volume *The Holy Spirit* was published in 1965. It deals with controversial topics like efficacious grace, the baptizing work of the Spirit, and spiritual gifts. Ryrie distinguishes between the baptism by the Spirit (a ministry of the Spirit that began at Pentecost and occurs but once in the life of every believer—at the moment of salvation) and the filling of the Spirit (which is subsequent to salvation and repeatable for every believer). An exponent of the noncharismatic view, Ryrie distinguishes those spiritual gifts that were foundational and therefore temporary (apostleship, prophecy, miracles, healing, and tongues) from those gifts that are permanent and appear in all generations. Ryrie argues for the cessation of tongues as a spiritual gift on the grounds that (1) the need for the gift ended with the completion of the canon, and (2) the middle voice of the verb "they shall cease" in 1 Corinthians 13:8 suggests that tongues "would die out of their own accord."[18]

Dispensationalism Today

The name Charles Ryrie is synonymous with dispensationalism because of his association with Dallas Seminary, and also because of the publication of *Dispensationalism Today* in 1965. This work is the definitive source for contemporary dispensationalism. In it Ryrie seeks to allay many misconceptions. In 1945 Oswald T. Allis had published *Prophecy and the Church,* which charged that "dispensationalism has been becoming increasingly in recent years a seriously divisive factor in evangelical circles. . . . [It is] a serious departure from the historic faith of the Church as set forth in the Scriptures. The result is a situation that is deplorable. It is more than deplorable; it is dangerous."[19] Allis wrote "to expose the danger in [dispensationalism's] teaching regarding things to come . . . and to prove it

15. Charles C. Ryrie, *The Grace of God* (Chicago: Moody, 1963), 11.
16. Ibid., 76.
17. Ibid., 80–81.
18. Charles C. Ryrie, *The Holy Spirit* (Chicago: Moody, 1965), 92.
19. Oswald T. Allis, *Prophecy and the Church* (Philadelphia: Presbyterian and Reformed, 1945), vii.

to be unscriptural."[20] Daniel Fuller and Clarence Bass later joined the attack on dispensationalism.[21] In *Dispensationalism Today* Ryrie addressed these charges, howbeit in an irenic tone. Indeed, the last chapter is a plea for tolerance. Ryrie wrote *Dispensationalism Today* for two purposes: "(1) to try to correct the misconceptions about dispensationalism and thus to allay the suspicions about it and (2) to give a positive presentation of dispensationalism as it is being taught today."[22]

Of course, the primary question remains: What is a dispensation?[23] Ryrie defines a dispensation as "a distinguishable economy in the outworking of God's purpose." By stressing that a dispensation is an economy rather than an age or a period of time Ryrie distances himself from C. I. Scofield, who defined a dispensation as "a period of time during which man is tested in respect of obedience to some *specific* revelation of the will of God."[24] The key biblical word underlying the concept of dispensations is *oikonomia*, which means "stewardship." Carefully analyzing the parable in Luke 16:1–13, where the word occurs three times, Ryrie cites the following characteristics of a stewardship or dispensation: (1) there are two parties, the one in authority delegating responsibilities and the other obligated to carry out those responsibilities (v. 1); (2) there are specific responsibilities (v. 1); (3) the steward is accountable (v. 2); and (4) when the steward is unfaithful, a change in the system may be made (v. 2). Ryrie explains a dispensation both from God's view

and from ours: "From God's viewpoint a dispensation is an economy; from man's it is a responsibility to the particular revelation given at the time."[25] Each dispensation comprises a test, failure, and judgment. When humans fail the test, God judges and inaugurates a new dispensation. Ryrie charges covenant theology with failing to acknowledge the obvious: "Covenant theology with its all-encompassing covenant of grace glosses over great epochs and climaxes of history lest they disturb the 'unity of Scripture' and introduce something so new that a dispensation might have to be recognized."[26]

Ryrie identifies three essential tenets of dispensationalism: (1) Israel and the church are distinct; (2) Scripture must be interpreted literally (Ryrie speaks of the "normal" or "plain" meaning) without spiritualizing or allegorizing the text (allowances can be made for figures of speech); and (3) the underlying purpose of God in the world is not our salvation but his glory.[27] Ryrie also identifies at least three dispensations specifically mentioned in Paul's writings: "In Ephesians 1:10 he writes of 'the dispensation of the fullness of times,' which seems to be a future period. In Ephesians 3:2 he designates the 'dispensation of the grace of God,' which was the emphasis of the content of his preaching at that time. In Colossians 1:25–26 it is implied that another dispensation preceded the present one in which the mystery of Christ in the believer is revealed." Ryrie concludes, *"There can be no question that the Bible uses the word dispensation in exactly the same way the dispensationalist does."*[28] What are these three dispensations? Law, grace (or the church age), and the millennial kingdom. These are also the

20. Ibid., 262.

21. Daniel P. Fuller, "The Hermeneutics of Dispensationalism," Th.D. diss., Northern Baptist Theological Seminary, 1957—Fuller builds on his dissertation in *Gospel and Law: Contrast or Continuum?* (Grand Rapids: Eerdmans, 1980); Clarence B. Bass, *Backgrounds to Dispensationalism* (Grand Rapids: Eerdmans, 1960).

22. Charles C. Ryrie, *Dispensationalism Today* (Chicago: Moody, 1965), 9.

23. Ibid., 22–47.

24. *Scofield Reference Bible* (New York: Oxford University Press, 1945), 5.

25. Charles C. Ryrie, "Dispensation, Dispensationalism," in *Evangelical Dictionary of Theology*, ed. Walter A. Elwell (Grand Rapids: Baker, 1984), 322.

26. Ryrie, *Dispensationalism Today*, 41.

27. For an exposition of this third tenet see Charles C. Ryrie, *Transformed by His Glory* (Wheaton, Ill.: Victor, 1990).

28. Ryrie, *Dispensationalism Today*, 27.

only three dispensations specifically identified in Dallas Seminary's doctrinal statement. Although many dispensationalists tenaciously hold to seven dispensations, Ryrie believes that the number and names of the dispensations are "relatively minor matters."[29]

In responding to the charge of recency (viz., that dispensationalism was first formulated by John Nelson Darby and the Plymouth Brethren in the nineteenth century), Ryrie traces dispensational concepts to Justin Martyr, Irenaeus, Clement of Alexandria, and even Augustine. French philosopher Pierre Poiret (1646–1719) developed a sevenfold scheme of dispensationalism in a six-volume systematic theology, *L'Économie divine*. In addition, John Edwards (1637–1716) and Isaac Watts (1674–1748) both developed sophisticated schemes of dispensationalism long before the Plymouth Brethren.

In comparing and contrasting covenant theology with dispensationalism, Ryrie points out that it is covenant theology that is recent; it is post-Reformation.[30] It is not found in the theology of the early church nor of the Reformation leaders. Nor, says Ryrie, does it have a basis in Scripture; rather, it is a deduction from Scripture. Moreover, he sees covenant theology as based on the faulty hermeneutic that interprets the Old Testament by the New Testament. "There is," avers Ryrie, "everything wrong about imposing the New Testament on the Old."[31] Ryrie also chides dispensationalism's opponents for misrepresenting its position on the critical issue of the terms of salvation. He cites in particular John Wick Bowman and Clarence Bass.[32] Ryrie summarizes: "The *basis* of salvation in every age is the death of Christ; the *requirement* for salvation in every age is faith; the *object* of faith in every age is God; the *content* of faith changes in the various dispensations."[33]

The Salvation-Lordship Debate

In 1988, with the publication of *The Gospel according to Jesus*, John MacArthur launched an assault on proponents of the view that one can accept Christ as Savior without making him Lord of one's life.[34] In particular, MacArthur attacked Dallas Seminary founder Lewis Sperry Chafer and professors Zane Hodges and Charles Ryrie. The criticism aimed at Ryrie centered on his discussion "Must Christ Be Lord to Be Saviour?" which had appeared in *Balancing the Christian Life*.[35] Ryrie was responding to, among others, J. I. Packer, who, in critiquing methods of gospel presentation, had asked: "Is this way of presenting Christ [i.e., merely as Savior and not also as Lord] calculated to convey to people the *application* of the gospel, and not just part of it, but the whole of it? . . . Or will it leave them supposing that all they have to do is to trust Christ as a sin-bearer, not realizing that they must also deny themselves and enthrone Him as their Lord (the error which we might call only-believism)?"[36] Ryrie argued that "the message of faith only and the message of faith plus commitment of life cannot both be the gospel; therefore, one of them is a false gospel and comes under the curse of perverting the gospel or preaching another gospel (Gal. 1:6–9), and this is a very serious matter."[37] The logic of the position that salvation is impossible without granting Christ lordship leads necessarily to the conclusion that there are no, so to speak, uncommitted or carnal believers, but Ryrie cites Peter (Acts 10:14) and the converts at Ephesus (Acts 19) as examples.

29. Ibid., 48.
30. Ibid., 177–91.
31. Ibid., 187.
32. Ibid., 110–11.
33. Ibid., 123.
34. John F. MacArthur, *The Gospel according to Jesus* (Grand Rapids: Zondervan, 1988).
35. Charles C. Ryrie, *Balancing the Christian Life* (Chicago: Moody, 1969), 169–81.
36. J. I. Packer, *Evangelism and the Sovereignty of God* (Chicago: Inter-Varsity, 1961), 88–89.
37. See Ryrie, *Balancing the Christian Life*, 170–73.

What should one conclude? That Peter and the others were never saved? Or did they lose their salvation when they rejected the lordship of Christ?

Ryrie focuses attention on the meaning of "Lord" (*kyrios*). Does usage of "Lord" signify that we have made Christ "Master" of our lives? Ryrie admits that sometimes it does; but when used in relation to salvation, it simply affirms Jesus' deity. Consider as evidence the controversy that was stirred up when Jesus, an ordinary man from a poor carpenter's family, was called *kyrios*. The term obviously meant more than "Sir" or "Master"; it was an affirmation that Jesus is God. He is the God-man. That is also the emphasis in Romans 10:9. Ryrie concludes, "It is the confession of Jesus as God and thus faith in the God-Man that saves from sin."[38]

The issue for Ryrie is the purity of the gospel. He is concerned that nothing be added to the gospel of salvation by grace through faith. If conditions are attached, where do the conditions stop?

> If the gospel of the Lord Jesus includes lordship over my life, it might very well also include the necessity of believing He is my Creator, Judge, coming King, Example, Teacher, and so forth, on and on, to include every attribute of Deity and every aspect of the perfect humanity of the Lord Jesus. . . . The emphasis the Bible gives to these words [Lord Jesus] is on His being the God-Man, Man in order to die, and God to make that death effective for the remission of sins. Where do you stop if you start adding something else to this which is the gospel revealed in the Bible?[39]

A further confusion in the debate centers on the word *disciple*. What does it mean? According to Ryrie, "a disciple is one who receives instruction from another; he is a learner."[40] Given this definition, a disciple may be an unbeliever like Judas or may

desert Christ (John 6:66). MacArthur, on the other hand, equates discipleship with salvation. There are, then, conditions for salvation. "Salvation is for those who are willing to forsake everything. . . . We *do* have to be willing to forsake all (Luke 14:33). . . . People with genuine faith do not refuse to acknowledge their sinfulness. They sense that they have offended the holiness of God, and do not reject the lordship of Christ. They do not cling to the things of this world. Real faith lacks none of these attributes. Saving faith is a commitment to leave sin and follow Jesus Christ at all costs. Jesus takes no one unwilling to come on those terms."[41]

With the publication of MacArthur's *Gospel according to Jesus*, to which Packer and James Montgomery Boice had contributed forewords, the battle lines were drawn. In 1989 Ryrie responded to MacArthur's charges with *So Great Salvation*, to which Warren Wiersbe contributed the foreword. The issue for Ryrie is still the nature of the gospel. From 1 Corinthians 15:3–8 he concludes that "the Gospel that saves is believing that Christ died for our sins and rose from the dead. That is the *complete* Gospel, and if so, then it is also the true full Gospel and the true whole Gospel. Nothing else is needed for the forgiveness of sins and the gift of eternal life."[42]

A Systematic Theologian

In 1972 Ryrie brought out his *Survey of Bible Doctrine*, an overview of systematic theology for the lay reader. Written without technical jargon, the book explains the basic elements of Christian doctrine in lay language. Ryrie's thesis is clearly stated in the introduction: "God intended you to understand what the Bible teaches. This does not mean that you will comprehend all its truths at first reading or even in a lifetime, but it does mean that you can expect to learn a great deal. God used language

38. Ibid., 175.
39. Ibid., 177.
40. Ibid., 178.

41. MacArthur, *Gospel according to Jesus*, 78, 87.
42. Ryrie, *So Great Salvation*, 40.

which He meant to be taken just as normally and plainly as the words in this book."[43]

In 1986 appeared *Basic Theology*, a more comprehensive work which quickly sold over sixty thousand copies. Ryrie's central presupposition in this volume (as in his other works) is the inerrancy of Scripture. "This stands as the watershed presupposition. If the Bible is not true, then trinitarianism is untrue and Jesus Christ is not who He claimed to be. And we cannot be certain that what we learn from the Bible about the Triune God is accurate unless we believe that our source itself is accurate. Thus the belief in the truthfulness of the Bible is the basic presupposition."[44]

But how shall the Bible be interpreted? Ryrie argues for a literal interpretation because we normally express our thoughts literally, and that, in fact, is the way God has communicated to us. "If one does not employ normal [i.e., literal] interpretation, then objectivity is lost to the extent that he does not use it consistently. Switching the hermeneutical base from literal to allegorical or to semiallegorical or to theological inevitably results in different, inconsistent, and often contradictory interpretations."[45] Other elements of sound hermeneutics include grammatical and contextual analysis, comparison with other passages of Scripture, and recognition of the progressiveness of revelation.[46] That is Ryrie's stated hermeneutical system, and that has been his practice.

In *Basic Theology* the reader will find definitive statements of Ryrie's view of inerrancy, interpretation, the nature of the gospel, charismatic doctrine, the distinctives of the church, and eschatology. *Basic Theology* will probably prove to be his magnum opus, not only because it summarizes his theology, but also because it is written in his highly readable style.

A Commentator on Contemporary Issues

Another indication of the breadth of Ryrie's interests is his *You Mean the Bible Teaches That . . .* (published in 1974 and enlarged and reissued in 1991 as *Biblical Answers to Contemporary Issues*). Here he addresses contemporary and controversial issues like civil disobedience, capital punishment, women's liberation, divorce, situation ethics, and abortion. His purpose is "to try to focus on the major aspects of problems which confront people today."[47] Ryrie does not have easy answers nor does he opt for popular conclusions. But he is thought-provoking.

In discussing divorce, Ryrie explains the exceptive phrase of Matthew 19:9 as relating to the marriage of close relatives, which was prohibited by the Mosaic law (Lev. 18:6–18). He had developed this thesis earlier in *The Place of Women in the Church*. While many interpret the exceptive phrase as a reference to adultery, Ryrie notes that adultery cannot be in view since the penalty for adultery was death (Lev. 20:10; Deut. 22:22). Ryrie concludes that Christ taught the indissolubility of marriage.[48] Ryrie's inference that scripturally there is no justifiable divorce will prove unpopular amid our divorce-ridden society. He does offer, however, compassionate counsel and words of wisdom: "The church should receive such people and minister to their special needs and seek to help them find a proper place of usefulness. An ounce of prevention is worth a pound of cure! Perhaps we are spending too much time today seeking to find the innocent party . . . it is far more important to

---

43. Charles C. Ryrie, *A Survey of Bible Doctrine* (Chicago: Moody, 1972), 9–10.
44. Ryrie, *Basic Theology*, 16.
45. Ibid., 113.
46. Ibid., 114–15.

47. Charles C. Ryrie, *You Mean The Bible Teaches That . . .* (Chicago: Moody, 1974), 9.
48. Ibid., 45–56. Ryrie's thesis has been amplified by a former student of his; see J. Carl Laney, *The Divorce Myth* (Minneapolis: Bethany, 1986).

indoctrinate young people in scriptural standards concerning marriage."[49]

Of those who avow civil disobedience based on the unconstitutionality of a law, Ryrie asks: "But who decides if a law is clearly unconstitutional? Is it up to each individual, or do we abide by the decisions of the courts?"[50] Civil obedience does not stand in isolation; it is part of the larger picture of constituted authority. As the church is subject to Christ, servants to their masters, wives to their husbands, children to their parents, church members to their leaders, so believers are to be subject to their government. Ryrie concludes, "When civil law and God's law are in opposition, the illustrations of the Bible sanction, if not obligate, the believer to protest or disobey. But when a believer feels he should disobey his government, he must be sure it is not because the government has denied him *his* rights, but because it has denied him *God's* rights."[51]

In discussing women's liberation, Ryrie reminds his readers that "Christianity was a women's lib movement long before current groups ever devised a plan."[52] Christianity elevated the status of women. This becomes apparent when one considers the position of women in Greek and Roman society. "Jesus Christ introduced a new appraisal of women. He offered them spiritual privileges equal to those given to men, but He did not sanction equal spiritual activities."[53] Therein lies the distinction between the functioning of men and women in the Christian church. "In various ways, women served the new churches but apparently always in a secondary place. The apostles were all men. The missionary activity was done by men. The writing of the New Testament was the work of men. The leadership of the churches was in the hands of men. Equality of spiritual position for women

did not mean equality of spiritual ministry."[54] So how can women serve in the church? The only possible place of leadership is deaconess, but the relevant texts (Rom. 16:1–2; 1 Tim. 3:11) are unclear on the matter. Ryrie summarizes: "(1) the primary and honored place of the Christian woman is in her home, which takes precedence over all other opportunities; (2) her position in the body of Christ is equal to that of every other believer; (3) her function as far as office and activity is restricted, recognizing the leadership and ministry of the church as the responsibility of men."[55]

Though *You Mean the Bible Teaches That . . .* is but a small volume, it clearly reveals Ryrie's position. He is willing to accept a difficult conclusion if he is convinced that it is the biblical teaching. He is willing to assume a stance that runs contrary to popular opinion (even popular *evangelical* opinion). There is no question that his authority is the Bible. Perhaps that is the secret to the success of Ryrie's writings. Though his readers may not agree with him on every issue, they are aware the man writes with an unshakable conviction of the normativeness of God's Word. The Bible is his authority. It has the final say.

The Ryrie Study Bible

A hallmark of Charles Ryrie's academic achievements is *The Ryrie Study Bible*. First introduced in 1976, it is now available in various editions (NIV, NASB, KJV, NKJV, Portuguese, and Spanish). Unlike *The Scofield Reference Bible,* which is theologically oriented, *The Ryrie Study Bible* is more exegetically oriented in that Ryrie seeks to illuminate verses for the reader through explanatory notes. These notes provide historical, geographical, grammatical, etymological, political, cultural, and theological information. While Ryrie remains firmly committed to his theological views, he explains other positions. In the introduc-

49. Ryrie, *You Mean,* 56.
50. Ibid., 15.
51. Ibid., 19–20.
52. Ibid., 34.
53. Ibid., 36.
54. Ibid., 38.
55. Ibid., 43.

tion to the Book of Revelation, for example, he discusses different interpretive approaches to the book, though he clearly states that he holds the futurist view. Charitable toward opposing interpretations, *The Ryrie Study Bible* sometimes does not take a position where it could. Accordingly, it has even been accepted by charismatics.

Like many of Ryrie's other writings, the *Study Bible* has plowed new ground, providing the average reader with helpful introductory information on each of the books of the Bible (author, date, historical background, purpose, content, outline). In one volume Ryrie offers a concise commentary, word studies, and doctrinal helps. The chain that had anchored the Bible to the pulpit, and that Martin Luther broke, has been broken further, giving the reader a clearer understanding of God's Word.

Charles Ryrie has made a unique and important contribution to twentieth-century theology. His ability to communicate to the layperson undoubtedly stands without peer. Few theological volumes written in this century have communicated truth as effectively to the ordinary individual as have Ryrie's works. Part of his legacy is his example of crystalizing and clarifying the complex topics of theology. Many Christians have been guided into an understanding of Christian doctrine through books like *A Survey of Bible Doctrine* and *The Holy Spirit*. Many more will undoubtedly be helped by his *Basic Theology*. Ryrie's writings serve to clarify the teachings of Scripture "that the man of God may be adequate, equipped for every good work" (2 Tim. 3:17 NASB).

Ryrie's legacy also challenges the Christian reader to serious thinking about how biblical teaching relates to the contemporary world. He has grappled with how the Bible applies to the serious issues of the day: the role of women, divorce, legalism, the nature of the gospel, the charismatic movement. He has not necessarily arrived at popular conclusions, but he has drawn the reader back to the Scriptures. For Ryrie the authority is not society or experience, but the Bible. This engenders confidence in his writings as well as encourages average Christians to study the Bible on their own for theological answers. What could be of greater satisfaction to a theologian?

Primary Sources

Ryrie, Charles C. *The Acts of the Apostles.* Chicago: Moody, 1961.

_____. *Balancing the Christian Life.* Chicago: Moody, 1969.

_____. *Basic Theology.* Wheaton, Ill.: Victor, 1986.

_____. *The Basis of the Premillennial Faith.* Neptune, N.J.: Loizeaux, 1953.

_____. *The Bible and Tomorrow's News.* Wheaton, Ill.: Scripture, 1969. Reprinted as *The Final Countdown.* Wheaton, Ill.: Victor, 1982.

_____. *Biblical Theology of the New Testament.* Chicago: Moody, 1959.

_____. *Dispensationalism Today.* Chicago: Moody, 1965.

_____. *First and Second Thessalonians.* Chicago: Moody, 1959.

_____. *The Grace of God.* Chicago: Moody, 1963.

_____. *The Holy Spirit.* Chicago: Moody, 1965.

_____. *The Living End.* Old Tappan, N.J.: Revell, 1976. Reprinted as *The Best Is Yet to Come.* Chicago: Moody, 1981.

_____. *The Miracles of Our Lord.* Nashville: Nelson, 1984.

_____. *Neo-orthodoxy.* Chicago: Moody, 1956.

_____. *The Place of Women in the Church.* New York: Macmillan, 1958. Reprinted as *The Role of Women in the Church.* Chicago: Moody, 1970.

_____. *Revelation.* Chicago: Moody, 1968.

_____. *Ryrie's Concise Guide to the Bible.* San Bernardino, Calif.: Here's Life, 1983.

_____. *The Ryrie Study Bible.* Chicago: Moody, 1976.

_____. *So Great Salvation.* Wheaton, Ill.: Victor, 1989.

_____. *A Survey of Bible Doctrine.* Chicago: Moody, 1972.

_____. *Transformed by His Glory.* Wheaton, Ill.: Victor, 1990.

_____. *What You Should Know about Inerrancy.* Chicago: Moody, 1981.

_____. *What You Should Know about Social Responsibility.* Chicago: Moody, 1982.

_____. *What You Should Know about the Rapture.* Chicago: Moody, 1981.

_____. *You Mean the Bible Teaches That. . . .* Chicago: Moody, 1974. Reprinted as *Biblical Answers to Contemporary Issues.* Chicago: Moody, 1991.

J. I. Packer

Roger Nicole

On July 22, 1926, J. I. (James Innell) Packer was born in Gloucester, England. His father was a clerk for a railway company, and his mother was a schoolteacher. Their home was nominally Anglican but without deep religious commitment. Discussions with a Unitarian friend, the reading of some of C. S. Lewis's works, and the conversion of one of Packer's friends had a positive influence; and subsequent contact with the Oxford Inter-Collegiate Christian Union led him to faith. He gave up his position of clarinetist with the Oxford Bandits, a jazz band, in order to attend Bible-study sessions on Saturday nights.[1]

While an undergraduate at Oxford, Packer made the discovery of the Puritan writings, specifically those of John Owen and Richard Baxter. They challenged him to combine a staunch doctrinal commitment with a firm evangelical lifestyle and due emphasis upon an outgoing evangelistic ministry. In 1948, after the completion of a B.A. degree in classical studies, Packer accepted a post teaching classical languages at the Anglican Theological Seminary of Oak Hill near London. This one-year appointment gave him opportunity to teach philosophy and a course on Ephesians as well. A call to ministry that he had sensed earlier was confirmed here with a specific direction toward teaching. During that year he attended regularly the Sunday evening services at Westminster Chapel, where Martyn Lloyd-Jones's powerful preaching made a lasting impact upon his life.[2]

With a view to ordination, Packer returned to Oxford to study at Wycliffe Hall. He received a B.A. degree in theology in 1950 and an M.A. in philosophy in 1952. That same year he was ordained to the ministry in the Church of England and also made the acquaintance of his future wife,

1. Christopher Catherwood, *Five Evangelical Leaders* (Wheaton, Ill.: Harold Shaw, 1985), 170.

2. Ibid., 173.

379

"Kit" Mullet, a nurse from Wales, who was at that time working in a London hospital. They married in 1954 and eventually adopted three children—Naomi, Ruth, and Martin.

In 1954 Packer also received his D.Phil. from Oxford University. His thesis of 499 pages is entitled "The Redemption and Restoration of Man in the Thought of Richard Baxter." Even though Baxter's views were the focus of his thesis, Packer did not subscribe to every one of them, particularly the idea that Christ made satisfaction for the sins of all, which was made explicit in Baxter's posthumously published *Universal Redemption of Mankind by the Lord Jesus Christ* (1694). Indeed, Packer made a resolute endorsement of limited atonement in his introductory essay to a new edition of John Owen's *Death of Death in the Death of Christ*.[3]

From 1953 to 1955 Packer served as curate to William Leathem in Birmingham. In 1955 he was called to be a tutor at Tyndale Hall, an evangelical Anglican seminary in Bristol. There he had opportunity to manifest his gifts to an ever-widening circle both within and outside the Church of England. Among the beneficiaries of his contributions were the annual Puritan Studies Conference held at Westminster Chapel and the Theological Studies Conference of Inter-Varsity Fellowship.[4]

In 1958 Packer's first book appeared. *"Fundamentalism" and the Word of God* immediately secured the attention of the evangelical public and marked him as one of the most gifted and effective writers of the orthodox faith. It opened for him an immense potential not only in the British Isles, but in the United States, Canada, Australia, and ultimately worldwide. Thus, in addition to his various resident positions, he was a visiting professor at a large number of seminaries, notably Gordon-Conwell, Westmin-

ster, Fuller, Columbia, and Reformed in Jackson and in Orlando. He also ministered at many conferences and institutes, such as the International Council on Biblical Inerrancy, the Philadelphia Conference on Reformed Theology, the Pensacola Biblical Institute, the International Council for Reformed Faith and Action, the Evangelical Theological Society, and the Ligonier Conference.

In his next volume, *Evangelism and the Sovereignty of God* (1961), Packer gave a brilliant demonstration of the consistency of Calvinism with the evangelistic drive. At about the same time he accepted a call to serve at Latimer House, which represents the evangelical Anglican point of view at Oxford. He served first as librarian (1961–63) and then as warden (i.e., director, 1963–70).[5]

During the 1960s Packer was faced with two major controversies. First there was the question of the possible reunion of the Methodists with the Church of England. Evangelicals as well as Anglo-Catholics were opposed to such a union, the former on doctrinal grounds, the latter on ecclesiastical grounds. Packer emphasized the benefits of unity in faith, love, and evangelistic efforts. In 1963, after an initial proposal had been defeated in the Church of England, Packer was appointed as a member of a commission to study the matter further. He took this occasion to remind both Anglicans and Methodists of their historic foundations in the Thirty-nine Articles (or John Wesley's abridgment thereof to twenty-four) and to stress the importance of doctrinal unity. At this point there seemed to be some measure of agreement with some leading Anglo-Catholics, notably E. L. Mascall; and a volume entitled *Growing into Union*, in which Packer was one of four essayists, was published jointly in 1970.[6] This irritated greatly the evangelical

---

3. J. I. Packer, Introductory Essay to *Death of Death in the Death of Christ*, by John Owen (London: Banner of Truth Trust, 1959), 1–25.

4. Catherwood, *Five Evangelical Leaders*, 176.

5. Ibid., 186.

6. C. O. Buchanan et al., *Growing into Union: Proposals for Forming a United Church in England* (London: S.P.C.K., 1970).

community, particularly those who were members of Free Churches; they seemed to be unable or at least unwilling to understand that this book represented a courteous debate rather than a surrender to a quasi-popish view.[7]

The second controversy broke out in 1966, when Martyn Lloyd-Jones, convinced that there was no way of bringing the Church of England back to a sound doctrinal position, made an urgent call to evangelicals within that church to leave. He pleaded with them to join with Free Church evangelicals and thus be liberated from what he viewed as compromising associations. This caused great distress to men like John Stott and Packer, who were persuaded that their ministry was to be pursued from within the church. At the National Evangelical Anglican Congress at Keele (1967) the position of the evangelicals was carefully considered. Packer subsequently edited a volume of essays entitled *Guidelines: Anglican Evangelicals Face the Future.*[8] Unfortunately, the two controversies caused a serious estrangement between Packer and Free Church evangelicals and made his work much more difficult. It was especially painful for him to be at odds with Lloyd-Jones, whom he described as "the greatest man he had ever known."[9]

In 1970 Packer left Oxford to accept the position of principal of Tyndale Hall in Bristol. When three seminaries were united into one called Trinity College, Packer was named vice-principal (1972). These positions permitted continuation of his teaching ministry and some pursuit of scholarship. An early fruit thereof was *Knowing God,* which was published in 1973 to almost instantaneous acclaim. Within less than twenty years more than one million copies were sold in English, and translations have appeared in French, German, Korean, Chinese, Japanese, Spanish, Norwegian, Finn-

ish, Polish, and modern Hebrew. *Knowing God* clearly manifests Packer's masterful gift of dealing with theological questions in a way that is understandable to lay people and has strong practical spiritual impact. This surely is a book in the best Puritan tradition.[10]

In 1979 Packer accepted a call to serve as professor of historical and systematic theology at Regent College in Vancouver. This opened up for him additional opportunities for an international ministry, while distancing him somewhat from the painful frictions experienced in Britain.[11] Worthy of special mention is his involvement with the International Council on Biblical Inerrancy. He served on the editorial committee for each of the three summit meetings in Chicago (1978 on the nature of inspiration, 1982 on hermeneutics, and 1986 on application) as well as the two conferences intended for the Christian public at large (1981 in San Diego and 1988 in Washington). In the same vein was his book *Beyond the Battle for the Bible* (1980).

Since 1984, Packer has produced four additional major works, each of which includes in a very convenient form previously published articles or lectures which had become very hard to lay hold of: *Keep in Step with the Spirit* (1984); *Hot Tub Religion* (1987); *A Quest for Godliness: The Puritan Vision of the Christian Life* (1990); and *Rediscovering Holiness* (1992). For years he has been at work on a comprehensive systematic theology that he is uniquely qualified to write. Highly appreciated as a teacher at Regent College, he has also continued to be very much in demand as a lecturer and preacher.

Major Themes

The Doctrine of Scripture

The prominence of Scripture in Packer's thought was already evident in *"Fundamentalism" and the Word of God,* whose opening

7. Catherwood, *Five Evangelical Leaders,* 187–89.
8. J. I. Packer, ed., *Guidelines: Anglican Evangelicals Face the Future* (London: Falcon, 1967).
9. Catherwood, *Five Evangelical Leaders,* 190.
10. Ibid., 193.
11. Ibid., 203.

chapter gives an overview of the criticisms that Gabriel Hebert, Alan Richardson, and A. M. Ramsey have leveled against the evangelical position and practice. These criticisms are shown to be mutually incompatible and based on misapprehensions of the evangelical movement.[12] The next chapter clarifies the true nature of evangelicalism in contrast to the liberal desupernaturalization of Christianity. It also shows why "fundamentalism" is not an appropriate designation for British evangelicalism.[13] In the chapter on "Authority" Packer shows that Jesus, the apostles, and the early church were completely united in their view of Scripture as the Word of God, the supreme norm of faith and practice.[14] And the chapter entitled "Scripture" constitutes a restatement of the evangelical doctrine of inspiration; among Packer's emphases are that (1) divine authorship of the Bible is consistent with the personal characteristics displayed by the human authors therein; (2) Scripture is the Word of God expressed in propositional revelation both infallible and inerrant; and (3) a proper interpretation will manifest the unity of Scripture, which is a mark of the Holy Spirit's control.[15]

Packer proceeds to show that "Faith" is the proper response to God's revelation in Scripture; the witness of the Holy Spirit to the believer generates conviction, not merely assent.[16] There follows a discussion of "Reason," wherein Packer shows that the evangelical view does not minimize the role of the human rational faculties. On the contrary, they are essential for (1) *receiving* revelation couched in human language, (2) *applying* its truths to life at our level, and (3) *communicating* it in witness and preaching. In performing these functions, however, reason must be the servant of Scripture, not its master. Reason does not have the right

to judge what is acceptable and what may be rejected.[17] This is precisely where liberalism has gone wrong. By refusing to submit from the start to the biblical doctrine of inspiration and by giving priority to historical criticism liberals have committed a principial mistake which is bound to vitiate their conclusions.[18] Liberalism "discounts the authority of Christ, . . . expresses an attitude of intellectual impenitence, . . . denies the rule of the Creator over His world, . . . and presupposes an apologetic strategy which is fundamentally wrong."[19] It is, in short, "bad Christianity."[20]

After this first, and very important, salvo Packer continued to give close attention to the doctrine of Scripture. In *God Has Spoken* he considers the need of revelation ("The Lost Word"), general and special revelation ("God's Spoken Word"), inscripturation ("God's Written Word"), and finally illumination ("God's Word Heard").[21] In *Beyond the Battle for the Bible* he examines contemporary developments and issues (particularly the relationship of evangelical theology to the biblical-theology movement and the discussions within the Roman Catholic Church).[22] He also articulates with precision the relationship of the Bible and the church (the headings here are "The Bible over the Church" and "The Church under the Bible"). A review of three recent books (1975–79) closes the volume.[23]

In addition to Packer's three volumes dealing with the doctrine of Scripture, a great many articles on the subject have ap-

12. J. I. Packer, *"Fundamentalism" and the Word of God* (Grand Rapids: Eerdmans, 1958), 9–23.

13. Ibid., 24–40.

14. Ibid., 41–74.

15. Ibid., 75–114.

16. Ibid., 115–25.

17. Ibid., 126–45.

18. Ibid., 146–68.

19. Ibid., 160–62.

20. Ibid., 160.

21. J. I. Packer, *God Has Spoken* (Downers Grove, Ill.: Inter-Varsity, 1979).

22. J. I. Packer, *Beyond the Battle for the Bible* (Westchester, Ill.: Cornerstone, 1980).

23. G. C. Berkouwer, *Holy Scripture*, trans. and ed. Jack B. Rogers (Grand Rapids: Eerdmans, 1975); Harold Lindsell, *The Bible in the Balance* (Grand Rapids: Zondervan, 1979); Jack B. Rogers and Donald K. McKim, *The Authority and Interpretation of the Bible: An Historical Approach* (San Francisco: Harper and Row, 1979).

peared in periodicals or in symposia. These would constitute a good-sized book, even if the overlapping were eliminated. It is good news that such a book is in process of compilation.

The Doctrine of God

A second major theme is the doctrine of God. *Knowing God* is dedicated to this topic. It emphasizes the blessing of knowing God, not merely knowing about him. Packer also emphasizes the blessing of knowing God as triune. He then devotes individual chapters to some of the attributes of God: immutability, majesty, wisdom, veracity, love, grace, righteousness, wrath, goodness and severity, jealousy. Packer summarizes the biblical evidence for each attribute and then discusses in a very practical way its impact on our lives and piety. The book concludes with chapters on propitiation, adoption, guidance, serenity in adversity, and ultimate Christian optimism (Rom. 8). The intensely biblical character of this material, its careful organization, and the practical applications to life go far to explain the exceptional success of this work. Here is theology made comprehensible and interesting to lay people, and at the same time challenging to those who study in seminary. It is written with indisputable earnestness and abounds in practical application of the truth. An especially notable feature is the frequent use of quotations from hymns.[24]

The doctrine of God is also the focus of *Evangelism and the Sovereignty of God*, which was written to dispel the erroneous but widespread notion that Calvinism, with its emphasis on the priority of God's decision and action, paralyzes evangelism and mission. The key to a proper stance here is to understand that God's priority does not rule out human decision and action: "To evangelize is to present Jesus Christ in the power of the Holy Spirit, that men shall come to put their trust in God through Him, to accept Him as their Saviour, and serve Him as their King in the fellowship of His Church."[25] There is no question here of neglecting the lordship of Christ in the gospel call, for the concept of divine sovereignty regulates the message and method of evangelism, provides the motivation for it, and is the grounds for confidence in its effectiveness. A powerful argument in a very concise form!

The Work of the Holy Spirit in Human Lives

Keep in Step with the Spirit begins with an overview of some common but incomplete perspectives on the work of the Holy Spirit: it provides power for living, performance in service, purity of value and action, presentation for decision. These elements must be seen in combination rather than in isolation, declares Packer, and others—perception, pull, personhood, and especially presence—should be added. This balanced survey of the work of the Holy Spirit leads to a special discussion of the way of holiness and a critique of inadequate views of sanctification.[26] The last one hundred pages of the book are devoted to a study of the charismatic life. Packer displays here a generous appreciation of the strengths in the charismatic movement as well as a keen perception of its potential exaggerations and distortions.[27] A moving chapter "Come, Holy Spirit," summarizes the Spirit's importance for our lives and churches today.[28] A brief appendix argues that "the wretched man" of Romans 7 represents one aspect of Christian experience.[29]

Rediscovering Holiness is a practical return to this particular aspect of the Spirit's

24. J. I. Packer, *Knowing God* (Downers Grove, Ill.: Inter-Varsity, 1973), 27, 57, 69, 97, 113, 119, 120, 121, 122, 123, 124, 133, 175, 179, 189, 194, 195, 198, 209, 220, 229, 240, 249, 250, 252.

25. J. I. Packer, *Evangelism and the Sovereignty of God* (Chicago: Inter-Varsity, 1961), 37–38.

26. J. I. Packer, *Keep in Step with the Spirit* (Old Tappan, N.J.: Revell, 1984), 74–169.

27. Ibid., 170–234.

28. Ibid., 235–62.

29. Ibid., 263–70.

work.[30] Packer forcefully argues that holiness is necessarily implied in the experience of salvation. It is an ever-deepening blessing in repentance, Christ-likeness, spiritual strength, and endurance of hardship. A truly edifying book constellated with apt quotations from hymns.

In *Hot Tub Religion* Packer deals with crucial questions that frequently beset Christians: What is God's plan? Who can claim to know him? What does holiness require? How will God guide me? Is there divine healing? What should I expect of God when I am sick or depressed? How should I react to the condition of the church? Here we have ten very practical chapters carefully grounded, as always, in Scripture and integrated with Reformed theology.[31]

Christian Doctrine as a Whole

Packer is also concerned with Christian doctrine in general. *I Want to Be a Christian*, for example, is an adult catechism with a luminous commentary on the Apostles' Creed, the Lord's Prayer, and the Ten Commandments.[32] The meaning of baptism and conversion is also carefully explained.

God's Words consists of pithy studies of seventeen Bible themes: revelation, Scripture, the Lord, the world, sin, the devil, grace, the Mediator, reconciliation, faith, justification, regeneration, election, holiness and sanctification, mortification, fellowship, death.[33] The Scripture index has upward of twelve hundred entries, some of them with multiple references!

Concise Theology: A Guide to Historic Christian Beliefs is a series of ninety-four brief studies of the main points of Christian doctrine arranged in the order usual in systematic theology.[34] Each study, comprising from one to three printed pages, provides a positive statement of doctrine with abundant scriptural references. These studies are to be incorporated in the New Geneva Study Bible, which will feature the Reformed interpretation of Scripture, even as the Geneva Bible did in the sixteenth century. The ninety-four studies fall into four major divisions:

1. God Revealed as Creator (29 studies)
2. God Revealed as Redeemer (23 studies)
3. God Revealed as Lord of Grace (34 studies)
4. God Revealed as Lord of Destiny (8 studies)

This very concise presentation, which does not embroil itself in theological controversies, provides a very lucid and readable statement of Reformed doctrine. It whets the appetite for Packer's systematic theology.

The Puritans

Packer has often openly acknowledged his great indebtedness to the Puritans. It is not surprising, then, that *A Quest for Godliness: The Puritan Vision of the Christian Life* is his largest book (367 pages of rather fine print).[35] There are six major divisions, each of which contains three essays:

1. The Puritans in Profile
2. The Puritans and the Bible
3. The Puritans and the Gospel
4. The Puritans and the Holy Spirit
5. The Puritan Christian Life
6. The Puritan Ministry

Some twenty-three pages of notes indicate the scholarly tenor of this well-researched work. For years Packer has been well

---

30. J. I. Packer, *Rediscovering Holiness* (Ann Arbor: Servant, 1992).

31. J. I. Packer, *Hot Tub Religion* (Wheaton, Ill.: Tyndale, 1987).

32. J. I. Packer, *I Want to Be a Christian* (Wheaton, Ill.: Tyndale, 1977).

33. J. I. Packer, *God's Words: Studies of Key Bible Themes* (Downers Grove, Ill.: Inter-Varsity, 1982).

34. J. I. Packer, *Concise Theology: A Guide to Historic Christian Beliefs* (Wheaton, Ill.: Tyndale, 1993).

35. J. I. Packer, *A Quest for Godliness: The Puritan Vision of the Christian Life* (Wheaton, Ill.: Crossway, 1990).

known for a seminary course in this area, and now its major elements are available in print.

Basic Approach

Analytic, Scriptural, Historical

That Packer takes a systematic approach is evident in works like *"Fundamentalism" and the Word of God, Evangelism and the Sovereignty of God,* and *Knowing God.* He is very careful in analyzing the various components of any major tenet, somewhat as a prism sorts out the various colored rays which together constitute white light. Each component is explored and delineated with reference to Scripture. The correlation between the various components is carefully noted so that none is emphasized to a degree that minimizes any other. When tension appears, when our finite minds are transcended to the point where we do not perceive how elements which seem to be in conflict actually coexist in the realm of the infinite, Packer does not insist on providing a rational reconciliation. He is ready instead to posit an "antinomy," thus maintaining both aspects of the truth without impairing either one of them. Examples in point would be the divine inspiration and human authorship of Scripture; the all-encompassing sovereignty of God and the reality of human and angelic decisions; the conjoining of the divine and human natures in the perfect unity of the person of the incarnate Christ; the unity of the divine nature and the "threefoldness" of Father, Son, and Holy Spirit; the coexistence in the Godhead of perfect love and perfect justice.

For Packer the Scripture is always the foundation and the place of ultimate appeal. He does find comfort, however, in showing that his interpretation of Scripture is not without precedent, but harmonizes with certain historic affirmations of God's people, particularly in the early church and at the time of the Reformation. His grasp of the stream of the history of Christian doctrine reinforces his conviction that he has rightly understood the teaching of Scripture, and that the Word of God is not shrouded in obscurity but perspicuous. Those who desire to know and do God's will can find in Scripture the way of salvation and of a godly life. Packer is, then, rightly professor of historical and systematic theology at Regent College. For he thinks and lives in communion with the stalwarts of the early church, with Augustine, with Anselm, with Martin Luther, John Calvin, and the English Reformers, with the Puritans of the seventeenth century, and with the evangelical theologians of later ages. This is not his foundation, but it is a reassuring sign that he has understood aright what the Bible teaches.

Apologetic

Packer is resolutely Christian, Protestant, evangelical, and Puritan. Therefore he is prepared to dispute the views of non-Christians, of Roman Catholics and other sacramentalists, of modernists, and of formalists. In so doing he maintains a serenity that prevents him from caricaturing or misrepresenting those he opposes. Yet he perceives with devastating acuity the crux of the difference, and he is prepared to concentrate his attack there.

Packer is very gifted in causing objections to or criticisms of his evangelical views to boomerang, showing that it is the objectors who are in the wrong. For instance, Packer shows that some of those who accuse the evangelicals of having a docetic or monophysitic view not only are wide of the mark, but reveal a Nestorian outlook which leads them to make that charge.[36] And critics who accuse evangelicals of bibliolatry have actually forged for themselves an authority that supplants the authority of God.[37] Moreover, those who bring a charge of obscurantism against the evangelical position are guilty themselves, for they ignore the fact "that the Bible teaches a positive doctrine of its origin and

36. Packer, *"Fundamentalism,"* 83–84.
37. Ibid., 62, 171.

nature, which Christ incorporated in His own teaching."[38]

Irenic

Packer has broad affinities with many Christians who differ with him on some particulars, while agreeing with the major thrust of his approach. Thus he is not sectarian or provincial, but has worked happily with many interdenominational endeavors. He has refused to castigate the Church of England for its well-known toleration of many different strands of doctrine and of worship. This is the main topic of his pamphlet *A Kind of Noah's Ark*, which was published in 1981.[39]

Packer's irenic spirit is also admirably illustrated in his attitude toward charismatic life and teaching. Witness, for instance, the discussion in *Keep in Step with the Spirit*. He begins by carefully defining the charismatic movement in terms of five distinctive emphases: (1) major postconversion enriching of personal Christian experience; (2) speaking in tongues; (3) other spiritual gifts (including healing and prophecy); (4) worship in the Spirit (with more freedom than in liturgical worship); and (5) certainty that charismatic renewal is central to God's present purpose for the church.[40] Packer then lists and discusses twelve aspects of the movement which he deems positive and commendable: (1) Christ-centeredness; (2) Spirit-empowered living; (3) expression of emotion; (4) prayerfulness; (5) joyfulness; (6) every-heart involvement in the worship of God; (7) every-member ministry in the body of Christ; (8) missionary zeal; (9) small-group ministry; (10) church structures that express the life of the Holy Spirit; (11) communal living; and (12) generous giving.[41] Then, and then only, does he list negative aspects that may damage the contribution of the movement: (1) elitism; (2) sectarianism; (3) emotionalism; (4) anti-intellectualism (with some distaste for seminary training); (5) illuminism; (6) charismania; (7) super-supernaturalism (miracles are constantly expected); (8) eudaemonism (health-and-wealth gospel); (9) obsession with demons (and excessive exorcism); and (10) conformism.[42]

It is clear from this summary that Packer has made a special effort to study and understand the charismatic movement. He is glad to acknowledge wholesome features, even though some of them may have slipped into occasional excesses. He is also clear-sighted in discerning dangers and insufficient safeguards in some forms of the movement. Surely this is material that non-charismatics would do well to read and ponder, lest they miss some part of the full gospel of Christ; charismatics also would do well to consider the dangers listed here in order to be sure that their life and worship do not derail in the manner described.

Evaluation

In both the themes and basic approach he has chosen, in his biblical moorings and historical perspective, in theological grasp and practical application, in the depth of his thought conjoined with lucidity of expression, J. I. Packer has given us a splendid example of what a theologian should be and can be. Among his great strengths we must reckon the keen analytic ability that he applies to the consideration of any issue that he deals with; his willingness, even earnest desire, to validate any element of truth, no matter where he may find it; the resulting careful balance that he maintains between elements of the truth which are in tension and whose ultimate consistency lies beyond the purview of finite human reason; his even-tempered and gracious attitude toward those who differ with him; his uncompromising, steadfast adherence to the fundamentals of the Christian faith; his intense

38. Ibid., 144.
39. J. I. Packer, *A Kind of Noah's Ark: The Anglican Commitment to Comprehensiveness* (Oxford: Latimer, 1981).
40. Packer, *Keep in Step*, 176–81.
41. Ibid., 185–91.

42. Ibid., 191–97.

desire to see the faith implemented in lives dedicated to the glory of God; his clear perception of the missteps and lacunae in the position of his opponents, together with an almost uncanny ability to make their strictures boomerang. With all this he combines a delightful sense of humor and a sharp psychological perception, both of which are not immediately apparent, but are obvious to those who are privileged to be well acquainted with him. Surely if soundness is considered as a paramount qualification for a theologian, Packer must be numbered among the greatest theologians of our generation.

Primary Sources

Packer, J. I. *Beyond the Battle for the Bible.* Westchester, Ill.: Cornerstone, 1980.

_____. *Concise Theology: A Guide to Historic Christian Beliefs.* Wheaton, Ill.: Tyndale, 1993.

_____. *Evangelism and the Sovereignty of God.* Chicago: Inter-Varsity, 1961.

_____. *"Fundamentalism" and the Word of God.* Grand Rapids: Eerdmans, 1958.

_____. *God Has Spoken.* Downers Grove, Ill.: Inter-Varsity, 1979.

_____. *God's Words: Studies of Key Bible Themes.* Downers Grove, Ill.: Inter-Varsity, 1982.

_____. *Hot Tub Religion.* Wheaton, Ill.: Tyndale, 1987.

_____. *I Want to Be a Christian.* Wheaton, Ill.: Tyndale, 1977.

_____. *Keep in Step with the Spirit.* Old Tappan, N.J.: Revell, 1984.

_____. *Knowing God.* Downers Grove, Ill.: Inter-Varsity, 1973.

_____. *Knowing Man.* Westchester, Ill.: Cornerstone, 1979.

_____. *A Quest for Godliness: The Puritan Vision of the Christian Life.* Wheaton, Ill.: Crossway, 1990.

_____. *Rediscovering Holiness.* Ann Arbor: Servant, 1992.

_____. *Your Father Loves You.* Wheaton, Ill.: Harold Shaw, 1986.

Secondary Source

Catherwood, Christopher. *Five Evangelical Leaders,* 169–204. Wheaton, Ill.: Harold Shaw, 1985.

Donald G. Bloesch

Donald K. McKim

When twenty seminary professors were asked who is the most brilliant, creative evangelical systematic theologian today, Donald G. Bloesch's name topped the list.[1] For thirty-five years Bloesch has taught at the University of Dubuque Theological Seminary and during that time has become one of the most prolific American theologians. He has written or edited some 25 books and over 275 published articles and book reviews. His two-volume *Essentials of Evangelical Theology* has been hailed as a pioneering work; an important seminary textbook and guide for evangelical Christians, it has been translated into several languages. Bloesch has charted his own course as an evangelical leader and has been widely involved in speaking and lecturing throughout the country at a variety of theological institutions as well as to church and renewal groups. His work has had substantial influence as a model of evangelical theology, which he views as entailing "a definite doctrine as well as . . . a special

kind of experience."[2] His writing blends his concern for the historic evangelical faith with a zeal for spiritual experience of that faith, which takes the form of "an acknowledgment of the claims of Jesus Christ and an obedience to his commands."[3]

Early Experiences

Donald Bloesch was born on May 3, 1928, to Herbert and Adele Bloesch in Bremen, Indiana. Both of his grandfathers had come from Switzerland to the United States as missionaries to German-speaking immigrants. One was sent by the Basel Evangelical Missionary Society and the other by the

1. Leslie R. Keylock, "Evangelical Leaders You Should Know: Meet Donald G. Bloesch," *Moody Monthly* 88 (March 1988): 61.

2. Donald G. Bloesch, *Essentials of Evangelical Theology*, 2 vols. (San Francisco: Harper and Row, 1978–79), 1:ix.

3. Ibid., 1:2.

St. Chrischona Pilgrim Mission. Herbert Bloesch was a minister of the Evangelical Synod of North America, which in 1934 merged with the Reformed Church in the United States (German) to form the Evangelical and Reformed Church. This denomination later merged with the Congregational Christian churches to form the present-day United Church of Christ. The Evangelical Synod of North America had been established out of the Old Prussian Union in Germany—a mixture of Lutheran and Reformed traditions. In America, it maintained the Lutheran pietist heritage, which continues to be a vital force for Bloesch.[4]

The call to Christian ministry came to Bloesch during his high-school years and after his confirmation (a two-year process of Bible and catechetical study). He enrolled at Elmhurst College, a denominational school which H. Richard and Reinhold Niebuhr had also attended. At Elmhurst, while majoring in philosophy and maintaining a strong interest in sociology, he was introduced to liberal theology. Bloesch recalls writing a paper espousing an adoptionist Christology, an early heresy which taught that Christ was a man gifted with divine powers who became the Son of God at his baptism.[5]

Though Eden Seminary was the usual choice of Elmhurst preministerial students as well as the school from which his father had graduated, Bloesch in 1950 accepted a full scholarship from Chicago Theological Seminary (CTS). While at the seminary, Bloesch never took a course in sociology of religion, even though he planned to concen-trate in that area of study. Liberal theology was predominant at the seminary and at the University of Chicago, where Bloesch enrolled in the doctoral program after his graduation in 1953.

At the university Bloesch was exposed to the neonaturalism or process theology of the faculty, and especially of Daniel Day Williams. From various guest professors such as Daniel Jenkins, Markus Barth, Wilhelm Pauck, and Jaroslav Pelikan, Bloesch also received an introduction to the theology of Karl Barth. He developed strong interests in Emil Brunner, Rudolf Bultmann, Paul Tillich, and Reinhold Niebuhr as well. Though it consisted largely of undergraduate students, Bloesch was attracted to the Inter-Varsity Christian Fellowship chapter at the university. He comments, "I sensed in that group a spiritual bond I did not have with even the neo-orthodox students at CTS."[6] As Bloesch neared completion of his doctoral dissertation, Williams, his thesis advisor, left the school. Bernard Meland, his replacement, was not interested in Bloesch's topic, and so Bloesch began a new thesis, this time on Reinhold Niebuhr's apologetics.

During graduate study, Bloesch served as pastor of St. Paul's Church in Richton Park, Illinois. After receiving his Ph.D. in 1956, he studied for a year at Oxford University, where he became fascinated with Anglo-Catholicism and began to examine Christian renewal movements in Switzerland, France, Italy, and Germany. Some of this research later appeared in his first book, *Centers of Christian Renewal*.[7] He reacted negatively to the ascetic rigorism found in some forms of monasticism. He recalls being told of a mother superior who was regarded as the most holy person in the convent because she slept in the coldest room. Bloesch comments, "Somehow, I felt something had gone wrong!"[8]

---

4. Bloesch notes that "whereas the Reformers place the accent upon *Christ for us,* [Pietism, Puritanism, and evangelicalism] seek to give equal emphasis to *Christ with us* and *Christ in us*" (*Crisis of Piety* [Grand Rapids: Eerdmans, 1968], 43). See also Donald G. Bloesch, *The Evangelical Renaissance* (Grand Rapids: Eerdmans, 1973), ch. 5; idem, *The Struggle of Prayer* (San Francisco: Harper and Row, 1980).

5. Donald G. Bloesch, "My Theological Journey," tape recording, University of Dubuque Theological Seminary, 25 October 1984.

6. Quoted in Keylock, "Evangelical Leaders," 63.

7. Donald G. Bloesch, *Centers of Christian Renewal* (Philadelphia: United Church Press, 1964).

8. Bloesch, "My Theological Journey."

Bloesch's return to the United States brought a one-year appointment at the University of Dubuque Theological Seminary, a Presbyterian institution with an ecumenical student body and a one-hundred-year history of preparing pastors for churches in the Upper Midwest. Later Bloesch discovered that "the administration hired me partly to be a liberal counterpart to a neo-orthodox theologian on the faculty. They assumed that because I had gone to the University of Chicago, I would be liberal."[9] Except for several stints as a visiting professor at various schools, Bloesch has taught at Dubuque since 1957, where his friendship with Arthur C. Cochrane, a major interpreter of Barth's thought, has been a strong influence on his theological journey. Bloesch was made full professor in 1962. Doane College conferred a D.D. degree on him in May 1983.

In November 1962, Bloesch married Brenda Mary Jackson, whom he met while in Geneva and who holds a Ph.D. in French literature from the University of London. After a period of teaching, Brenda redirected her energies to assisting her husband as a researcher and copyeditor. His exceptional output of publications is facilitated by her work in their remarkable partnership.

Evolutionary Trajectories

Herbert Bloesch had imbibed a moderate liberalism during his seminary career. His son's liberal teachers at Elmhurst College were disciples of the great nineteenth-century liberal theologian Albrecht Ritschl. As the younger Bloesch matured, however, he became critical of liberal theology for its this-worldly optimism, downplaying of sin, interpretation of Jesus as the maturation of the human spirit, and accommodations to culture (what Karl Barth called neo-Protestantism). Bloesch was especially disturbed by Meland's *America's Spiritual Culture*, which argued that the key to theological re-

newal was to make theology particularly American, to create an indigenous American theology. Meland went on to compare this favorably with the attempts of the German Christians during the National Socialist era to wed Christian theology to nationalism.[10]

Today, Bloesch believes that while theological liberalism has made contributions, one must be discriminating. Fundamentally, liberal Christianity "tends to read Scripture in the light of the wisdom and experience of modern culture. The truth of Scripture is judged on how it accords with the spirit of modernity." Bloesch is therefore "convinced that religious liberalism is basically incompatible with evangelical Christianity, though this is not to deny that it contains Christian elements."[11] Bloesch is not totally antiliberal, for he does believe in the liberal spirit which embraces dialogue and openness to truth wherever it is to be found. But he does reject what he sees as liberalism's antisupernaturalism, its downplaying of the mystery of faith, and its reduction of Christianity to ethics.[12]

After three years in seminary, Bloesch considered himself an existentialist theologian. He remembers being impressed by Bultmann's *Jesus and the Word* and the major writings of Paul Tillich, whose *Protestant Era* and three-volume *Systematic Theology* appeared during Bloesch's student years. Bloesch saw Tillich as a possible alternative to the process theology of his

---

9. Quoted in Keylock, "Evangelical Leaders," 63.

10. Bloesch characterizes the German Christians as having "sought to read into the faith their own ideological commitments" (*Is the Bible Sexist?* [Westchester, Ill.: Crossway, 1982], 78). He sees parallels in "those theologies and movements that seek a resymbolization of the faith and appeal to natural revelation" (ibid., 120 n. 29). Here Bloesch is targeting process theology, radical feminism, and the new religious Right. See also Donald G. Bloesch, *Crumbling Foundations: Death and Rebirth in an Age of Upheaval* (Grand Rapids: Zondervan, 1984); his most sustained discussion is in *The Battle for the Trinity* (Ann Arbor: Servant, 1985), ch. 6.

11. Donald G. Bloesch, *The Future of Evangelical Christianity* (New York: Doubleday, 1983), 4.

12. Bloesch, "My Theological Journey."

professors. As he continued to study, how- ever, Bloesch became increasingly dissatis- fied with this form of existentialism. Many years later he would explain:

> I have not dismissed the need for an exis- tential encounter with God. But I have sought to relate it more closely to the in- spired Word of God. I see Holy Scripture as a definitive word from God that in- cludes information about God as well as about humanity and the world. I wish to present a theology that is solidly grounded in the gospel as attested in Holy Scripture. We have the living Word only in the form of the written Word and the proclaimed Word.[13]

In opposition to Tillich's method of cor- relation, which sees the task of theology as correlating contemporary questions with theological understandings, Bloesch opted for Barth's emphasis on proclamation or confrontation. This follows in the path of the classical theologians Augustine and Anselm, whose theological method can be described as faith seeking understanding. Seeing Tillich's and Barth's approaches as mutually exclusive, Bloesch chose to re- main true to Barth. "You can't have both," he says.[14]

Through the years Bloesch has been sub- stantially influenced by Barth, whom he lists as one of his theological mentors.[15] In both seminary and graduate school, Bloesch found Barth's thought to be "a via- ble alternative to the neonaturalism of Wie- man, Meland, Daniel Williams, and others, which dominated the scene at that time."[16] Yet this has not been an uncritical appro- priation. Early on, Bloesch rejected Barth's objectivist view that salvation occurs totally outside ourselves in the advent of Jesus Christ, and that the whole world is con- verted and liberated because Christ repre- sents all humanity.[17] Bloesch's second book, *The Christian Life and Salvation,* which represents the continuing pietist in- fluence on him, was written in part to counter Barth's view.[18] For Bloesch, "salva- tion is realized both in the cross of Christ and the decision of faith, but only those who have faith can legitimately claim that they were already redeemed at the cross of Calvary."[19] Thus, "the world is not yet rec- onciled or redeemed, but the community of the faithful partakes now in both reconcili- ation and redemption."[20] In a later work, *Jesus Is Victor!* Bloesch presents a fuller view of Barth's teachings on salvation. While he finds much to applaud, he has sig- nificant qualms as well.[21] This is also true of Bloesch's assessments of the whole of Barth's theology—he expresses both "ap- preciation and reservations."[22]

Bloesch's appreciation of Barth has dis- tinguished him in important ways from other evangelicals who have seen much more to criticize and far less to praise in Barth.[23] Actually, Bloesch has never been a fundamentalist and holds views that differ significantly from those of others in the evangelical movement.[24] Bloesch's criti- cisms of fundamentalism as well as some forms of conservative evangelicalism in- clude: (1) obscurantism—emphasizing, for

---

13. Quoted in Keylock, "Evangelical Leaders," 63.
14. Bloesch, "My Theological Journey."
15. Ibid.
16. Donald G. Bloesch, "Karl Barth: Appreciation and Reservations," in Donald K. McKim, ed., *How Karl Barth Changed My Mind* (Grand Rapids: Eerd- mans, 1986), 126.
17. Donald G. Bloesch, *Jesus Is Victor! Karl Barth's Doctrine of Salvation* (Nashville: Abingdon, 1976), 36 n. 16.
18. Donald G. Bloesch, *The Christian Life and Sal- vation* (Grand Rapids: Eerdmans, 1967).
19. Bloesch, *Evangelical Renaissance,* 87; see also idem, *Jesus Is Victor!* ch. 3.
20. Bloesch, *Jesus Is Victor!* 121.
21. Ibid., ch. 7.
22. See Bloesch, "Karl Barth: Appreciation and Reservations," 126–30; he used the same rubrics in *Evangelical Renaissance,* ch. 4.
23. For varying views see Gregory Bolich, *Karl Barth and Evangelicalism* (Downers Grove, Ill.: Inter- Varsity, 1980).
24. Bloesch, *Future of Evangelical Christianity,* 25– 29.

example, scientific creationism and the young-earth theory, which arise from a literalistic reading of the early chapters of Genesis; (2) rationalism—making the bar of reason and science the norm for truth; (3) separatism—drawing people away from the established churches; (4) patriarchalism—tying the faith to ideology and always relegating women to "second and third and fourth place"; and (5) political conservatism—allying, for example, with the Moral Majority.[25]

Throughout his teaching and writing career, Bloesch sought an alternative vision beyond liberalism and fundamentalism. In doing so, he became increasingly aware of the dangers in aligning the Christian faith with ideologies of either the political Right or Left. Just as he criticized fundamentalism and conservative evangelicalism for affiliations with American political conservatism, so he recognized that classical liberal theology had been undercut by its ties to the economic and political interests of the German upper-middle class in the late nineteenth and early twentieth centuries. The secularism of contemporary American culture he saw as

> a capitulation to the *Zeitgeist*, the "spirit of the age." It means not simply an openness to the values and goals of the world but the enthronement of these values and goals. Secularism represents a rival religion, an absolutizing of what had previously been regarded as penultimate concerns: the things that have to do with the maintenance of life in this world. . . .
>
> [Secularism] often takes the form of ideology, a theoretical justification for a sociopolitical program serving the interests of a particular class or party within society. Among the current ideologies striving to be king of the hill are socialism, classical liberalism (now called conservatism), welfare liberalism, fascism, feminism, gay liberationism, anarchism, and pacifism. Ideologies make social restruc-

25. Bloesch, "My Theological Journey."

turing an ultimate concern and thereby become secular salvations.[26]

Bloesch's long exposure to process theology has led him to regard it as "admirably adapted to the *Zeitgeist*, the spirit of the times." This is chiefly because "process theology locates authority in cultural experience." It "fits into the American temperament and culture more than Reformed theology ever could," since it seems congruent with the influential transcendentalist tradition of Ralph Waldo Emerson, Henry David Thoreau, Walt Whitman, and William James, who emphasized the interrelatedness of all reality, individualism, and free will. These concepts are also found in democratic liberalism, an ideology with which process thought is allied. In addition, "the process view that being is to be understood in terms of doing fits in well with such values of the modern technological society as productivity, efficiency and utility."[27] In making such critical comments about process theology, Bloesch acknowledges that theology in general is susceptible to similar dangers:

> We should keep in mind that all theology has an ideological taint, including Reformed theology. . . . Christians should at all times endeavor to transcend ideological bias, and we can be partly successful in

26. Bloesch, *Crumbling Foundations*, 37–39. See also Donald G. Bloesch, "The Challenge Facing the Churches," in *Christianity Confronts Modernity: A Theological and Pastoral Inquiry by Protestant Evangelicals and Roman Catholics*, ed. Peter Williamson and Kevin Perrotta (Ann Arbor: Servant, 1981), 205–6; idem, "The Ideological Temptation," in *Freedom for Obedience: Evangelical Ethics in Contemporary Times* (San Francisco: Harper and Row, 1987), ch. 13—here Bloesch says that an ideology "presents a picture of the world that gives legitimacy to the cultural values and goals [a particular class or group in society] holds most dear. While its focus is on social-empirical reality, the workaday world, it colors one's understanding of every aspect of life" (p. 250).

27. Donald G. Bloesch, "Process Theology and Reformed Theology," in *Process Theology*, ed. Ronald H. Nash (Grand Rapids: Baker, 1987), 36, 52.

this task because we are in contact with a God who transcends human culture even while he is actively at work within it. Yet we should always be circumspect in our claims, especially in the political and social arena, knowing that we are probably more children of our times than prophets to our times.[28]

Bloesch's determination to be anti-ideological is apparent in his various writings on the church and its mission.[29] Thus he writes in his major work on evangelical ethics: "The church in our time can only become truly prophetic when it awakens to the reality of the ideological temptation. Only when it successfully begins resisting the beguiling promise of ideological support will it be free to speak the Word of God with power and boldness."[30] Bloesch agrees with Reinhold Niebuhr that "the only viable way of combating ideology is to place our faith in a God who infinitely transcends human culture, even though he condescends to our level in a self-disclosure through historical events."[31]

Bloesch sees the crucial choice today as being between a prophetic church and a merely cultural church:

The first is anchored in an infallible divine revelation in history; the second appeals to the aspirations and hopes of the culture in which it finds itself. In a cultural church, religion is appreciated for its social utility, for the psychic and cultural benefits it provides, rather than for its truth. In a prophetic church, religion moves us to surrender the illusions and pretensions of the culture and to live only by the promises in Holy Scripture. . . .

[In avoiding the ideological temptations of both the Left and the Right, a prophetic church] will find itself at odds with both civil religion and popular cultural religion. It will see through the appeal to traditional values and to the national heritage, for its God cannot be used to promote either a national spiritual revival or an egalitarian cultural ideal realizable by social legislation and education. It will champion a transcendent religion that does not simply shore up human values but gives primacy to the kingdom of God.[32]

The church gives primacy to the kingdom of God when the main thrust of its preaching is "the Gospel of reconciliation and redemption which involves the announcement of judgment as well as grace manifested in Jesus Christ."[33]

Bloesch declares that "two dangers that confront the church today are divorcing the kingdom of God from politics and economics and maintaining that the kingdom is realized through politics and economics."[34] He advocates a middle course. His own social concern has been strong and has encompassed a number of issues. In his view, "embracing the Gospel means being willing to give a public testimony to the freedom of Christ and the law of grace in the face of the political religions of nations, races, and classes." This "entails not only taking up the cross in service to the unfortunate in society but also engaging in political programs

28. Ibid., 52; see also Bloesch, *Battle for the Trinity,* 83.

29. Donald G. Bloesch, "The Mission of the Church: Spiritual or Secular?" in *Crisis of Piety,* ch. 4; idem, *The Christian Witness in a Secular Age* (Minneapolis: Augsburg, 1968); idem, *The Reform of the Church* (Grand Rapids: Eerdmans, 1970); idem, *The Invaded Church* (Waco: Word, 1975); idem, *Essentials,* 2:155–73.

30. Bloesch, *Freedom for Obedience,* 270. Bloesch makes clear that "it is not only liberal Christianity but evangelical Christianity that has become vulnerable to ideological subversion. Evangelicals today tend to rely on slogans (such as biblical inerrancy and the four spiritual laws) rather than on hard study of the theological and social implications of the gospel. The virtues of the technological society—utility, productivity, and efficiency—are uncritically accepted by most evangelical churches and seminaries" (pp. 272–73).

31. Bloesch, *Freedom for Obedience,* 270, citing Reinhold Niebuhr, *The Nature and Destiny of Man,* 2 vols. in 1 (New York: Scribner, 1951), 1:194–202, 214–20; see also Bloesch, *Battle for the Trinity,* 83.

32. Bloesch, *Freedom for Obedience,* 272, 274; see also 239–40.

33. Bloesch, *Essentials,* 2:161.

34. Ibid., 2:167.

for social change."[35] Indeed, "social service (*diakonia*) sometimes take chronological priority over the preaching of the Gospel since, if our hearers are in dire physical distress or material need, they will not listen to our message until these immediate concerns are dealt with."[36] Accordingly, social witness has been recognized by Bloesch and other evangelicals as part and parcel of their heritage.[37] Social justice, he writes, is "a fruit and consequence of the righteousness of the kingdom which already grips the faithful and impels them to action."[38] It is "a fruit and faith and love and a means to faith and love." Social justice is a "necessary fruit," yet "progress toward social justice must never be confused with the coming of the kingdom . . . of God, [which] is present only where people enter into the higher righteousness, the fellowship of sacrificial love (the *koinonia*)."[39]

Clearly, Bloesch is determined to maintain both the spiritual and the social dimensions of the church's mission; he ever keeps in mind, however, that the social springs from the spiritual focus on Jesus Christ:

> In fulfilling the great commission of our Lord, we should avoid both the spiritual-

ization of the gospel (reducing it to spiritual values or moral principles) and its politicalization (confusing it with a program for social change). As the church confronts the burning social and moral issues of the day, it must strive to preach the whole counsel of God, and therefore a gospel that will have political relevance. But the message itself should be centered on God's gracious act of reconciliation in Jesus Christ, whereby the sin and guilt of the world are taken away for all those who repent and believe.[40]

While some have seen Bloesch's theological journey as an evolution from liberalism to conservatism, he himself traces his steps from Pietism to liberalism to conservatism to radicalism.[41] Elements of all these traditions continue in his theology. His evolutionary trajectory has led him to embrace selective dimensions of each and to synthesize those perspectives he believes to be true to the Christian gospel, which he considers "the very heart and soul of evangelical theology."[42]

Wide-ranging, Mediate Writings

While Bloesch's writings cover a multitude of topics, they all display the emerging emphases of his theological vision. We can, in general, classify his books in three balanced categories: formal theology, the church and renewal, and contemporary issues. His theological studies include *The Ground of Certainty: Toward an Evangelical Theology of Revelation* (1971), *Jesus Is Victor!* (1976), *Essentials of Evangelical Theol-*

35. Ibid., 2:168. Bloesch had earlier written, "It is well to recognize that service entails more than charity. It also includes social action, i.e., the application of power on the part of Christians to change social conditions" (*Reform of the Church*, 168).

36. Bloesch, *Essentials*, 2:168.

37. See *The Orthodox Evangelicals*, ed. Robert Webber and Donald G. Bloesch (Nashville: Nelson, 1978), which constitutes an appeal to evangelicals that arose from a May 1977 conference in Chicago. The "Call to Holistic Salvation" states, "Wherever the church has been faithful to its calling, it has proclaimed personal salvation; it has been a channel of God's healing to those in physical and emotional need; it has sought justice for the oppressed and disinherited; and it has been a good steward of the natural world" (p. 14). Bloesch wrote the chapter explicating the "Call to Spirituality" (pp. 146–65). Bloesch elsewhere noted that he speaks as "a socially concerned evangelical, one who sees that the Gospel is a stick of dynamite in the social structure" (*Essentials*, 1:xi).

38. Bloesch, *Freedom for Obedience*, 84.

39. Ibid., 85.

40. Ibid. This is related to an earlier statement: "Our chief motivation for spreading the Gospel, however, is not to overturn oppressive social structures or disturb the existing social order but instead to witness to God's incomparable grace in Jesus Christ and thereby save souls from sin, death, and hell" (Bloesch, *Essentials*, 2:170).

41. Bloesch, "My Theological Journey." In another self-evaluation Bloesch writes, "My theology is hopefully radical as well as conservative, since I seek to return to the roots of the faith and to the infallible standard of faith, Holy Scripture" (*Essentials*, 1:x).

42. Bloesch, *Essentials*, 1:4.

ogy (1978–79), *The Struggle of Prayer* (1980), and *Freedom for Obedience* (1987). The church and renewal is emphasized in *Centers of Christian Renewal* (1964), *The Christian Life and Salvation* (1967), *The Crisis of Piety* (1968), *The Christian Witness in a Secular Age* (1968), *Christian Spirituality East and West* (1968), *The Reform of the Church* (1970), *Servants of Christ: Deaconesses in Renewal* (1971), *Wellsprings of Renewal: Promise in Christian Communal Life* (1974), *Light a Fire* (1975), and *The Invaded Church* (1975). Current theological issues are addressed in *The Evangelical Renaissance* (1973), *The Orthodox Evangelicals* (1978), *Faith and Its Counterfeits* (1981), *Is the Bible Sexist?* (1982), *The Future of Evangelical Christianity* (1983), *Crumbling Foundations* (1984), and *The Battle for the Trinity* (1985). The first volume of Bloesch's *Theological Notebook*, his spiritual journal, was published in 1989.[43]

In many ways, Bloesch's writings attempt to find a middle way between extremes, for example, between the theological Left and Right, between liberal theology and fundamentalism. He in fact begins his major work on ethics with the statement, "I have endeavored in this study first of all to present a viable alternative to legalistic ethics on the one hand and situational and relativistic ethics on the other."[44] Bloesch seeks to mediate extreme positions by introducing a spirit of ecumenical cooperation. In the preface to his work on evangelical theology he notes, "I try to be irenic wherever possible: where bridges can be built that will contribute to Christian unity it is incumbent upon us to do so."[45] In the foreword to *The Future of Evangelical Christianity*, which is subtitled *A Call for Unity amid Diversity*, he explains his role: "I try in this book to build bridges between the various strands of evangelicalism and also between evangelical Protestantism and the Catholic churches."[46] This orientation, however, does not hinder Bloesch from fully forging his own views, for his next sentence reads: "At the same time, I point out where bridges cannot be built, where compromise is out of the question." While Bloesch seeks balances, he is not bland.

Enduring Themes

The breadth of Bloesch's writings makes summary in short compass impossible. Yet some foundational themes in addition to the dimensions outlined above have continued to orient his theological and ethical thought.

Theological Method

Bloesch is currently writing an extensive work that will deal formally with his theological method.[47] His aim is to "transcend the cleavage between fideism and rationalism" and to develop "a methodology that has its source of inspiration in Scripture, not in some philosophy extraneous to Scripture."[48] This aligns Bloesch with the classical tradition of Augustine and Anselm, whom he sees as "true to the central thrust of the Bible when they propounded 'faith seeking understanding' as the method of scientific theology." For Bloesch, theology does not begin with a pure fideism, a leap of faith. Instead, he follows Barth in viewing divine revelation as the point of departure. This revelation "can be apprehended to be sure only with the eyes of faith. Yet the light of faith is a light

43. For a fuller bibliography see Bloesch, *Future of Evangelical Christianity*, 190–92; idem, *Battle for the Trinity*, 121–34.
44. Bloesch, *Freedom for Obedience*, 1.
45. Bloesch, *Essentials*, 1:x.
46. Bloesch, *Future of Evangelical Christianity*, ix. Cf. his statement in the Introduction to *The Struggle of Prayer*: "This book attempts to open up a dialogue between the evangelical and mystical traditions" (p. 2).
47. This is the first of six volumes to be published by Inter-Varsity Press in which Bloesch will deal more thoroughly with issues raised in his *Essentials*. The first volume will consider authority and method in theology; the second, Scripture and revelation. Another volume will focus on the church and sacraments.
48. Bloesch, *Future of Evangelical Christianity*, 121, 122.

that also illumines our reason, so that a re-born reason is capable of understanding the truth of revelation, not exhaustively but adequately. [Thus,] Christianity does not contradict rationality, for the Word of God is also the Logos or wisdom of God, but it does oppose rationalism, which seeks to bring revelation into accord with the canons of human logic."[49]

Bloesch's method has freed him from the quagmires of "rationalistic apologetics," which he sees as "still very much in evidence among neoevangelicals."[50] It has also resulted in his rejecting attempts to reduce Christian theology to a Christian philosophy or philosophy of religion which would have as its concern nothing more than an overall view of the world.[51] While philosophy of religion is "an integral part of theology," it is not, Bloesch maintains, a "preparation or foundation for faith but rather a supplementation of faith." It serves "not to persuade the unbeliever of the credibility of the faith," but "to help the believer to understand his faith better." Also, "like theology itself it should be seen in the context of faith seeking understanding."[52]

Revelation and Reason

Bloesch's views on the relation of revelation and reason are closely linked to his theological method. While "reason is involved in faith from the very beginning, because faith is a rational commitment as

well as a decision of the will," Bloesch cautions that "at the same time, we should beware of seeking a rational or philosophical basis for faith." This is because "reason is a useful instrument in explicating the truth of revelation, but it cannot prepare the way for the reception of this truth." Though "the whole of creation reflects the light and glory of God (cf. Ps. 19:1–4; Rom. 1:19, 20)," Bloesch warns that "we must steer clear of any natural theology that supposes valid knowledge of God on the basis of this general light in creation."[53] He rejects natural theology, agreeing with Barth's view that while there is an inescapable presence of God in all creation, "general awareness of this divine presence cannot yield an adequate or valid knowledge of the true God, because the fall into sin warps our noetic faculties as well as corrupts our moral sensibilities."[54] And while "it is incumbent upon us to present to the world a reasonably coherent, intelligible gospel, and theological reflection is geared to this end," Bloesch emphasizes that "our theological method is reason in the service of revelation to the greater glory of God."[55]

The Authority of Scripture

Another of Bloesch's enduring themes is the authority of Scripture. He notes that "evangelical theology appeals to the authority of Scripture because it sees Scripture as

---

49. Ibid., 122.
50. Ibid., 30. Bloesch sees tensions within evangelicalism between rationalists and fideists (p. 58). Two evangelical rationalists who disagree with Bloesch's views on, for example, propositional revelation, the use of logic and reason, and inerrancy are Ronald H. Nash, *The Word of God and the Mind of Man* (Grand Rapids: Zondervan, 1982), 95–96, 122, 124–31; and Carl F. H. Henry, *God, Revelation and Authority*, 6 vols. (Waco: Word, 1976–83), 3:475–76; 4:186, 281–82. For a discussion of these issues see Nicholas F. Gier, *God, Reason, and the Evangelicals* (Lanham, Md.: University Press of America, 1987).
51. Bloesch, *Essentials*, 1:19.
52. Donald G. Bloesch, *The Ground of Certainty: Toward an Evangelical Theology of Revelation* (Grand Rapids: Eerdmans, 1971), 58.

53. Bloesch, *Future of Evangelical Christianity*, 121. Bloesch wrote elsewhere that "revelation is mediated through the world of nature, but it does not arise out of this world" (*Ground of Certainty*, 192).
54. Bloesch, "Karl Barth: Appreciation and Reservations," 127. It is Bloesch's view that God's revelation "both renews and redirects reason." The human perspective "is not simply broadened but also drastically revised," so that one has "a radically new perspective, a wholly new vision" (*Ground of Certainty*, 192–93).
55. Bloesch, *Essentials*, 1:18. Bloesch had earlier written: "My position is much closer to fideism than to rationalism in that I see faith as determining reason and not vice versa. . . . I uphold not a mere fideism but a trinitarian fideism, one that has its source not in the leap of faith but in divine revelation. Faith should be understood in this context not as a venture in the darkness but as an intelligible response to the gift of Jesus Christ" (*Ground of Certainty*, 187).

the written Word of God."[56] Bloesch rejects the position of "many liberals that the Bible is fundamentally a human account of a particular people's experiences of God or the product of a heightened religious consciousness." This leads to an "ebionitic view of Scripture."[57] On the other hand, he also rejects the position of "many within the camp of orthodoxy and fundamentalism, that the Bible is predominantly a divine book and that the human element is only a mask or outward aspect of the divine." This leads to "a docetic view of Scripture." The belief "that the Bible is an exact reproduction of the thoughts of God . . . denies its real humanity as well as its historicity."[58] For Bloesch, Scripture is "more than a human witness to revelation: it is revelation itself mediated through human words. It is not in and of itself divine revelation, but when illumined by the Spirit it becomes revelation to the believer."[59] Like the Protestant Reformers, Bloesch notes the "indispensable role of the Holy Spirit." While "the truth of revelation is objectively given in biblical history," revelation "also encompasses the interior work of the Holy Spirit by which this truth is gratefully acknowledged and received (cf. Eph. 1:17, 18; Gal. 1:12)."[60]

Bloesch affirms the plenary inspiration of Scripture; he believes that "the Scripture in its totality is inspired" and that inspiration is "both conceptual and verbal, since it signifies that the Spirit was active both in shaping the thoughts and imagination of the biblical writers and also in guiding them in their actual writing." Yet he strongly maintains that "verbal inspiration must not be confused with perfect accuracy or mechanical dictation."[61] He acknowl-

edges that there are "culturally conditioned ideas as well as historically conditioned language in the Bible," and that "the prophets and apostles were men of their times though the message that they attested transcended their age and every age."[62]

We need to recognize, says Bloesch, that the conflict over whether Scripture contains errors is rooted in disparate notions of truth:

> Truth in the Bible means conformity to the will and purpose of God. Truth in today's empirical, scientific milieu means an exact correspondence between one's ideas or perceptions and the phenomena of nature and history. Error in the Bible means a deviation from the will and purpose of God, unfaithfulness to the dictates of his law. Error in the empirical mind-set of a technological culture means inaccuracy or inconsistency in what is reported as objectively occurring in nature or history. Technical precision is the measure of truth in empiricism. Fidelity to God's Word is the biblical criterion for truth. Empiricism narrows the field of investigation to objective sense data, and therefore to speak of revelation as superhistorical or hidden in history is to remove it from what can legitimately be considered as knowledge. The difference between the rational-empirical and the biblical understanding of truth is the difference between transparency to Eternity and literal facticity.[63]

Use of the term *inerrancy* to cover "purely historical and scientific matters, even when the treatment of these in the Bible does not bear upon the message of faith, [suggests] literal, exact, mathematical precision, something the Bible cannot provide."[64]

---

56. Bloesch, *Essentials,* 1:51.

57. Ibid., 1:52. The Ebionites in the early church so stressed the humanity of Jesus that they lost sight of his divinity (p. 79 n. 1).

58. Ibid., 1:52. The Docetists in the early church did not fully portray the humanity of Christ, emphasizing only his divinity (p. 79 n. 1).

59. Ibid., 1:52.

60. Ibid., 1:54.

61. Ibid., 1:55; see also 1:76.

62. Ibid., 1:64.

63. Bloesch, *Future of Evangelical Christianity,* 120.

64. Bloesch, *Essentials,* 1:66. Bloesch continues: "The extrabiblical criterion of scientific exactitude is imposed on the Scriptures, and certainty is thereby made to rest on objective, external evidence rather than on the internal witness of the Holy Spirit (as with the Reformers)." He agrees with G. C. Berkouwer that "inerrancy in the biblical sense means unswerving fi-

Bloesch concludes that those who "base the authority of Scripture on the inerrancy of the writing and then try to demonstrate this according to the canons of scientific rationality" have gone astray.[65]

Bloesch contends that both sides in the fundamentalist-modernist controversy, the residual effects of which still continue within evangelicalism, were mistaken. In his view, "the truthfulness and reliability of Scripture can only be properly measured in the light of its own criterion, the Gospel of the cross, embodied in Jesus Christ, and attested to in both the Old and New Testaments."[66] The Scriptures are

> infallible because their primary author is God himself, and their primary content is Jesus Christ and his salvation (cf. John 5:46, 47; 2 Tim. 3:15). Yet we have the infallible, perfect Word of the living God enclosed and veiled in the time-bound, imperfect words of sinful men. . . . It is only when people of faith are given spiritual discernment that they can perceive the priceless treasure of God's holy Word in the earthen vessel of the human word.[67]

Thus Bloesch espouses what he calls a sacramental approach to the Bible. He sees Scripture as God's revelation as well as "a divinely-appointed means of grace and not simply an earthly, historical witness or sign of grace. . . . Scripture is inseparable from the revelation which produced it and which flows through it but . . . the words of Scripture in and of themselves are not divine revelation."[68]

In Bloesch's view, the task of interpreting Scripture, hermeneutics, includes use of the tools of literary and historical criticism. But the interpreter must move on to "theological exegesis, which means seeing the text in the light of its theological context, relating the text to the central message of Holy Scripture."[69] More specifically, Bloesch advocates a christological hermeneutic, since theological exegesis seeks to relate "the innermost intentions of the author" to the "center and culmination of sacred history mirrored in the Bible, namely, the advent of Jesus Christ."[70] Bloesch's approach "has much in common with historical orthodoxy, but one major difference is that it welcomes a historical investigation of the text." Yet such investigation "can only throw light on the cultural and literary background of the text; it does not give us

---

delity to the truth, a trustworthy and enduring witness to the truth of divine revelation. It connotes not impeccability, but indeceivability, which means being free from lying and fraud."

65. Bloesch, *Essentials*, 2:270.

66. Ibid., 1:68. Bloesch later notes that "the bane of much of modern evangelicalism is rationalism which presupposes that the Word of God is directly available to human reason" (1:75).

67. Ibid., 1:69. Bloesch comments: "The Bible contains a fallible element in the sense that it reflects the cultural limitations of the writers. But it is not mistaken in what it purports to teach, namely, God's will and purpose for the world. There are no errors or contradictions in its substance and heart. It bears the imprint of human frailty, but it also carries the truth and power of divine infallibility."

68. Ibid., 2:274. The term *sacramental* denotes that Scripture has "two sides, the divine and the human, and the human is the instrumentality of the divine" (2:270). Bloesch contrasts the sacramental approach with two others: the scholastic approach "understands revelation as the disclosure of a higher truth that nonetheless stands in continuity with rational or natural truth [so that] the Bible becomes a book of revealed propositions which are directly accessible to reason and which contain no errors in any respect"; and the liberal-modernist approach understands revelation to be inner enlightenment or self-discovery. For his call for a sacramental understanding of biblical authority, see Bloesch, "Challenge Facing the Churches," 209.

69. Bloesch, *Essentials*, 1:70–74 (the quotation is from p. 71). P. T. Forsyth, whom Bloesch quotes frequently, calls theological exegesis "the highest criticism" (as over against higher criticism). This means, says Bloesch, "seeing every text in the light of the Gospel, the theological center of the Bible" (1:72).

70. Donald G. Bloesch, "A Christological Hermeneutic," in *The Use of the Bible in Theology: Evangelical Options*, ed. Robert K. Johnston (Atlanta: John Knox, 1985), 81. This means "there is definitely a place for typological exegesis," properly carried out (p. 85; Bloesch, *Essentials*, 1:73). Bloesch associates his approach with Karl Barth, Jacques Ellul, and Wilhelm Vischer, among others.

its divinely intended meaning."[71] Bloesch credits Barth with helping him realize that higher criticism "takes us only so far, that it must be supplemented and fulfilled by theological criticism, which is carried on only by faith seeking understanding."[72]

Evangelical Theology

Throughout his career Donald Bloesch has sought to present the fulness of the evangelical faith. He sees the term *evangelical* as denoting "that segment of Christianity that makes the proclamation of the biblical gospel its chief concern, that appeals to this gospel in its biblical setting as the final arbiter for faith and practice."[73] His systematic theology, *Essentials of Evangelical Theology,* defines "evangelical" as relating to the gospel message and the catholic heritage and focused on the revealed Word of God.[74] He believes that "evangelical Christianity is the true orthodoxy. Yet it is not an orthodoxy bent on preserving its own sacred traditions but one that uses these traditions to advance the cause of the gospel in the world today."[75]

Essentials of Evangelical Theology deals with controversial themes that have proven barriers to Christian unity in the past. Volume 1 includes chapters on the sovereignty of God, the primacy of Scripture, total depravity, the deity of Jesus Christ, substitutionary atonement, salvation by grace, and (justification by) faith alone. Volume 2 considers the new birth, scriptural holiness, the cruciality of preaching, the priesthood of all believers, the two kingdoms (God's and Satan's), the church's spiritual mission, the personal return of Christ, and heaven and hell. In the chapter "How Distinctive Is Evangelicalism?" Bloesch highlights themes

he believes distinguish evangelical religion from nonevangelical religion: the supreme authority of the Word of God, the transcendent God, the radical pervasiveness of sin, the uniqueness of Jesus Christ, the free gift of salvation, and inward religion. These themes have frequently appeared in his other writings through the past three decades. For Bloesch the hallmark of evangelical faith is

the cross of Christ, the doctrine of salvation through the righteousness of Christ procured for us by his sacrificial life, death, and resurrection. It is the cross that gives authority to Scripture, and it is the cross that reveals and confirms the Messianic identity of Jesus as the Son of God. We cannot know the meaning of the cross apart from the Bible or the preaching of the church, but these are only instruments of the Spirit, who alone gives the proper interpretation as we hear the Word from the mouth of its ministers.[76]

Bloesch is committed to evangelical theology and the evangelical faith as authentically expressed by the church catholic, the Protestant Reformation, and the revival movements of the eighteenth and nineteenth centuries. One of his chief concerns is that this faith be soundly articulated today in confessional statements as well as in practical Christian action. An ecumenical thrust is evident in his fostering dialogues among different wings of the universal church. Indeed, he believes that "a viable doctrine of the church for our time will involve us in a passionate concern for church unity."[77] He also insists that "doctrine, life and experience . . . be held together in a catholic balance, [for] if any one of these is neglected we are on the slippery slope to heresy."[78]

71. Bloesch, "Christological Hermeneutic," 82.
72. Bloesch, "Karl Barth: Appreciation and Reservations," 127.
73. Bloesch, *Future of Evangelical Christianity,* 4.
74. Bloesch, *Essentials,* 1:12, 15.
75. Bloesch, *Future of Evangelical Christianity,* 5.

76. Bloesch, *Essentials,* 2:238.
77. Bloesch, *Future of Evangelical Christianity,* 129.
78. Ibid.

The goal of the Christian life is, in Bloesch's opinion, conformity to the image of Christ. Regrettably, much of current spirituality falls far short; "what is missing . . . is the ethical or prophetic note."[79] As a result, Bloesch has taken pains to address contemporary ethical issues. For example, he has refused to take an absolutist stand on abortion, called for a bilateral nuclear freeze, and as early as 1960 signed, along with six other colleagues from Dubuque Seminary, "A Statement concerning the Use of Mass Extermination as a Means of Waging War."[80] On other important issues for evangelicals, Bloesch has supported the ordination of women to the ministry of Word and sacrament, while resisting any revisions in language that refers to God.[81]

Donald Bloesch's theological works have placed the evangelical world in his debt. It is true that his distinctive stances have been labeled too conservative by some and too liberal by others. Yet, as he himself has shown, such labels are imprecise; and his themes and emphases have endured despite them. Perhaps he would prefer to be assessed by his own self-description: "I identify myself as an evangelical because I definitely share in the vision of the Reformers, Pietists and Puritans of a church under the banner of the gospel seeking to convert a world under the spell of the powers of darkness to the kingdom of our Lord and Savior, Jesus Christ."[82]

79. Ibid., 134.

80. For Bloesch's stand on abortion, see *Future of Evangelical Christianity*, 135; for his discussion of "The Folly of War," see *Freedom for Obedience*, ch. 14. The Dubuque Statement, which was reissued by the surviving signatories in February 1980, can be found in Arthur C. Cochrane, *The Mystery of Peace* (Elgin, Ill.: Brethren, 1986), 167–69.

81. Bloesch, *Is the Bible Sexist?* 53. Resisting both radical feminism and patriarchalism, Bloesch supports a "qualified, biblical feminism" (p. 97). For the debate on language see ch. 4, and Bloesch, *Battle for the Trinity.*

82. Bloesch, *Future of Evangelical Christianity*, vii.

Thomas Oden

Daniel B. Clendenin

S ome eyebrows might rise at the inclusion of Thomas Oden in a handbook of evangelical theologians. Yet the selection of this longtime professor of theology at a thoroughly liberal United Methodist seminary and graduate school (Drew University) is not at all odd but for several reasons is altogether fitting. One even suspects the inclusion brings him an unfeigned sense of joy and satisfaction. Oden carries what for some (but hardly all) is the sine qua non of evangelical identity—membership in the Evangelical Theological Society, which he assumed in 1990.[1] When asked by this author why he joined the society, Oden responded that he felt he belonged there, that, indeed, to employ the metaphor of his plenary address to the society, this was one further step on a long journey home. Another reason for including Oden is that his massive three-volume systematic theology has earned critical ac-

claim.[2] The wide-ranging subject matter and sheer number of his publications place him in the category of the prolific.[3] Finally, Oden is included because of his remarkable and uncommon pilgrimage from ardent liberalism to classic orthodoxy, or to what he refers to only slightly tongue-in-cheek as a postmodern paleo-orthodoxy.

Life

Thomas Clark Oden was born October 21, 1931, in Altus, Oklahoma, the son of an

1. At the 1990 annual meeting of the Evangelical Theological Society in New Orleans, Oden gave an address entitled "The Long Journey Home," which was later published in the *Journal of the Evangelical Theological Society* 34 (1991): 77–92. For Oden's definition of "evangelical," see Thomas Oden, "Back to the Fathers," interview by Chris Hall, *Christianity Today,* 24 September 1990, p. 31.

2. Thomas Oden, *The Living God* (San Francisco: Harper and Row, 1987); idem, *The Word of Life* (San Francisco: Harper and Row, 1989); and idem, *Life in the Spirit* (San Francisco: Harper and Row, 1992).

3. In addition to the books listed in the bibliography, Oden has written over sixty articles, two unpublished novels (*Dayspring* and *Amos*), and a book of poetry (*Runes*).

attorney and a music teacher. In a recollection of how his father's death brought the true meaning of Christmas home to him, Oden expresses gratitude for a homelife steeped in vibrant evangelical faith.[4] His father's long-term friendships with blacks, his ministry to Mexican Americans, his efforts in setting up a mission to Indians, and his legal expertise in starting Western Oklahoma State College for low-income people, all made an indelible and wonderfully positive impression on Oden's life, perhaps most of all because, as Oden recalls, "all four interests were deeply rooted in a realistic evangelical faith that manifested itself in regular Bible study, daily family prayers at breakfast, [and] teaching Bible classes for over fifty years."[5]

In 1949 Oden entered the University of Oklahoma, where in 1953 he took a B.Litt. From there he matriculated at Southern Methodist University's Perkins School of Theology, where he earned a B.D. in 1956. Ordained by the Oklahoma Conference of the United Methodist Church (deacon in 1954, elder in 1956), Oden served in various parish ministries from 1951 to 1964. In 1956 he entered Yale University, where he took an M.A. (1958) and Ph.D. (1960), working under the supervision of Hans Frei and H. Richard Niebuhr. His Yale dissertation, "The Idea of Obedience in Contemporary Protestant Ethics," was directed by Niebuhr and published in a revised form as *Radical Obedience: The Ethics of Rudolf Bultmann.*[6]

A year of postdoctoral study took Oden to Heidelberg as a Danforth cross-disciplinary fellow (1965–66), during which time he taught at the Psychiatrische-Neurologische Klinik of Ruprecht-Karl Universität and the Ecumenical Institute at the Château de Bossey in Switzerland. His primary teach-

ing career has consisted of service at three institutions: as an instructor at Perkins School of Theology (1958–60); as an associate professor and professor (1960–70) at Phillips University; and as Henry Anson Buttz Professor of Theology at Drew University (1971–). Lectureships and visiting professorships have taken him to such illustrious institutions as Moscow State University, Oxford, Edinburgh, Duke, Emory, Princeton, and Claremont. He has also given of his talents to the Ethics and Public Policy Center of Washington, D.C., the White House Dialogue on Urban Initiatives (1985), and Public Information Office briefings (1984–86).

From Modernism to Classic Orthodoxy

Although Oden has written about a dozen books that deal primarily with psychotherapy (see the bibliography), the focus of our review will, naturally, be on his contributions to theology. By his own account Oden now distances himself somewhat from his early works on psychotherapy, preferring the special delight that the study of God has brought him in recent years.[7] He has indicated in several autobiographical pieces that his theological pilgrimage falls into two distinct periods: (1) an earlier period devoted to modernistic liberalism (both theological and political) and its hermeneutic; and (2) a conversion and even reversal to classic Christian orthodoxy. In several places he refers to these two periods as "then" and "now."[8]

"Between 1945 and 1965," Oden recalls, "every turn I made was a left turn."[9] An early devotee of pacifism, Sigmund Freud, and Rudolf Bultmann, he attended seminary out of social idealism rather than any

---

4. Thomas Oden, "My Dad's Death Brought Christmas Home," *Christianity Today,* 11 December 1981, pp. 20–22.

5. Ibid., 21.

6. Thomas Oden, *Radical Obedience: The Ethics of Rudolf Bultmann* (Philadelphia: Westminster, 1964).

7. See, e.g., the moving passage in Oden, "Long Journey," 86–87.

8. The following analysis is taken from Oden, "Long Journey," "Back to the Fathers," and "Then and Now: The Recovery of Patristic Wisdom," *Christian Century,* 12 December 1990, pp. 1164–68.

9. Oden, "Back to the Fathers," 28.

commitment to biblical Christianity. Despite his recent conversion to postmodern orthodoxy, even today he affirms that it was Bultmann more than any other scholar who made the Bible come alive for him. His early studies reflect a strong commitment to the German thinker's program of existentialism and demythologization. In *Radical Obedience: The Ethics of Rudolf Bultmann*, for instance, Oden surveys the "malaise . . . inadequacies and unfulfilled expectations" in the ethics of Reinhold Niebuhr, Paul Tillich, Karl Barth, and Dietrich Bonhoeffer; and in their stead he proposes that Bultmann, although not without his weaknesses, offers "some promise for a fresh beginning point," a "significant corrective," and "some new keys for the improvement, modification, and elaboration of the current issues in Protestant ethics, now in something of a quandary."[10]

"Then," as Oden likes to describe this period before his conversion to patristic theology, he aimed for what today we would call political correctness, as was expected of members of the liberal guild. This attitude manifested itself above all in attempts to formulate new insights (theological boredom being a constant threat), a focus on humanistic psychology (several of his first books deal with the interface of theology and psychotherapy), enslavement to the most recent theological fad, hypertoleration, and a desire to please academic peers. "Then" he was a perfect eisegete, co-opting the Bible to find proof texts for his own ideological precommitments. Exhibiting what C. S. Lewis once called the "chronological snobbery" of modernism, he eschewed with chauvinistic contempt any patristic texts as oppressive. "Then" Oden distrusted "anything that faintly smelled of orthodoxy."[11] In sum, he was passionately fixated on modernity and its four funda-

mental elements: hedonic self-actualization or narcissistic hedonism, autonomous individualism, reductive naturalism, and moral relativism. In Pauline language, he describes his former self as "blown by every wind of doctrine." But Oden is careful to add two key qualifiers. First, he does not mean that he was unconverted, alienated from or lacking faith in God. Rather, he was "lacking attentiveness to apostolic testimony and the sanctification of time through grace."[12] Nor does Oden mean to imply that, having reversed his theological trajectory, he has now ceased to be a modern man; indeed, he writes that he has never been more alive to the world than in recent years.[13]

In the late 1960s and early 1970s Oden began to question his entire worldview and its assumptions. Practical experiences and what amounted to scholarly shock therapy combined to force a radical reversal in his entire theological hermeneutic. First, in a practical and experiential sense, Oden became disillusioned, even frightened, at the destructive consequences of the four elements of modernism listed above. Close friends had ruined their lives with sexual experimentation and substance abuse. The abortion issue became a watershed for Oden when he realized that innocent human beings were being destroyed. The antinomianism and anarchist tendencies exhibited at the 1968 Democratic National Convention, where people threw excrement at the Chicago police, scared him. These practical experiences all contributed to a "gracious disillusioning" of all his fundamental assumptions about modernity.[14]

On a scholarly level Oden recalls an encounter with his former mentor, Will Herberg of Drew University, who chided him for his neglect of patristic and medieval lit-

10. Oden, *Radical Obedience*, 13–14, 23–24. In chapter 5 Oden lists seven inconsistencies in Bultmann's thought; for Bultmann's response see pp. 141–47.

11. Oden, "Long Journey," 85.

12. Oden, "Then and Now," 1165.

13. Ibid.; see also Thomas Oden, *Two Worlds: Notes on the Death of Modernity in America and the Soviet Union* (Downers Grove, Ill.: Inter-Varsity, 1991), 17.

14. Oden, "Back to the Fathers," 28.

erature. To that point he had concerned himself almost entirely with contemporary sources. He writes:

> If I had to assign a date to my entrance into the "post-modern" world, I think it would be the day when I had to choose the books I most needed, and most certainly wanted with me [for a sabbatical year away from home], and discovered to my astonishment that if push came to shove I could do without the twentieth-century material altogether, but that I could not seem to do without Hippolytus, Thomas Aquinas, Nicholas of Cusa, *Theologia Germanica*, Maimonides, Pascal and Kierkegaard.[15]

The year was 1976. Oden describes as a "shock" and "moment of recognition" the realization that his "consciousness had shifted away from the idolatry of the new."[16] In particular, it was in reading *On the Nature of the Human* by Nemesius (bishop of Emesa in Syria, fl. c. A.D. 400) that it "dawned on me that ancient wisdom could be the basis for a deeper criticism of modern narcissistic individualism than I had yet seen."[17] Reading the *Commonitorium* of Vincent of Lérins (fl. c. A.D. 425) and discovering his threefold test for orthodoxy (that which has been believed "everywhere, always, by all") provided a new and essential methodological or hermeneutical Archimedean point. "From then on it was a straightforward matter of searching modestly to identify those shared teachings."[18]

In what he calls his "now" period, Oden discovered that most of his ostensibly modern questions had already been addressed by the ancient exegetes. Justin Martyr's *Dialogue with Trypho* presaged modern Jewish-Christian dialogue; Chrysostom's reflections on voluntary poverty adumbrated Peter Berger's call for a knowledge elite; read-

ing Cyril of Jerusalem's catechetical lecture on the resurrection helped Oden to value the wisdom of Wolfhart Pannenberg rather than Bultmann on the historicity of the resurrection. Now he has traded humanistic psychology for personal reflection in the light of the incarnate Word who alone brings human fulfilment. Now he ponders why blatant heresy is so easily endorsed. He basks in the warmth of two millennia of orthodox consensus and "happily embrace[s] the term paleo-orthodoxy if for no other reason than to signal clearly that I do not mean once-fashionable neo-orthodoxy."[19] This paleo-orthodoxy is "post everything," for "the further one 'progresses' from ancient apostolic testimony to God's word the more hopeless becomes the human condition."[20] Now he preaches not about himself or his own sentimentalities, but from the canonical text. Instead of fearing rejection by his peers in the guild of modernity, the awareness of eschatological judgment has freed him to obey the final Judge. He has experienced nothing less than a complete hermeneutical reversal; his former commitment to the matrix of modernism and its formulations has given way to a view of all things theological through the lens of "ancient, consensual, classic Christian exegesis of holy writ."[21]

A Program of Classic Orthodoxy

As early as 1979, with the publication of *Agenda for Theology*, Oden had formulated his basic theological program, which since then, because of its basic nature, has not changed.[22] In that work he diagnosed the terminal illness of modernity and prescribed an antidote of consensual orthodoxy. This postmodern return to ancient orthodoxy leapfrogs the recent past to the

15. Thomas Oden, *After Modernity—What?* (Grand Rapids: Zondervan, 1990), 25.

16. Ibid.; Oden, "Back to the Fathers," 29.

17. Oden, "Then and Now," 1164.

18. Oden, "Long Journey," 85.

19. Ibid.; here he explicitly repudiates his book *The Promise of Barth: The Ethics of Freedom* (Philadelphia: Lippincott, 1969).

20. Ibid.

21. Oden, "Then and Now," 1165.

22. Thomas Oden, *Agenda for Theology* (San Francisco: Harper and Row, 1979).

patristic period, much as the Renaissance disdained the so-called Dark Ages, choosing instead to revive and even emulate the classics of ancient Greece and Rome.[23] In *After Modernity—What?* which is a revision of *Agenda for Theology,* Oden adds four chapters but holds to his twofold thesis: (1) modernity has collapsed; and (2) the only viable answer to this disaster is a return to collective, consensual Christian orthodoxy.

But what are modernity and orthodoxy? Oden usually refers to the four elements of modernity that have already been mentioned: narcissistic hedonism, autonomous individualism, reductive naturalism, and moral relativism. He has, however, given us a more extensive definition.[24] Modernity idolizes, at any cost and with cultic fervor, the "just now." It is xenophobic toward the past; it loathes yesterday. Strict scientific empiricism is its final court of appeal in all questions of truth. Oden distinguishes three senses or stages of modernity. In the broadest sense, modernity is simply the hegemony of an intellectual ideology that has prevailed since the French Revolution. Others sometimes refer to this as the Enlightenment mind-set. Modernity is also an intransigent epistemological predisposition, found especially among intellectual elites, that uncritically elevates modern ways of attaining knowledge over premodern formulations. Most particularly, modernity entails "a later-stage deterioration of both of the preceding viewpoints."[25] Elsewhere he speaks of "the acid destructiveness of modernity," a "desperate game" to find a substitute for apostolic testimony that has been lost.[26] Oden's own frightening experiences in the late 1960s are but one example of many that expose the dead end into

which modernity has led us—AIDS, increased poverty, abortion on demand, and a spiraling drug crisis. Most recently Oden has referred to modernity as a malady or malaise epitomized by Karl Marx, Friedrich Nietzsche, Freud, and Bultmann.[27]

As for defining the medicine of orthodoxy, Oden is fond of citing Lancelot Andrewes, a sixteenth-century Anglican: "One canon, two testaments, three creeds (the Apostles', Nicene and Athanasian), four (ecumenical) councils, and five centuries along with the fathers of that period."[28] Oden also employs the geometric metaphor of a circle with a "wide circumference": Holy Scripture, the "incomparable textual center of orthodoxy," is supplemented by the three venerable creeds, the seven ecumenical councils, and the eight great doctors of the East (Athanasius, Basil, Gregory of Nazianzus, Chrysostom) and West (Ambrose, Augustine, Jerome, and Gregory the Great).[29] In theory he extends the wide circumference of orthodoxy up to the end of the seventeenth century, with special dispensations granted for a few thinkers like Søren Kierkegaard and John Wesley, but in practice Oden rarely ventures beyond Chalcedon.[30] But if orthodoxy so defined is never less than a textuary tradition, it is also much more for Oden. Orthodoxy is "a living community, not merely a set of ideas."[31] In fact, the vital and unifying center of this historically variegated tradition, which variegation he never denies, is "life in Christ" or "some form of interpersonal encounter with the living Christ."[32]

Systematic Theology

Having spelled out Oden's twofold thesis of the demise of modernity and the necessity of a revival of orthodoxy, we will now illustrate it from three of his works, one each

---

23. We are reminded of Raphael's painting *The School of Athens* (1511), where portraits of the artist's contemporaries represent, among others, Plato, Aristotle, Sophocles, and Euclid.

24. Oden, *After Modernity,* 43–58.

25. Oden, *Agenda,* 46.

26. Oden, "Then and Now," 1167; see also Oden, *Two Worlds,* 15–16, on the death of modernity and the rise of postmodernity.

27. Oden, *Two Worlds,* 36–41.

28. Oden, "Back to the Fathers," 28.

29. Ibid., 30.

30. Oden, "Then and Now," 1167.

31. Oden, "Back to the Fathers," 30.

32. Oden, *After Modernity,* 180–81.

from the areas of systematic theology, biblical exegesis, and, a lifelong scholarly interest, pastoral counsel.[33] Oden's systematic theology follows a trinitarian sequence, its three volumes being devoted, respectively, to God the Father, Jesus Christ, and the Holy Spirit. Readers are treated to a veritable encyclopedic synthesis of the early Fathers. Oden strives to imitate what he sees as their theological method of being "self-consciously *un*original in desiring not to add anything to an already sufficient apostolic faith but only to receive and reappropriate that faith creatively in their particular historical setting and language." No doubt, continues Oden, "some may think it mildly amusing that the only claim I make is that there is nothing whatever original in these pages."[34]

In *The Living God*, the first volume in the trilogy, Oden makes two significant methodological reversals in an effort to follow patristic sequencing. First, he subordinates the study of theological method to theology proper; thus Part I addresses the nature and attributes of God, while the study of method must wait until Part IV. Second, study of the attributes of God precedes consideration of the questions of his existence and his triune nature (Part II). Classical Christian exegesis assumed the existence of God, but the proofs thereof are not without some meaning; Oden suggests that in their cumulative impact they confirm faith and so serve "a modest but important function."[35] Oden then rejects the idea that the doctrine of the Trinity is a later Hellenistic intrusion; rather, it developed from Old Testament "preindications" and the explicit teachings of the New Testament, and was later amplified by the Fathers.[36]

Part III turns to the work of God in creation and providence. Scripture affirms that the creation was made *ex nihilo* (Heb. 11:3), while human beings were not made out of nothing, but out of the dust of the earth (Gen. 2:19). Oden thus hints at theistic evolution, but he never really delves into the question. His is a theology of affirmations not questions, and thus it is enough for Oden to write that "the Christian doctrine of creation is not focused primarily upon scientific description of what happened perhaps thirty thousands of millions of years ago. Christian faith in creation is compatible with accurate scientific description, but not identical."[37]

Almost like a postscript or addendum, Part IV takes up the matter of theological method. Throughout his first volume Oden has hinted at the Wesleyan quadrilateral of Scripture, tradition, reason, and experience, but only now does he formally explain it.[38] These four sources of theology are interdependent, and together they in turn "depend upon and exist as a response to their necessary premise: revelation" in the history of Israel and Jesus Christ.[39] Scripture is unique as the primary theological source, while tradition, reason, and experience follow both temporally and dependently as secondary sources: the Word remembered, made intelligible, and experienced.

The Word of Life, the second volume, tackles Christology. It illustrates the direct impact that Oden's theses regarding modernity have on his theologizing. Modernity, having been "fully corrupted by its own premises," is dead and gone. "We are now living in a postmodern, postcritical situation, wherein the assumptions of modernity are no longer credible apart from tiny, introverted elites."[40] For Christology this means the rejection of typical historical-

33. The material that follows is drawn from Daniel B. Clendenin, "Learning to Listen: Thomas C. Oden on Postcritical Orthodoxy," *Journal of the Evangelical Theological Society* 34 (1991): 97–102.

34. Oden, *Living God*, xiii.

35. Ibid., 134–42.

36. Ibid., 194–208, 220.

37. Ibid., 231.

38. Ibid., 330–39; for previous hints of the quadrilateral, see pp. 26, 54, 130, 179.

39. Ibid., 330.

40. Oden, *Word of Life*, 527.

critical attempts to reconstruct the real Jesus, replete as they are with a total lack of self-criticism, unquestioned philosophical precommitments, and exaggerated competence. Still, Jesus Christ did live in history, and Oden has no desire to barter away historicism only to embrace fideism. Thus he does not disavow historical inquiry that remains a means and not an end in itself. Oden reminds his readers, however, that it "cannot yield saving faith . . . [nor] save one from sin," and in a sense "the reform of Christology cannot proceed without offense to historicism."[41]

The critical questions which constantly attach themselves to Christology provide Oden an occasion to include in *The Word of Life* a "Personal Interlude: A Path toward Postcritical Consciousness," which explains why his christological methodology must begin with the premise of "the implausible pretensions of the critical study of Jesus."[42] He recounts the fundamental redirection he took upon reading Nemesius: "Something clicked. I learned that I must listen intently, without reservation. Listen in such a way that my whole life depended upon hearing. Listen in such a way that I could see telescopically beyond my modern myopia. . . . Only in my forties did I begin to become a theologian."[43] The Christology which results from this perspective, he observes wryly, is "Vincentian and not Bultmannian." Thus Oden's long tome rehearses an orthodox Christology that has been unanimously received by East and West, by Catholic, Protestant, and Orthodox believers. Oden admits that many will find it amusing (although he considers it "a sober, ironic fact") that *The Word of Life* is simply "an introduction to its annotations."[44] That is not an exaggeration. True

to his promise, Oden launches an avalanche of long quotations from biblical and patristic sources. Parts I and II set forth the consensual orthodoxy on Jesus Christ as true God and true man, one person with two natures. Parts III and IV examine the work of Christ as Prophet, Priest, and King.

Biblical Exegesis

Oden's writings in the area of biblical exegesis, like his systematic theology, sum up classic orthodoxy. In the introduction to his commentary on *First and Second Timothy and Titus*, he serves notice that it is unusual in two ways. First, instead of treating the text in a verse-by-verse manner, he has organized the three epistles topically according to five major themes: the authority of the apostolic tradition, the heart of Christian preaching, pastoral care, the right ordering of ministry, and some conclusions. No footnotes clutter the text, the few Greek words used are always transliterated, and practicality is assured by frequent discussions of what Oden calls "preaching questions," ranging from issues of race and gender to worship, liturgy, and the intergenerational transmission of faith.

Second, the commentary is unusual in a more fundamental and important sense, according to Oden, for it is "grounded in the classical, consensual tradition. . . . The underlying conviction is that the better interpreters of the Pastorals are classical Christian exegetes."[45] Indeed, "most of what is enduringly valuable in contemporary biblical exegesis was discovered by the fifth century."[46] Why is this so? Oden insists that it is not because classic exegetes were chronologically nearer to the historical events, but because they were more attentive to the text, which is to say, they came to the text to listen and not to ask questions. They came not to lord it over the text, but to bow before it. The text, not the theologian, asked the questions. Like the classic exegetes it is Oden's intent to treat

41. Ibid., 529–30.

42. Ibid., 217–28; see also Oden, *After Modernity*, chs. 7–8 ("The Broken Promise of Critical Method" and "The Limits of Historical Method"); and idem, *Two Worlds*, ch. 5 ("Toward a Postmodern Critique of Modern Criticism").

43. Oden, *Word of Life*, 219–20.

44. Ibid., xiv.

45. Thomas Oden, *First and Second Timothy and Titus* (Louisville: John Knox, 1989), 2–3.

46. Oden, *Word of Life*, xi.

the Pastorals, and all of the Bible for that matter, as "the veritable address of God" and to "*listen* for the plain sense of Scripture."[47] So it comes as no surprise that, contrary to almost all critical studies of the Pastorals, Oden affirms their Pauline authorship, because, except for Marcion, this was never questioned for eighteen centuries. Accordingly, "the case against Pauline authorship reeks with difficulties."[48]

Having committed himself to a classic exegesis of the three texts, Oden admits that the offense of the gospel will scandalize modernity and all its self-important hubris. Commenting on 2 Timothy 1:8 he writes with both candor and passion:

> Academic theology remains ashamed of this apostolic testimony. I teach in a seminary. I know how embarrassed we professors are about the gospel and how hard we work to try to make the gospel conveniently acceptable to the modern mind. We will do almost anything to get wider university applause. We are ashamed of the fact that God hates sin, that we are sinners, that human history remains a history of sin, that God has suffered vicariously for us in order to redeem us from our sin. We are even ashamed of our own dear Loises and Eunices—our grandmothers and mothers. We cannot believe that they had greater integrity and strength than we have.[49]

To take another example. In regard to verse 10 of the same passage, Oden remarks that a renewal of Christianity demands a recovery of the meaning of the resurrection. But an obstacle blocks our path: "We have been cheated by modernity. Modernity has blinded our historical perspective. It has cut us off from the past. It has fixated our attention upon naturalistic explanations, upon reductionistic assumptions about the meaning of anything to which one can point."[50] This censorial modernity, how-

ever, has "now come to a senile end." We need not worry whether orthodox Christianity can survive modernity, for the tragic irony (and Oden takes no delight in this) is that "modernity is not even surviving itself. Modernity has not survived these times. All we have left is postmodernity. Modernity has long been in the process of radical disintegration."[51]

Pastoral Counsel

Pastoral Counsel is the third volume in Oden's Classical Pastoral Care series.[52] The purpose of the series is "to present in plain English the most indispensable texts of pastoral writers prior to the beginning of the eighteenth century"; that is, it gives a historical overview of the best Christian wisdom on the subject of the care of souls.[53] As in the companion volumes, the chapters of *Pastoral Counsel* cover broad themes: the conditions of a helping relationship; metaphors for pastoral counsel; the analogy of God's own care for people; timing in pastoral counsel; the dynamics of language and silence; the work of admonition, discipline, and comfort; the nurturing of responsible freedom; anticipations of modern psychotherapy; and the dynamics of human willing. The text is in fact an anthology of sorts. Primary readings from the past, most of which are less than a page in length, are preceded by short introductions by Oden.

Like Oden's works in the areas of systematic theology and biblical exegesis, the Classical Pastoral Care series builds on the thesis of the death of modernity and the necessity of a return to the wisdom of antiquity. Christians have a rich heritage of pastoral wisdom that needs to be reclaimed. It is not only remarkable but unconscionable that this heritage remains neglected and

47. Oden, *Timothy and Titus*, 16; see also 66, 92.
48. Ibid., 15.
49. Ibid., 128; see also 73.
50. Ibid., 130–31.

51. Ibid., 133.
52. Thomas Oden, *Pastoral Counsel* (New York: Crossroad, 1989). The other volumes in the series are *Crisis Ministries* (1986), *Becoming a Minister* (1987), and *Ministry through Word and Sacrament* (1988). (*Crisis Ministries*, though the first to be published, is actually the last volume in the series.)
53. Oden, *Pastoral Counsel*, 1.

even spurned by modern chauvinism that assumes that what is current is both superior and normative.[54] Seeking to correct this tragic myopia, the Classical Pastoral Care series prefers earlier texts to later ones.[55] Earlier texts provide a canon of cumulative wisdom to which we would do well to listen. In fact, many if not most so-called modern insights of psychotherapy were well understood by the ancients and can be found in their writings at least in embryonic form. Further, ancient wisdom often confounds the pretensions of modern psychology. For example, contrary to Carl Rogers and others, the ancient pastoral counselors followed up their diagnoses with admonition and advice.[56] Their giving priority to Scripture relegated human reason to a humbler role.[57] And whereas modern counsel tends to be individualistic (recall the four elements of modernity), the counsel of the Fathers stressed the need for community.[58] Moreover, the consensual tradition would disapprove of the tendency of modern psychology to separate psychology, theology, and ethics.[59] It would also radically question the modern assumption of the goodness of people and the corollary of historical optimism.[60]

Oden's Classical Pastoral Care series adds a new twist at this point in that it finds points of congruence between past and present. Though "classical Christianity remains ironically 'ahead' of modernity in its balance of complementary values and virtues so prone to imbalance in modern discussions,"[61] the primary emphasis in *Pastoral Counsel* is not to overthrow current psychological wisdom, but to show its continuity with the past. For example, ancient orthodoxy foreshadowed modern ideas of transference, Rogers's dictum that the therapist manifest an unconditional positive regard for the client, Freud's emphasis on self-disclosure, Immanuel Kant's postulate that the sense of moral obligation presupposes the freedom to obey or disobey, recognition of the importance of body language, the classification of personality types and temperaments, behaviorist insights about habits, and primitive dream theories.[62] Ambrose even anticipated the psychiatrist's couch![63] So great is the congruence between past and present that Oden devotes an entire chapter of *Pastoral Counsel* (ch. 8) to documenting rudimentary ways in which the classics anticipated, for instance, reinforcement techniques, psychoanalysis, the notion of religion as projection, and modern methods of caring for the emotionally ill.

Evaluation

Oden's proclamation of the death of modernity and the consequent vacuum of meaning today is born of pathos and not joy. He does not write polemically or with bitterness. His posture is irenic throughout. Nor does his listening to the consensual voices of the past lead to an "uncritical credulity or archaism or idolatry of tradition."[64] His affirmative position on the role of women in ministry would be hard to document in the early church, and he even hints that modern caregivers might need to demythologize ancient accounts of demons like that found in Athanasius's *Life of St. Anthony*. No one can complain that modern critical studies are neglected by Oden, for as an insider he has paid his dues to the critical guild. He warns of both excessive conservatism that would overvalue the past and excessive progressivism that would neglect it.[65] He does not romanticize about a

---

54. Oden, *Becoming a Minister*, 1, 8.
55. Ibid., 3–4; see also Oden, *Pastoral Counsel*, 2.
56. Oden, *Pastoral Counsel*, 72, 160.
57. Ibid., 103–4.
58. Ibid., 182.
59. Ibid., 199.
60. Ibid., 209.
61. Ibid., 226.

62. Ibid., passim; Oden, *Becoming a Minister*, 2.
63. Oden, *Pastoral Counsel*, 251.
64. Oden, *Timothy and Titus*, 23.
65. Oden, *Living God*, 362. In a similar vein, Oden suggests in his *Two Worlds* that modernity has collapsed in America because of excessive individualism, and in the Soviet Union because of excessive collectivism.

patristic golden age in which heterodox opinion never questioned orthodoxy. In Christology, for example, Marcion, Celsus, Praxeas, and Lucian, not nineteenth-century historical critics, were the first to raise many of the most pertinent questions. He understands that the classical consensus he so cherishes is only proximate.

Oden does little to help his readers with the necessary task of contextualization. He is most helpful exegeting the texts of the classical theologians, and least helpful in exegeting society and bringing the two together. That does not mean he considers this work unimportant; rather, it is simply a task he leaves to others. Further, Oden is so intent on letting the ancients speak for themselves that his method is deliberately long on recitation and short on explanation. He realizes that some will consider his calculated method boring, but he sees it as essential.[66] In the preface to *The Word of Life* he admits to feeling "the eccentric longing" of Henry Vaughan's "Retreat":

> O how I long to travel back
> And tread again that ancient track! . . .
> Some men a forward motion love,
> But I by backward steps would move.

Oden has no illusions about the reception of his distinctive methodological program: "Some may feel that this argument, if taken seriously, would set theology back a hundred years. I would hope not—I would prefer a thousand or more."[67] Henry Vaughan would have liked that.

Primary Sources

Oden, Thomas. *After Modernity—What?* Grand Rapids: Zondervan, 1990.

_____. *After Therapy, What? Lay Therapeutic Resources in Religious Perspective.* Springfield, Ill.: Charles C. Thomas, 1974.

_____. *Agenda for Theology.* San Francisco: Harper and Row, 1979.

_____. *Becoming a Minister.* New York: Crossroad, 1987.

_____. *Beyond Revolution.* Philadelphia: Westminster, 1970.

_____. *Care of Souls in the Classic Tradition.* Philadelphia: Fortress, 1984.

_____. *The Community of Celebration: Toward an Ecclesiology for a Renewing Student Movement.* Nashville: National Methodist Student Movement, 1964.

_____. *Conscience and Dividends.* Washington, D.C.: Ethics and Public Policy Center, 1985.

_____. *Contemporary Theology and Psychotherapy.* Philadelphia: Westminster, 1967.

_____. *Crisis Ministries.* New York: Crossroad, 1986.

_____. *The Crisis of the World and the Word of God.* Nashville: National Methodist Student Movement, 1962.

_____. *Doctrinal Standards in the Wesleyan Tradition.* Grand Rapids: Zondervan, 1987.

_____. *First and Second Timothy and Titus.* Louisville: John Knox, 1989.

_____. *Game Free: A Guide to the Meaning of Intimacy.* New York: Harper and Row, 1974.

_____. *Guilt Free.* Nashville: Abingdon, 1980.

_____. "The Idea of Obedience in Contemporary Protestant Ethics." Ph.D. diss., Yale University, 1960.

_____. *The Intensive Group Experience: The New Pietism.* Philadelphia: Westminster, 1972.

_____. *Kerygma and Counseling: Toward a Covenant Ontology for Secular Psychotherapy.* Philadelphia: Westminster, 1965.

_____. *Life in the Spirit.* San Francisco: Harper and Row, 1992.

_____. *The Living God.* San Francisco: Harper and Row, 1987.

_____. *Ministry through Word and Sacrament.* New York: Crossroad, 1988.

_____. *Pastoral Counsel.* New York: Crossroad, 1989.

_____. *Pastoral Theology: Essentials of Ministry.* San Francisco: Harper and Row, 1983.

_____. *The Promise of Barth: The Ethics of Freedom.* Philadelphia: Lippincott, 1969.

_____. *Psychotherapy.* Philadelphia: Westminster, 1965.

_____. *Radical Obedience: The Ethics of Rudolf Bultmann.* Philadelphia: Westminster, 1964.

66. Oden, *Word of Life*, 112.
67. Ibid.

_____. *Should Treatment Be Terminated?* New York: Harper and Row, 1976.

_____. *The Structure of Awareness.* Nashville: Abingdon, 1969.

_____. *TAG: The Transactional Awareness Game.* New York: Harper and Row, 1976.

_____. *Two Worlds: Notes on the Death of Modernity in America and the Soviet Union.* Downers Grove, Ill.: Inter-Varsity, 1991.

_____. *The Word of Life.* San Francisco: Harper and Row, 1989.

_____, ed. *The Parables of Kierkegaard.* Princeton, N.J.: Princeton University Press, 1978.

_____, ed. *Six Papers on Church Renewal.* Nashville: National Methodist Student Movement, 1962.

_____, A. Godin, and A. Chapelle. *Expérience thérapeutique et révélation: Un symposium.* Louvain: Nouvelle Revue Théologique, 1965.

Millard J. Erickson

L. Arnold Hustad

Millard John Erickson is an unusual combination of scholar, educator, and pastor. Currently research professor of theology at Southwestern Baptist Theological Seminary, he has become known as a significant evangelical and Baptist theologian and prolific author.

The youngest of four children, Erickson was born on June 24, 1932, in Stanchfield, Minnesota, just north of Minneapolis.[1] He was raised in a church of the Baptist General Conference, which originated among Swedish immigrants. This religious legacy, fostered especially through his grandparents and parents, led him early in life to personal Christian commitment.

Although he had intended to study science at the University of Minnesota, Erickson felt led into Christian vocation and attended Bethel College in St. Paul, where that call was confirmed. After two years he

transferred to the University of Minnesota in an effort to broaden his exposure to the academic world. In 1953, he graduated with a major in philosophy and minors in psychology and sociology.

Erickson's theological education began at Bethel Theological Seminary and continued at Northern Baptist Theological Seminary in Chicago, where he received a B.D. in 1956. Two years later, his interest in philosophy led to an M.A. from the University of Chicago. His Ph.D. in systematic theology was conferred in 1963 by Northwestern University in a joint program with Garrett Theological Seminary, where he studied under William Hordern.

Further shaping Erickson's theology was his pastoral experience. He became pastor of Fairfield Avenue Baptist Church in inner-city Chicago upon graduation from

---

1. Much of the following material was derived from Leslie R. Keylock, "Evangelical Leaders You Should Know: Meet Millard J. Erickson," *Moody Monthly* 87.10 (June 1987): 71–73; David S. Dockery, "Millard J. Erickson," in *Baptist Theologians*, ed. Timothy George and David S. Dockery (Nashville: Broadman, 1990), 640–44; and personal conversations with Erickson.

seminary and was ordained in that church in 1957. In 1961 he moved to Olivet Baptist Church in suburban Minneapolis. Though a few years later he shifted to the academic arena, he has, since leaving the full-time pastorate, maintained contact with lay people through over forty interim pastorates in almost as many churches. Noting that the theologies of Paul Tillich, Karl Barth, and Rudolf Bultmann were developed in the context of the church, he has consciously interacted with congregations in the process of developing his thought.[2]

Erickson's teaching career began in 1964 as an assistant professor of Bible and apologetics at Wheaton College. In 1967, he assumed the chairmanship of the Department of Bible and Philosophy. During this time he adapted his doctoral dissertation, which was published in 1968 as *The New Evangelical Theology*.[3] In 1969, with his wife Virginia and their three daughters, Erickson moved to Bethel Theological Seminary to teach theology, and in 1984 he became dean of that institution. He began his present position at Southwestern in 1992.

Except for his obvious Baptist loyalties, Erickson is not easily identified with any particular theological camp. It might be said, however, that *The New Evangelical Theology* sketches the context for his theological development. He looks at the new evangelicalism from various standpoints—historical, doctrinal, apologetic, and ethical—placing emphasis upon key players such as Harold Ockenga, Carl Henry, Billy Graham, Bernard Ramm, Vernon Grounds,

and Edward John Carnell. Though largely positive in his critique, he notes among the movement's weaknesses the lack of a fully rounded theology that is in touch with contemporary problems.[4] In many ways, his own writing has been an effort to fulfil that need.

Erickson acknowledges several influences upon his thinking. An apologetic tone in portions of his writings seems to have been influenced by Carnell, and in particular by his *Introduction to Christian Apologetics*. It is significant that Erickson's *Christian Theology* is dedicated to three individuals. Bernard Ramm is credited with stimulating Erickson's interest in theology. William Hordern instilled an appreciation for views other than one's own. Also acknowledged is Wolfhart Pannenberg, with whom Erickson spent a sabbatical leave in 1976 at the University of Munich.[5] Behind these influences, however, lies a Christian devotion shaped in part, no doubt, by the Pietism of his Baptist roots.

Ethics

Somewhat overshadowed by Erickson's extensive production in systematic theology is his contribution to Christian ethics. His academic interest in ethics developed in part out of the necessity to teach the course on social ethics at Bethel Seminary. A result was the publication of *Relativism in Contemporary Christian Ethics* in 1974.[6] Written after the popularity of situation ethics had dissipated, this work analyzes dimensions of ethical relativism that remain

---

2. E.g., he acknowledges members of the Cross of Glory Baptist Church in Hopkins, Minnesota, for assistance in formulating certain sections of *Christian Theology*: "This fine suburban congregation served as my church laboratory for the theological concepts which I was developing. Particularly in the Sunday evening feedback sessions and the Wednesday Bible studies, I was impressed again with the theological interest and competency of lay persons" (Millard J. Erickson, *Christian Theology* [Grand Rapids: Baker, 1986], 12–13).

3. Millard J. Erickson, *The New Evangelical Theology* (Westwood, N.J.: Revell, 1968).

4. Ibid., 224.

5. Erickson, *Christian Theology*, 11–12; see also Millard J. Erickson, "Pannenberg's Use of History as a Solution to the Religious Language Problem," *Journal of the Evangelical Theological Society* 17 (1974): 99–105.

6. Millard J. Erickson, *Relativism in Contemporary Christian Ethics* (Grand Rapids: Baker, 1974); see also idem, "Human Engineering and Christian Ethical Values," *Journal of the American Scientific Affiliation* 30.1 (March 1978): 16–19; idem and Ines E. Bowers, "Euthanasia and Christian Ethics," *Journal of the Evangelical Theological Society* 19 (1976): 15–24.

implicit in culture. Intended for popular consumption, the book was judged simplistic and incomplete by some reviewers.[7] It does offer, however, an alternative Christian method that many have found to be of help in dealing with moral problems.

Erickson points out that ethical relativism was at least in part the product of several developments in general culture as well as in theology. These developments undermined the belief in commonsense absolutes and, in the ethical realm, resulted in systems such as situation ethics, as popularized by Joseph Fletcher. Fletcher had contrasted two approaches to ethics. Legalism assumes a prefabricated morality, as if one could find in a book a fixed law to govern each situation. Antinomianism, at the other extreme, eliminates all rules or maxims, relying perhaps upon some intuition or direct revelation from the Holy Spirit. Rejecting these extremes, Fletcher opted instead for a situational approach, affirming love as the only intrinsic good. Thus, only this one absolute norm need be applied to any moral situation. Yet it is not to be applied prescriptively. There is no prefabricated morality, for love is applied according to the situation.

Erickson's critique of situation ethics enumerates a host of difficulties. Yet he notes that it correctly recognizes the diversity of life, with which no legalistic system can adequately contend. As an alternative, Erickson proposes an approach that is based on principles found in God's revelation, which is an expression of his good will. The Bible teaches objective, normative values whose application depends upon the set of circumstances in the given situation. Some of these principles are quite general, such as the glorification of God. Others are more specific, such as the necessity of mutual trust if human relationships are to succeed. To reach an ethical conclusion, we must follow several steps:

1. Determine the relevant principles.
2. Combine these principles to form some type of rule or directive.
3. Refine the rule from general to specific.
4. Determine the application of the specific rule; that is, subsume the individual case to the rule.
5. Decide upon a method of disposition of those cases that do not seem to be subsumable under any rule.[8]

One noteworthy aspect of Erickson's approach is the distinction between good and right. While good is the ideal at which we should aim, in some cases the only possibility is to choose the lesser of two evils. To do so may be right, though it falls short of the ideal.

Erickson's interest in ethical and social concerns, especially as related to systematic theology, is evident in his chapter on "The Universality of Humanity" in *Christian Theology*. He affirms that all humans, despite their differences, share the ability to know and respond to God. That God's image encompasses both sexes, all races, all economic statuses, all age groups, including the unborn, has inescapable moral implications.[9] An interesting inclusion in this chapter is a section on the unmarried. Remaining unmarried throughout life ought not be regarded as second-class status. In fact, it appears that Jesus never married, and Paul urges readers in Corinth, whether married or single, to remain as they are. Thus, neither state is inherently inferior. Both groups can find fulfilling ministry within the church. Erickson concludes that since all humans partake of God's image, all should be treated with impartiality and concern.[10]

A further evidence of Erickson's regard for ethical issues appears in his discussion of the social dimensions of sin. In response to corruption in society, he advocates per-

---

7. See, e.g., Allen Verhey, review of *Relativism in Contemporary Christian Ethics*, by Millard J. Erickson, *Calvin Theological Journal* 9 (1974): 257–60.

8. Erickson, *Relativism*, 139.
9. Erickson, *Christian Theology*, 542–56.
10. Ibid., 558.

sonal regeneration combined with nonviolent reform.[11] Application to specific issues, however, is left to the reader.

Systematic Theology

The bulk of Erickson's writing has been in systematic theology. His topical studies in this area include *Contemporary Options in Eschatology, Salvation,* and *Responsive Faith.*[12] Most celebrated, however, is his comprehensive *Christian Theology,* which was first published in three volumes (1983–85), and then in a one-volume edition (1986). *Christian Theology* is a response to what Erickson himself, early in his career, identified as a "pressing need for an up-to-date conservative systematic theology text."[13]

Christian Theology is intended as a resource for contemporary students, just as Charles Hodge, Augustus H. Strong, and Louis Berkhof wrote for their generations. It has been used widely as a textbook in colleges and seminaries as well as by pastors and others interested in evangelical doctrine. A three-volume series of Readings in Christian Theology is designed to supplement the text.[14] It is not our aim here to survey the entire sweep of Erickson's theology, for much of it does not differ significantly from conventional evangelical thought. There are, however, certain distinctive contributions which are worth exploring.

The task of the systematic theologian is to describe, analyze, and criticize the doctrines of Christianity. More succinctly, theology is the study or science of God.

While not eliminating a unique status for theology, Erickson does argue that it meets the traditional criteria to be considered scientific. For example, theology has a definite subject to investigate. It deals with objective matters and has a distinct methodology. Its propositions are coherent. Further, theology shares common ground with other sciences. It is subject to the basic principles and canons of logic. Theology is capable of being communicated and employs methods utilized by other disciplines, such as history and philosophy. It even shares subject matter with other disciplines, though it deals with that subject matter in a unique way. For example, theology, like some branches of science, considers the human an object to be analyzed, but in so doing it employs its own distinct frame of reference.

Vital to understanding Erickson's theology is its relation to biblical studies. Careful to define biblical theology as "simply theology which is biblical, that is, based upon and faithful to the teachings of the Bible," Erickson asserts that systematic theology of the right kind "is not simply based upon biblical theology; it is biblical theology. Our goal is systematic biblical theology. . . . The systematic theologian draws upon the product of the biblical theologian's work. Biblical theology is the raw material, as it were, with which systematic theology works."[15] Indeed, *Christian Theology* is replete with scriptural references. They are not treated as mere proof texts, but as integral elements in the theological venture.

Theological Method

One of Erickson's significant contributions to evangelical theology is his regard for method. Elaborated in the opening chapters, and implicit throughout *Christian Theology,* is a specific procedure for actually doing theology, as well as contemporizing it. Since Erickson considers theology an art as well as a science, this procedure need

11. Ibid., 658.
12. Millard J. Erickson, *Contemporary Options in Eschatology: A Study of the Millennium* (Grand Rapids: Baker, 1977); idem, *Salvation: God's Amazing Plan* (Wheaton, Ill.: Victor, 1978); and idem, *Responsive Faith* (Arlington Heights, Ill.: Harvest, 1987).
13. Erickson, *New Evangelical Theology,* 85; see also p. 224.
14. Millard J. Erickson, ed., *The Living God* (Grand Rapids: Baker, 1973); idem, *Man's Need and God's Gift* (Grand Rapids: Baker, 1976); idem, *The New Life* (Grand Rapids: Baker, 1979).
15. Erickson, *Christian Theology,* 25.

not be rigidly nor sequentially followed. Yet a clear, logical order akin to Erickson's nine-step approach is recommended:[16]

1. *Collection of the biblical materials relevant to the particular doctrine being investigated.* The exegete must be careful from the start not to use tools or methods that preclude what the documents assume. For example, a method which denies supernatural occurrences such as miracles would be inappropriate for the conservative exegete.

2. *Unification of the biblical materials.* On the assumption that the many biblical writers were consistent, unifying statements on the doctrinal theme can be developed.

3. *Analysis of the meaning of the biblical teachings.* The biblical terms and concepts should be explored to discover what they really mean.

4. *Examination of historical treatments.* Lessons may be learned from the way in which theologians in the past treated the issue under consideration.

5. *Identification of the essence of the doctrine.* This is a pivotal step in Erickson's methodology. It involves separating the permanent content of the doctrine from the cultural and temporary form in which it was expressed. This means, as Erickson describes it, "separating the message to the Corinthians as first-century Christians living in Corinth . . . from the message to them as Christians."[17]

6. *Illumination from sources beyond the Bible.* Though the Bible is the major source for systematic theology, Erickson contends that there are other resources. Since God makes himself known in general revelation, the insights of psychology, for example, may enlighten our comprehension of salvation.

7. *Contemporary expression of the doctrine.* Stating the essence of the doctrine in contemporary form is an attempt to answer in an intelligible fashion questions raised by one's culture. This does not require alteration of the content. Erickson provides a helpful analysis of this step in the process. Since the Christian message was originally declared in a specific context, it must be "decontextualized" before it can be recontextualized for another setting. This recontextualization may involve, says Erickson, three different dimensions. First is what he calls the dimension of length: the message is brought from the context of the biblical era to the twentieth century. The dimension of breadth involves expressing the truth for a contemporary culture other than one's own. Finally, the dimension of height considers the level of complexity and sophistication of those to whom the message will be communicated.[18] For example, though the truth is invariable, the theologian and the layperson will deal with it at different levels.

8. *Development of a central interpretive motif.* By selecting a central theme around which to organize the various doctrines, we can bring a unity to theology as well as enhance our ability to communicate it. Erickson develops his theology (though not always explicitly) around the theme of the magnificence of God, which suggests both his greatness and the excellence of his moral nature.

9. *Stratification of topics.* Finally, the more crucial doctrines should be distinguished from those that are less crucial. Erickson notes that the second coming of Christ is a major belief. Of lesser significance is the issue of whether the church will be removed

16. Ibid., 66–79.
17. Ibid., 71.

18. Ibid., 76.

from the world before the great tribulation.

The nature of systematic theology is not fully encompassed by this procedure, however. Erickson recognizes the latitude afforded the systematic theologian to make statements which may not be directly taught by Scripture. He describes various types of theological assertions and notes that the level of their authority is correlated to their source. Direct statements of Scripture, of course, hold the highest priority. Direct and probable implications therefrom, because of their inferential nature, have somewhat less authority. Inductive conclusions from Scripture yield only probabilities, and conclusions inferred from general revelation, if they are to carry weight, must be tied to explicit biblical statements. Because gaps in our knowledge will inevitably remain, Erickson believes that there is even a place for overt speculations, "which frequently include hypotheses based upon a single statement or hint in Scripture, or derived from somewhat obscure or unclear parts of the Bible."[19] This privilege includes a responsibility, however, to issue a warning that one is speculating.

Another noteworthy aspect of Erickson's theological method is his concern to contemporize the Christian message. Following William Hordern, he distinguishes between transformers and translators.[20] Transformers assert that many traditional Christian beliefs depend on the outmoded ancient worldviews which spawned them. Furthermore, humans have radically changed, so that the message is no longer suitable to meet their needs. Accordingly, the content of the message must be altered or transformed; an example is the Death of God theology in the mid-1960s.

By contrast, the translator seeks to retain the biblical message, but to reexpress its content in an intelligible and meaningful form for the modern person. This approach, with which Erickson identifies, ascertains the permanent essence of the doctrine and separates it from the temporal forms in which it was given. To assist us, Erickson lists several criteria for determining the unalterable message. For example, that which is permanent is marked by a constancy across cultures. Here he cites the principle of sacrificial atonement, which is found in both the Old and the New Testament.

From Erickson's methodology it is clear that he views systematic theology as far more than simply collecting Scripture verses that focus on certain themes. That broader scope is evident in his definition of theology as "that discipline which strives to give a coherent statement of the doctrines of the Christian faith, based primarily upon the Scriptures, placed in the context of culture in general, worded in a contemporary idiom, and related to issues of life."[21]

Theological Distinctives

The Magnificent God

To know God, in Erickson's view, we must know God in the way in which he has revealed himself. God has communicated himself through universal revelation, knowledge that is general in content and accessible to all persons at all times. He has also revealed himself through particular revelation, including Scripture and the incarnation of Christ. The Bible, the supreme source of our understanding God, is rendered accurate through the Holy Spirit's supernatural influence, which is called inspiration. A corollary of inspiration is inerrancy, which indicates that the Bible, "when correctly interpreted in light of the level to which culture and the means of communication had developed at the time it was written, and in view of the purposes

19. Ibid., 80. See p. 1234 for an example—Erickson's own speculation regarding degrees of reward in heaven.
20. Ibid., 113–24.

21. Ibid., 21.

417

for which it was given, is fully truthful in all that it affirms."[22]

Though God's self-revelation is not exhaustive, it is adequate to communicate the nature and qualities of God, as well as his relationship to creation. We are told, for example, that God is both plurality and unity, both three and one. This is no contradiction, for God is not three and one in the same respect. Scripture also indicates God's attributes, his permanent qualities. These attributes, which Erickson classifies under the rubrics of God's greatness and goodness, are not to be considered apart from his essence. They are simply various facets of God's unified being.

One aspect of Erickson's understanding of the nature of God deserves special attention. The immanence and transcendence of God, which Erickson terms the nearness and distance of God, are not treated as attributes, but as descriptions of God's relationship to his creation.[23] The immanence of God designates his presence and activity in the universe, including human nature and history. God is involved in the activities of individuals as well as human institutions. He is also at work within the processes of nature. Erickson appears to narrow the gap between the natural and the supernatural. While God occasionally works through miracles, or unusual acts which are clearly supernatural, even some of what are normally considered natural events should be considered God's doing. For example, God may heal miraculously, but the skill of the physician used to bring the patient to health may also be viewed as God's activity. It is part of God's general revelation.

Since God is involved in the processes of nature, we may ascertain something about him through the orderliness of the universe. Nature ought also to be appreciated, since God is at work within it. A further implication of God's immanence is that God may work through non-Christian people or

through heathen nations, as is evident in the Old Testament. Some acts of non-Christians, then, may be genuinely good, though not meritorious. Accordingly, "when no compromise of biblical truth is involved, the Christian and the church may at times cooperate with non-Christian organizations to accomplish part of God's plan."[24] God's immanence also provides points of contact with the unbeliever through which the gospel may be disclosed.

Emphasis upon God's immanence alone, however, may identify God too closely with his creation, and thus lose sight of his personal character. God's immanence must be balanced with his transcendence. The transcendent God is independent from and superior to his creation. Erickson's understanding of transcendence appears to draw on two proposals of Søren Kierkegaard. First, the distinction between God and humanity is not a matter of mere degree, but of quality. Consider as an analogy that regardless of how much one refines cotton, it will never become silk. Though he rejects Karl Barth's infinite extension of the distinction, Erickson affirms a differentiation in kind between God and humans. This yields several theological implications. For example, God is the ultimate ground of all value and truth. Further, being transcendent, God will on some occasions work beyond what would naturally result from a set of circumstances. In view of his uniqueness in kind, reverence and worship of him are appropriate. In addition, salvation is clearly a work that only God can accomplish. It does not elevate us to divine status, but restores us to what we were intended to be. Thus, the distinction between God and humans is not merely moral or spiritual, but also metaphysical.

The second proposal of Kierkegaard on which Erickson draws is dimensional beyondness. The traditional model of transcendence is limited by inadequate spatial designations such as "up" and "down." But

22. Ibid., 233–34.
23. Ibid., 302–3.

24. Ibid., 311.

God dwells on an entirely different plane or level of reality. This is what permits us to think of immanence and transcendence simultaneously: "God is in the same place we are, yet he is not accessible to us in a simple way, for he is in a different dimension."[25] Even as someone without a radio receiver cannot access the frequencies immanent within a room, so we cannot geographically find God, though he is near to us. His presence must be understood in terms of a spiritual dimension. God is both near and far, both immanent and transcendent. Neither may be emphasized over the other, for both are expressive of his relationship to creation.

In addressing the subject of what God does, Erickson suggests that one way of organizing systematic theology is by the primary work of the respective members of the Trinity. The Father's work is featured in creation and providence, the Son's in redemption, and the Spirit's in the application and completion of redemption.[26] Erickson's most creative proposal is his response to the classic question of whether God's plan or human action is logically prior. Does God decide exactly how we are going to act, or does he base his decisions of what will happen on what he foresees we will do?

Historically, Calvinists have affirmed that human decisions and actions are a consequence of God's plan. The Arminian, however, suggests that the plan of God is conditioned by human decision. In Erickson's view, which he calls a moderately Calvinistic model, God's decisions are unconditional—he does not choose us on the basis of what he foreknows we are going to do. To the Arminian's reliance on Romans 8:29 ("whom [God] foreknew he also predestined") as a proof text, Erickson responds that "foreknowledge" here means far more than an advance knowledge of what will happen. It also carries with it the idea of favorable disposition or selection.

Yet the logical priority of God's plan does not exclude human freedom. Erickson holds to the notion of "compatibilistic" freedom: human free will is compatible with God's sovereignty. True to form, Erickson provides an explanation of this apparent contradiction. He distinguishes between God's rendering something certain and rendering it necessary. The former is a matter of God's plan that something *will* happen; the latter is a matter of his decreeing that it *must* happen. Since God does not render our choices and actions necessary, we are free to do whatever pleases us. However, since God renders them certain, we are not entirely in control of what holds appeal for us. Our choices are based upon certain characteristics which we cannot alter on our own. In a choice between liver and steak, says Erickson, he may be free to choose liver. However, since he has no conscious control over his distaste for liver, he will choose steak.[27]

The conditions under which I make my choices are governed by God. Knowing what my choices would be, God chose me in particular, out of all the infinite possibilities of genetic combinations, to bring into being. In addition, my choices are influenced by the circumstances which he brings into my life. Thus my actions are rendered certain, though not necessary. Erickson denies that his view is Arminian, for Arminianism maintains that God merely confirms the human choices and actions which he foresees. In Erickson's view, foreknowledge enters the picture earlier, so to speak. God foreknows all human possibilities and, accordingly, chooses to bring into existence precisely those individuals who will do what he desires.

That God has rendered all things certain does not mean, of course, that he is pleased with all that is done. Erickson distinguishes between different senses of God's will. God's "wish" is his general intention, the values with which he is pleased; God's

---

25. Ibid., 316.
26. Ibid., 846.

27. Ibid., 356–57.

"will" is his specific intention in a given situation, what he decides shall actually occur. For example, it is God's wish that we should not sin. However, like parents who may at times not intervene even when their child's action is contrary to their wishes, God's will may permit a sinful course of action.

Erickson anticipates the conclusion of some that if God renders all things certain, it makes little difference whether we evangelize. Will not those who are elect be chosen anyway? Erickson's response is that it may be God's plan that our witness to the gospel is the means by which an elect individual will come to salvation. Furthermore, we do not know who is chosen by God, nor can we be certain that our efforts at evangelism are not in fact fulfilling another part of God's plan.[28]

Humankind and Sin

Erickson believes that God created humans directly and completely; he did not make them out of some lower creature. While a certain measure of evolutionary process took place within the framework of the "days" in Genesis 1, that process was not without limits. Each day was begun by a creative act of God. Thus, both the physical and spiritual natures of humankind were specially created.

What elevates humans above animals is the image of God. Traditionally, there have been three views of the way in which humans reflect God. The relational view speaks of the image as the experience of a particular relationship with God. According to this position, which was espoused by Emil Brunner and Karl Barth, the image is not something humans possess, nor something they are. It is a relationship with God, either positive or negative. Another option is the functional view, according to which the image is something that the human does. Here the image is frequently identified with the creational mandate given in Genesis 1:26 that humans are to have do-

minion over the earth. Erickson rejects both options in favor of the substantive view. The image is something that the human is, not a specific relationship or function. The relational and functional views actually focus on the consequences of the image rather than on the image itself.

Of what does the image consist? This question has been argued by theologians for centuries. Refusing to limit the image to simply one dimension, Erickson turns to the two alternative views which he has rejected. Although humanity's relationships and functions are not the image of God, they are its manifestations, its consequences. These consequences are best portrayed in the perfect example of humanity. In Jesus we find perfect fellowship with and obedience to the Father, and love for humanity. Jesus portrayed what God had intended his likeness in humans to be.[29]

To understand Erickson's view of humanity, we must also understand his notion of our constitutional makeup. Of what are humans composed? Erickson dismisses both trichotomism and dichotomism, notions popular throughout church history. Scripture, he notes, seems to regard humans as unitary beings. The biblical terms *body* and *soul* cannot be readily dichotomized into an embodied and a disembodied state. On the other hand, Erickson is not a monist after the fashion of John A. T. Robinson. He does not find persuasive either Robinson's linguistic arguments for indivisibility or his philosophical argument that human dualism is untenable.

Instead, while acknowledging that Scripture usually regards the human being as a unity, Erickson points out that it also speaks of an intermediate state between death and resurrection; during that period the human is clearly disembodied. The resurrection to come, as Paul teaches in 1 Corinthians 15, will remedy the situation, for each person will receive a perfected body. Thus, Erickson espouses a "conditional

28. Ibid., 361–62.

29. Ibid., 514–15.

unity." The normal state of the human is an embodied, unitary being. That unity is broken down at death, however. Eventually, at the moment of resurrection the individual will assume a body that has some points of continuity with the old body, but is also a new or reconstituted or spiritual body.

Another key tenet of Erickson's view of humanity is that we are not now fulfilling all that God intended. Sin, says Erickson, "is any lack of conformity, active or passive, to the moral law of God. This may be a matter of act, of thought, or of inner disposition or state."[30] One intriguing aspect of Erickson's discussion responds to various theories of original sin. Assuming that there is some precondition in all of us that leads to sin and depravity, he turns to the question of the manner in which humans are affected by the sin of Adam.

Erickson adopts the Augustinian view, which sees Adam's connection with us in terms of a natural or realistic headship.[31] All of us were germinally in an undifferentiated form in Adam. Thus, when he sinned, we sinned as well. There is nothing unfair in our being encumbered with Adam's corruption and guilt since, in a sense, we sinned with him. Erickson's interpretation of Romans 5:12–19 supports this contention. Clearly, in verses 12, 15, and 17, Adam is identified as the one through whom sin and death came into the world. The last clause of verse 12, however, appears to indicate another source: "death spread to all men because all men sinned" (RSV). The question is whether this means that individual sin has led to our personal guilt. Erickson notes that the tense of the verb "sinned" is a simple aorist. Had Paul intended to indicate that sin and corruption resulted from our own individual sins, he likely would have used a present or perhaps imperfect tense. However, since the aorist

commonly refers to a single past action, we ought to consider the sin of Adam and the sin of "all men" the same.

Erickson extends his discussion to the difficult case of infants and children. If all are born in sin, are all who die in infancy or childhood condemned to eternal death? Evangelicals have frequently proposed, often with little support, that there is an age at which we become accountable for our sin. Before that time God will simply intervene by his grace. Erickson, however, notes the parallel in Romans 5 between Adam and Christ. One might expect that if guilt and condemnation are conveyed to us without any conscious choice on our part, the same would be true of redemption. Evangelicals, however, have rejected that idea. The imputation of Christ's work is based upon a conscious decision of faith. Perhaps then, says Erickson, the imputation of sin is based upon a conscious decision at which point we become responsible for our sin. Until then, there is merely a conditional imputation of Adam's guilt. The conscious decision may not occur at a particular age, nor even when one first sins. Rather, we become responsible, and thus guilty, when we approve of or acquiesce to our corrupt nature.[32]

Christology

Erickson's most extensive doctrinal monograph to date—*The Word Became Flesh: A Contemporary Incarnational Christology*—was published in 1991. His interest in christological method had been evident a decade earlier, when he contrasted Christology done from above with Christology done from below.[33] Christology from above includes the methods of Barth, Bultmann, and Brunner, who focused more upon the account of the church's proclamation re-

30. Ibid., 578.
31. This correlates to the traducian view of the origin of the soul, which holds that, in addition to our physical being, we receive our soul from our parents as well.

32. Ibid., 638–39.
33. Millard J. Erickson, "Christology from Above and Christology from Below: A Study of Contrasting Methodologies," in *Perspectives on Evangelical Theology*, ed. Kenneth S. Kantzer and Stanley N. Gundry (Grand Rapids: Baker, 1979), 43–55; see also Erickson, *Christian Theology*, 661–81.

garding Christ than upon the historical Jesus. Christology from below, represented by Ernst Käsemann and more recently Wolfhart Pannenberg, stresses historical investigation as the basis for belief in the deity of Christ.

The issue, suggests Erickson, is the value of faith for grounding reason, and thus may be perceived as the problem of the relationship between reason and historical faith. Whereas Christology from above is essentially fideistic, and Christology from below is primarily Thomistic, Erickson adopts the Augustinian model: both reason and faith. Thus, "faith precedes but does not remain permanently independent of reason. Faith provides the perspective or starting point from which reason may function."[34] Faith and reason are interwoven so that faith in Christ opens the way to understanding the historical Jesus, and the historical Jesus undergirds faith in Christ. It could be argued that this method is in evidence in *Christian Theology*.

In *The Word Became Flesh*, the author's attention turns to the task of developing a statement of Christology which will do for this generation what the Chalcedonian fathers did for theirs. Gathering the pertinent biblical and philosophical data, he grapples with the inner logic of the incarnation. Certain suppositions are immediately apparent. First, Erickson rejects a purely functional Christology. The New Testament is interested in ontological concepts as well as in more functional concerns.[35] Following Reginald Fuller, Erickson notes as well that the Hebrews were not as nonmetaphysical as some have thought. Further, a function is meaningless if it is not grounded in ontology.[36] A second supposition is that, like all other doctrine, Christology is and must be

contextualized. Those who berate the Chalcedonian theologians for doing theology from the view of fifth-century Greek thought fail to recognize the contexts out of which their own theology issues.

It is vital, then, to establish a metaphysical worldview as a framework in which to formulate a biblical Christology. For Erickson, a theistic worldview that is cognizant of current philosophical schemes but grounded in biblical revelation is most adequate.[37] He focuses on several theological themes as he forges a worldview that will enable him to explore the logic of the incarnation:

1. Even as a work of art reflects the artist, so creation reflects its Creator. There is a continuity between God and nature which made creation receptive to his presence in the incarnation.

2. God is not impassive, unmoved by events in the world. God is active and dynamic, though within the context of his constant nature. Again, there is an affinity between God and creation as is evidenced even in vicarious suffering with his creatures. This harmony renders the incarnation less problematic.

3. The image of God in the human also eases the difficulties presented by the doctrine of the incarnation. The likeness is evident in several common qualities as well as in personality itself.

4. Scripture indicates that the human Jesus was sinless. This effectively answers the challenge that God could not have united with a sinful human. Unencumbered by depravity, Jesus was actually more human than anyone since Adam and Eve before the fall.

The cumulative effect of these considerations reduces the perceived distance be-

---

34. Erickson, "Christology," 54.

35. Erickson, *Christian Theology*, 703.

36. Millard J. Erickson, *The Word Became Flesh: A Contemporary Incarnational Christology* (Grand Rapids: Baker, 1991), 510–11; see also Reginald H. Fuller, *The Foundations of New Testament Christology* (New York: Scribner, 1965), 247–50.

37. Erickson, *Word Became Flesh*, 524–30.

tween humankind and God, who became incarnate.[38] Erickson still has not, however, sufficiently answered the question of how an omniscient and omnipresent God could unite with a human who was not all-knowing and who was limited in his body to one spatial location at a time. Further, unlike humans, God is sinless and cannot be tempted. This is a question of whether the inherent limitations of each nature can be compatible with the other.

To metaphysically explain the incarnation, Erickson proposes that Christ did not divest himself of certain attributes of God and certain attributes of humanity. Instead, God added to each nature the attributes of the other. Thus, the form of God was retained, but to it was added the form of a servant (Phil. 2:7). Adopting a view similar to that of Stephen Davis, Erickson distinguishes between God in abstraction and God in incarnation, and between being human in abstraction and being human in incarnation. The manifestation and function of the attributes of both deity and humanity are different when they are united. Erickson uses the admittedly imperfect analogy of the combination of sodium and chlorine atoms into common table salt: "The qualities of the compound are quite different from those of either of the elements making it up."[39] Furthermore, the presence of the image of God in humans permits us to conceive of the two natures not as different qualities, but as partial and complete versions of the same thing.

A frequent barrier to understanding the incarnation is that we begin with the traditional concepts of humanity and deity, and assume that they are incompatible. Instead, what we ought to begin with is the fact that both God and humankind are most fully known in Jesus Christ.[40] It ought also to be recognized that Christ voluntarily accepted the inherent limitations of each nature,

submitting, for the time being, to a position of dependence upon the Father.[41]

An illustration of the manner of Christ's limitations during the incarnation is that, though as deity he possessed complete knowledge, it was resident only in his unconscious. After all, he grew in knowledge as does every child. Omniscience was accessible to him only as the Father permitted it. Thus it is correct to say that Christ was omniscient, though, in submission to the Father, access was limited. Other nettlesome difficulties, including omnipresence and the temptation to sin, are dealt with in somewhat similar fashion.

Coming to terms with Christ's incarnation may be furthered by the fact that it is continuing. Erickson points to biblical statements such as 1 Timothy 2:5, which affirms that Jesus remains the only mediator between God and humans. Though Christ retains his human nature, he now possesses a perfected humanity which "imposes even less restriction upon the functioning of the divine nature."[42] There is greater compatibility between deity and glorified humanity. The context for the foregoing conclusion is Erickson's formulation of the relationship between the resurrection and ascension. Differing with some evangelicals, Erickson maintains a two-stage exaltation of Christ. Since there are significant differences between the appearances of Jesus immediately following the resurrection and the appearance, for example, to Saul, the ascension must have completed the transformation begun in resurrection. Christ's body before ascension certainly transcended many natural laws, though it maintained scars from the crucifixion, and may even have required physical food. Resurrection, however, ought not to be considered as primarily a physical phenomenon, but as a triumph over sin and death. The ascension, which completed Christ's transformation, was not essentially a transfer from

38. Ibid., 541–48.
39. Ibid., 556.
40. Erickson, *Christian Theology*, 736–37.

41. Erickson, *Word Became Flesh*, 558.
42. Ibid., 576.

one place to another, but a spiritual reinstatement to the Father's right hand.

Salvation, the Church, and Eschatology

Erickson's development of the doctrines of salvation, the church, and eschatology is rather standard evangelical fare. However, their integral position within his theology requires at least brief comment.

Erickson's view of the atonement as penal and substitutionary sets the stage for his understanding of individual salvation and its collective dimensions in the church. Christ's sacrifice can legitimately be described as propitiatory, for there is no contradiction between God's love and a wrath that must be appeased for the remission of sins. Since there is nothing that humans have done or can do to persuade God to save them, God's grace is a necessity. Consistent with his moderate Calvinism, Erickson reiterates that God's plan, and more specifically salvation, depends upon his prior decision.[43] Those who respond are not under necessity to do so, but it is certain that they will, since God makes the offer so appealing.

Erickson's temporal arrangement in *Christian Theology* of the aspects of salvation suggests a logical progression, though it may in part be pedagogic. Salvation is initiated through the subjective aspects of effectual calling, conversion, and regeneration, in that order. The objective aspects, including our union with Christ, justification, and adoption continue through sanctification, which aligns our moral condition with our legal status. Finally, since God renders things certain, there is perseverance; though believers could fall away from God, it is sure that they will not.[44] Salvation culminates in both moral and physical glorification.

The inclusive term for salvation is union with Christ. All the other constituents are really subdoctrines. Justification, for example, is judicial union with Christ. Righteousness is imputed to us as we are incorporated into Christ. When God looks upon believers, he sees them together with Christ. This union also creates a spiritual vitality in the individual believer. Experiencing the life of Christ within actually effects transformed behavior.[45]

On the collective level, Erickson's doctrine of the church is developed biblically and is clearly fashioned by someone with pastoral concerns. The basic functions of the church include evangelism, edification, worship, and social concern. Lying at the heart of all these functions is the proclamation of the gospel.[46] Erickson's views of church life are predictably in concert with his ecclesiastical heritage and identity. In church government he is congregational. Baptism he regards as a sign of and confession of our union with Christ. Though he demonstrates some latitude concerning mode, he points out that the form most expressive of the believer's experience is immersion. The Lord's Table is a commemorative symbolizing of the death of Christ as a sacrificial offering to the Father in our behalf; it further symbolizes the unity of believers in love and concern for one another.[47]

Finally, Erickson's first publication in the field of eschatology was his *Contemporary Options in Eschatology: A Study of the Millennium* (1977). It issued from a survey course taught at Bethel Seminary. Though objective and irenic in tone, Erickson does

---

43. Erickson, *Christian Theology*, 925. For a lay-level discussion of the doctrine of salvation, see Erickson, *Salvation*.

44. Erickson, *Christian Theology*, 992–97. According to Erickson, the warnings, as in Hebrews 6:4–6, that are addressed to genuinely saved people who could theoretically fall away, actually render it certain that they will not.

45. Ibid., 953. For Erickson's interaction with current issues regarding the doctrine of salvation, see Millard J. Erickson, "Is Universalist Thinking Now Appearing among Evangelicals?" *United Evangelical Action* 48.5 (Sept.–Oct. 1989): 4–6; idem, "Lordship Theology: The Current Controversy," *Southwestern Journal of Theology* 33.2 (Spring 1991): 5–15.

46. Erickson, *Christian Theology*, 1059–67.

47. Ibid., 1122–24.

espouse posttribulational premillennialism. In *Christian Theology* this view is more fully expressed.

Of interest is Erickson's notion of bodily resurrection: more than mere physical resuscitation, it involves a transformation of some kind that utilizes the old body. An analogy is the petrification of a log: "While the contour of the original object is retained, the composition is entirely different."[48] So while the resurrection will certainly be "bodily" in nature, our new bodies will be more spiritual than physical. Further, our resurrection bodies will be more like Jesus' present body than like the body he possessed between resurrection and ascension.

Resurrection is anticipated for both the righteous and unrighteous. The righteous will enjoy forever the presence of God, perfected knowledge, and the removal of sin and evil. The unrighteous will experience God's absence, perhaps physical suffering, and certainly mental distress from loneliness and the recognition that their banishment from God's presence is permanent. Though heaven and hell may be considered places, they ought even more to be considered states of existence.

Evaluation

Since much of Erickson's work is of recent vintage, an extensive analysis of his thought is yet to be undertaken. The difficulty of such a task is compounded by the comprehensive nature of many of his works, some of which were intended as textbooks. With the publication of *The Word Became Flesh*, however, he has provided an intensified view of a pivotal doctrine in his theology.

Though some reviewers have been uneasy with a few of Erickson's proposals, no significant challenge has surfaced. For some, he may be too Calvinistic; for others, too moderately so. Several have questioned portions of his Christology, for example, his

view of Jesus' resurrection.[49] Most of the response to Erickson's endeavors, however, has been quite enthusiastic.

Indeed, there is much to appreciate. His numerous writings display a scholarly awareness of pertinent issues, and a capacity to interact with a broad theological spectrum. Rather than merely embracing traditional interpretations, he has courageously explored the rational boundaries of doctrine without compromising biblical authority. Valued as well is his functional theological method, firmly rooted in biblical truth and evangelical tradition, and accessible even to those without technical expertise. His lucid and erudite style has gratified many who have been introduced to the theological venture through his textbooks and lectures.

Though known primarily as a theologian and seminary professor, Millard Erickson is at heart a pastor whose ministry focuses on equipping others to minister. Yet it is improbable that he will in that capacity gather to himself a following of disciples. More likely, his impact will be felt by a generation of pastors and scholars who will read his work, appreciate his wisdom, but follow his Lord.

Primary Sources

Erickson, Millard J. *Christian Theology*. Grand Rapids: Baker, 1986.

_____. "Christology from Above and Christology from Below: A Study of Contrasting Methodologies." In *Perspectives on Evangelical Theology*, edited by Kenneth S. Kantzer and Stanley N. Gundry, 43–55. Grand Rapids: Baker, 1979.

_____. *Contemporary Options in Eschatology: A Study of the Millennium*. Grand Rapids: Baker, 1977.

_____. "Immanence, Transcendence, and the Doctrine of Scripture." In *The Living and Active Word of God*, edited by Ronald Youngblood and Morris Inch, 193–205. Winona Lake, Ind.: Eisenbrauns, 1983.

48. Ibid., 1199.

49. Dockery, "Millard J. Erickson," 653.

_____. "Lordship Theology: The Current Controversy." *Southwestern Journal of Theology* 33.2 (Spring 1991): 5–15.

_____. *The New Evangelical Theology.* Westwood, N.J.: Revell, 1968.

_____. "Pannenberg's Use of History as a Solution to the Religious Language Problem." *Journal of the Evangelical Theological Society* 17 (1974): 99–105.

_____. "Principles, Permanence, and Future Divine Judgment: A Case Study in Theological Method." *Journal of the Evangelical Theological Society* 28 (1985): 317–25.

_____. *Relativism in Contemporary Christian Ethics.* Grand Rapids: Baker, 1974.

_____. *The Word Became Flesh: A Contemporary Incarnational Christology.* Grand Rapids: Baker, 1991.

Secondary Sources

Dockery, David S. "Millard J. Erickson." In *Baptist Theologians,* edited by Timothy George and David S. Dockery, 640–44. Nashville: Broadman, 1990.

Keylock, Leslie R. "Evangelical Leaders You Should Know: Meet Millard J. Erickson." *Moody Monthly* 87.10 (June 1987): 71–73.

Clark H. Pinnock

Robert K. Johnston

Clark Harold Pinnock was born in Toronto on February 3, 1937. Brought up in a liberal Baptist congregation, Pinnock recounts that as a child he had little interest in the church.[1] However, he did have, in his words, a "Bible-believing grandma and a like-minded Sunday School teacher" who were instrumental in his conversion in 1949.[2] They instilled in Pinnock a love for God and a confidence in the Bible which would prove ongoing.

As a conservative evangelical teenager in a liberal church setting, Pinnock early became "aware of the need to be alert to defections from the true faith and to maintain a theologically sound testimony."[3] He attended Youth for Christ meetings in Toronto and worked one summer at the Canadian Keswick Bible Conference. He recalls that a lecture on biblical criticism puzzled him as to how such theories could enhance one's confidence in the reliability and authority of Scripture. Thus, already in his early years as a Christian, themes that would remain central in Pinnock's theology were apparent—his criticism of liberalism and his recognition of Scripture's centrality.

In addition to youth organizations and Bible conferences, Pinnock was introduced in the 1950s to various ideas that helped shape North American evangelicalism. In particular, at an Inter-Varsity bookstore he bought the works of such Calvinistic writers as J. I. Packer, John Murray, Paul King Jewett, Martyn Lloyd-Jones, Carl Henry, and Cornelius Van Til. Pinnock would later come to question the Reformed perspective, but through his student days and on into his first teaching position, Pinnock continued to believe "that Calvinism was just scriptural evangelicalism in its purest expression."[4]

---

1. Clark H. Pinnock, "Baptists and Biblical Authority," *Journal of the Evangelical Theological Society* 17 (1974): 193.

2. Clark H. Pinnock, "I Was a Teenage Fundamentalist," *Wittenberg Door,* December 1982–January 1983, p. 18.

3. Pinnock, "Baptists and Biblical Authority," 193.

4. Clark H. Pinnock, "From Augustine to Arminius: A Pilgrimage in Theology," in *The Grace of God, the Will of Man: A Case for Arminianism,* ed. Clark H. Pinnock (Grand Rapids: Zondervan, 1989), 17.

In 1960 Pinnock graduated with honors from the Ancient Near Eastern Studies program at the University of Toronto and was awarded both a Woodrow Wilson Fellowship to Harvard and a British Commonwealth Scholarship to England. Choosing the latter, he studied New Testament with F. F. Bruce at Manchester University, completing his doctoral dissertation in 1963 on the Pauline concept of the Holy Spirit. During this period and his subsequent work at Manchester as an assistant lecturer in New Testament studies, Pinnock came under the influence of Francis Schaeffer, even working for a time at Schaeffer's retreat, L'Abri. Schaeffer's strong influence would be apparent in Pinnock's apologetics for some time, and the debt to Bruce is still noticeable.

His formal education complete, Pinnock went to the United States in 1965, accepting a position at New Orleans Baptist Theological Seminary, first in New Testament studies and then, after two years, in systematic theology. In New Orleans, Pinnock wrote *A Defense of Biblical Infallibility* (1967) as well as *Set Forth Your Case* (1967). The former booklet argued for the necessity of belief in the Bible's authority, inspiration, and inerrancy. The latter, with a nod to Schaeffer, defended biblical faith against the inroads of modern culture. *A New Reformation: A Challenge to Southern Baptists* followed in 1968, a strongly worded warning to Southern Baptists to maintain belief in the evangelical truths of an inerrant Bible. Pinnock's booklet *Evangelism and Truth* (1969) completed his major writing during this period; it linked apologetics and Scripture directly: "Evangelism is the declaration of a specific *message*. It is not holding meetings, or getting results. It is communication of the Good News. Therefore *evangelism and truth* are inseparable. . . . As soon as confidence is weakened in the integrity of our source material, evangelism is weakened to a corresponding degree.[5]

From the inception of his writing career, Pinnock has argued for biblical truth, recognized the importance of apologetics, and polemicized against liberals who would relativize the faith. At stake for Pinnock has been the clarity and effectiveness of gospel proclamation. These themes have remained central for Pinnock throughout his career, even if his initial militancy has softened and his viewpoint broadened.

From 1969 to 1974 Pinnock taught at Trinity Evangelical Divinity School near Chicago, and from 1974 to 1977 at Regent College in Vancouver. Robert Price has labeled this period the second phase of Pinnock's career, when he came to recognize that evangelicals not only need to defend the gospel, they need to practice it.[6] It is not that Pinnock's interest in apologetics and the biblical revelation waned. Indeed, during this period he wrote *Biblical Revelation: The Foundation of Christian Theology* (1971) and *Reason Enough: A Case for the Christian Faith* (1980; the book is based on magazine articles appearing first in 1976 and 1977). But added to these foci was a third general area of interest—renewal of vibrant and obedient Christian living within evangelicalism.

The source of Pinnock's new emphasis on life in Christ can be traced to 1967, when he and his wife Dorothy attended a home prayer meeting and, in his words, "glimpsed the dimension of the Spirit which the New Testament describes but is so often absent in churches today."[7] By the 1970s Pinnock was writing articles in support of this Neo-Pentecostalism. Pinnock's openness to the power of the Spirit would develop still further in the years beyond, particularly as he experienced healing in his one functioning eye. He comments, "I know from personal experience that one such incident can be worth a bookshelf of

5. Clark H. Pinnock, *Evangelism and Truth* (Tigerville, S.C.: Jewel, 1969), 18–19.

6. Robert M. Price, "Clark H. Pinnock: Conservative and Contemporary," *Evangelical Quarterly* 60 (1988): 164–74.

7. Clark H. Pinnock, *Three Keys to Spiritual Renewal* (Minneapolis: Bethany, 1985), 51.

academic apologetics for Christianity (including my own books)."[8]

A second change occurred in 1970 as Pinnock studied the Book of Hebrews and came to the conclusion that the deterministic logic of Calvinism is flawed. Instead, a modified Wesleyan-Arminian position is called for (*Grace Unlimited*, which he edited in 1975, argues for this position). Pinnock's neo-Arminian stance has continued to enlarge. "Driven by Scripture itself," he has reconsidered the doctrines of predestination and double predestination, election, total depravity, and Christ's atoning work. In the early 1980s his Arminian pilgrimage extended still further into the territory of Christian theism itself. Pinnock came to believe that Augustine, influenced by Greek philosophy, had distorted the biblical picture of a personal God to one who was "timeless, changeless, passionless, unmoved and unmovable."[9] Such error needed redress.

Thirdly, influenced by Jim Wallis and other students at Trinity, as well as by the writings of John Howard Yoder, Pinnock adopted in the early 1970s a more radical politics, even voting for Communist candidates in one municipal election. As a contributing editor of *Sojourners* (formerly *Post-American*), Pinnock called for the liberation of North American Christians. Such radicalism was recanted in the 1980s as Pinnock came to believe that the positive tendencies of democratic capitalism are the best hope for the poor.[10] But whereas such conservatism had taken the form of quiescence early in his career, in the last decade it has motivated Pinnock to argue for Christian involvement in government—for such causes as the right to life, the family, an adequate defense, limited government, and the needs of the

poor. In an ironic twist, as Pinnock has become increasingly Arminian in his soteriology, he has become more Calvinistic in his political theology. Christ is to be the transformer of culture.

In 1977 Pinnock was appointed associate professor of systematic theology at McMaster Divinity College in Hamilton, Ontario. He returned home, both figuratively and literally, to continue the theological battle. At McMaster, Pinnock has developed his most mature thought, extending and reworking themes and interests from earlier periods in his career. In *The Scripture Principle* (1984) Pinnock rethinks biblical authority in light of its own witness to itself, its human character, and its spiritual dynamic. This book is less rationalistic and bombastic than his earlier writing, and it moves away from a position of strict inerrancy, arguing instead for one that is more nuanced. Speaking in 1987 to the Southern Baptists at their Conference on Biblical Inerrancy, Pinnock commented, "The reason I defended the strict view of inerrancy in my earlier years was because I desperately wanted it to be true. I wanted it to be true so badly that I passed over the obvious problems."[11] In *The Scripture Principle* he attempted to address those problems. Yet though he came to some new insights ("I hope we all have and that none of us are standing still"), he also was quick to assert "in no uncertain terms that I have not changed one whit in the matter of holding to the Bible as the inspired Word of God written and as the absolutely trustworthy norm of the church, and whatever changes I may have undergone were in the way of points of clarification as to what it means to believe that."[12]

In *Three Keys to Spiritual Renewal* (1985) Pinnock seeks to encourage the revitalization of the church. How is it, he asks, that

---

8. Clark H. Pinnock, "A Revolutionary Promise," review of *Power Evangelism*, by John Wimber and Kevin Springer, *Christianity Today*, 8 August 1986, p. 19.

9. Pinnock, "From Augustine to Arminius," 23.

10. Clark H. Pinnock, "A Pilgrimage in Political Theology: A Personal Witness," in *Liberation Theology*, ed. Ronald H. Nash (Milford, Mich.: Mott Media, 1984), 103–20.

11. Clark H. Pinnock, "Parameters of Biblical Inerrancy," in *Proceedings of the Conference on Biblical Inerrancy, 1987* (Nashville: Broadman, 1987), 96.

12. Clark H. Pinnock, "What Is Biblical Inerrancy?" in *Conference on Biblical Inerrancy, 1987*, 74.

evangelicals can be so numerous and have such little effect? Renewal will come as we get "our message straight, and our religion vital, and our obedience worthy of the gospel." To do this, says Pinnock, we must wage battle for the gospel truth: "Our theology and our preaching must be biblically sound." Second, we must experience the Spirit more profoundly: "It is not enough to be biblically sound if we are not spiritually alive at the same time." And lastly, we must be more serious in practicing our discipleship: "The whole point of God giving us his Word and his Spirit is in order for us to live out the gospel in the world and carry out the mission to the nations."[13]

Tracking the Maze (1990) is Pinnock's most comprehensive attempt to date to articulate his theology systematically. But here, too, Pinnock's concerns remain largely contextual and apologetic. Seeking to move beyond both modernism and fundamentalism to what he labels at one point "postmodern orthodoxy," Pinnock tries to balance creativity and fidelity, context and text. In order to accomplish this via media, Pinnock proposes that our theological thinking must turn away from both timeless propositions and contextual relativity to viewing the Christian narrative as the story of God's intervention in history for the salvation of humankind. Abstract theology is important, but in a secondary way: "Truth and meaning for Christianity lie with the narrative before it is expressed in the doctrinal form. Theology exists to serve the story and not the other way around." When we focus upon narrative, Scripture becomes more functional: "The Bible points us to the story of salvation and facilitates it coming alive in our experience as it is mixed with faith." In other words, the message for Pinnock is bipolar, inviting us "to attend to definite content while relating it to human existence."[14]

Continuity as an Evangelical Apologist

Do Pinnock's life and work have an overarching coherence? Can one find in his first twenty-five years of scholarship (more than a dozen books, one hundred articles, and forty book reviews) a unity of thought and design? Some have looked at the theological and personal pilgrimage of Clark Pinnock and have concluded that there is an instability in his character.[15] Others have seen distinct periods in his thought.[16] Still others believe his movement to Arminianism is a paradigm shift which has slowly affected Pinnock's total theology.[17] Recognizing the validity of at least the last two of these hypotheses, I believe it is nonetheless more helpful to view Pinnock the theologian in terms of continuity, not discontinuity. He has been from his youth an evangelical apologist and remains so.

What is it that brings focus to Pinnock's work as a theologian? His overarching concern has been for the three basic commitments that mark evangelicalism: (1) a commitment to the authority of Scripture (*A Defense of Biblical Infallibility; A New Reformation; Evangelism and Truth; Biblical Revelation; The Scripture Principle*); (2) personal, vital commitment to Jesus Christ as Lord and Savior (*Truth on Fire: The Message of Galatians; Grace Unlimited; The Grace of God, the Will of Man: A Case for Arminianism*); and (3) a commitment to disseminate the Christian faith with zeal (*Set Forth Your Case; Live Now, Brother; Reason Enough*). Pinnock's agenda has always been to provide an evangelical perspective within contemporary theology (*Toward a Theology for the Future; Three Keys to Spiritual Renewal; Tracking the Maze; Theological Crossfire: An*

---

13. Pinnock, *Three Keys*, 9–11.

14. Clark H. Pinnock, *Tracking the Maze: Finding Our Way through Modern Theology from an Evangelical Perspective* (San Francisco: Harper and Row, 1990), 61, 153, 182, 172.

15. Roger R. Nicole, review of *The Scripture Principle*, by Clark H. Pinnock, *Christianity Today*, 1 February 1985, p. 71.

16. Price, "Conservative and Contemporary."

17. Ray C. W. Roennfeldt, "Clark H. Pinnock's Shift in His Doctrine of Biblical Authority and Reliability: An Analysis and Critique," Ph.D diss., Andrews University, 1990, pp. 349–72.

Evangelical-Liberal Dialogue [coauthored with Delwin Brown]).

Pinnock has himself defined what it means to "write as an evangelical theologian":

This means that my insights come from the perspective of one who stands within the stream of historic Christianity, and confesses the great truths of incarnation and atonement, of salvation by grace through faith, and of our everlasting hope only in Jesus Christ. I am committed to the infallibility of the Bible as the norm and canon for our message, and stand staunchly against the modern revolt against all these truths.

Finally I am not writing theoretically or abstractly. I feel keenly about my subject matter here. As a theologian I work where the battle for gospel truth rages fiercely. As a church member and deacon, I long for the church to come alive unto God. And as a Canadian citizen I grieve over the decline of North America into the secular abyss and thirst for its Christian reconstruction.[18]

Here is Pinnock's career goal—to help the church to worship God "with freedom, to experience the truth of the Bible in fresh ways, and to be able to share the Gospel in a more effective and natural manner."[19]

Pinnock writes self-consciously to define and clarify North American evangelicalism. As he does so, he always employs an apologetic style. Context and audience set the boundaries and dictate the tone of his writing. In a brief written response to Rex Koivisto, who had detected what he thought was a shift in Pinnock's understanding of biblical inerrancy, he observed:

Context has a great effect on me, as I suppose it does on others too. When I find myself confronted by unbelief as respects the truths of the Bible, my reaction is always to oppose it most vigorously. This is just as true in 1981 as it was in 1967. But when I

find myself confronted by internecine rivalry in which it appears to me that evangelicals are cutting each other up over code words that they never really define, then my reaction is to oppose that. I do not find this behavior at all inconsistent.

Pinnock admits that in response to new situations and perspectives, his thinking has evolved. In fact, he is pleased that there has been growth. But he is convinced that he has not reversed himself. His concluding remarks to Koivisto are cogent: "I have had to introduce course corrections into my work. I have had to listen more carefully to what the Scriptures actually say and teach. I have had to reduce certain emphases and experiment with others. . . . [But] I am not aware of having changed . . . in any vital respect."[20]

Although the trajectory of Pinnock's thought has remained steadfastly evangelical, the tone of his apologetic has changed markedly, particularly in response to different contexts. Perhaps William Hull has captured best Pinnock's movement from a combative to an irenic theologian. At the 1987 Southern Baptist Conference on Biblical Inerrancy, Pinnock argued that inerrancy should be redefined as an irenic rather than a destructive force in Baptist life. In responding to that argument, Hull recalled his introduction to Pinnock at the Louisiana Baptist Convention some twenty years earlier. There Pinnock had unleashed "a withering attack on [his] most cherished friends in Southern Baptist theological education." Now, Hull said somewhat incredulously, "that same speaker has just delivered an equally impassioned speech on the same subject, but this time his presentation is marked by prudence, charity, and forbearance."[21] What is to explain the old and

18. Pinnock, *Three Keys*, 11.
19. Ibid., 55.

20. Clark H. Pinnock, "A Response to Rex A. Koivisto," *Journal of the Evangelical Theological Society* 24 (1981): 153–54.
21. William E. Hull, "Response" (to Pinnock, "What Is Biblical Inerrancy?"), in *Conference on Biblical Inerrancy, 1987*, 84.

new Pinnock? Pinnock again provides his own colorful key:

> The Preacher tells us, "There is a time for peace and a time for war" (Eccles. 3:8). In the 60's I believed it was time to say that the SBC was threatened by religious liberalism. It was and it is to a great extent. But in the 80's I believe I must say the threat has been turned back and the new danger is one of going too far in mopping up. It is not necessary to injure and maim godly evangelical pastors, professors and church workers just because we have the political power to do so.[22]

Pinnock's change from combative to irenic apologetics is apparent in the titles of two of his major apologetic works, *Set Forth Your Case* (1967) and *Reason Enough* (1980). The moderation in tone is also evident in *Theological Crossfire: An Evangelical-Liberal Dialogue* (1990), where co-authors Pinnock and Delwin Brown engage in constructive conversation in the hope that liberals and evangelicals alike can learn from their model. The vitality of the church, Pinnock believes, is tied to our ability to listen, learn, and change. He does not want so much to win the argument with Brown as to advance the search for understanding and truth.

But Pinnock is still capable of combat. He remains straightforwardly opinionated. It would be wrong to think that all the fire has gone out of his challenge to religious liberalism or that his critique of contemporary theology has lessened. For example, it is Pinnock's judgment that "the current tendency to relate theology to struggles of the present day, while commendable if it were to represent a desire to apply the Scriptures, [is actually] a recipe for Scripture-twisting on a grand scale."[23] And he con-

cludes in *Tracking the Maze* that "religious liberalism is in a rather weak condition and not very appealing to new converts." Accordingly, he believes that it is a "sell-out" to side "with the very forces of unbelief that threaten to destroy Christianity and western culture."[24] Such criticism might seem to evangelicals and moderates to be matter-of-fact and perhaps deserved. But James Barr hears Pinnock with another ear: "The amicable-seeming quotations appear in the end to be window-dressing. For whenever Pinnock gets the idea that someone is an actual liberal he loses control of himself . . . there seems to be no logic or reason in the shifts between Dr. Jekyll Pinnock and Mr. Hyde Pinnock."[25] Barr, a theological liberal who has felt the bite of Pinnock's continuing apologetic tone, thus responds in kind.

Clearly, Pinnock believes that what he calls "The Great Defection" must continue to be challenged. Commenting on his liberal church upbringing, he wrote in 1985:

> I remember feeling appalled at the omission of the central gospel themes both in my church and in other churches like it. . . . It has been about thirty years since I was saved, and I have never been able to shake off the feeling of outrage at the arrogance of the liberal decision to revise the New Testament message to make it acceptable to modern men. I suppose that my deepest concern as a theologian today is to expose and refute this deadly error.[26]

There is no doubt, then, that Pinnock remains today the evangelical apologist he was twenty-five years ago.

Theological Emphases

Biblical Authority

Throughout his career as an evangelical theologian Pinnock has insisted that the Bi-

22. Pinnock, "Parameters of Biblical Inerrancy," 101.
23. Clark H. Pinnock, "How I Use the Bible in Doing Theology," in *The Use of the Bible in Theology: Evangelical Options*, ed. Robert K. Johnston (Atlanta: John Knox, 1985), 29.

24. Pinnock, *Tracking the Maze*, 125, 140.
25. James Barr, review of *The Scripture Principle*, by Clark H. Pinnock, *Virginia Seminary Journal*, July 1986, p. 37.
26. Pinnock, *Three Keys*, 18.

ble has binding authority. Thus he asserts in *The Scripture Principle* that "the Bible, not modernity, is normative, and our thoughts are to be shaped by its teaching, not the reverse. Only by acknowledging this can we prevent revelation from being buried under the debris of human culture and opinion and from disappearing as a liberating Word from outside the human situation. A stance of determined faithfulness to Scripture is what our day calls for."[27] Lacking such commitment, the church will lose both its direction and its sense of mission.

Initially, Pinnock linked his understanding of biblical authority to the doctrines of divine inspiration and consequent inerrancy. To counter the noncognitive, subjectivist ideas of revelation that were current in liberal Christianity, Pinnock argued that the Bible's "divine inspiration has rendered the book 'infallible' (incapable of teaching deception) and 'inerrant' (not liable to prove false or mistaken)."[28] In his monograph entitled *A Defense of Biblical Infallibility* (1967) as well as in his book *Biblical Revelation* (1971), he defended the authority and reliability of Scripture. At once polemical and didactic, Pinnock's writings sought both to expound and to vindicate his position.

Three of Pinnock's arguments warrant mentioning. First, the Bible teaches that it is both inspired and inerrant (Matt. 5:17–18; John 10:35; 2 Tim. 3:16; 2 Pet. 1:20–21). Second, Christ viewed the Old Testament as authoritative and authenticated the New. Finally, Pinnock argued that plenary, verbal inspiration was the historic doctrine of the church until the modern defection resulting from the hubris of the Enlightenment. In general, Pinnock followed B. B. Warfield's deductive approach. Faithful to Christ, we should adopt his view of the Bible as inerrant and treat the particulars of

the text in that light.[29] Trusting the Bible as God's inspired Word, we should accept its claims to truthfulness and inerrancy. Pinnock stressed that the "inductive difficulties encountered in the text cannot change the fact that the Bible claims not to err."[30]

Even in his earliest work, however, Pinnock recognized that the definition of inerrancy must be based in an adequate hermeneutic. It needs to be nuanced according to the phenomena of the text itself. And so, to his deductions concerning biblical inspiration, Pinnock added from the beginning several important inductive qualifications. He recognized that modern historiography was unknown in biblical times. The writers often used the language of simple observation; thus they spoke, for example, of the sunrise. In addition, figurative and mythological language are at times evident in Scripture (Job 9:13; Isa. 27:1). Old Testament citations are often loosely rendered in the New Testament. And so on. Pinnock concluded that infallibility is "restricted to the intended assertions of Scripture."[31] Recognition of this restriction dissolves many of the purported errors in the Bible.

Pinnock's acknowledgment of difficulties in the biblical text was circumscribed at first. He rejected the notion that apparent inconsistencies in the sources quoted by biblical writers suggest error. He also dismissed the allegations that the Bible contains historical blunders, accommodations to the moral standards prevailing in biblical times, scientific inaccuracies, and pseudonymous writing intended to deceive the reader. Although such theories had been proposed, these "assured results" of scholarship were for Pinnock "little more than the current popular hypotheses grounded upon the dubious assumption that Scripture may contain errors."[32] Posit instead the Bible's own

27. Clark H. Pinnock, *The Scripture Principle* (San Francisco: Harper and Row, 1984), 213.

28. Clark H. Pinnock, *A Defense of Biblical Infallibility* (Philadelphia: Presbyterian and Reformed, 1967), 1.

29. Clark H. Pinnock, *Biblical Revelation: The Foundation of Christian Theology* (Chicago: Moody, 1971), 178–79.

30. Pinnock, *Defense of Biblical Infallibility*, 18.

31. Ibid., 13; see also Pinnock, *Biblical Revelation*, 71.

32. Pinnock, *Defense of Biblical Infallibility*, 30.

teaching concerning its infallibility, declared Pinnock, and even the more difficult problems lose much of their edge.

During Pinnock's first decade of scholarship, the modernist threat shaped much of the argument regarding biblical authority, encouraging him to concentrate on the Bible's ground of authority, divine inspiration. But in the mid-1970s the growing spirit of suspicion and hostility present in intraevangelical discussions about inspiration caused him to refocus his attention on matters of interpretation. Rather than let the escalating argument between conservative and progressive evangelicals divide the church and undercut its mission, the two groups, argued Pinnock, needed to recognize their basic commonality. Dissension could only prove debilitating and disgusting.

As the evangelical argument over Scripture turned sour, Pinnock began to reexamine his strict view of inerrancy. In a series of articles written in the second half of the 1970s, he recast his arguments for biblical authority, while committing himself to a broader use of the term *inerrancy*.[33] Strict

inerrantists, Pinnock came to believe, wrongly based their assumptions regarding Scripture on the model of prophetic inspiration ("Thus saith the Lord"). Such an understanding concerning the creation of many of the biblical books, for example, the Wisdom writings, was simply untrue. Pinnock concluded that though Jesus and the apostles held to a high view of biblical inspiration and authority, their approach to the use of the text was far more flexible and practical than inerrantists typically have allowed. Should we not permit the same latitude? Indeed, is not the detailed view of inerrancy more a false deductive argument from the nature of God than something inductively garnered from a study of the Bible itself?

As Pinnock argued for a broader, more functional understanding of biblical truth, he also began to be more candid about difficulties found in the biblical text. Scripture is totally reliable, even inerrant, in all that it teaches and affirms. But, wishing to respect the text exactly as it presented itself, Pinnock was now prepared, if the text presented a difficult feature, "to admit that it does and not try to resist it."[34] Viewed correctly, this inductive approach avoided the strained exegesis which prevailed too often within evangelicalism. Viewed constructively, it facilitated approaching the text with simplicity and trust by directing attention away from the small difficulties and focusing the reader instead on Scripture's intended proclamation. The perfect errorlessness of nonextant autographs was an abstraction that, for Pinnock, died the death of a thousand qualifications. More importantly, it failed to prove the dynamic authority of the present text.

Pinnock allowed observations concerning the conflation of Old Testament historical accounts and the New Testament's freedom in citing the ipsissima verba of Jesus as well as Old Testament quotations to nuance his definition of biblical inerrancy even further. That is, he now viewed in-

33. Clark H. Pinnock, "The Inerrancy Debate among the Evangelicals," *Theology, News and Notes*, special issue (1976): 11–13; idem, "Inspiration and Authority: A Truce Proposal," *The Other Side*, May 1976, pp. 61–65; idem, Foreword in *The Debate about the Bible: Inerrancy versus Infallibility*, ed. Stephen T. Davis (Philadelphia: Westminster, 1977), 11–13; idem, "Fruits Worthy of Repentance: The True Weight of Biblical Authority," *Sojourners*, December 1977, p. 29; idem, "Three Views of the Bible in Contemporary Theology," in *Biblical Authority*, ed. Jack B. Rogers (Waco: Word, 1977), 47–73; idem, "Evangelicals and Inerrancy: The Current Debate," *Theology Today* 35 (1978): 65–69; idem, "Biblical Authority, Past and Present, in the Believers' Church Tradition," in *The Believers' Church in Canada: Addresses and Papers from the Study Conference in Winnipeg, May 15–18, 1978*, ed. Jarold K. Zeman and Walter Klaassen (Waterloo, Ont.: Baptist Federation of Canada and Mennonite Central Committee [Canada], 1979), 75–86; idem, "The Ongoing Struggle over Biblical Inerrancy," *Journal of the American Scientific Affiliation* 31.2 (June 1979): 69–74; idem, "The Inspiration and Interpretation of the Bible," *TSF Bulletin* 4 (Oct. 1980): 4–6; and idem, "'. . . This Treasure in Earthen Vessels': The Inspiration and Interpretation of the Bible," *Sojourners*, October 1980, pp. 16–19.

34. Pinnock, "Response to Rex A. Koivisto," 154.

errancy "in a *qualified* sense, relative to the intended assertions of the text."[35] This need to nuance the definition of inerrancy had long been recognized by Pinnock (any student of F. F. Bruce could hardly have thought otherwise). But throughout the seventies and eighties Pinnock spent considerable energy at the task of qualifying inerrancy in the light of the scope, purpose, and genre of the biblical passage under consideration. Recognizing that a text should be judged according to its specific intention, Pinnock now maintained that "the Bible *contains* errors but *teaches* none."[36]

When understood inductively in this nuanced way, inerrancy is "a good deal more flexible than is supposed," according to Pinnock; "it does not suspend the truth of the Gospel upon a single detail as is so often charged."[37] Pinnock's qualifications concerning Scripture's inerrancy were internally derived and textually oriented. He continued to reject externally formulated theological categories (e.g., the faith and practice of the church) as means by which to judge the intention of a specific text; so too, the "good reasons" of the interpreter were given no authoritative status. Instead, Pinnock sought to let the genre and historical context of each passage serve as the chief indicators of its scope and purpose.

In *The Scripture Principle* (1984) and again in *Tracking the Maze* (1990) readers can see the expanded results of Pinnock's commitment to accepting biblical texts as what they appear to be. He comments, "I felt I ought to be more willing to respect the Bible's right to teach me in ways which it determines rather than in ways I impose."[38] Pinnock's conclusions are at times at variance with traditional evangelical opinion. It is apparent why the conservative wing of

evangelicalism is uncomfortable. For example, Pinnock is now open to understanding the opening chapters of Genesis as saga and certain other texts as legend (Elisha's axhead and the fate of Lot's wife), to viewing Jonah as didactic fiction, to dating Daniel's final form to the Maccabean period, to seeing some of the numbers in the Bible as inflated, to regarding certain elements in Matthew as Midrashic embellishment, and to treating Paul's personal advice (e.g., 1 Cor. 7:25–26, 39–40) as just that, nonbinding opinion. Pinnock is not dogmatic about any of these possibilities, often mentioning them simply as questions arising from the text. But it is clear that he has opened himself to modern biblical scholarship in ways he had previously rejected.

Pinnock realizes that some will question how such interpretations of the biblical text fit with any typical notion of inerrancy. But his desire to maintain a strong commitment to Scripture's authority and reliability has not lessened. Scripture remains for Pinnock inerrant in all that it affirms. It is only his understanding of what exactly is affirmed that has changed.

The real problem in the inerrancy debate, suspects Pinnock, is that many conservatives are not using inerrancy simply to signify the truth of God's Word, but also to encourage conformity to a certain set of theological beliefs: "beliefs about women in ministry, the charismatic renewal, creationism, theories of eschatology and atonement."[39] Such positions ought to be discussed, argues Pinnock, on the basis of the interpretation of relevant biblical texts rather than being imposed under the banner of inerrancy. That is to say, inerrancy must be disentangled from hermeneutics.

Believing the Bible to be the indispensable source of God's truth, Pinnock has spent much of his academic career seeking to clarify its nature and authority. He has done this against a backdrop of serious polarization between liberal and conservative

35. Pinnock, "Inerrancy Debate among the Evangelicals," 12.
36. Ibid.
37. Ibid.
38. Clark H. Pinnock, "Response to Delwin Brown," *Christian Scholar's Review* 19.1 (1989): 75.
39. Pinnock, "Parameters of Biblical Inerrancy," 100.

forces. As Pinnock has reworked his understanding of inerrancy, he has recognized among liberals a tendency to ignore the Bible's truth claims. But among evangelicals there are problems as well. There are a propensity to overvalue Scripture's self-claims and a concomitant tendency to undervalue its humanity. Taking care to emphasize both the truth claims and the humanity of Scripture, Pinnock adds a third element to his understanding of biblical authority: the role of the Holy Spirit. Pinnock hopes that this third prong of his theology of Scripture will prove comprehensive and satisfying to liberals and conservatives alike.[40]

In *Biblical Revelation* (1971) Pinnock had argued that the Holy Spirit is Scripture's best interpreter, for he is its author. The Spirit does not obviate the need for sound exegesis; rather, he creates that inner receptivity which allows God's Word to be understood and believed. It was Pinnock's conviction that without the Spirit's witness the biblical text would remain confusing. The Word and the Spirit must work in tandem. Any "appeal to the Spirit apart from Scripture is sub-Christian fanaticism," reasoned Pinnock. But "to appeal to Scripture apart from a humble dependence on the Spirit is presumption."[41] Pinnock thus conjoined Word and Spirit in a typically Reformed manner. But it must also be noted that Pinnock, like most American evangelicals, did not initially emphasize the Spirit's role nor give the Spirit much operational room. It was almost as if, having tipped his cap to the Spirit, Pinnock felt free to return to a proper rational explication of the Word.

In *The Scripture Principle* (1984), while he continues not to affirm an authority for the Spirit which is somehow separate from the Word, Pinnock is concerned to help evangelicals develop a fuller appreciation of the work of the Spirit in regard to the Word. In contrast to his earlier writings, Pinnock now argues that the Spirit has a role in providing assurance that revelation is authentic and true, and that Scripture is trustworthy and authoritative. Reason and historical investigation alone are not capable of fully testing the truth of Scripture. While there is evidence for the credibility of Scripture, the ultimate confirmation of the Bible's authority comes from the Spirit's testimony.

According to Pinnock, evangelicals need also to recover an appreciation of the role of the Spirit in relation to both the interpretation and the application of Scripture. The evangelical penchant to defend the objective truth of Scripture has led all too often to inerrantists' downplaying the significance of the Spirit. Not wishing "to sound like Barth," they avoid "sounding like Paul," too. "Whatever the reason," writes Pinnock, "stress on the Spirit is noticeably lacking in the literature of inerrancy."[42]

With regard to interpretation, the historical meaning of a text should be ascertainable by all, but it is the Spirit who causes the reader to be receptive to the text's "surplus of meaning." The plain meaning of a text does not help us understand the rich figurative language in Scripture, which cannot be adequately paraphrased, nor the place of the text within the "messianically structured canon." It would be wrong, then, to think that the Bible takes the form of a systematic theology. Rather, it is a narrative, the story of the grace of God in action. As a result, "the truth it yields is not cut-and-dried," but "balanced and nuanced."[43] The Spirit provides the wisdom to understand.

40. Pinnock, "Treasure in Earthen Vessels," 16–17: "I believe that the doctrinal model or key which could enable us to heal the rift contains the three elements found in a significant statement of Paul's: 'We have this *treasure* in *earthen* vessels to show that the transcendent *power* belongs to God and not to us' (2 Corinthians 4:7).

"The Bible is a rich treasure, the Word of God, mediated to us in a human vehicle and capable of being, in the power of the Spirit, the place where we can hear God speak to us today."

41. Pinnock, *Biblical Revelation*, 216.

42. Pinnock, *Scripture Principle*, 154.

43. Ibid., 169–70, 175–76.

Pinnock also sees the Spirit as fundamental to appropriate biblical application. Although we may be able to comprehend a biblical text at one level, "there is also a large role for the Spirit here, in that we need God's guidance in knowing how to put the Scriptures into effect in our situation today." Beyond understanding what a given text says, Christians need "the direction and discernment that the Spirit gives" as to which of the possible applications is to be made in the present situation.[44]

A balanced view of the Spirit's role has helpful implications for all three aspects of Pinnock's understanding of Scripture: (1) because the Spirit authenticates Scripture, it is not necessary to inflate the claims of inspiration; (2) given the Spirit's role, the humanity of the text is easier to accept, for our trust in it does not depend on our ability to explain all of its difficult features; (3) recognition of the Spirit's empowering presence in the text helps readers avoid inappropriate legalistic interpretations and applications of the Bible.[45] Pinnock summarizes the Spirit's effect: "The Bible can be little more than a museum of old antiques, but when the Spirit gets hold of it, the inspired information deposited in the Text becomes activated in our experience. The Bible in the power of the Spirit is a means of grace whereby the liberating force of Jesus' message can become real in human life today."[46]

Personal Salvation

Pinnock is best known for his discussion of Scripture. But equally if not more important to evangelical theology has been his strong call to understand soteriology in more Arminian terms. In two collections which he edited—*Grace Unlimited* (1975) and *The Grace of God, the Will of Man: A Case for Arminianism* (1989)—as well as in *Tracking the Maze* (1990), Pinnock has developed

this line of thought. While remaining staunchly evangelical, he has been willing to reconsider the traditional Reformed categories and to pose non-Augustinian alternatives. Here again we observe Pinnock's penchant to stand apologetically over against his context. He has been a leader in what Robert Brow has labeled the "Evangelical Megashift."[47] But evangelical thinking in this vein, writes Pinnock in his response to Brow, is not really new at all: "What is new is that the dominance of Calvinist thinking in evangelical theology is being challenged by a wave of Arminian thinking breaking on its shores. So the real issue is one of control: Will the Augustinian old guard that dominates the structure of official evangelicalism gracefully surrender some of its power to a resurgent wave of Arminian thinking? Or will it fight to retain control?"[48]

Central to Pinnock's understanding of soteriology are two foundational truths: (1) God's genuine desire to save all humanity; and (2) humankind's freedom to accept or reject God's offer of salvation. The essence of the Christian message, the gospel of Jesus Christ, is God's intervention in history for the salvation of humankind. For Pinnock, "this message is naturally bi-polar because it invites us to attend to definite content while relating it to human existence."[49] Not only has God acted in grace, but we must respond in faith.

The content to which we must attend and respond is God's gracious, all-embracing historical plan—the Good News that God is reconciling humankind and restoring his creation and all humanity to what they were originally intended to be. "It is a newscast," writes Pinnock, "the best news the world has ever heard, the epic comedy with the happy ending. This story holds together the Bible in all its diversity."[50] Be-

44. Ibid., 170–71; see also p. 197.
45. Clark H. Pinnock, "Reflections on *The Scripture Principle*," *TSF Bulletin* 9 (March–April 1986): 10.
46. Pinnock, "Treasure in Earthen Vessels," 19.
47. Robert Brow, "Evangelical Megashift," *Christianity Today,* 19 February 1990, pp. 12–14.
48. Clark H. Pinnock, "The Arminian Option," *Christianity Today,* 19 February 1990, p. 15.
49. Pinnock, *Tracking the Maze,* 153.
50. Ibid., 155.

ginning with God's decision to bless Abraham and through him all the peoples of the earth (Gen. 12:3), the narrative culminates in Jesus Christ, the Savior of the whole world (1 Tim. 2:4; Titus 2:11).

In Jesus we discover God's unlimited grace. God does not desire to save only some (2 Pet. 3:9), nor does he delight in the death of the wicked (Ezek. 18:32). "The world needs to hear the unconditional good news of Jesus Christ," writes Pinnock, "which is the proclamation of God's desire to save and transform the world."[51] "In Jesus Christ God has declared himself for the salvation of all sinners, and there is no 'secret will' of his that has decided otherwise. Jesus Christ is the revelation of God's 'secret plans,' and it was for the whole world that he was delivered up."[52] Any "pseudo-gospel which leaves out most of the human race" has no appeal for Pinnock, for he believes it will have little apologetic force in contemporary society.[53]

God's plan of salvation is being enacted in history, but that history is not, in Pinnock's view, "just a play in which God puts himself on the stage and creatures are merely what is performed."[54] No, there is a divinely intended reciprocity between God and humankind. There is a real dialogue, a two-sidedness in the drama of redemption. Such mutuality cannot be programed or fully controlled. God refuses to mechanize his creatures, allowing them, instead, to remain independent and free—even "free to create new situations which God himself has not willed."[55] Human freedom is one of the deepest of all intuitions and perceptions, and its reality finds confirmation in the Bible. God puts life and death before us, but we must choose (Deut. 30:19). For Pinnock, what is notable about Abraham was his response to God's call (Gen. 15:6; Heb. 11:8). "Salvation in the Bible is by the grace of God and is *conditioned* on an obedient response, apart from which it is not actualized."[56]

In such ways Pinnock argues for understanding the Christian story as a genuine life together between God and humankind, a life which rises for both God and humankind "only out of a love born in freedom."[57] Challenges to such an understanding, thinks Pinnock, come mainly from the traditionalist side. Since the early centuries, classical theism has pictured God as impassible (incapable of being affected by anything outside himself), immutable (incapable of change in any respect), timeless (outside of time and history), and omniscient (having an exhaustive foreknowledge of everything that will ever happen). But Pinnock believes that in classical theism human freedom, though not usually denied in a formal sense, is "nullified by an overpowering model of deity that ruins the flow of the Christian story. What we need is 'free-will theism' to preserve the dynamism of God and the liberty of human beings."[58]

Pinnock maintains that misunderstanding the nature of God has become the greatest contemporary hindrance to belief in the Christian story. (Again Pinnock's strong apologetic stance is noteworthy.) "Why should [people] believe in a God they see to be remote, arbitrary, unemotional, strict, sexist and so forth?" he asks.[59] We need, instead, to turn to a scriptural, neoclassical theism. The "form of theism received from great theologians like Augustine and Anselm . . . does not stand beyond criticism

51. Clark H. Pinnock, "A Comment on 'Is There Anything Which God Does Not Do?' by George Mavrodes," *Christian Scholar's Review* 16.4 (1987): 393.

52. Clark H. Pinnock, "Responsible Freedom and the Flow of Biblical History," in *Grace Unlimited*, ed. Clark H. Pinnock (Minneapolis: Bethany, 1975), 105–6.

53. Pinnock, *Three Keys*, 26.

54. Pinnock, "Responsible Freedom," 107.

55. Ibid., 108.

56. Ibid., 106.

57. Gabriel Fackre, quoted in Pinnock, *Tracking the Maze*, 194.

58. Pinnock, *Tracking the Maze*, 194.

59. Clark H. Pinnock, *Reason Enough: A Case for the Christian Faith* (Downers Grove, Ill.: Inter-Varsity, 1980), 118.

for a biblically-oriented evangelical."[60] Just as Augustine read the Bible in the cultural context of his day, we need to be "reading the Bible afresh but in the twentieth-century context. . . . Influenced by modern culture, we [need to be] experiencing reality as something dynamic and historical and . . . consequently see . . . things in the Bible we never saw before."[61]

The way forward, Pinnock believes, is to speak of specific ways in which the God of the Bible is "unchangeable" and "also of ways in which God is able to change, as in his personal relationships with us and with the creation. . . . Immutable in his self-existence, the God of the Bible is relational and changeable in his interaction with his creatures."[62] God experiences real sorrow, sadness, and joy. We must also affirm with the Bible that God operates within time and history. Time is no threat to the divine, for God is everlasting; but he also looks back, relates to the present, and projects the future. Finally, Pinnock believes that God is omniscient in the sense that he "knows everything that can be known, but that free choices [cannot] be known even by God because they are not yet settled in reality. Decisions not yet made do not exist anywhere to be known even by God."[63] His exhaustive knowledge of past and present does give predictive prophecy a relative validity, but the outcomes remain genuinely open.[64]

Such a reformulation of Christian theism has some connections with process thought. But Pinnock clearly rejects process theology. While learning from its critique of traditional theism, he rejects process theology's overreaction to monarchical models of God. One cannot be ambiguous about God as Creator, nor should one see God as in an eternal struggle against the evil power of this world. Such "thin soup" does not adequately portray the God of the Bible. Perhaps it is best to view Pinnock as "Between Classical and Process Theism," as the title of his article in a volume on process theology suggests.[65]

To describe Christian salvation in a way that is both scripturally faithful and contextually compelling, Pinnock has been forced to reformulate classical theism. He has increasingly struggled with the subject of religious pluralism as well, and is presently working on a book addressing the issue. How are we to understand the Christian story amid a world of religions? The world has become a global village which forces this question upon us with real urgency. In "The Finality of Jesus Christ in a World of Religions" (1988), Pinnock seeks in a preliminary, nondogmatic way to correlate the demands that come from his Christian tradition with his experience of modern life. He describes this process as "passionate and stressful."[66]

Pinnock makes a threefold proposal. He notes first that "when Luke quotes Peter's statement 'Jesus Christ is Lord of all!' (Acts 10:36) he is enunciating basic Christian grammar. . . . Although it undoubtedly creates a problem for us in the area of religious pluralism, this conviction about Jesus' Lordship is nonnegotiable for Christians." But Pinnock notes as well that in confessing the finality of Christ as Peter did, we also confess Jesus as the *Universal Savior*. Christ died for all; Jesus is the means of God's saving love. Thus, "this particularism carries with it universal implications."[67]

60. Clark H. Pinnock, "The Need for a Scriptural, and Therefore a Neo-Classical Theism," in *Perspectives on Evangelical Theology*, ed. Kenneth S. Kantzer and Stanley N. Gundry (Grand Rapids: Baker, 1979), 37.
61. Pinnock, "From Augustine to Arminius," 27.
62. Ibid., 24.
63. Ibid., 25; see also Clark H. Pinnock, "God Limits His Knowledge," in *Predestination and Free Will*, ed. David Basinger and Randall Basinger (Downers Grove, Ill.: Inter-Varsity, 1986), 141–62.
64. Pinnock, "God Limits His Knowledge," 157.
65. Clark H. Pinnock, "Between Classical and Process Theism," in *Process Theology*, ed. Ronald H. Nash (Grand Rapids: Baker, 1987), 309–27.
66. Clark H. Pinnock, "The Finality of Jesus Christ in a World of Religions," in *Christian Faith and Practice in the Modern World*, ed. Mark A. Noll and David F. Wells (Grand Rapids: Eerdmans, 1988), 153.
67. Ibid., 154–55, 157.

Although this grand vision, the greatest story ever told, is nonnegotiable for Pinnock, it entails certain difficulties. In Pinnock's colorful words, "If the Lord is not content to sup with only 10 percent of the fallen race because 90 percent of them historically speaking have never heard the gospel, what are the arrangements for the seating of the guests? What about the other religions, and what about the fate of the very numerous heathen?"[68] Here the second part of Pinnock's proposal for understanding our pluralistic world comes into play. We must recognize the role of God's universal or general revelation; "the supreme revelation in Christ is not the sole revelation of God." Pinnock labels general revelation "the Melchizedek factor." When Abraham, God's representative, met Melchizedek, he recognized that here was a man who really knew God through alternate means (Gen. 14:18–20). Just as with this king of Salem, so God visits all humankind with general revelation and common grace in order that they will seek and find him. Thus the world of religions can be preparatory to the gospel.[69]

But what of the majority of the human race who have lived only under the influence of God's general revelation? What of people who are spiritually "Before Christ" even if they are chronologically "Anno Domini"? Is salvation possible only where the gospel is preached and accepted? The answer for Pinnock is both yes and no. The third part of his proposal is that God takes account of faith in him even when it occurs in the context of general revelation. Moreover, those who have responded to the light they have been given will be afforded the opportunity to encounter Jesus Christ. Texts like 1 Peter 3:18–20 and 4:6 provide hope for the unevangelized even after death. God will give an opportunity to those who sought him but never came into contact with the gospel. "All that I feel justified in concluding," says Pinnock tentatively, "is

that everyone will have an opportunity to be saved so that the possibility of salvation is universally accessible."[70] Anything less would be inconsistent with God's unlimited grace.

Apologetics

Pinnock urges us "to be sound in biblical doctrine, alive in our relationship with God, and serious in carrying out the mission God has given us."[71] We have considered Pinnock's agenda with regard to the first two of these commitments. It remains to consider Pinnock as Christian apologist, doing battle for gospel truth. We have seen that his arguments concerning Scripture and salvation are addressed primarily to the Christian community, where liberals and fundamentalists alike have, in his opinion, skewed the Christian message. An evangelical theology, if it is to be truly valid, must run the risk of displeasing both the conservatives, who are content to rehearse thoughtlessly the slogans of the past, and the radicals, who seek liberation from biblical norms in order to shape a system to suit their own taste.[72] But Pinnock as an apologist addresses those outside the church, giving reason for what he believes.

Pinnock defines an apologist as "one who is prepared to defend the message against criticism and distortion, and to give evidences of its credibility."[73] The apologist attempts to show that the gospel message is true in what it affirms. In *Set Forth Your Case* (1967), *Live Now, Brother* (1972), and *Reason Enough: A Case for the Christian Faith* (1980), as well as in a half dozen articles over the same period, Pinnock did just that.

68. Ibid., 157.
69. Ibid., 159, 162, 164.
70. Ibid., 162, 167.
71. Pinnock, *Three Keys*, 11.
72. Clark H. Pinnock, "Prospects for Systematic Theology," in *Toward a Theology for the Future*, ed. David F. Wells and Clark H. Pinnock (Carol Stream, Ill.: Creation House, 1971), 93.
73. Clark H. Pinnock, "Apologetics," in *New Dictionary of Theology*, ed. Sinclair B. Ferguson, David F. Wright, and J. I. Packer (Downers Grove, Ill.: InterVarsity, 1988), 36.

Indebted initially to Francis Schaeffer, Pinnock worked in the genre of cultural apologetics. Beginning with the "existential dilemma of unbelieving man," particularly as expressed in contemporary literature and the arts, he attempted "to establish connection links between questions raised in literature and the answers contained in the Bible." He sought, if not wholly successfully, "to get inside the perspective of the writer and not impose a set of categories extrinsic to the literature in question." By taking this approach, Pinnock thought that he and other apologists might be able to explain the gospel to the modern individual in ways that were relevant. As he argued, "The price of Christian cultural isolation is irrelevance; the reward for cultural awareness is the gaining of a hearing."[74]

The early Pinnock viewed contemporary culture as most typically positing the death or absence of God. The result for Jean-Paul Sartre, Franz Kafka, and Samuel Beckett was a crisis in values: "Man committed to nothing is a frightening phenomenon. As Beckett put it, 'Two times anything equals zero.' Or as Schaeffer sums it up, 'Matter plus time plus chance equals nothing.'"[75] There had taken place a death of hope, and with it, a loss of the human. The answer, argued Pinnock, was to be found in the truth of the gospel as spelled out in the Scriptures.

Pinnock did not build his apologetics solely on Schaeffer's model, however. Even in *Set Forth Your Case* (1967) Pinnock saw the need to combine cultural with evidentialist apologetics. Pinnock's early mentor in this regard was John Warwick Montgomery. In a 1986 article, Pinnock criticized Schaeffer for building his whole apologetic on a "biblical presuppositionalism" which would have one accept the Bible "as inerrantly true because it would be pragmatically wise to do so and because it would

give us a rational system of truth to depend on."[76] A theology built in this fashion was for Pinnock "a mere castle floating in mid-air" and ultimately no different from the modern "upper-story" theologies Schaeffer himself attacked.[77] There needed, instead, to be a sound rational and historical basis for one's faith.

Pinnock realized that in seeking "objective evidence of the truthfulness of the Christian message," he was challenging contemporary opinion.[78] As he said in the appendix to the 1971 edition of *Set Forth Your Case*, the "bane of modern theology has been the insistence that the acts of God are visible only to the eyes of faith."[79] By contrast Pinnock sought to validate the gospel by a historical approach to Christian evidences. There are supernatural indicia, both the acts of God and his prophetic words, that the ground on which the Christian faith rests is firm. Above all, "Jesus has presented himself as divine Messiah and the resurrection has dramatically authenticated his claims."[80] Pinnock did not believe that such evidence could convince people to accept the Christian faith. Only the Spirit can do that. But evidentialist apologetics can function as a form of preevangelism, preparing people to make an intelligent decision for Christ.[81]

In *Set Forth Your Case* (1967) Pinnock's evidence for the faith includes the historical trustworthiness of the New Testament, the historicity of Christ, the fact of the resurrection, the inerrancy of Scripture, theistic proofs for God's existence, and the spe-

74. Clark H. Pinnock, "Cultural Apologetics: An Evangelical Standpoint," *Bibliotheca Sacra* 127 (Jan.–March 1970): 59–61.

75. Ibid., 62.

76. Clark H. Pinnock, "Schaeffer on Modern Theology," in *Reflections on Francis Schaeffer*, ed. Ronald W. Ruegsegger (Grand Rapids: Zondervan, 1986), 184.

77. Pinnock, "Cultural Apologetics," 58; idem, "Schaeffer on Modern Theology," 184–85.

78. Clark H. Pinnock, *Live Now, Brother* (Chicago: Moody, 1972), 20.

79. Clark H. Pinnock, *Set Forth Your Case*, rev. ed. (Chicago: Moody, 1971), 132.

80. Clark H. Pinnock, *Set Forth Your Case* (Nutley, N.J.: Craig, 1967), 43.

81. Ibid., 8, 43.

ciousness of the myth of evolution. Pinnock believed such data certain, and he argued dogmatically. But in his *Reason Enough: A Case for the Christian Faith* (1980) he softened his stance, seeking only to present strands of evidence. His claims of certainty were diminished. Presenting a cumulative argument, he cited five circles of evidence—the pragmatic, with its existential drive toward meaning; the experiential, with its intuition of the reality of God; the cosmic, which attempts to understand the world; the historical, which adduces events of the past as a basis for faith; and the communal, which calls attention to the social impact of the gospel. These circles or strands overlap and together form a strong defense for the Christian faith.

There are in *Reason Enough* an openness and humility with regard to its evidential cogency. The modern historical sensibility concerning Jesus' life is noted. And, having abandoned the position of strict inerrancy, Pinnock now speaks of, for example, "the factual evidence for the truth of the Christian message."[82] He concludes his presentation with a discussion of the problem of doubt, whether arising from spurious issues (e.g., Karl Marx's attack on religion) or real issues (e.g., the problem of evil). Pinnock still sees himself "in the role of a fair-minded lawyer seeking to convince you the jury of the truth of the Christian message through the presentation of the evidences at my disposal."[83] But now he does not aim at presenting "rational proof," but mere "reasonable probabilities," for he believes that God "approaches us gently with clues and reminders of who He is as if to woo and win us."[84]

Evaluation

Throughout his career Pinnock has written self-consciously as an evangelical theologian. Rejecting both fideistic traditional-

ism and reductive liberalism, he has sought for theology a fidelity to the Scriptures in the context of modernity. As Pinnock argued in his inaugural lecture at McMaster Divinity College in 1977, evangelical theology must be both conservative and contemporary.[85] That is to say, "we should strive to be faithful to historic Christian belief taught in Scripture, and at the same time, to be authentic and responsible to the contemporary hearers."[86]

In assessing Pinnock's work as an evangelical theologian, it is not enough, however, to note his commitment to be both biblical and contextual. One must also take notice of the fundamental "over-againstness" of his writing. Pinnock the evangelical has remained Pinnock the apologist. He has consistently spoken out when he believes that the Christian faith is being skewed or threatened by others. The list of his opponents is lengthy. Pinnock has opposed liberals among the Southern Baptists by arguing for inerrancy; he has opposed liberals in the wider church for compromising the facticity of the Jesus event. Given the closed-mindedness of many evangelicals, he has pled for space for Neo-Pentecostalism. In the face of evangelicalism's Reformed theological establishment he has argued for a neo-Arminian soteriology. He has pitted his evidentialist apologetics over against both secularism and presuppositionalism. He argued first for radical politics when the evangelical church seemed quiescent and then for democratic capitalism when progressive evangelicals became enamored of politically correct liberalism. He has questioned classical theism as too static a model, argued against strident inerrancy when the evangelical church was threatened with division and a deflection of its mission, and opposed liberals and conservatives alike on the subject of the place of other religions.

82. Pinnock, *Reason Enough*, 91.
83. Ibid., 17.
84. Ibid., 18.

85. Pinnock, *Three Keys*, 85.
86. Clark H. Pinnock, "An Evangelical Theology: Conservative and Contemporary," *Christianity Today*, 5 January 1979, p. 23.

Pinnock's chief significance as an evangelical theologian is that, like the boy in "The Emperor's New Clothes," he has been willing to question what has on authority been accepted as true and to risk alternatives. At times his alternatives can be questioned. Has Pinnock given adequate criteria for determining what in Scripture is legend? Does his qualification of divine foreknowledge square with the biblical data? Can one really speak of degrees of biblical inspiration, the specific affirmations being more inspired than the rest of Scripture? Have the paradoxical truths of divine sovereignty and human freedom been separated unnecessarily? In arguing passionately against the theological establishment (whether evangelical or liberal), Pinnock occasionally is unconvincing, if not mistaken. But more often than not, Pinnock's confrontations reveal truth, to the benefit of even the emperor.

Pinnock's penchant for battle and his passion for biblical truth have brought change within his evangelical theology. Both text and context have provided new light. Over the last twenty-five years Pinnock has become less rationalistic, more open to the world, more accepting of the contribution of biblical criticism, less Calvinistic, and more receptive to the Spirit's work. Yet the basic contours of his evangelical thought have endured. At the 1990 meeting of the American Academy of Religion, Pinnock presented an appreciative paper concerning the contribution Bernard Ramm had made to evangelical theology. He commented that liberals have asked, "Why has Ramm made so few changes?" And conservatives, "Why has he made so many?" These comments could easily be redirected at himself. Criticized by both Left and Right, Pinnock is playing a prophetic role in the church.

Primary Sources

Pinnock, Clark H. "Between Classical and Process Theism." In *Process Theology*, edited by Ronald H. Nash, 309–27. Grand Rapids: Baker, 1987.

_____. *Biblical Revelation: The Foundation of Christian Theology*. Chicago: Moody, 1971.

_____. "The Finality of Jesus Christ in a World of Religions." In *Christian Faith and Practice in the Modern World*, edited by Mark A. Noll and David F. Wells, 152–68. Grand Rapids: Eerdmans, 1988.

_____. "God Limits His Knowledge." In *Predestination and Free Will*, edited by David Basinger and Randall Basinger, 141–62. Downers Grove, Ill.: Inter-Varsity, 1986.

_____. "How I Use the Bible in Doing Theology." In *The Use of the Bible in Theology: Evangelical Options*, edited by Robert K. Johnston, 18–34. Atlanta: John Knox, 1985.

_____. "The Need for a Scriptural, and Therefore a Neo-Classical Theism." In *Perspectives on Evangelical Theology*, edited by Kenneth S. Kantzer and Stanley N. Gundry, 37–42. Grand Rapids: Baker, 1979.

_____. "Parameters of Biblical Inerrancy." In *Proceedings of the Conference on Biblical Inerrancy, 1987*, 95–100. Nashville: Broadman, 1987.

_____. "Prospects for Systematic Theology." In *Toward a Theology for the Future*, edited by David F. Wells and Clark H. Pinnock, 93–124. Carol Stream, Ill.: Creation House, 1971.

_____. *Reason Enough: A Case for the Christian Faith*. Downers Grove, Ill.: Inter-Varsity, 1980.

_____. *The Scripture Principle*. San Francisco: Harper and Row, 1984.

_____. *Three Keys to Spiritual Renewal*. Minneapolis: Bethany, 1985.

_____. "Three Views of the Bible in Contemporary Theology." In *Biblical Authority*, edited by Jack B. Rogers, 45–73. Waco: Word, 1977.

_____. *Tracking the Maze: Finding Our Way through Modern Theology from an Evangelical Perspective*. San Francisco: Harper and Row, 1990.

_____, ed. *The Grace of God, the Will of Man: A Case for Arminianism*. Grand Rapids: Zondervan, 1989.

_____, ed. *Grace Unlimited*. Minneapolis: Bethany, 1975.

Secondary Sources

Price, Robert M. "Clark H. Pinnock: Conservative and Contemporary." *Evangelical Quarterly* 60 (1988): 157–83.

Rakestraw, Robert V. "Clark H. Pinnock." In *Baptist Theologians*, edited by Timothy George and David S. Dockery, 660–84. Nashville: Broadman, 1990.

Roennfeldt, Ray C. W. "Clark H. Pinnock's Shift in His Doctrine of Biblical Authority and Reliability: An Analysis and Critique." Ph.D. diss., Andrews University, 1990.

Alister E. McGrath

Michael Bauman

Alister Edgar McGrath was born on January 23, 1953, in Belfast, Northern Ireland, the only son of Edgar McGrath, a county health officer, and the former Nancy McBride. Despite a Christian background, it was not until his student days at Oxford University that McGrath, through the Oxford Inter-Collegiate Christian Union, became a Christian at the age of eighteen. His spiritual journey is best recounted in his own words:

> Although I was brought up as a Christian, I have to confess that I could never understand what relevance Christianity could have for anyone. How could accepting a few ideas as true change your life? How could believing that there was a God up there somewhere have any relevance to the real world? Between the ages of thirteen and eighteen, I attended a very religious high school—the Methodist College, Belfast, in Northern Ireland. Christian worship was very much part of the regular programme of the school, and there was no way that I, or anyone else for that matter, could avoid it. It turned me off Christianity completely.
>
> Initially, my reaction to Christianity was one of indifference. I couldn't see why anyone should be interested in it, and was

content to leave matters there. But I began to develop more definitely atheistic views as time progressed. In the first place, I studied the natural sciences in some detail. Initially, up to age fifteen, I specialized in chemistry, physics, biology and mathematics. Then, until the age of seventeen, I chose to specialize in pure mathematics, applied mathematics, chemistry and physics. Eventually, I became deeply influenced by the spirit of scientific materialism, and felt that God had no useful place or purpose in the universe.

> But I also began to get interested in Marxism. I think it was when I was fifteen or so that I really became interested in its ideas, and their potential religious importance. God was just some kind of religious narcotic, designed to dull the senses of those who couldn't cope with life. But *I* could! And so I dismissed belief in God as some kind of wish-fulfilment, a crutch

that inadequate people leaned upon. I also found myself especially interested in the writings of Theodor Adorno, who developed the idea that students were the heirs to the workers as the force that would bring about the new socialist world order. The events of 1968—when the student world was shaken by the Paris revolts—seemed to usher in a new revolutionary era. I very badly wanted to be part of it.

But life went on. In the fall of 1970, aged seventeen, I began to study in depth with a view to gaining admission to Oxford University. I sat the special examinations late that year. Just before Christmas, I received the news that I had been awarded a major scholarship to study chemistry at Wadham College, Oxford—the home of two of the greatest chemists in England, and also a college which possessed important historical associations with Marx and left-wing causes.

I went up to Oxford in October 1971, full of excitement. Here was a new world to discover. However, I was beginning to have my doubts about Marxism. There were just too many unanswered questions. 1971 was probably the heyday of Marxist influence at Oxford, and my doubts seemed out of place. Nevertheless, I began to rethink things—including Christianity. I was invited to a meeting of the university Christian Union, and went along out of interest. It was considerably less dreadful than I had expected. In fact, I found it interesting, even *attractive*, in a way that puzzled me. It was as if I had discovered a gap, a spiritual void, in my life. I decided to learn more.

I had never given all that much consideration to Christianity, which I had tended to regard as little more than some form of spiritual narcotic to deaden the pain of life—quite unnecessary for someone like myself, who was perfectly capable of coping with things. I found myself re-opening old questions I thought I had buried, and allowing myself to listen to ideas I had never really taken seriously. While I cannot place an exact date and time to my conversion, I am sure that a significant part in that story would be due to some talks given by a visiting speaker at Oxford about half-way through that first term.

The name of that speaker was Michael Green. By the time he had finished speaking, I knew that Christianity had something far more satisfactory—and far more *moral*—than Marxism to offer the world, myself included. I became a Christian, and can honestly say I have never looked back since then. If I had to identify one thing that I got right in life, it was that decision to commit myself to the living and loving God.

But I was determined to be a *thinking* Christian. My initial temptation was to abandon my study of the sciences, and study Christian theology instead. But I was advised to wait. After completing my undergraduate and research degrees in the natural sciences, I began to study theology seriously, eventually taking a degree in the subject at Oxford (1978). At that stage, the Oxford University Faculty of Theology could fairly be said to have been dominated by a gentle liberal Protestantism. Perhaps a number of its members may have seen their educational objectives to be to encourage students to abandon their evangelicalism, and become liberal Protestants, like themselves. At any rate, I found that my youthful views on the nature of Christianity were often ridiculed as unworthy of serious consideration.

I realized that I had lost confidence in my evangelicalism. In effect, I had become a liberal, and went on to train for ministry in the Church of England at Westcott House, Cambridge, then firmly established as the flagship of liberal catholicism within the Anglican seminaries. My change of mind seemed confirmed by events in 1977, which witnessed the publication of *The Myth of God Incarnate* and James Barr's *Fundamentalism*, works which finally persuaded me that evangelicalism totally lacked serious intellectual content, and had been completely rejected by mainstream academic life. I firmly believed that I could not be a thinking Christian and an evangelical. Things have changed a lot since then; but in those days, there were few evangelicals in high places in Oxford. At the same time, I also took up a research fellowship at St. John's College, Cambridge, which allowed me time to develop my theological scholarship.

I kept thinking about my faith throughout my period at Cambridge, and on into my three-year curacy at a suburban parish in the city of Nottingham, in England's East Midlands (1980–83). I found myself plagued by doubts about my commitment to liberalism. It became increasingly clear that liberal Anglicanism often amounted to little more than a conglomerate of transient theological responses to events in the academic world. It seemed as if it had no hard theological or spiritual core. As I struggled with the issues thrown up by my preaching and pastoral work, I found myself continually wondering whether liberalism actually had anything to say to the world, other than uncritically endorsing its latest trends.

After much mental and spiritual wrestling and soul-searching, I decided that evangelical Christianity had far more to commend it than any of its rivals. It was not merely biblically-based; it was pastorally relevant and spiritually exciting. And increasingly, I came to realize its intellectual coherence and strength. I regained my confidence in evangelicalism, and felt that I ought to encourage others to do so as well. And so I took up (1983) a teaching position on the faculty of Wycliffe Hall, Oxford, now firmly established as the Church of England's leading evangelical seminary. In teaching historical and systematic theology to my students, I believe that I am equipping them for the full task of ministry and preaching in the modern world. It has been a pleasure and a privilege to work in so stimulating and supportive an environment, which has formed the background to just about every book that I have written.[1]

In a personal conversation (4 July 1990) McGrath noted that his parish work at Nottingham affected him much as parish work at Safenwil had affected Karl Barth: it ended his flirtation with theological liberalism. Through this experience McGrath discovered that "unless theology is grounded in the everyday life of the people, it fails to

1. This autobiographical sketch was specifically written for the present volume.

make any sense." After receiving his B.D. from Oxford for research in late medieval theology, he became lecturer in historical and systematic theology at Wycliffe Hall. He has also served as chaplain (1983–87) at St. Hilda's College, Oxford, and as examiner (1983–86), and later as chief examiner, of candidates for Oxford's certificate in theology. He has twice been awarded a British Academy research grant (1985, 1988) for study in the Swiss Reformation. As an outgrowth of his abiding interest in German theology, from 1985 to 1989 McGrath served as the joint secretary of the Oxford-Bonn Theological Seminar. And in 1989 he was appointed theological consultant to the House of Bishops regarding relations between the Church of England and the evangelical churches of Germany. He was elected the 1990 Bampton Lecturer, the youngest to serve in that capacity in this century, and the only evangelical. That same year he was the Ezra Squier Tipple Visiting Professor of Historical Theology at Drew University.

Luther's Theology of the Cross

In order to get a grasp of McGrath's contribution to evangelical theology, we will take a brief look at four of his major works: *Luther's Theology of the Cross* (1985); *Iustitia Dei* (1986); *The Making of Modern German Christology* (1986); and *The Genesis of Doctrine* (1990). His first book, *Luther's Theology of the Cross*, is significant in three ways. First, he reverses the tendency in modern scholarship to begin by identifying theological themes or notions in Luther and then to work backward in an attempt to discover the same ideas in late medieval thought. McGrath works the other way around. He first traces the shape of late medieval theology and then moves forward to discover in what ways Luther relates to the great questions of late medieval thought. McGrath's approach is better, because it places Luther in his proper historical and theological context and recognizes that the Reformation in general, and Luther's thought in particular, arose as the result of a historical process. Only in this way can one properly evaluate "Luther's transition from being a typical theologian of the late Middle Ages to the pioneer of a new reforming theology."[2]

Second, McGrath argues that Luther's theological breakthrough, which centers on the doctrine of justification, ought to be dated early in the Reformer's career. While this thesis is not entirely new, McGrath's volume makes the most comprehensive English-language case for it.

Third, McGrath points out that Luther's theological breakthrough, though focused on the doctrine of justification, is actually a theological *program*. Once one works that program through, McGrath contends, one ends up with the *theologia crucis*, or theology of the cross, "one of the most powerful and radical understandings of the nature of Christian theology which the church has ever known."[3] Luther's theology of the cross is present, in seed form, in his theological breakthrough. This insight, McGrath says, is the principal contribution of his book. Prior to *Luther's Theology of the Cross*, scholars tended to regard Luther's breakthrough and his theological agenda as separate items.

McGrath characterizes "the prevailing state of the Christian church" in the late Middle Ages as "possessed of a tired spirituality, morally bankrupt, doctrinally confused." The confusion of which he speaks concerned the doctrine of justification. To the question, "What must I do to be saved?" the church of that day gave an uncertain answer. "This confusion," McGrath writes, "undoubtedly did much to prepare the way for the Reformation, in that the church was simply unable to respond to Luther's challenge [on this issue] when it finally came."[4]

Luther's cause was aided also by the proliferation of reform movements (such as the Brethren of the Common Life) within the church at that time and by the intense interest of the humanists (like John Colet, Jacques Lefèvre d'Étaples, and Erasmus) in the writings of Paul, which together made the late medieval church ripe for spiritual and theological renewal. Thus, as McGrath observes, "the fuel for the Reformation had been piled up for many years: it happened to be Luther's posting of the ninety-five theses on indulgences [in 1517] which eventually sparked off the conflagration which proved to be the greatest intellectual and spiritual upheaval yet known in Europe"—and this even though "most of Luther's theses were quite unexceptional" to the Roman hierarchy.[5]

McGrath argues that Luther was intent upon nurturing a threefold reformation within the Church of Rome: a reformation of morals, of spirituality, and of doctrine. Of these, Luther believed the last to be most crucial. According to McGrath, Luther's project was shaped under the joint influence of (1) Renaissance humanism and its emphasis upon the *studia humanitatis*, (2) the nominalism of the *via moderna*, and (3) the *schola Augustiniana moderna* of Luther's own monastic order.[6] To these three important elements of late medieval thought, which McGrath characterizes as the "headwaters of the Reformation," he adds Luther's own considerable theological genius.[7]

The *studia humanitatis*, though doing little to provide Luther with the substance of his reform, did provide him with its means.[8] While McGrath properly declines to label Luther a humanist, he does identify four important affinities between Luther and his humanist counterparts: their mutual rejection of scholasticism, their mutual desire to return to the early Fathers of the

---

2. Alister E. McGrath, *Luther's Theology of the Cross: Martin Luther's Theological Breakthrough* (New York: Blackwell, 1985), 2.

3. Ibid., 1.

4. Ibid., 12.

5. Ibid., 15–16, 19.

6. Ibid., 27.

7. Ibid., 26.

8. Ibid., 52.

church, their mutual desire to return to Holy Scripture, and their mutual interest in rhetoric.[9]

Having been taught the epistemological nominalism of the *via moderna* at Erfurt, Luther adhered to it throughout his life. Moreover, according to McGrath, Luther's early formulation of the doctrine of justification employed the *via moderna*'s important distinction between, on the one hand, God's absolute power with respect to the initial set of possibilities open to him and, on the other, his ordained power with respect to the subset of possibilities he determined to actualize.

Regarding the *schola Augustiniana moderna*, McGrath argues that by Luther's time there had arisen within Luther's order a unique theology of justification which combined "much of the authentic theology of St. Augustine" with "the results of the application of logico-critical methods, such as the dialectic of the two powers of God, associated with the *via moderna*."[10] To this school of thought, especially during his days at Erfurt, Luther was closely aligned.

Before his decisive theological breakthrough, Luther "held a doctrine of justification which was firmly set within a well-established medieval theological tradition. All that was required of man was that he humbled himself before God, in order that he might receive the gift of grace which God would then bestow upon him."[11] By thus seeing Luther in continuity with late medieval theology, McGrath argues, one can more readily appreciate his break from it when it occurred.

That breakthrough concerned, first of all, Luther's concept of the righteousness of God (*iustitia Dei*), which McGrath, unlike many previous scholars, tends to date early rather than late in the Reformer's career. McGrath does so by emphasizing Luther's early texts, like his *Dictata*, rather than his autobiographical reminiscences as an old

man. As McGrath reconstructs it, while Luther began his theological career within the pale of the *via moderna*, by about 1514 he began a spiritual and doctrinal journey that by 1518 led to the *theologia crucis*. As a consequence of Luther's new answer to the question of what was meant by Paul's phrase "the righteousness of God," the entire substance of Luther's theology "had to be reworked, leading eventually to the theology of the cross. . . . The old wineskins of the theology of the *via moderna* were simply incapable of containing the new wine which Luther introduced."[12] That theological reworking included a number of significant changes in Luther's teaching, among which are the twin notions that we are passive in the work of justification and that we are held captive by sin and are incapable of attaining righteousness apart from grace. Any contrary notion Luther denounces as Pelagian.

McGrath identifies five distinctive features or ideas of Luther's theology of the cross: (1) it is a theology of revelation, and as such stands in opposition to all theologies of speculation; (2) this revelation is indirect and concealed from all but the eye of faith; (3) this revelation is found most arrestingly in the cross of Christ, and not in human moral activity and human reason, which the cross shatters; (4) the eye of faith detects the hidden God in the passion and cross of Christ, the sole reliable source of knowledge of God—to search elsewhere is to fall prey to the *theologia gloriae*, the only alternative to the *theologia crucis;* and (5) God makes himself known through suffering, whether that of Christ or that of the Christian.[13] To this final characteristic idea of the theology of the cross, Luther attaches his doctrine of *Anfechtung*, the soul-shaking despair by which God disabuses us of our self-sufficiency and readies us to turn from ourselves to Christ.[14]

9. Ibid., 50–51.
10. Ibid., 67.
11. Ibid., 92.
12. Ibid., 99.
13. Ibid., 149–51.
14. Ibid., 152.

McGrath correctly discerns the central role played in Luther's theology of the cross by the hidden God, the *Deus absconditus*, who reveals himself most plainly in the apparent clash of contraries; for example, his strength is made known through weakness, his wisdom through our folly, and his love through judgment. For Luther, the *Deus absconditus* is hidden both in and behind his revelation.[15]

Iustitia Dei: A History of the Christian Doctrine of Justification

The first full-length treatment of its kind, McGrath's two-volume *Iustitia Dei* is "a bibliographical essay which records, correlates, and where possible extends the present state of scholarly work on the development of the Christian doctrine of justification." In volume 1 he outlines the development of the doctrine of justification within the Western theological tradition to the eve of the Reformation, and in volume 2 he traces it from the Reformation through the modern period. In so doing, McGrath intends, among other things, to correct two errors: (1) the misconstruing of the nature of late medieval theology, and (2) the imposition of a historically naive interpretation of Pelagianism upon the theologians prior to Luther—errors which McGrath addressed in less detail in *Luther's Theology of the Cross*.

As McGrath sees it, the doctrine of justification is the theological epicenter of the Christian church. It "encapsulates the essence of the Christian faith and proclamation, locating the essence of Christianity in the saving action of God towards mankind in Jesus Christ."[16] That saving activity entails three propositions: (1) God is righteous; (2) man is a sinner; and (3) God justifies man. "The quintessence of the Christian doctrine of justification," says

McGrath, "is that these three propositions do not form an inconsistent triad."[17] Having thus defined the subject matter of his inquiry, McGrath carefully delineates the multiple nuances of the concept of righteousness in Hebrew, Greek, and Latin before turning his attention to the relevant portions of the works of Augustine, whom he considers the fountainhead of Western theological speculation on this topic.[18]

Unlike many theologians before him, Augustine rejected the Greek notion of αὐτεξούσιον and its Latin equivalent, *liberum arbitrium*, which before his time had dominated Christian thought on justification. He also rejected the correlation commonly perceived to exist between human moral effort and justification.[19] Instead, as his lengthy quarrel with Pelagianism demonstrates, Augustine believed that an individual's justification is ultimately based upon God's eternal decree of predestination, that human faith is a gift from God, and that human free will is compromised by sin and unable to lead to justification unless it is liberated by grace.[20] According to McGrath, Augustine held that humans have free will, but not the power to accomplish good—"The free will is not lost, nor is it non-existent: it is merely incapacitated and may be healed by grace. In justification, the *liberum arbitrium captivatum* becomes *liberum arbitrium liberatum* by the action of healing grace."[21] "Central to Augustine's doctrine of justification," McGrath stresses, "is his understanding of the 'righteousness of God,' *iustitia Dei*. The righteousness of God is not that righteousness by which he is himself righteous, but that by which he justifies sinners. The righteousness of God . . . is so called because, by bestowing it upon man, God makes him righteous."[22] Like some of the Greek theo-

15. Ibid., 165–66.
16. Alister E. McGrath, *Iustitia Dei: A History of the Christian Doctrine of Justification*, 2 vols. (New York: Cambridge University Press, 1986), 1:2.

17. Ibid., 1:5.
18. Ibid., 1:17.
19. Ibid., 1:18.
20. Ibid., 1:25.
21. Ibid., 1:26–27.
22. Ibid., 1:28–29.

logians, Augustine conceived the scope and intention of justification to be "the restoration of the entire universe to its original order, established at creation."[23]

Augustine's theology exercised considerable sway over much of the subsequent speculation concerning the doctrine of justification. In many ways medieval thought on this issue "may be regarded as a systematic attempt to restate and reformulate Augustine's theology to meet the needs of the new era then developing."[24] This was done by translating the Pauline/Augustinian taxonomy of the aspects of salvation into the language of legal and moral discourse.

The characteristic medieval concept of justification, McGrath observes, "refers not merely to the beginning of the Christian life, but also to its continuation and ultimate perfection, in which the Christian is made righteous . . . through a fundamental change in his nature, and not merely his status."[25] This view, the systematic development of which began in earnest in the twelfth century, stands in contrast to the later Reformation conception, which carefully distinguished between justification and such other aspects of salvation as regeneration and sanctification. So different are the medieval and Reformed conceptions of justification that we must be careful not to tie them too closely together or to locate the notions of the latter too fully in the former.[26] Having issued this warning, McGrath suggests that the early medieval views of the *iustitia Dei* can be classified under three headings: the subjective, the objective, and the Pelagian. The subjective view, which McGrath connects to Ambrosiaster, identifies the *iustitia Dei* as the "righteousness by which God is himself righteous"; the objective view, originating with Augustine, identifies it as the righteousness that God gives to the justified sinner; and the Pelagian identifies it as "the divine at-

tribute by which God rewards man according to his just deserts."[27]

Turning to Anselm's later view, McGrath notes that both the *Proslogion* and the *Cur Deus homo?* assert that God's mercy is rooted in his justice, and that God wills and does only what is in strictest agreement with his nature, a consideration which ought to be the controlling factor in our contemplation of the divine activity. This view gave way to the theory of *ius diaboli*, which contends that God was obligated to respect the devil's rights to our fallen race. Christ's death on the cross for our sin was, so to speak, a payment to Satan.

Aristotelian notions of justice made their way into scholastic theology by the mid-thirteenth century, thinkers such as Albertus Magnus and Thomas Aquinas being their most notable proponents. In Thomas's case they surfaced as opposition to the voluntarist conception of *iustitia Dei*, which, as expounded by theologians like Duns Scotus and Gabriel Biel, insisted upon "the priority of the divine will over any moral strictures by declaring that God's will is essentially independent of what is right or wrong. . . . The divine will is thus the chief arbiter and principle of justice, establishing justice by its decisions, rather than acting on the basis of established justice."[28] Thomas averred, by contrast, that the ultimate standard of justice is *sapientia*, right reason. "For Thomas, the deliverance of mankind through the death of Christ is the most appropriate mode of redemption, and can be established as such on rational grounds."[29] The voluntarist notion, he believed, was both arbitrary and blasphemous.

With regard to the subjective appropriation of justification, "the medieval tradition followed Augustine of Hippo in insisting that man has a positive role to play."[30] The precise nature of that role, however, was

23. Ibid., 1:36.
24. Ibid., 1:38.
25. Ibid., 1:41.
26. Ibid., 1:51.

27. Ibid., 1:51–52.
28. Ibid., 1:64.
29. Ibid., 1:63.
30. Ibid., 1:70.

the subject of continued debate, centering primarily around three issues: (1) the nature of human free will, (2) "the necessity and nature of the proper disposition for justification," and (3) the proper understanding and application of the axiom that "God will not deny grace to the man who does his best."[31] This discussion developed in conjunction with an equally important elaboration of sacramental theology, which understood justification as a process beginning in baptism and continuing in penance.[32] By tying justification so closely to the sacramental life of the church, medieval theology began more strongly to assert that there is no justification outside the church.[33]

After discussing the concepts of grace and of merit, McGrath directs his attention to the medieval debate surrounding the dialectic between divine freedom and divine obligation. For theologians of the *via moderna,* the soteriological upshot of this debate was that "the present established order, although radically contingent, is totally reliable. God is not obliged by any external constraints to justify man: however, having determined to do so by a free and uncoerced act of self-limitation, he abides by that decision."[34]

McGrath turns next to various perspectives on the relation between predestination and justification. He begins with Augustine's view, which is, in essence, "that man's *temporal* election, or justification, is the consequence of God's *eternal* election, or predestination."[35] Gottschalk later expanded Augustine's view into double predestination, which was ardently opposed by both John Scotus Erigena and Hincmar of Rheims.[36] Later still, Duns Scotus argued that "predestination was an act of the divine *will* rather than the divine *intellect*," the soteriological implications of which led

William of Ockham to speculate that "reprobation is based upon a quality within man, rather than an act of divine will."[37] Johannes Eck, Luther's noted opponent at Leipzig, tended to "refer predestination to justification" by insisting that one may be assured concerning predestination by performing good works.[38]

McGrath then delineates five major schools of thought concerning the doctrine of justification: the early Dominican school, the early Franciscan school, the later Franciscan school, the *via moderna,* and the heterogeneous Augustinian school.[39] He closes the first volume of *Iustitia Dei* with a brief account of both the continuities and discontinuities existing between the theology of the Middle Ages and that of the Reformation. The continuities he identifies largely as issues relating to the mode of justification; the discontinuities pertain primarily to its nature.

Volume 2 documents the development of the doctrine of justification within the Christian tradition from 1500 to the present, a period of remarkable diversity of opinion on this issue. According to McGrath, the Protestant doctrine of justification is characterized by three prominent features: (1) the definition of justification as "the forensic *declaration* that the believer is righteous . . . rather than the process by which he is *made* righteous"; (2) the "deliberate and systematic distinction between *justification* and *sanctification* or *regeneration*"; and (3) the view of justifying righteousness "as the alien righteousness of Christ, external to man and imputed to him."[40]

McGrath describes the young Luther's understanding of the righteousness of God as "essentially identical to that of the *via moderna.*"[41] By 1515–16, however, Luther had made a decisive break with this theol-

31. Ibid., 1:70, 83.
32. Ibid., 1:91.
33. Ibid., 1:99.
34. Ibid., 1:124.
35. Ibid., 1:128.
36. Ibid., 1:130–33.

37. Ibid., 1:134, 137.
38. Ibid., 1:144.
39. Ibid., 1:158–79.
40. Ibid., 2:2.
41. Ibid., 2:4.

ogy on at least three fundamental points: Luther insisted that we are passive rather than active in our own justification; he insisted that human will is incapable of attaining righteousness apart from grace; and he rejected as Pelagian the notion that on our own we can do whatever there is in ourselves.[42] Luther also asserted that "iustitia Dei is not to be understood as the righteousness by which God is himself just, but the righteousness by which he justifies the ungodly."[43] As McGrath encapsulates it, Luther's essential insight is that "God himself bestows upon man the gift of *fides Christi*."[44] The gospel has the effect of destroying all pretense of human righteousness by insisting that we must lay hold of a righteousness that is not our own—the *iustitia Christi aliena*.[45]

After a brief comparison between the thought of Luther and Augustine on this point, McGrath turns to the early Lutherans' doctrine of justification. He describes, in turn, the Augustinianism of Andreas Karlstadt and Johann Bugenhagen, the forensic overtones of Philipp Melanchthon's views, and the Osiandrist, Stancarist, antinomian, Majorist, and synergist controversies. McGrath then begins his survey of the early Reformed views on justification by noting the Erasmian moralism of Huldrych Zwingli, Martin Bucer, and Johannes Oecolampadius. There follows a discussion of John Calvin's explicitly forensic conception that "man is not made righteous in justification, but is accepted as righteous . . . on account of the righteousness of Christ outside of man." This view McGrath labels "extrinsicism."[46]

In delineating the subsequent shape of the new scholasticism within Protestant orthodoxy and its attendant confessionalism, McGrath focuses on the theology of Theodore Beza, Calvin's successor at Geneva,

and the influence his theology had on the five articles of the Synod of Dort (1619) and on such prominent covenant theologians as Franciscus Gomarus, Johannes Wollebius, Zacharius Ursinus, and Johannes Cocceius. Their stance, in turn, was countered by the hypothetical universalism of Moses Amyraut of Saumur.[47] What the Canons of Dort were to Reformed thought in the seventeenth century, the Formula of Concord was to Lutheran theology. McGrath compares the theology of these two confessional traditions under three heads—the nature of justification, the objective grounds of justification, and the subjective appropriation of justification—and concludes that while the Lutheran and Reformed understandings of the first issue are similar, they differ significantly on the second and third.[48]

The emergence of Pietism as a reaction to Lutheran orthodoxy McGrath characterizes as a consequence of insistence upon the active nature of faith. This in turn gave rise to the doctrine of Christian perfection and to Pietism's threefold rejection of vicarious atonement, imputed righteousness, and deathbed conversion, beliefs it considered inimical to piety.

Meanwhile, of course, Roman Catholic theologians were not idle. In examining developments within pre-Tridentine Catholicism, McGrath focuses on the "radically theocentric doctrine of justification" espoused by Juan de Valdés; on Gasparo Contarini's view that the "sacrifice of Christ upon the cross was more than adequate as a satisfaction for human sin"; on Johannes Gropper's "double righteousness" view, which some mistakenly label *duplex iustitia;* and on Italian evangelism, an undogmatic movement characterized early on by strongly Augustinian and individualist beliefs.[49] Tridentine thought itself asserted that "free will is not destroyed, but is weakened by the Fall"; that "man is called

42. Ibid., 2:6.
43. Ibid., 2:7.
44. Ibid., 2:8.
45. Ibid., 2:12.
46. Ibid., 2:36.

47. Ibid., 2:43.
48. Ibid., 2:44–51.
49. Ibid., 2:54–61.

through prevenient grace, without reference to his merits"; and that "faith is to be seen as the beginning of human salvation, the root of all justification, without which it is impossible to please God." Trent also carefully identified the causes of justification: the final cause, the glory of God and eternal life; the efficient cause, the mercy of God; the meritorious cause, the passion of Christ; the instrumental cause, the sacrament of baptism; and the formal cause, the righteousness of God.[50] In the wake of Trent, various controversies erupted within the Roman communion, of which McGrath singles out three for special attention: Baianism, Molinism, and Jansenism. Despite the divergent views represented in these controversies, post-Tridentine theology is characterized by two overarching features: the Roman Catholic Church "continued to regard justification as a process," and it permitted the term *justification* itself to be "gradually eliminated from the homiletical and catechetical literature of Catholicism."[51]

Though drawing inspiration from their continental counterparts, the English Reformers, such as William Tyndale, John Frith, and Thomas Cranmer, propagated their own distinctive views on justification, which McGrath describes as "essentially Augustinian." They omitted "any reference to the concept of the imputation of righteousness," and understood humans "to be *made* righteous *by fayth onely*, with good works being the natural consequence of justifying faith." In time this Augustinianism was tempered by "a Melanchthonian doctrine of justification *per solam fidem.*"[52] Later in the sixteenth century, however, Richard Hooker's more Calvinistic views on this particular issue gained prominence. He maintained, for example, that "God bestows upon man justifying and sanctifying righteousness . . . at one and the same time: the distinction between the two lies in the

fact that the former is external to man, and imputed to him, while the latter is worked within him by the Holy Spirit." Further, this justification ought to be "conceived Christologically, in terms of the appropriation of the personal presence of Christ within the believer through the Holy Spirit."[53]

Before turning his attention to John Henry Newman, McGrath examines the Arminianism of the Caroline divines, the experimental predestinarianism of their Puritan counterparts, and the federalism of Heinrich Bullinger and others. Newman's views, McGrath insists, rest upon "an historical analysis of the doctrines of justification associated with Luther (and, to a much lesser extent, with Melanchthon), with Roman Catholic theologians such as Bellarmine and Vasquez, and with the Caroline divines." Unfortunately, "Newman's historico-theological analysis appears to be seriously and irredeemably inaccurate [and to] rest upon a fallacious interpretation" of all three sources, as well as on a concept of "the real presence of the Trinity within the soul of the justified believer," a notion apparently drawn from the Greek Fathers.[54] That Newman's analysis is indeed mistaken McGrath establishes with precision and in detail.[55]

Modern discussion of the issues involved began with "the rise of anthropocentric theologies of justification." Characteristic of the Enlightenment, these theologies tended to emphasize "the autonomy of man as moral agent" and exhibited great "optimism concerning the capacity of natural human faculties," thus calling into question the doctrine of original sin that previously underlay all orthodox speculation on the matter.[56] In England these ideas were advanced first by philosophers like Edward Herbert (Baron Herbert of Cherbury) and John Locke. They were succeeded by ratio-

---

50. Ibid., 2:81–83.
51. Ibid., 2:97.
52. Ibid., 2:98–102.

53. Ibid., 2:104–5.
54. Ibid., 2:122–23.
55. Ibid., 2:125–34.
56. Ibid., 2:136.

nalists of various stripes and hues as well as by evangelicals and pietists.

In Germany the sequence was different. There rationalism followed Pietism and was deeply influenced by it. While the Enlightenment proved destructive of the orthodoxy of many, it was itself unable to withstand the withering critique aimed at it by such thinkers as Immanuel Kant and Friedrich Schleiermacher. Kant's "analysis of the concept of moral autonomy in the light of the principle of radical evil . . . demonstrated the superficiality of the moralism of the Enlightenment," as did Schleiermacher's "rejection of the equation of religion and morality [and his] demonstration of the heteronomous character of man's soteriological resources."[57] In their wake, Albrecht Ritschl reintroduced a more objective soteriology based upon "the centrality of God's redemptive action in history, with its associated (and subsequent) human response and obligations." Ritschl viewed religions in general and Christianity in particular as fundamentally soteriological. Through the intrusion of Hellenistic metaphysics, however, Christianity had become corrupted into a christologically oriented religion.[58] Thus Ritschl not only was critical of Enlightenment soteriology, but also objected to orthodox formulations, especially their "judicial approach to justification and the concept of original sin."[59]

Liberalism followed Ritschl, and Karl Barth followed liberalism—with a vengeance. Barth's theology, as McGrath describes it, is "an extended reflection upon the fact that God has spoken to man—*Deus dixit*—abrogating the epistemological chasm separating them in so doing."[60] Barth's theological system, as a result, is a progressive unfolding of the inner meaning and manifold implications of the fact that God has spoken. As such, it stands in contrast to the anthropocentricity of liberal-

ism. But, observes McGrath, in Barth's system soteriology becomes a necessarily secondary consideration, one dwarfed by the fact of revelation.[61] Nevertheless, Barth's modest soteriological concerns do bear a "remarkable degree of continuity" with the Enlightenment, Schleiermacher, and Ritschl, as well as "a close affinity with the theological framework of the liberal school, despite substantial differences."[62]

McGrath draws three important conclusions from his study of justification:

1. There is a general consensus of the church that the human situation has been transformed through the action of God in Christ.
2. Although humans are generally understood to be involved in their justification in some manner, the action of God in transforming their situation is based upon the grace of God alone.
3. The development of the doctrine of justification has been neither linear nor continuous, but sporadic and episodic, as well as both relevant and urgent.[63]

(Because space is limited, and because enough has been said already to indicate the nature and scope of McGrath's contribution to the study both of the Reformation and of related ages, issues, and movements, we shall only briefly mention three other significant texts. *The Intellectual Origins of the European Reformation* is a detailed historical account of the theological and philosophical roots of Reformation thought; it points out both the continuity and discontinuity between early Protestant beliefs and their late medieval antecedents. *Reformation Thought: An Introduction* aims to introduce students to Reformation-era theology and its relevance for today. *A Life of John Calvin* traces the origin, development, and

57. Ibid., 2:158.
58. Ibid., 2:161.
59. Ibid., 2:165.
60. Ibid., 2:172.

61. Ibid., 2:176.
62. Ibid., 2:179.
63. Ibid., 2:189–90.

influence of Calvin's theology and political thought.)[64]

The Making of Modern German Christology: From the Enlightenment to Pannenberg

McGrath's *Making of Modern German Christology* is "intended to introduce to English-speaking readers the main themes, problems and personalities associated with the development of the Christology of modern German-speaking Protestantism," as well as to "bring up to date the Christological debate within English-speaking circles."[65] Here McGrath specifically mentions his own Church of England—which he believes has largely ignored contemporary questions and concerns and failed in its responsibility to proclaim Christ to the modern world. McGrath selects the Enlightenment as the *terminus a quo* of his study because many scholars now view the Enlightenment as "the most significant development in the intellectual history of the Christian faith—far surpassing the Reformation in this respect."[66] The central christological problem of the Enlightenment and post-Enlightenment eras, McGrath insists, "is not the ontological problem which dominated the patristic period, but the question of the relationship between revelation and history."[67] By replacing metaphysics with historical understanding, modern Christology has tried to bring the revelation of God in Christ under historical scrutiny. It insists that because this revelation has "taken place within universal history," it must "be open to historical enquiry."[68]

According to McGrath, the Enlightenment reliance upon human reason as the final arbiter of truth represented a "cognitive crisis." "The world of the *Aufklärung*," he writes, "was essentially a rational cosmos in which man, as a rational being, works towards his own moral perfection through conforming himself to the rational structure of the cosmos." Having declared themselves epistemologically and morally autonomous, Enlightenment thinkers fell into conflict with orthodoxy, which declared that "man's intellect was blinded so that he could not see into the divine mind, and his will perverted so that he could not function as an autonomous moral agent."[69]

Given its emphasis on reason, the Enlightenment transformed Christ into a mere teacher and exemplar, one who embodied "the fully realized potential of every rational individual." Christianity, like Christ, became "essentially ethical in character."[70] In his *Von dem Zwecke Jesu und seiner Jünger*, Hermann Reimarus argued that Jesus was merely a disillusioned apocalyptic Jew whose views had "a purely limited temporal reference and relevance." The resurrection was a fraud perpetrated and perpetuated by the apostles, who also elevated Jesus to supernatural status. Thus, Reimarus wrote, one could—and should—"distinguish between the Jesus of history and the later beliefs of the apostolic church."[71]

Like Reimarus, Gotthold Lessing attacked the apostolic picture of Christ, insisting that "even if there were reasons for supposing that a supernatural event had taken place in the history of Jesus, . . . [it is] impossible to deduce a doctrinal or metaphysical truth from a factual or historical event." This led to Lessing's now famous declaration that the "accidental truths of history can never become the necessary truths of reason." The most one can expect from history is a mere corroboration of "the truths which reason itself [has] discov-

64. Alister E. McGrath, *The Intellectual Origins of the European Reformation* (Cambridge, Mass.: Blackwell, 1987); idem, *Reformation Thought: An Introduction* (Cambridge, Mass.: Blackwell, 1988); idem, *A Life of John Calvin: A Study of the Shaping of Western Culture* (Cambridge, Mass.: Blackwell, 1990).

65. Alister E. McGrath, *The Making of Modern German Christology: From the Enlightenment to Pannenberg* (Cambridge, Mass.: Blackwell, 1986), 1, 216.

66. Ibid., 1.
67. Ibid., 2.
68. Ibid., 3.

69. Ibid., 11.
70. Ibid., 13.
71. Ibid., 15.

ered"; history "[cannot] be permitted to establish them in the first place."[72]

The *Aufklärung* was set in retreat by two very different movements—the empiricism of British writers like David Hume and the romanticism of German writers like Novalis and Friedrich Scheiermacher, whose fundamental axiom concerned the way individualized human sentiment is oriented toward the infinite. Profoundly christocentric, Schleiermacher's *Glaubenslehre* is "constructed around the antithesis of sin and grace—that is, around man's need for redemption, and the actuality of this redemption in Jesus Christ."[73] To Schleiermacher, human God-consciousness, not reason, was the irreducible foundation of religious belief. This led him to conclude that "Jesus may only be approached through the experience of his benefits as mediated in the historical continuity of the community of faith." Christology, then, was not a function of Enlightenment reason, but a "reflection upon historically and socially mediated experience."[74] While the theologians of the *Aufklärung* conceived of Christianity and human destiny rationally, Schleiermacher preferred to express them religiously, in terms of God-consciousness. By means of his critique of rationalism, Schleiermacher "opened the door for the new Christological developments of the nineteenth and twentieth centuries."[75]

The unique brand of idealism advocated by Georg Hegel, Schleiermacher's contemporary, exercised considerable influence over christological studies in the mid-nineteenth century. Hegel's fundamental contribution hinged upon his distinction between *Vorstellung* ("representation") and *Begriff* ("concept"). This distinction enabled him to critique various forms of religious expression without sacrificing philosophical rigor. For Hegel, "the supreme religious *Vorstellung* from which theological and philosophical speculation may begin . . . is empirically and objectively grounded in the history of Jesus of Nazareth."[76] Though such *Vorstellungen* occur in all religions implicitly, in Christianity they are explicit, thus rendering Christianity the substance of which all other religions are merely the shadow. As McGrath explains, the *Vorstellung* of the incarnation is transformed into the *Begriff* of theology by means of a process of reflection. This reflection, however, inevitably increases the epistemic distance between history and concept.

Later, David Strauss, Ferdinand Baur, and Ludwig Feuerbach transformed Hegel's mental distance into a chasm. Strauss did so by subjecting the Gospels to historical examination based upon naturalistic assumptions. His historical criteria served to identify and to set aside the supposedly mythical elements in the Gospel accounts. According to Strauss, "because the idea of 'resurrection' includes the obviously supernatural idea of the return to life of a dead man, a rational observer is forced to conclude 'either Jesus was not really dead or he did not really rise again.'"[77] Strauss simply replaced the *Vorstellung* of incarnational history with the *Begriff* of his own speculations, which he believed to be as existentially satisfying as and considerably more precise than myth.[78]

Although greatly influenced by Schleiermacher's *Glaubenslehre* as a young man, Baur later grew to reject its Christology as insufficiently historical. It was his contention that "unless theology begins with the historical Jesus, in terms of a critical analysis of the gospel accounts, he will never be found." For Baur, "the key to a correct understanding of the significance of Jesus of Nazareth lay in a critical study of Christian origins."[79] The Gospel of John was the text that polarized Baur and Schleiermacher. For the latter, John's Gospel "was the

72. Ibid., 16.
73. Ibid., 19–20.
74. Ibid., 20–21.
75. Ibid., 26.

76. Ibid., 33.
77. Ibid., 37.
78. Ibid., 38.
79. Ibid., 39–40.

most nearly continuous, complete and historically reliable portrait of Jesus," while for the former the fourth Gospel was "a source for the theology of the early church, rather than a source for the history of Jesus of Nazareth."[80] Baur differed not only from Scheiermacher, but also from Hegel. "For Hegel," McGrath explains, "Christianity was primarily about a concept (*Begriff*); . . . for Baur, Christianity was primarily about a *person*," a person of history.[81]

After a brief survey of Feuerbach's reductionistic anthropotheism, McGrath focuses on liberal theologians from Albrecht Ritschl to Adolf von Harnack and on the pictures of Christ that they developed. Ritschl's point of departure was his insistence that "Christ's *person* must be determined from his *work*," a notion based upon Ritschl's conviction that Christianity is concerned primarily with the action of God and the action of humans in relation to one another.[82] According to Ritschl, Christ's uniqueness consists largely in his status as the historical founder of the Christian community. His primacy is historical rather than ontological. But "although Jesus may be viewed as a man objectively, faith recognizes him as having the religious value of God."[83] Thus Christ has a unique status within the community of faith. But this unique status does not imply that we have direct or immediate contact with God. The presence of God is always a mediated presence, mediated in the community of faith. As McGrath explains, "the presence of Christ is to be understood as the spatio-temporal extension of the ideas and principles represented in his person within the community of faith."[84]

The quintessential liberal portrait of Christ was not Ritschl's, but Harnack's. Harnack distinguished carefully between the religion of Jesus and the religion about

him that arose later. McGrath identifies in Harnack's version of the religion of Jesus "three circles of thought, each of which contains the whole proclamation of the gospel: the coming of the Kingdom of God; the fatherhood of God and the infinite value of the human soul; the higher righteousness and the commandment of love."[85] The religion about Jesus, as it developed over time, was a "gradual adulteration of the original Palestinian gospel through the infiltration of Greek philosophy."[86] The historian of theology's task, declared Harnack, is to identify the irreducible element in the gospel by eliminating from it the unnecessary accretions added over the centuries. The principal example of this Hellenization in the realm of Christology is the Chalcedonian definition of the two natures in Christ. To reverse the process of theological accretion, the historian of theology has to employ proper historiographic principles. "Harnack thus replaced the traditional dogmatic criterion of the *doctrines* of Christianity with the historical criterion of the *nature* of Christianity, by which the fundamental principles (*Grundzüge*) of the gospel might be established and verified through a critical historical analysis which isolated the distinctive essence (*das Wesen*) of Christianity from the temporary historical forms in which it manifested itself."[87]

Harnack's liberalism was short-lived, being superseded by the work of Johannes Weiss, Martin Kähler, and Ernst Troeltsch. In his brief *Die Predigt Jesu vom Reiche Gottes* Weiss rediscovered, as it were, the eschatological nature of Jesus' message. As Weiss understood it, Jesus preached an apocalyptic kingdom which God himself would bring about in the near future. Jesus did not initiate the kingdom, Weiss argued; he merely preached repentance. His penitential ethic was the way by which his followers would prepare themselves for the coming of the kingdom. The kingdom of

80. Ibid., 40.
81. Ibid., 41.
82. Ibid., 57.
83. Ibid., 58.
84. Ibid., 56.

85. Ibid., 68 n. 43.
86. Ibid., 60.
87. Ibid., 59.

God was "thus the motive for ethics, rather than its embodiment."[88] The kingdom of God was not the result of human insight and development over time, insight gained from liberal reflections on the teachings of Jesus; rather, the kingdom "comes as a catastrophe from heaven."[89]

Kähler's *Der sogenannte historische Jesus und der geschichtliche, biblische Christus* was designed "to establish an invulnerable area of faith in the midst of the crisis which he correctly perceived to be developing."[90] By exposing the hitherto unacknowledged dogmatic presuppositions of both the *Aufklärung* and the liberal school, Kähler effectively challenged their Christology. Their efforts, Kähler insisted, were "a blind alley."[91] To be properly understood, Christ must be viewed as a suprahistorical being rather than as a merely historical figure. To view him as the latter leads only to Arianism or Ebionism. This reduces Christian piety from "worship of God to worship of a hero."[92] Kähler, by contrast, avoided all such consequences because he was far more interested in what Christ did than in what Christ was. That is, Kähler's focus was soteriological, not ontological. He believed the "pseudo-scientific Christ" of the life-of-Jesus movement to be "devoid of existential significance."[93]

But it was Troeltsch who was the undoing of the liberal Christ. Troeltsch noted that the Ritschlians based their ideas on a "discredited supernaturalism," whereas his own work was based upon a "consistent historicism . . . which . . . alters everything until it finally explodes the entire structure of theological methods employed until the present."[94] In his view, the radical application of the historical method leads to the dissolution of dogmatics because it exposes

as spurious the connection between sober history and dogmatic speculation. In light of what he believed to be his withering critique, Troeltsch thought liberalism had to die. In large part it did.

The vacuum was filled by the dialectical theology of Karl Barth and the dialogical theology of Emil Brunner. In Barth's view, one had to choose between the Jesus of history and the Christ of faith. Unlike Harnack, he chose the latter. He did so as a reaction to the nineteenth-century *Zeitgeist*. His *Römerbrief* (1919) stressed both the otherness of God and the hopelessness and irrelevance of historicism, especially regarding God in Christ. Barth believed that "God's revelation can no more be pinned down in human history than a bird in flight. . . . In Jesus, God becomes a secret, making himself known as the unknown, speaking in eternal silence."[95]

In contrast Brunner held that "God reveals himself within the historical process, and supremely in the work of Christ."[96] God's revelation of himself is both personal and historical. Furthermore, it is "necessarily Christocentric."[97] This christocentric revelation, Brunner warns, must be understood biblically rather than philosophically.[98] We must eschew the false objectivism of the early church, which relied too heavily on Greek philosophy. For Brunner, religious truth is personal, not propositional; and it is an act of God, not something from the world of ideas.[99] In his later years, Barth rejected his Kierkegaardian dialecticism and adopted a view closer to Brunner's, differing primarily on anthropological grounds, grounds that rendered Brunner's God-human dialogue a divine monologue only and Barth's Christology far less history-bound than Brunner's.[100] The differences, McGrath contends, are consid-

88. Ibid., 72.
89. Ibid., 73.
90. Ibid., 76.
91. Ibid., 78.
92. Ibid.
93. Ibid., 79.
94. Ibid., 83.

95. Ibid., 96.
96. Ibid., 102.
97. Ibid., 103.
98. Ibid., 101.
99. Ibid., 103.
100. Ibid., 105–6.

erable—they "mark the end of a road" and necessitate regarding Barth's theology as premodern.[101]

By the early 1940s the influence of the dialectical/dialogical theology of Barth and Brunner began to wane, being eclipsed by Rudolf Bultmann's kerygmatic/existentialist theology, which declared that a modern individual cannot accept the mythological framework of the New Testament proclamation of Christ. One needs "to reinterpret the mythology of the New Testament anthropologically, or *existentially.*"[102] Bultmann had in mind the existentialism of Martin Heidegger. McGrath explains:

> Bultmann's theology may be regarded as an ellipse constructed around two foci: first, the programme of demythologization, or existential interpretation, of the New Testament; second, the idea of *kerygma*, the proclamation of a divine word addressed to man, occasioning a crisis and demanding an existential decision on his part.... For Bultmann, the *kerygma* is the word of proclamation through which the Christ-event confronts the individual here and now. The word of God becomes a *personal* word of God, addressed to the individual, striking his conscience and demanding a decision.... The *existentially significant* Christ is not "Christ according to the flesh," but the "preached Christ," the Christ who is present in the *kerygma.*[103]

The Christology of Paul Tillich was also influenced by Heidegger, his onetime colleague at Marburg. Tillich held that "the event upon which Christianity is based has two aspects: the fact which is called 'Jesus of Nazareth,' and the reception of this fact by those who received him as Christ."[104] Because Tillich posited such a radical disjunction between faith and history, his Christology was more idealist than biblical

or historical. At best, McGrath concludes, we are "presented with a philosophy of existence which attaches itself to the existence of Jesus of Nazareth in the most tenuous of manners."[105]

According to later Bultmannians like Gerhard Ebeling, faith cannot and should not be seen as *fides historica*, for "faith is an existential attitude, and most emphatically does not have an object.... Faith concerns what gives existence stability."[106] In Ebeling's construction "the only historical fact on which Christology is based is the cross"; nothing else in the Gospels is to be regarded as objective history.[107] Thus "Jesus is not the *content* of faith," but "its evoker, or cause, ... he is the *ground* of faith."[108] Ebeling's theology, then, is existentialist. It is also kerygmatic in that he believes that "the crucial aspect of Christology is that the *event* of the cross has become the *word* of the cross."[109]

But Bultmann's unhistorical Christ soon began to elicit objections, first from Ernst Käsemann and Joachim Jeremias, but most significantly from Wolfhart Pannenberg.[110] Rather than grounding his Christology in a philosophical analysis of existence or in an ancient kerygma, Pannenberg chose to ground it in universal history, which is itself an indirect revelation of God. McGrath explains, "For Pannenberg, revelation is essentially an historical event interpreted as an act of God."[111] Because the significance of a revelatory event can be fully understood only from the standpoint of the end of history, it must be interpreted proleptically. Accordingly, ancient apocalypticism looms large in Pannenberg's theological agenda both because it informs the historical background of Jesus' life and teaching, and because it provides the eschatological per-

101. Ibid., 110–15.
102. Ibid., 129.
103. Ibid., 133, 138, 140.
104. Ibid., 145.

105. Ibid.
106. Ibid., 146.
107. Ibid., 147.
108. Ibid., 148.
109. Ibid., 149.
110. Ibid., 162.
111. Ibid., 165.

spective from which to view events before the end of time. "In that the end of history is disclosed in the resurrection of Jesus, and in that history discloses the acts of God which can only be fully interpreted as revelation from the standpoint of the *end* of history, Pannenberg is able to argue that the resurrection establishes Jesus as the final revelation of God."[112] Thus, for Pannenberg, "Christianity ultimately rests upon an *event,* rather than an *idea.*"[113]

McGrath completes his survey of modern German Christology by examining the work of Jürgen Moltmann and Eberhard Jüngel. Moltmann's approach is based on the idea that "Christology is *totally* eschatological."[114] Ours is a religion of expectation based upon the death and resurrection of Christ. Moltmann sees the death of Jesus as a statement about God, for in the cross of Christ "the Father suffers the grief of the loss of his Son, and the Son suffers the agony of God-forsakenness. The Father delivers up his Son on the cross in order that he may be the Father of all those who are delivered up; the Son is delivered up to this death in order to become the Lord of both the dead and the living."[115] So then, "the *historical* event of the crucifixion gives solace and strength to those presently suffering, and the *eschatological* event of the resurrection of the one who was crucified points to the final eschatological resolution of human suffering."[116] Echoing Moltmann's distaste for metaphysical theology, Jüngel also focuses upon the cross of Christ. He "locates the origin of all heresy in the refusal or reluctance to recognize God in Jesus Christ. Theology is therefore concerned with the unfolding of the knowledge of God which is to be had from the crucified Christ."[117] However, "it is not clear, at points, whether Jüngel is suggest-

ing that God is *identical* with, or that God *identifies himself* with, the crucified Jesus."[118]

In summing up, McGrath notes that modern German Christology has had three dominant concerns: "(1) history; (2) the nature of the New Testament sources for Christology; and (3) the apocalyptic nature of the New Testament sources."[119] Under the influence of these three overriding concerns, "Christology has undergone a radical change in the last two centuries, perhaps even greater than at any previous period."[120] The most important modern theologians do not focus on the issues that occupied their ancient and medieval predecessors. McGrath says that those (predominantly English-speaking) theologians who do not address the modern questions have failed to proclaim Christ to today's world. The chief purpose of his writing *The Making of Modern German Christology* has been to bring them into the discussion.[121]

The Genesis of Doctrine

The Genesis of Doctrine is in part a historical analysis of "how the phenomenon of doctrine arose, how it has been understood, and how the past has been restructured and reappropriated by Christian theologians, especially in the modern period."[122] But the book is not purely historical in character; it also employs a creative dialectic which is, on one hand, historical and descriptive and, on the other, theological and prescriptive.[123]

"Reappropriation of the doctrinal heritage of the Christian tradition," McGrath observes, "is perhaps one of the most difficult tasks confronting contemporary theology." Too often theologians approach this

112. Ibid., 173.
113. Ibid., 176.
114. Ibid., 186.
115. Ibid., 190–91.
116. Ibid., 191.
117. Ibid., 196.

118. Ibid., 195.
119. Ibid., 212.
120. Ibid., 215–16.
121. Ibid., 216.
122. Alister E. McGrath, *The Genesis of Doctrine: A Study in the Foundations of Doctrinal Criticism* (Cambridge, Mass.: Blackwell, 1990), viii.
123. Ibid., ix.

task uncritically. The result is either "an uncritical *affirmation* of the Christian tradition" or "an uncritical *rejection*" of it. To evaluate this heritage properly, McGrath contends, one must turn to the discipline of doctrinal criticism, which "seeks to evaluate the reliability and adequacy of doctrinal formulations of the Christian tradition by identifying what they purport to represent, clarifying the pressures and influences which led to their genesis, and suggesting criteria—historical and theological—by which they may be evaluated, and, if necessary, restated."[124]

McGrath begins by taking a look at George Lindbeck's *Nature of Doctrine* and its threefold classification of existing theories of doctrine: cognitive-propositionalist theories emphasize "the manner in which doctrines function as truth claims or informative propositions"; experiential-expressive theories view "doctrines as noncognitive symbols of inner human feelings or attitudes"; and cultural-linguistic theories focus upon the rule or regulative aspects of doctrine.[125] In response McGrath develops his own view of the nature and history of Christian doctrine, positing a fourfold delineation of doctrine as social demarcation, interpretation of scriptural narrative, interpretation of experience, and truth claims, a schematization he believes more fully captures "the polymorphic and polyvalent character of doctrine."[126] Without "prejudging the question of what doctrine *ought* to be," McGrath sets out under these four headings a historical description of what doctrine actually was and is.[127]

First, because "there is an obvious need for a religious group to define itself in relation to other religious groups and to the world in general," Christian doctrine serves as a social demarcation. It helps a given religious group to satisfy their "need for social definition" and ideological legitima-

tion.[128] In other words, doctrine "assists in defining both the limits of, and the conditions for entering, a religious community." It also helps to define "communities of discourse."[129]

Second, doctrine functions as a communal interpretation of Christianity's foundational narrative, the Gospel accounts of the life and ministry of Jesus of Nazareth. As such, Christian doctrine helps to preserve the church's identity, self-consciousness, and values.[130] In so doing, doctrine serves as the bearer and interpreter of tradition, thus illuminating the present and opening up options for the future.[131] "Doctrine provides the conceptual framework by which the scriptural narrative is interpreted. It is not an arbitrary framework, however, but one which is suggested by [the Gospel] narrative, and intimated by scripture itself."[132]

Third, despite the fact that words cannot fully express or define religious experience (indeed experience of any kind), Christian doctrine is concerned to communicate the communal experiences of the church. Though "human words, and the categories they express, are stretched to their limits as they attempt to encapsulate, to communicate, something which tantalizingly refuses to be reduced to words," and though "Christian doctrine . . . is obligated to express in historical forms, in words, those things which by their nature defy reduction to these forms, there is a fundamental resonance between words and experience."[133] This resonance arises from "the communicability of emotion and feelings *through* words, despite their innate ineducability *to* words. The communal Christian experience may be communicated verbally to those who have yet to discover it, in such a manner that an individual may, in the first

124. Ibid., vii.
125. Ibid., 14.
126. Ibid., 33.
127. Ibid., 37.

128. Ibid.
129. Ibid., 38.
130. Ibid., 52.
131. Ibid., 53.
132. Ibid., 58–59.
133. Ibid., 67–69.

place, experience it, and in the second, recognize this experience for what it is."[134]

Fourth, "there is an ineradicable cognitive element to Christian doctrine. . . . It purports to be a representation, however provisional, of the way things really are, in response to the questions arising from the history of Jesus of Nazareth." Thus, while "it is impossible to represent God exhaustively at the cognitive level, [it is] possible to represent him adequately for the purposes of Christian proclamation and existence."[135] Christian doctrine constitutes "a communal claim to possession of significant true insights concerning God and humanity. It is the intellectual self-expression of a living and thinking community."[136] "To speak of doctrine as 'truth,'" McGrath explains, "is rightly to draw attention to the fundamental Christian conviction that doctrine has to do with veridicality, rationality, and comprehensive elucidation."[137] Following Brunner, McGrath also affirms that Christian "truth is something which *happens*," and that it involves an encounter with Jesus Christ, the source of Christian truth.[138]

To set the stage for his own theoretical model for properly understanding and employing the history of doctrine, McGrath traces how the authority of the past was both understood and appropriated in the Renaissance, the Reformation, and the Enlightenment, and by modern historians of dogma (from Baur to Harnack). McGrath's model resembles, but does not imitate, Harnack's:

> While the suggestion, implicit within much *Dogmengeschichte*, that doctrine is an outmoded form articulating Christian insights must be regarded as implausible, the assertion that history must be permitted to criticize doctrine remains valid, to the point of being of crucial importance in

the contemporary task of evaluating and reappropriating the doctrinal heritage of the Christian tradition. The intellectual and historical credentials of this heritage must be investigated, with a view to ascertaining how and why a given doctrine gained its plausibility within the community of faith, with a view to eliminating those found to be deficient.[139]

McGrath's view relies heavily upon the Marxist framework of Walter Benjamin's "Theses on the Concept of History"; indeed, McGrath lauds Benjamin as "possibly the most important cultural theorist within the Marxist tradition."[140] Benjamin's basic principle "is that the present moment involves the intermingling of the past and present. . . . The past injects an impulse into the historical continuum, which is appropriated at specific subsequent periods, if ignored by others. . . . [Though] the past is dead, in the sense that it is chronologically discharged—yet the present moment is able to salvage at least part of its heritage, and assimilate it. There is a sense of solidarity with the past."[141] McGrath is drawn to Benjamin's Marxist model because it "incorporates the notion of historical development . . . with the pervasive and observable tendency of the present to 'recollect'—in the dual sense of 'remember' and 'pick up again'—the past. . . . The past is not regarded as dead; rather, it is viewed as a source of creative impulses, running parallel to the continuum of history, which may impose themselves upon that continuum."[142]

A chief benefit of adopting Benjamin's model is its implication "that the phenomenon of reappropriation of the *doctrinal* heritage of the past involves no special claims for Christian theology; rather, it illustrates a general tendency of human historical and

134. Ibid., 70.
135. Ibid., 75.
136. Ibid., 72–73.
137. Ibid., 78–79.
138. Ibid., 74, 79.

139. Ibid., 151.
140. Ibid., 166. For the text of the theses see Walter Benjamin, *Gesammelte Schriften*, 3 vols. (Frankfurt am Main: Suhrkamp, 1972–80), 2:691–704.
141. McGrath, *Genesis*, 168.
142. Ibid.

cultural reflection."[143] Moreover, Benjamin's model is capable of being reworked christologically. "The memory of Jesus of Nazareth," McGrath explains, "embodied in specific historical forms and traditions, pervades the historical continuum, and is capable of being 'recollected' or 'remembered' throughout history. It is the generative event of the history of the communities of faith. . . . The history of doctrine may therefore be approached as a process of recollection, of recalling the fundamental impulse of Christian faith and communal reflection."[144]

Because truth, as the Christian community of faith understands it, centers on an event—the Christ event—Christian doctrine arises in response to the history of Christ. Thus "Christianity is characterized by its tendency to insist that 'God' is Christologically specified." We Christians "are constrained in our thinking about 'God' by the transmitted history of Jesus of Nazareth."[145] Individual Christians "do not begin their quest for knowledge [about God] de novo, as if they were isolated from society and history. . . . The Christian faith does not come into existence in a conceptual vacuum, but is both generated and informed by a corporate tradition—the proclamation of the community of faith. . . . Indeed, underlying the affirmation 'I believe in Christ' may be detected a latent 'I believe in the church.'"[146]

McGrath by no means advocates an uncritical acceptance of tradition; in fact, he insists that it is "open to verification or falsification."[147] But he does reject the cavalier dismissal of the past by the Enlightenment, a dismissal he characterizes as sociologically naive, phenomenologically inaccurate, and ideologically conditioned. The Enlightenment rejection of history and tradition is self-stultifying: "There are no tradition-independent standards of argument or reason available by which the Christian tradition may be evaluated. All inquiry begins from some specific social and intellectual past. . . . All criteria have a history."[148]

McGrath concludes by insisting that theological reconstructionism proceed by means of "critical evaluation and reappropriation of the doctrinal heritage of the Christian tradition."[149] This tradition is handed both *down* and *over* to us. Thus the doctrinal heritage of the Christian faith is "both a gift and a task, an inheritance and responsibility. What our forebears in the Christian faith passed down to us must be appropriated, in order that we may wrestle with it within our own situation, before passing it on to those whose day has yet to dawn."[150]

McGrath is currently at work on a projected three-volume systematic theology that will explore the ways in which the cross functions as the centerpiece of Christian thinking. Volume 1, *The Cross of Christ and the Glory of God*, deals with the foundations of Christian theology, namely Scripture, Christ, and the cross. Volume 2, *The Cross of Christ and the Redemption of the World*, will focus on the relation between the person and the work of Christ, as well as on the nature of redemption. Volume 3, *The Cross of Christ and the Community of Faith*, will be a detailed discussion of the way the cross shapes the Christian church, especially its worship, its ministry, and its hope. In addition, McGrath has been commissioned to write a biography of J. I. Packer.

McGrath's considerable reputation as a popularizer of theology rests upon the success of his *Understanding Jesus, Understanding the Trinity*, and *Understanding Doctrine*, which are vivid, entertaining, and enlightening.[151] Energetic scholar, effective teacher,

---

143. Ibid., 169.
144. Ibid., 170.
145. Ibid., 175.
146. Ibid., 177–78.
147. Ibid., 185.

148. Ibid., 192–93.
149. Ibid., 198.
150. Ibid., 200.
151. Alister E. McGrath, *Understanding Jesus: Who Jesus Christ Is and Why He Matters* (Grand Rapids: Zondervan, 1987); idem, *Understanding the Trinity* (Grand Rapids: Zondervan, 1988); and idem, *Understanding Doctrine: Its Purpose and Relevance for Today* (Grand Rapids: Zondervan, 1990).

committed churchman, McGrath has already made his mark on modern evangelical theology. Because he is still young and so prolific, our summary of his work can be only an interim report. We eagerly anticipate those contributions yet to come.

Primary Sources

McGrath, Alister E. *The Genesis of Doctrine: A Study in the Foundations of Doctrinal Criticism.* Cambridge, Mass.: Blackwell, 1990.

_____. *The Intellectual Origins of the European Reformation.* Cambridge, Mass.: Blackwell, 1987.

_____. *Iustitia Dei: A History of the Christian Doctrine of Justification.* 2 vols. New York: Cambridge University Press, 1986.

_____. *A Life of John Calvin: A Study of the Shaping of Western Culture.* Cambridge, Mass.: Blackwell, 1990.

_____. *Luther's Theology of the Cross: Martin Luther's Theological Breakthrough.* New York: Blackwell, 1985.

_____. *The Making of Modern German Christology: From the Enlightenment to Pannenberg.* Cambridge, Mass.: Blackwell, 1986.

_____. *The Mystery of the Cross.* Grand Rapids: Zondervan, 1988.

_____. *Reformation Thought: An Introduction.* Cambridge, Mass.: Blackwell, 1988.

_____. *Understanding Doctrine: Its Purpose and Relevance for Today.* Grand Rapids: Zondervan, 1990.

_____. *Understanding Jesus: Who Jesus Christ Is and Why He Matters.* Grand Rapids: Zondervan, 1987.

_____. *Understanding the Trinity.* Grand Rapids: Zondervan, 1988.